WITHDRAWN

 W9-CAO-205

WITHDRAWN

**Illinois Central College
Learning Resources Center**

SOUTHERN DAUGHTER

Margaret Mitchell, Spring of 1935

SOUTHERN DAUGHTER

The Life of Margaret Mitchell

DARDEN ASBURY PYRON

New York   Oxford
OXFORD UNIVERSITY PRESS
1991

Oxford University Press

Oxford   New York   Toronto
Delhi   Bombay   Calcutta   Madras   Karachi
Petaling Jaya   Singapore   Hong Kong   Tokyo
Nairobi   Dar es Salaam   Cape Town
Melbourne   Auckland

and associated companies in
Berlin   Ibadan

Library of Congress Cataloging-in-Publication Data
Pyron, Darden Asbury.
Southern daughter : the life of Margaret Mitchell /
Darden Asbury Pyron.
p. cm. Includes index.
ISBN 0-19-505276-5
1. Mitchell, Margaret, 1900–1949—Biography.
2. Novelists, American—20th century—Biography. I. Title.
PS3525.I972Z82 1991 813'.52—dc20 [B] 90-20833
ISBN 0-19-505276-5

All quotations from *Gone with the Wind* are taken from
the 1936 edition, published by the Macmillan Company, New York.

2 4 6 8 9 7 5 3 1

Printed in the United States of America
on acid-free paper

This book is for my darlings,
Jane Worrall
Jo Scott
and John Mattison Geer
and for their mother
Marguerite McGee Geer
for old time's sake

. . . and the greatest glory of a woman is to be least talked about by men, whether in praising you or in criticising you.

Thucydides, "Pericles' Funeral Oration," *The Peloponnesian Wars*, II, 46.

For I am the first and the last
I am the honored one and the scorned one
I am the whore and the holy one
I am the wife and the virgin. . . .
I am the barren one, and many are her sons. . . .
I am the silence that is incomprehensible. . . .
I am the utterance of my name

Thunder, Perfect Mind, from Elaine Pagels, *The Gnostic Gospels* (1979)

Preface

I was born lucky. Besides a good gene pool, I was blessed with honorable parents, virtuous brothers, and an extended family of grandmothers, aunts, uncles, cousins, in-laws, niece and nephew who have supported me in every scheme I ever launched, laughed at my jokes, and marveled at my wit and charm. I love them very much. I married the woman I wanted, and she gave me the three healthy, handsome, and loving offspring to whom I have dedicated this book. In college and graduate school, I lucked out with good teachers and inspiring friends. In Charlottesville, too, I rediscovered the Society of Friends, and Quakers from Philadelphia to the Florida Keys have brightened my life for twenty-five years. I am grateful.

Of the great good fortune of my life, nothing has quite matched my landing a job at Florida International University back in 1971. In the first place, virtually no academic jobs existed that year, and still four years away from finishing my dissertation, I was hardly, as they say, the most marketable commodity. Through some benevolent Providence, however, the dean of the college, Butler Waugh, and his associates, Dick Dwyer and Harry Antrim, offered this very fresh graduate student the position of acting chairman of a brand-new history department. I still marvel at their audacity—and only a little less at my chutzpah in accepting. Those three men, each in a very different way, continue to sustain me. As one of the two smartest people I have ever known, Dwyer especially kept me on my marks while making me laugh for nearly twenty years as well.

As for my fellow historians in this department, I can hardly imagine a better group of people. Three of them, succeeding me as chairman, proved especially loyal and committed. I have been equally fortunate in colleagues in other departments here, too, especially in English and Women's Studies. For twenty years, these folks have proven faithful friends, challenging intellectuals, and inspiring teachers. They have goaded me to my best efforts while seeing me through the sloughs that invariably plague research, scholarship, and writing, not to mention the other woes that dog middle age. They read my first forays into literary history, Southern intellectual history, the Southern cultural awakening, and biography, and my work is better for their criticism. I also owe to them, not least, my discovery of *Gone with the Wind*, which proved the most fortuitous turn of all of my career.

Inspired by one of my colleques to read Margaret Mitchell's Civil War epic for the first time in 1974, I discovered that no one had "done" either the novel or its author. With extraordinary name-recognition that hardly wanes with time, Margaret Mitchell produced the most famous novel in the English-speaking world, which led to the most famous film of all time. It seems almost inconceivable to me now that such a character had won no sustained intellectual or academic inquiry prior to 1980. Her archives at the University of Georgia were as rich as they were huge, and a little digging turned up wonderful collections elsewhere, completely untapped. She was one of the most phenomenal letter writers of this century, and the complexity of mind, spirit, and personality in her correspondence challenges me yet; as indeed it should continue to inspire other biographers, cultural critics, and literary historians.

Mitchell was a perfect subject for biography. She lived in one of the most important cities in the American South and her family had shaped Atlanta's history for three generations before her birth in 1900. Her genealogy provides a microcosm of Atlanta, Georgia, and Southern history for one hundred years. Mitchell also lived at a critical juncture in American intellectual and social history and an even more crucial time in regional history. Although rarely associated with the Southern literary renaissance, she lived and breathed the values that shaped the most remarkable generation of Southerners since the Civil War. She possessed wonderful connections in her friends, and while few of them achieved fame, their lives have provided me a new perspective on what I call the Young South Movement. Here I name another evidence of my good fortune: Discovering and speaking with the survivors of Mitchell's generation opened a whole world to me, and I consider having found so many of her relatives and associates alive, well, and saucy as ever they were in 1925 another of the great lucky strokes of my career.

An omnivorous reader, she was thoroughly steeped in the currents of both national and Southern culture. She wrote hundreds of essays, articles, and reviews for the *Atlanta Journal* in the four years of her employment there between 1922 and 1926, and she read virtually all the standard journals, magazines, and reviews of her time, from *The Saturday Evening Post*, to *Harper's*, *The Saturday Review*, *Vanity Fair*, and the important "little magazines" of the Southern literary awakening, like *The Reviewer*. One of the last signed pieces she contributed to the *Journal* was a review of William Faulkner's *Soldier's Pay*. She proved a bellweather of her time. While she later repudiated the just-emerging tenets of literary modernism, her reading and writing introduced her to every tendency in the contemporary world, from detective stories and murder mysteries to the hard sciences. Cataloguing the books she read, rereading them myself, and chronicling their impact on the novelist's thinking has certainly proved one of the most pleasurable aspects of researching and writing this biography. It has provided me the excuse to explore all of Hemingway, Fitzgerald, and Faulkner, but also the rationale for reading far more obscure and unstudied folk whom I might never even have heard of otherwise, like Michael Arlen, Havelock Ellis, Marie Conway Oelmer, Wilhelm Stekel, James Branch Cabell, the Duchess d'Orleans, Corra Harris, and a score of others.

At every intersection of Mitchell's life, I discovered some new connection with her time that opened new vistas on her age and its intellectual currents; but finally, apart from her place in history and culture, the daughter of Eugene and May Belle Mitchell always engaged me. She never once grew tedious. The vivacity and intensity of her personality shines through everything she did, said, or wrote. Her novel is only the most famous manifestation of this power. Although I had read *Gone with the Wind* more times then I could count, I sat down once to read the book exclusively for grammar, syntax, word usage, and other linguistic phenomena. Invariably, however, I would discover that I was on page 10 or 20 or 30 of a chapter, having last noted an adverb or recorded a paragraph length on page 3. Swept along, willy-nilly, into her drama, I would have to go back and start again. That's the way she was.

I have read her jokes and stories over and over again, in some cases for over a decade. They still make me laugh. Margaret Mitchell was an extremely funny person. I think she could have made Calvin Coolidge grin—once at Smith College she actually tried. She could charm the pants off the staidest stockbroker and, literally, win the affection of hardened criminals. She was not always funny, however, nor always charming. She could prove implacable and unforgiving, and most of all, capable of purple rage and anger. She herself spoke of having two personalities—not the least fascinating aspect of her life—but whether Margaret Good or Peggy Mean, her life never lost its edge for me. General Richard Taylor, C.S.A., son of General Zachary Taylor, U.S.A., wrote in his memoirs that the Civil War resulted in part from Southerners' refusal to be bored. Margaret Mitchell lived the maxim. And as a Southerner born and bred myself, I have no greater source of pleasure in having hit upon such a subject for my research.

I directed my first attention to Margaret Mitchell by way of her novel, and I wrote my first article on her book in 1975. In 1977 I conceived of a book devoted to her epic, and I published that collection of essays as *Recasting: "Gone with the Wind" in American Culture* in 1983. As soon as I plunged into the novel, however, I realized the importance of Mitchell's life, and I contemplated some sort of biographical study as early as 1977. I conducted my first biographical interviews that year. In the thirteen or fourteen years that have passed since I first began, I have accumulated the most numerous debts. I have named some of them already, for the general and sometimes specific support, for example, rendered by my colleagues and family. This hardly scratches the surface.

Although I labored over my first book while beginning this one, a real turning point in this study came in the summer of 1980 when I participated in an NEH Summer Seminar with John Reed at the University of North Carolina. That was a perfect time, and I am delighted to acknowledge my appreciation to John, my fellow seminarians (especially Charles Wilson and Ruth Banes, now lifelong friends), the National Endowment for the Humanities, the University of North Carolina, and the North Carolina Department of Archives and History.

Nineteen eighty-three found me back at Chapel Hill in another N.E.H. seminar, this time with George Brown Tindall, a fellow graduate of Furman University whom I consider in all respects a light unto the Gentiles. He has proven altogether as faithful in my cause as John Reed. I wrote the first draft of the first chapter of this book for George, and although space requirements prohibited its inclusion in the final manuscript, it proved a great exercise, and I still value George's deft criticism. This seminar also brought a host of new friends, not the least John Haley, who worked diligently to keep me aware of issues of race in my work.

Tindall's seminar proved most extraordinary of all in that the University of North Carolina actually hosted three N.E.H. seminars dealing with aspects of regional culture in the summer of 1983. While I established a natural relationship with John Reed's group, Louis Rubin actually allowed me to present a paper in one of his sessions. This was the summer of "The Po' White Trash Song" when the various members of all these groups gathered to make our own folklore. My roommate that summer, my F.I.U. colleague and friend Tucker Arnold, wrote the song and helped make these two months a special treat. I add here that subleasing Joel Williamson's basement apartment launched another friendship that has grown with time. I offer, then, the same enthusiastic applause as with John Reed's seminar in 1980 to all those people and institutions who made this summer special indeed.

As I began the chore of actually writing up my findings in 1983, I could have done nothing, of course, without data. This introduces a still wider category of people and institutions whose assistance I am delighted to acknowledge. My university has sustained my research in both funds and time free from teaching. Florida International University has granted me a half-dozen monetary stipends for travel and other expenses and awarded me a Provost Grant and year-long sabbatical for completing and polishing this book. I take this opportunity to thank my deans, Jim Mau and Art Herriott, in particular, for their support. I could hardly have survived my sabbatical, much less have fed my babies, if Oxford University Press had not come through with a generous advance when it first awarded me a contract in 1987. Thanks to the venerable Press and to my friend at court, Sheldon Meyer.

As for the actual collection of data, I have been able to tap some of the best facilities in the United States. First and most significantly, I could not have even started without the archives of the Hagrett Rare Book and Manuscript Library at the University of Georgia, the repository of the bulk of Margaret Mitchell's papers. Up through this writing, in the winter of 1990–1991, the staff continues to offer every kindness. Every researcher should be so fortunate to find such folks. While my research has outlived (in some cases literally) most of the people I first worked with in Athens, Larry Gully has seen it all, he deserves special credit. So does Tom Camden, the present head of the collection.

Although much smaller than the collection in Athens, the Mitchell material at the Atlanta Historical Society has proved very valuable in its own right, while the staff and environment have been equally pleasant and generous. More important than the Mitchell papers specifically, the Historical Society's general collection, books, maps, city directories, and other material on Atlanta's and Georgia's past proved a godsend. The Mitchell material in Special Collections at Emory University's Woodruff Library is smaller still, but it also contains the author's correspondence with Harvey Smith in an otherwise "dark age"—1925 to 1933—one of the two single most revealing exchanges in her surviving epistolary oeuvre. (The other is her letters to Allen Edee at the Atlanta Historical Society, edited by Jane Bonner Peacock and published as *A Dynamo Going to Waste: Letters to Allen Edee, 1919–1921*. For her heroic and sensitive research, Jane Peacock also wins my special praise.)

With its marvelous collection of Mitchell manuscripts contained in the Macmillan Company Collection, the Rare Books and Manuscripts Division of the New York Public Library proved an invaluable source of information, too; while the staff demonstrated all the professional virtues associated with that great institution. The Atlanta Public Library, Special Collections, allowed me to reproduce photographs in their archives and consult their other material. I am grateful.

Three very important collections of Mitchell material remain in private hands, and I am deeply indebted to Roland Zane, Elinor Hillyer von Hoffman, and Courtenay Walthall Ross McFedyen for sharing these with me. I add, too, that I cannot describe my pleasure and excitement on watching these doughty octogenarians pull out their boxes of material for the first time. In the case of Mrs. von Hoffman, that shoebox had not been opened in half a century. The discoverer of King Tut's tomb could not have felt more euphoric than I did that day. I felt the same way when I first turned the pages of Courtenay McFedyen's 1917 scrapbook and unboxed Frances Marsh Zane's letters from her sister-in-law.

While I could read, study, and draw conclusions from all this material in all these collections, I could not use it without the permission of Stephens Mitchell, and then, with his death, the Mitchell estate's. To Mr. Mitchell, then, and his executors, I owe the most monumental thanks.

In the course of finishing this book, I have interviewed a score or more of people and corresponded with almost that number. More than anything else, the time I spent with these folks brought Margaret Mitchell back to shimmering life for me. They were almost invariably fascinating and engaging people in their own right. I owe them much. The late Stephens Mitchell, the novelist's brother, was free with his time—and his gin and tonic. Besides the actual information he imparted, I delighted in the chance to see and know the family furniture in his home—the same that had graced Margaret Mitchell's apartment, her mother's home, and her grandmother's house. This was the same furniture that Phillip Fitzgerald had bought originally for his farm at Rural Home a century and a quarter before.

One cannot count all the Mitchell Stephens cousins, but several of them gave me great stories and insights into my subject and her times. By accident, I ran into Willis Timmons, the novelist's first cousin, at the Atlanta Historical Society one day, and this son of Aline Mitchell Timmons, Eugene Mitchell's sister, gave a great interview. Other Mitchell cousins have been free with their time as well, either on the telephone or in personal interviews; among them Marie Stephens Fox, daughter of John Stephens, and David and Stephens Crockett, sons of Ruth Stephens Crockett. Although confined to a wheelchair and struggling at every breath, Stephens Crockett delighted me for an afternoon with his great stories about the Stephenses and Fitzgeralds. Another Stephens connection, Fontaine LeMaistre, allowed me to use a photograph in his mother's possession of his great-grandmother, Annie Fitzgerald Stephens. I appreciate that favor enormously.

Although no blood kin, Roland Zane, the husband of Frances Marsh (John Marsh's sister), shared his wife's marvelous collections and recollections with me, while he gave me more information than any other single source about the Marsh family, John Marsh in particular, and some of the peculiar aspects of the Mitchell-Marsh union. His sharp and critical mind made me regret leaving his Washington apartment.

I also appreciate Craig Zane's helpful intervention with his father.

Mitchell's friends were legion, and many of them survived to tell their own great stories about Mitchell and Southern life among the gentry in the first half of this century. Of all these, I owe the most to Harvey Smith. I count him my friend and worthy of a book in his own right. He entertained me like a prince in his Greenwich Village apartment, wrote marvelous letters about his youth, and allowed me free access to his own personal papers, including the critical original version of Mitchell's " 'Ropa Carmagin" story. While he differs about my specific interpretations of some of his stories, my book owes a considerable amount of what sparkle it possesses to his rich anecdotes. The letters he donated to Emory University were among the greatest discoveries I made. Making them even more important, Smith himself had annotated them with information (sometimes as long as or longer than the letter itself) that created a whole new base of information and judgement. Finally, he put me on to still other people, who gave me still more information; specifically, Elinor Hillyer von Hoffman and Ruth Townley Smathers. Mrs. Townley Smathers took the time to write a great and very illuminating letter of Atlanta's social life in the twenties, and Elinor von Hoffman, in addition to allowing me access to her Mitchell letters, gave me two extended interviews and elaborated her answers in critical letters as well.

Augusta Dearborn Edwards, according to the author herself, had helped save Mitchell's sanity after 1919, and this sparkling woman filled in many blanks of my information about the writer. So did two of the first people I interviewed, Frank Daniel, Mitchell's long-time friend from her newspaper days, and Edwin Granberry, one of the original reviewers of her novel who, with his wife Mabel, remained a very close friend until the novelist's death in 1949.

Over the telephone I interviewed four of Margaret Mitchell's fellow debutantes and old-time friends, the two Turman sisters—Lethea Turman Lockridge and Helen Turman Markey—and Caroline Tye Ferguson and her sister Ethyl. From them I gained otherwise obscure data about the hows and whyfores of Atlanta's debutante clubs. I relish in particular the conversation with the funny and engaging "Beaut" Ferguson.

Courtenay McFedyen and her daughter, Courtenay Leet, gave me lunch, the scrapbook, and three hours of their lives on a beautiful May day in 1985. I spent half an afternoon with wonderful Julia Memminger Riley, Mitchell's dear friend from the interwar period. This descendant of two of Charleston's most notable families, the Memmingers and the Draytons, regaled me with the most outrageous stories of Mitchell and her own family history. She charmed me completely and also led me to discover Harvey Smith. I also lucked out in discovering Willie Snow Ethridge and her notable husband Mark. They also gave me lunch, plied me with more gin and tonic, and filled an afternoon with recollections of their old fellow journalists, the Marshes. The novelist-historian Clifford Dowdy also answered my questions and volunteered still more answers to questions that I didn't even know to ask.

None of Mitchell's old friends from pre-fame days remained as faithful as Anne Guidicci, née Couper, and while this scion of the noblest Georgia coastal family died long ago, her two remarkable daughters, Anne Fettner and Jo Cauthorne, spent much time with me recounting their own recollections of Mitchell, their mother, and the culture that produced both women. Anne Fettner also gave me access to her own family archives, and seated in her Brooklyn apartment amidst family treasures that originated in the Couper mansion on St. Simons Island, I got the same rush I did watching Elinor von Hoffman open her shoebox of letters. I discovered these two women, extraordinary in their own right, through another Couper connection, one of my oldest and most favorite colleagues here at this university, James Maxwell Couper, whom I discovered by accident to be of "those Coupers." His mother, Frances Ellis, was another of Margaret Mitchell's debutante group, and Jim's recollections have also enriched my knowledge and understanding of Atlanta culture.

Virtually the embodiment of Atlanta history, Franklin Garrett of the Atlanta Historical Society not only gave me good anecdotes about the Mitchells, but he proved a perpetual font of information about the city of his birth and all its inhabitants. Like Garrett, Richard Harwell also wore two hats for me: He had known Mitchell personally in addition to his better-known professional relation—editing her letters, anthologizing articles, and presiding over the Mitchell papers at the University of Georgia. Rick Harwell was my friend, and he helped me enormously.

I have written numerous people over the years requesting specific information or recollections of one kind or another, and the response has amazed me. The Alumni Office at the University of Kentucky kept me supplied with great information on the Marsh family. Harvard University did the same with Clifford Henry. Columbia University did the same to help me track down the first outside reader of the manuscript, Charles W. Everett. So, too, did the authorities at the United States Naval Academy, which enrolled two Upshaws. My old friends in Raleigh at the North Carolina Department of Archives and History where I had written my first experiment on female biography years before gave me my first direct contacts with the Upshaw family; and Berrien Upshaw's two half-sisters, Mrs. Herbert Lamson, Jr., and Mrs. Courtenay Egerton, wrote fascinating accounts of their father's strange first son; while their brother William and his wife, Sydney B. Van Lear, gave me still more personal data about the clan. Mrs. Lamson and

Mrs. Egerton also shared letters from their father to Margaret Mitchell, otherwise missing from the Mitchell-Marsh papers, and included other valuable information that helped me make sense of Berrien Upshaw's tortured life.

I owe still other debts. As a new university, F.I.U. suffers from a weak library collection, but a great staff helps fill the breach. My research has outlived half the library's interlibrary loan staffers, but all those people did Trojan labors for me. I name Jenny Wheeler as representative of all of them. Among the other librarians, Rose Sparks was always there to answer my questions about microfilm, and if Marge Beary had charged for her bibliographical labors, I'd be broke. She was wonderful.

Another category of folks has helped me over the years in whipping my research into literary form. Where would I have been without my friend and former student James Coleman Price! On his own time and money, and with only the remotest promise of ever getting reimbursed, he flew from Miami to Atlanta and reproduced every single article that Margaret Mitchell ever wrote for the *Journal*. If I did finally reimburse him for his expenses, I honor now publicly his loyalty and devotion. My friends Judy Green and Elena Maubrey have seen this manuscript in almost every version of its long life. Besides forming a kind of one-woman Pyron claque, Elena Maubrey has typed, proofread, and lightened my load in innumerable ways over the past four years. God bless her. Mary Jane Elkins cut through impossible chapters with grace and penetrating comments about improvement. Sheldon Meyer made me think I was a good writer and played my part in increasing my advance from Oxford; he still edits with style and grace as well. Oxford's Gail Cooper fits my ideal of an editor and proved my luck still held as my book went into production. With the rare distinction of being simultaneously Southern, cultured, smart, and sober, she picked out the grossest of my errors, moderated my judgements, and offered fresh insights into Mitchell's life. A native of my hometown, she knew the region as well as I did, and had her own estimable connections to Miss Mitchell's epic. She was special indeed.

No one has surpassed Bill Harbaugh's enthusiasm and encouragement over the life of this book. In addition to his estimable and penetrating criticism of the manuscript itself, his once-monthly calls over the years have been a tonic when I was low, and the perfect end to days when things were going well. I count myself especially fortunate in his friendship.

As Gail Cooper told me once, "Spelling is not your long suit," and Winslow and Charlotte Shea, my fellow Quakers and devoted proofreaders, saved me from myself, while offering more substantive criticisms about my book as well. My faithful friend Bill Robertson, who helped save my own life back in 1978, lugged my manuscript, then in its 1,600-page form, around with him on his vacation in 1989, and he has offered penetrating and provocative responses to that work and Mitchell's, too, over the years. In still more general ways, a host of students, particularly ones in my seminars and classes on the historical novel, Southern history, and biography, kept me alive to different ways of interpreting texts and lives, and they proved a great forum as well for testing new ideas. I can't name them all, but I hope they recognize themselves in these pages.

And then I return again to my colleagues, those presently members of my department, but especially the Old Guard—Eric Leed, Brian Peterson, Joyce Peterson, Howard Rock, and Mark Szuchman—who have read and commented on my work over the years. Tom Breslin, my old comrade-in-arms from Charlottesville, came to Miami soon after I did, and I consider myself fortunate in his continued excitement about this book.

F.I.U.'s History Club and Marilyn Hoder-Salmon's Women's Study Center here have provided other means of sharing my work with a larger audience. Furman University, my alma mater, allowed me the same opportunity, as did the Page-Barbour Lecture Series at the University of Virginia and the Atlanta Historical Society on two separate occasions, in 1986 and 1989. My friend Staige Blackford, the worthy editor of *The Virginia Quarterly Review*, has allowed me still another forum for testing ideas.

A host of other people have played a more or less conscious part in whatever merit this book possesses. Among my academic friends, I list Anne Jones at the University of Florida; George Tindall and John Reed in Chapel Hill; Charles Wilson at Ole Miss; Helen Taylor at Bristol (England) Polytechnic Institute; Sue Curtis of Purdue; Van Melton of Emory; and Mike Ebner at Lake Forest College. Plenty of nonacademics have inspired me, too, sometimes without any inkling of their efforts: among them, Caroline Barker, another estimable librarian here; Sheila Bailey in Athens; John Sansing of Washington and Lucille Howell Sansing of Kent Island; Georgia, Ray, and Chris Hollifield of Yancy County, North Carolina; Myrtle and Belle Hollifield of Seven Mile Ridge, same state. Herb Bridges, an awesome collector of Mitchelliana, has lent general support, but he has also allowed me to use his vast archive of photographs. His contribution rescued me at a crucial moment. Sam Heyes did a great piece on Annie Fitzgerald Stephens for the *Atlanta Journal and Constitution* in 1986, and he was also generous with his time in answering my questions about his unpublished research. He also put me on to Sonny LeMaistre and the only extant photograph of Annie Stephens.

While I began this preface with general references to my loyal family, I conclude with more specific thanks. Both of my brothers, Scott and Christopher, allowed me bed and board on innumerable trips to

Atlanta and New York. My niece, Christine Pyron Novac; my mother, Jo Scott Pryon; and my sister-in-law, Jo-Ann, have provided the same services among many others over the years. My nephew, Brigham Asbury Pyron, a talented photographer, reproduced items from the collection of the Atlanta Public Library despite his busy schedule. Warley Geer Van Atten has read my work, and her enthusiasm still flatters me. My loving appreciation to all of them.

In over a decade of labor, still others have contributed their bit to this book, sending me notes, clippings, and bibliographical references, offering anecdotal material of one kind or another, and enriching my understanding in still other ways. If I have omitted their names, I have appreciated their contributions nonetheless.

Writing this book was a challenging and ever-engaging way of spending what one of my colleagues referred to as "my middle years." I hope my next books take less time, but I could never expect them to be half the fun nor open half the challenges and delights as this one.

Coral Gables, Florida   D.A.P.
February 1991

Contents

PART IV FAME

PART V REACTION

SOUTHERN DAUGHTER

Prologue
City of the Tribe

🌀🌀🌀🌀🌀

The big holiday of the year then was the 26th of April, the day that Gen. Johnston had surrendered this district of the Confederacy. The town was crowded with people. It was like an ancient tribal gathering. . . . The city was a Confederate town. That was its history.

STEPHENS MITCHELL [1]

*P*erched in the tall pine tree high in her backyard or ensconced in the tower of her parents' Victorian mansion, the tiny child with the strawberry blonde ringlets and the enormous blue eyes commanded the whole world. From her heights, Margaret Mitchell could see everything.

On the east side of Atlanta, Jackson Hill formed a long, high prominence that ran exactly parallel to the Peachtree Street ridge only a half-mile to the west. The Mitchell-Stephens property on Jackson Street dominated the crest of this hill and the slope upward to the south. It provided—then as now—a perfect view of the entire city of Atlanta. The great dome of the State Capitol dominated the panorama off to the left. One could barely see, hard by, the square, pinnacled towers of the Church of the Immaculate Conception where her mother's family had worshiped for fifty years. In the same direction, but out of sight, stood the Methodist churches where her father's people had attended for an even longer time. The child could not see the trains from here, but their comings and goings rattled the day and night while their smoke and soot darkened the air of the south end. Nor could she make out the industrial plants—like the Fulton Bag Works—that lay in the same direction, but she could see their pollution in the creeks and smell it in the air.

On the other side of the valley, between Jackson Hill and Peachtree, the child could also see "the new city rising," as her older brother called it. Sitting on the honeysuckle-vined front steps of her mother's house, she had only to glance up from her book and look a little to her left to see the cluster of towers that sprouted around Five Points, the main intersection downtown. The local entrepreneur Joel Hurt had dazzled the citizenry with the eight-story height of his Root-designed Equitable Building in 1893. The slender Flatiron Building graced the skyline four years later. In 1900, the Century Building joined these two. Nearby rose the chunky Empire and Grant-Prudential buildings. After 1906, the Candler Building dominated the scene, and nothing matched its height and mass until completion of the Hurt and Healey Building in the first world war.

For all the architectural activity in the center of this panorama, the bustle terminated less than ten blocks north of Five Points. Only a mile from the Capitol, the vaguely comical, twin dunce-cap spires of the Marist Sacred Heart Church, built in 1897, marked the end of the urban scene. As the mockingbird flew, this church, where the girl worshiped every Sunday, lay less than a half mile from the child's front porch. Dome to spires, this cityscape comprised only about a seventy-five-degree portion of the whole scene.

Beyond Sacred Heart, other spires and occasional steeples cut the air, but tree-lined residential areas dominated the rest of the view to the north. This domestic landscape in turn gradually gave place to the wilder woods that hedged the landscape. These actually penetrated the city itself through the numerous ravines and gulches that characterized the natural terrain. Not much lay beyond A. G. Rhodes' 150-acre establishment out Peachtree, but even this estate still fell within two miles of Five Points. The chief residential areas were much closer in. Her grandfather R. C. Mitchell's great house on Ivy Street was an easy walk from downtown; so was her great-uncle Frank Rice's grander showplace just around the corner on Baker. The girl could see these places from her upstairs bedroom.

Few of the tree-shaded homes on Jackson Hill matched the classiest Peachtree residences, but most held up honorably in comparison with the other best houses in the city. In 1904, the child's Grandfather Mitchell threw up a massive pile on an enormous lot only four blocks from her own house; his retirement home, which matched his status as one of the city's wealthiest and most prominent citizens. Just south of her own house, only three hundred feet up Jackson Street, her Grandmother Stephens' grand edifice crowned the crest of Jackson Hill. With its wide veranda, lofty chimneys, whimsical cupola, and enormous, oak-studded yard, Annie Fitzgerald Stephens' mansion set the tone for the street itself. The houses up and down this boulevard mirrored its late–nineteenth-century architectural profusion. The girl had only to glance across the street to glimpse the most exuberant mode: with its multicolored slates and shingles, gingerbread and gimcrack, turrets, gables, and stained glass, the Lewis house displayed the richest expression of the whole street's style.

Jackson Street epitomized Victorian Atlanta; but the view changed radically as the little girl peered through the banisters of her upstairs porch past the architectural frippery of the close-set houses across the street into the long slough that separated Jackson Hill from the Peachtree Street ridge just west. The land fell precipitously away into a jumble of shanties and shacks, muddy lanes and unpaved alleys. This was Atlanta's "black bottom" that ran for blocks north and south along Butler Street at the valley's lowest part. It was home to thousands of the city's poorest, who rose early each morning to ascend the twin ridges for their jobs every day.

It was black Shermantown—Darktown—in contrast to the granite monuments of Five Points and the Victorian profusion of Peachtree and Jackson. The same was true of the southern prospect. If she climbed the steep rise to the corner of her grandmother's property, she watched the hill drop as sharply here as it did to the west. Jackson Street descended rapidly in the south towards an intersection with Old Wheat and Auburn avenues. Running east to west at the bottom of another valley, these streets defined another black bottom. Home of higher-class Atlanta blacks than Shermantown, "Sweet Auburn" boasted Negro businesses, schools, and churches. Even the best here, however, still stopped well short of the elegance at the crest of Jackson Hill.[2]

Urban center, polluting industries, lavish residences, steepled churches, and black shanties, the city bustled at young Margaret Mitchell's front door; yet even so, it ended, literally, at her backyard. In Mitchell's girlhood, Jackson Street marked Atlanta's easternmost development. Beyond its line of dwellings lay mostly fields of sedge, broken woods, and country tracks. Nor had urban development effaced completely the old Confederate breastworks that meandered from the old redoubt beneath her Grandfather Mitchell's new mansion through the huge back lot behind her Grandmother Stephens' house. With its fierce abatis, this line of trenches had marked the city's inner defenses when Sherman besieged the place in 1864, thirty-six years before the youngest Mitchell child was born. In the expansive field back of Mrs. Stephens' house, children of the new century sported and staged mock battles where a generation before their grandfathers had fought much more deadly earnest games. Captain John and Annie Stephens' mansion had itself survived those terrible times. Its walls and floors had absorbed the cries and blood of Southern soldiers: the Confederates had used it as an advance hospital during the dreadful Battle of Atlanta. And less than a half a mile from the family stable, the child trotted her pony through the broken terrain that had witnessed the

Confederate debacle of July 22, 1864, when Sherman had finally invested the town.

All this was Margaret Mitchell's world for her first twelve years. Much longer, its values influenced her outlook. Conflict defined its nature. Abuzz with commerce, the city proved cosmopolitan enough to support two Catholic parishes and an old, active Jewish community. Urbanity, however, was often more apparent than real. Agriculture and tradition girdled the city even as the ruined Confederate breastworks circumscribed it geographically. Tradition yowled against the future. Atlanta was also Tom Watson's Georgia, and the virulent negrophobia, violent anti-Jewish prejudice, and rabid anti-Catholicism of this Democratic-Populist demagogue reflected itself powerfully even in the urban core. Well into the 1920s, the Ku Klux Klan controlled the city government. The country claimed its patrimony repeatedly from the city; sometimes the bourgeoisie fought back, sometimes they joined the foe. Conflict was a way of life. The ridges went against the bottoms; Victorian propriety jousted with the black subculture for the city's soul; transient crackers snarled at both sides. Complex and paradoxical, Atlanta told a tale with the most mixed morals. No one part captured the full truth. The young Margaret Mitchell imbibed these contradictions, and they in turn defined and exaggerated the conflicts in her own life and values.

PART I

CHILD

I

Rebels, Patriarchs, and Ladies

🕮🕮🕮🕮

For you I would disobey my father.
                        EUGENE MITCHELL TO MAY BELLE STEPHENS[1]

*H*igh on the hill, the big house glittered in the brisk November night. In their silver candlelabra, innumerable candles glowed and flickered through the windows. Excitement hung in the air as the rich carriages of Atlanta's élite deposited the guests at the Stephenses' door to be greeted by the Captain and his small, round wife. It was November 8, 1892, and the Stephenses were celebrating the marriage of their eldest daughter, Mary Isabel, to the young, well-connected Atlanta lawyer, Eugene Muse Mitchell.

The *Atlanta Constitution* called it "one of the most beautiful and brilliant home weddings ever witnessed in Atlanta." The Stephenses spared no expense. They had sent to Florida for the greens, palms, and Japanese bamboo that decorated the mansion along with the local white chrysanthemums. They had invited scores of guests, and the parlors could not hold the crowds. The excess overflowed onto the grand enclosed piazza, which had been "transformed into a witching fairey land by silvergray moss and brilliant autumn leaves." Not the least interesting part of the ceremony, the bride, dressed in the height of late Victorian fashion, also wore the same "wreath of pearls" that had decked her mother in her wedding ceremony in Atlanta when the village was a Confederate town twenty-nine years before.[2]

For all the excitement of the festivities, the bridal pair faced hard competition for this company's attention. The wedding coincided with a presidential election day, and the voting culminated the most thrilling and ominous canvass in Georgia since Reconstruction. Tom Watson's angry populist campaign in rural Georgia and the threat of black insurgency had excited the gentry's darkest fears and chilled the wealthy who crowded Captain and Mrs. Stephens' home.[3] And this was a very political congregation, as the Mitchell-Stephens nuptials allied two of the most important political families in the city. The groom's father and uncle, R. C. Mitchell and Frank Rice, had dominated the city government for twenty years, as aldermen, mayor pro tem, state senator, and member of some of the most important committees and commissions in Atlanta's history. Only a little less significant, the bride's father had served six terms as police commissioner. The close family friend Hoke Smith helped hold the state for the conservative Democrats, and president-elect Grover Cleveland would reward him with a Cabinet post come March, but no one would have dared predict this outcome as the young couple recited their vows that evening, and the guests buzzed with news of the campaign.

For the Stephenses and Mitchells, political and economic authority coincided, and this wedding summarized that convergence. So it had been for more than a generation, but for still more generations these two families had represented a microcosmic history of Atlanta, Georgia, and the South. Shaped by a distinctive regional culture, they in turn shaped the minds and characters of their children. As both individual characters and conduits of tradition, family dominated Margaret Mitchell's life and imagination. Her values and spirit make sense only in light of who and what the Stephenses and Mitchells were—and who and what they were not.

Eugene Muse Mitchell sprang from quintessentially Southern roots.[4] Farmers, planters, preachers, patriots, and politicians, the Mitchells and their allied kin—the Sweets, Munnerlyns, Dudleys, Thompsons, Rices, and all the rest—had helped shape regional culture from its foundation in the seventeenth century. They left their record from the shores of the Chesapeake to the rich soil of northern Florida, from the Tidewater rice plantations of South Carolina to the cotton lands of Texas. No family, however, had closer ties to the city of Atlanta. Mitchells lived there before Atlanta *was* Atlanta. According to legend, Eugene Mitchell's circuit-riding Methodist grandfather, Isaac Green Mitchell, performed the first wedding in the village when the settlement still went by the name of Marthasville. This preacher Mitchell's brother, Alexander, had established the first cotton brokerage house in the town by 1843, and their mother passed her last years here as well, so that the young groom could boast of being a fourth-generation Atlantan even though the town itself dated only to 1837.

By 1856,the family solidified its connections to the town when I. G.

Mitchell gave up the circuit and settled permanently in the pulpit of the Methodist Protestant Church downtown at the intersection of Garnett and Forsyth streets. In his photographs, Eugene Mitchell's grandfather looked the part of Jeremiah in a frock coat. He preached a fire-and-brimstone puritanism and followed a "conservative, even reactionary politics," according to his family. Although he opposed both slavery and secession, once Georgia left the Union, he transferred his fierce evangelism to the Confederate cause. Even after the Federals seized the town in September of 1864, he still blistered Yankees from his pulpit. On account of his militancy, so the story ran, the invaders singled out his church, his home next door, and his other properties for special destruction. He also numbered among that hapless group of citizens whom Sherman expelled from Atlanta to the woods at Rough and Ready, soon after the city fell.

This Methodist divine spawned a large and celebrated family, the most notable and notorious member being Eugene Mitchell's own father. Russell Crawford Mitchell personified the epic generation that fought the war and then rebuilt the South after Appomattox. Born in 1837, he attended the Methodist Protestant Bowdon College (now West Georgia College) in Carroll County, but soon rebelled permanently against his father's religious faith; indeed, against faith altogether. His grandson remembered him as "a virtual heathen."[5] Within a year of leaving college, he struck out for Texas, where he took up law. Radically secessionist before Fort Sumter was fired upon, he hankered for a fight just as furiously afterward. With First Manassas, he organized his own infantry troop. Elected captain, he directed the unit to fight in Virginia, but the troops voted for Missouri. Denied his wishes to serve with Joe Johnston, Robert E. Lee, and Stonewall Jackson, he resigned his commission in a fury. After he resigned his captaincy, he enlisted as a private in I Company, First Texas Infantry, under the command of John Bell Hood, a general hot enough to satisfy the most aggressive Rebel's wishes. He served as partisan, spy, and guerrilla raider, but he also participated in eleven full-scale battles, the bloodiest in the early phases of the war. At the most dreadful of these, Antietam, he sustained two terrible head wounds, and his compatriots left him for dead near the Dunkers Church. His willfulness sustained him, and the story of his survival became the stuff of legend.[6] As an old man, he retold the story often for his grandchildren as he traced the scars of the bullets on his scalp. "Grandpa's hand would guide your fearful fingers to the spot. 'Feel it, child. Do you feel it?' " his grandson Stephens Mitchell quoted the aged veteran. "I defy any child to hear that story while feeling the grooves cut by the minie ball in the old gentleman's skull and not grow up with the idea that the Mitchells were tough!"[7] Stephens' sister absorbed the same moral: the Mitchells are fierce and ornery; walk lightly in their presence.[8]

After Antietam, Russell Mitchell made his way back to Georgia, where he recuperated with a favorite brother in Thomasville. Resuming active service in Atlanta just as Sherman began his inexorable drive to take the city in the summer of 1864, he participated in all the terrible battles at that time and retreated with Hood to Tennessee in the disastrous days of the winter of 1864. As Hood's command disintegrated after the battle of Franklin, Mitchell joined up with General Nathan Bedford Forrest in Alabama. He fought to the very last in the dying hours of the Confederacy in April 1865.

During his convalescence in South Georgia, Russell Mitchell had met a local girl across the state line in Quincy, Florida—Deborah Margaret Sweet, the handsome daughter of one of the county's richest families. As the war ended, he returned to claim her hand. More than love attracted him to north Florida, however. The war had spared the rich plantation country here, people were starved for goods, and cotton had never sold higher. Opportunity beckoned. In six months, the ex-Confederate parlayed a fifty-cent hard cash investment into a considerable fortune. He proved as indomitable a capitalist as he had been a soldier. On the day of his marriage, he lost all of his investment in the destruction of a river steamer full of goods, but the catastrophe failed to daunt him. Back in he plunged. With still more credit, he bought cotton at eighteen cents a pound, found a New York market at fifty-one cents, and soon was rich again. But the contentious former Rebel courted trouble as persistently as he wooed Mammon. His grandson told the tale:

> After a few months of industry in the cotton business, my grandfather got into a dispute with a Mr. Gibson who had a good deal of influence with the local commander of the U.S. Army of Occupation [in North Florida]. The dispute led to a fight, and Mr. Gibson was badly hurt. He reported the affair to the authorities of the Army of Occupation, and grandfather had to flee.[9]

He escaped Yankee retribution for refuge in Atlanta. From there he sent his brother to fetch his bride. When she arrived, they deliberated their future, whether to remain in business in Atlanta or return to Texas and the law. In an extraordinary understatement, Mrs. Mitchell acknowledged that her husband "seemed to have the knack of making money." She recommended they stay in the Gate City. They did. His future confirmed his wife's judgment. By 1866, he had formed a partnership with two brothers-in-law, Frank P. Rice and Anthony Murphy. When they discovered a Federal army sawmill on the auction block, the three decided to go into the lumber business. As a lawyer, Russell Mitchell was elected by the other two to make the deal. "Margaret always liked this part of the story," her brother related:

Grandpa looked the mill over mighty carefully. It looked good to him. He asked a few cautious questions of the Yankee officer, who eyed him warily. "Were you a soldier?" the officer asked him. The officer looked up and asked, "What outfit?" "First Texas Infantry." "Well I have never seen better troops. I don't like bombproofs nor hideouts. If you have your parole and have taken the oaths, you can have the mill." Grandpa saluted him, and he rose and shook Grandpa's hand.[10]

The partnership prospered wildly. Murphy sold out to his kinsmen, the two reorganized as Rice and Mitchell, and they invested aggressively in real estate. Nineteenth-century property maps reveal "R. C. Mitchell" or "Rice and Mitchell" in virtually every city ward. Some of their style emerges from Frank Rice's entry in the *Atlanta City Directory*, where in dark, oversize letters that dwarf the other entries on the page, he names his occupation, simply,

CAPITALIST.

The two men created a formidable political alliance as well. Rice initiated his political career in 1871 with the first of many terms as alderman and member of the city council. For years, his district also returned him repeatedly to the House and Senate of the state legislature.[11] Mitchell, meanwhile, won election to the city council in 1872, and in the tumultuous presidential election of 1876, he served on the three-man Democratic campaign committee along with two other citizens who weave in and out of the Atlanta Mitchell story, then—city attorney and soon judge, William T. Newman; and future Cabinet member, governor, and senator, Hoke Smith, then barely twenty-one.[12] Mitchell oversaw the arsenal. Harking back to the brawls and scrapes in Florida and Texas, he prepared "to shoot it out, if that became necessary," his grandson recalled. It did not. And the forty-year old ex-Confederate might even have been a little disappointed.[13] From 1877 to 1880 he served as alderman; that last year as Atlanta's mayor pro tem. Although tendered the nomination for mayor in 1884, he declined.

On moving back to Atlanta permanently in 1865, Russell Mitchell had built on Jackson Hill just up the street from where the Stephenses would live. His eldest son, Eugene, was born here. By 1870, as his fortune grew, he moved to the most fashionable district downtown where he commissioned a grand place on Ivy Street just around the corner from his brother-in-law's palatial residence. He never surrendered the Jackson Hill property, however, and in 1904 he erected a baronial mansion on the site of his very first dwelling, which aptly illustrated his social power and economic influence in the capital.

Stephens Mitchell described his grandfather as bold and reckless. A "tall, muscular, athletic man," his grandson wrote, R. C. Mitchell stood over six feet and weighed 190 pounds. With coal-black hair and eyes, "he stood erect and had a very straightforward manner."[14] Great muttonchop whiskers added to his domineering mein, while the two long scars across his pate bore perpetual testimony to his battlefield heroics. He was the perfect image of the nineteenth-century patriarch. He was prolific as well. Twice married, he begot twelve children between 1866 and 1894 by these two unions. All but one child survived past infancy. He died in 1905, one of Atlanta's first citizens, at his new mansion on Jackson Hill. Fittingly enough, the new dwelling sat in the middle of the block that had been "enclosed with an enormous redoubt" during Sherman's siege. The yard yielded harvests of cannonballs and bullets for years, palpable reminders of the awesome history this generation had created.

The family into which this soldier-capitalist married—the Sweets—replicated the Mitchells' model. In 1896, Eugene Mitchell took a genealogical research trip to Florida to interview his Sweet forebears, and he found heroes there to match his legendary father. His maternal grandfather, William Sweet, had fought the Indians during the Seminole War and served the Confederacy as well. A member of the Georgia militia, he had guarded Yankee prisoners at the notorious Andersonville camp but found the work too tame for his glory-seeking spirit. Although old by common soldier standards then, he welcomed still more active duty in the crisis of Sherman's Atlanta siege. He fought in the rearguard action after Hood's retreat in the fall of 1864 and was nearly fifty when a Yankee minie ball smashed his left lung at the battle of Coosawhatchie, where, with a tiny remnant of the Home Guard, he contested Sherman's entry into South Carolina in the last months of the war.[15] Even as boys, his sons also duplicated his battlefield heroics. They awed Eugene Mitchell. He thus memorialized his Uncle Charles, one of Deborah Sweet's brothers: he was "among nature's noble men. When a boy of sixteen, he was promoted to be ensign of his regiment for gallantry on the field of Chickamauga."[16]

These legend-making characters proved the most formidable act to follow. Measuring up to the formidable men who fought the Civil War was one of the critical issues for an entire generation of Southerners, but it marked Eugene Mitchell's life especially. He found no compensation in his mother. She was ill and almost constantly pregnant between his birth in October 1866 and her own death at forty only twenty-one years later. In nineteen years she gave birth to ten children. Early in her marriage she had also contracted tuberculosis. This scourge finally killed her, as it did six of her children. Her eldest was only twenty when her family buried her in Oakland Cemetery. Cool, austere, and unsentimental, she never made nurturing a virtue, even at her best.

With such a monumental father and a mother so otherwise preoccupied, Eugene Mitchell was born to scrap for attention and affection.

Sensitivity about his size complicated the issue. Very small by any standards, he stood a head shorter than his father. A sense of being literally and physically shortchanged ran through his life, with all the side-effects of such a feeling. He brimmed perpetually with resentment and fought constantly as a boy. He lacked ease and grace in social circumstances—"a poor politician," his son called him. Extremely sensitive about his own integrity, he furiously resented authority. While he focused his hostility chiefly on religion as a young man, his rebellious skepticism also challenged his teachers, and the fight culminated in his expulsion from school. He nursed the slight for years.

For all his resentments and gracelessness, the boy was also very bright and studious. He loved literature, read voraciously, and excelled in both modern and classical languages. He finished first in his class at the Means Private School in Atlanta in 1881. At age fifteen, he already qualified as a sophomore when he entered the University of Georgia. The boy's achievements pleased his father; at the same time, the son's ambition unsettled the parent. "He stood his examination for that class without missing a question," the patriarch wrote his sister. "He is one of the youngest boys out of 151 in college. It is conceded that he is a very fine scholar and one of the brightest in college. I think he aims to contest for the highest honor"; he then added, "But I think he is very young to aspire so high."[17] In keeping with this qualification, the parent had also opened his letter with one more reference to his first-born's size. If Eugene Mitchell feared and even resented his father, he came by his anxieties honestly.

In college, Eugene's classmates called him "the long haired, short legged genius," and he compiled the best academic record up to that time at the University of Georgia.[18] Until he died, he always wore his Phi Beta Kappa key as a reminder of the distinction. He was valedictorian for his class, and class poet. He led his fraternity, too. The patterns of his youth persisted, however, and he remained as prickly and prideful, as resentful and reserved as he had ever been. These traits, in turn, soured his successes. Sober and proper, he wrote home at the beginning of his senior year, "I have now located a good quiet boarding house where there are only a few boys and all of them are very studious and none rowdy. When I want society, I can seek it elsewhere."[19] He seldom did. Honors notwithstanding, then, he considered his student years a failure.

According to family legend, Eugene Mitchell aspired to the academy and belle lettres. His father wanted him to practice law. He obeyed the patriarch's injunction. After completing his B.A. in 1885, he remained in Athens to take his J.D., which he completed in only one year. Not yet twenty, he opened his own law office in Atlanta in 1886 with a Mitchell cousin, Wellborn M. Bray, a former Confederate artillery officer. In his professional activities for the remainder of his career, he continued the family tradition of allying with relatives. In 1893, his younger brother Forrest Gordon Mitchell (named after the two Confederate generals) passed the Georgia bar, and the two siblings formed a partnership that lasted until 1919, when Eugene Mitchell's son, Stephens, joined the firm in a partnership that lasted until the senior Mitchell's death in 1944.

For a young lawyer trying to make his way, times were especially hard in the South between 1886 and the great depression of the 1890s. This complicated life further for the sons of Confederate heroes. While the fathers preempted the fields of military and political heroics, the economy limited their fortunes, too. Like his Grandfather Mitchell—and in contrast to so many of the other forebears he chronicled—Eugene Mitchell claimed to have "no gift for making money." Stephens Mitchell related that the depression of 1893 destroyed his father's daring. Afterward, the son insisted, Mitchell sought only "a competence" and forfeited the dream of wealth and fame.[20] Perhaps the hard times did harden his conservatism but the trait of deprivation already existed in his character. It was, thus, in flush times well before the panic hit that he wrote his prospective bride about his "poverty" and the necessity of devoting all his time and energy to work.[21]

Unlike his father, who lost and gained money without a backward glance, Eugene Mitchell constantly fretted about cash, minimized his capital, and exaggerated his debts. He dwelt constantly on the theme of his ancestors, like Anthony Sweet or his own father, being "mighty businessmen"; these characters measured his own inadequacies.

What in his youth made him scrappy and contentious made him tight, suspicious, and withdrawn as an adult. Among those who knew him as a man, Eugene Mitchell left an invariable impression. Inflexibly conservative, severely decorous, socially reactionary, and relentlessly proper, the picture of the narrow legalist dominated every impression of him. In his family memoir, Stephens Mitchell recollected his father as "intensely reserved," painfully shy, humorless, and devoid of imagination. One younger colleague remembered most Mr. Mitchell's extreme reserve and decorousness.[22] Among Margaret Mitchell's childhood friends, one called Eugene Mitchell "the perfect Southern gentleman,"[23] while another, rather more irreverently, considered him stiff and impersonal, somewhat intimidating, and a humorless "stick-in-the-mud."[24] Eugene Mitchell found his solace in the punctilio of his profession, the solemnity of his study, the rigidity of manners, the arch-propriety of regional high culture, and the conventions of Victorian privacy and domesticity. Not least, he found his supreme comfort in Mary Isabel Stephens—"May Belle" from her infancy—the woman who on that splendid evening in the fall of 1892 became his bride.

No less than the Mitchells—even more, perhaps—the Stephenses and their allied kin were the stuff of legend.[25] They always stood apart. Most critically, their religion separated them from their fellow Southerners. Their Catholicism had brought them to Calvert's Maryland in the seventeenth century, and they persisted in their faith in the new nation. They maintained their own communities and communion even when they left Maryland. The McGhanns, for example, trekked southward down the frontier from the Chesapeake with their Protestant neighbors, but they settled and intermarried with fellow Catholics along the way. By the early nineteenth century, they had established themselves in a small community in the heart of the new cotton lands at Taliaferro County, Georgia. Visited occasionally by traveling priests, they kept the faith in the interval in part through the "classical" school they founded there. While sustaining their separate religious identity, this institution also provided a second source of distinction—their commitment to learning and knowledge. Indeed, this provided a bridge to even the most committed local Protestants, who found few comparable schools elsewhere in the social order.[26]

In addition to religion and education, immigrant and ethnic status also distinguished Margaret Mitchell's maternal ancestry. Twice in the nineteenth century, in successive generations before the Civil War, sons of Eire married into Mitchell's Anglo-American Catholic line.[27] These unions revitalized the family's commitment to the mother church and the old faith, but Phillip Fitzgerald in the 1820s and John Stephens in the Civil War era brought with them a vigorous ethnic identity, and their Irishness added a new source of peculiarity to the family legacy. It set them apart from the Southern norm, but it also exaggerated the family's clannish self-consciousness, sense of its own distinction, and the feeling of being at odds with the world. These two Irishmen helped shape the most fundamental stuff of Margaret Mitchell's imagination.

Phillip Fitzgerald was born in Tipperary in 1798; soon after his birth, however, his family fled the island in the wake of the aborted uprising of 1798. The boy grew up in France, and he never professed any sentimental attachment to the "auld sod" at all. "He was glad to be done with it, and that was that," one of his daughters remembered.[28] By his early twenties, he departed for America. Landing first in Charleston, South Carolina, he joined older siblings who had migrated before him. By 1831 he made his way into the backcountry and settled in the village of Fayetteville, the seat of Fayette County, deep in the Georgia interior. In the mid-1830s, Phillip Fitzgerald abandoned the village and trade for the country and cotton. He relocated one more time, to the still-more-interior Clayton County, where he settled permanently on a parcel not far from the village of Jonesboro.

In his migrations in the Southern interior, Phillip Fitzgerald had discovered the isolated settlement of Catholics at Locust Grove in Taliaferro County, Georgia; and in 1837, aged nearly forty, he married one of its daughters, Eleanor McGhann. Born in 1818, she was twenty years his junior when she returned with him to his new home. The couple produced an extraordinary progeny of seven girls without a single son surviving infancy. The phenomenon took on quality of a legend. All these girl children were a curse that Phillip Fitzgerald's acquisitiveness had incurred, or so ran the story:

> In the course of his land buying, Phillip became the owner of two parcels with a desirable farm lying between them. This last was to everyone's mind the ideal site on which to build the plantation house. The owner of the farm was a poor man, and unlucky. Several successive years of poor crops took all he had and brought in the sheriff. The farm was sold at auction and Phillip bought it in. The woman whose home it had been stood by, her children around her. She looked at Phillip and her eyes were as hard as his: "You'll never raise a man child on this land," she said, and spat. Phillip and Eleanor never did. They enlarged and improved the old house and they filled it with daughters.[29]

Cursed with girls or not, Fitzgerald prospered in the tremendous cotton boom before the Civil War. By 1854, he owned over 3,000 acres of land and thirty-five slaves at his large farm, which the family called Rural Home.

Compared with the great plantations in the richest areas of the coast and the Piedmont, the Fitzgerald holdings looked like small potatoes. The mere existence of such an estate in this particular area, however, makes Phillip Fitzgerald all the more notable. This was not plantation country. In this period, Clayton County lay on the farthest frontier of cotton, slave, and plantation culture. Small-scale subsistence farming dominated the local economy, and the family story about the cracker's curse preserved the vestiges of yeoman resentment against the planter class that existed even before the Civil War. It flowered into open rebellion in the populist revolt afterward. The Irishman played his part in that conflict, too.

Phillip Fitzgerald survived the death of slavery to build a new fortune after Appomattox. His ambition now clashed even more directly with his neighbors' politics. As cotton culture, railroads, and all the other agencies of an international economy finally smashed the old ways of the small independent farmers, Phillip Fitzgerald helped lead the charge, despite his age. Family lore recorded one version of the conflict. The tale also offers evidence of the interplay between Mitchell's family and the quintessential young New South politico from Atlanta, Hoke Smith. Smith represented the regular Democrats, and appeared in Clayton and Fayette against the agrarians, who far outnumbered the regulars. He spoke to a clearly hostile audience, and the "drunken toughs," in the family's recollection, confronted Smith with drawn pistols. Old Phillip Fitzgerald saved the day. Although close to eighty then, the tiny old man "climbed up the front of the platform like a monkey, drew a Bowie knife from his boot and said coldly, 'I'll cut out the heart of anyone who touches this young man.' No one had the courage to tackle him, so Phillip remained seated on the platform, his legs dangling, his knife in his hand, while the nervous young Hoke Smith continued his speech."[30]

In his ambition, enterprise, intelligence, Irish heritage, puritanical Catholicism, and devotion to the Southern way of life, Phillip Fitzgerald seems unique in the regional tradition, but one of his daughters discovered a husband who very nearly duplicated all these characteristics. John Stephens made his own powerful, primary impact upon his family, but he also reinforced his father-in-law's intellectual and cultural legacies.[31]

Born near Parsonstown (now Birr), in King's County in 1833 to Catholic gentry, John Stephens grew up in Ireland, but, like Phillip Fitzgerald, he left Europe as a young man and joined an older brother in Georgia who ran a store in Augusta. Shortly afterward, he moved to Tennessee, where in 1856 he completed a bachelor's degree at Hiawassee College. He remained in the Volunteer State four more years, after President James Buchanan appointed this fiercely committed Democrat postmaster of Morganton, Tennessee. With the secession crisis he returned to his family in Augusta and, with the outbreak of the war, joined the Ninth Georgia Infantry. Rising to the rank of captain, he spent much of the war in or near Atlanta in the Quartermaster Corps. He remained there after Appomattox, too.

No less than R. C. Mitchell, this Ireland-born Confederate thrived during Reconstruction. "As John Stephens knew how to keep books and there were few men of the type known today as 'certified public accountants,'" wrote his granddaughter, "he did not face the problem of many ex-Confederates with no training for anything except cotton farming with slave labor. He made $200 a month, in gold."[32] While Phillip Fitzgerald had made his way with the help of siblings, John Stephens had no kin in Atlanta; but in a pattern typical of enterprising immigrants, he formed partnerships with other Irishmen, John Flynn, for example, in the hardware and grocery business. With his stake established, he branched into the standard sources of Atlanta wealth after the war: building, land speculation, and property development. He was one of the prime movers behind the growth of Atlanta's east side, where he resided most of his life. He built numerous rental units on his properties and also founded, after the fashion of the times, a trolley company to serve the area and encourage its population. Lines of the Gate City Railway Company ran all the way along Jackson Street to Ponce de Leon Springs, which, with such other notable Atlanta capitalists as W. D. Grant, Captain Stephens also helped develop. By the 1880s he was rich indeed. And like his father-in-law before him, he also turned his wealth to public service (and vice versa) when, in acknowledgment of the heavily Irish population of the police force, this wealthy son of Eire served six terms on the very important Atlanta Police Commission.[33]

Like Phillip Fitzerald, Stephens devoted himself passionately to books, learning, and intellectual culture. He fully shared the nineteenth century's commitment to education as the key to human potential and happiness.[34] He combined all these qualities with powerful and essentially puritanical religious convictions. Indeed, the pious rationality and systematic thought of St. Thomas Aquinas offer the key to his temper and to the ideas he pressed upon his family. As puritanical and humorless as his father-in-law, John Stephens was even touchier and more sensitive to slights.[35] In this, he also resembled his future son-in-law. He stood no taller than Eugene Mitchell, either. He proved as stubborn and inflexible as the younger man as well, even in his own family circle. One of his nephews recalled his fierce personality years later. Clarence Stephens Durham considered his Uncle John "a very prompt and stern man—to use your Grand Mother's words—the hardest-headed man she ever saw," he wrote to Margaret Mitchell a half-century after his youth.[36]

Clarence Durham's remarks about his uncle John offer a nice introduction to the Captain's still-more-formidable spouse. Annie Fitzgerald Stephens had no problem in complaining to the world about her stubborn husband; indeed, she had few problems about complaining about anyone and anything. A headstrong daughter, a formidable wife, and a fearsome mother, she imprinted her character and values on her family as indelibly as her men did. As she lived until 1934—many of these years in the Mitchell household—Annie Stephens affected her granddaughter's life both directly and indirectly, through her influence on May Belle Mitchell. She was a hellion from birth.

Born on December 22, 1844, Annie Fitzgerald fell in the middle of the covey of Fitzgerald daughters. None exceeded her will, determination, and fierceness. She alone of this brood, for example, refused the others' cloistered education, her grandson Stephens Mitchell related:

> She had stubbornly refused to accept the advantages given her sisters who had gone to Charleston convents for their education. Phillip Fitzgerald might work harder than all his thirty-five slaves to make his plantation prosper, but he insisted that his seven daughters should be convent-reared in the French way. One by one they left the plantation for Charleston. All but Annie Elizabeth, Grandmother. She made up for this later by sending her daughters to school in Canada. All but Mother, who stood out for an American education.[37]

She challenged the invading Yankee armies with the same fury that fueled her adolescent rejection of convent school. As a Confederate refugee in Reconstruction Macon, for example, she decided she needed protection, one family story ran, from drunk Yankees, loose freedmen, and vagrant Confederates. She not only "walked through the whole Yankee army to get to the Federal general's tent," she actually won around-the-clock protection for her home—and secured Yankee rations in the process.[38]

Unlike her men, she cared little for literature and writing. Only one letter in her hand survives. At the same time, her energy, ego, and determination matched or even exceeded theirs. She was contentious, aggressive, domineering, and outspoken. Family stories recounted numerous examples of her explosive temper and iron will. The memory of her nephew Clarence Durham suggests she was a harridan in the house; Stephens Mitchell's memoir delineates the same traits:

> Certainly there was nothing sentimental about Grandmother Stephens. Short, blond, plump as long as I knew her, she had the quick, authoritative step, the high held head and flat back of a Major General. Determination was in the set of her lips and jaw, arrogance in the curve of her nostrils and shrewd intelligence in the flash of her blue eyes. Temper was there too. . . .[39]

Annie Stephens kept the city of Atlanta waiting on her whims. When her husband was a major stockholder in the Gate City Railway Company, she always instructed a child to hold the car when she had not completed her toilette. "The car would wait, and the passengers with what patience they could command until Grandmother bustled down the path and shoed her spick and span brood aboard." She refused to alter her habits when her husband lost the line. "I can still remember her sending out the cook with orders to hold the car while she finished dressing, and how violently enraged she was when the motorman paid no heed to her command, and his car rattled derisively by. . . ." She filled her house with her oaths of rage and vengeance, Stephens Mitchell recounted.[40]

Property obsessed her. She never surrendered her interest in her father's country property, and from her newlywed days to her death in the Great Depression, she forayed regularly to the farm to tend the crops and boss the tenants.[41] She did the same with her urban properties as well. As her husband's health and fortune declined, hers rose. Trying to corner the cotton market in the Panic of 1893, John Stephens had lost heavily in the depression that followed. His health suffered, too. He died three years later. His wife thrived in picking up the pieces and expanding what was left. Her grandson recalled that, even after

John Stephens lost his trolley company, Annie Stephens retained one of the old streetcar nags, and she relished hitching the horse to a carriage to "drive around town to keep an eye on Grandfather's properties and to collect the rents."[42]

One would not have wished to be her tenant. She drove everyone. She also thrived on litigation, and the Fulton County Courthouse records still memorialize her numerous suits, many against her own children.[43] One of her grandsons recalled still grander suits fought through the federal courts after the Civil War, arising out of her desires for compensation for damages sustained in that conflict.[44] She harried her own family as relentlessly as she pushed her renters. One story, perhaps apocryphal, goes that after her maiden sister's death, she hired men to haul out the family heirlooms from Rural Home while everyone else was at the graveside.[45] According to her grandson Stephens Crockett, she also broke her father's will in her own favor. He had supposedly stipulated that his plantation was to be a permanent refuge for all the family who were in distress. After her husband's death, Annie Stephens determined that she fit the category and fought successfully for a grander share of Phillip Fitzgerald's estate. All this culminated in the bitterest wrangles, exclusions from wills, and even coffin removals and disinterments.[46] Her honor was as touchy as her husband's, and she made it a point to repay slights she perceived from any quarter. Thus, one legend ran, when the city's greatest dowager, Mrs. William Lawson Peel, staged a great reception at the D.A.R. Hall, Annie Stephens showed up in her gardening gloves, as an insult to match some earlier one she felt she had received from Mrs. Peel.[47]

The puritanical John Stephens wed this virago in Atlanta in 1863, and she survived Sherman's Georgia campaign in the city. After the war, the couple established themselves in a large brick tree-shaded mansion that dominated the northwest corner of the intersection at Jackson and Forrest streets on the east side of the city; the Mitchell property lay less than two blocks away. As the Captain's fortunes waxed during Reconstruction, they moved. Jackson Street was graded to the hill's crest at about 1879, and about this time the Stephenses bought the huge old house that crowned the ridge's summit. They remodeled it with all the finery of high Victorian style, and by 1882 they moved in.[48] At these two places, chiefly, the couple produced twelve children, six of whom survived to adulthood. The first arrived in 1864, while the city endured the worst of the Civil War. Unlike the fictional Beau Wilkes, however, Phillip Stephens, named for his maternal grandfather, did not live out the year, nor did his brother who followed him in 1865. Four more daughters arrived before Mary Isabel, the author's mother, was born in 1872, but these four also died before maturity. Five more children followed: John, Eugenia, Edythe, Alexander, and Ruth.

While Annie Stephens produced offspring with the ease of a brood mare, she lacked all nurturing instincts, by all accounts. She won, indeed, a legendary reputation as a wretched parent. With all these children tugging on her skirts in any case, she failed the opportunity to inculcate the graces in her children, her granddaughter wrote long afterward. Regularly she imported her two maiden sisters from the countryside to manage the children. And when "Mamie" and "Sis" returned to Rural Home, she just as regularly shipped her offspring out to them. This circumstance applied especially to Mary Isabel, the sickly third surviving Stephens child, who required far more physical attention than her parent could ever give, even had she made nurturing a virtue.[49]

For the first ten years of her life, May Belle Stephens spent almost as much time with her grandparents and spinster aunts at Rural Home as she did with her mother and father in Atlanta. She thrived there. The Fitzgeralds adored her quite as much as she loved them. Phillip Fitzgerald softened to this one grandchild. As a grown woman, she fondly recalled the old man's affection. She was only four when he taught her to read.[50] The unmarried aunts also proved willing tutors. Devoutly Catholic in a land of Protestants, Sarah Fitzgerald, in particular—"Aunt Sis," to generations of nieces and nephews—inculcated her faith in this special child. She also introduced May Belle to the classics, music, and painting; and not least of all, she instructed her in "gentleness of demeanor, dignity of carriage, kindness of heart and gaity of temper."[51] This Sarah Fitzgerald, like her mother, Eleanor McGhann (of the native-born Catholic branch of the family)—and indeed, like May Belle herself—possessed a special "gift of laughter," a singular trait among these generally somber folk.[52]

While the children's visits to Rural Home stretched into weeks or sometimes months, Annie Stephens also planned still lengthier separations. While she herself had little affinity for school, she, like her father, insisted on a convent education for her girls, at least the oldest batch. As they reached their teens, she packed her three eldest surviving daughters off to convent school in Canada. At thirteen, May Belle joined her sisters at Villa Maria Seminary in Bellevue, Quebec. During a two-year interlude in Canada, the girl corresponded regularly with her family, and these letters allow a rare glimpse into her character and the dynamics of the interfamily relations that shaped the personality of the most important figure in Margaret Mitchell's life.

Even as a thirteen-year old, the child stamped a clear personality on all she wrote. Intelligence dominates her missives, and this virtue confirms both her father's notions of the girl as well as the chief impression she made in maturity. "You are blessed with intellectual gifts," her parent told her over and over.[53] "You are interesting because you are bright." He praised her sharp, analytical intelligence, her ability to see the point of any argument, and her skill at expressing ideas clearly. "An interesting talker," too, he added.[54] She lived in the world of ideas and books, and literary and historical allusions crowd her letters. She wrote unselfconsciously of the lessons she gleaned from Madame de Stael and poetry. She especially delighted in the Irish balladeers like Thomas More. Considering herself thoroughly Irish, May Belle repeated how she shared "the story of Robert Emmet, of Tara and the Bards" with her schoolmates. She feared she might have bored her friends with her renditions of Irish literature and history, but she could not control her enthusiasm over "my Father's and my Grandfather's country—the country of a Burke, a Curran, and of an Emmet."[55]

While the girl (like her father) alluded to her ability to charm others with her talk,[56] seriousness and sobriety mark these letters themselves. She wrote gravely of morality, duty, and obligation. Intent on moral reform, she determined to turn over a new leaf, she insisted to her father, "on which I will record nothing but what is good. This I do for your and Mamma's sake."[57] Even winning the academic palm of honor provoked her sense of loss and burden. "I have never been perfectly happy but twice in my life," she told her father afterward. "I always feel a longing for something that I have not—I describe it as a vacuum and if I expect too much from anything, I am sure to be disappointed, then I feel it more than ever." She resolved, she said, "to become a Stoic, heedless of joy or sorrow," but she stopped herself: "This kind of reasoning is not suitable for a girl of thirteen. I know it and try not to think of such things but I can control all my other faculties better than my thoughts."[58]

She came honestly, of course, by her sober morality. Her father constantly admonished her along the same lines. "We should only learn what is good, think only of what is pure and proper," he told her.[59] He advised bookish consolation for her moral and intellectual anguish. Read those books that edify the mind and elevate the spirit, he instructed. In the same vein, he disdained light, escapist reading. "You can read History, Philosophy, too. Do not waste your time in those little Novels—even if Catholic—," he added, "Ask Mother Superior to let you have access to Standard works. Say that I desire it."[60]

To an extraordinary degree, John Stephens treated this child as an intellectual equal. He traded ideas on literature, poetry, and music with her and recommended business and science courses to expand her mind. "I want you to understand business principles for yourself," he insisted.[61] He shared his political ideology with her and assumed her thoughtful response. Just before her return to Atlanta, he expressed the fear that she had absorbed snobbish ideas from her French friends. He reminded the fifteen-year-old then of "our simple Republican way of living. You used as a child to admire the views of Thomas Jefferson. You know he said that all were free and equal . . . hence on your return you must be a good Democrat."[62] He laid still other political obligations upon the girl. In admonitions she would echo to her own offspring, he also demanded from her bravery, courage, daring, and forthrightness. Over and over he instructed her "never submit to injustice without a protest." Only "slaves and sycophants" submit. Fight "with your whole force," he demanded; "to do otherwise would be an outrage on morals and conscience."[63]

John Stephens's advice created dilemmas for his daughter, if not himself. In all his counsel about courage, resistance, and honor, he had drawn no gender distinctions. On the contrary, his admonitions actually held out a model of otherwise male virtues for the girl. At the same time, such advice confounded Stephens's Southern, Victorian, and Catholic notions of sex, gender, and the sphere of true womanhood. He wanted it both ways. The contradiction surfaced as she prepared to come home. He fondly anticipated her expanded intellectual potential, but he added that he hoped she remained "a little girl in feeling."[64]

The sentiment was ominous. The paradox emerged directly in another letter as he lectured her on the relationship of women and politics. For all his insistence on resistance, courage and honor, he utterly repudiated extending to women the franchise and denied their participation in the political order. He argued that they should understand politics and government systems; they should even help shape them. They must never, never sully themselves, however, by actually voting, canvassing, or running for office. Woman's purity alone kept society on its course; maintaining her place in the home must be the unchanging standard in a chaotic world. "Woman is Guardian Angel of the home," he told her; the sailor's "Polar Star." If that star went "sloshing around," he fulminated, how could the mariner steer his course? The contradiction went further. Men and women occupied different spheres and had entirely different roles to play in life, he instructed her; and he quoted scripture to prove this scheme was ordained of God "for the happiness of each and the good of the whole." At the same time, he insisted that she must appreciate and honor her part through free intellectual inquiry. "I want you to have a broad mind, to understand the position which each Sex 'Should, Could or Might' fill, and then from Conviction drop into the true Sphere of Womanhood." With all innocence, he thus posed the most debilitating dilemma for his own most precious treasure.[65]

May Belle Stephens and her family had calculated on her spending three years at Villa Maria. Her two more pliable older sisters completed this course. When they graduated in 1887, however, and she faced the prospect of staying in Canada by herself, she balked. Family tradition had it that she rejected both sequestered education and foreign training on ideological grounds; against her mother's wishes, in any case, she carried the day for returning to Atlanta and completing a secular education. She returned to Georgia in 1887 and completed her schooling at the Atlanta Female Institute, with honors. At this point she disappears from the literary record. She reappears again, but only in shadow form, between 1890 and 1892, in letters written by her devoted suitor and future husband, Eugene Mitchell. His letters survive; hers do not.

For all his devotion, her lover's ardent correspondence fails generally to reveal specifics about his beloved. From his references it is obvious that she read constantly, attended church regularly, and comported herself as might be expected from any member of late–nineteenth century polite society in Atlanta. She attended rounds of parties and social engagements and spent long vacations at popular resorts in the mountains of North and South Carolina. It was on such trips, indeed, that she received Eugene's romantic letters.

Eugene Mitchell seldom addressed himself to concrete issues she might have raised in her letters. Once he reacted against her self-assessment that she was too intellectual or rational—"too lacking in feeling." Judging from their differences about long engagements and more generally from Eugene's pleas for "a little romance" in their relationship, she does, indeed, seem even more detached than he. In the same way, certain of his responses suggest she acknowledged much more objectivity than her lover their differences in religion and temperament, and that perhaps she doubted the ability of love to conquer all. If such responses suggest a more general pattern of detachment and objectivity, they only confirm the qualities that permeate her childhood correspondence with her father.

One other element emerges from Eugene Mitchell's correspondence with his eighteen-year-old bride-to-be that had the greatest consequences for him, for her, and for her image for her children. Literally, he idolized her. The young lawyer did not invent the Lady on the Pedestal, but the icon served particularly well special circumstances in his character. If his own mother proved physically unable to supply the nurture he required or the proper refuge from a lordly father, he doubled all his desires and needs and fastened his hopes for their fulfillment upon his own lady. High Victorian culture and peculiar regional values bolstered this inclination. The Stephenses' daughter may or may not have been a saintly cynosure of virtue, as her young man constantly insisted, but, seeing her this way, Eugene Mitchell helped guarantee the image. In one letter, the young man compared himself to the hero of Thomas Carlyle's *Sartor Resartus*. Teufelsdröckh had felt imprisoned in the iron processes of a material universe. Without faith or religion, he despaired. Even so, his lady, Blumine, and her love had liberated and uplifted him. "Did not her presence bring with it airs from heaven? . . . Pale doubt fled away to the distance; Life bloomed-up with happiness and hope," Carlyle wrote about his hero. "The past, then, was all a haggard dream; he had been in the Garden of Eden, then, and could not discern it! But lo, now, the black walls of his prison melt away, the captive is alive, is free."[66]

As for Teufelsdröckh, so for the restless, anxious young agnostic Southern lawyer, Eugene Mitchell. May Belle Stephens became Blumine. She liberated him. His heart's door had been locked; "you found the key," he told her.[67]

More immediately and tangibly, May Belle Stephens also provided another form of liberation for the young man. She was both the end and means of his breaking away from his domineering father and asserting his independence within the patriarchal system. His father "bitterly opposed" his marrying, he told her:

> He believes (I judge) that I should remain single and devote myself to my younger brothers and sisters. He has as much told me that if I choose to get married I need not look to him for help. My father might be called rich (for this city) and though his family is large, he could leave all his children in good circumstances. But I feel reasonably certain that it will be only at his death that I will receive any share in his estate. I must look to myself and above for my fortune.

And he closed: "For you I would disobey my father."[68] And so he did on that brilliant November evening in 1892.

Eugene Mitchell's early devotion never waivered. Later letters brimmed with the same affection and sentiment. His own life bears stronger witness to his adoration and dependency. When he was fifty-three and she forty-seven, the influenza epidemic deprived him of his Blumine. Something went out of him forever. A score of years later the thought of her death still tempered his happiness: "I am blessed now and have been for many years blessed with everything a man's heart should desire except the companionship of May Belle who died 22 years ago," he wrote a cousin. "But Margaret is so much like her," he concluded, "that it lightens the loss."[69] His comparison proved both threat and challenge to his only daughter.

II

Jimmy

The day seldom passed that the young lady who accompanied us didn't turn her horse and race for home. She realized, even if I didn't, that the company of quarrelsome old gentlemen was no place for a lady. . . . At the age of six, I was not concerned about being a lady.[1]

MARGARET MITCHELL

*T*he bride was twenty, the groom twenty-six when they returned from their wedding trip to the West. A baby arrived the next year. Named after his paternal grandfather, he lived only a few months. The infant's death coincided with the severe economic depression that struck in 1893 and John Stephens's death three years later. These were hard times. Things brightened slowly. In 1896, the same year as Captain Stephens's death, May Belle and Eugene Mitchell produced a healthy baby, Alexander Stephens Mitchell, named to honor both Mrs. Mitchell's family and a Georgia lion of the Confederacy, Alexander H. Stephens, a special hero of the Mitchell family. Four years later, the couple had a final child, Margaret Munnerlyn, named for her Mitchell grandmother and a Sweet great-great-grandmother. She arrived propitiously on her parents' eighth anniversary, and on another presidential election day as well.

The young couple spent the first decade of their marriage in the large cottage at 296 Cain Street. The house lay about 200 feet east of Jackson Street almost at the Stephenses' back door. This was only one of several rental houses on the huge lot bounded by Cain on the south, Jackson to the west, and Highland on the north. On the north end of the block, for example, stood two large houses that Captain Stephens had built around 1890. In 1902, the Mitchells moved into the northernmost of these. The next year, they purchased the house next door, and by the summer of 1903 the family took up residence in their own home at 179 Jackson Street. Margaret Mitchell grew up here.

The big house sat well above the street on a stone-walled embankment above the sidewalk. Jackson Street dropped sharply away on the north and continued a very steep rise to the south towards the hill's crest, dominated by Annie Stephens's Gothic mansion. Although much more modest and restrained than most of the other dwellings on the street—John Slaton's place up the block, the Lewises' directly across Jackson Street, or the Stephens place itself—the Mitchells' house still boasted a Victorian profusion of ornament. With thirteen rooms, it stood three stories tall with a steep, gabled roof surmounted with a still higher square tower. Long and narrow, its short side fronted Jackson, and a generous porch dominated the entrance and south sides. To please his wife, Eugene Mitchell ordered the place painted bright red with yellow trim. May Belle Mitchell kept an equally colorful garden. While she trained honeysuckle to twine all about the porch to make a natural arbor, she cultivated beds of fragrant roses and brilliant red-orange canna lilies in the yard and lined the neat brick walks around the house with violets and other spring and summer flowers.[2]

The Mitchell's youngest child was only two and a half when the family settled in at 179 Jackson Street. Not long after, she survived the first of a series of accidents that plagued her throughout her life. Mrs. Mitchell had left the children alone in Stephens's care. While her brother read, Margaret played with her cat, Piedy. Too near the fireplace's open grate, her skirt caught fire. Her screams brought Stephens flying. He beat out the flames with difficulty, but neither child was hurt. The episode terrified them both, though neither, Stephens added, was "so frightened as Mother when she returned." Once over the shock of the charred petticoats, the children's tears, and her own emotions, May Belle Mitchell had a characteristically unconventional response. "That day," the older brother wrote afterward, "all Margaret's pretty dresses were put away except for special occasions. From that time until she started to school Margaret dressed in boy's pants and shirt." To cap the image off, literally, she tucked her blonde hair into a tweed cap when she went out. Thus attired, she made a great impression on the neighborhood. Dressed as a boy, she acquired a male identity. Thus neighbors came to call her "Jimmy," after her fancied resemblance to a lad in a newspaper cartoon in the *Journal*. "Though she was small and exquisitely made, she was really a sturdy child," Stephens testified, "and the boy's clothes suited her."[3]

The costume is as appropriate as it is biographically significant. The little girl delighted in competitive play, and her Jimmy persona meshed nicely with the athleticism and rough-and-tumble sporting sense that dominated her preschool years. Jackson Hill provided the perfect field for the child's energies.

When the Mitchells moved to 179 Jackson Street, nothing separated their yard from the oak-dotted property of the Captain's widow. By 1906, or so, Mrs. Stephens put up another house between the two, which she provided for still another daughter, Ruth; her husband, David T. Crockett; and their two boys, Stephens and David; but even this dwelling failed to alter perceptibly the spaciousness of the block itself. The Stephens property line lay two hundred feet behind Jackson, and this huge block allowed the children a free play zone. In addition, little development had disturbed the back half of the city block towards Boulevard, another 200 feet in the rear. Over forty years before, this crest had boasted the city's inner defenses against the Federal armies; on this site now, the neighborhood children staged their own war games. Here they pitched a "pavillion-type tent" that made "a splendid general's headquarters," Stephens Mitchell recalled, and a jumble of abandoned pine girders made a still more heroic fort.[4] They loved to dig, and Stephens remembered that "if Grandma didn't interfere too much," the children could "build tunnels and castles and even throw up a set of breastworks" themselves for their military games.[5] The Crockett boys also remembered the prizes that their female cousin buried on the property and the Gold Bug–like treasure maps she drew for them.[6]

This huge lot also provided the space for pick-up ball games. Mitchell first made her reputation as a baseball player here, and her family preserved wonderful pictures of her play in the middle of the action. In her short gingham skirt and long hair braided on top of her head, she pals with her two younger cousins, David and Stephens Crockett, in one photograph and in another tags one of the boys out at first base. Still later, tennis courts went up, and she learned a new sport.

On Jackson Street, the girl also established a notable reputation as an equestrian. Mrs. Mitchell insisted both children learn to ride, and soon after moving to the towered house on Jackson, they acquired "a small plains pony . . . the usual roan and white pied color," which was a source of Mrs. Mitchell's anxiety and irritation for years.[7]

By age six, she rode by herself. Every afternoon found her on her own, and she collected a motley crew of other horsemen on her rides. Among her troop she numbered a *beau age* belle and ancient cavalry veterans, one of whom looked and acted the part of a stage Confederate, complete with jimswinger coat, gray goatee, and the habit of "gallantly kissing the ladies' hands—even my own grubby six-year-old hand," Mitchell related as an adult. "Their families and my mother encouraged us to ride together in the belief that we'd keep each other out of mischief." No such luck. As the old boys got more and more wound up refighting old battles, their language became saltier and saltier. It finally sent the belle off in a fit of embarrassment, but the six-year-old jogged right along, unfazed; she relished every story and anecdote—and every oath and every profanity, too. She never lost her own love of swearing.[8]

The girl had other passions. She adored all animals and kept a regular menagerie. Besides horses and ponies in the stable out back, and a cow in the vacant field, the family zoo included dogs, ducks, turtles, and, at one time, even two alligators. She may or may not have played with dolls, but "an infinite variety of cats" allowed her every opportunity of playing house and mother.[9] Cat tales run through every account of her childhood, and afterward she recalled her "long suffering" mother's toleration of her pets. The animals thronged the house and yard and charmed her when all else failed. When teary at a portrait session, the three-year-old lit up when the photographer produced a tiny kitten. "On this occasion she was led to believe it was the cat's picture that was desired, not hers, and she was delighted to assist."[10] In the tall pine tree in the sideyard where she and Stephens had built a treehouse, she rigged up a wicker elevator for hauling Piedy's progeny up to her perch—much to the animals' annoyance, according to Stephens.[11] After Piedy died, Hypatia and Lowpatia joined the household. The latter won fame for a special trick: "Margaret taught him to stand up and salute with his right paw beside his ear. When he performed this in a proper military manner, he was rewarded by being fed cantaloup, his favorite delicacy."[12]

This pleasant childhood world was not free from horrors. In 1906, when she was five, she lived through one of the most violent race riots in regional history. White berserkers controlled Atlanta for three days at the disorder's height. The heavily black east side spawned some of the worst troubles as white gangs roamed the city searching for victims. With her mother spending the month at a sanatorium in the north, she was alone with her father, and Eugene Mitchell left a record of the affair that included his child's response to the disorder. When the rumor circulated that "negro mobs had been formed to burn the town, cut the water pipes, etc.," the Mitchell's neighbor John Slaton (who lived in the Victorian confection across the intersection from Annie Stephens) "went down the street warning every man to get his gun and be ready at a moment's warning." Without firearms, Eugene Mitchell stood guard with the only weapons he could find, his ax and an iron waterkey. As he guarded his family with these odd implements of destruction, his five-year-old daughter advised him "that Mr. Daley's sword might be a good thing. I adopted the suggestion," he reported with some small pride.[13] Twenty years later, Mitchell herself still vividly recalled her terror at the pop of guns and pistols late in

the night as the riot ran down. "They fought all day just a block behind our house," she related. The battle consisted of besieged Negroes,
police, and white rioters. "I also recall that no sight has ever been so
sweet to these eyes as when I crawled out from under the bed where I
had prudently taken refuge to see the milita tramp up Jackson Street
and camp on our lawn and the street."[14]

Even in her first six years, her world extended far beyond Atlanta's
Jackson Hill. In the summers, the mother and her children abandoned
the city's stifling heat for the cool mountain air of north Georgia or
the bracing sea breezes of Wrightsville Beach in North Carolina. The
child also traveled with her parents on pleasure trips to New York and
the North, and on at least one notable occasion in 1905 and probably
other times as well, she passed the summer with her mother at a health
sanatorium in New Jersey, where the both of them underwent "the
milk cure" to help the ailing mother's fragile health.

The most memorable and pleasurable experiences for the child outside of Atlanta, however, came in visits to the Fitzgerald homestead at
Rural Home, out in the country at Orr's Crossing in Clayton County.
With their niece Agnes Ransford, the maiden great-aunts, Sadie and
Mamie, kept up the place until their deaths in the 1920s. The Mitchell
children passed many summers there, and these vacations formed an
essential part of their memories. "We ran barefoot, rode the farm horses
and mules, picked fruit, and occasionally helped with the cotton picking," Stephens Mitchell recalled.

> After the mid-day dinner you rested in a shaded room, with a book if you
> could not sleep. Then you bathed and dressed fresh for supper. After-
> wards you played some more and then sat out on the porch and listened
> to the hoot owls and waited for the cool wind that would come at last
> out of the shaded wood lots. Then it would be time to go down to the
> well with a pan to fill with cold spring water in which to wash your feet
> before going to bed.[15]

The girl delighted in these days. Years later, reading Marjorie Kinnan Rawlings' *The Yearling* triggered anew her memories of these visits to the Southern countryside and running "wild in the woods" as a
child. Rawlings' novel evoked especially the sharp smells of one special childhood escapade:

> I remember especially the way the swampy bottoms of the Warrior River
> smelled and the steaming sweat on me and the colored boys when we
> crawled through the underbrush hunting wild hogs, and the river smell
> and the rotting vegetation and the sharp smell of a wild boar at far too
> close quarters.[16]

Wild-hog hunting with country black boys—this was high adventure!

At Rural Home, the children lived daily with history and tradition. The past imposed itself everywhere. The aunts were full of stories, and the land itself breathed legend. Kith and kin dominated every visit. Yet tradition hardly resided at the family's country seat alone. In the city, too, the bosom of the clan embraced, literally, multitudes. Family was everywhere. "On Jackson Hill we lived closely surrounded by grandparents, aunts, uncles, cousins of every degree and age, and hordes of visiting kinfolks," Stephens Mitchell testified.[17] Mitchell's hawkeyed Grandmother Stephens always lived just down the block or just around the corner. In 1904 the Mitchell grandparents also returned to Jackson Hill and brought with them their younger children, who, if aunts, were hardly older than Margaret and Stephens. Older siblings accompanied them, too, including her father's brother and law partner, Gordon Mitchell. By 1908, May Belle Mitchell's sister and her family had moved in next door and provided more kin and cousin-playmates. Mitchell's great-aunt, Isie, sister to Annie Stephens, also made her home on Jackson Hill with her numerous brood.

But all this barely scratches the surface of the Mitchell-Stephens clan connections. Eugene Mitchell had eleven brothers and sisters. All lived to adulthood. Five of them produced children of their own. Mrs. Mitchell also had eleven siblings, and five of these had children, too. These ten blood aunts and uncles produced more than a score of first cousins in Atlanta and environs for the Mitchell children.

There is more. As fairly typical Southerners of their generation (and later, too, in fact), the family did not distinguish much between aunts and uncles, or great-aunts and uncles, or between first and third or even fifth cousins. The tendency to include in this family web the non-blood collateral kin into which these people married expanded the familial pattern even more remarkably. Even failing to count the offspring of Eugene Mitchell's maternal line, the Sweets, who mostly remained in Florida, or most of John Stephens's siblings, whom the Irish diaspora scattered to the winds, Margaret Mitchell's family connections are simply incalculable.

While non-Southerners or even many modern Southerners might boggle at the custom, all these people knew where they fit in the most spidery family charts. They knew each other as real people, too, and made spaces for each other in their daily lives. Even those not kin might as well have been for everyone knew who everyone else was and where he or she belonged in the scheme of things for generations. Any one, if pressed, possessed at least sketchy knowledge—often more—of the grandparents or even great-grandparents of their friends. William Faulkner nicely caught the spirit of this broad notion of community and kinship in his *Absalom, Absalom!*. As Miss Rosa Coldfield retold the tale of the stranger Sutpen's first appearance in Jefferson, she also described the norm of the Southern social order:

> our father knew who his father was in Tennessee and who his grandfather had been in Virginia and our neighbors and the people we lived among knew that we knew and we knew they knew we knew and we knew that they would have believed us about whom and where he came from even if we had lied. . . .[18]

Put down on paper, as demonstrated in Eugene and Stephens Mitchell's often dry genealogies, the family history lacked power. In the oral tradition, however, it hummed with authority. Indeed, the primitive significance of all this kin network went hand-in-hand with the continuation of an equally primitive oral tradition. Together, family and oral tradition formed one of the South's most potent legacies for the freckle-faced girl on Jackson Hill.

Far into the twentieth century, Southern culture flourished in oral knowledge. With a high illiteracy rate, as in any premodern social order, regional society nurtured word of mouth as a standard means of communication. Preaching and political oratory spoke especially to people's needs. The forms of oral presentation also permeated written modes. Southerners instinctively minded assonance and alliteration; their words formed natural rhythms on the page; their language evoked senses prior to thought. The oral tradition served as both cause and effect of other values. Conservative in its nature, it stressed form, manner, and gesture over content: how one talked or told a tale was as important as the tale one told. Meanwhile, tales and stories remained critical means of conveying truth. The simplest facts came embedded in rich narrative, complete with elaborate dialogue.

In such a society, the disciplined memory assumed the most critical importance. Those with the best and most memories possessed the greatest power. In this regard, it is no accident that Margaret Mitchell and her family stressed good memory as a special characteristic of their clan. They considered it a genetic trait. Margaret Mitchell prided herself on her own phenomenal power of recollection. The old folks, with the most recollections, were preeminent. "What memories they had!" Stephens mused.

> Let two or three of them get together on the porch in an evening, and to the creak of the rocking chairs and the gentle swish of their palmetto fans they would reminisce. One of them had only to ask, "What ever happened to Cousin Lula May?" for another to break in, "Do you remember the time she. . . ." And there would follow a story. One story invariably suggested another.[19]

The tales were everywhere.

The power of the oral tradition certainly existed prior to 1861, but the Civil War greatly exaggerated this impulse towards a story-told reality and a literal "legendary truth" in the postbellum world. Like the Trojan Wars, the "War for Southern Independence" provided an epic source and object that focused and concentrated the narrative and oral impulse of the South. Margaret Mitchell provided a glimpse of this alternative, narrative reality when she half-joked that she was ten before she realized the South had lost the war, or when she related that she thought it all had happened just before her birth. The oral tradition collapses time. She learned the Civil War in her cradle, she wrote. "I heard so much when I was little about the fighting and the hard times after the war that I firmly believed Mother and Father had been through it all instead of being born long afterward. . . ."[20]

And then there were the Sunday calls.

> When we went calling on the older generation of relatives, those who had been active in the sixties, I sat on the bony knees of veterans and the fat slippery laps of great-aunts and heard them talk about the times when Little Alex [Confederate Vice-President Stephens] was visiting them and how much fried chicken Father Ryan could put away and how nice thick wrapping paper felt when put between the skin and the corset in the cold days during the blockade when woolen goods were so scarce. And how Granpa Mitchell walked nearly fifty miles after the battle of Sharpsburg with his skull cracked in two places from a bullet. They didn't talk of these happenings as history nor as remarkable events but just as a part of their lives and not especially epic parts. And they gradually became a part of my life.[21]

The oral sense of history made tradition immediate, bold, and timeless. The tangible, material presence of the past added further flesh to this palpable reality. The war was as real as the minie balls the children turned up at their Grandfather Mitchell's place or in the backlot where the Southern breastworks ran. It was as hard as the rows upon rows of white markers at Oakland cementery and as unyielding as the stone lion that guarded them. It was as close as a five-minute pony ride to the gullies and ravines just east of Jackson Hill where Sherman's troops had finally seized the railroad and sealed Atlanta's fate. The old ways lived. The ritual life of the city celebrated their power. Confederate Memorial Day ritualized tradition's authority in Atlanta. On April 26, the anniversary of the·final surrender of all Confederate armies, Atlanta reaffirmed its living links with history with parades and oratory. Everyone attended. Everyone knew each other, in truth, like family. With all the crowds and the pervasive sense of unity, Stephens Mitchell remembered, "it was like an ancient tribal gathering."

The crucial moment was the passing of the aged veterans with their timeworn battle flags:

> all of a sudden . . . you would hear a silence descend. And when you looked up, you saw this great mass of blood-red flags, held high with their white stars, and a long line of old men shuffling along. And nobody said a word, but tears just flowed down everybody's cheeks. That was your nation that you were crying over, and you knew it. . . . This was still conquered territory, and you could feel it. And it never would get out of your bones.

"The city was a Confederate town," he said in truth; "that was its history."[22]

Through such ritual enactments and in the telling and retelling of old tales, a tribal past imposed its hegemony over the present. The process made it ever new. Old R. C. Mitchell's wounded flesh ran red again, and Annie Fitzgerald stepped anew amid the Yankee hordes in Macon during Reconstruction. In constantly rehashing skirmishes and battles, aged veterans made "might-have-beens" "might-be's." Willy-nilly, the children absorbed the lore.

What did it mean to grow up amid this omnipresent past of aging flesh and blood? William Faulkner, born in 1897, again captured some of the spirit in *Absalom, Absalom!* as Quentin Compson mused upon his state:

> he would seem to listen to two separate Quentins now—the Quentin Compson preparing for Harvard in the South, the deep South dead since 1865 and peopled with garrulous outraged baffled ghosts, listening, having to listen, to one of the ghosts which had refused to lie still even longer than most had, telling him about old ghost-times; and the Quentin Compson who was still too young to deserve yet to be a ghost, but nevertheless having to be one for all that, since he was born and bred in the deep South the same as she was—the two separate Quentins now talking to one another in the long silence of notpeople, in notlanguage. . . .[23]

As an adult, Margaret Mitchell reflected that "the old days" seemed more real to her than her own,[24] and not unlike Faulkner's Quentin—or indeed, most members of her generation of Southerners—modernism wrestled with tradition for her spirit; two Margarets struggled for primacy in her own personality. If regional tradition, the Confederate war, and the legacy of Appomattox created one set of conflicts, circumstances of her own home and childhood exaggerated that battle and created new sets of conflicting loyalties within the child's character.

Stephens Mitchell once noted that he and his sister experienced a completely normal family life. He told the truth, but other truths lie within his observation, obscured by the curiosities of a peculiar, high-

Victorian Southern household. Family culture, gender roles, and mother–daughter relations in particular created special circumstances for the Mitchell girl.

When Margaret Mitchell recollected her childhood, her father figured in almost none of her memories. As a kind of classic late-Victorian gentleman, father, and husband, he defined his first role in life as the material provider for his family. His own economic insecurities exaggerated this inclination. He lived in a world of work and kept long hours at his office. Cultural commitments stole his time as well. Although Eugene Mitchell disliked the public world, he took seriously the obligations demanded of a man of his name, his class, and his status. As a very young man he had served on the county executive committee and joined the Young Men's Democratic league.[25] He also helped found, and accepted the honorific presidencies of the Atlanta and Georgia Bar Associations. If he took politics seriously, all this tested the limits of his political engagement. His appointment to the Atlanta School Board better illustrates his public commitments. The old family friend Hoke Smith had used the school board to launch a political career in the 1890s and to renew it again in 1904.[26] For Mitchell, it served as an end in itself.

His real commitments were less public and political than private and cultural. His work on behalf of Atlanta's libraries exemplifies most perfectly his efforts to integrate his essentially private values with public obligations. He helped found the Young Men's Library Association and headed the organization and managed its finances for many years. From 1899 to 1903, he served as trustee of the public library in Atlanta. More than any other single individual he helped secure Carnegie monies for that institution. His love of literature and books led him back to history, too. As chairman of the history committee of the Young Men's Library Association, he initiated the collection of books on Georgia and Atlanta history that became the basis of the Atlanta Public Library's Georgiana collection.[27] In much the same way, and operating under similar social and cultural influences, he co-founded the Atlanta Historical Society, led it as president, and edited its bulletin on local history. Although Mitchell did not become a legal scholar, he increasingly came to indulge his old passion for history as quasi-scholarship. He pursued his historical and genealogical researchers with the same kind of punctilio that characterized his law practice: he produced fact-heavy records of Atlanta's past and long chronicles of names and dates of his own family's history.[28]

Between his work and his public service, Eugene Mitchell was often away from home. When there, he regularly sequestered himself in his library. He loved his children, and he adored his only girl, but he expressed sympathy, affection, warmth, or humor rarely, if ever, towards his offspring. He appears as cool and formal in his children's recollections as he does in the memories of legal and business acquaintances. While his son described him as "intensely reserved," and almost genetically obstinate and suspicious, his daughter depicted him consistently as scholarly and dutiful, formal and aloof, "reserved and unenthusiastic."[29] She once called him "the most brilliant man I'll ever know,"[30] but generally she identified his intelligence with the precision, meticulousness, and fastidiousness associated with drawing up a proper contract. For all her admiration, however, Eugene Mitchell hung only on the periphery of his daughter's childhood. He figured in her imagination not at all. He could not have differed more in this regard from the role his wife played in shaping his children's character.

May Belle Mitchell dominated her household and her children's lives. She was a most extraordinary character in her own right, and glimpses into her personality as a child and young woman preview her impact on all those whose lives she touched as an adult. Everyone who ever knew her affirmed the same characteristics: her extraordinary intelligence, her personal charm, her Christian charity, her religious piety, her uncompromising morality, and her political enthusiasm. She was a completely remarkable woman.

Unlike her husband's, May Belle Stephens's education stopped when she finished high school, but her learning, intelligence, and erudition matched his. She was, by general consensus, "a woman of splendid education and brilliant qualities of mind," as her obituary described her.[31] She read very widely, including the high-culture journals of both the United States and Europe. She spoke French as fluently as English. She possessed a natural turn for science, and she particularly excelled in mathematics. Along with her reputation for intellectual brilliance, she won esteem for her rectitude. Long after her death, one of her kinsmen recalled her uncompromising morality. "You know, Maggie," the cousin quoted her, "I do not care much what Stephens and Margaret do as long as they are truthful—to me that means everything!"[32]

Eugene Mitchell regarded his lady as a cynosure of virtue, but in truth her sympathy and selflessness recognized few bounds. Even rumors of sickness or distress set her compassion in motion. When disaster really struck—as in the great Atlanta fire of 1917, she appeared, as always, dispensing aid, hope, and cheer as if she had no interests of her own.[33] When World War I erupted, she behaved similarily, making her home an open house for soldiers.[34] Her daughter recounted still other instances of her "insatiate giving."

> She was constantly taking up with strange people on street cars and trains and having exciting and animated arguments with them. She stopped the car at Five Points, if necessary, to call to old negroes who had worked for her or her family and held long, public conversations with them on their love lives and their miseries. She never turned any hungry or needy

person from her door and I've seen her peel off her gloves on cold days to put on the blue hands of poor children and only restrained [her] by my wails from giving her muff too. And lots of times, we walked home from town because she'd given her last cent and car fare to someone who needed it.[35]

One family legend went that such generosity cost her her life: when the influenza epidemic struck in 1918, she wore herself out nursing others, and in a weakened state her body could not resist that plague.[36]

May Belle Mitchell practiced public as well as private virtue. While her husband took up his public duties reluctantly, she thrived on these responsibilities. Through her leadership of Atlanta's Woman's Study Club, she established a model of intellectual life for women in the Georgia capital. She poured still greater energies into her religious activities. A devout Catholic, she led crusades both within and without the church. Steeped in theology and in good literature as well, she had no patience with weak sermons and doctrinal sloppiness; she criticized both at the Church of the Sacred Heart, which she had joined soon after its founding in 1897. Her "high handedness" alienated the clergy. She disregarded their objections. The church, she insisted, was big enough to use the talents of intelligent, committed women, whether or not this ran against the prejudices of the priesthood.[37]

She moved easily from these campaigns within the church to fighting the external enemies of her faith. A very self-conscious Catholic, she sprang immediately to the colors when Catholicism came under terrific fire in Georgia on the eve of World War I. By 1905, Thomas Watson of Thompson, Georgia, had assumed the role of a racist tyrant of Georgia Democratic politics. Demanding strict accountability on matters of race, he required another test of loyalty in his vicious campaigns against Jews and Catholics. The Watson-inspired "convent inspection act" finally galvanized Georgia Catholics to action. They launched a counterattack at May Belle Mitchell's parish church in August 1915. The following year they institutionalized their opposition as the "Catholic Laymen's Association." Even though prohibited from membership initially, because of her sex, Mrs. Mitchell helped charge the group. She left no record of her response when, three years after the initial meeting, in August 1918, the organization voted to open membership to women. The body had convened once again at Sacred Heart to reach this decision. She could not possibly have been a passive observer in this decision. As a fighter, a woman, and a faithful Catholic, in any case, the decision surely gratified her sense of justice.[38] "She believed in the role of the lay apologist," her son remembered, "and she, with those like her, made a bright chapter in the history of the church in Georgia."[39]

Her political activity within and on behalf of the church introduces a still more important element of her public life. She had won her political captain's bars long before she joined the campaign against Tom Watson's crude anti-Catholicism. By that time she had logged fifteen years as a veteran in the trenches of the campaign for women's right to vote. About the time of her daughter's birth, Mrs. Mitchell made women's suffrage the great cause of her life. Stephens Mitchell related that some of his earliest memories (he was born in 1896) were "of Margaret, strapped on her mother's back, so that [she] could attend her equal rights meetings."[40] From about 1900 until her death in 1919, nothing absorbed her energy so completely.

She came to the women's suffrage movement initially from a concern for practical justice. Her political disabilities barred her, she charged, from exercising rights over her own property. Her son repeated her argument from suffrage meetings:

> All I have to say, and all there is to say, is that every woman whose name is on this list of my organization pays taxes on real estate in the city of Atlanta, in the county of Fulton and in the state of Georgia. If you can stretch your neck a little bit, you can look down on Decatur Street and see the drunken bums being thrown out of the saloons on the sidewalk. And because they are men, though they haven't paid a dime and the city and the county have supported them all their lives, they are entitled to vote and we are not. Is that fair?[41]

Mrs. Mitchell's concerns coincided with the chief interests of the Georgia women's rights movement.[42] By 1899—about the time she joined the campaign—the Georgia Women's Suffrage Association formally offered economic equity as the chief justification for extending the franchise. The theme grew with time. In 1902 and 1909, when the Atlanta City Council was considering charter revision, the suffrage advocates collected data on women property owners in the city to advance their cause. Even if her name does not appear in the sketchy history of this campaign, documents chronicled other aspects of her participation in the movement. The *Atlanta Constitution* of January 1915 recorded her presence at a reception for the Georgia Woman's Suffrage League. This was one of the largest events of a week of women's politicking, and May Belle Mitchell played a central role. The paper listed her among the League's officers, and she stood in the reception line to welcome the guests from over all the state. The local press also recorded that "Mrs. Eugene Mitchell gave a splendid talk on 'Why She Was a Suffragette,' " at the annual meeting of the organization.[43]

In her offsprings' recollections, military images pervaded her response to masculine inequity, and in keeping with the metaphors, she professed no faith in liberalism and scorned an easy, Millsan equality between the sexes. On the contrary, she assumed an aggressive, aristocratic position that replaced modernism and equality with a forceful medieval notion of female knighthood. The Industrial Revolution, she insisted, had really enslaved females. Women became "just so many cheap hands, cheaper than the men. . . . Don't talk to me about liberation in modern society," she exclaimed. "We've got to go back three or four hundred years and treat women as they were treated then. What chance would Joan of Arc have to lead an army today?"[44]

In confirmation of her own metaphors, her children reverted often to military figures to describe their parent. Utterly decorous and rigorously disciplined, she lived life as if at a "soldier's post," her son insisted. Ramrod stiff, her back never touched the back of a chair.[45] In the same way, he associated his mother with soldierly fortitude in the face of chronic ill-health.[46] Although Stephens failed to peg the admonition directly to his mother, a later reminiscence rings with her determined fearlessness. "We were taught a stoic philosophy," he wrote: " 'What can't be cured must be endured'—that was the way they paraphrased Marcus Aurelius and all the other Stoics." And he turned to the most fatalistic book in the Bible for what he considered a family motto: "The race is not to the swift, nor the battle to the strong, neither yet bread to the wise, nor yet riches to men of understanding, nor yet favour to men of skill; but time and chance happeneth to them all."[47]

May Belle Mitchell did not spare other women from her campaigns either. She condemned those, for example, who failed to support women's political liberation, but she also mounted a factional campaign within the women's suffrage movement itself. "She did not treat well with the rival branch of the suffragettes," her son explained.[48] In a generational as well as ideological revolt, she helped initiate the crusade against the Old Guard in the Georgia women's movement about the time of World War I. From the first feminist stirrings in 1890, Mrs. Mary Latimer McLendon had dominated the women's movement in Georgia. Beginning in 1905, this very well-connected figure in state politics was re-elected every year, for sixteen terms, to the presidency of the Georgia Women's Suffrage Association, until her death in 1921. In 1913, however, the women broke ranks. Rebelling now against the pre–Civil War generation of matriarchs like Mrs. McLendon and her sister, the future United States senator from Georgia, Mrs. Rebecca Latimer Felton, May Belle Mitchell's generation sought a larger role for themselves and a more active, liberal policy as well. The Latimer sisters had founded their campaign on the explicit racism of the agrarian revolt, and they possessed the strongest connections with back-country populism.[49] In this regard, their challengers repeated in a later generation the confrontation of Phillip Fitzgerald and Hoke Smith with the populist radicals. May Belle Mitchell assumed her grandfather's part, while Hoke Smith's sister, Mrs. Frances Smith Whiteside, took her brother's role against the negrophobic agrarian harridans. These paladins did not duplicate their men's success. Failing to oust the antebellum—if not antediluvian—Latimers from the regular organization, the team of Whiteside and Mitchell launched the Georgia Equal Suffrage League as an alternative to the matriarchal tyranny of the political grande dames. The new organization elected May Belle Mitchell president. In 1914, the Mitchell-Whiteside activism spawned the Equal Suffrage Party; this, in turn, in 1919 grew into the League of Women Voters.[50]

If a public figure to reckon with, May Belle Mitchell exercised even greater authority within her family circle. While Stephens Mitchell, for example, often referred to his father in his numerous essays, interviews, and memoirs, his mother dominates his recollections: her name appears more than half again as frequently as the father's in these accounts. Still less self-consciously, the son generally conflated "parent" and "mother" in the specific absence of a gender reference.[51] He acknowledged her power explicitly, too, and in one notice he suggested both the nature and direction of her authority: "She insisted that we fight for our rights, even though we were bested. Time and again she said that courage was the only virtue worth worrying about, for it comprehended all the others. Her influence over both of us was very strong."[52]

This extraordinary woman exercised the most potent effect upon her only daughter. Long after her death, May Belle Mitchell lived and even grew in Margaret's imagination. Years later, for example, the daughter's correspondence still brimmed with references to her. As with her brother's memories, these allusions celebrate the parent's intelligence, virtuosity, morality, and grace. At the same time, however, her memories possess an edge that his lack. If she considered her mother the standard of female virtue, that ideal measured the girl's failures as well as her successes. Most of the daughter's references hint at these dual meanings, as when she related how she admired her parent "excessively" or insisted that her mother set "an impossibly high standard."[53] Describing her parent to one of her closest friends in the 1920s, she both began and closed her catalogue of her mother's virtues with ambivalent comparisons to herself. Look at me and you will see my mother, she asserted; no sooner had she made the identification, however, than she qualified it by reciting how really intelligent, kind, and attractive her mother was—in contrast to herself. After delineating May Belle Mitchell's merits, she repeated the qualification as if she had never made it at the outset: "I realized when I re-read this array of virtues that I was very conceited, in the first paragraph of this page, in saying that I'm like her, for I'm not. I couldn't be but I have tried—."[54]

Mitchell's attitude towards this ideal figure also shaded regularly to still darker emotions. Disguised mostly as humorous hyperbole, fear and anger lurked beneath the surface of her celebration.[55] If the daughter genuinely adored her "tower of ivory," conflict, discipline, punishment, and literally disease seep constantly through her praise.

Of all the subtly double-meaning references to her mother, few reveal more than what she claimed to be her first memory. A 1945 article in the *Atlantic Monthly* prompted the recollection. By Gretchen Finletter (the sister-in-law of Sidney Howard, who wrote *Gone with the Wind*'s film script), "Parents and Parades" memorialized the trials and tribulations of a daughter of a militant turn-of-the-century feminist. The essay detailed Finletter's ambivalent response to a powerful, aggressively opinionated mother and chronicled a daughter's innocent skepticism about women's suffrage and even feminism itself. "In school we were told ambiguously that we must lead useful lives, but in the suffrage world words were not minced; we were told we had to have careers, and to fight to hold them, and do even better than the men." The challenge depressed the child. "I was not very old and it seemed to me that if I ever got through school, which was already becoming difficult, I should not then be happily quit of it all, but should have to go on and on. . . . Did I really want to be a great lawyer?" she fretted. "Should I be happy removing an appendix? I began to feel guilty and troubled." Such ambitions also ran counter to a fundamental part of the life of her imagination. Like other little girls, she related, she played house and fantasized about having babies. "Now all this was to be denied me. I wished my mother didn't care so," she grieved. "A lot of the other ladies seemed so unaware, and though I felt they had none of my mother's spirit, their children seemed less weighed down by their future responsibilities."[56]

The circumstances of Gretchen Finletter's life duplicated those of Margaret Mitchell in Atlanta, and the essay prompted a memorable response. "My earliest memories are of my mother and the woman's suffrage movement," she began her note of appreciation to Finletter.

My mother was small and gentle but red-headed, and nothing infuriated her as much as the complacent attitude of other ladies who felt that they should let the gentlemen do the voting. . . . The first time I was ever permitted to stay up later than six o'clock was on the tremendous occasion of a suffragette rally which was to be presided over by Carrie Chapman Catt. (It may have been Miss Susan B. Anthony or Miss Amelia Bloomer. It's been so long ago I can't remember!) The cook went home sick, all the relatives had gone to the meeting, and there was no one to look after me. Mother tied a Votes-for-Women banner around my fat stomach, put me under her arm, took me to the meeting hissing blood curdling threats if I did not behave, set me on the platform between the silver pitcher and the water glasses while she made an impassioned speech. I was so at my eminence that I behaved perfectly, even blowing kisses to gentlemen in the front row. I was kissed by Mrs. Catt (or perhaps Susan

B. Anthony), and called the youngest suffragette of Georgia and the future of our cause. I was intolerable for days afterward and, only after being spanked, was permitted to witness a parade such as your sister described. Please tell her how much I enjoyed her articles and how many happy childhood memories they recall.[57]

Mitchell's images are telling. Although she first introduces her mother in the inoffensive terms of "small and gentle," the figure that develops is closer to a harpy. Furious and passionate, this figure attacks other women. Taking the child to the meeting against her will in any case, she hisses like a snake, threatens like a witch, and curdles her blood with fear. Seated (in curiously Freudian imagery) between the pitcher and the water glasses, the story's little girl gets her vengeance: she upstages the mother. Indeed, her own perfect behavior contrasts with the mother's "impassioned speech"—the child's manner being defined essentially as sexual play, blowing kisses demurely to men in the front row. At the same time, her youth and innocence win the affection and approbation of the suffragette matriarch whose name is memorably and repeatedly forgotten but who appears logically as a kindly, forgiving double of the wrathful mother. But the wrathful one still wins after all. The moment of glory ends in punishment. Indeed, in Mitchell's version the glory and assertion even cause the punishment. The mother spanks the pride out of the child; discipline restores her balance.[58]

If violence and confrontation lay just beneath the surface of Mitchell's first memory, conflict and parental rebuke also characterized another, even more important, episode with her mother. It was the most critical episode of her childhood. Ultimately, she declared it the most important event of her whole life. In the fall of 1907, May Belle Mitchell enrolled her daughter in the first grade at Forrest Avenue Elementary School. The child balked. A monumental confrontation followed. Mitchell gave several versions of the affair, but every variation repeated the same essential facts and contained the same dynamics.[59] As with her first memory, this one also repeats the pattern of a willful child and a furious parent.

In "Parents and Parades," the article that moved Margaret Mitchell to recount her memory of the suffrage rally, Gretchen Finletter had discussed the early feminists' preoccupation with education and the anxieties their ambition created in their daughters. In this regard, May Belle Mitchell virtually caricatured the feminist mother, as her daughter reconstructed the confrontation over schooling. Education for a woman was everything, and the mother was determined to force this lesson on the child by illustrating the inevitably grim and unpredictable future. So she hitched the horse and buggy, drove out the road to Jonesboro, and pointed out along the way the ruins of once-proud houses where fine people had once lived. In one version of the story, Mitchell related that her mother had populated these crumbling mansions with equally sad and dependent aged virgins: "Charming, embroidering, china-painting one-time belles, who, after the war had deprived them of their means, degenerated pitifully."[60] All these people had lived securely once, but their world had exploded. "And she told me that my own world was going to explode under me someday, and God help me if I didn't have some weapon to meet the new world."[61] That weapon was education.

Mitchell recalled her mother's lesson within a Dantesque setting of exploding worlds, ruined landscapes, and hellish heat. Her mother had launched her offensive "on the hottest September day I ever saw," and her rhetoric matched the weather. The sinister hulks, gaunt chimneys, overgrown fields, and weed-choked gardens illustrated the child's future. Had May Belle Mitchell harangued the feminists? She directed the same force now against her daughter. The mother may or may not have approached the affair as a kind of test, but the daughter understood it so beyond all doubt, and it defined the earliest crisis of her life—an indelible matriarchal rebuke. The jeremiad left a permanent mark, and twenty years later Mitchell integrated the whole diatribe into the novel she was writing. In Chapter 43 of *Gone with the Wind*, Rhett Butler condemned Ashley Wilkes and repudiated him as a coward and a weakling. This monologue, the author asserted, simply rephrased her mother's furious sermon on that hot September day in 1907. Periodically the world turns upside down, the fierce homily began, and in the disorder, only fighters survive. The scrupulous, the weak, and cowards meet an inevitable fate. "They don't deserve to survive because they won't fight—don't know how to fight," the mother had insisted. And so Rhett Butler:

This isn't the first time the world's been upside down, and it won't be the last. It's happened before and it'll happen again. And when it does happen, everyone loses everything and everyone is equal. And then they all start again at taw, with nothing at all. That is, nothing except the cunning of their brains and the strength of their hands.[62]

While the fiction omitted the feminist context, gender formed the basis of the Margaret Mitchell's mother's moral. If only strength and cunning count when worlds explode, women's lack of physical power forces them to rely exclusively on their mother wit. In order to survive, then, women have no alternative but to cultivate their intelligence. Only education, the mother hectored, stood between the six-year-old and the disasters that surrounded her in the rural Georgia landscape. "So for God's sake," she railed, "go to school and learn something that will stay with you. The strength of women's hands isn't worth anything but what they've got in their heads will carry them as far as they need go."[63]

While the issue of education defined a chief manifestation of May Belle Mitchell's feminism, the form of the story, as the daughter reconstructed it, carried its own truth. The incident reveals a more general conflict of wills: the parent asserting, the child resisting, the matriarch reasserting her authority. This sequence underlined a critical aspect of the Mitchell mother–daughter relations in any circumstance. "Margaret always fiercely resented being asked what she was doing, had done or was about to do," Stephens Mitchell insisted. "This trait was strong in her even as a small child." The brother believed his mother "always respected her daughter's right to privacy," although he added that the parent always kept "a prudent watch over her and her activities."[64] Stephens, however, underestimated both the mother's tolerance and his sister's provocation. For all May Belle Mitchell's grace, kindness, and forbearance, her daughter's stubbornness, secrecy, and general deportment rankled her, and the mother exploded easily into hot anger. One childhood friend judged the child calculated her behavior to "get the goat" of her "very proper, very Victorian" mother,[65] and the daughter herself recalled goading her parent into furious outbursts.[66]

The schoolday story hides still other truths. In one version of the narrative, Mitchell indicated that she had provoked her mother's rage when she insisted she did not need an education because "she would just grow up and marry a wealthy gentleman."[67] Although her mother might have understood and feared this rationale, the six-year-old's real motive for rebellion lay elsewhere. As a figure of enormous (even if ambiguous) power, May Belle Mitchell shielded and protected her daughter. If the daughter resented and resisted her mother's authority, she also craved that protection. She felt helpless on her own.

For all her rough-and-tumble competitive play, for all her physical daring, the child was actually "shy and self-conscious," Stephens Mitchell insisted. She "had started life self-conscious, stand-offish, and silent," he said, "a diffident, shy child." More significant, he recalled specifically that "she would hide behind Mother's skirts and refuse to speak to strangers."[68]

May Belle Mitchell would not abide the trait. Demonstrations of timidity infuriated her. Stephens Mitchell said his sister frequently spoke about her childhood shyness and the inevitable punishment it provoked. "Mother would take her upstairs and apply the slipper, telling her she must talk to people who were polite enough to notice and speak to her. She must respond. Not to do this was rude. And with Mother, rudeness ranked with sins which cried to heaven for vengeance."[69] Actually, the parent imposed a whole catalogue of manners on her household, and any breach elicited the same response, at least for the youngest. Stephens related how his sister always recalled their mother's emphasizing her verbal rules with a smack of her slipper.[70] As much as the substantive issue of education, then, the child's introversion caused conflict with the mother.

Stephens Mitchell deemed his mother's response successful, even if perhaps he harbored some slight misgivings:

> I don't believe our elders thought a child that was sound in body and reasonably intelligent could present any problem that could not be corrected by prompt, vigorous application of the hairbrush. Mother used her slipper on Margaret. . . . I don't know how the modern child psychologists would view this method of correction. I only know it worked with my sister. By the time she was old enough to start school she no longer suffered the agony of shyness. She was never pert or pushing, but she could always hold her own.[71]

May Belle Mitchell did push her girl. But she pressed two worlds upon the child. On the one hand, she forced her to attend the hated classes in deportment with the Misses Hudson and the dancing lessons of the equally loathsome Professor Seaglo's. She must know the rules and perform her part as belle and proto-lady. On the other hand, she demanded that her daughter "do what the boys do."[72] Horsemanship proved one of the more masculine virtues she insisted upon; so was marksmanship. According to Stephens, "Mother took her out to the Springs and had her practice with a rifle. Mother believed everyone should know how to handle firearms."[73] More generally, of course, by boasting she had taught her daughter "to stand on her own feet," the parent implied still more masculine-linked characteristics of independence, autonomy, and assertiveness. This other side still shows through in photographs. A half-dozen snapshots scattered over a fifteen-year period reveal Margaret in the same pose—arms akimbo, feet widespread, she defiantly faces the camera's lens.

Guns and roses did not always blend easily, but the parent persisted, and, as the brother related, the lessons took, if only after a fashion. Perhaps from respect for that famous "#3 slipper," the daughter learned to hide her deference and fear, but the sense of personal vulnerability persisted. It manifested itself repeatedly in all manner of circumstances at often curious times throughout her life. Among her most intimate friends, shyness remained the first impression they had of her, and, indeed, was the very basis of the intimacy.[74] In school, she compensated for her reticence by developing, if anything, a brassy front. And here the story returns to the confrontation on the Jonesboro road in 1907. The mother, of course, carried the day. Her cataclysmic vision on that hot September day "frightened and impressed" the six-year-old, and she allowed herself to be enrolled. But Mrs. Mitchell only won a halfway victory. Her daughter remained rebellious, and education remained a bone of contention between the two. One of Margaret's school chums called her " 'pertiferous', always in trouble, always being sent home." Shooting spitballs across the room won the same punishment year-in and year-out, even as the girl calculated such behavior, according to her friend, to offend her mother.[75] There were other problems. In glaring contrast to her mother's mathematical talent, numbers proved disastrous for her.[76] She spelled with careless abandon. And in contrast to her parent's "copperplate" script, she never lost the bold, distinctive scrawl of her earliest hand, with her eccentric style and form of punctuation—"x" for periods, and dashes strewn like chaff before the wind. Typically, in ruling little notebooks for her stories, her lines would jut and fly at every angle.[77]

The girl never liked school. At the same time, education remolded her life. In school she learned to read, and she fell in love with books. In later years, Mitchell always returned to the age of six as a watershed of one kind or another; nowhere is this more apparent than in the beginning of her passionate affair with literature. When Stephens Mitchell conjured up his sister's childhood image, books seemed her identifying device.

> When I think of Margaret back in those days on Jackson Hill, I usually see her in a starched dress, her short blonde hair brushed back from her face, sitting on the top step of the porch deep in Grimm's Fairy Tales; later on when she was ten and wore her hair in braids bound round her head, she still chose that place to sit and read. Then the book might be one of the Waverly novels, or one of Dickens'. She had read almost all the English classics by the time she was twelve.[78]

Nothing pleased her more than reading, and literature allowed escape like nothing else. She passed countless hours lost in books. Even her reading, however, occasioned more conflict with her mother. Her parent wanted her to read "good books"; the child wanted to read what she wanted. If May Belle Stephens had truckled to her own father's wishes to read only that which edified, she would impose the same values on her child. The confrontations followed the same old pattern: a willful child versus committed parents and resolution in a punishing mother. Margaret related several versions of one such story. "Most of my 'classical' reading was done before I was 12," she told one correspondent, "aided by five, ten and fifteen cents a copy bribes from my father, and abetted by the hairbrush or mother's number three slipper. She just about beat the hide off me for not reading Tolstoy or Thackeray or Jane Austen, but I preferred to be beaten."[79] Defending herself against charges of cribbing Scarlett from *Vanity Fair* gave the occasion for another version of tale. "Mother used to give me a nickel for each of Shakespeare's plays, a dime for Bulwer-Lytton (And I was underpaid!), a dime for Dickens, fifteen cents for Nietzsche and Kant and Darwin," she related in classic hyperbole. " 'Vanity Fair' was in the fifteen cent class but I couldn't or wouldn't read it. . . . I never could get past the place where Becky threw away the book. Even after being spanked I made no progress. . . ."[80]

As much as reading, learning to write also distinguished her seventh year. With this skill, her life was never the same again. And, unlike her reading, she could always write in privacy and avoid immediate conflict with avenging agents of Victorian virtue. Even so, fiction played a critical role in her life even in her childhood.

According to Stephens Mitchell, his sister wrote hundreds of stories in her childhood. Of these, very few survive. Only four written before she was twelve exist in archival sources. This sampling indicates her talents. Most obviously, she possessed a powerful, natural sense of narrative. She was a storyteller born. Her brother wrote that she plotted fictions from the time she learned to hold a pencil and dictated stories even before she went to school. Growing up in a literally storied society, she remained, always, first a talker and a yarn-spinner.

Her fiction absorbed the oral tradition's clear, linear movement. She structured her stories with precise beginnings, middles, and ends, each with its own rhythm and tempo. She played imaginatively with the narrative line as well. In "Two Little Folk," her earliest story, written probably in 1907 or 1908, the protagonists, ordinary people at the beginning, indulge in bizarre behavior in the middle, while the ending makes it right by revealing that they were ducks all along.[81] "Knighthood," composed when she was probably eight or nine, possesses more traditional linearity. With a conventional plot, this story tells of a beautiful and "very rich" lady who lived in a valley between two high mountains. While everyone loved her, a "wild rough knight" worshiped her, but she did not love him. Rejected, he decided to seize her by force. A "good but poor knight" lived nearby, heard about the plot, and defended the lady. The story ended (with all its childish errors): "Both knight drew there swords and rushed togeth. The good knight hit the bad one such a blow that he was killed. The lady fel in love with her rescueuer, and they were married."[82]

Such vicorous verbs as "draw" and "rush" illuminate another gift. Her language matched the vigor of her plots. She wrote as if by ear. Her use of dialogue is equally powerful. Although it is rare among child writers, she used speech and talk often; rarer still, she drafted it to serve the artful purpose of moving the plot along and developing character. An uncompleted story, "The Little Pioneers," best represents this talent; just so, it also captures her sense of aggressive narrative and dramatic action. It was written around 1910. Its leading character is introduced forcefully but indirectly through dialogue as venturesome, daring, and heroic. Thus a secondary actor shouts the opening lines to the protagonist: "Hold on, Margaret, hold on. Can't you wait for a fellow?" The heroine, named "Margaret Mitchell," has raced ahead of her companion as they gallop across a western plain in search of a lost character, "Eugene." An impending Indian raid adds urgency to their search. The character never turns up, but the raid itself allowed the young writer to sketch a dramatic scene that utilized all her talents for vivid imagery and action.[83]

Aside from the surface narrative, the content of "The Little Pioneers" reflects values and characteristics of Mitchell's childhood. The chief character bears far more than the creator's name. She represents the real child's love of horses and reckless horsemanship, her physical skill and daring, and her delight in competition and beating the boys at their own games. Mitchell peopled the story exclusively with the friends and family that crowded her own life on Jackson Hill. Her uncle, David Crockett, husband of her mother's sister, commands the fort in the narrative, while his two children, Stephens and David, her first cousins, are the heroine's boon companions. Its omissions signal as much as its inclusions. The missing Eugene suggests her absent father. But even more significantly—except for the protagonist, she purged her fictional world of females. Indeed, the story is aggressively masculine. Even the protagonist embodies male-linked characteristics, such as physicality, aggression, force, daring, and association with the outside physical world itself. The heroine rides literally beyond the pale as the story opens, but even the enclosure of the fort is male domain, especially when the Indian attack begins. Her depiction of that raid, smoke-crowned and arrow-pierced, encapsulates the world of war, the very essence of violent masculinity—and excitement. And this relates to still deeper elements in her character.

Mitchell had related that when she was six she rode daily with rough, profane old veterans of the Civil War. The tale confirmed her delight in freedom of both speech and action, particularly aggressive action; it associated such liberty with men and identified her own kinship with the license, violence, and stubbornness of the "old boy" veterans of Confederate cavalries. She pointedly alienated women from this world. Encouraging the child to ride as a means of "avoiding mischief," her mother had washed her hands of the troublesome girl. As the conversation became more violently masculine, even the belle finally fled. "She realized, even if I didn't, that the company of quarrelsome old gentlemen was no place for a lady. . . . At the age of six, I was not concerned about being a lady."

The *beau age* Miss and the hardened old veterans defined the polarities of gender culture in the South, but Mitchell's six-year-old Jimmy persona allowed her run with the hare and hunt with the hounds. If she could not participate in the male talk, her "Jimmy" could still accompany the men. And if she did not have to flee to guard her reputation, she still won sex-based deference as the old gentlemen gallantly kissed even her small grubby hand. Mitchell's Jimmy here is a classic type defined by the regional patriarchy: the naïf or pre-pubescent innocent who cannot be held accountable for her social breaches. Such a character or role, in one expression or another, crops up over and over again in Mitchell's life. Playing such a part resolved dilemmas women experienced in the Southern patriarchal order, even if its ambivalence created countercurrents of its own. The author herself discovered these soon enough, and this suggests another dimension of the crisis at age six.

Mitchell's brother had said his sister dressed in boy's clothes until she started school. School spelled a new discipline. Back came petticoats, bows, and sashes. Jimmy was obscured. She struggled to preserve this old identity even while compromising, inevitably, with the social dictates of the belle—personified in her own May Belle. As awareness of the world of feminine discipline and self-effacement closed in, writing allowed the preservation of her personal authority, in truth, as author. As writer, she maintained her Jimmy. Writing allowed her to recapture the "old boy" liberties of her Jimmy years in constantly making and unmaking worlds of fiction. She literally "made the book" in these years. She not only wrote stories but bound them in proper form as well.[84] Fiction encouraged her to make and remake herself, too; it provided a fresh stage upon which she might play with different roles and guises for herself, including male personae.

A final work of Mitchell's late childhood marks a new phase in her literary commitments. Written probably in 1911 or very early in 1912, the nameless tale is distinguished first by its length. Of about 18,000 words originally, the narrative exists in a fragment containing about one-third that number in five full chapters and part of a sixth. It is structurally and narratively complex as well. Even in its mutilated state, it demonstrates Mitchell's literary ambitions.[85]

A romance of the Civil War, the story traces the numerous adventures of the protagonist, a Yankee officer behind Confederate lines. It draws on many conventions of the Civil War romance, such as the heroism of hand-to-hand combat, the tragedy of a brothers' war, and the healing of the nation's wounds in romantic love. Conventionally, the hero falls in love with a Rebel belle, but Mitchell twists another convention here by making her hero Southern after all, even though he remains blind to the nature of who he really is.

Matters of identity and divided loyalty pervade the tale. Thus, the fragment begins with hand-to-hand struggle to the death between the hero and a Rebel; yet they are soon revealed as former friends and classmates. The hero escapes an enemy patrol only by donning his dying friend's uniform and identity. This is the first of two such episodes when the hero slays or wounds old friends from Dixie. Each provokes a violent internal crisis about what he does and why, and who, indeed, he is. An episode of amnesia underlines these themes. His role as spy sums up such complexities: unaware of his real identity, the Southern-born protagonist—as a Yankee—roams Dixie in a purloined Rebel uniform.

Although these qualities are exaggerated by its mutilation, the child conceived the tale as highly episodic and complex. With sharp cuts and abrupt transitions, the story line whips and curls in unexpected directions. The author introduced gross changes of circumstance and time from chapter to chapter; then, in a more leisurely way, allowed the characters to fill in the missing story or stories by their reconstructive dialogue. By this means, Mitchell tells the tale, but her characters relate their own stories, too. Dialogue moves the plot along, and the adventure becomes a story about things being told. With all its numerous plots and subplots, its young author may or may not have knitted the various themes together in the lost concluding chapters, if indeed she completed them at all. The individual episodes do engage one's interest, however, as they stand. For all the stylized settings and conventional types, her actors live and breathe with their own memorable identities. Even as a ten- or eleven- or twelve-year-old, she commanded a talent for gripping narrative.

The manuscript's mutilation obscures the personal meaning of the work, yet certain biographical themes do emerge. Although the character at the center of the fiction is a male, women, femininity, and domesticity now compete (if still not on equal footing) with Mitchell's old biases towards men and the world of masculine endeavor. This suggests her own discovery of such motives; these themes soon flowered in her later adolescent fiction. The emphasis on issues of divided loyalty and conflicting identity likewise intimate that her writing had absorbed realities of her personal development. Finally, the story's ambition and complexities indicate a growing sense of authority and command; they suggest a new, self-conscious identity as a writer or artist. In this new awareness of herself, she inscribed a fiction to an old Jackson Hill companion even as she prepared to leave that neighborhood behind her: "To my *dear* friend, Frances Noyes, my first long story is dedicated."[86]

In such ways as these, Mitchell's Civil War romance marked new departures in her literary commitments. That is fitting. Her life took new turns at this time, too. Belledom beckoned, and with it, still more momentous changes in her life.

III

Shero

🌿🌿🌿🌿

I remember something your mother said. She had come out to the Seminary to see one of the other teachers and stopped to talk to me. "Margaret puzzles me. I don't know whether she is headed for success or failure, but in any event she will be her own honest self."

MRS. EVA WILSON PAISLEY TO MARGARET MITCHELL [1]

S oon after the riot of 1906, Eugene and May Belle Mitchell determined to abandon Jackson Hill. They bought a lot in the burgeoning north side and prepared to build. Atlanta was changing, and the Mitchells' move represented the most fundamental alteration in the city's demography, life, and culture. The old Fourth Ward had mixed rich and poor, residences and businesses, blacks and whites. Not the Eighth. While virtually no one lived here in 1900, by 1910, 14,000 people called it home; almost all of them were white. Although blacks averaged 40 percent of the city's total population and comprised 60 percent of the Fourth Ward's inhabitants, only 1,000 of them lived in the Eighth in 1910. As far from barbarous whites as blacks, this district also boasted 60 percent of all Atlantans listed in the *Social Register* in 1908. Despite the Eighth Ward's enormous population increase by 1920, the percentage of Social Register people had soared to almost 74; 28 percent lived in prestigious Ansley Park alone. [2]

In 1911, the Mitchells began construction on a new house. The workers finished their job the next year, and in 1912 the family abandoned Jackson Street for 1149 Peachtree Street. Although only about three miles separated their new home from the old, the move meant leaving the neighborhood where the child had lived all her life, the houses where she had been born and nurtured, the streets and alleyways that she knew as intimately as the parlor in the Victorian house itself. The new house meant abandoning the ponies, cows, wide fields of sage out back, forts, treehouses, and other haunts of childhood play. The move coincided with other changes in the family. Eugene Mitchell's career changed at this time, too. Pressed financially (in his own mind, at least), he resigned his longtime place on the school board and turned more exclusively to his private legal practice in 1911. In the fall of the same year, Stephens Mitchell left home for college at the University of Georgia in Athens. With that, his sibling became the primary focus of her parents' attention, not always to her benefit. Peachtree Street, Stephens Mitchell averred, signaled the end to childhood altogether.[3]

All this spelled crisis, and as often happened in her life, accidents and physical disabilities followed close behind. The first of these, catching her skirts afire, had coincided with the move to 179 Jackson Street in 1903. As her family prepared to move again, she experienced another major accident. She was riding the family's large, fast horse, and the mount went down with her. The fall injured her leg and she suffered multiple cuts and bruises. Afterward, her father sold the animal, and they never owned another.[4] The new house even lacked a stable. As she loved horses and riding was her favorite sport, the accident redoubled the idea of her twelfth year as a turning point as she herself now attained *beau age.*

The new house represented all the changes. How it differed from the old! Set back only a little from the street, with two spindly poplars flanking the walkway, its fifty-foot façade stretched almost the width of the lot. Two pairs of tall Doric columns supported its flat, balustraded porch roof. Stark white here replaced the brilliant reds and yellows of the house on Jackson Street. Only the great, elaborate, window-lit Palladian entrance provided much ornamentation. After the neoclassical style of McKim, Meade, and White, the house proved Mrs. Mitchell's fantasy: the white, pillared, Colonial Revival house was "exactly the house Mother had wanted to live in. It was in every detail the complete fulfillment of her dreams," wrote her son.[5]

The Mitchells occupied one of the first two dwellings on the block. In 1912, the area was still new-suburb raw. "From our house," Steve Mitchell remembered, "you could look west across the vacant land and see woods running from West Peachtree Street right on to the river."[6] The severely symmetrical façade of the Mitchells' house gave way in back to an uncleared, ungraded, jungled ravine. From the trickling watercourse at its bottom, this brambled wood extended up again through the back neighbor's equally deep lot and thence to the order and regularity of The Prado, the main street of the city's most prestigious suburb, Ansley Park. The rugged terrain, dark growth, and marshy bottom of the back lot allowed no space for the gardens, lawns, pastures, and stables of Jackson Hill. Yet it did provide the Mitchell child her own space. Just back of the house, before the steepest drop, so the story ran, she planted a small garden of privet hedge, and in this "sacred circle" she escaped the house to read and compose her stories. In the house, she made her room a similar retreat.[7]

The north-end boom was just beginning when the Mitchells moved, and soon houses sprouted like summer mushrooms all along this section of Peachtree and beyond what would soon become Pershing Point where the two main Peachtrees (Peachtree and West Peachtree) merged. Every new dwelling brought its gangs of kids. Jackson Hill had thronged with children; so did Peachtree and Ansley Park. Stephens called their roll: the Jernigans, McCulloughs, Powerses, Kirkpatricks, Bucknells, and Buchanans; all figured in the Mitchell story.[8] More followed every year: like her Crockett cousins who moved there shortly; Dot Bates, who would serve in Mitchell's wedding; Courtney Ross, who lived around the block in Ansley Park. Mitchell left a vivid impression on all of them. In the musty-smelling basement of her house, which overlooked the dense growth out back, she gathered gaggles of these children and spun the stories that still had the power to spook after twenty-five years. One child of 1913 vividly recalled the terror of the "hair-raising ghost stories" Mitchell used to tell. As a prominent New York investment banker, DeWitt Alexander later remembered: "Many the time after they were over, I would take to the middle of the street and run from Peachtree to Prado in less time than it takes to write about it."[9]

If Mitchell awed the neighborhood with her dramatic narratives, she also turned to drama itself soon after moving to Peachtree. Especially between 1912 and 1917, drama became the chief focus of her adolescent creative energies. She wrote, directed, produced, and performed in a wide variety of plays, pageants, and skits, like *The Cow Puncher, The Fall of Ralph the Rover, In My Harem, A Darktown Tragedy, Phil Kelley, Detective, Bayou Royale, The Regular Hero, The Exile, Mexico,* and *The Greaser.*[10] While not all of her productions were intended for large audiences or even public audiences at all, the new house adapted wonderfully to use as a stage. Throwing open the French doors between the two front rooms and the large central hallway, Mitchell created a space to accommodate a very grand audience indeed.

Like the Jackson Hill stories, except more so, the plays allowed Mitchell the opportunity to remake the world, master an environment, and adopt new identities. In *Phil Kelley, Detective,* she created a special role for herself as "Zara the female crook and one of the gang" that suggests a whole complex of problems associated with male and female, good and evil, and the individual and society. More generally she leapt into the breach of such problems by featuring herself as the male lead. Thus, typically, one resident of the Peachtree neighborhood recalled the

> elaborate and convincing dramatizations of "Birth of a Nation" enacted in the lot back of Erskine Jarnegin's [sic] house (and us drawing straws to determine whose turn it was *this* time to make the noble leap off the six-foot-high cliff and be seduced, usually as I recall, by one Margaret Mitchell in the role of the Little Colonel). . . .[11]

Mitchell herself recalled a similar role in what developed as the most memorable production of these years, her dramatization of *The Traitor: A Story of the Fall of the Invisible Empire,* by Thomas Dixon. Dixon's turn-of-the-century novels, *The Leopard's Spots* and *The Clansman,* represented the negrophobic, plantation-Reconstruction romance at its peak, and these two works provided, in turn, the basis of D. W. Griffith's great 1915 cinematic epic, *Birth of a Nation.* Inspired by both Dixon's and Griffith's visions of Southern history, the girl in late 1915 and early 1916 produced her own dramatic rendering of *The Traitor,* a later Dixon work. She took the lead, and preserved a whole series of photographs of herself in costume. With her hair slicked back, her father's fedora in her hand, and looking for all the world like a cocky adolescent boy, she posed against the great Palladian doorway of her parents' house. When Mitchell was famous, Thomas Dixon himself wrote a commendation of her novel, and she replied with her own version of this production. She had to play Steve, she protested, because "none of the little boys in the neighborhood would lower themselves to play the part where they had to 'kiss any little ol' girl.' " In her recollection of the play, these "small fry" boys provoke a humorously harrowing series of complications as well. Most critically, they upstage the hero/heroine at the climax: "Just as I was about to be hanged, two of the clansmen had to go to the bathroom, necessitating a dreadful stage wait which made the audience scream with delight, but which mortified me intensely." Immediately after describing her "mortification" on the stage, she told of another in real life. "My mother was out of town at the time," she related:

> On her return, she and my father, a lawyer, gave me a long lecture on infringement of copy-rights. They gave me such a lecture that for years afterward I expected Mr. Thomas Dixon to sue me for a million dollars, and I have had a great respect for copy-right ever since then.[12]

Her parents may or may not have actually strictured the fifteen-year old on account of her copyright violation, but otherwise this moral of the tale confirms a classic image in Mitchell's memory: of the hectoring mother and the cowering child. Her version of the play, however, contains other curiosities. While she peopled the story of her production with little boys, for example, only girls had actually participated. This was hardly a casual error, either, for the belles of her circle had organized a regular sorority for the production of their plays, and "The Sewing Club," as they called themselves, effectively put out signs, "No Boys Allowed." "We sew a little and giggle a lot," one of the members sang merrily at the time. "Sometimes we give a play (à la "The Traitor") and then a gay time begins."[13]

The Mitchell child had organized her club within a year after her move to the north side. The group consisted of eight girls, mostly much younger than their ringleader at 1149 Peachtree. Leila Kirkpatrick was three years her junior; she lived just south on Peachtree. So did Erskine Jernagin and Maude Powers, who were two years younger. "Erkie" Jernagin had helped stage the production of *Birth of a Nation* at her house, according to Lucille Little, a later addition to the circle. Jean Lambdin was among their number, and the two wacky Buchanan sisters, Elizabeth and Eugenia. They were younger, too, and lived only doors away from Mitchell on the same side of Peachtree Street. Years later Mitchell remembered that Eugenia had performed as the black mammy in *The Traitor*.[14] Finally, there was "Court" Ross. Born in 1899, the oldest in the group, she lived at 47 The Prado, just around the block from the Eugene Mitchells in Ansley Park proper. No less than Margaret Mitchell, she also led the group. She played an important part in Mitchell's life, as well.

Courtenay Walthall Ross's family embodied the culture of the most aristocratic antebellum tradition as it survived and even thrived into the twentieth-century South. One ancestor was Mirabeau Lamar, president of the Republic of Texas. Her great-uncle was Lucius Quintus Cincinnatus Lamar, Confederate soldier, ambassador, Cabinet member, U.S. Senator, and Associate Justice of the Supreme Court. Her maternal grandfather was Edward Cary Walthall, a Richmond-born Confederate officer who concluded his career with thirteen years of service as Mississippi's representative in the United States Senate. The Rosses moved in the same circuit, and when Court's father, a prominent attorney in Memphis died, her mother allied with still another notable family when she wed J. P. Billups, a Southern railroad executive.[15] From Virginia to Mississippi, West Tennessee to Georgia, her family was connected to an intraregional power structure that dominated the South both well before and well after the War Between the States. Court Ross grew up in saucily irreverent knowledge of all this power. Her aristocratic insouciance did not dim with time. As an old woman, when queried about the Rembrandt Peale portrait on her dining room wall of Mississippi Senator Sargeant Prentiss—was he an ancestor, too?—she cackled her answer; "No, Grandfather Walthall won it in a crap game when he was senator."[16]

After the Billups wedding, Court Ross and her siblings moved with their mother and stepfather to Atlanta in 1912. Immediately they assumed a natural place among the city's gentry. Their fine house on The Prado only made their status manifest. Yet Ross felt ill at ease. "I felt shy and awkward on moving to Atlanta," she remembered. "Margaret was rather timid, too, and I suppose this is why we were drawn together from the very first. She had just moved, too, you know."[17] Second children, the scions of privilege, wealth, and status; near neighbors, close in age, and both new to the neighborhood, the two clung together like shells of a clam. Being the daughters of very determined, very proper, and very powerful Southern ladies also bonded the girls. Court Ross loved, but simply did not like, the imperious matriarch of her household, while Mitchell felt more subterranean antagonism toward her powerful parent. The two girls effectively swapped their parents. While Mitchell admired Mrs. Billups, Court adored the mother of her friend.[18]

Separately, and more often, together, the pair gave their mothers fits. They won a reputation as the "Peck's bad boys" of Ansley Park. Even at the famed *beau age*, they still challenged the rules of proper ladylike deportment. Thus, at thirteen, they joined a boys' baseball team. Court pitched; Margaret caught. As if that were not enough, they allied with a local "roughneck" lad and billed themselves "The Dirty Three," "D. T." for short.[19] They got into other scrapes regularly. On one occasion, they filched a neighbor's pony cart, took it for a spin, and managed to wreck it in the process, with Margaret bruising herself badly.[20] Their theatricals proved another source of parental annoyance. If Mitchell herself recalled her mother's agitation about *The Traitor*, Court Ross remembered other instances of Mrs. Mitchell's disapprobation when, for example, she objected to her child's appearing in blackface in a play.[21]

While their productions in the front parlor might have disquieted the adults, the pair also gave private performances that demonstrated other aspects of their adolescent insouciance and rebellion. The "soirees that you and Courtenay used to have all by yourselves," as one friend recalled them, mightily impressed their peers.[22] Still another of the circle recalled these "melodramas entirely impromptu—no, no, in those days they were SOIREES—at your house."[23] These affairs were not, actually, all impromptu. One three-page script survives that suggests the blooming adolescent fantasies that titillated the Sewing Club late in the evening at one or another of the girls' homes.

Mitchell called her sole surviving adolescent play, "(Seen) Scene at a Soiree."[24] Very short, only three pages long in manuscript, "Soiree" is a play about a play. Actually (and more accurately), it dramatizes the "backstage preparation" for one of the Sewing Club's productions. Only at "Soiree's" conclusion can the "real drama" commence, but the theatrical, of course, is done by then. The play contains three roles, and the dramatis personae bear real people's names: Courtenay Ross, Mitchell herself, and the new girl from across the street, Dorothy McCullough. The characters also build on the real personalities of the three girls. Thus, the oldest and the leaders of the Sewing Club, Ross and Mitchell, dominate the play and dialogue. Younger by two years or more than the "stars," Dorothy McCullough plays the passive character, while in real life she also maintained a reputation for innocence and naïveté.[25] More specifically, Court and Mitchell play male parts—the hero and the villain, respectively—Dot McCollough, the hapless heroine or "shero."

The narrative action of the play revolves around the nature of the "play" to come. The characters debate the setting of the production, more important, they dispute who will play what parts and how: who will be the villain, who will be the hero, who will be the female lead. Although Mitchell has assigned the roles before the dialogue begins, the villain—the author herself—rebels against the part; she wants to be the heroine. Court offers a compromise, to swap the role of hero and villain. Margaret refuses. She will have one extreme or the other, nothing in between.

"Soiree's" parts caricature gender roles. The villain in particular represents elemental masculinity in the skit—in his initiation of the action, the domination of the dialogue, and the command of the means of violence in the skit. Just so, the "shero" burlesques femininity. At the outset, the female part exists chiefly as the object of debate between the male protagonists. Both literally and figuratively, Shero is dumb: she rarely speaks, and when she does, she betrays no mind or sense of who or where she is. Passive, she is victim, too. Halfway through the play, she is discovered to be unwittingly pregnant.

Costume and props play a critical role in the drama. The characters' debate about their roles hinges on what they wear and carry, and the characters do not exist apart from how they dress. Clothes denote fundamental substance. Puttees therefore mark the villain; white serge pants, the hero. Clothing signifies power even as its absence denotes victimzation. Thus, as "Soiree" opens, the guileless heroine enters the action with her clothes, per the stage directions, literally falling off. Bare, she is soon confirmed bearer, the victim of male sex. In this way, appearance suggests a kind of substance in the drama. The author appreciated even at age fifteen that, as a woman at least, one must always "cover up"—whether to acquire power or to avoid victimization. Paradoxically then, disguise defines identity.

This notion of disguise also introduces another motive of the play relating to ambiguity and hidden meaning. The title itself established the idea. "(Seen) Scene at a Soiree" plays with the grammatical distinction between verb (to see) and noun or object (scene). By the same measure, it fuzzes the relationship between the active and the passive and between the subject and the object. The initial introduction of the cast confirms the conundrum. Thus Courtenay is described as "hero" but also also as "cussworthy imbecile"; Margaret is the "villain" but also the "sanctified cherub." Dot McCullough appears in ambivalent terms as the "shero," but the author also added a mysterious qualification—"of an enlarged 'ego.'" A subplot of the play is to clarify this mystery of meaning. The "enlarged ego" turns out to mean that she is pregnant. This description also ultimately recasts the heroine's character. While innocent and passive, she is also revealed as "loose." Virginity overlays promiscuity in her character in much the same way that villainy coexists with virtue within the divided masculine character. Finally, the punning language of the skit validates these themes. Mitchell packed almost every line with double entendres and sly sexual innuendo. To cite an additional example other than the ones of "scene/seen" and "bear/bare/bear," the hero and villain debate the setting for the future "play," and with knowing winks, the villain charges the heroine to "lay" the scene. Mitchell's language itself disguised her meaning even as it revealed, as Emily Dickenson said, "truth slant."[26]

Paradox, ambiguity, contradiction, inversion, and "truth slant" dominate the author's fictional imagination from the play's beginning. Mitchell stretched language, challenged conventions, and inverted the order of the world. She played with the very nature of reality. Endings became beginnings. Girls became men. Fact became fancy, but fancy connoted fundamental truth as well.

Besides the richness of the content, the playlet possesses other merits. It demonstrates the girl's mastery of language. As in her earlier stories and narratives, the dialogue of this skit is brisk and sprightly. It moves the action aggressively. More generally, Mitchell worked language skillfully. She used highly tactile words, and her usage exists in dynamic tension with the content as she underscored or undercut the visual images presented on the stage or in stage directions. She wrote very well.

"Soiree" suggests all manner of forces at work in Mitchell's adolescent life, and it foreshadows still more far-reaching influences in her later career. Costume and disguise were not by any means the least of these, nor the jokes and whimsy that often covered the most serious intent. The skit also suggests how art and writing absorbed and recast her oldest childhood tensions. Was she Belle or Jimmy? Was she a girlishly shy creature or a grizzled veteran? Was she the helpless child of an omnipotent mother or the mother of art in her own right? Was she hero, villain, or witless female lead? Writing allowed resolution. If art resolved conflicting claims within her character, real life proved far less malleable to the Mitchell belle. Adolescence tested her severely.

The tension of the relationship with her parent persisted. Mitchell still struggled with her mother. If six had proved a crisis year for her, twelve would be a comparable watershed. She referred repeatedly to this age as a time of particular conflict with her mother. The girl's shyness set now like concrete, to intransigence. As she budded into womanhood, she resisted her mother's influence and challenged her authority. The author herself illustrated the conflict in her humorous hyperbole. She had a not-too-far-distant Mitchell ancestor, she related, who had but one liability: "He could not endure to have any questions asked about his business, either private or public. Nor did he suffer any questions about his activities." His one eccentricity provoked "great though suppressed indignation among the females of his family. As you can imagine," she continued,

> such an eccentric was not bragged about in my presence when I was young. However, when I had turned twelve and had goaded mother about something she burst out with the fact that there was only one person in the family I have ever showed the slightest resemblance to and it was the bewhiskered old wretch who didn't want anyone to know about his business and who couldn't bear to have a house full of women gabbling and quacking about his activities.[27]

Here again, as with the ancient cavalrymen, Mitchell associated herself with a "bewhiskered old wretch"—in this case, a Mitchell male— in general contrast to domestic femininity and "gabbling, quacking women." Significantly, her mother plays the role of female "goose" to her hardbitten masculine identity.

If the author did not name the cause of this spat in her thirteenth year, she did specify another at this age. She was, she insisted twelve when she revolted against her mother's authority in literature. From this age on, she gave herself over to romances and adventures, dime novels, and cheap thrillers. By her own confession, she consumed pulp culture with a passion for the rest of her life. All this was at the opposite pole from her parent's literary values, and recrimination and guilt occurred almost inevitably over the subject of reading matter. She did not lie when she told a Catholic priest that her mother would have forbidden her to read *Gone with the Wind* before she was eighteen. "She did not permit me to read *Tom Jones, Moll Flanders*, and other books of that type until I reached that age."[28] Nor, however, did she lie and say she obeyed her mother's rules. If to the Catholic priest she tut-tutted adolescents' poring through her novel, to the much more worldly Stephen Vincent Benét she rejoiced in children's nibbling her forbidden fruit. When Benét compared her book to the books one read as a child, she glowed with pleasure. "I'd feel mighty happy if I knew that some small girl was ruining her eyes reading my book under cover by flash light!" It reminded her of her own childhood rebellion against her parent's taste, and she reveled in the recollection of smuggling books to bed and reading them by flashlight, away from her mother's prying.[29] Forbidden fruit was very tasty. Sneaking forbidden books echoes hidden themes of her "Soiree"; likewise, it suggests the rebel-versus-mother motif much farther underneath the surface of that play; and finally, it presages Mitchell's later fascination with pornography when she was grown.[30]

If conflict with her mother persisted in her adolescence, school also remained a problem. According to Stephens Mitchell, the parents—more precisely, Mrs. Mitchell—had planned a secular education for the children: public elementary schools, college prep, and then college in the North. Without much choice the girl began this program more or less dutifully after the crisis of 1907 passed. After moving to Peachtree in 1912, she completed the sixth grade at Tenth Street School. In her year-end school photograph, she glares out as saucily as any normal twelve-year old. The following year, 1913–1914, she attended the private Woodbury School near her new home, and in the fall of 1914, when she was thirteen going on fourteen, her parents enrolled her in Washington Seminary as they had always planned. Then the struggles began in earnest. She fought on two fronts—academic and social.

Washington Seminary was an old, prestigious finishing school for girls founded by supposed kin of the first President, hence its name. At the peak of the social scale in Atlanta, well above the public high schools, it fell, however, rather short of the still more prestigious private schools outside the city, like the Cathedral School in Washington, D.C., where the city's wealthiest and most urbane families often sent their girls to board.[31] Housed in a huge neoclassical mansion surrounded by a noble portico with more than a score of Corinthian columns, the Seminary was located just north of the Mitchell house. While it evoked the look associated with the Old South tradition, it ran something along those lines as well. Although well into the 1930s the institution still genuflected to the conservative Baptist Puritan morality of its founders, snobbish social values competed with academic standards as the dominant characteristic of the student body.[32] Although a girl might pass easily with the female equivalent of a "gentleman's C," Seminary teachers also offered a rigorous intellectual program to those who cared. While teachers came and went, "Miss Nora Belle," "Miss Sharpe," "Our Miss Emma," and Mrs. Eva Wilson Paisley were school fixtures; they challenged the best students. They got very mixed results from the troublesome, diminutive Mitchell girl and from her companion in impishness Courtney Ross.

Academic discipline still came very hard for Mitchell. Her dislike and despair about calculating assumed almost mythic proportions. "They had to dynamite that worthy institution to get me out of geometry," she jested, half in earnest.[33] Her failure acquired special meaning for her, as she generally compared her own shortcomings in the subject with her mother's skill. She won low C's in French and barely passed her Latin, [34] although she loved mythology. Her grown-up love of Frazer's *Golden Bough* was early manifested in the uncharacteristically meticulous notebook she kept at Washington Seminary on Greek and Roman gods, heroes, and classic myths.[35] Although she excelled in history and maintained a high B to a low A average,[36] her commitment failed her even here upon occasion. She submitted a paper for the annual United Daughters of the Confederacy award and won the prize. She had not prepared it properly, however. She "fell back," she said, on her memory, Henry Grady's famous "New South" speech, and gleanings from Myrta Lockett Avery's *Dixie After the War.* Her "humiliated family" discovered her plagiarism, and her cheating won her "the last of many lickings," she recalled, that she received in childhood.[37]

Her performance in English deserves treatment by itself. The girl loved the liberty of reading, writing, and literature; she loathed the discipline of grammar, syntax, and spelling. The disparity spelled trouble, and a very notable teacher, Eva Wilson Paisley, closed the gap. She played a special role in Mitchell's life.

An unconventional woman of great power, Paisley left a shadow of her authority in a memoir cum meditation she wrote long after abandoning Atlanta and the Seminary. *Sanctuary: A Finding of a Life* chronicled her retreat, à la Henry David Thoreau, to a small, isolated cabin in the wilds of Maine, where she survived on her own for a decade in her late middle years after leaving Georgia.[38] The author of the book confronts despair and evil full in the face; she does not flinch. A fatalistic, Ecclesiastes-like sensibility pervades the text, and if nothing else, the tone links the teacher with the stoical model that May Belle Mitchell adopted even as a girl. So does her paean to the world-defying courage of the individual. "The greatest enemy to a stability of thought is fear—fear of being singular, asking for the gray of a blue jay's breast when that color is not recognized by the Avenue," she wrote. Her figures of speech also echo May Belle Mitchell's:

> Suppose that maid, Joan, had allowed herself to be held back by the limitations of traditional guard rails. Posterity wouldn't be writing her name. I am sure she stayed out in the thickening shadows until her thinking was done; and when, at last, she slipped through the door of her father's humble home, that thinking had become resolution. She had no advice from an Associated Press, no patter from the radio, not even a town crier to bawl the news. Alone with herself, thought reached its star.[39]

Paisley exemplified for her student "the courage of the individual, the fortitude of the human mind, the bottomless resources of the spirit."[40] She admired her teacher inordinately; she feared her equally. Even after twenty-five years, the then-famous author related how the sight of her teacher's old, familiar script had fanned her old anxieties.[41] In the mingling of devotion and terror, her attitude towards Mrs. Paisley reflected her response to her mother, and in her correspondence with her old teacher, the novelist's language tended to blur the distinction between them. "Margaret puzzles me," Mrs. Mitchell had told the teacher. The daughter, now grown, continued the reference. "I wonder how you ever had the patience to put up with me. I recall that mother frequently expressed that same thought."[42] Was it the mother who lacked patience, or was the mother sympathizing with the teacher? The author's language makes no distinction.

Mitchell's correspondence with her old teacher captures another aspect of her character, too. She longed for commendation, but she anticipated condemnation. Expecting and even courting criticism, she then assumed praise to be defective, corrupted, and corrupting, too. "Praise from you is just about the highest praise I can get," she wrote. "You will never know how hard I used to struggle to get praise from you. Now I thank the Lord that you were sparing of it for it would have ruined me." In college, she blushed, she had actually wrung compliments from a professor. They failed to satisfy, she told her former teacher. Moreover, she judged the teacher herself inadequate because of her tributes. "I recall my sense of shock when I went to college and a good-hearted professor proclaimed me a youthful genius on the strength of the world's worst theme," she related. "I know she should have realized how rotten it was. Most of all, I knew you would have realized it. . . . So I didn't have any respect at all for her and I learned precious little from her."[43]

The girl was in a narrow box. Expecting her teacher's criticism, she determined to give her something to criticize. Inattentive and talkative, Mitchell and her pal Ross disrupted class constantly. In colossal understatement, the teacher remembered the two as "not always as attentive as I might have wished."[44] In desperation, Paisley isolated the two at the front of the class to control their tongues and their behavior. An old snapshot got it nicely as the two girls whispered and sniggered on the verge of some new devilry. Something of Mitchell's schoolgirl incorrigibility emerges even from the former teacher's warm and gentle commendation of her student's epic. She had not expected finesse and nuance, she related, but she knew that she "would find straight-forward thinking and great dramatic quality." She put it kindly, based upon her memories of the girl at Desk 44.

The teacher held the girl accountable for her misconduct; she held her just as firmly to the highest standards of English composition.

Careless work won the revered teacher's public censure. "Margaret, you could write if only you would work hard," one other student remember Paisley saying. "You have ability but you are so careless about the construction of your sentences. Remember, my dear, that a sentence is the complete expression of a thought in words. It must be cohesive, concise, and coherent."[45] Mitchell confirmed the same stories. Once, she related, she had turned in work that she believed revealed "authentic genius." Mrs. Paisley rejected it with public humiliation. "You read it before the class with appropriate remarks about just how bad it was." Mitchell also reconstructed, in her own hyperbole, the remarks that appeared upon the margins of her themes. Her teacher had observed, according to Mitchell, "that after three years I had not absorbed even the elements of unity and coherence. While as for emphasis and proportion, I would not know them if I met them in the road."[46]

If a demanding teacher and cool personality, Eva Paisley actually liked both Court and Mitchell. Given her biases, as betrayed in *Sanctuary*, she certainly preferred these insouciant belles' creativity and originality to the culture-stamped belledom of the school. She took a personal interest in both of them. "She seemed to take personal affront when we did not do well," Ross remembered. "If for some reason or another we were not doing well, she would take us aside and admonish us ever so gently, 'Now, my dear, why don't you try to improve?' "[47] She wrote Ross sweet notes with at least a touch of homoeroticism:

> A little line to a little girl who is looking at the doughnut and not the hole. You will smile when you learn that I had serious thoughts of picking you up someday and showing you the shady side. My dear cute girl, I hope this Christmas holiday will be a beautiful rest in every way and you will come back to me my old "Ross" of last year.[48]

Paisley liked Margaret equally. One of Mitchell's literary efforts so delighted her, for example, that she delivered it as a public reading, "an amusing satire, 'American Patriot,' " as the newspaper described it.[49] She took the girl's part in other ways. For all her criticism, both public and private, and despite her student's " 'pestiferousness' " in class, Mrs. Paisley acted as Mitchell's patron and protector. Thus, when the yearbook editor rejected a Mitchell story, Paisley intervened. Perhaps it was with her influence, certainly it was with her approval, that Mitchell won the editorship of the annual in her senior year. This rebel yahoo needed all the help that she could muster. Her social relations at Washington Seminary proved even more problematical than winning A's.

Her brother summarized the problem. Despite her social and economic advantages, "she had not made a social success at her school," he wrote.[50] Stephens Mitchell's assessment reflects something of his family's fatalistic predisposition to disparage their successes, but his sister, rightly or wrongly—like her father before her—felt socially ill at ease, especially among the typical Seminary girls. Mary Lamar Ross personified this perfect type, according to her sister Courtenay. A "pretty young lady with her bouncy gold brown curls and sophistication," Mary Ross had no rough edges and won her way effortlessly at school.[51] The prettiness, grace, and social ease of such girls set Mitchell's teeth on edge.[52] She glared at these perfect specimens and delighted to upstage them. These young women dominated the school, and Mitchell challenged them where she could. While she lost her bid to join the school social sorority, she and Ross "teamed up as bona fide school politicians," the friend remembered; they won lesser class offices, dominated one of the literary societies, and organized the school drama club.[53]

The theater provided a great opportunity for Mitchell and her mate to steal the show literally. In the school production of *The Merchant of Venice*, Court and Margaret missed the leading roles but upstaged the stars as Gratiano and Old Gobbo.[54] Years later, Lucille Little, an old running mate from these days, huzzahed about "the classic pageants in which Courtenay Ross and M. M. as Launcelot Gobbo and pal stole the show even from the cool and stately May queen (hooray!)"[55] There were other theatrical thefts as well. The earliest Mitchell memory of Elinor Hillyer's, who would later win a special place of friendship, was of Mitchell playing Bottom in an outdoor production of *Midsummer Night's Dream*, the ham's perfect role.[56] She played Julius Caesar, too.[57] In an operetta, *The Japanese Girl*, the fifteen-year-old Margaret "took the part of the Mikado. Imagine!" Court wrote in wonder—maybe at her friend's tin ear.[58] In *The Class President*, written perhaps by Mitchell herself, she played the protagonist's roommate, at "a college in the east," who challenged "the class snobs."[59] The plot was up her alley: the fiction described the reality of the girl's Washington Seminary ambitions. The Turks against the Belles.

The rivalry between Mitchell's set and the Seminary "snobs" centered around the literary societies. Mitchell and Ross dominated the Washington Literary Society; their enemies organized in an alternative, the Alice Chandlers headed by Anne Hart—later Anne Equen—who crops up as regularly as a canker sore in the author's life. The two clubs competed for pledges, and "much excitement and friendly rivalry ensued."[60] The clubs also challenged each other to formal debates;[61] most critically, however, they contended for control of the school literary magazine. Besides the prestige, the editorship determined whose literary efforts would be published. Mitchell remembered this as the apex of her ambition. "How I politicked to be editor," she recalled. "I so wanted a story of mine to be printed in the annual."[62] She lost the contest for the editorship in her junior year, and her rival, Anne Hart, now editor, duly rejected her story. Much later, the victorious editor included her own version of this episode:

> In those days aspiring young writers submitted manuscripts in a contest in which the best story was chosen and featured in the school annual. . . . Peggy Mitchell wrote a story. Proudly she entered it in the contest. Promptly it was rejected. . . . The decision of the judges was not unanimous. The teacher held out for Peggy's story. . . .[63]

Only the intervention of the magazine's advisor—that was Mrs. Paisley—guaranteed a place for Mitchell's effort, an essay titled "Little Sister," in the 1917 school annual, *Facts and Fancies.*

This fight remained a critical affair in Mitchell's imagination. Investing it with even mythic significance, she made it the subject of a very long, ambitious fiction. Mitchell translated the infighting and rivalries between her rebel friends and the girls of the establishment into a fourteen-chapter, 400-page-long novel. Now vanished, *The Big Four* dealt, in one late reader's innocuous terms, with "the rivalry of some school girls over the editorship of a school publication."[64] That hardly does justice to the schoolgirl's motives.

Mitchell's novelistic rendering of the Seminary fight is gone, but the story, "Little Sister," survived as her contribution to the school yearbook. Anne Hart Equen had concluded her narrative about the literary contest with a third party's moral about the unnamed Mrs. Paisley's judgment: " 'Could she in her wisdom have seen the spark of genius?' "[65] If no work of literary genius, "Little Sister" has much to recommend it as a youthful literary effort. Along with "Sergeant Terry," published during her own editorship the next year, this story clarifies the direction of her literary apprenticeship. Together, they also offer fresh insights into the values that governed her imagination.

In her skit, "Soiree," Mitchell's characters had discussed various settings for the drama, including both hell and Mexico. In "Little Sister," Mitchell combined the two.[66] Although revolution had unsettled Mexico since 1910 and wrought havoc in Mexican–American relations, Pancho Villa's atrocities in Sonora and at the border had blackened headlines in the United States for a year in 1917 when the two debating societies had argued whether the United States should annex the convulsed republic. The violence fascinated Mitchell. She had made Mexico the subject of two plays already, and she used the events of the Epic Revolution to tell her own tale in 1917.

"Little Sister" chronicles an outlaw raid against an isolated American family in northern Mexico. It is told from the perspective of the sole survivor, a ten-year-old, blue-eyed, freckle-faced child who goes by the generic title "Little Sister" but whose name is "Peggy." The story opens after the raid. The child has lain in the mesquite all through the night. For hours she has waited, "hugging her father's big rifle to her breast." As the child watches, the author retells the story of the raid. The family had consisted of Father, Mother, Big Sister, her fiancé Bob, and the little sister. Without any warning, bandits had stormed this little island of domestic tranquillity. Sweeping into the house, they shot the father first as he protected his wife; she got the second bullet. Springing to his girl's defense, Bob died next. Not so his intended. With her protection gone, she proved ripe pickings for Alvaro and his gang. "Pretty and sweet, the embodiment of every grace and virtue," this classic virgin fell helpless victim to the barbarians' violent passion. Their lust, however, effectively spared the youngest child. As the bandits took the virgin, the little sister, in her youth and physical insignificance, managed to escape. As she fled in mindless terror, she stumbled over her father's rifle; she picked it up only because it had hindered her flight. She spent the night hiding in the bushes above the house, shielding her ears futilely against her sister's screams. Then the turning point. "With ominous suddenness, Big Sister's voice was still and the child was left alone in silence and the dark." The darkness and silence transformed the child. She lost all feeling, all emotion. She became the principle of revenge. She became, effectively, the rifle itself, her vision limited to what appeared in the sight's cross-hairs. Insensate now to sound or suffering, she lived only for murder. At this point, the narrative catches up with the tale. Dawn approaches; Alvaro emerges from the cabin. His hand upraised for silence, he listens for sounds that fail to penetrate the protagonist's consciousness. The story ends in killing. It meant her own death, she knew, "but she cared nothing."

> With infinite care, Peggy slid the gun up to the level of her eyes and found the man across the sights. Coldly, dispassionately, she viewed him, the chill steel of the gun giving her confidence. She must not miss now— she would not miss—and she did not.

The tale is simple enough, but it demonstrates some art. Mitchell not only allows the reader to complete the narrative, for example, but she clues readers to two very different endings. Thus, once again, she builds ambiguity into her fiction's very structure, as in "Soiree." The child assumes her shot is suicide as well as murder, that her bullet will provoke an answering fusillade. The risk excites her reckless courage. But Mitchell allowed a different reading, too. The child's obsession has deafened her: she misses what the bandits hear,—indeed, what draws them from the house—hoofbeats in the distance. Without saying so, Mitchell permits the reader to believe the child might well be saved, yet insofar as the reader identifies with the protagonist, even more, with her monomania, those hoofbeats are truly incidental. In rather the same way, Mitchell exercises literary economy by suggesting scenes and actions without actually describing them—as in the sister's rape. Thereby she encourages the reader to fill in or complete the fictional shorthand. By this means she creates tension within the confines of a simple story and a conventional "perils of Pauline" plot. She compacts an enormous amount of action and energy into less than two printed pages. She curries a complex sense of drama and dramatic action from the tale.

Complexity exists on other levels, too. Hidden in the romance of a bandit raid lies another story: the child's development and change. Mitchell chronicles the little sister's transformation from girlish innocence, mindless emotionalism, and reactive flight, to cold self-determination, brutal fearlessness, and immovable will. This transformation depends upon the destruction of the home and domesticity; more specifically still, the ruination and death of the big sister. The silence and the dark give birth to a new character. Big Sister's screams, agony, and death, then, finally produce this new creature. Only with this virgin's sacrifice does the character grow. Gender governs this transformation. The child's innocence, passivity, mindlessness, emotionalism, and vulnerability are linked with females; action, self-direction, will, rationalism, and force with males. The story's Peggy exchanges her "female" feelings—specifically panic, terror, and passive flight—for "male" initiative, rational action, and force. As the child shucks fear and feelings, feminine-linked passivity vanishes, too. She becomes pure calculation and pure action. If femininity, as in "Soiree," falls ripely to masculine aggression, the protagonist, in her growth, acquires male attributes or male properties. In "Soiree" and "Little Sister," firearms—pistols and rifles—have the same significance. Survival as a character depends on the father's weapon, which Peggy cherishes at her breast and whose chill steel inspires her. In the process, she loses both her childhood and her sex. She loses time as well, or gains timelessness. Her fearful tears of the night before, by morning, seem to have been shed "a million years before."

The gender morality of "Soiree" and "Little Sister" is much the same. In both, woman *qua* woman is victim, passive and helpless. Man, conversely, is violator; more striking still, he is associated with the mechanized, unfeeling violence of weapons and machines. To survive, much less to grow, a woman must have these tools, yet their acquisition challenges her sexual identity. In "Little Sister," male weaponry signals the end of Peggy's female identity just as surely as it destroys the other women's lives. In neither "Soiree' nor "Little Sister" does the good male or hero offer a positive or redemptive model. The Hero in "Soiree" is no real option; just so, "Bob" and "Father" prove impotent to protect their women or themselves. Childhood can: the play and story suggest that a kind of asexual or prepubescent youth can resolve the paradox. In the short story, the child is small and insignificant, but she possesses the potential for action and violence, like the villains. "Soiree" does something of the same, as the "villain" is also described as a "sanctified cherub." By this light, the girl-child has room for action and activity denied to women. As with the lesson from "Soiree," a childish or childlike guise, then, might offer an excuse or legitimation for action, force, and creation otherwise prohibited to women. Prepubescent willfulness might then become a means by which a woman finds a niche for action. In this way, the fictional Peggy in "Little Sister" relates directly to the "Jimmy" figure of Mitchell's own childhood, and her Jimmy lived and found new vitality through the fictional Peggy. There were other ways of dealing with such dilemmas in real life and in fiction. Mitchell tried them. A second story published in 1918 demonstrates a literary alternative to the Jimmy-Peggy figure.

Under Mrs. Paisley's aegis, Mitchell won the editorship of *Facts and Fancies* in her senior year. She herself, then, accepted her second story, "Sergeant Terry," for the high school annual of 1918.[67] Although dealing with many of the themes about sex, gender, and family that characterized her other writings, this story relies on much more stereotypical roles and much more conventional patterns in both form and content. Like "Little Sister," it draws on a topical subject; this time, the European war. Unlike "Little Sister," however, it is far removed from actual scenes of fighting. Mitchell sets "Sergeant Terry" on the domestic front during World War I. It spins the story of a girl who falls in love with a soldier, loses him, then gets him back again. Unlike "Little Sister" or even "Soiree," this story is conventionally linear and ends with an equally conventional, O'Henry-like conclusion. It is not open-ended like the others. Mitchell leaves little here to the reader's imagination. The setting is constricted, too: she limits the action to an urban streetcar. In keeping with this, the story has very little action and almost no dialogue. She pulls the action inside and gives the reader thoughts and inward monologues. On a trolley crowded with soldiers, the girl discovers from a cast-off newspaper that a submarine had torpedoed the troop transport that was bringing her lover home. He had, however, actually sailed on an earlier vessel, and unbeknownst to either of them, they are seatmates on the streetcar. The story concludes, of course, on the happy note of their mutual rediscovery.

No hidden tale of character development lies beneath the surface of this fiction. The first story recorded the destruction of home, family, and passive femininity, and it chronicled the liberation of the heroine into an amoral world of masculine violence. It only hinted at some remote salvation of the girl-child through the far-off beat of cavalry hoofs. "Sergeant Terry" reverses this order. Only jesting with such destruction, the second story celebrates the most saccharine ideal of home: "a wee sweet bungalow," a cozy fire, gay chintz curtains, and "a canary bird that sang all day." Salvation for this girl, unlike the Peggy of "Little Sister," lies exclusively in getting a man, a house, a home. Her exclusive identity lies there. Without them, she has no identity at all. She is No Body. And indeed, the story's merit lies in its structural and literary confirmation of the protagonist's lack of individuation, initiative, and creativity.

Mitchell makes this character a kind of generic female. Like the murdered mother and brutalized sister of the other story, the protagonist never even gets a name. She is merely "Girl"—poor, weak, and helpless. The author's words define the image. The "slim girl" stumbles forward "in a worn serge dress, her soft eyes staring wide and dazed from under a dropping hat brim." This description appears even before she realizes she is an unwed "widow." With the discovery of her "loss," the imagery intensifies. White-faced, she looks but does not see. She is misunderstood and speechless. Actually, she manages only one phrase in the whole story, a mechanical, but suggestive, "Thank you." Although the "shabby little figure" thinks, her mind is like a squirrel. It is frantic, anxious, random, and confused, just like the female figure in "Soiree." Like the big sister in the earlier story and the Shero in "Soiree," she is a victim, a powerless object, vulnerable, and without strength or character outside of the home and connection with her man. The repeated image of the caged canary affirms the figure.

If Mitchell denied the girl a public voice or even a coherent inner one, she allowed the story meaning through another character who stands outside the conventional plot line. She assigned this figure the narrative voice, and both began and ended the tale with his musings. He has a name; the girl does not. Moreover, he preempts the very title from the no-name protagonist, whose protagonism, indeed, is crippled and constricted. Sergeant Terry McGovern truly governs the tale. He provides the meaning and moral of the story. The tale's strengths lie all with him. Even so does his authority exaggerate the girl's weaknesses at every juncture. In contrast to her and her isolation, he and the other soldier-comrades on the trolley suggest force and violence, but even more, life, vitality, self-control, and rational action. They think and speak clearly and definitively. Mitchell's language supports this characterization: they smile, they joke, they laugh, they roar, they shrill, they command. They express themselves in exclamation points. The girl, meanwhile, shrivels and diminishes when confronted with this vitality. In this fiction, the males animate themselves. So totally passive, the girl cannot react positively, even to their stimuli. Thus full of life, Sergeant McGovern has no fear of death or the deathlike fears that freeze the girl. "A fellow died one way or another," he muses. "It didn't matter how so long as he died."

Terry McGovern has no real story of his own; he stands objectively outside the narrative flow. He is a literary Adam who names things in the tale. Even so, Mitchell allows him a humanity and even flowering that she denies the girl. Introduced as the ribald, forceful rogue whom the other men naturally defer to, the very image of dominant sex, he transcends his own sexual stereotypicality through his compassion for the girl at the story's end. He gains, thereby, something of female tenderness, feeling, and emotion without sacrificing any of his male virtues, such as rationalism and fearlessness. In this way, masculinity acquires a positive aspect absent in "Little Sister" and only suggested in "Soiree."

Although the first story vastly excells the second in imaginative quality and literary structure, Mitchell works in both with the same underlying problems and issues. These carry through, in turn, the contradictions of private womanhood versus public masculinity that she treated with poignant, lascivious humor in "Soiree." In all, womanhood is defined by domesticity, passivity, selflessness, privacy, sequestration; masculinity by action, consciousness, force, and will in the public world. Males provide meaning, even for the home; outside the domestic circle women are helpless and vulnerable unless they acquire males (as in "Sergeant Terry") or male attributes (as in "Little Sister" and "Soiree"). In this scheme, men, like Sergeant McGovern, might assume female sensitivities; this, however, does not mean the alteration of their fundamental characters. Her female characters lack this option.

Such notions affect the very nature of language and speech. Even as a child, Mitchell knew it. Thus, in acknowledging that the public world is male, Mitchell recognized that the public voice, language, and speech belong to men as well. Pen resembled pistol.[68] How then might a woman write without compromising her sex? What is her legitimate voice? This is the nub of Mitchell's fiction and defines a central element of all three narratives. In none of these three stories do her women really speak. Although Dorothy talks in "Soiree," her words come in fits and starts; she cannot address the main line of the narrative, and she fails to understand what is happening to her, or the central issues of the play. In the two short stories, Mitchell explicitly describes the protagonists as mutes. They have lost their voices. Peggy fails to speak at all; the Girl speaks once, a pitiful "Thank you." How do they express themselves, then? How are their stories finally told? Dorothy's "enlarged ego" is an unborn baby. Peggy speaks through the bark of her father's weapon; and in the final story, Sergeant McGovern provides a substitute narrative, the language, in effect, for the silent girl. What does it mean for a woman to be writing stories of voiceless heroines?

Like any adolescent, Margaret Mitchell wrestled with the sense of who and what she was. Unlike most, however, she persistently transformed the struggle into fiction. During these years, her consciousness as an artist grew to acquire a life of its own. She scribbled constantly, even when she failed to carry through her projects. She conceived of arresting opening lines; she contemplated plots and settings; she listed scenes and words that magnetized the senses. She saw herself as writer even when she assumed her failure at the craft. For instance, she scrawled at the end of one adolescent fiction: "There are authors and authors but a true writer is born and not made. Born writers make their characters real, living people, while the 'made' writers have merely stuffed figures who dance when the strings are pulled. That's how I know that I'm a made writer." In short, she conceived of herself as writer, even while she dismissed her true talent.[69]

Even if it did not remove the tension of her life, her art transformed it. Her identity as a female assumed primary importance now as she struggled both against and towards the powerful model provided by her mother, and as she responded in like manner to the Southern ideal of the belle as she found it personified in the girls at school. Self-consciously she tested the options for a female in her social order. If she admired the freedom, initiative, and even violence that characterized the traditional public world of men, other currents tugged another way. The Shero tide ran strong. As suggested in her "Sergeant Terry," the European war, immediately at least, exaggerated the role of traditional femininity in her prose. It would influence her life similarly. Even so, the war years liberated her, too. Amid such conflicting currents it is little wonder Margaret puzzled Mrs. Mitchell. The girl battled against herself.

IV

"Where Do We Go
from Here?"

ᗑᗑᗑᗑ

When mother untied the apron strings and I went away to Yankee-
land on my own, I shall never forget my state of mind. . . . I seemed
to feel something within my innermost me uncoiling and stretching
and awakening, a consciousness of myself, of power, of my own
awakening personality swelling to such a point that I had to sternly
restrain myself from wallowing on the soft campus grass and yelling. . . .

MARGARET MITCHELL TO HARVEY SMITH[1]

*T*he conflagration roared northward faster than a man could walk.
It began in a pile of discarded mattresses at the "negro pest
house" just north of the railroad tracks in the middle of the block
near Decatur, Fort, and Hilliard streets around one o'clock on May 21,
1917. The wooden shingles and cheap pine boarding of the miserable
rows of shotgun shanties in Buttermilk Bottoms fed a firestorm.

Within a half hour after the pesthouse alarm, the fire swept to the
crest of Jackson Hill. John Slaton's wonderful Victorian house at 142
Jackson Street was only a memory by 2:30. Catercorner across the street,
the Widow Stephens's house had survived the Battle of Atlanta, the
Confederate retreat, and Sherman's devastation. When did it explode
in flames? When did the Crocketts' house go? And when the towered
house at 179 Jackson that had been the scene of all Margaret Mitchell's
childhood memories? By three, the holocaust had stripped the block.

ᗑ 74 ᗑ

Only gaunt chimneys, smoldering ruins, and blackened trees remained. The Mitchells and Stephenses lost as many as twelve houses, among them all the great edifices associated with their early history on the hill.[2]

When the last flames died, ruin confronted the city. From Decatur Street in the south, all the way past Ponce de Leon in the north, for over a mile, the fire had cleared a swath over five blocks wide. It devasted over 300 acres of prime urban properties. It charred $5.5 million in property. It left 10,000 homeless, mostly the poorest of Atlanta's blacks, but the rich suffered, too.

The city mobilized. Yet relief seemed as hopeless as fighting the fire had been. A tent city was set up in Piedmont Park to house the refugees, and the City Auditorium served a similar function. In keeping with her nature, May Belle Mitchell had sped here quickly after the disaster started. She took her sixteen-year-old Margaret with her. At midnight, Mrs. Mitchell was still there "helping feed the hungry and comfort the terrified." The daughter followed her parent's lead. Someone charged her with matching lost goods with missing owners, and she worked through the night and returned the next morning and then again later to oversee her job.[3] Her efforts hardly affected the chaos.

For the third time in its history, Atlanta was put under martial law. While Sherman had done it first in 1864, the awful race riot in 1906 had provoked the second suspension of civilian rule. By 4:00 on the afternoon of the fire, the streetcars of the Georgia Railway and Power Company were shuttling hundreds of soldiers downtown from Fort McPherson at the city's edge. While the soldiers joined the firemen's fight to quench the blaze, they remained to forestall looting. Khaki-clad men patrolled half the city. Unlike during the military rule of 1906, however, the citizenry had grown used to soldiers by the time of the great fire. By 1916 the threat of a German war had prompted military expansion, and Fort McPherson was drawing hundreds of uniformed men to the city. The new installation at Camp Gordon attracted thousands more, as Atlanta became a major training facility for the entire Southeast. Only the month before the fire, the United States had declared war on Germany; the military had mobilized with extraordinary rapidity; and the troop numbers had swelled further.

The fire, the soldiers, and the Great War came together to work the greatest changes of all in the city's life. The soldiers left their mark everywhere and symbolized still larger change. Similarly, in a small way at least, the Great Fire prepared them—and Atlanta—for the horror of the greater conflagration across the North Atlantic. Mitchell's life changed, too. Men, romance, the North, college, death: the time from the summer of 1917 until her mother's death in January 1919 witnessed changes altogether as profound in her biography as the fire that obliterated the places of her youth.

In 1917 and 1918, local and international disasters shadowed life, but things continued. They continued even during the fire itself. While the flames had swept the city, the junior class at Washington Seminary had not canceled its reception for the graduating seniors that afternoon. Marie Stoddard's parents provided an orchestra and elaborate decorations at their home on Piedmont Drive. Court and Margaret stood in the receiving line with the other class officers. They stood long; they received few. "Although we did our best to see the funny side of it, I must admit we all looked powerful nervous," Court noted in her scrapbook. "Who wouldn't when they didn't know if their house was still standing or had gone down in the flames?"[4]

Life went on. Indeed, the shadows lurking in the background even intensified the insistence upon gaiety. The national and international excitements coincided with the schooltime liberation of Mitchell's senior year, and the young woman lived high. She and her companion Court savored their literary victories at school and threw themselves carelessly into the whirl of outings, parties, and dances that filled the days and nights. They danced a tarantella. And they had as many partners as they chose.

Males buzzed around Peachtree and The Prado like bees around summer flowers. No space on any dance card went unfilled for either girl in this delicious year. The men from Georgia Tech were always close at hand with favors. All through the winter of 1917–1918, lights glowed late at 47 The Prado for the college flyboys' parties that Ross and Mitchell threw: "Just little informal dances to help amuse the Tech aviators—but oh! such fun!" Ross burbled.[5] Within a week of the fire, Court memorialized another one of these "would be" dances, as they called them. While the guest list included many of her oldest chums and pals, new names also joined the most familiar. She recorded fresh suitors, among them Berrien K. Upshaw, as the young man scrawled his name grandly—and almost illegibly—in her autograph book.[6] The sixteen-year-old boy was big for his age, and he wooed Court ardently.[7] The rawboned lad, however, faced impossible odds. His suit faltered beside the sophisticated college boys and the Tech aviators, but the soldiers drove all competition from the field.

In the manic year of 1918, everything revolved around the young army officers. "When Steve and Margaret had their little party at the Piedmont Driving Club it seemed like *every* soldier-boy from Ft. McPherson was on hand," Court Ross scribbled in her scrapbook. "Everything is military, even at dances."[8] Atlanta held open house. Almost a half century later, Stephens Mitchell still savored the memory of these affairs.

> The site of most of these parties would be our home or the Capital City Club roof garden or the Piedmont Driving Club, which during that sum-

mer were lovely, really lovely. The outdoors, the wind that blows across Atlanta, the starlit nights, orchestras under the stars, great groups of young people, all of them having a good time—that would be a striking scene for anyone. . . . That season we danced to "Poor Butterfly," "The Girl on the Magazine Cover," "Long, Long Trail," "Where Do We Go from Here," and "Over There."[9]

While Mrs. Mitchell hosted grand levées throughout the season, she also made her house a kind of a proto-U.S.O. Fretting over the lack of heat in the military barracks during the winter of 1917–1918, she regularly invited in scores of the young men at a time, warming them up, according to her daughter, with "hot coffee, cakes, and sometimes a huge turkey or ham."[10] She found other needs to fill for the soldiers, too. In her daughter's recollection, she virtually ran a taxi service out to Camp Gordon, where they regularly visited Stephens. After graduating from the University of Georgia in 1915, the Mitchell boy had gone north to take his law degree at Harvard; with the outbreak of the war, however, he quit his studies, enlisted in the army, and found himself assigned to camp in his own hometown prior to joining the American Expeditionary Force (AEF). His mother and sister visited often, "and we usually hauled twelve soldiers to town everytime we went out to see Stephens." Once, she said, they had given a lift to F. Scott Fitzgerald. He was not famous then, of course, but she did not forget his distinctive face, and she remembered him from pictures after he achieved a reputation.[11]

For the girls, patriotism blended nicely with romance. "There was a social duty on the young men to go to war," Stephens Mitchell recalled nostalgically, "and there was a social duty on the young ladies to see that the soldiers had as nice a time as they could."[12] That was an easy chore: the men pleased easily, and the girls possessed rare talents for delighting. "Most of the young officers in the regiments at Ft. McPherson were young university students or recent graduates," wrote Steve Mitchell:

> Margaret could entertain these young men. She had a big house, servants, a car that would hold seven people, and, if you crowded enough, quite a few more. She was a good dancer and, just as important, a good conversationalist, and she also had the gift of listening to other people.

It was true, even if Court Ross's suitors might have contested Steve Mitchell's conclusions about his sister, that "There was no girl in Atlanta more popular with the young officers."[13]

"I . . . could have dated up two weeks in advance had mother permitted it," the young woman wrote later; still, she deprecated her appeal: "The only charm I had was a hot line."[14] That was good enough.

For the first time she exercised the full panoply of her charm. She delighted with her talk. She possessed a very wide-ranging and intensely curious mind; she could pick up almost any theme or topic of conversation. For a sixteen- or seventeen-year-old, she was experienced, too, having traveled widely as a child. She read, of course, still more extensively. Moreover, she bridged gracefully the gaps between her own experience and that of others. "Hot line" does not do justice to her talents. What a fascinating talker she was! Her old friend from the twenties, Harvey Smith, smiled to recollect "the charm with which she could envelop the most minor incident in retelling it." He continued:

> Unlike many great conversationalists, Peggy was not a monologist; she allowed others to talk at great length. . . . She was sincerely interested in so many things and so intensely interested in some that her attitude towards conversation with people who interested her was one of making a sincere effort to put them at their ease, make them feel charming and important and to learn as much as possible about them. . . . As soon as Peggy could discover or imagine the trend of one's secret wish as regarded one's self, she played up to it quite openly and laid on the flattering picture so heavily that those around were often annoyed but never the subject.[15]

In their blend of youthful cockiness and wartime anxiety, the fresh lieutenants flourished like green bay trees beneath such lavish husbandry. For many a lonesome young officer, the delightful Southern girl embodied all the charm associated with the region. Enchantment lit the scene like Japanese lanterns at a summer garden party, and many a Yankee lad succumbed to the "soft Southern nights of Atlanta, the drives, the dances, our house with its wide terraces, the moonlight with the strolling Negro guitar players under the deep shadows of the oaks," and all the rest in Steve Mitchell's recollection.[16] While more than one soldier fell in love with Margaret Mitchell, in the lovely spring of 1918 the seventeen-year-old girl reciprocated the affection of one of them, a New York aristocrat, Lieutenant Clifford Henry.

Long, long after, she professed never to have gotten over this romance. She treasured the boy's photograph all her life, and sent his parents flowers on the anniversary of his death until the time she died herself. She also conceived of him as something of a holy spirit who guided and protected her. Who was this young man who so galvanized her fancy? In browning photographs, he stands with other uniformed soldiers, but neither height nor build distinguish him. Still, he has a certain presence. While the other young officers clown at the camera, he remains consistently, quietly sober. Uncapped, his thick blond hair and heavily lidded eyes always set him clearly apart from the others.[17]

Full lips add to the general impression of brooding good looks. Some of his photographic reserve sprang, perhaps, from aristocratic diffidence. He personified, in any case, the silk-stockinged New Yorker. His parents divided their time between their Manhattan residence and a house in that enclave of aristocracy, Card Sound, Connecticut. Very much like the Roosevelts, with whom he went to school—Theodore Roosevelt would write his eulogy—his family represented old wealth and status. Born in 1896, Clifford Henry prepped at Trinity, the oldest in the country, before entering Harvard in 1914. He was an ordinary boy in Cambridge except for his military commitments. His military professors encouraged him to join the regular army. In the fall of 1917, he followed their advice, withdrew from school, and after a three-month training course at Fort Leavenworth, won his lieutenant's bars in February 1918. In mid-May, the army transfered him to Camp Gordon at Atlanta, where he instructed American doughboys in the bayonet. He remained there less than two months before shipping out to Europe.[18]

Where and when exactly did they meet? The girl left no record. What was the attraction? Even as a maid the girl was not inured to class and status; the young man had both. He was reserved and shy, innocent and guileless; those appealed, and so did his literary, poetic bent. Combined in a handsome man in a dress uniform, they spelled romance. He was barely twenty-two in the summer of 1918; she was just seventeen and in the full flower of her own youthful fantasies. Above all this hung the dread excitement of the war: his troopship was to depart New York on July 17. *Carpe diem,* the world sang. Sometime in July, probably just before he left for New York and then Europe, the young lieutenant gave her a large, old family ring, and they exchanged promises to wed. They shared an idyllic spring. Court captured the mood nicely from the perspective of a year later. Under a snapshot of her best friend's beau—by then long buried in French soil—she wrote: "Last summer—Oh! Good old days!"[19]

Amid the bliss, Eugene Mitchell sounded the only discordant note. News of the Henry liaison sent shock waves through the Mitchell household when the father heard the news. His caution and conservatism grew yearly, and the events of 1917–1918 troubled him deeply: the war, the loss of family properties in the fire, the economic decline attendant on both, and the new liberality that unsettled the old way in his city. The engagement capped his anxieties. Mr. Mitchell expressed grave fear about his daughter's vulnerability; perhaps he dreaded his own as well. The costly doings by his coolly dutiful wife must have troubled his intensely conservative nature even as the crowds of strangers in his home subverted his set routines. And here was one of these strangers threatening to run off with his daughter. He lost his temper. Two months after Clifford Henry had sailed to Europe, the prospective father-in-law still fumed and fretted, and he poured out his anger, anxiety, and frustration to his wife. Who is this man? he stammered. Where does he come from? What is his family? What are his prospects and resources? How can he support her? What of Margaret's reputation?

May Belle Mitchell could hardly have differed more in her attitude towards her daughter's love affair. She summarized her response in a long letter that addressed—and then dismissed—each of her husband's concerns. Her tone bears special notice as well. Where he was fussy and nervous, she was cool and rational. Where he panicked, she insisted on objectivity and distance. One of the two long, surviving letters in her hand from her adulthood, this missive reaffirms all the qualities apparent in her life from the time she went away to school in Canada over thirty years before; just so, it confirms the qualities that her daughter both adored and hated. Gently patronizing in meeting her husband's panic, she regarded him from her Olympian height and reprimanded him softly. "Dear, you must have had no youth or forgotten it," she chided,

> if you attach so much importance to the affections of seventeen years. The Henrys as far as I have seen are good people, well-travelled, educated, how much or how little money I do not know, but respectable. The boy is over in Europe, perchance for life. Why worry over what can't happen for four or five years and 99 to 100 will not happen at all. Can you remember how many girls Stephens has been in love with since he was seventeen? Youth has ways of its own for education. I will tell the Henrys when I see them that they must not say anything of Margaret to anyone, so as to leave both their son and Margaret freedom to change their mind if they so desire. Margaret herself is not ignorant of the natural manner of seventeen to change its mind. So put your mind at rest about this affair, as there can come no harm from it.[20]

It indicates her character that this letter allows no distinctions between the romantic liaisons of her son and of her daughter. If the father tried to make his daughter a special case, the mother disallowed it. She affirmed the same idea of equality about her daughter to her prospective in-laws at this time as well. She warned the Henrys: "I have taught my daughter to stand on her own two feet."[21]

For all its other relevance, this letter also indicates May Belle Mitchell took her daughter's side for once, despite the pair's old conflicts. The year 1918 proved special in this regard. The two never seemed closer. In late August the mother and daughter launched on a long, leisurely journey to New England, and the trip provided a special bond between them. Taking a train for Savannah, they boarded a coastal steamer for New York. Shipboard photographs from this time affirm their pleasure: they stand on deck with shining faces. New York pleased them more than ever. They visited museums. They shopped. They dined at the Waldorf. They applauded Broadway plays. They delighted in one another as they strolled Manhattan's avenues.[22] Four months later, May Belle Mitchell lay dying, and as she tried to summarize her conflicted relationship with her daughter, she recalled these pleasant days for her only girl. "Goodby, Darling," she closed, "and if you see me no more, it may be best that you remember me as I was in New York."[23]

Besides the joys of New York City, the two experienced a final bonding in the summer of 1918 that made these days satisfying for the mother especially. They had initiated this trip north in the first place to enroll the girl in college, and insofar as education and college capped her ambitions for her child, the mother's pleasure could have been no greater. She had anticipated this moment since her daughter's infancy. Her strategy assumed legendary proportions in family lore. "Margaret was to attend an elementary public school, then Washington Seminary, and finally one of the women's colleges in the north," Stephens summarized her plan.[24] No one in the family quite shared the mother's enthusiasm. Her "newfangled ideas of education" ran counter to the Fitzgerald family tradition in general and Annie Stephens's prejudices in particular. The venture also generated opposition still closer to home. From the lofty perspective of twenty-two years and two winters in Cambridge, Massachusetts, Steve Mitchell fulminated against Northern schooling for a well-bred Dixie belle. College "was the ruination of girls," he warned his family. Northern colleges? They were even worse.[25] Eugene Mitchell left no record of his opinion, but later he specifically discouraged her from returning to school. Moreover, his ferocious defensiveness about his daughter generally sustained the biases of his more liberal son. And the daughter herself? If she felt little more enthusiasm about college than she had about school in general, she submerged her doubts in the face of her parent's fervor. The mother was not to be deterred. May Belle Mitchell did all the planning in any case. By mid-summer, she had made her selection. Her daughter would matriculate at Smith College in Northampton, Massachusetts.

If Mrs. Mitchell had known of Smith before, she knew it best through her neighbors, the Drury Powers family. Maudie, a younger sister of the clan, had been a charter member of the Sewing Club, but Mamie, the older girl, was a Smith freshman when Mitchell enrolled. The Powers women had toured the Northeast exploring colleges in 1917. Mamie Powers related that she had fallen in love with the town and campus; her mother, however, had "more practical concerns and so did Mrs. Mitchell." Both mothers, she later said, "were interested in the fact that Smith was founded in 1871 with funds left by Sophia Smith of Hatfield, Mass., who strongly believed that women should have equal educational opportunities with men."[26] Sophia Smith's goals spoke directly to May Belle Mitchell's deepest passion. She was convinced. She required no campus visit.

The girl retained her doubts about schooling and education, and they flowered soon enough. In the fall of 1918, however, she subordinated her misgivings to her mother's passion. She focused her anxieties, not on college, but on living in the North. Yankee folk and Yankee ways set her teeth on edge. So did her own Yankee relatives. Indeed, experiences with her maternal kin confirmed her biases and exaggerated her foreboding. In September, Mitchell and her mother spent several weeks in Greenwich, Connecticut, visiting with May Belle Mitchell's sister Edythe and her very wealthy husband, Edward Ney Morris. Among folk such as Scott Fitzgerald chronicled in *The Great Gatsby*, the Atlanta girl felt strange and awkward. "It's a barbarous country," she fumed from her aunt's mansion in Greenwich; "it's only money, money, *money* that counts," she told her father. Although engaged to a scion of this very society, she rejected the possibility of living in this world "even if Rockerfellow himself proposed to me." (Her spelling had not improved since Boulevard Grammar School.) She smelled hypocrisy everywhere. Thus, lunching at an ambassador's mansion in Greenwich, she contrasted the lavish display of wealth with the table talk of national sacrifice. She resented the situation all the more when she decided her hosts expected her to shell out her own small change for buying flea market trinkets to "aid the war effort." "Patriotism!" she exploded. "Why the devil don't the people give up a servant, a car, a club—something that really counts and quit yelling patriotism and selling 50 cent things when they are supporting a useless retinue . . . ? It makes me sick," she groaned, "but I can't say anything."[27]

The stay at her aunt's confirmed her apprehension. Would college be different? "I'm going to try to like the place I must live in for nine months," she told her father, "but it will be rather difficult. Perhaps Northampton is different from Greenwich. I hope so anyway for I want to get a place where the individual and not the millions count."[28] She soon found out. Within a week of writing this letter to her father, she was unpacking her trunks at her residential dormitory at 10 Henshaw Street in Northampton, Massachusetts—a college freshman.

As she had predicted (effectively), she remained at Smith only nine months. And as she anticipated, little went smoothly in her year away from home. In the first place, the times were out of joint in the fall of 1918. With nearly 800 entering freshmen, Smith had never enrolled a larger number of students, and the school lacked facilities to accommodate them all. More than two thousand women thronged the campus. Sheer numbers necessitated housing many off campus and about town—as with the thirty-five young women who boarded at Mrs. Pearson's house at 10 Henshaw Street "Ten Hen," as the girls called it. The school's size and the fragmentation exaggerated difficulties for the Atlanta girl. After all, she had graduated with a class of only forty girls in her hometown where everyone of consequence had known each other for generations.

Other circumstances multiplied the disruptions. The Spanish influenza epidemic of 1918, which would end by killing 20 million people worldwide, struck Northampton in the fall. Exactly two weeks after school opened, on October 3, medical authorities quarantined the college, and the administration canceled all classes. Some courses floundered until the Christmas holidays.[29] In the disruption of academics, the students engaged in make-work activities of one kind or another for the war effort. They raked leaves, crated vegetables, and picked tobacco. These efforts accomplished little, and the women themselves saw them mostly as excuses for social outings.[30]

Two weeks after the quarantine lifted, news of the Armistice dominated affairs in Northampton, and the ensuing celebrations disrupted classes once again. Mitchell marched in Northampton's peace parade, but even after the Armistice the war continued to unsettle normal routines. The students knitted socks, rallied for Armenian relief, campaigned for Red Cross and bond drives, sang army songs, and reflected on their families, friends, and lovers overseas.[31] Christmas break began on December 20; the flu hit again; and the second semester began in disruption, too. In this disjointed world, books and studies seemed peripheral.

For all the dislocations, the girl signed up for standard courses, and like most freshmen, she had no higher goal than finishing—if that. The issue bears noticing only in the context of her later stories about her vaunted—and thwarted—aspirations in going away to school. Especially in the thirties, after she became famous, Mitchell circulated tales that she had gone to college to study psychology. She elaborated the story over time. She would be a psychiatrist or a neurologist. She would study with the greats in Europe; in Vienna, even. Others picked up the tales and they circulated as fact.[32]

She fabricated it all.

The legend of her neurological ambition, however, bears at least a tangential relationship to reality. It is important for what it reveals as well as for what it hides. At the outset, it does suggest a kind of metaphorical truth. In the twenties and thirties, Mitchell read tracts and volumes on neurological medicine for fun. She loved psychology and psychologizing. She studied psychoanalytic theory for her own delight.[33] She analyzed character deftly. She penetrated human motivation with rare ease and instinctive intelligence. Perhaps, then, the stories reflect what she might have been, what she might have wanted, had she been a different person, from a different place, a different time, or even the other sex. Psychology might have been the natural outlet for a rare, distinctive talent. As a Southern girl in 1918, even at a

Northern college, however, she could hardly have known this as a real option. If her very education was such a tenuous thing—and it certainly was—how much more impossible would have been these other dreams? She did not, in any case, express any such hopes at the time. She did have other ambitions, however, even if less obviously vaulting than studying with Sigmund Freud.

If the girl left no evidence whatsoever of a desire to study psychiatric medicine, she littered the record with her hopes of writing professionally. One housemate from Ten Hen remembered the conversations: "She continually talked of wanting to write. I did too and we had frequent gab fests about it."[34] An old beau with similar ambitions offered similar testimony. " 'When I get through here, I am going to find out if I really can write,' " he remembered her saying.[35] Mitchell memorialized these career ambitions herself. Soon after she left Smith, she grieved bitterly about "giving up college and forever all dreams of a journalistic career to come home and keep house. . . ."[36]

At Smith, Mitchell's courses reflected these literary biases; not scientific ones at all. In contrast to her tales of medical and scientific goals, chemistry nearly killed her, and math remained her nemesis.[37] Meanwhile, she breezed through her literature courses and won the praises of her composition teachers.[38] Literature delighted her outside of class quite as much as in. Her rooommate, Madelaine "Red" Baxter cherished memories of the two of them ensconcing themselves in the only two bathtubs on their floor, and, "with hot water dripping constantly and parboiling our skins to lobster red," the two took turns reciting poetry, each trying to stump the other.[39] Much later, Mitchell found little to celebrate about her academic career at Smith. Student publications rejected her work, she remembered, and Smith had done nothing for her in a literary way. Even her teachers' praise lacked balance, she thought, and she failed to profit by it.[40]

The Southern girl had other problems with her courses. Although she considered history her best subject, she did poorly after a terrible run-in with her professor. Race provoked the conflict. Smith was no bastion of racial equality; it did, however, admit a few black women every year, "all excellent students and quiet, fine girls," one alumna boasted. The class of '22 had one or two. One of these proved the fuse for the student–teacher confrontation. At the beginning of the term, the Atlantan discovered that she shared her history class with one of these young women. In the recollection of her then-roommate, Florence Grandin, Mitchell exploded. Storming back from class, she slammed her books on the table and pronounced her anathemas on the teacher with "a few damns and hells" thrown in for good measure:

> She had talked to Miss Ware after the class was over and asked her to change [her] to another class. This Miss Ware refused to do. Peggy . . .

vowed and declared that she would go and see the dean or the president if she had to, but she was not going back into that class! I never really knew just whom she did see, but by some artful strategy she won her point, and the first of the week she was changed to another history class. That she used real strategy could not be doubted, either, as she was attending a New England college whose policy it had been for some time to accept one or more negro girls in each entering class.[41]

Twenty years later, Mitchell had her own version of this affair. When she protested the presence of the other young woman in the class, the teacher flunked her steadily, she remembered, even though the dean already had approved her transfer. She challenged the teacher with hypocrisy. She wanted to know if Miss Ware "had ever undressed and nursed a Negro woman or sat on a drunk Negro man's head to keep him from being shot by the police." Finally, she also related the cause, or so she thought, of her professor's animosity. She had informed her mother of the episode, and Mrs. Mitchell told her that this very teacher "was a daughter of a New England family of good social position in the north which came to Atlanta as teachers of Negroes after the war, which though never cut were never accepted—[and they] left after a few years with a bitter hatred of Southerners."[42] Mrs. Mitchell's explanation had at least some basis in fact. She associated Professor Dorothy Ware with the family of Edmund Asa Ware, the Yale-educated Yankee reformer who was inaugurated the first president of black Atlanta University in 1867. This knowledge, however, gave the Smith freshman cold comfort in the fall of 1918. On the contrary, it only heightened her discomfort about living in the North.

Socially? How did Mitchell survive among the Yankee girls in general? She left her mark. Most of them remembered best her humor. "The most vivid memories I have of Peg Mitchell are highlighted by laughter and hilarity," one of her two true friends recollected. "She was full of fun, had a keen sense of humor, was a good mixer with old and young alike," her roommate Florence Grandin reminisced; while still another housemate described her as "very bright, quick, and animated—ready to laugh, not at people ever, but with them always." She planned elaborate practical jokes—a tradition she continued back in Atlanta, to the vast amusement of her friends.[43] She clowned and strutted.[44] In the process of these performances, she won something of a reputation for a lack of seriousness. One housemate put it kindly. She was, Martha Cole wrote to Mrs. Parker, "one of the most colorful girls in the group."[45]

She shared the age's reputation for rebellion, too. "To us it was an escapade to smoke a cigarette; or to ride up to Florence with a man other than our own father or a friend's father; or even to go to a movie in Hamp unchaperoned!" one housemate exclaimed.[46] The young Atlantan shared in all such underground activity. She regularly indulged her passion for the movies, slipping in and out after hours, carefully avoiding Mrs. Pearson's eagle eye. While she had no boyfriends in the first semester and precious few the second, she did act as accomplice in her housemates' trysts.[47] She smoked in spartan secrecy. She swore and cursed memorably. In short, she violated, in one close friend's fond memory, every standard of the stereotypical self-effacing Southern lady.[48] Years later, Mitchell looked back on all these high jinks in a letter to her friend Red Baxter, her most cherished companion of all from her year at Smith: "You are still skeptical of the pleasant guff smug people hand out. . . . You still cry 'spy!' (if not something unprintable) on fake sentiment. . . . Both of us were non-conformists even then, and perhaps were somewhat of a trial to our contemporaries and elders."[49]

Mitchell left still other impressions on her fellows. "I remember her as rather dynamic and aggressive and even her speech, in spite of her southern accent, had a clipped, incisive quality. She had self-assurance which in a less gentle, friendly person, would have amounted to brashness," Martha Cole recalled. The "Yankee qualities" of her personality struck her, too: "her lack of pretense in herself and her hatred of it in others."[50] Other faces sometimes showed as well. Some housemates considered her retiring or enigmatic. She was "a shy little person" who "looked like a little girl dressed up in adult clothes." This same young woman remembered Mitchell closeting herself for a day when some bad news arrived and "emerging later looking a little sad, but going about her daily routine."[51] Similarly, while her first roommate noted her gaiety and laughter, Florence Grandin also believed that "anything that hurt her, or that she felt deeply, she could not talk about."[52] The assessment hit the mark. True, too, much was happening that she felt deeply, of which she could not speak.

The young Atlantan was not happy in Northampton, and there was very much she could not talk about. In her diary, she characterized herself as "a lonely, hurt little girl."[53] She felt isolated and alienated among the other girls. "I never found my level," she ruminated two years after she left Smith. "I was a misfit at 10 Hen. My roommate . . . and Red Baxter were about my only friends." "I was too young to have gone off to college," she told a friend. "I'm sure if I ever have a daughter I won't send her to Smith till she's 19 or 20—unless she has had a great deal more practical experience with the world, the flesh and the devil than her mother had at 16 or 17!"[54] She was, in short, miserable. Years later, reflecting on her year away from home, she believed she had flirted with a nervous breakdown. The very fact of leaving home and going away to college in the North provoked a major crisis. In her first weeks at Smith, she experienced the most intense mixture of liberation and limitation, independence and alienation, euphoria and depression. Years after the fact, at least, this is how she recorded her reactions.

A decade after she packed her last trunks for home, the young writer, then in the very middle of creating her epic novel, tried to reconstruct her chaotic state of mind at Smith in the first semester.[55] Even after all that time, she had not made sense of all her reactions; they remained a jumble of clashing extremes. Euphoria was her initial response on going away to school. She described in orgiastic terms her reaction "when mother untied the apron strings," as she phrased it. This liberated and expanded sense of self so possessed her, she wrote, "that I had to sternly restrain myself from wallowing on the soft campus grass and yelling extatically [sic] after the initial frenzy passed." With the passing frenzy, however, depression settled in. Indeed, her expanded sense of self also liberated sleeping terrors. For two years before going off to school, she had been finding answers to all manner of problems and difficulties in her life. She reached "many conclusions that were diametrically opposite opinions I had held all my short life." She had not dealt with the problems, however; she had shoved them into "the Pigeon holes" of her unconscious. Now, suddenly, away from home and on her own, "the unconscious unpigeonholed itself." Wild thoughts assaulted her from every direction. "I began to be afraid that I was losing my mind because so many bewildering thoughts and feelings seemed to pop out of nowhere, answers to things that had puzzled me for years." She could not express her terror, even had she possessed a confidant. She had none in any case. She was voiceless and terrified. "At night I tramped the dark campus and communed with myself whether or not I was crazy."

The writer herself never pulled all the loose ends of her college crisis together to her own satisfaction, but consciously or not, she left a clue to both the sources and the significance of her woes at the very beginning of her letter. She had prefaced her description of her orgiastic sense of freedom with liberation from her mother. Only when her mother released her, she related, did she feel herself "uncoiling and stretching and awakening," did she experience "a consciousness of myself, of power, of my own awakening personality." If separation from her mother spelled liberation, however, it also prompted the anxiety that followed. Even almost a decade after the crisis, Mitchell could still not bring herself to make the full connection of her own mixed feelings about her mother and herself; in a tangled, convoluted way, however, she acknowledged that intensely conflicted relationship as the source of her dilemmas that fall of 1918 as she tramped the dark campus questioning her sanity. In her 1927 analysis of the crisis, she professed that the source of her depression and despair still eluded her, but in the middle of her discussion of her crisis, she made an odd judgment that suggested her deeper understanding. "If I wasn't crazy, why did

Truth and Honesty seem suddenly the most important things in the world wasted on allegorical characters in 'Every Woman'?'' The expression is odd from any angle. What did she mean by all the peculiar references to virtue, "allegorical characters," and "Every Woman?" Unraveling the sentence helps illuminate a thought that Mitchell disguised even from herself. The expression would seem to read: Virtue and merit are real; they do not reside solely in the Ideal Type or Perfect Forms; the individual exists outside these forms. Critically, however, Mitchell casts all this in gender-specific terms. For a female, she would say, merit exists outside the strictures of True Womanhood; indeed, she allows that Perfect Ladyhood actually wastes or ruins virtue for individual women.

Although she phrased these issues as abstractions and enigmas, they hit the core of her values. As a child of Dixie and a woman growing up with the region's radical idealization of womanhood, her references reveal a fundamental crisis about her cultural identity as a Southerner. Regional mythology, for example, associated allegorical virtue with True Womanhood in the most aggressive way and then extended these to define the goal and essence of Southern culture and regional distinctiveness itself. For an individual woman, then, to challenge the Lady threatened the entire social structure. More to the point, however, the problem hit hardest insofar as May Belle Stephens Mitchell embodied and personified the daughter's image of the ideal. The young woman's individual liberation therefore entailed a whole train of personal, psychological, social, and cultural consequences that threatened every aspect of her identity. No wonder she feared for her sanity.

While Mitchell groped with a fundamental element in her psychological and cultural life in her first months away from home, other catastrophes compounded her sense of crisis. In mid-fall, Clifford Henry's parents notified her of their son's injuries. Soon after they informed her of her fiancé's death. She left no record of her response. That, perhaps, was one of those hurts that she felt too deeply to discuss in any circumstances. She did, however, describe another crisis in her first semester. Away from her family for the first Christmas in her life, she passed the season with her rich Aunt Edythe, and the visit proved a disaster that agitated her for years.

In the fall of 1918, the Mitchell women had stayed with the Morrises before traveling to Northampton. The girl had not been happy in Greenwich. The longer, return visit over Christmas made the earlier episode seem idyllic. She did not like this aunt, whom she considered insecure, pretentious, and vain. After fifteen years passed, she liked her even less. In her re-creation of the affair a decade and a half later, she characterized Edythe Stephens Morris as the very devil, and she classed her stay with her among her life's traumas.[56]

Things started off wrong and got worse rapidly. In the high-handed manner that generally characterized the Fitzgerald and Stephens women, the aunt decided that nothing about the girl was right, and she set about correcting all the errors. "My clothes were wrong, my manners boorish, my conversational frankness something to be curbed," the author wrote bitterly. The social horrors she created for her niece, however, were Mitchell's angriest complaint. Her Aunt Edyth used her pitilessly, Mitchell insisted, to advance her own social standing. Specifically, on New Year's Eve, Mrs. Morris set her up with the fastest set of Greenwich youth, who then promptly dumped the girl for a foray into New York. "She forced me on the people she wanted to crash and if I live to be a million I will never forget the unhappiness and mortification which I suffered at their hands," she wrote. "I can see now that they didn't want me any more than they wanted her and resented having me pushed on them. But then, young and bewildered, I only thought that I was at fault and that I was very unattractive and crude and a family disgrace. . . ." They abandoned her completely in a company where she knew not another living soul. "Like childbirth," she related, "this is an agony no male can ever fully appreciate. I had been weighed and found wanting." She fled weeping to the ladies' room, where some displaced Southerners recognized her accent and rescued her. The story ran a final chapter when Mrs. Morris blamed the girl for driving off her date.

Her mother's sister pricked something deep in Mitchell's life, and as the writer adjudged the affair long afterward, she used much the same language to describe her reaction as she had to define her college crisis of the fall. Here, however, the shadow of her mother falls much more clearly. While she blames her aunt completely for the affair, she implies, at least, criticism of her sainted mother, too. Thirteen years after May Belle Mitchell's death, the daughter still could not censure her own parent, but her aunt's words challenged May Belle Mitchell's values, in this reconstruction, as much as the Mitchell girl herself. As she explained the affair, her aunt's diatribe

> made me look inside myself and ponder my education and wonder vaguely if she was right or not. But I was only sixteen [sic] and had been brought up to believe that grown ups knew it all. I had the greatest respect for Mother's opinion and she had told me to obey my aunt. And I was very distressed at the thought that I was so crude and common that I had disgraced her and hoped that Mother would never hear of my conduct. I never wrote Mother about it all. I didn't dare and I had no one with whom I could discuss it all and my standards of conduct that heretofore seemed so firm were wobbly and I didn't know what impulse to trust and what to repell. . . .

Had her mother raised her right or not? Did the saint have dirty hands? Or had the daughter earned the aunt's—and mother's—stricture? This puzzle lay beneath the surface of the Christmas story, and it helped inspire the author's passionate rendering of the episode. In confirmation of the riddle's power, Mitchell made the exact same question a paradigm in the novel she was writing at the very moment she made this judgment about her own personal affairs. Moreover, if the circumstances differed, Mitchell used the same ambivalent language for her heroine's dilemma as she had employed to describe her own circumstance. "Nothing her mother had taught her was of any value whatsoever now and Scarlett's heart was sore and puzzled," she was writing. "Scarlett thought in despair: 'Nothing, no nothing, she taught me is of any help to me! . . . Oh, Mother, you were wrong!'"[57]

In this passage, Mitchell's fictional heroine was ruminating on her own condition; she was doing so, however, in the critical context of that mother's death. So was the author. In the middle of the crises of her freshman year, three weeks after the Greenwich catastrophe, May Belle Mitchell died.

A new outbreak of the flu had delayed the school's opening in Northampton, and Mitchell had remained with her Aunt Edythe for another fortnight after New Year's. She had barely unpacked her new clothes when on January 22 she received a somber message from her father that her mother was ill. She had contracted a severe case of influenza on January 18; her condition deteriorated daily. The girl sped home. She arrived on the twenty-sixth. Her mother had died the day before.

Three days before she died, as May Belle Mitchell waged the last battle of her life, she dictated a long letter to her daughter. Nothing demonstrates her character better; nothing suggests more clearly her relationship with her daughter. To the last and *in extremis*, she remained cool, rational, and admonitory. In full possession of her senses, she died as the good stoic, the model she had adopted even as a child. It signaled the ultimate measure of her commitment to self-denying life at a soldier's post. The letter is critical for still other reasons. Mrs. Mitchell sought here to make a final impression and leave a final word. In trying to summarize her wishes for her child, she also reviewed and judged her own life. In so doing, this most pivotal character in Margaret Mitchell's biography provides an ultimate glimpse of the divided legacy she passed on. "Dear Margaret," she dictated to her son,

> I have been thinking of you all day long. Yesterday you received a letter saying I am sick. I expect your father drew the situation with a strong hand and dark colors, and I hope I am not as sick as he thought. I have pneumonia in one lung and were it not for flu complications, would have more than a fair chance of recovery. But Mrs. Riley had pneumonia in both lungs and is now well and strong. We shall hope for the best but remember, dear, that if I go now it is the best time for me to go. I should

have liked a few more years of life, but if I had had those it may have been that I should have lived too long. Waste no sympathy on me. However little it seems to you I got out of life, I have held in my hands all that the world can give, I have had a happy childhood and married the man I wanted. I had children who loved me, and, as I loved them, I have been able to give them what will put them on the high road to mental, moral and perhaps financial success, were I to give them nothing else. I expect to see you again, but if I do not I must warn you of one mistake that a woman of your temperament might fall into. Give of yourself with both hands and overflowing heart, but give only the excess after you have lived your own life. This is badly put. What I mean is that your life and energies belong first to yourself, your husband and your children. Anything left over after you have served these, give and give generously, but be sure there is no stinting of love and attention at home. Your father loves you dearly, but do not let the thought of being with him keep you from marrying if you wish to do so. He has lived his life; live yours as best you can. Both of my children have loved me so much that there is no need to dwell on it. You have done all you can for me and have given me the greatest love that children can give parents. Care for your father when he is old, as I cared for my mother. But never let his or anyone else's life interfere with your real life. Goodbye, darling, and if you see me no more it may be best that you remember me as I was in New York.

Your loving mother.[58]

One last time she tried to set things straight. In consciousness of her own motherhood and womanhood, in her special sense of obligation to her woman-child, and, not least, in her lifelong concern with women's issues, Mrs. Mitchell wrote to her daughter as her ultimate audience and court. As she held up the mirror of her own values to her child, she was also speaking to the mirror.

Assuming her daughter's criticism, the dying woman confronted the question of her own success or failure. She gave a positive answer. Domesticity, a husband, and loving children are everything the world could give, she related, and this was what she had wanted. But the impression was not exactly right. She knew it. Instinctively, she stretched a finger to fix it up. Simply put, she admitted that she had wanted something more for her own child than this. By her own description, the object of her motherly ambitions had not been the passive one, to teach them to accept "what the world can give"; on the contrary, it was to set them on the high road to public success and to inspire them actively to make their own way in the world. It was the same goal that had fired Gretchen Finletter's mother—and produced the consequent anxiety in Gretchen Finletter herself. Give and give, the parent advised, in deference to traditional roles for women; but acknowledging new notions of self and achievement, she also insisted, "give only the excess after you have lived your own life."

With this strong counsel, now the mother knew that she had definitively altered the image she first created. Hair straggled untidily from beneath her feminist chignon. And now she could not get the image straight again. "This is badly put," she admonished herself. She tried to restate the issue: "What I mean is. . . ." But things got blurrier. She smudged the clear advice to follow one's own ambitions. Thus, she radically modified "your own life" to mean "yourself, your husband and your children." She was then back again to the old model of giving and giving. This correction, however, reveals another flaw: the sense that selfless generosity might be actually at the expense of those within the family circle. "Be sure there is no stinting of love at home," she warned. Was this the mother's fear for the daughter? Was it her anxieties about herself, that her own activities came at the expense of her own family? It names, in any case, another dimension of the woman's struggle between "self" and "other." The dying woman had no problem, however, releasing her child from filial obligations. She discharged her daughter—or so she tried—from any debts and obligations she might have felt to her. You have more than duly compensated me, she says. And so she charged and discharged the woman: You have satisfied your debts to your parents; you do not have to marry if you do not choose; be on your own, you are on your own. Others have had their lives, "live yours as best you can." And she repeated: "never let . . . anyone else's life interfere with your real life."

As May Belle Stephens herself had known, the advice was far easier to offer than to follow. Her own religious training had helped her avoid the severest consequences of the conflict between self and other. Her daughter lacked that discipline: nowhere in her letter had Mrs. Mitchell talked of God or religious doctrine or the consolation of church or faith. Then, too, against the mother's admonition for autonomy, the daughter would always see the selfless model of the Angel in the Home when she thought of womanhood. Thus, even on her deathbed, the mother perpetuated the woman's dilemma of giving and holding back. Even by that time, the daughter knew already the tension of this conflict. It lay in no small measure behind the crisis she had felt earlier as she walked Northampton wondering if she was going mad.

The daughter's struggle for autonomy focused chiefly on independence from her mother, and May Belle Mitchell's death at this juncture forestalled the possibility of the daughter's dealing directly with her powerful parent in her own terms. She made only one major gesture in this direction. If she could not reject her mother directly, she could reject her mother's religion. As the most lasting element of her crisis in her freshman year, she jettisoned "the religious Catholic code under which I had been brought up." This was her mother's church. Through thick and thin, Mrs. Mitchell had never waivered in her religion. Mitchell first questioned her parent's faith during her year at Smith, and soon abandoned the church entirely after returning to Atlanta. She even came to sound something like Tom Watson in her snide denunciations. "Peggy was a maverick because of religion," one friend testified. "She used to talk about the Catholics the same way some people talk about New York Jews."[59] She remained as faithful to her skepticism as her mother had been to Catholicism.[60] This was as far as she could go in conscious rejection of her parent's model. The effort was too painful. Indeed, she gave up trying. She "gave up analyzing," she wrote, and determined to ride her moods "like surf riders take the crest of waves."[61]

Mitchell always imagined herself as something of an emotional orphan, but her mother's death guaranteed this state; she froze, by her own reckoning, into something like permanent childhood.[62] This is the way that Mitchell herself framed the issue as she spoke about her mother: "I knew her only as a child and as an adolescent knows an adult. I never knew her as one grown woman knows another. I should have liked very much to have known her after I was grown up." To the same correspondent, however, Mitchell's beloved and feared Mrs. Paisley, Mitchell also insisted that people remain children and never really grow up at all. "The queer thing about growing older is that one does not grow older. People just think you do because of your outward appearance."[63] For all this, girlhood possessed its own potency. It was, after all, "little girls," and motherless ones at that—like the "Peggy" of her earliest published fiction—who might avoid the prisonhouse of True Womanhood. And, indeed, that murdering, motherless child of "Little Sister" was not far from her mind in her year at Smith. Maybe that mute, avenging killer constituted one of the mad thoughts that swooped and darted at her sanity at this time. If so, she snatched this one and controlled it. It was this year away from home that she adopted a new name. Henceforth she would be Peggy Mitchell.

The author had played around with names as she had applied to college. On her Smith application form she had substituted the name "McKenzie" (an aunt's middle name) for the Munnerlyn of her birth certificate. She did not stick by that change, but she adopted the name Peggy now permanently for her own. No one had ever called her this before. Her family, especially her mother, eschewed such intimacies; her father and brother never surrendered to the fancy.[64] The name was hers all the more. She made it synonymous with herself, especially her writing self. Henceforth, this was how she introduced herself, and all the friends she made from Smith onward always called her by the diminutive. Yet another level exists in this rechristening of herself. However much the diminutive bespoke little-girlhood, it possessed other powerful connotations for her. It was short, in her lexicon, for Pegasus, Bellerophon's winged mount through whose power he slew the Chimera. She made the steed, minus the rider, her symbol, most notably, for example, in commissioning a bookplate with the device.[65] Peggy,

Pegasus, and power. The contradictions defined the dilemmas of her time at Smith, the ambivalence of her relationship with her mother, the future of her creative impulse, the difficulties of her years to come.

Where would she go from here? Would she fly? She battled chimerae aplenty in any circumstances.

PART II

MAID

V

First or Nothing

I only know one thing, that there are few troubles in this world that a woman, directly or indirectly, is not connected with. The French adage is right—"Cherchez la femme."

MARGARET MITCHELL TO ALLEN EDEE [1]

When she stepped off the train on Sunday, January 26, Steve received her with the news. When they got back to the house, the place was thronged with people; the college freshman took up her duties greeting all of them. May Belle Mitchell's passing brought out the mourners like night the fireflies. Besides family, friends from the suffrage movement, and fellow parishioners from Sacred Heart, poor-white folks came in from the rural districts and millworkers from the south side and west end with offerings of some kind, too, "and they insisted on seeing me because they wanted to tell me what mother had done for them, medicine when they were sick, shoes so that the children could go to school, advice when young daughters were going astray." Still other folk appeared as well.

> Negroes streamed in and out of the kitchen, most of them bringing me some poor little present, a hot corn pone, a slice of pie, a dish of greens with the grease congealing in white clumps. And they all said, as the white people had said, "Your Ma was sho a lady a real great lady. . . ."

After the mass at Sacred Heart, the funeral cortège wound its long way down Peachtree to Oakland Cemetery. There, in the heart of winter, they interred her in the plot with her beloved father and next to her older sisters, who had died thirty years before. "I did not even have time to cry," the daughter said.[2]

In keeping with ancient Southern tradition, people returned with the family to the house; but quiet soon returned, and the girl debated her future. She considered staying in Atlanta, but finally, she determined to return to Northampton. She was back by the first week of February. If she shared any of her grief with the other girls, it made no impression on them. The same held true for the boyfriends she made in her second semester. She resumed her studies and continued the same general pace she had established in the first semester. But things had changed permanently.

After the fact, Mitchell always linked her mother's death, the necessity of leaving school, and the obligation of returning home to care for her brother and father. In this sequence, the prime cause produced its inevitable effects. She exercised no choice in the matter; circumstances beyond her control dictated her actions, she always insisted. Her justification, however, reflects only partial truth. From another perspective, her mother's death came at the end of a sequence as much as at the beginning of one, and it liberated as much as it imposed new duties.

In the first place, it allowed her a rationale for quitting school. The enthusiasm for education had been her mother's, not hers. Margaret Mitchell liked school no more in 1918 than she had in 1907. She felt awkward around the other girls, and Yankees *still* put her teeth on edge. Academics offered no solace; neither did extracurricular activities. College was a bust before that dreadful news in January. In this regard, her mother's death was only one more incident in the disaster of her college year. This was precisely how she described it at the time. "Sometimes I get so discouraged I think there is no use keeping on here," she told her brother in March.

> It isn't in studies, for I'm about a "C" student—but I haven't done a thing up here, I haven't shone in any line—academic, athletic, literary, musical or anything. Of course, I suppose my year has been rather broken up with the flu and Clifford's and Mother's death but in a college of 2500 there are so many cleverer and more talented girls than I. If I can't be first, I'd rather be nothing.[3]

If her mother's death only confirmed the gloom that had racked her all year, that catastrophe also liberated her. Had the little girl succumbed to the matriarchal authority so long ago on what she later called the "Road to Tara"? Had she surrendered to her mother's wishes again in the matter of college in the North? Now she could act on her own initiative; she could assert her own will and desires without fear of her mother's censure. Indeed, she could violate her parent's fondest wishes without fear of retribution. Assertion, however, had its price. The girl could jettison college; she could not discard so easily eighteen years of admonitions that had identified women's achievement with education. By the fall of 1919, the dropout was already experiencing guilt and frustration about her willfulness. "I know perfectly well that I need more education and that I am a terrible fool and that hard study and discipline would be extremely beneficial to me," she echoed her mother; "but alas, it cannot be. Lord knows how I will end up. It worries me sometimes when I think of it."[4] The next year, the issue of education weighed even more heavily on her, and schooling became tangled in her mind with a series of other issues, not least her sense of success and failure. "I've done a pile o'thinking," she wrote in the summer of 1920:

> More than ever is the call for more schooling, more than ever the desire to know if I'm worth anything is strong. . . . It's heart rending to see the days slip by and the girls go back to school. So I've made up my mind that sometime, somehow, I'm going away, *somewhere!*[5]

She played for years with the idea of finishing her college work. Smith beckoned, if very, very faintly. Columbia seemed an option for a time. Even Wellesley. So did local Oglethorpe.[6] Something always intervened. She never did go back; yet she never reconciled herself to not finishing, either. The failure perpetually disquieted her, even when she had otherwise achieved "success" as the world defined it. In this sense, her mother's earnest promises became a plaguing curse.

Much the same forces came into play in Mitchell's decision to return home, specifically, to become mistress of her father's house in 1919. In the first place, this violated her mother's most explicit advice and desires. In her deathbed letter to her daughter, May Belle Mitchell had warned her specifically against assuming responsibility for Eugene Mitchell and his household. The prospect of her daughter's playing nursemaid to this patriarch, even one she loved, distressed her deeply, and she tried to steel the girl against the father's needs. "He has lived his life; live yours as best you can," the dying mother admonished. By returning home, then, the girl repudiated her mother's will; at the same time, assuming her mother's place in the Mitchell household provided a means of re-creating for herself some of her mother's authority. For all her strictures about the "high road" to public success, the source of May Belle Mitchell's power for her children lay in her dominion over hearth and home. Insofar as her daughter craved influence, what more legitimate place to obtain it than in the very home her parent had made, in the very seat she had occupied? The daughter wanted to be "first or nothing." If she was nothing, by her own measure, at Smith, home offered another field for her ambitions. Taking her mother's place satisfied her ambition for "first or nothing" in still another way. Mrs. Eugene Mitchell was both anonymous and heroic. She combined power and self-effacement. She was both first and nothing. The dual claims to authority and self-abnegation galvanized the imagination of the daughter. Home might resolve these conflicting claims for her even as it had seemed to do so for her parent.

In any case, when the spring semester ended at Smith, Margaret Mitchell packed her bags permanently for home. She left Northampton on June 5. Charlie, the driver and yard man, met her at the terminal as her train pulled in from New York. Late Atlanta spring offered consolation for the dismal winter, but the house itself was cold and empty. Steve, her father, and her Grandmother Stephens greeted her somberly. In life, May Belle Mitchell had buffered each of them from the others and had checked their excesses. No one served that function now. If Steve went coolly and methodically about his tasks, the other two members of the household took up the slack of emotion. Still ailing from the influenza that had killed his wife, Eugene Mitchell grieved disconsolately, and he demanded old routines still more insistently. He was never an easy man; his wife's passing made him worse. Even more set in her ways than her son-in-law, Annie Fitzgerald Stephens had survived war, invasion, economic catastrophes, social upheavals, and the deaths of babies, adolescent children, and a spouse of thirty years. At seventy-five, she took new disasters as new challenges. In residence at 1149 Peachtree Street, the Widow Stephens claimed that establishment as her own imperium. Was the house cold? It also simmered. The future glowered at the eighteen-year-old girl. She soon discovered the length of her domestic tether.

As pretender to her mother's rule, the young woman faced enormous problems. The big white house on Peachtree Street itself conspired against her. It was her mother's in almost every way. May Belle Mitchell had been the one to press for the move from Jackson Hill. She had been the one to insist upon the cool, neoclassical exterior. The furniture was hers; its placement, too. She filled the place with her own family heirlooms, like the huge old Empire sideboard that had graced the Fitzgerald dining room at Rural Home. But it was hers, of course, in other ways. She commanded the table. She filled the larders. She oversaw the servants. More, as woman, wife, and mother, she dominated and defined this house as Home. Now she was gone. Yet her spirit remained almost as powerful as her presence had been. It lurked in the corners and filled the air. Taking up this burden was harder than it looked. Little went right. The most basic requirements of housekeeping gave her eighteen-year-old successor fits. Had this world turned as her mother nodded? Even when the new mistress yowled, it hardly seemed to budge.

In later years, mistress of her own tiny apartment, Mitchell joked that God never intended her for housekeeping. She had, in truth, no talent for or inclination toward domestic management. On the contrary, she rather thrived on mess. Her disorder even established a certain standard among her college friends.[7] The habits persisted back at home. "This room is a wreck," she noted in the spring of 1920 from her littered bedroom. "It reminds me of Room 23 at Ten Hen, so complete is the chaos."[8] In contrast to her chores at Smith, Mitchell's household duties now included oversight of an entire establishment. She bore responsibility for the kitchen and marketing, for all the clearing and maintenance, but also for gardening and the grounds. Domestic help freed her from actual physical labor, but managing servants proved another kind of burden. Yes, she soon discovered the length of her tether.

In the spring of 1919, the young woman had found a true friend in a graduating senior from nearby Amherst College, Allen Edee; and after she returned to Atlanta, she wrote him regularly. These epistles chronicle her growing disenchantment with managing her father's house. At first, especially, she found householding exciting, she told Edee. While it kept her busy from early morning to almost midnight, she still considered it "good fun if you don't weaken."[9] The fun palled quickly. "I'm in the parlor on the sofa now, directing at intervals the polishing of the floors and furniture for Sunday," she wrote in March of the following year. "Probably the butler will quit if I work him too hard. I've got a rep of being a slave driver already."[10] After a year of this routine, it held no charms at all for her—nor, it would certainly seem, for the servants. "Frankly, Al," she wrote her old friend,

> I wouldn't call housekeeping a bed of roses, especially when the house has to be painted, walls papered or canvassed, house cleaned, etc. The butler, who thought he was merely for ornamental purposes, received the shock of his youthful career when I walked in Monday, coupling my "Hello, folks," with "Wash the windows, wax the floors, polish the furniture." After two days of labor (both for me and him—it was hard work making him work!), he privately thought I was the meanest white woman God ever made. Anyway, I fired him today and I'll have the deuce of a time getting another.[11]

She came to loathe the work.

No less than for the house itself, she assumed responsibility for all her father's and brother's domestic needs. This proved no less burdensome. Their health and well-being was as much her job—in her mind and theirs—as keeping the place clean and tidy. "I couldn't leave them alone and unprotected—to say nothing of undarned and unfed," she mused on occasion.[12] On another, when her father ate himself into the hospital, she remarked that her men "all seem to carry their digestion in their women folk's names and if they get sick it's the women's fault for leaving the food around."[13]

She found no sympathy in her family for her labors. Indeed, the Mitchell males did not perceive her life as burdensome at all. There was not much, really, to running the house, her brother remarked blandly. "Her duties were not arduous," he volunteered. After all, he added, she did have Susie the cook and Charlie the chauffeur–yard man.[14] They actually compounded her difficulties. "The Mitchells had plenty of money, but old man Mitchell was tight," one old friend remembered. "He didn't want Peggy to have the house done over, he was so close, but finally she did it anyway."[15] His concerns affected the daily and weekly maintenance of the house, too; for example, in his constant complaints about the thermostat setting and lights left burning. One visitor from these years recalled the establishment as "a cold, kind of shivery old house because it was so big and her father didn't warm it up so much."[16]

Although Eugene Mitchell adored his daughter, he complicated her life in a score of ways. Compulsively fastidious himself, he held her to an Olympian standard of tidiness and order. In an article she wrote later about household management, his image illuminates her picture of the "typical male." He swears to leave home at even the sight of a mop or broom, but "if only a cobweb is sighted in a distant corner or the windows clouded with dust, he cries aloud that he is living in indescribable squalor." In the same essay, she named other difficulties that echo her father's character. When a woman loses some item, she might grieve her loss, but there the issue rests—not so, the male. "A woman would never summon in the household and call on heaven to bear witness that the male contingent of her family have entered into a foul conspiracy to hide all her underwear and sox, as men are wont to do on similar occasions."[17] Not least, the father also expected her to run still more personal chores. "Xmas is almost here," she groaned in 1921. "And I wish to God it was over. Father expects me to buy 20 presents for his relatives, and I'm down to 101 pounds as a result."[18] Such tasks proved to be only more examples of the numberless obligations that fragmented her days, frayed her nerves, and drained her strength. Even so, her domestic duties were only one portion of the responsibilities she assumed on becoming mistress of her father's house.

When Mitchell returned to Atlanta in the spring of 1919, she made no distinctions between her domestic and social obligations as mistress of the Mitchell establishment. As she defined it, she really had only one job: "to come home and keep house and keep my family and home intact and take Mother's place in society."[19] She insisted repeatedly that her social activities fell into the same category as darning socks, managing servants, and feeding her family. She protested that taking over her mother's social duties "was just about the only unselfish thing I can remember having done in my life. To me, it meant giving up all the worthwhile things that counted—for nothing! For a rapid, rushed existence in a slightly uncongenial companionship." [20] If she saw her social duties as one more burden, however, she still led the most active social life. If she really lacked affection for society, she compensated with the energy of her commitment. Perhaps she still felt shy and awkward, but she screwed up her courage, adjusted her cockade, and leapt into the social battle.

Although ostensibly in deep mourning, she plunged into the middle of Atlanta's social season immediately upon returning home in June 1919. She underwent an appendectomy that summer, but the debility slowed her only briefly. By the early fall, as the social season commenced in earnest, she had hoisted every sail. She served as one of the Georgia "Maids of Honor" for the Confederate Veterans' reunion between October 7 and 9. Two weeks later, she hosted a large reception for Dr. William Allan Nielson, the former president of her alma mater, when he came south for the "All South Smith Rally." In the three weeks that followed, she remarked in passing to Al Edee that she had also participated in the first of the great dinner-dance festivities that inaugurated the debutante season and arranged a "four-hundred-couple bridge party for some charity." [21] She maintained this tempo the entire first season she was home. The next year actually increased the pace while it also altered significantly the nature of her engagements. She debuted.

Debuting was a significant if fairly late innovation in regional social history. [22] In Atlanta, the wealthiest and most prominent families began presenting their daughters formally to society in rounds of parties within twenty years of Appomattox, but debuting ceremonies reached their apex between the 1880s and the Great Depression. Debuts confirmed membership for the élite while fulfilling the more obvious purpose of encouraging endogamy or intermarriage within the gentry class. At the same time, the ceremonies ritually demonstrated the gentry's authority to a wider world.

Debutante clubs lacked written codes and formal structures, and the absence of literary evidence makes them difficult to trace. Evidence exists, however, to reconstruct the broad outline of the rituals. Coming out the same year as Margaret Mitchell, Caroline and Ethyl Tye confirm the pattern of how the clubs worked. The Tyes represented old and rich Atlanta, although, like so many of the gentry families, they often violated conventions and stereotypes. Like the Mitchells, they stressed education, and both sisters went away to school—one at Sophie Newcomb in New Orleans, the other at Barnard College in New York City. At 740 Peachtree Street, the Tyes lived only a few blocks closer to town than the Mitchells, and the ballroom on the second floor of their big house echoed with the cheer of many grand parties that season.[23] The perpetually merry Caroline, nicknamed "Beaut," later wed Ira Ferguson, and she left her own record of the ceremonies:

> Only the oldest families presented their daughters; all the parties were held at homes. There were no "hired stags," only two boys and the girl's father. There was no formal organization to the debutante club, families simply got together. Also there weren't any "foreigners," only native Atlantans. And there was no such thing as commuting debutantes, either. It lasted a season and a girl was there the whole time. It was a chance to be formally introduced to one's mother's friends and contemporaries.[24]

The rituals served the needs of the regional gentry, yet the hoi polloi relished them as much as or more than the participants, at least judging by the amount of coverage in the newspapers. Every lavish party and every aristocratic shimmy received its journalistic due every year, from October through March. Margaret Mitchell herself captured some of the popular fascination in an article she wrote for the *Atlanta Journal* four years after she had completed her own rite of passage:

> What is there about the magic word "debutante" that sets a girl apart from her fellows as unerringly as the spotlight picks the star from the chorus? After all, she is just a girl, subject to the same desires and impulses as most other girls, thinking things out along the same lines.[25]

The young reporter never professed to know the source of the magic, but it worked just the same. Her own group of girls demonstrated the appeal almost classically. On September 26, 1920, the *Atlanta Constitution* ran the first photographs that introduced the debs of that year to the masses of newspaper readers in the city. It pictured Mitchell and her pal Ross, her old buddy Dorothy Bates, Lethea and Helen Turman, Virginia Walker, Frances Ellis, and Dolly Hart, the sister of her once and future antagonist, Anne Hart.[26] This group of eight grew and shrank over the next half year of the social season. The very week this picture appeared, for example, Court Ross informed her mother that she was getting married, with or without her approval. With her wedding on October 21, 1920, to her soldier fiancé, Lieutenant Bernice McFedyen, she fell immediately off the list. Rosylyn Amorous came later but went in a similar fashion. By April 10, only Frances Ellis, the Turmans, Mitchell, and Virginia Walker remained of the original crew. The old group had been augmented, however, by the addition of the lively Tye sisters and two other girls.[27] Regardless of this shifting personnel, the Atlanta papers carried almost daily reports of the comings and goings of the debutante set.[28]

From the beginning of her debutante year, Margaret Mitchell's social career ran a rocky course. According to one source, her father pressed her against her own wishes into debuting to honor what he deemed his wife's wishes for the daughter.[29] As the clubs remained the special purview of women, however, his wife's death deprived his child of her chief sponsor. She found her champions, but they came with liabilities. Annie Stephens filled the gap somewhat; so did Mrs. Stephens's very, very aristocratic sister, Mrs. Laurent De Give.[30] Even at her best, however, the graceless Annie Stephens had created powerful enemies among Atlanta's matrons. At the same time, the girl and her grandmother clashed with greater and greater frequency over matters of social deportment, and the old lady threatened to withdraw her support completely.

Other disadvantages marred her presentation to society. Religious prejudice worked subtly against her. If her De Give relatives were Catholic, their religious eccentricity might be forgiven in light of both their wealth and their connection with actual *ancien régime* aristocracy.[31] Not so the more ordinary Stephenses. As her brother put it, their religion detracted from his sister's "marriageability."[32] To add to these problems, the debutante harbored her own reservations about the enterprise. She considered it something of a joke. "Debut! Poo! Poo!" she scoffed to her friend Edee.[33] After evenings of parties, she often returned home, kicked off her shoes, and traded cynicisms with her brother about the late evening's company. "First you assume that all rich people are good people," the two agreed; "and then, with that as an axiom, all the means by which they become rich are blessed and sanctified." All Atlanta citizens knew their place as surely as if they possessed a number according with their economic rank, Steve chortled. His sister added, "Did you ever see so many horse-faced people in your life and so many dumb-bells?"[34]

Her jaunty cynicism masked other emotions. Debuting touched some of her oldest fears. Society frightened her. She felt isolated and alone even in the city of her birth. Very early after her return to Atlanta, she had referred to Atlanta as "an unknown country where I knew no one except Dad and Steve and had to make my own way." The old alienation she had felt at Smith received new life.[35] Her anxiety led her to insist that Court Ross begin the season with her, even though she knew of her friend's coming marriage. A newspaper reporter, known as "Polly Peachtree," captured her diffidence, too. "Piquant, vivacious and cultivated, Margaret Mitchell justly claims some real achievement along literary and dramatic lines," reported the gossip columnist of the Hearst *Sunday American*, "for since childhood she and Courtenay Ross have written, staged and acted plays and lived charmingly in the realm of a vivid imagination which was but another link in the delightful friendship of the two." The young woman refused, however, to claim these honors: "When you urge her to talk of herself . . . she will at once tell you a funny story, or something about 'Court's' approaching wedding or in some other charming way divert attention from herself." And so "Polly Peachtree" judged her "the shy and shrinking violet of the club." It seemed very odd: "Was this the breadth of vision which her college life engendered? Or is it just Margaret's unselfishness in loving to exploit the attractions of those she loves?" the reporter wondered.[36]

When Court Ross left debuting for the altar, the shrinking violet changed. Was she cynical? Was she still shy? Did she loathe the pretense? No matter. She repeated the pattern of her school days. Did she expect criticism? She would give people something substantive to criticize. When she made up her mind to play the belle, she played in earnest. It was all or nothing. She had the gambler's motto: in for a dime, in for a dollar. Debut? By God, she would debut.

The newspapers recorded the change. The rotogravure section of the *Journal* depicted her dressed in trainman's mufti, clambering over a railroad locomotive. She donned an elegant, patterned—and also very low-cut—gown, for both her formal and informal debut photographs, and thus attired, she struck poses even more provocative than the dress. The newspaper published one of them: she stands in the corner of the entrance of her father's house; chin down, she turns her huge eyes seductively upward towards the camera and casts the most alluring smile towards the photographer—and of course towards the hundred-thousand readers of the *Atlanta Journal*, too. The papers also chronicled her political debut. Organizing the rebel/debutantes, she arranged an interview between newspaper reporters and the dissidents, she and the disaffected Tye sisters. Dominating the session, the young woman pronounced solemnly on a whole range of topics otherwise forbidden to the belle. She pooh-poohed marriage: "not essential to salvation," she ejaculated. She moved still farther into forbidden territory with her discussion of jobs, career, and money. "We are coming down off the auction block," the young woman declared. "Three of us that is. Helen, Lethea and I have torn off the price tags—we'd said that $5,000 a year was our lowest price—and we are going to work." Doing what? the reporter queried. And Mitchell affirmed her oldest ambition: "Oh, I am going to write comedies and short stories," she snapped back smartly.[37]

This startling young belle "was in for anything that smacks of the revolutionary," observed the reporter, and she dressed for battle. "When a girl is making a social career," she told a delighted reporter, "clothes are a uniform to be worn like a soldier's. . . ."[38] When she issued her feminist manifesto, she wore "a plain little tailored suit with a plain tailored blouse, a little bow tie, low heeled oxfords and a small close-fitting hat," and could easily be mistaken, the reporter continued, "for some energetic young person who is just setting out to reform the world."[39] A change in tactics dictated the change, but the military figures of speech persisted. Thus when she discovered "an ancient black velvet dress that I thought was given to the cook years ago," she reveled in the "sweet memories of the damage it did its country in the last war, 1917–1918," and she laid plans for its new career in new campaigns.[40]

The young woman launched the most notable sortie of her debutante year at the last great affair of the social season. As a gesture to social responsibility, the debutantes of the 1920–1921 season scheduled a charity ball for March 1 at the Georgian Terrace. They settled on the theme of "France." As they divvied up their various tasks and roles, it fell to Peggy Mitchell's lot to offer the evening's central contribution to fun and scandal. She chose to demonstrate the latest rage (supposedly) of Paris low life, the Apache dance. Any youth devoted to the movies, *Dancing Fool* or *The Four Horsemen of the Apocalypse*, currently playing in Atlanta, knew the way it went. Mitchell loved movies, she adored dancing, and she danced very well indeed. Fate called.[41]

Elevating misogyny to terpsichorean art, this routine represented the French notion of an Indian brave's cruelty to his squaw. With cigarette dangling from vicious lips, he slings his maiden this way and that; she slides away only to crawl back in supplication. The dance involved considerable slapping and other mayhem alternating with histrionic poses. All in all, Mitchell loved it. She wanted it just so, and she and her partner, Sigmund Weil, a friend from Georgia Tech, practiced diligently. The society editor was privy to what was up, and recorded the rehearsals with some delectation. "They threw one another around like rag dolls," she reported; "Margaret would hit the floor with a thump." Her father had boggled at it, according to the same report. He considered the routine "a little too—strenuous is the only word," the journalist smirked.[42] But Eugene Mitchell had lost his authority long before.

They delivered a sensational performance. Not everyone applauded. As the music died and Weil led his partner from the stage, eyebrows arched all around the room. "I thought this was supposed to be an Indian dance," wailed one horrified matron; "did you see how he *kissed* her?"[43] "What can Eugene Mitchell be thinking of to allow it?" echoed another scandalized response, as if poor Eugene Mitchell did not feel their agitation twice over.[44] The wild shenanigans and manic high jinks of the rebel deb soon had all Atlanta gabbling. A reporter summarized the affair laconically: "One other debutante offering herself and all she was on the altar of charity was constantly 'hors de combat' because of the strenuosity of the Apache dance—Margaret Mitchell, you know."[45]

The newspapers loved the affair, and the young woman constantly satisfied the journalists' desire for copy. Weeks after the benefit ball,

Medora Field, the society editor of the *Atlanta Journal*, still relished writing of the deb who "created a sensation among the mid-Victorians with her Apache dance."[46] Even two months later, the affair still generated public interest, and the *Journal* ran a photograph of Mitchell and Weil in a reprise of the performance posed before the house at 1149 Peachtree.

The young woman had poked a hornet's nest. The issue was not merely her performance at the Georgian Terrace, but more generally the persona she projected and her cultivation of the press. The old regional adage ran that a woman's name should appear only three times in the papers: at her birth, her marriage, and her death. Although honored much more in the breach than the observance, the rule still had power as a model. Peggy Mitchell scorned it. Just so, she defied the arbiters of social conduct. She chalked her mark on Peachtree, then dared anyone to cross it. Plenty were delighted to accept her challenge. "Between the older and the younger generation swords were drawn,"[47] she recollected long afterward. This was war. Women defined decorum, and women defined the enemy in the social season of 1920–1921.

Although May Belle Mitchell's ghost haunted her daughter's escapades, the foe was not all phantom. Mrs. William Lawson Peel lived and breathed, and she did no more than caricature the iron maidens of Atlanta's social order. This particular social virago, in one contemporary's colorful recollection, was "the undisputed arbiter of society in Atlanta during my childhood. She was rude and ruthless enough to make enemies and for there to grow up about her a whole system of Peeliana which was very amusing."[48] Sweeping in De Give's Opera House or the City Auditorium on opening night, this indomitable personage left an indelible impression, with her choker pearl necklace, her elaborate furbelows, and—not least of all—her tall satin shepherd's crook.[49] She cuts a comic figure in retrospect; she was a holy terror in her time. Mrs. Peel was the kind of character Margaret Mitchell certainly had in mind when she commented on the first photographic stills she received from Hollywood after the filming of her novel had begun in 1939. "One still sent me by Mr. Selznick showed Mrs. Merriwether at the bazaar and, I give you my word, I practically cringed before her," the author laughed. "She looked like a combination of all the dowagers who harassed me in my young days driving me to wait on tables at Georgia Products dinners and to sell tickets on tag days."[50] If the grande dames always "scared the liver and lights" out of her (to use her phrase), their young captains and lieutenants outdid the Marschallins. The battle culminated a year after her debut. Soon after the conclusion of the social season, Mitchell, with her fellow debs, began her probationary year as a member of the Junior League. This provided her antagonists their opportunity.

The Junior League represented the Atlanta matriarchy institutionalized. Organized by Idolene Campbell, a debutante of 1916, soon after her coming out, the Atlanta Junior League had, by 1921, established a clear, indisputable place in Atlanta's social scheme. Much more than the debutante clubs, it possessed a clear structure, rules, and order. Connected with a national organization, it was, effectively, the political arm of Atlanta ladyhood. It was as racially pure, economically sanitary, and socially élite as the Piedmont Driving Club, or more so. It served as the women's equivalent of that great bastion of the male gentry—to confirm the rules, impose order, and maintain the status quo. Was membership for a debutante usually pro forma? Yes. But not for the motherless Margaret Mitchell. She had drawn blood in the war over her social career, and she now paid the price.

In the earliest surviving reference to it, Mitchell summarized the Junior League fiasco for her sister-in-law in 1926: "In my gone and forgotten deb days, I was a probationer of the League, did a year's work in the hospital among what is laughingly referred to as Social Diseases and never made the League because I was a wild woman."[51] Mitchell had insisted on doing her volunteer service working at Grady Hospital in the black and charity wards. This pushed altruism beyond the limits of the acceptable forms of service for the ladies. They grumbled. She rejoiced in their antagonism. In later days, she regaled her friends with tales of how these doings scandalized her aunts and family, and she made the funniest stories about outraging "that old crowd of old hens who sat on the terrace of the Georgian Terrace tearing people apart," one friend of those days recalled. "The old group still ran things. We belonged to the old group but the young crowd was picking up all the 1920's and 1930's ideas. Everyone still preached to us to be Ladylike, but we had other ideas."[52]

She antagonized the young matrons even more thoroughly than the dowagers. The conflict, according to her brother, went back to old confrontations at Washington Seminary. The clashes between the two literary societies echoed to a later day, and "led to much bitterness," he wrote. "There are people in Atlanta who have always disliked Margaret Mitchell and will always dislike her. Margaret," he added, "never forgot who her enemies were."[53] Her enemies remembered, too. Indeed, the Mitchells believed that peers actually launched the offensive. Anne Hart had led the opposition to the Mitchell-Ross faction in the squabble over the editorship of the Washington Seminary school annual. She had debuted the year before Mitchell and her sister Dolly had come out with Mitchell's group. She had joined the Junior League in due order and helped lead the organization in the year of Peggy Mitchell's probation. In the Mitchells' opinion, this contemporary led the blackball campaign.[54] Whatever the circumstance, however, the Junior League rejected this one probationer in the spring of 1922.

Regardless of the source of conflict with this organization, this squabble actually represents the norm of the girl's life between 1919 and 1922. After her return to Atlanta, the young woman had fought constantly. She challenged the servants; she disputed her father and her brother; she battled her grandmother. She also dueled with more elusive enemies. Indeed, these outward conflicts reflected a no-man's-land of inner strife. Her body itself became a battleground.

In 1903, Mitchell had caught her skirts on fire while playing near an open fire. Eight years later she fell in a riding accident. Other than these, nothing particular or unusual emerges from the record regarding her health. After 1919, however, sickness, disease, accidents, and physical disabilities of one kind or another became the hallmark of her life. The magnitude—more, the number—of her ailments afterward become a critical aspect, even the dominant element of the impression she gave of herself. Almost every letter that she wrote after this time makes reference to some new ailment or the recurrence of some old debility. As remarkable as the references themselves, the manner and form of the references bear equal import. It was an extraordinary record.

The problems began almost immediately upon her returning home in 1919. Two months after she moved back, she suffered an attack of appendicitis. As if in contagion, she suffered the operation almost simultaneously with her friend Court Ross. The problems accelerated through the year that followed. In the winter, she recorded a six-week bout with the flu. In the first week of May 1920, she complained that she had "either torn a ligament or misplaced or displaced, whichever it may be, a joint in my hip—sacroiliac something-or-other." The physician prescribed bed rest. "If I'm real good, he'll give me a plaster cast and that will mean six weeks." Eight weeks after this diagnosis, she related that she had done it again. In swimming at the end of June, she reported, she had jumped into shallow water, kicked a brick, and broken her foot. "Like a fool, I didn't have it set, and danced, swam, drove and hiked for all I was worth, which didn't improve it a-tall. Finally it gave out and so did I."[55]

Accidents continued throughout the year and into 1921. In the summer, she looked back on "about four bad accidents last winter" with a bed-stay of two or three weeks for the worst of these.[56] Another riding accident proved the most notable. On a weekend visit to the University of Georgia in the fall of 1920—was it on a date with Berrien Up-shaw?—her mount went down with her, and she reinjured her foot and leg. She gave up riding for good afterwards.[57] It did internal damage as well, she insisted. This became, indeed, a kind of model accident for her, as it set off a series of other ailments and complaints that troubled her the rest of her life. Thus she attributed to this accident what she called "adhesions of the intestines." She was in and out of St. Joseph's Hospital all summer in 1921 with the condition, which she described as "just about everything below my waistline was out of place and growing to everything that they shouldn't." If she was supposed to take it easy, her campaign against strenuousness ended almost before it started. By the close of 1921 she recorded more broken bones and then complicated the injury with still more furious escapades: "I went on a possum hunt the other night, and in the dark three of us rolled down into a ravine," she told Allen Edee. "I'm a bit sore."[58] This required more doctor's visits "to get another bandage on these infernal ribs." In addition to all these, she suffered from persistent and near debilitating insomnia.[59]

While every letter recorded some new ailment she never whined or grieved about these disabilities; on the contrary, she sketched an antithetical image of herself. She presented herself in the most robust terms, as a baseball player, a football quarterback, or better still, a jockey.[60] She described herself as "a miniature Dempsey." She protested her athleticism, strength, and stamina. These two images—of failing flesh and heartiness—coexisted in a single letter, and she even joshed about the conflict. When once in their correspondence Allen Edee had referred to her as "a tough little devil," she challenged the characterization immediately. "Indeed! Sir, how dare you? Why I'm a fwagile li'l fing." Just as quickly, however, she changed the impression. "No," she corrected herself at once, "I'm exceptionally husky and muscular for a shrimp of my size." Was she a baby-talking, fragile little thing or a husky miniature Dempsey who spoke in clipped prose? Both images demanded her loyalty. Mitchell herself acknowledged the conflict and worked out her own solution to the contradiction.

In the future, charges of hypochondria and the like sent the writer into rages. In this earlier period, however, well before Mitchell herself was reading Freud and before "accident-prone" had seeped into the popular parlance, the young woman had no qualms about coupling her physical ailments with her mental disabilities. She did so over and over. Her psyche, she volunteered, betrayed her otherwise healthy body. "I go to pieces under heavy nervous strain"; that, of course, reacts on me physically and I go under. And believe me, Al, I had been living on terrible tension for a month and something had to break," she wrote to her old friend in early March 1920.[61] Something had to break? Better yet, everything had to break.

Things got worse steadily, and Mitchell repeated this analysis in even starker terms two years later. By that time, late 1921, she was losing the struggle against what she called her "black depression." She had stopped writing letters, even. "I won't saddle anyone with a rambling letter of hard luck and bitterness," she explained. "I decided that if I couldn't write cheerful letters, I'd wait until I could." She related, incidentally, how she had cracked a couple of ribs the month before and

rebroken them soon after, but these complaints paled beside the problems with what she termed "morale"; indeed, psychological affliction
produced the physical debility, she judged.

> As long as I'm in a normal, tranquil state of mind, I'm perfectly all right.
> But just let me get upset or mad or cry or be happy—and bingo! Every
> muscle seems to go slack and the jolly old pep goes, and in the reaction
> that comes on I'm too exhausted to give a damn . . . just let Dad begin
> to fuss at me about something or let me forget and go on one of my old
> swearing rages . . . and then it's goodby for a while for me! . . . When I
> left St. Joseph's, the doc told me to 'lay away my emotions in cotton
> wool' for a year. Well, Al, mine was never a tranquil temperament, and
> to lead a stolid, unemotional existence is not an easy task for me! After
> I've cut loose on a grand 'emotional spree,' as Doc Leslie calls 'em, and
> hated somebody gloriously for a couple of hours—and the reaction hits
> me—it's like another Margaret coming to the surface. I just don't care—
> nothing seems to matter. My reason can plead with my lethargic second
> self that I'm a damn fool—that I have everything that matters. . . . And
> yet, old dear, when the gloom descends, all that isn't any consolation.[62]

Over and over she would make these connections: Emotional reaction deadened her vitality, physical debility resulted, and waves of
depression flooded her spirit. She read a letter that provoked her tears
and wrath. "The result 'shot me,'" she insisted. The same day, she
"held two hands and listened to two hard-luck stories that make the
world seem singularly rotten and brutal. There's so much suffering
and sorrow in the world and so little I can do, and I do want to help
so much." Sympathy drained her. She lost will and energy with every
expression of feeling. It seemed even to diminish her physically. In the
middle of this very litany of sorrows, she ejaculated, "It's hell to be
small." What of her miniature Dempsey? Her very self diminished, and
she shrank into some anonymous, prenatal state:

> Just now, I have such an odd feeling of mental lethargy stealing over me.
> Tonight I'm so very tired of planning, worrying, feeling, sympathizing
> for people. How nice it would be just to lie in someone's arms like a
> child, cuddled close against their shoulder, every aching muscle relaxed,
> every keyed-up nerve loosened, no worry, no responsibility—only peace—
> to drift and drift.[63]

Depression settled in like the leaden skies of a Southern winter. "I'm
as acutely unhappy as it is humanly possible to be and remain sane,"
she wrote, just past her nineteenth birthday. Why? She did not know;
but peace never came:

> I keep life filled and speeded up so that I can cheat myself into believing
> that I am happy and contented, but oh! Al, when night comes and I go

to bed and turn out the lights, I lie there in the dark, I realize the absolute futility of trying to kid myself . . . there is something missing in my life. For a year now I have been trying to figure out what it is, for it is vital to happiness—but I can't find out.[64]

She fought the world, the flesh, and the very devil, but in the midst of family fights, social conflicts, household burdens, and all her other nameless woes, the young woman still tracked her muse, one way or another. She still wrote. Indeed, her writing both lightened and formalized her pain. Deep into the night she made her insomnia functional as she composed voluminous letters to friends, scribbled diary entries, and labored over short stories and other fiction. Very little of what she wrote in this time survives. Only one correspondent preserved her missives in this period.[65] Her diary also disappeared, except fragments. If she destroyed all her fictions, one survived in palimpsest; she described it in a letter to Allen Edee. The context reveals as much about her values as the story itself. Both confirm the ways her writing absorbed the conflicts of the years after her mother's death.

In the spring of 1920, she worked industriously on one short story, and over the course of three letters to her friend Allen Edee, she described it in detail. If Mitchell created such fictions perpetually, this one is especially important because even in outline form it alone survives of all her literary efforts between "Sergeant Terry" of 1918 and her journalistic writing that commenced about New Year's Day, 1923. It is important for other reasons. As she summarized it to her old friend, it restated some of the oldest themes of her girlhood fiction, but still more critically, it underlines her fictional rendering of the struggles of her life after her mother's death.

On March 4, 1920, Mitchell alluded initially to the story with only a passing reference.[66] In a second letter, nine days later, she described the plot in much more detail. She elaborated the narrative still further and finally in a letter of March 26. Taken together, these references allow a reconstruction of the tale, at least in outline. They also permit a glimpse into the author's attitude about her fiction and, finally, suggest relationships between her fiction and her life.

The story, on the surface, chronicles a traditional *ménage à trois*. A maid falls in love with a penniless youth, but she marries another for the sake of material security. At the wedding, the rejected lover kisses the bride in such a way as to make her realize her folly. The kiss dashes her hopes for the future and triggers a terrible sense of loss. Here, however, the author hit a literary stump; her difficulty prompted her first reference to the fiction. She knew how the story ended—with her heroine's frustration—but how was the heroine to be kissed so as to provoke this sense of misery? She carried her dilemma to her old friend Edee.

Up to this point in her description, Mitchell chronicled a traditional romantic threesome, but the rejected lover dominates her re-creation of the story. His public action—the wedding kiss—initiates and focuses the tale's dramatic tension. In kissing the bride, he intends to finish the heroine as a "physical being," to make her "dead in the flesh," and to "kill the physical side." The bride, for her part, is passive and defenseless. All the same, she has earned her punishment. Having recognized true love, she rejected it for the material security of the elderly groom.[67] Her error won proper retribution.

Prompted by Mitchell's queries of March 13, Allen Edee offered some suggestions about just how the rejected suitor should respond to the faithless woman. And now the author revealed that the male's actions and motives were actually quite irrelevant to her problem. If getting the man's attitude right were the only problem! she fussed. "I could do it beautifully from the masculine angle," she declared.[68] What then was the problem? What did she mean in her earlier complaint about the difficulty of "writing something you have never felt and cannot comprehend"? It was not the kiss itself she could not describe, nor the male attitude, she protested; it was, rather, the girl's response that baffled her. She summarized the issue:

> I can't write such a kiss from a girl's viewpoint. You see, Al, this story is written from the viewpoint of a girl's diary, and that makes it difficult to describe the kiss. I don't believe anyone ever had truthfully portrayed a girl's mental processes during a love scene—or just exactly what she thought and felt when kissed. It seems almost a betrayal of one's sex to write such things![69]

This gloss on her story changes the perspective entirely. As diary entries, the characters and actions in this fiction live only insofar as the protagonist imagines them. Existing exclusively in the heroine's mind, they are thereby "fictional" on two levels: Mitchell imagines her heroine imagining them. She filters them through female consciousness twice over—her own and her protagonist's. Despite the author's ostensible interest in "the masculine angle" and a traditional romantic threesome, then, she actually creates a kind of female geometry. The bride herself occupies one angle. In the other corner, her material or self-interested self substitutes nicely for the otherwise vague man she married for physical security. The "true love" in the final corner? He represents, in Mitchell's definition, a manifestation of the heroine's own creativity—a kind of spiritual side that both censures and inspires the girl.

In Mitchell's retelling of her story, her heroine has two mutually exclusive—and antagonistic—sets of interests. She is divided against herself. The material or physical wars against the spiritual. The heroine is looking out for her material well-being in rejecting her "poor man" and real love. Before that, however, she has already effectively decided to deny her own spiritual nature, which he represents. This rejection, in turn, provokes the train of punishment, of which the male acts primarily as the agent. The punishment, moreover, only redoubles the protagonist's original dilemma: retribution for her error is no more than to own the divided nature that prompted her problem in the first place. Whichever way she turns, the heroine finds herself in double jeopardy. This, then, is the profounder "situation from which there was no logical escape." The heroine's frustration is, effectively, the story's real object. By the same token, as the dominant motive of the tale, frustration starts the story, too. In this context, Mitchell's difficulty with the kiss itself defines less the problem of a specific act than of the more general quandary of delineating the cause of the heroine's frustration.

The implications of this analysis reach deep into the author's life; they illuminate some of the most obstinate problems of Mitchell's creative impulses. The content of the story's triangle might change, but the triangular conflict persists: it now depicts the heroine's self locked in antagonism with, and endless longing for, its own obscure desires. This new triangle, in turn, reflects the shadow of a third—the relationship between Margaret Mitchell and her own mother. Mitchell's recreation of her earliest memory depicted the feminine triangle one way, a charming child confronting the split image of a mother—a hissing witch up here, a kindly matron over there. In other cases, the image of the mother remained constant while the child divided her part between the intransigent wretch and the helpless innocent.

The author's identity permeates her heroine's. The bride cannot seize the initiative and write/right her problems. The author will not, cannot make her writer write. Mitchell cannot write herself. In this impossible circumstance, the story writer abandons the dilemma that she created for her heroine. With the promise or threat of "betraying one's sex," the young author moved from the protagonist's dilemma to her own. By interjecting her own personal, extra-literary authority here, Mitchell forecloses her heroine's search and stops the story short of a conclusion.

Mitchell and her heroine were not the same, but they shared much. Both were writers: if the fictional one was an unselfconscious diarist, the real-life author was an ambitious proto-professional. Both were baffled in their tasks. Mitchell admitted thwarting her character, but this action mirrored her own immediate circumstances. Frustration bracketed every reference to her art in these years. Her first allusion to her narrative set the stage. She had been sick and anticipated going out, but the weather prohibited it. It had rained for days. She had gone through all the books in the house; she had nothing to read. Her fiction remained. She could not finish it. She had created a plot that she could not move; she had imagined a circumstance she could not describe. Having trapped her heroine, she herself responded like an animal in a cage, "tramping up and down the library, pausing at intervals to flatten my nose against the French windows and curse the rain."

The protagonist of the story is not only a writer. She is Woman Writing. The immobility of her pen spells the end of her. Mitchell felt the same compulsion about writing and much the same identity as writer. The failures of her own pen heralded the same fate as her fictional subject's. Frustration? Deadly frustration. This is where both authors' tales commenced and closed in these frantic years. Still she struggled with her little story, but life was too tangled. "I swear I've never had as much trouble with any story as this one. I have written and rewritten this page a score of times, but I can't get it right. . . . Nothing seems right. I'm in despair." Even so was her immobilized, nerve-racked heroine. And just so did these difficulties mirror the difficulties of her life at home. Householding stole her time. Chores fragmented her hours. Her "menfolk" expected her attention. Jane Austen would have recognized her plight. "I haven't much time to concentrate on writing anyway," she continued. "The phone's always jangling, or somebody coming in, or orders to be given and work to be superintended, or business to be done for Dad or Steve, for they are too busy to attend to anything outside of the office." Two weeks later, nothing had changed as she wrote one last time of her tale, amid her own deepening sense of gloom. "Poor story," she sighed. "It hasn't moved a line since I wrote you concerning it! In the first place I was a little at sea, and then, too, I wanted to finish another story first. I haven't much time for consecutive writing anyway."[70]

Nothing ever changed. Maybe it was all a bad job, anyway. Maybe some other environment might nurture her ambition more than this one. Maybe she could find another outlet for her ambition. Maybe men could satisfy her where she could not satisfy herself. She played with this option even as she struggled with her fictions.

VI

The Baby-Faced Vamp

Really there's nothing in the world to boost a girl's morale like the knowledge that there's a gempmum fren' all ready to seduce her if she gives him one half the chance. This knowledge was all that kept me going lots of times when I wanted to slump. . . . . They always ended by getting disgusted when my virtue remained adamant under assault or else they wanted to marry me which was worse. . . . I think a man who makes improper proposals is a positive necessity in a girl's life—just as much of a necessity as a man whose intentions are honorable and who believes you the personification of all ignorance and innocence.

MARGARET MITCHELL TO FRANCES MARSH[1]

*B*y 1922, her charm had become legendary and her romantic conquests a matter of public record. "Suffice it to say, she has in her brief life, perhaps, had more men really, truly 'dead in love' with her, more honest-to-goodness suitors than almost any other girl in Atlanta," gossip columnist "Polly Peachtree" wrote that year. "For she is a beauty. Then, too, she has a pretty wit, a sparkling manner and a fearlessness which is most engaging."[2] Men adored her.

She possessed a singular beauty; indeed, she was hardly a beauty at all by conventional standards. Tiny, only four feet eleven inches in low heels, she fought to keep her weight above 100 pounds. Other than a squarish jaw and a pointed chin, her face lacked structural distinctiveness; indeed, it possessed the most extraordinary malleability. Depending on her mood and dress, she is hardly recognizable from photograph to photograph: in a middy blouse, she passes for a schoolgirl; in a low-cut evening gown, she looks like the vamp personified; she appears almost matronly in a black satin dress, hat, and gloves; whereas white serge pants change her appearance just as completely. The motorcycle hat, puttees, and holstered pistol transformed the impression altogether.

She had wide cheekbones, and, when she crinkled her eyes, she appeared almost oriental. Although she had inherited her mother's clear, almost transparent white skin, her enormous eyes, fringed with long dark lashes, remained her most striking feature. They seemed to change color from friend to friend or mood to mood. Some saw grey, some violet. People generally settled for dark blue. Her hair seemed to change color, too. Some people called her a redhead, but chestnut or deep auburn brown described it better. Even at the height of the flapper bob's popularity, she never cut it. She kept it long but pulled up and pinned back in soft folds. On several notable occasions, it fell loose with the most dramatic effect.

She was well-proportioned and prided herself on her good figure. While she dressed like a high-style if miniature mannequin, she also carried herself very well and boasted an athlete's physicality. She could dance all evening, yet arise the next day early to swim, to camp, and to hunt possum that night. Yet even her physical grace and energy paled beside her social charm. No one matched her talent for good talk and lively conversation. Infinitely curious about everything, she possessed an intelligence and wit to match. People frequently noted her "forthrightness," "frankness" and the liberality of her talk, but she could offer the keenest—and otherwise most outrageous—observations without ever (or almost never) offending. She knew all the "pleasant butter and soft soap and meaningless flatteries most southern girls have up their sleeves," she wrote; indeed, she elevated flattery to an art form.[3] Men fell upon her like wolves.

Men adored her, and she, in turn, needed men. Males, however, exerted the most ambivalent attraction for her. While she relished male company and flaunted her collection of suitors, marriage failed to interest her. Sex repulsed her. These divergent impulses created the fiercest cross currents in her life, just as they underlined the divergent tendencies in her own character. Men and sex, sex and men: from her first romance in the summer of 1918, they represented the tangle in her life, and in the process of her affections, she tangled many an admirer's life as well.

Her brief affair with Clifford Henry represented one aspect of her attitude towards love. She idealized that affair without any physical side at all. When her friend Allen Edee referred slyly to the sexual aspect of the romance, she claimed he had "dirtied up" the affair. Their love, she fumed "had in it no trace of physical passion." She described it as "the feeling that just misses the platonic and comes before the realization that in maturer love, passion has an indispensable place." This was one man, she cried, "who revered me because I was not common," and she cherished "the childish ideal that somewhere there is a man who will love and respect me far more because I have kept above the cheapness of passing passion."

That physicality had to enter love seemed sad or almost tragic in her view of things. "Of course I realize that death spares us many disillusionments and that the boy I promised, *in all faith*, to marry would have returned different and a man," she mused.[4] The remark is critical: "different and a man." She never had to face that problem with Cliff Henry. His death both deprived her and saved her. The tragedy lay not merely in his death, but in that he would have returned with physical appetites at all. His death permanently preserved the illusion of his (now literally) disembodied love. He became pure spirit after St. Mihiel. Indeed, Mitchell made him over, literally, as a protecting ghost, and she told at least one long story about how this wraith rescued her from a dangerous situation with one overzealous lover.[5] Her Clifford-Galahad defended her from such rakes; more critically, this spirit protected her from herself, from that "other Margaret" who led her into scrapes and jams or harried her towards her own destruction. "Will you believe me when I tell you that I am never alone—except when I'm up to some mischief in which I have no business?" she told her friend Allen. "I seldom make a mistake, and when I do," she added, "it is because I trusted my judgment and not Clifford's."[6] This phantom recalls another version of her old divided self, the good, chaste Margaret, battling the hell-raising Peggy; even so, it echoes the influence of her dead parent, too. She made the latter connection herself. Her affection for Cliff Henry, she insisted, "has had more influence for good in my life than anything besides my mother."[7] Indeed, with their virtually simultaneous deaths, she conflated their spirits.

With Henry in Europe and then dead, men and sex figure hardly at all in her year at Smith. Her roommates marveled at her vast overseas mail and her collection of soldiers' photographs, and her closest friend Red Baxter recalled that "all men were putty in Peg's hands,"[8] but another housemate sketched a more accurate picture: "Peg was popular with men but not what might be called a heavy dater."[9] Indeed, the girl survived the fall without any apparent male company at all. Her first dates came at Christmas when she holidayed with her rich Aunt Edythe in Greenwich, the visit that realized her worst nightmares about boys. Forced on unwilling escorts and then abandoned at a party where she knew no one, she described the New Year's Eve affair as one of the unhappiest and most mortifying experiences of her life.[10]

New Year's at her aunt's in Greenwich had been a horror; her mother's illness, death, and funeral shattered the rest of the winter. In the dreadful spring of 1919, gloom's maw yawned. Just then, another man appeared, and Allen Edee proved to be the most important suitor of her year away from home. She was fighting the blackest depression, she told him later, when he sauntered into her life. "I was up against something that seemed almost occult to me and I just about desperate. You arrived at the psychological moment."[11] In her profound slump, as she called it, she found in Allen Edee the perfect "gempmum fren' " to "keep her going."

Two years her senior, the young Midwesterner from Pawnee City, Nebraska, was just finishing Amherst when he met the Smith freshman in her second semester. Dark, suave, and wryly self-possessed, he impressed Mitchell immediately. He was at once, as Mitchell scribbled in her diary, sardonic and gentle, blasé and tender.[12] Both sides satisfied her needs. She set her cap for him.

Mitchell practiced a self-conscious technique for snaring men. She would "lay low, look wide-eyed innocence and see what happens."[13] She used the same approach with the Amherst boy. "I try to get a line on this suavely smiling man but admit defeat," she wrote in her diary. "All I can do is attempt to impress him that I am only a sweet young thing." While she protested her real innocence, he voted her "a 'hard proposition and an experienced flirt.' " Watching the performance, one of her housemates muttered, "Watch Al fall for the baby-faced l'il 'vamp.' " The freshman overheard the remark, and it gave her "a thrill of wicked satisfaction," she wrote later.[14]

Edee succumbed.

The pair hit it off immediately as Mitchell continued to play the role that attracted Edee in the first place. She cultivated him by playing the ingenue and sweet young thing to his "ultra-sophisticated young senior who understood women and loved to make cleverly cynical remarks about them."[15] She was the naïf and wide-eyed innocent before the expositions of his "Don Juan-ish subjects" and his "Bohemian ideas on life in general." Yet her correspondence shows that she patronized and coddled quite as often as she "played the baby." In her letters, she might have apologized for her "motherly advice," but she made no apology for—rarely even deigned to notice—all her other passing references to "my child," "my boy," "old boy," "dear boy"—forms of address that dominated her letters.

If she performed the roles of both helpless child and mother-wise matron with Edee, she shied away from the intervening woman's part that connoted sexuality or physicality of any kind. Sex figured in their relationship only as a topic of conversation; even in this vague guise, however, it unsettled the Atlanta girl. She particularly disliked what she called Edee's "bolshevisticly-Byronic" ideas of love. "I was always vaguely suspicious of them," she said. His theory of life and love "never appealed to me nor did I fully understand it," she told him afterward.

> There was one of your pet theories on morality that used to annoy me terribly. It was your Greek philosophy of the immorality of all things destructive and the goodness of all creative forces. Dear me, how often I have mentally frothed at the mouth about that! Really, I felt deeply upon the subject as it was all at variance with my Puritanical upbringing.[16]

Her "Puritanism" also accounted for the fury with which she responded to one of Allen Edee's otherwise innocuous philosophical musings as they strolled the campus in the spring of 1919. " 'To know life thoroughly one must live deeply and know many experiences,' " he had intoned. She exploded. "I suppose by 'experiences' you mean women. By George, I'll never be a part of any man's experience!" she snorted. A year later, she still seethed to recall her "helpless rage" as she had glowered up at Edee's "coolly smiling face" after this exchange.[17]

Mitchell saw him as "a pal to stand by" or "the pal who made life livable [for] a miserable, unhappy kid"; "comradely affection" governed her emotions.[18] Edee pressed for something less platonic. On one outing, at Old Sugarloaf Mountain, a favorite courting spot for Smith girls and Amherst boys, they petted, and the couple sneaked back to Northampton long after curfew at Mrs. Pearson's.[19] However innocent, the episode distressed her. Her diary recorded "the loss of self-respect that only a breaking of principle can produce," and months later her guilt still rankled in her letters to her friend. "I suppose you think I 'neck' every man who takes my fancy. You think that because I liked you and showed it that it is impossible for me to pursue successfully my 'conservative' career."[20] The affection proved to be an anomalous aspect of their time together. She never allowed such liberties again, even when they parted. This was her triumph, and she recorded it as such in her diary. "I knew as he bent to kiss my hand, that I was mistress of this last situation even tho he had dominated many in the past." And she smiled to think that even her victim sensed her authority. "[I] knew, too, that a dim realization that would take months to fully mature was beginning to dawn on him." "I shall never forget it," she gloated.[21]

The baby-faced little vamp, the ingenue, the sweet young thing, versus the "hard proposition and an experienced flirt": by the spring of 1919, the young woman had the parts down to an art. The flapper world of postwar Atlanta proved to be a perfect setting to demonstrate her talents. She did. And in the three crazy years that followed, she ensnared half of male Atlanta with her beguiling mix of innocence and worldliness. She kept a veritable stable of suitors. Soon after returning home, she described one batch of men competing for her favors: "One, age 30, Southerner of 15 years' experience in slinging lovely bull; one enterprising youth, age 24, strictly practical and efficient; and last but by no means least, a youthfully exuberant cave man of 19 summers." At one time or another, she related, she accepted the marriage proposals of all three.[22]

Two years later, only the setting, number, and personnel of her suitors had changed. Now five men, she related, demanded her attention. She was sick in the hospital, and all of them appeared simultaneously at her bedside. She made a tale of it:

> I didn't know the boys were going to come to town till they turned up and somehow bribed the nurse to let them in. None of them knew that the others were coming, so it was kind of a surprise party all around. Sick as I was, the whole thing amused me because it was the first time I had ever seen them all together when there wasn't an air of constraint. . . . I thanked them all for the way they'd helped me and yanked me out of trouble during these last six months. Winston addressed the company as "fellow sufferers gathered here in a common cause," and asked if I had come any nearer to making up my mind. I said no, that I loved 'em all and appreciated what they had done for me but I didn't have any intention of marrying any of them. That didn't seem to worry them much, for they made a motion that I be elected "community fiancée." The motion was seconded and carried and the five kissed me goodnight—to my enjoyment and the intense horror of the nurses.[23]

The wild debutante Peggy Mitchell thrived on men, and she treasured every masculine heart she humbled. She played the game, however, for her own amusement, and she protested over and over her innocence, virtue, and chastity in describing all her *affaires de coeur*. "I said I was going south to be the most conservative girl in town and that I was going to be the kind of girl 'they'd' want to marry. Well, dear boy, I have and I've made a success of it," she crowed to Al Edee. "I told you I'd never mush over any man till the man I was going to marry came along, and I haven't." It was just a game, but males always seemed to misinterpret her, she grumbled. "Men don't seem to realize that a girl can care for a man, (or lots of men!), flirt with them, pet and baby them and never mush over them," she fumed.[24]

The young woman's protestations of innocence did not convince Allen Edee. He jibed her continually about her "cutie career." She invariably bit his bait. If he accused her of using feminine wiles unfairly against men, she had a quick, if somewhat ambiguous, retort:

> When a girl knows the male psychology as thoroughly as I do—when she knows the thousand and one small tricks by which a girl can "inno-

cently" run a man wild or sweep him off his feet—when she knows these things and is small and helpless to boot, and she doesn't use these afore-mentioned tricks—well, I'd say she played fair![25]

She regularly fell back on this rationale, insisting that her suitors misconstrued her motives and took advantage of her weakness. Had she consented to wed the nineteen-year old caveman? She absolved herself of responsibility; she did not love him, but he overpowered her and gave her no choice:

> He came out to see me and stayed ages till I was so tired and weak that I was dizzy. Naturally, I didn't tell him so, but I must have been a pretty soft and helpless looking proposition because he lost his head and, pick-ing me up in his arms (appendicitis and all), he proceeded to caveman me in the old and approved style. . . . I was pretty much unnerved by that time, and moreover, I had a particularly feminine curiosity to see what would happen if I did promise. So I said I'd marry him if he would only put me down and not kiss me.[26]

Was he playing fair? she protested. Certainly not! She could not pos-sibly be bound by a promise extracted under such circumstances:

> I was on the verge of hysteria, so he left, believing I'd keep my promise. Well, I didn't let him come near me till I was able to stand up and scrap. So then I called him out and told him what I thought of a man who took advantage of a girl's weakness to extract a promise. Comprenez? Well, I wouldn't exactly say I was engaged to him, would you?[27]

Her arguments did not wipe the smirk from Allen Edee's face. Nor did she enhance her credibility with the casual aside about satisfying her "feminine curiosity to see what would happen" if she did promise to wed the boy. Edee mocked her protests. Four months later she still burned at Edee's jibes, and she told him a slightly different version of "l'affaire caveman Bill." "It wasn't that I cared for him but because I was so sick and weak that at that moment he represented the only way out of a bad situation."[28]

For all the young woman's protestations, sex did fascinate her. Rape, seducers, and seduction shadowed even her discussion of her sexual purity. When Allen Edee had taxed her with teasing men beyond en-durance, she protested, "I've drawn a line that men can't pass except by force." In the same letter, she testified that no man had kissed or held her except that "he was stronger than I. . . . Since I left Hamp no man has been able to penetrate the wall separating superficiality from real feeling."[29] Despite her protests to the contrary, Mitchell's actions invited the crossing of that line and the breaching of that wall. She did lead men on, and later she frankly conceded it:

> I used to have an elegant time in my early youth . . . by giving a life like imitation of a modern young woman whose blistering passions were only held in check by an iron control. It frequently succeeded so well that all thoughts of seduction were tabled and rape became more to the point.[30]

Here, then, is the other side. If sexual chastity, the aversion to sex, and the dislike of men as sexual creatures all fit a clear pattern in Mitchell's life, then aggressive males, masculine aggression, and sexual violence filled another. She dreamed of satyrs. Her friend Harvey Smith recalled their long conversations on the subject, drawn from their favorite elicit reading. "Her ideal man, she said, was right out of Havelock Ellis, a swashbuckling British army officer in India who would perform any sexual act with anyone—or so it seemed with anything!"[31] In later years she laughed that John Marsh alone of all her suitors never tried violent seduction. "It used to worry me an awful lot," she joked, "and I wept many tears for fear I was losing my sex appeal."[32] Her jest remained half true. She nurtured fantasies about the rapist. His sinister and leering form changed place with the mild countenance of her asexual Galahad. The conflicting elements in her own character attracted their opposite number among her masculine companions, and the two Margarets became inextricably intertwined with both Galahads and satyrs. She found men enough willing to play the parts, even well-born Southern men, and the "other Peggy," of the "restless, emotional nature and . . . reckless diablerie" encouraged this behavior in her men friends.

Life was all confusion, and one particular episode of her romantic adventures summarizes all the conflicting elements of her life in these manic years.

The dashing young woman, of course, had numerous men friends in this time, but this particular episode involved only two, "Dan" and "A. B.," as she called them in her correspondence. They represented the old split in her image of men between saint and the rapist. Dan personified the former. She liked him, but he was a Yankee, and "the family, of course, objected to him on general principle, so of a necessity I didn't see much of him." As things turned out, Dan had fallen for another girl, who, to the boy's dismay, "didn't give a snap of her fingers for him, except as a friend." He went to Mitchell for counseling. "Well, Al, he opened up and told me some of the sweetest, dearest thoughts a man could have and some of the purest ideals a man could try to live up to," she began. He did not get what he expected:

> I should have been proud to be made his confidante, but instead I turned loose the most cynical stream of ridicule I had in my repertoire. I was feeling in one of my "what's-the-use-anyway?" moods, so I went joyfully into the task of ruthlessly smashing every ideal I could. Well, I got a

letter from him that night and I never want to get another such. It simply scorched.[33]

If Mitchell gave one version to Allen Edee, she repeated the affair in still fuller detail to Courtenay Ross. She particularly elaborated the agonies that Dan's letter caused her. She "stood naked under a merciless lash." "I was in a mental hell," she grieved:

> The very soul of me cringed. When you've taken a man who is self-confessed fast as lightening, with no faith in God or respect for women, and have put ideals and faith into him, you've reasons to be proud. . . . Why I, like a damn fool, in a mood of cynicism, should have turned loose and ridiculed all that he held sacred, all his newborn ideals, all that is sweet and pure in women, all that was good in God, I don't know—but I did—and God! But you should have seen that letter! . . . The man I had pulled out of the mud sat in judgment on me and flayed me with an unyielding hand. At the end he spoke of the ideals I had given him and the faith in the infinite goodness of God. In other words, he called me a cold and soulless wretch. . . . Ye gods! and I who had been on a pedestal.[34]

Dan named the fundamental contradiction in Mitchell's life. She had worn a halo and personified saintliness, selflessness, and pure ladyhood. But she had acted like the devil, just the same, in her most cynical, sardonic mode. Dan called her on the contradiction and compelled her to confront the split within herself. She could hardly do that, and his letter plunged her into the depths of profoundest gloom. Her failure drained her so completely she even felt physically diminished. At this very moment, while she hovered at the brink of despair, the Dan story segued into her romantic adventure with the would-be "rapist," "A. B."

While Dan desired only Mitchell's friendship, A. B. wanted the young woman herself. If Dan was a penitent rake, A. B. strode onto the stage a wolf in Galahad's armor. "I always distrusted him," she told Edee, "but the family liked him because they knew his people well and because—oh! well, because he had the elements of success and looked a gentleman. I couldn't explain to my mid-Victorian family that I knew he was fast, and that—oh! dear I could tell a girl!"[35] A. B. had most persistently courted her. Indeed, he was taking Mitchell out on the very evening that Dan's epistle had arrived. And this coincidence formed the very crux of the Mitchellian tangle. Mitchell's letter to Edee had told only half a story; Court's letter chronicled both tales and how they intersected.

As A. B. rang the doorbell, Dan's letter still "burned into my brain," she said. "I could think of nothing else." It governed the "near tragedy," as she called it, that soon followed. She looked gorgeous that evening, she admitted, probably, she added, "because I didn't give a damn how I looked." The Dan affair had thoroughly distracted her. Still, she remembered her costume completely and described it to her oldest friend—and also its apparent effect on the cad in question:

> I was wearing that "lo and behold!" black evening dress, and I looked better than I ever have. (Pardon conceit, bum, but I did. . . .) I was desperate. Not only was that letter iron in my soul, but A. B. annoyed me horribly. Ever know a man who makes you acutely conscious that your dress is too low? That's A. B. Suddenly I began to loathe him. I took sidelong glances at him, noting his sensual mouth and closely cropped moustache and meeting his assured, faintly sneering eyes. I hated him. His very nearness made my flesh crawl. I knew I would have a fight with him when we got home, and the thought sickened me. I couldn't talk to him, so I cut loose and began to flirt outrageously with the other men at our table. . . . I hoped A. B. would get mad but it never fazed him.[36]

At 3:00 A.M. the dance ended, and her escort took her home. Insinuating she was drunk, he refused her request to leave:

> He only smiled (how I hated his smile!), shut the door and piloted me, weakly protesting, into the parlor. The fire had died down to red coals, the room was warm and shadowy. Nothing seemed real. I was too tired to think. He took off my coat, pushed me down on the sofa and stood and watched me.[37]

He finally promised to leave if she allowed a kiss. "Kiss you, hell! Go home," she exploded. He stayed to propose they wed. His proposal prompted another outburst. "I'm not going to marry you because you are too damn sensual," she retorted, but her temper excited him. " 'I love to hear you say naughty words,' " he grinned. " 'When you try to be rough, you are so feminine!'. . ." He then went wild, according to the young woman. He disgusted the object of his affections: "I felt absolutely dirtied up everywhere he touched me." She summarized what followed. "It was the evening dress, I guess, and the fact that both straps slipped down at this inopportune time," she said guilelessly.

> When at last I went up to my room and looked in the mirror, I nearly fainted! One strap had let the dress drop horridly low, giving a wickedly rakish air. My hair was completely down, and I looked for all the world like "Act I, Scene II. Why Girls Leave Home!"

She concluded: "I hate men." She might as well have cursed her gown; even so, she then promptly modified her pronunciamento: "No I don't, there are some decent, clean, self-controlled men. And speaking of strong men—" she then launched into a paean to Cliff Henry. "Oh! Court,

Court!" she wailed. "If I could *only* forget! If I could only be free again! But I never shall. I gave my word once and it seems as if it will hold thru eternity. I shall never be free from him til some man. . . . The rest of the sentence vanished with the lost page, but ellipses fit the sentiment to perfection.[38]

This episode is classic in almost all its details. Here are the two models of masculinity that fired her imagination: the sex-mad satyr, A. B.; and Dan, the kindly, repentant Lancelot. Here, too, appear the two Margarets: the reckless, flirtatious ingenue and the innocent victim. This doubling, however, has still another manifestation that affected the very form in which she spun the tale. While she had shared the sad Dan part with Edee, she had reserved the lurid details of the molestation scene for her girlfriend's eyes alone—or so she thought. The very pages of the letter—they and only they—that contained her juiciest revelations, however, never got to Courtenay Ross. Mitchell sent them, not to her female confidante, but to another "gempmum friend," Edee. This was, of course, a slip of the most extraordinary magnititude, for all along her old boyfriend had teased and challenged her about her "cutie career." Her revelations provided him endless fun and opportunity to mock her ideals of chastity, purity, and selfless virtue. This mockery, in turn, allowed and even necessitated Mitchell's reassertation of her ideals of woman's virtue, true love, and all the rest. It also provided the occasion for her reaffirmation of all men's lack of sympathy, understanding, and compassion for womanhood. It was a perfect mix-up.

The episode has other significance for Mitchell's life. The young woman once testified that nothing boosted a girl's spirits "like the knowledge that there's a gempmum fren' all ready to seduce her if she gives him one half the chance. . . . I think a man who makes improper proposals is a positive necessity."[39] When the blues slammed home, she continued, only this knowledge kept her going. The lower her spirits, the greater the need for sexual boosting—and a year after her mother's death, her morale was low indeed.

As indicated by her intense reaction, Dan's letter touched other sources of anger and depression: anxiety about home and school, what she wanted, who she was. The future scared her witless and she longed for blessed surcease, "like a child, . . . no worry, no responsibility—only peace—to drift and drift." It was a return to babyhood she visualized, or even farther back to some prenatal state. If it was the uncompromising devotion of a mother she really longed for, she desired an impossible goal. Her mother was no nurturer to begin with, and May Belle Mitchell was two years dead in any case.

If she longed for loss of self, however, she also battled that same impulse. The young woman admitted her "moods of black depression" alternated with "a restless, emotional nature" and "restless diablerie."[40] "Too much surplus energy," she snorted. "When I get out of this house again, I shall probably raise the devil as a result of the aforementioned energy. Overcharging the batteries, I should call it."[41] "I can't do any constructive work along any line with a date every night and something going on every day," she cried. "I can't concentrate. I feel like a dynamo going to waste. I have possibilities, if energies are just turned in the proper channels."[42] Yet the mania had its awful purpose. "I keep life filled and speeded up so that I can cheat myself into believing that I am happy and contented." "If I don't keep busy and dated up I always get into mischief—so I rush around as much as possible."[43] But "dating up," as demonstrated in the A. B. affair, produced its own mischievous consequences. "I'm just waiting to get well and get into trouble," she wrote soon after her appendectomy. "Well, so much for my reckless career," she concluded, still protesting that she would "be minus a bridle for a long time yet."[44]

She ran in a frantic, debilitating circle. No wonder that her grandmother raged and her father was worried to furious distraction.

What lessons did Mitchell herself draw from the affair with Dan and A. B.?—Why girls leave home. It was truer than she knew. She was ready to escape her home in any case. A. B. appeared to be a potential agent of her ambiguous liberation. How much longer could she avoid the bride's bridle?

The "only way out of a bad situation," she had reflected when she accepted the cave man's marriage proposal. More bad situations pressed her daily. Depressed in general, and miserable as the homemaker in someone else's home, Mitchell did consider men as a way out of her black circumstance. Over and over she used her suitors as means of equalizing what she considered the unfair power of her family—her father, her grandmother, and even her brother—and the miseries of domesticity. When the pressure of domestic life mounted, she threatened regularly to escape by way of marriage. Did her parent object to the company she was keeping? She would keep the friends she wanted! she stormed. She would do what she wanted—or else; the "else" being to elope. "When Dad and Grandma kept nagging me about 'ruining my social career,' I rose and registered an oath in Heaven that if they didn't let me see my friends in peace, I'd elope with the first man who would have me." Not even a convent would be secure enough; beyond surveillance of her family, she would probably "elope with a garbage man, just to be annoying," her brother commented.[45] The more she threatened, however, the more she exaggerated her family's fears about her lack of judgment; this provoked more "meddling" in her affairs, which put more pressure on the young woman, and prompted her to threaten still more often elopement or other forms of matrimonial mayhem.

Still, however, she resisted this course. Completely aside from sex, she considered marriage a nightmare, which is plain even when she veils her antipathy in genuinely funny prose.

> I've skidded along the edge of matrimony a few times since I've been home but never seriously, because as you say, Al, it's a serious proposition to belong to one man for the rest of your natural life or till you relieve the boredom by putting arsenic in his soup. It's quite a different thing to see a man twice a week on dress parade, when you both sit circumspectly on opposite sides of a squashy sofa and discuss nails in the barrel industry or the price of cheese, *but*—three times a day for three hundred and sixty-five days a year—and just think, Al, he might live more than a year. How unspeakably terrible! It's not to be considered![46]

Describing an actual wedding elicited a similar cynical riposte—and probably mirrors something of the tone she used with poor moonstruck Dan.

> There's no thrill comparable to the one that comes only when "Here Comes the Bride" sounds from behind the palms, and the bridal party, heralded by two hysterical infants scattering flowers, comes stalking grimly in. The groom is maudlin with fright and maintains a pretense of composure only by the aid of whispered curses from the best man. Of course, the bride looks beautiful then, if she never looks pretty again, and everybody whispers, "Isn't she sweet?" Some way they get thru the hectic performance and then everybody kisses the bride, and in the confusion, the best man manages to kiss all the bridesmaids. Everybody wolfs a lot of indigestible grub, and after commenting, "*Such* a sweet wedding. What can she see in him?" they go home.

She concluded with a Dorothy Parker-like sigh: "Lord! Weddings are enough to try the most iron nerves! I always weep at weddings—weep from the sheer horror of imagining that it might be mine! There on the 'Altar of Love,' I renew my vows of celibacy!"[47]

She fought her fate in other ways. "I want to marry and help my man and raise healthy, honest children," she averred. "My only problem is I can't love any man enough. I've tried—oh, so very hard, but it's no go."[48] She described the horns of her dilemma. "I realize that my happiness lies in a husband and children." She continued immediately without a break or bridge, however, "I don't believe in happiness. I know I can never be really happy, but my best chance lies in love. And I can't love." She knew what Allen Edee would say to this, and she dealt with his protests in advance:

> Perhaps you'll say "the right man hasn't come along." Al, there isn't any such thing as one "right man." Anyone of a thousand men raised in the same circumstances and environment and class, used to the same refine-

ments and education, will be the same. I'm not incapable of love; in fact, I have vast capabilities for love. I could love a man and drive him till he made good. I love children. Now, I have penchant for the bizarre and wild that I've had to ride most of my life, but I guess I could ride it better if I were married. Heigho! Sometimes I wonder how 'twill turn out! No old dear, I'm engaged to no man, and furthermore, I'm "heart whole and fancy free." Let the picture remain where it is, please.[49]

She pleaded less to Allen Edee than to some nameless deities to let the picture be. Artemis, the protector of virgins, served her ill. Mitchell herself could not let the single picture "remain." However much she resisted, she was pushed and shoved towards matrimony. In her death-bed letter, her mother had said she did not have to marry, and the young woman had her ambition, if vague and distant, to write—comedies, short stories, novels, journalism; or to design clothes. Neither her society nor her immediately family, however, put much stock in such objectives, and she had no training or preparation for these ends. She possessed no models, either, for a real, independent career outside the home. While her mother had pressed her towards the "high road" of public success, domesticity remained Mrs. Mitchell's own real dominion. Then, too, the pressures of her daily life—housekeeping and socializing—undermined these goals for the daughter. If school and college offered some possibility of escape, all manner of issues vitiated that ambition. Even when most hopeful about continuing her education, she still muttered darkly that "something will happen to make school impossible." "Lord knows how I'll end up."[50]

The Lord knew. Marriage offered that very something. Everything in the social order pushed her towards the altar. It allowed the possibility of escaping her father's—and her mother's—home, with all the special burdens of carrying on where her dead parent had left off. Marriage was the obvious end of all the courting ritual, too, however much the girl herself objected. Her friends' careers acknowledged this, despite her own denials. With predictable regularity, her pals peeled off into the married state: Court in October 1920; Helen Turman exactly a year later; Lethea the following year.

Life was all confusion. Whichever way she turned offered equally unappealing solutions. As her own will failed, the suit of an aggressive male once more offered a way out of her dilemma, and in the summer of 1922, she accepted the inevitable when she announced her engagement to Berrien Kinnard Upshaw.

She had known him since 1917 when he was a gangling sixteen-year-old ogling Court Ross. He had come back into her life in 1920 and persisted since then. He had been among the five suitors who visited her in the hospital room at St. Joseph's in 1921. And among that number, he did not seem too high on the list. What recommended him among this company? Witty Jimmy Howat was devoted to her. He made tears of laughter stream down her face with the funny little cartoon book he made for her; it contained a sequence of photographs of both of them, captioned with Howat's equally witty dialogue.[51]

Dr. Hudson was smooth, urbane, and sophisticated, a veteran of the British cavalry in the Great War. His sardonic humor especially appealed to her. In contrast, Winston Withers was bluff and hearty, an old Camp Gordon beau (like Howat), and a cattle rancher from Greensboro, Alabama. Withers had "put a man in the hospital for trying to kiss me," Mitchell boasted.

While one acquaintance considered Henry Angel only a "pleasant and ineffectual" old friend from her grammar school days,[52] he also amused her, and she joked that she had rewarded him with a rare kiss "when he told me that I helped him give up 'likker and wild women.' "[53]

These four did not exhaust Upshaw's only competition. Frank Stanton mooned over the vivacious young woman, too. From an old Atlanta family that had known the Mitchells and Stephenses for generations, he was as kind and thoughtful as he was intelligent. With their mutual and intense concern with literature and poetry, they seemed a natural match. It never jelled. Still others came and went. One of them, a twenty-four-year-old, rather unlikely Kentucky country boy penned lines that almost any of them might have written. He described their affair as "a form of liberal platonism. . . . Peg has made a success at that sort of relationship as she has the largest and oddest collection of men friends, real *friends*, pals, of any girl of twenty I have ever encountered. I am proud to join the circle." "We have made a solemn promise not to fall in love with each other;" still, he supposed that "eventually like the others I will be secretly in love with her, covering up an apparently hopeless passion. Ah well. Ho hum," He concluded wistfully. "The friendship of a girl like Peg is worth having and I value it."[54]

Who was this B. K. Upshaw who had won this rare bird in contest with a very host of suitors and gallants, and perhaps against her own better judgment?

"Red" Upshaw was not Old Atlanta. Old Atlanta therefore assumed he was some sort of interloping alien. He might as well have been from Mars—or Nebraska. He was, however, Georgia-born and Atlanta-bred, a native Southerner whose family had lived in North Georgia for as long as the Mitchells, Turmans, Tyes, or any of the Atlanta gentry. The Upshaws arrived late in Atlanta, however, and left early. William F. Upshaw had brought his family to the Georgia capital around 1905. While the Upshaws did not live in the posh districts of North Peachtree and Ansley Park, their community on Gordon Avenue was solid upper-middle class. They moved up, too. In 1912, they relocated to the more fashionable district of East Lake out the Decatur Street line. A successful businessman, Mr. Upshaw was the chief executive for the

Aetna Life Insurance Company in Atlanta, but in 1916 a promotion took him and his family out of Georgia altogether when he moved to Raleigh, North Carolina. If Atlantans did not know the Upshaws, the good citizens of Raleigh knew them well. They wrote their own page there in local history.[55]

Berrien was the eldest son of William and Annie Berrien Upshaw. Born in March 1901, four months after Mitchell, he was only four when the family left their native town of Madison, Georgia, for the capital. His father sent him away to prep school, but he grew up in the city. He first appears in a public record in June 1917 at a party hosted by Court Ross.[56] The sixteen-year-old boy was visiting the city from his parents' home in Raleigh where they had moved the year before. In 1918, he moved back to Georgia when he enrolled as a freshman at the University of Georgia in Athens. He stayed a year. On June 26, 1919, he won an appointment to the United States Naval Academy, the first of two Upshaw brothers to be so honored. While his half-brother William graduated and made the Navy his life, Berrien led a much more checkered military career. He did not last long at Annapolis. He resigned, for academic reasons, in January 1920, and returned to Athens for another semester. He won readmission to the Academy in the summer, and that term began with a tour of duty on the West Coast. His tenure this time was shorter still. He resigned less than four months later, on September 1, 1920, this time, permanently.[57] He re-enrolled at the University of Georgia one more time, but he failed to complete his B.A. there as well. Within the year, he returned to his hometown, and the city directories list him as "agent"; for whom or what is not clear.[58] Employment, indeed, was always a problem. As his stepmother related, "Berrien could always find a job but never kept one long."[59] When Upshaw returned to Atlanta, he was just twenty.

His first love, Court Ross, remembered him as a peculiar fellow. Perpetually moneyless, he haunted her house but could never afford to treat her. As a consequence, their dates consisted mostly of long walks that cost neither anything but time. The memory of these walking dates stayed in the woman's memory, including the chief topic of conversation. Here was a local Georgia version of "Alibi Ike," the comic literary figure invented by Ring Lardner. "He was always whining and complaining. He couldn't stay in any school, and it was always somebody else's fault he had to leave." In Court's memory, he had little force or character. "I dated him out of my Christian duty," she laughed long afterward.[60] Aggie Dearborn drew similar conclusions: "Neither my sister nor I could see what [Margaret] saw in Red to make her marry him beyond a physical attraction and perhaps maternal feelings."[61] The two vivacious Turman sisters thought him "dull and on the gauche side. None of the men we dated thought him worthy of her attentions." Helen Turman recollected: "To me he was a hanger on who contributed little to any occasion. Peggy was so vivacious I never thought she realized his dullness."[62] Still another debutante, Yolande Gwin, echoed this opinion: "I wouldn't say he was an attractive looking man— certainly not. I don't think he had a lot of personality. I did not know him well, but he just didn't look the type of man who had a lot of personality. He would say hello and let it go at that."[63] He won romantic fame for athletics as Mitchell described him as "an ex-Annapolis, ex-U. of Ga. football player," but his football record remains obscure, and may even be spurious. If he played for either institution, no record of his participation survived in either Annapolis or Athens.

Physically, he possessed a certain presence without being handsome. He was tall and very fair-complected, with dark carroty-colored hair— hence his nickname. He did have very sharply defined features, a high forehead, high cheekbones, and a striking profile. He was always thin, however, and with very deep-set eyes, he had, even by 1920–21, acquired something of a sepulchral look of the tuberculosis that eventually undermined his health—along with alcohol. Even to his family, his face resembled nothing so much as a skin-shrouded skull.[64]

What of his personality? Not unlike the woman he would marry, he had two sides, but he held them together with even greater difficulty than she. At best he was erratic, at worst psychotic. His mother, like May Belle Mitchell, died in the 1918–1919 Spanish influenza epidemic when he was only seventeen. His father, a widower with four sons, remarried soon after. His stepmother was a generous and kindly woman by all accounts, including her ex-daughter-in-law's, and she extended her benevolence to him. He never reciprocated. He had been the eldest son of the first marriage, and his stepmother thought him spoiled.[65] He did not, however, get along well with his father. Berrien, wrote his parent, "labored under the delusion that I was his archenemy." Even in the best of times, Colonel Upshaw continued, he considered his son "more or less nervous and eccentric." While his other children from both marriages made notable successes of their lives, this child alone did nothing right. "Berrien's life so far has been quite a disappointment to me," Mr. Upshaw wrote flatly in 1936. He might have made the same judgment any time after 1918. The boy excelled in nothing, his father observed, except "his ability to woo and marry about the finest girls in the world."[66] Eventually he ran through three wives. All filed for divorce. He contested none of them. From 1916 until his death in 1949, he lacked any real home. He floated across the country, from Atlanta, to Raleigh, to Asheville, to Honolulu, to Phoenix, to Galveston, and then back again. In the coastal Texas city he finally ended his life by leaping from a hotel window in January 1949. Tuberculosis and alcohol plagued him perpetually.

Mitchell's family remembered him as dangerously unstable.[67] His only child (by his second marriage), William, left the impression of his father as "sadistic and cruel."[68] Mitchell herself charged him with beating her on two occasions.[69] While his roommate and friend, John Marsh, never referred to his violence, he did characterize him as excitable, headstrong, and prone to "wild ideas."

If the adventurous and erratic side of Red Upshaw's character appealed to her, another did, too. "She felt sorry for him," assayed Courtenay Ross.[70] Aggie Dearborn believed her friend needed to mother the boy. The answer is not farfetched, even if another truth lurks behind this. Mitchell certainly had an affinity for males whom she could "care for . . . , pet and baby." She possessed a powerful impulse to nurse and mother a man. Already by 1922, her fiancé had established an unenviable record for failure, and perhaps she saw in him the husband she could "drive . . . until he made good." Her earliest references to him support this judgment. She considered him "nice," a rare term in her vocabulary. She used the expression when describing their first date in the spring of 1920 at the University of Georgia. The young man had just returned to Athens from his abortive term in Annapolis, and he had invited Mitchell over from Atlanta for a fraternity weekend in the college town. Mitchell described it both before and after. "I'm slated for a Sigma Nu house party, and to be perfectly frank, I'm scared to death," she scribbled to Al Edee as she rode the train to Athens on April 28:

> I've never seen my bid but four times in my life and three of those times were before the war! In fact, the last time I saw him was to say hello when I met him out with Courtenay. He's awfully nice, but I can't yet see why he asked me. "Time will tell." He's such a good friend of Court's that I feel as if I'd been knowing him for years.[71]

That weekend in Athens turned out gloriously, according to the Atlanta belle. It impressed her beau still more forcefully. It convinced him he should marry her. A month later, he insisted that she accept his fraternity pin. She offered numerous objections for refusing but finally accepted on one curious condition: "That I'd return it when he got home." She didn't. She couldn't . . . she had lost it. Like sending Court's letter to Edee, this represented another one of those striking slips that cropped up so often in the young woman's life. Her inability to return the pin, of course, meant that as a matter of honor, she remained bound to the young man. Once again, the circumstances seemed to dictate her action: it was all beyond her control.[72]

Did she ever find Upshaw's pin? She never said. She stood him off for two more years in any case. In the interval, he did not go away. Nor did the other courtiers. Indeed, by 1922, Upshaw discovered a most unlikely chief competitor. John Marsh met Margaret Mitchell in the winter of 1921–1922. She bewitched him immediately. "I have spent about as much time with her as the law allows," he wrote his sister in January to explain the inadequacy of his correspondence. "It is a distinct novelty for me to have [a] girl in this nouveau riche city that I can take an interest in, and I have been reveling in the sensation."[73] Through Mitchell, Marsh also met Red Upshaw. John Marsh was over five years Upshaw's senior, but the younger man beguiled him almost as much as the vivacious girl. The two suitors decided to become roommates. It was an odd threesome, indeed. Marsh captured some of its eccentricities in the comments he made on photographs of the three of them he sent to his sister Frances:

> I am enclosing a picture or two which may be of interest. The dramatis personae are Miss Peggy Mitchell, Mr. Red Upshaw, one of her lovers and my room mate, and Mr. Marsh. Scene—The Mitchell front porch. Time— Any Sunday morning or afternoon or any other afternoon or evening. Theme—I could love the one or the other if either dear charmer were gone. Moral-Don't weaken.[74]

In April 1922, Frances Marsh came to Atlanta to visit her brother, and the Marsh-Upshaw courting partnership alarmed her. "They would toss a coin to see who might have the first half of an evening with her, who, the latter half," Frances Marsh related. "I remember John taking Peggy home at ten P.M. to a waiting Red. John bent over her hand, kissed it and said, 'Red, I now surrender to you the woman we both love.' "[75] The gesture typified John Marsh's suit. Their evenings together consisted, in his terms, of "exchanging philosophies of life and conversationally turning the pages of family picture albums." Their courtship never progressed beyond "swapping favorite books and treasured souvenirs of the past." He made no physical advances whatsoever. "John never tried to rape me. He confesses at this late date," she wrote his sister, "that he desisted only because every one else was doing it and he blandly hoped to shine by contrast."[76]

By the spring, this double suit was provoking considerable talk around the town. Photographs of the three appeared on the newspapers' society pages, and at least one columnist devoted an article to the subject:

> Inseparable friends for a long period and equally under the spell of a certain charming Atlantan, they have served her hand and foot for many months, have continued in their friendly appreciation of each other and successfully hidden every trace, if trace there be, of any small pangs of jealousy which her smiling too often in first one direction or the other might have occasioned.

The same article pondered the exquisite agony of the maid in question, "the horrible indecision as to which of the friends feels most deeply, seems her most devoted admirer and is altogether the one of her choice—if choice must be made."[77]

"If choice must be made," the gossip columnist had concluded her story of the two suitors. Sometime in early summer, the choice was made. The mystery does not altogether go away, and the gossip columnist who first wrote about the engagement expressed it well: "I could almost explode a bomb and create less excitement than if I were to tell you just which of the Atlanta beauties has confided to me the fact of her engagement." Polly Peachtree blamed the decision on "some strange trick of Cupid."[78] John Marsh seemed actually to provide one of Cupid's arrows. He himself demanded no alteration in the status quo from either his beloved or his roommate. Given Red Upshaw's excitability, however, Marsh's very presence challenged the younger man.

That seemed the point of Frances Marsh's story, at least. In the spring of 1922, she visited her brother in Atlanta and stayed with the Mitchells. At one of the big parties of the season, Red cornered her and told her, " 'John thinks he is going to win but I'm pulling the big guns.' I am assuming he was using his sex appeal which he had a lot of," she concluded.[79] However much or little sex appeal Red Upshaw had, John Marsh had none, but the older man's competition inspired the younger. In any case, six months after John Marsh began hanging around 1149 Peachtree Street—over two years after Mitchell had first dated the tall redhead, the young woman decided on the younger of the Castor and Pollux team.

Perhaps Mitchell wanted to play Zelda to Red's Scott, or Scott to his Zelda, for that matter; but their life worked out even more oddly than the Sayre–Fitzgerald coupling. Upshaw proved not malleable at all, while his excitability and willfulness became an even greater burden than she bore already in the daily rounds of keeping up her father's house. She was running away with the garbageman of her father's nightmares.

VII

The Lion's Den

There had been some skepticism on the Atlanta Journal Magazine staff when Peggy came to work as a reporter. Debutantes slept late in those days and didn't go in for jobs.

MEDORA FIELD PERKERSON ON HIRING MARGARET MITCHELL[1]

*A*s she descended the stairs, did she remember her cynical asides about typical weddings?—hysterical infants scattering flowers, a terrified groom, the ever-so-sweet bride, the inedible grub, and all the rest? She planned her own wedding, at least in part, with such ideas in mind. "There was never another wedding like it," remembered her old friend Caroline Tye:

> Everyone was just agog. The house was decorated in the traditional way with smilax, traditional white and green but instead of carrying it through with the traditional lilies, Margaret carried a great big bunch of red long-stemmed roses! Atlanta never saw anything like it before or since.[2]

The bride chose a Protestant ceremony, too. Reverend Douglas of St. Luke's Episcopal Church read the service. It sealed her final break with Catholicism. The decision set the Stephenses scowling and added one more complication to the troubled relations between the Mitchells and their in-laws. Other little curiosities marked the ceremony. With the exception of her brother, all the groomsmen had been her suitors. Indeed, she was about the only thing they had in common. Winston Withers had courted her for over a year. He was one of the five who had crowded her hospital room the year before. In the wedding photograph, he stares glumly at the camera. The best man had been the groom's chief competitor for the bride, and he looked even more forlorn than Withers.

The formal notices that appeared on Sunday morning, September 3, 1922, the morning after the wedding, were odd, too. Doubly so. In the first place, the rejected suitor John Marsh had written them.[3] The content also distinguished them. It ignored all the most notable elements of the bride's career—her family standing, education, literary bent, whirlwind debut, and her extremely active social life in the three-year period before the wedding. Instead, it dwelt exclusively on her "enviable record of war work"—completely fabricated. While it remarked upon her service in the Red Cross canteen in Atlanta (appropriately enough), it invented other service, such as her employment in ammunition factories in New Hampshire and Massachusetts. And instead of the abortive social rounds that dominated her recollection of the short time she spent with her Aunt Edythe in Connecticut, Greenwich became the place "where she joined the women's ambulance corps rendering service for many months. After this, she served as a farmerette with the Harvestry Co-op in the Connecticut Valley." Thus her nine months at Smith were telescoped into one minor episode of about a week's duration of frolicking make-work when the school had effectively closed for two weeks in the fall of 1918.[4] It was very curious, and the announcement signaled an odd beginning to the ill-fated match.

For all its anomalies, the ceremony itself proceeded without a hitch. Besides her two little first cousins as flower girls, three old friends attended her: the former Martha Bratton, now Mrs. Franklin Stevens Chalmers; Mrs. Thomas J. Kelly, Jr.; and Augusta Dearborn. Dorothy Bates Kelly she had known forever, and Aggie Dearborn had saved her life after Courtenay married and moved away. They wore lavender dresses and carried bouquets of garden flowers. Other than her own bouquet of red roses, the bride wore a more or less traditional wedding gown—white ankle-length satin with train trimmed with pearls and orange blossoms. At the height of flapper fashion, she also wore a headband that held in place a filmy net almost as long as her gown's train. The gentlemen of the party all wore formal evening dress: tails, white ties, white gloves. Berrien, for one, never looked better. He resembled nothing so much as the Arrow Shirt Man, the very model of masculine good looks in the twenties.

Although in no way so grand or formal as her parents' wedding almost exactly thirty years before, the house looked very elegant for the ceremony. The bride had arranged it herself. She had improvised an altar before the front door in the main hall and decorated it with palms, ferns, Easter lilies, other white flowers, and silver candelabra. The florist had draped smilax from the chandelier, over the doorway, and around the balustrade of the stairs, and had arranged wicker baskets of pink roses and pink gladioli elsewhere about the house. The guests entered through the French doors that opened onto the terraces on both sides of the great Palladian entranceway. They watched the ceremony from the two large rooms on each side of the hallway: the parlor on the south side, the library on the north.

After the ceremony, Mr. Mitchell hosted the reception at his home. The guests wandered through the "display room," where they examined the gifts—"large silver pieces, linens, table silver, and checks from relatives"[5]—before greeting the bridal party. The receiving line consisted of the bride, the groom, Mr. Mitchell, Grandma Stephens, the groom's stepmother, four of the bride's Mitchell aunts—Mrs. Gordon Mitchell, Mrs. Lucian McConnell, Mrs. Willis Timmons, and Mrs. Hugh Roberts—and finally Court Ross's mother, Mrs. J. T. Billups. Lethea Turman commanded the punch bowl.

The bridal couple departed early the next morning on their wedding trip. They spent the first part at the famous Grove Park Inn in Asheville and then wended their way across the length of North Carolina to the old Mitchell stomping ground of Wrightsville Beach. Along the way they made a long side trip to visit the Upshaws in Raleigh. On their return, about a month later, they took up residence with Mr. Mitchell and Stephens in the big house where they had wed. Disaster followed.

At the outset, the couple's residence at 1149 Peachtree Street placed a terrible burden on their marriage. Eugene Mitchell cast a long, deep shadow over the establishment. Tight, introverted, and suspicious, he had fussed about all his daughter's gentlemen friends for years. If he had groaned over the rich, aristocratic, Harvard-educated Clifford Henry, one can well imagine the silences that chilled the Mitchell dinner table in the fall of 1922 as he stared across the dinner table at the man that his daughter had added to his family. Berrien Upshaw was still a youth, not yet twenty-two, and he lacked the breadth and urbanity that the Mitchells prized. He had also flunked out of two colleges, including the one where his father-in-law had graduated with two degrees, Phi Beta Kappa, after only three years of study. And where the older man, despite his inherited wealth and status, had constantly strained every nerve to save, make his fortune, and provide his bride with worldly goods and status, his son-in-law seemed utterly unserious about such matters. Upshaw held only odd jobs.[6]

Mitchell had earlier described how she was given to reckless moods of diablerie alternating with fits of black depression. Upshaw betrayed the same tendencies. Had the groom's other "eccentricities," as his own father called them, begun to show? Was he projecting onto his father-in-law or bride the anger that he otherwise reserved for Colonel Upshaw? Was he boozing yet? In any event, little conflicts exploded regularly into major confrontations. Despite Mitchell's own untidiness (or perhaps because of it), Red's messiness became a particular bone of contention. "That's what I remember about her references to him: her complaining about how he would drop wet towels just anywhere about the house after he showered," her friend Elinor Hillyer recalled.[7] John Marsh had his own opinions about their conflict-ridden union:

> The two of them love each other very much but they are as dissimilar as it is possible for two people to be, with virtually nothing in common in temperament, viewpoint on life, likes or dislikes. . . . Their total lack of congeniality caused constant small clashes, that threw Red off his stride as far as his work was concerned and were threatening Peggy with a nervous breakdown.[8]

Between Christmas of 1922 and July of the following year, the circumstances became unbearable.[9] Matters of work, income, and financial support wrecked the marriage.

Although Mitchell always worried about money, Red's shadowy jobs and vacillating income exacerbated her deepest fears. On another level, he was not doing what a husband and provider was supposed to do, and his failure freed her to step into the breach. In the late fall, just after her twenty-second birthday, she decided to provide her own income. Her decision to look for a job, however, produced more complications within her household, because her action underscored her husband's failings as a man and proper husband. Within the context of the times, a working wife ran aggressively against the grain of masculine pride, and Red Upshaw now found still more cause, in John Marsh's words, for losing his stride so far as jobs went. To make matters worse, she publicized his shame by working for the newspaper and writing under her own byline. In mid-February, she heaped insult on injury by reverting to "Peggy Mitchell" as her *nom de plume*.

If Berrien Upshaw felt less of a man with such a wife, he compensated by acting out a still more aggressively male role by the late spring. That, at least, offers one explanation of his decision to launch a career in bootlegging and liquor-running. In describing the episode, John Marsh's very language underlined Red's masculine imperatives:

> Red's love of adventure and excitement and his desire to clean up some easy money caused him to embark on a career of "rum-running." He had been running whiskey into Atlanta from the Georgia mountains for about a week before Peggy found out about it, telling her he was traveling for his company. I was the only one who knew about it, and I wasn't able to dissuade him, he is such a headstrong character when he gets one of his wild ideas in his head.[10]

Had the tension in the house been bad before, now it became intolerable. But the episode does not end here. Only Red Upshaw's ill luck exceeded his ineptitude. In his typically laconic mode, John Marsh summarized the hopeless mess his friend and former roommate had created for himself. "Rather unfortunately, the same day Peggy told him she couldn't stand it any longer, the professional bootlegger Red was working with double-crossed him and got away with the $200 that was his entire capital stock." No fame, no name, no glory. Poor Red Upshaw now lost his cash, his wife, and even his bed. About July 10, after a terrific wrangle, the couple called it quits; the banished groom moved back in with his old roommate for a time, and prepared to "pull out for a month in the great open spaces," as John Marsh summarized the dénouement.[11] Four months later, Mrs. Upshaw filed for a divorce.

The Mitchell-Upshaw film had a final reel to run, and an important one; the main story, however, was complete. By the summer of 1923, when Mrs. Upshaw kicked her husband out of her house forever after ten months of marriage, she was already well under way with a new chapter of her life. Her life had already sailed off in altogether new directions when she took a job as a newspaper writer.

Entering journalism was one of the two most important decisions of Mitchell's life. Much pulled her towards that career; much worked against it. As far as jobs went, it was an altogether natural choice, but she took it on against tremendous odds. Her family and her culture scorned women's economic independence, and newspaper work had particular liabilities as well.

If society in general opposed working women, Southern culture radically exaggerated the bias. In 1927, for example, an organization of careerist women in the region concluded its defense of women in the professions with a ringing justification of motherhood and domesticity. It confirmed, effectively, that careers for women were an anomaly. The very existence and continuity of the modern world, the essay trumpeted, "depend upon good homemakers and mothers. . . . it should be assumed by our educational institutions that every woman will marry and have a family."[12] If liberal Southern women themselves made such assumptions, how much more did the traditional exponents of the patriarchal order press the matter!

Professionalism for a woman was virtually nonexistent. In after years, Mitchell fabricated stories about wanting to be a physician, a neurologist, or a psychiatrist. That idea came late to her, but she had proof, even as she invented it, of its hopelessness. In her newspaper career, she wrote for and about women, and she searched for independent professional women in particular. In three and a half years of investigation, she discovered two psychologists, apparently Atlanta residents, and one physician—and even this one was only passing through the South.[13] While she found a few businesswomen, some actresses, a couple of politicians, and a couple of editors, she turned up no lawyers,

no dentists, no college or university professors. The huge bulk of her
working women, even in 1925, were only a few notches above day la-
borers. Society sharply circumscribed legitimate employment for
women.

Social work offered socially acceptable employment, and plenty of
young women of the most impeccable Southern lineage entered the
field. Lucy Randolph Mason, later an organizer for the CIO, began her
career with a commitment to the YWCA in Richmond. With one of the
grandest names in Georgia, Katherine DuPre Lumpkin followed much
the same course.[14] By and large, however, such a career generally pre-
supposed a heritage of evangelical Christian piety. Mitchell lacked that
background to offset the class and social prejudices against a woman
of her time and status going into such work. Teaching, of course, remained the most legitimate option and more women entered this
profession than all others combined, yet neither by word or deed did
Peggy Mitchell ever express even the vaguest inclination in this direction. It is difficult indeed to imagine her comfortable in a classroom.
She hated being on one side of the desk; she evidenced no desire to
stand behind it. Also, while she got along famously with individual
kids, children as a category never interested her. All this, actually, gets
close to the heart of the issue. All these other "womanly" or mothering-
oriented jobs failed to appeal to her. She did not want to institution-
alize domesticity in her employment. On the contrary, she wanted out
of the house and away from the burdens it entailed. Journalism certainly satisfied these ends and others, but it had drawbacks, too.

On the plus side, journalism allowed her to exercise her oldest ambition. She had nursed the hope to write professionally for years. She
had written innumerable short stories and she talked enthusiastically
about producing comedies and dramas. At Smith, if not before, she
had first contemplated journalism as a proper medium for her talent.
Then, too, Atlanta offered an especially attractive field for a budding
journalist. The Georgia capital was a big city by 1920; by regional
standards, a genuine metropolis. The town sustained three major, highly
competitive newspapers. Such a press generated an almost insatiable
demand for copy, and for the writers to generate the copy. By increasing the turnover rate, low pay also swelled the numbers who sought
employment at the trade. Atlanta journalism was a turnstile. Thousands of work-hungry youths from all over Georgia—and, indeed, the
South—served a stint in some newsroom in the Gate City. The papers
spat them out as rapidly as they chewed them up. For all its appearance of a great metropolis with a great metropolitan press, however,
Atlanta and its newspapers remained tighty controlled by local élites.
This, too, however, worked to Margaret Mitchell's advantage. Her family had known the editors, publishers, and owners of the town's press
for decades; they had indeed been owners themselves. Her uncle, Frank

Rice, had helped found the *Atlanta Journal*, for example, along with the close family friend, the political boss, Hoke Smith.[15]

Less tangible forces encouraged her to enter journalism. If Mitchell aspired to a higher goal than cranking out weekly features for the society pages (and she did), journalism allowed her to write without fully acknowledging those higher aspirations. Journalism seemed, in short, a practical, fulfillable expression of the old-time hope. It was steady and regular. Its limits were well-defined: so much copy on given topics by such and such a deadline. However pitiful, the income was steady, too.

Still other issues weighted in the balance of her decision to take up journalism as a trade. Journalism was bastard literature. It was the most profane literary profession in more ways than one, and this influence cut two ways with the young aspiring writer. Journalists personified the low life. Its practitioners caroused with a vengeance. They won due fame for their ability to procure and consume home brew, corn liquor, and other controlled substances of the era. They haunted dives and juke joints. One cub reporter from these days recalled his early career and his friendship with the senior reporter "who about once a week insisted upon putting four drinks under his belt and the same number under mine and hauling me off to the Gayety burlesque show there to sit in a box (always in a box) and almost collapse with laughter when the fat-fannied femme waddled out."[16] Overflowing ashtrays, smoke-filled rooms, dirty coffee cups, cluttered desks, bawdy laughter, loud obscenities, hardbitten cynicism, reckless ambition, rare talent, slave-labor hours, and a boisterous camaraderie—the vulgarity of the profession actually appealed to the insouciant former debutante.

For all the attractions of newspaper work, much militated against this employment, too. She felt miserably inadequate for the trade, but the absence of any training or experience in journalism exaggerated her reservations about her own ability. Breaking off her education, she thought, had ruined her chances in the profession. Later, she described her skill-less plight to a high school student who paraphrased the novelist perfectly: "Miss Mitchell wanted to work but was trained for nothing in the world. She especially wanted to do newspaper work but she saw no chance."[17] She found no support within her family. Her father violently opposed this career. At one time she had wanted to take business courses to learn to type, but "Dad wouldn't let me," she related long after. "That was in those days beyond recall when nice girls didn't work—and before I stopped being a nice girl and became a reporter."[18] In classic understatement, Mr. Mitchell's daughter caught the drift of her father's horror when she summarized her life years later: "I made my debut and then went on to the Magazine Section of the Journal, somewhat to the consternation of my father."[19]

Journalism, certainly, was not fit for innocents; just the same, aristocratic Southern belles in particular flocked to newspaper work after the Great War. Overeducated for the social order and otherwise under-utilized, the gentry's daughters had experienced the same liberation as their brothers in the Generation of 1900, but they had far fewer outlets for their talents. With the professions closed to them, they crowded those avenues remaining. Journalism could use them. The explosion of the urban population in the region, the proliferation of newspapers, and the expansion of female readership especially—all these issues drew the ladies from their parents' Victorian parlors. A young woman might contribute to the social pages as a logical extension of her own engagement in the aristocratic whirl. The work was often short-term labor that demanded little skill. Any belle might do it for diversion. Augusta Dearborn, Margaret Mitchell's dearest friend, had performed just such a temporary gig as "social editor" for her hometown paper in Birmingham.[20] Over in Chattanooga, the threadbare aristocrat Caroline Gordon launched her own distinguished literary career at the same kind of job at the same time.[21] Almost simultaneously, up in North Carolina, another belle stalked into the offices of Josephus Daniels's *News and Observer* in Raleigh and demanded work. Nell Battle Lewis belonged to the richest, oldest, and best-connected family in the state. She had finished Smith a couple of years before, served in the Red Cross during the war, and in 1919 found herself at loose ends. Josephus Daniels assigned her the same chores as Aggie Dearborn down in Birmingham. She remained with the paper for thirty-five years to become one of the most notable advocates of regional reform—and then reaction—of her generation.[22]

Mitchell's dear friend Susan Myrick perfectly embodied the breed of lady rebel journalist. The dashing, gravel-voiced daughter and grand-daughter of Confederate officers, she sprang from noble lineage in central Georgia, but her family had fallen low in the world by her youth. Without much training or education, she had taken a job at the *Macon Telegraph*. The redoubtable publisher, W. T. Anderson, had set her to writing all manner of news and topical pieces. She did everything. According to intimates, she also slept with the publisher.[23] Her grandfather, General Stith Parham Myrick, may or may not have approved. Sue Myrick may or may not have cared.[24] By 1928, Myrick and Mitchell had become confidantes, and Mitchell characterized her friend in terms that might have applied to any number (if not most) of the company of Southern women journalists. Sue, she wrote, "can—and does—do everything from advice to the lovelorn and the cooking page to book reviews and politics and hangings. But the thing that recommends her to me is her common sense and her utter lack of sentimentality about what is tearfully known as 'The Old South.' "[25]

Running against almost every prejudice in the Southern code, such women made their way on spunk, gumption, and their own talent. Patriarchal values and the Southern social order discouraged women more or less discreetly, but masculine bias asserted itself overtly when subtler pressure failed, Peggy Mitchell soon discovered. Men, she found out quickly, did not like women writing. They considered journalism a male preserve, and they aimed to keep it so. Even within the generally misogynistic tendencies of journalism in the twenties, Atlanta papers won a special place. By 1922, Mitchell's old beau John Marsh had passed his journalistic novitiate, and he knew the nature of things among the papers in the Georgia capital. He described the situation to his sister, who craved to work in the newsroom. "All three of the Atlanta papers are opposed to girls or women as straight reporters," he acknowledged frankly. "The more I see of newspaper work the more convinced I am that a girl with talents is wasting herself as a reporter. . . . Other kinds of journalistic work pay so much better and are so much better suited for a girl." Several "gifted young writers" worked for the magazine section of the *Atlanta Journal*, he added, so maybe feature writing was the proper course for her.[26] Did he offer this same advice to his old girlfriend Peggy Mitchell Upshaw? If so, she ignored it. In late November or early December 1922, nine months after John Marsh warned his sister about prejudice against women reporters, Margaret Mitchell discovered the bias on her own.

Peggy Mitchell had been Mrs. Berrien Upshaw only two months when she caught the streetcar that stopped near her father's home on Peachtree Street to go downtown that day. She hung on a strap until she got to Five Points and disembarked at the old, hulking *Journal* building at Forsythe Street. Clutching some of her old articles and essays in sweaty palms, she trudged through the noisy building to the city room, where she laid her offerings before the editor. She had walked into a lion's den. And Harlee Branch was hungry. The city editor had a notorious reputation,

> a hard-driving, hard-shouting, hawk-eyed bundle of energy, who could spot a tipsy reporter or an error in a story seemingly a block away, and who could think of night assignments with almost demoniacal perception for a reporter who had a date. He kept his staffers on their toes by continually bellowing at the top of his very adequate lungs.[27]

He terrorized the old hands. Imagine his impression on the green, prospective cub. Twenty years later, Mitchell recaptured a little of her old terror on first confronting the newsroom tyrant: "I am a product of that era when city editors kept long-handled polo mallets beside their desks just to shatter the skulls of applicants for jobs," she recollected. She was not just any applicant, however. The polo mallets had a special object: the skulls and dignity of female job applicants.[28] The newsroom contained not one female. The city editor did not hire women.

Even years later, Harlee Branch saw no necessity to apologize for, much less deny, his prejudice. Actually, he remembered, he had liked the young woman's writing. He also had admired her chutzpah. But this was the lion's den:

> I was impressed by her earnestness and by the way she went about asking for a job. We talked it over and I wanted to give her a job. But there were no women reporters on the paper then except on the Sunday Mag and the Society section and we felt the time was not ready for the *Journal* to hire regular women reporters.[29]

Given the domestic circumstances that impelled her to take a job and the difficulties of initiating a career in the first place, Branch's rejection might have deepened her gloom and blackened her anxieties about herself as a writer, a person, and a woman. Even the weather conspired against her. In this dreariest of all seasons in the South, between Thanksgiving and Christmas, crisp, bright autumn gives way to late fall's long nights, leaden skies, perpetual drizzle, leafless trees, and rattle-brown landscapes. She summoned her courage again, however, licked her wounds, and, before mid-December 1922, made her way one more time downtown to the *Journal* building.

This time she bypassed the city room. Maybe by now she had listened to John Marsh. She was looking for Angus Perkerson, the founder and editor of the Sunday features magazine of the paper. For once, gender operated in her favor. One of Perkerson's writers had gotten married, and Mrs. Roy Flannigan was leaving the paper to tend the hearth. This was the way it was supposed to be, of course—a woman leaving work for home and husband, and not the other way around, as Peggy Upshaw was proposing. In any case, the young college dropout asked for the slot left vacant by the Flannigan marriage. Mitchell had her own version of this legendary encounter, which she managed, as usual, to turn into a funny story.

> I had no newspaper experience and had never had my hands on a typewriter but by telling poor Angus Perkerson outrageous lies about how I had worked on the Springfield Republican (How could I? And all my people good Democrats?) and swearing I was a speed demon on a Remington, I got the job.[30]

If the terrified job applicant did not lie quite so stupendously as she claimed, Augusta Dearborn confirmed that her friend did "borrow" experience from the Dearborn curriculum vita: Mitchell told Perkerson that she had worked in Aggie's old job on the *Birmingham Times*.[31] The mastery of the typewriter actually was the greatest whopper. Even after four years, she still managed to use only two fingers on the keyboard. They at least could really fly across her Remington by then.

No less than Harlee Branch, Angus Perkerson disliked women as employees, but he particularly disdained belles. As a former debutante, then, Mitchell walked into his office with two strikes against her. Twenty-seven years softened his skepticism but slightly: "I was a little bit worried about putting her on the staff, because she was a society girl, and I said to Medora, . . . 'Medora, I reckon we'll always be waiting for her to get to work.'"[32] His wife shared the anxiety. "Nobody expected an ex-debutante to get to work on time [8:00 A.M.]," she mused, "or to do much work when she did arrive. Atlanta's debutante group of 1920–21 more or less reflected the current Scott Fitzgerald era—the jazz age—This Side of Paradise. It was the fashion to be daring."[33]

Skepticism aside, the editor still offered her the job. Now, however, the young woman had to face the consequences of her success. Here she was, a rich society girl, "with no training for anything in the world," in her own estimation, with a very specific job to do. If she had written all her life, she had never produced a single line of newspaper copy. She had no knowledge whatsoever of the complex procedures of putting out a paper. And as for the complicated journalistic lingo, it might as well have been Swahili. She had lied about her experience, sweet-talked, wheeled and dealed. She now felt the burden of her innocence and ignorance; guilt came into play as well, at least in part. Within two or three years, she was venting her own spleen against the novices on the staff who resembled nothing so much as herself in 1922. Angus Perkerson himself could not have been more cynical. "Little Elsie Dinsmore," Mitchell dubbed one of these green hands, after the guile-less heroine from the series of Victorian children's books. This particular "creature of sweetness and light," Mitchell told her sister-in-law,

> knew it all, there was nothing we could tell her. She kept to her own sweet and untroubled ways and gently forgave us all the unkind admonitions we heaped upon her. We could not fire her because she was "of the management." We were amply repaid by the boners she pulled.

Now, with three years' hard experience under her belt, Mitchell catalogued the sins of all the novices on the staff. "They've all . . . been told they're geniuses who must never stoop to 'cheap reporter tricks,' all want to write colyums and 'I' stuff and none of them know enough to ask for initials and addresses."[34]

Horror at being another journalistic Elsie Dunsmore encouraged Mitchell's cynical characterization of these innocents in 1926. In 1923, it fueled her furious desire to master her craft. Did Angus rant and rave? Did the others smirk behind her back? She would demonstrate her merit by working twice as hard as everyone. Late to work? Never.

She was long there by the time the Perkersons arrived. She opened the place every morning. She left it empty, too, six days a week, when she finally flicked out the lights each night.[35] For the next three and a half years, the *Journal* building was even more than second home, and the *Journal* staff became another family. And what a home it was!

Consider first the noble edifice. The building was notorious. "Smoke-stained, rat-infested, roach-ridden," its grimy, five-story, red brick mass hulked above the railroad tracks at Forsyth Street downtown. The railroad yard marked everything about the place. The grimy engines still rattled through William Howland's memory decades later as he penned a tribute to his old friend.

> There were no diesel switch engines or locomotives in the 1920's. There were only smoke-belching, soft-coal burning steam locomotives. The southern side of the *Journal* building was shrouded constantly with nauseous clouds of black smoke from the puffing engines. In winter, with the windows closed, it was hard enough to breathe without strangling. In summer, when it was a question of open the windows or suffocate, it was next to impossible. It was not uncommon occurrence for a red hot cinder to fall on one's desk. And it required iron concentration to take news over the phone or to write news, with locomotive whistles bellowing, engine bells clanging, just outside the window.[36]

The offices of the Magazine capped the horror. "The Black Hole of Calcutta," Reporter Mitchell christened the quarters. The paper squeezed Perkerson's entire five-person staff into a tiny space on the backside of the third floor. It possessed a grand view of a narrow alley and an insignificant hotel, which did provide at least the office boys with some small pleasure as they shot bent paper clips with rubber bands through open windows at the unsuspecting guests in summer. In winter, its filth-grimed windows admitted no light at all into the dark and gloomy space. The office's furnishings nicely matched the visual miseries. It contained but one telephone and one extension, and staffers harried and hassled one another constantly over its use; the one work table groaned under piles of papers, clippings, and photographs; a comparable mess obscured every other flat surface in the office and overflowed onto the floor as well; the desks might have survived, if barely, Sherman's furious siege; the typewriters were almost as venerable. Mitchell used an ancient Underwood that was "bouncy, jumpy and jittery from senility." It even lacked a backspace key, "and since Peggy was a 'hunt and peck' typist," her friend Howland wrote, "that lack gave her plenty of trouble." The *Journal* provided the cub reporter only an old kitchen chair to sit in, and her short legs dangled hopelessly from its height.[37]

"Primitive" aptly describes the working conditions. The job was grueling, too. Beginning no later than eight o'clock each morning, the work day stretched into the night, six days a week. Perkerson expected a major article of about 1,500 words each week from his employees. In three and a half years on the staff, Mitchell wrote approximately 120 such bylined pieces. The work required major unsigned articles, too. Mitchell preserved evidence of this anonymous work in her scrapbook. While the demands of producing this sort of journalism did not decline with time, her interest in clipping this material did. She saved almost nothing from her last year and a half of work. Still, her files record about fifty unsigned pieces for 1923 and 1924. In addition, she contributed about twenty book reviews to the Magazine's "editorial" page. Nor did this exhaust the demand for copy. Sometimes Mitchell wrote the "lovelorn" column, filling in as the generic "Marie Rose." She did the same sometimes with gossip. While the notorious banned-in-Boston Atlanta novelist Frances Newman created the persona of "Elizabeth Bennet," after the Jane Austen heroine, Mitchell sometimes assumed this responsibility, too.[38] Nor did it end there. The paper ran syndicated, serialized stories, mostly romances, and the young reporter found herself filling in the blanks created by the chaotic process by which the Magazine prepared these adventures for the printers. Bill Howland described this process and how she came to produce this still more anonymous work. Along the way, of course, he underlined still other duties of her job:

> She also had to divide, paste up and proofread the long serial story which the Sunday Magazine then considered essential—and which it published in its own columns on Sundays and continued over into the regular paper on week-days. This complicated method caused parts of the serial frequently to become lost or jumbled. Peggy used to tell the story that once a whole chapter of a heart-throbbing romance was lost and she simply wrote a new one to fill in.[39]

There was more, as Howland described it.

> In those robust days, the Sunday Magazine staff was charged not only with getting out a 32-page magazine, but also with editing and producing a Sunday rotogravure picture section—"The Brown Section" as it was called. Peggy, like the other staff members, had to select pictures and write captions for them. Very popular rotogravure material was the baby pictures—and the Sunday Magazine's office tables were often piled high with surplus baby pictures. Part of Peggy's job was to soothe those whose progeny's pictures failed to appear in print. That often required diplomacy of a very high order.[40]

Still other non-writing tasks demanded her attention. Formally and informally, she played copy editor.[41] She helped proofread all the ma-

terial the Magazine published, as well. This job proved especially oner-
ous. If almost always funny, typos could be threatening, too. They had
other consequences besides provoking the wrath of Angus Perkerson.
She recalled one much later, as her friend Elinor Hillyer planned an
article on the imperious, puritanical, and very powerful Methodist divine, Bishop Asa Candler. The good bishop was great material, she told
her friend, but "from a purely malicious reason or two," she added,
"I'd like to see him in print." The "malicious reasons" involved her
pain in proofing three and a half years of his weekly contributions to
the Magazine and in providing unintentional subject matter for the
bishop's Sunday diatribes as well:

> I refer in the first place to the hours I spent with his copy, dear heart,
> knowing my cubbish head would fall if even a typographic error crept
> in. And oh! that hideous day when the compositors dropped a take from
> a "conjur" story of mine into [the] Bishop's article and had the Rev.
> speaking in broad, nigger dialect. I refer secondly to the time when I was
> riding home from work, minding my business and reading Dr. Steckle's
> "Frigidity in Women." Someone sat down by me, rudely began reading
> my book and began snorting and puffing and shuffling his feet. It was
> none other than the Bish and I furnished him material for 2 Sunday
> articles.[42]

She hated proofreading. Her abysmal spelling and punctuation complicated the job. She found her own ways of dealing with the problem,
especially early on. She was willing to learn from anybody. "When she
first appeared for work, she knew no more about reading proof than
an Australian bushman," Medora joked. "But she didn't want anyone
else to learn that she didn't know—so she got one of the veteran composing room proofreaders to show her."[43] She never lost her gratitude
for the favor. Years later, when this veteran died, Mitchell insisted on
attending his funeral, according to Medora, "because he had given her
many kindly and helpful suggestions in her early years when she was
ignorant of her new job and anxious to conceal this ignorance from
other reporters."[44]

Mitchell cultivated friendships over the entire building. She was
"perky and friendly enough to have been nicknamed 'Bubbles' or 'Smi-
ley,'" her one-time co-worker Erskine Caldwell recalled.[45] Like the
venerable proofreader, many offered her valuable assistance, especially in that arduous first year. She returned the favor with loyalty
that did not wane with time. And so it was throughout the paper.

The proofreaders, typographers, writers, and all the rest constituted
a kind of family. Their company helped compensate for the horrors of
the *Journal*'s working conditions. Was the building dismal? the work
oppressive? the tasks endless? Professional camaraderie made it bear-
able. Long after, Bill Howland celebrated the staff's élan:

The *Journal* of those days also had "esprit de corps" of the kind you read about but seldom find. The elevator man was someone you knew, better than present day workers know those whose desks are side by side with them. You addressed the telephone operators by their first names when you placed a call. At lunchtime, reporters, editors, top executives, press-room men in overalls and sweaty shirts, every other variety of *Journal* worker, crowded into the little cafe on the first floor, sat at rickety tables or milled about at the counter, shouted back and forth, told jokes, ate the rugged fare. It was a rowdy group, a free and easy group, and it might be that was what held them together. They cursed the *Journal* for the low pay, and they worked for the *Journal* with an enthusiasm that money could never buy. They cursed the long hours and, at the end of the long day, they had steam enough left over to work up elaborate prac-tical jokes involving the connivance of every department of the paper.[46]

A special spirit animated the staff, and in later times when most of the journalists recalled those days, Peggy Mitchell held a central place in their memories. "Some of the most vivid were associated with you," one old associate told her years later. "The most vivid recollections of the old days I have are associated with the moments when you wan-dered down from Perk's office, or we sat out in the luncheon joint wait-ing for John to show up (while you read books you were ashamed to be seen with), or you expounded on the abysmal dumbness of debu-tantes."[47] Mitchell herself recalled some of the camaraderie that lent these days a special aura:

> Do you remember that day when the Perks had the mumps and the county cops pulled an entire car load of CedarBrook Rye and I, as temporary editor dispatched the entire staff, you, the office boy, the drunken Snod-grass and the Rhodes scholar out to cover the story and you covered it so excellently—I recall you covered five quarts even if the office boy was nearly shot while handing them to you. Them was the days![48]

If time gave "them days" a golden glow, it was really a special time: the twenties were a golden age of journalism in the United States. It was especially appropriate for Hemingway, for example, to make the hero of *The Sun Also Rises* a foreign correspondent, the most exotic and attractive kind of journalist of all. In real life, characters like H. L. Mencken, Ring Lardner, George Jean Nathan, Grantland Rice, Damon Runyon, and Don Marquis shaped the values of a generation. The *Jour-nal* staffers felt special kinship with these currents in the twenties. They relished associations with some of the most notable people in Ameri-can journalism. The great sportswriter Grantland Rice had served an early tour of duty in the red brick hulk on Forsyth Street. Don Marquis had worked there, too. He captivated a whole generation with his won-derful poetic critters, Archie the cockroach and Mehitabel the alley cat. It was to honor him and his wonderful creations that Margaret Mitchell renamed the unspeakable cafeteria in the Journal Building "The Roachery." While Mitchell read Mencken faithfully, she also clipped and saved column after column of Archie and Mehitabel columns. Mehitabel's standard exclamation, "Wotthehell! Wotthehell!" struck her fancy. At the top of one of her clippings, "The Song of Mehitabel," she scribbled, "Don't you like Mehitabel's toujours gai philosophy?"[49]

The *Journal* also served as the springboard for others of Mitchell's own generation to achieve national fame, another source of collective pride. An old Atlantan (also a friend and fraternity brother of Berrien Upshaw), Lamar Trotti, went from the *Journal* to success in Hollywood. Still another child of the city's gentry, Frances Newman, launched her national career from her contributions to Major Cohen's paper. So did Erskine Caldwell. Indeed, in looking back over half a century, Caldwell considered Atlanta and the *Journal* very heaven in the twenties. With one morning paper and two afternoon journals, the competition kept the writers constantly *au point*. The *Journal*'s offices were just across the street from Heart's *Georgian*, he recounted: "Both papers raced to get editions on the street and tried to out-do each other with blazing headlines. It was a great railroad and hotel town in the Twenties (and Thirties) and was perhaps the leading convention city in the South. There seemed to be a constant flow of well-known politicians, business, and sports personalities ready and willing to make comments and give interviews. A real good newspaper town."[50]

The former debutante relished journalism, not least, for the occasion it offered her to play the low life. By 1919, her propensity for oaths and curses had already won her notoriety; the *Journal* exaggerated the tendency. She was forever "god-damning" this, "helling" that, and "sons-a-bitching" the other. "She was the vulgarist thing I ever heard!"[51] laughed her rather more conventional friend Willie Snow Ethridge. Mitchell's unorthodox language delighted her more unconventional friends. Harvey Smith's views hit the mark:

> Obscenity as expressed by Peggy was less obscene than by anyone I have ever known: it was either hilariously funny or in some way enlightening. It was never self conscious, furtive or suggestive. It was, like her slightly distorted admiration for a large alcoholic capacity, purely a product of her period: the post war flapper era of Scott Fitzgerald [and Zelda], of Tallulah, Michael Arlen, Cabell, Freud, Havelock Ellis, Lorelei Lee, Mencken, D. H. Lawrence and all the rest.[52]

"Talks with the vulgarity of newpaper women," Jonathan Daniels noted during his interview with her in 1937, and he illustrated the propensity with a story she told about her early career. He jotted it down in rough note form that still suggests the teller's tone and voice:

When I was coming on only way man could insult a woman was to try to pull off her pants and if she knew how to act it was sometime before he got out of the hospital—now adays young girl insulted because escort went into the gents room and came back with liquor on his breath—young thing like this came rushing home in taxi and threw herself on bed in tears and said she'd been insulted. When I said what I did about insults when I was coming along (about 1924) she said my generation (with mincing voice) was the coarsest since the restoration—

and he concluded, incidentally, "(Pants is her favorite word although she also likes S.O.B. using the initials)."[53]

Newspapering also fed her ambivalent fascination with sex. From very early in her adolescence, Mitchell had played around the fringes of the erotic and pornographic. Her playlet, "(Seen) Scene at a Soiree" flirted with the forbidden, "seeing that which should not be seen, saying that which should not be said." In the early twenties she found new outlets for the interest. She collected erotica, delighted in what she fondly called her "dirty book stores" in New York City, belonged to an informal group of Atlanta bohemians who shared her interest, and relished talking about the subject with special friends. Much of this came together for her in her delight and appreciation of that notable Southern writer James Branch Cabell, and his very odd and very scandalous 1919 classic, *Jurgen*, his modern version of knightly romance that partook in nearly equal parts of the Arthurian romances, Lewis Carroll's *Alice in Wonderland*, Sir James Frazer's *Golden Bough*, and Frank Harris's *My Life and Loves*, all, not coincidentally, among Mitchell's favorite books. Having defended the devil, even if unawares, the eponymous hero of Cabell's romance is granted immortality, and he passes back and forth through time, encountering every personification of womanhood known to legend, myth—and Freudian psychology. Women, sex, lust, life, and death dominate every page, often in the most purposefully bizarre combinations. What did it all mean? What was *Jurgen*'s intention, to offer social criticism, or make a joke? Was he producing an allegory or an obscene gesture? Where did one purpose start and the other end? Was life itself a tragic, cosmic joke? Was this Cabell's ultimate truth? The writer himself left the issue to his readers. And Cabell's ambiguity appealed to the Atlantan.

For all the covert obscenity of this modern romancer, Mitchell herself preserved an intensely moralistic view even of Jurgen's randiest capers. Rare among her scrapbook clippings, she preserved one review that she did not write herself: Of *Jurgen*, it maintained that Cabell had written the ultimate modern morality tale and that the Virginian was the ultimate moralist.[54] But finally, of course, there was all that sex and quasi-sex and sexual innuendo all wrapped up in art. *Jurgen* made it all seem fine. For that aristocratic Mr. Cabell, a Southern newspaperman no less, to be banned in Boston and praised by the godlike H. L. Mencken in Baltimore seemed the most awesome accomplishment to the young Southerner. She could justify her excitement in moral terms and even as high art.

If she loved Cabell, she also discovered other objects to whet or satisfy her interest in erotica. From Cabell, she branched out into other more or less High Cultural pornography. She treasured *Fanny Hill, Aphrodite, The Perfumed Garden,* and *Lysistrata,* especially the "edition suppressed because of the Aubrey Beardsley illustrations depicting most graphically the sad plight of the sex starved Spartans."[55] Haunting New York's pornography shops, she crowed over finding "Vol. I (unexpurgated) Frank Harris 'My Life and Loves'" and noted that she had also "ordered Havelock Ellis 'Man and Woman.'"[56] The Ellis was a special prize. She treasured the English psychologist and sexologist above all others—except, of course, for Cabell himself.

Mitchell owned more of Ellis's books than of any author except Cabell. She shared with Harvey Smith her affection for the odd Englishman, and the two spent hours poring over his texts and reading the material out loud to each other. She especially savored case studies: what Smith recalled as the information tucked darkly away in appendices and footnotes. "Little bits of lusty living that appealed to both of us would peep through these footnotes," Smith related. "The most popular one of all with Peggy was the very long one in the appendix to Havelock Ellis's Sex in Society, the story of a British army officer in the orient."[57] This was the satyr with lust so unbounded that he paid attention to neither sex nor species.[58]

The Austrian psychologist Wilhelm Stekel also had many of the same characteristics that attracted Mitchell to Ellis. As free of psychoanalytic jargon as the Englishman, his *Frigidity in Women* actually made an aggressive case for using common language to describe psychological problems. Also, his long case studies contained the most intimate revelations, in several cases in long, autobiographical form. It constituted, in effect, the kind of material that the Victorians had circulated underground and anonymously fifty years before. Mitchell knew his work, too.[59] The nineteenth-century German Krafft-Ebing met some of the same requirements. He titillated, but she and Smith disliked him because "he so obviously found his subject matter loathsome but toothsome."[60]

She exercized her hobby as she could, and she shared it even with friends who were not aficionados. "Yes, I knew she had a collection," Elinor Hillyer von Hoffman wrote:

> books brought to her from Paris by maybe one of her Atlanta Journal friends, or maybe Harvey himself, but I never saw them. Except one afternoon she let me read some of *Fanny Hill* to illustrate something she

thought funny in 18th or 19th Century presentation of the subject matter. And so it was. She had some post cards from Paris, which she also thought were funny—the expressions of the model's faces.[61]

"Sex worshippers," Mitchell dubbed the devotees.[62]

The material amused some of her wittier friends like Hillyer; it rather baffled simpler minds like her fellow bohemian aristocrat, Julia Memminger. "I knew about all that stuff, but none of it ever interested me. I never did know why she liked it so."[63]

Her newspaper work provided more occasion to exercise her fascination with the genre. In 1926, the paper sent a young reporter out to do a story on a cremation. Reporting back, the cub related that the subject of the interview had not only the ashes but the diary of a woman who had kept a "house of ill-repute" when Atlanta had been wide open years before. The idea of the diary put Mitchell in a gleeful mood, although she raged on hearing the young reporter remark that the Methodist possessor of the document intended to burn the journal. "Oh, the mental processes of the godly!" she groaned, and she laid her own plans for retrieving the madam's record:

> I'm going out and tell her a good line about how I think it would be a good moral influence to publish it, minus names (if it could possibly get by)—how it would keep the faltering footsteps of many a pure girl from etc.—etc. And I really mean it. I'm not moral, myself, thank the Lord but I do think a few more books published about the sordidness and lack of romance in prostitution would do a lot for the counter jumpers who fancy it an improvement on their honest professions. So I'm working the Methodist through the moral end of it and she's conferring with her husband. Even if they didn't give me the right to publish it I'd like to read it over the weekend. I imagine it involves nearly every well know person in Atlanta. John and I could enjoy a quiet Sunday at home with Blanche Betterouse's diary![64]

Journalism also encouraged her going to places where ladies had never been, doing things ladies never did, and talking to folks that ladies could never deign to notice. The *Journal* allowed and even encouraged the satisfaction of her curiosity about disreputable women and prostitution. Assigned to cover a murder in a sleazy flophouse, she bragged to another reporter, "I was the first virtuous woman who ever set foot inside the doors of that hotel."[65]

She flirted enthusiastically with breaking other taboos for Southern ladies as she nurtured her image as a hell-raising journalist. Although she hid the habit from her father as long as he lived, she smoked with a vengeance. While she never liked alcohol and drank seldom, she also acquired a reputation for holding her liquor: "At her house one night, I watched her pour it out and toss it down, and I decided to keep up," one friend remembered. "She didn't blink. I had my first hangover."[66] She despised Prohibition on both general and practical grounds, and it posed few hindrances for getting booze. Everyone had their sources of bootleg whiskey. The newspaper friends had their own local contacts for home brew, and, long afterward, she treasured memories of beaux calling on her with offerings of Mason jars filled with the potent clear liquid, or the variant of red hot-water bottles, sans stoppers, that carried the same fiery potion.[67] She left no evidence of using other controlled substances, but she certainly knew of cocaine and on one occasion at least made a joke of its use, by passing out vials of a white dust at a party and encouraging her guests to snort powdered sugar.[68]

This life thrilled her. Fired by a rare sense of community, inspired by their national idols, infused with the sense of their own prophetic role in regional culture, and titillated, not least, by their own sexual power and energy, the young rebel generation looked to one another as the collective spirit of change and progress, nowhere more intently than at the *Journal*. Margaret Mitchell cherished belonging to this rebel fraternity. It nurtured her sense of meaning, purpose and worth. It had its cost, however. It remained a fraternity, with all the limitations and paradoxes of that term for women.

On the *Journal*, as John Marsh had intimated long before, the camaraderie was explicitly and aggressively masculine. In reflecting on this time, her co-worker Bill Howland returned over and over to the theme; it constituted, in truth, the fundamental assumption of his memoir of journalism in the twenties. "Women reporters were tolerated and not sought," he boasted.

> Those were entirely masculine days for the city news staff. There was none of the tribe of sob-sisters or women reporters then on the *Journal* city staff. The staff was composed entirely of men—most of them about equally proud of their ability to drink hard as to work hard. They wrote hard, factual news stories—often of crime and punishment—but with an almost fanatical zeal for factual accuracy. . . . Those were the days of the straight, factual news story, without the emotional fancy and often superficial trimmings of the news writing today.[69]

These cynical, hard, hardbitten, and rugged men accepted Peggy Mitchell, despite her sex. She won "the respect and admiration of her colleagues, men and women, for the way she made good in a hard, masculine business, asking no favors and giving none. She did it by hard sense and hard work." Just the same, the highest praise Angus Perkerson could muster in retrospect for this mite of a person was: "She wrote like a man."[70]

Yet even the fraternity's admiration had its limits. Later Mitchell joked about the overt misogyny she encountered as a staffer. When she had achieved worldwide success with her novel, she wrote that she could still vividly imagine herself seated at her old desk, trying to work, while "listening to my editor's oft repeated statements that I wouldn't be sitting in that seat if it wasn't that men reporters always got drunk and didn't show up for work and always had women no better than they should be phoning him at all hours. . . ."[71]

Mitchell's friend Elinor Hillyer recorded another version of the disabilities women writers encountered on the *Journal*. She did not laugh. After leaving the Columbia School of Journalism, the young woman had moved back to Atlanta and taken Mitchell's job when she resigned in 1926. One of Perkerson's most prolific writers, after four years she still made the same pay as when she started. Her $25 weekly paycheck was actually the same salary that the *Journal* had paid her predecessor, Peggy Mitchell, when she had started eight years before in 1922. Making the circumstance more grievous still, Perkerson paid her less than her male counterparts. She asked for a raise. Perkerson gave her the same answer he did to any such request from his female staffers:

> He told me no woman writer should earn more than a man. We didn't have to work, he said. We could always catch a husband to support us. I couldn't take that line again. It was the middle of the Depression and I didn't have another job, but I quit then and there.[72]

Mitchell lived daily with such prejudice. Nor, of course, was Angus Perkerson the only lion on the prowl. The "crusty curmudgeons of the composing room" resented women workers. The "extremely individualistic independent photographers of those pre–candid camera days" provided still more obstacles for female writers. Howland described one of them, the "acrimonious William Sparks" who rode the women ruthlessly. Howland described him as "very strict with the *Sunday Magazine* women reporters, often lecturing them on what they should wear and how they should behave on assignments." His rancor notwithstanding, Mitchell managed to become his "special favorite" after all. She used her old-girl charm to deflect his misogyny. This very exercise of rational self-defense, however, underlined her peculiar place within the journalistic fraternity.[73]

The all-male city room remained a constant, visible reminder of the gender limitations in the profession. Those limitations were symbolic; they were real and material as well. The city room contained the dictionary. Mitchell's sex denied her access to the word itself. Howland thought the prohibition was very funny.

> A tiny reddish-haired, electric-eyed sprite from the *Sunday Mag* department from time to time would come in to look up words in the big dictionary beside the city desk. She was so small that she would have to

stand on tiptoe and lean over the big book, often exposing an inch or so of white skin above tops of her rolled stockings. When that happened in those days when legs were not the public ocular property they are today, there would be considerable mis-typing and slowing down in production on the part of the young reporters. This soon caught Mr. Branch's alert eye. He stopped it by calling our visitor to his desk, and saying in the most fatherly fashion: "Miss Peggy, I'll have to ask you to stop using the dictionary—you're upsetting my young men."[74]

The city editor denied her even professional visits to his department. It was doubly damaging. She needed to check spellings and meanings, naturally enough, but she still cherished her old ambition to do straight news-reporting. Actually, once the city editor did ask Mitchell to write for him. He liked her piece, and he invited her to come up permanently to his department. His request provoked her old confusion. After his invitation, Branch reported, she was "very nervous. She was afraid it wouldn't be good enough. But when she saw me showing her story to some of the men reporters and telling them they ought to do something as good as that, she perked up."[75] Just the same, she turned the offer down.

Mitchell recalled the same incident herself. A decade later, Branch himself had graduated to higher and grander stations as he took a job as the New Deal's Assistant Postmaster General. When *Gone with the Wind* appeared, he sent the author a warm congratulatory letter. The author gushed in reply, but some of her old anxieties and frustrations glowed beneath time's ashes. "I am sure you never realized the great admiration I had for you during the days when I was a reporter on the Atlanta Journal," she began:

> You probably did not suspect that the height of my ambition was to do some work on the staff of the daily as well as feature stories for the magazine. You have doubtless forgotten that several times you did call on me to cover stories for the daily, and I was made so happy and excited that I could hardly write them. Then, one day when you had sent me to interview a lady axe murderess who had refused to unburden her soul to crude male ears, you liked my story enough to say loudly so that the whole City Room could hear, "How would you like to come upstairs and work for me?" Nothing will ever again give me such a thrill, because I knew very well you did not care greatly about having women working on the City Staff. I didn't go to work for you, but I always remembered your words with great gratitude.[76]

The little stint with Branch had been important. She carefully saved the clipping of the murder report in her scrapbook. The article is singular. If she did write more before, or after, she did not preserve them. Given her fastidious collection of all her early essays and her special interest in newsroom writing, this probably was, then, her full contribution to Branch's department. Even if she wrote others, this one certainly appealed to her, and her letter to Branch clarifies her interest. "A lady axe murderess" was a figure the Girl Reporter might relate to. She could certainly sympathize with the woman's reluctance to "unburden herself to crude male ears," and the two of them—girl reporter and murderess—formed a female community against those aggressive, prying men, at least in her reconstruction of the interview.

The actual article was rather different from Mitchell's later reconstruction. It contained no comic element at all. The perpetrator of the crime was no ax murderer, and no lady either, at least by regional definition of the term. A working-class woman had shot her husband: in an alcoholic rage, the man was beating her. He grabbed a gun. She snatched the pistol from his grasp; it fired as he struggled to get it back. No week passed that some such crime of passion did not stain police blotters in Atlanta. Perhaps this is why Mitchell earned the story's rights in the first place; it was ordinary. She made it unique. In her interview with the killer, she discovered that the woman had worked for the police with female offenders. The counselor now found herself on the wrong side of the bars.[77]

Mitchell took a straight story and made it something special: she dug out the element that set this tale apart from all the others. It was this element, most likely, and Mitchell's imaginative hard work that impressed Harlee Branch. She effectively determined how to beat the boys at their own game. She would get there faster, work harder, craft her material more carefully, and invest more of herself in her writing. It was a race, however, that she could only win in fiction. The game was rigged. She determined not to run it. If Branch really offered her a job, if, to boot, he really meant it, Mitchell would have been the Christian in the lions' den for sure. At the Mag, at least, she had female companionship, and she could trade special intimacies with the other women. She could expect no such easy conversations in the city room. Moreover, she always had a friend at court in Medora Perkerson, her working boss and intermediary with the editor. Even so, she had to muster Daniel's courage every day to face her own roaring, tightfisted chief. She detested him quite thoroughly, and long afterwards she still grumbled about his lack of appreciation for her work.[78] If working for the Magazine generated such problems, it took no imagination to conjure the social horrors of the city room for a lone woman. When the chance came, then, she shrank.

Even had she felt no inner doubts about herself and what she wanted out of life, her writing, or a career, this decision would have been difficult. Nor is it clear that she wanted to accept, finally, the limits of city-desk masculinity. Angus Perkerson testified she wrote like a man. His declaration is actually misleading. Neither the form, content, nor

tone of Margaret Mitchell's *Journal* articles fit the conventional patterns of newsroom reporting. Perhaps she muffled her voice against
"crude male ears." Perhaps she muffled it from herself. Her own distinctive sensibility as a woman, however, found a natural outlet at the
Magazine. Perhaps her decision to turn down Harlee Branch involved
the maintenance of her own distinctive view. With all its liabilities,
her old job fostered that, and that voice still echoes clearly through
her pieces for the *Journal* Magazine. She wrote like a woman.

VIII

The Whole Story
⬥⬥⬥⬥

From first to last she was a good reporter in the traditional sense that she never made excuses and never fell down on a story. She was more than a good reporter in that her work was definitely creative and had that extra something which gives life and color to the simplest story.

MEDORA PERKERSON ON PEGGY MITCHELL[1]

*M*ore than floors separated the City Desk from Features, and Medora Perkerson captured something of the difference in a story she repeated about her co-worker. "You could always tell when she was stuck on a story, because she would get out her lipstick and make up her mouth."[2] The imagery is nice: when she could not make up the story, she made up her face; she fixed her mouth; she altered her looks. This was not Harlee Branch's territory. The demographics of the department confirmed it, too: almost all the staffers on the Magazine were females; all the writers were. For all Angus Perkerson's burring bluster, his wife, Medora, exercised her own hegemony here as well. It was a woman's world.

A photographer—was it the irascible, misogynistic William Sparks?—captured the feel of the place nicely, too, when he memorialized the staff on film. Angus Perkerson failed to sit. Rifling papers at the cluttered desk, however, his wife dominates the picture with her forthright gaze and ready smile. Beside the office boy on the right, the cocky young artistic editor stands above, gripping firmly the shoulders of two female staffers. If one of the women looks sullen at the touch, the other, Peggy Mitchell, ignores him. She also dramatically ignores the camera itself, but she attracts attention to herself even so. She certainly stands apart. Her vermilioned lips distinguish her, as does her pose. The others here are wrens beside this sulphur-crested cockatoo. Well-coiffed and haute coutured, she bends her head dramatically away from the camera, directing her gaze towards the galleys in her left hand. Pencil poised loftily in her right, she interjects herself into the very center of the image with the mock heroics of a journalistic Irene Castle.

With fey hand, delicate pinky, and downcast eyes, Peggy Mitchell burlesques femininity. The pose fits her labors. Features was, after all, incidental writing on the periphery of the newsbeat's real journalism. Writing for the Sunday Magazine travestied her ambition and her histrionic affectation mocked the enterprise. At the same time, the writer's celebration of pen and galleys in her pose truly underlines her real commitment: Writing was everything. The contradictory impulses pulled her this way and then that, and this was a measure of the burden she bore as a woman and a journalist. William Howland celebrated her as "Peggy Mitchell, Newspaperman"; Angus Perkerson insisted she "wrote like a man." They got much less than half the story. Both the style and content of her writing convey another message.

Mitchell herself believed that women wrote differently from men. "Tell it the way a woman would tell it," she once wrote a friend.[3] In this frame of reference she identified the personal, intimate, and otherwise obscure detail with women's style. She often repeated the idea to her husband. "When I am narrating some interesting event to Peggy," he related, "she says, 'Now tell it like a woman,' meaning give the details. Fill in the small items that together created the picture and enable the listener to participate in the event."[4] Although none of her numerous recollections of her old friend ever referred to gender in one way or another, Medora Perkerson's overall characterization of Mitchell's writing makes the same general connections. "She had the ability to characterize a person so that the reader saw him vividly—and she never missed a chance to brush in a few strokes of personality," Perkerson observed. "Some writers give you the story adequately enough, but you have to look at the photographs to see the person involved. The persons Peggy interviewed were depicted in words—the story could have gone without any illustrations at all."[5]

In further description of her friend's approach, Perkerson emphasized still other values traditionally associated with womanhood: the emphasis on feeling, sympathy, and affection; the sense of immediacy, vitality, and nurturing; the celebration of the small, obscure, and simple.[6] Her friend possessed a gift for words, Perkerson recalled, but "something deeper than that, an understanding and appreciation of human values and the artist's ability to give life and color to the simplest story and to represent the whole picture."[7] In keeping with still other aspects of a feminine sensibility, Perkerson's analysis collapsed distinctions between how Mitchell got a story, how she told the story, and how she wrote the stories. In much the same way, her descriptions blurred the lines between the subject of the story and the reporter. "Wholeness," she related, was the dominating impulse.

> Because she genuinely liked people, they opened up and gave her the stories she wanted. It seemed to me that lots of young reporters who came on the newspapers in those days felt they were superior to the stories they were assigned to write. Peggy never felt that way. Whether she was sent out to interview a preacher or a butcher or Tiger Flowers [a notable black Atlanta prizefighter], she always sought to get the real story and the whole story.[8]

Medora Perkerson never claimed that Mitchell "wrote like a woman," but her analysis of her friend's journalistic virtues could hardly have differed more from those touted in the newsroom. William Howland had idealized the straight news story, devoid of emotion and embellishment, which he despised. Perkerson, in contrast, praised her friend's creative inventiveness: Mitchell frilled her stories with "that extra something which gives life and color." The idea of "life and color" appears nowhere in Howland's litany of journalistic merit. Perkerson connected Mitchell's literary vitality to the writer's sympathy and compassion. Howland ignored both. Both the style and content of Howland's recollection underline a fairly traditional male model: the hard-hitting good reporter batters down a subject and rams through a story. At the same time, Howland's journalism emphasized "high society and high business folk," and ultimately, the Big Story. Perkerson's notions of Mitchell's writing stressed a different end—and mode—entirely. In the time-honored way of women, Mitchell concerned herself chiefly with the small and simple and with little people, according to her friend. Furthermore, the "girl reporter" never condescended to these folks, however lowly, Perkerson insisted. She established genuine bonds of affection, feeling, and kinship between herself and them. She committed herself to them; they, in turn, "opened up" to her. To elaborate Perkerson's shorthand: People relaxed their guard and volunteered their tales; Mitchell then retold them as if indeed they had happened to her firsthand. Her sense of personal identification allowed her to see and feel as if she were her subject. Bonding with her subject, she challenged the lines between reporter and reported, between teller and tale, and even the narrative and the audience. She was voice of her subject but the eyes of her reader all at once. Here, then, was inclusiveness—wholeness at its most complete.

By distinguishing Mitchell's sympathetic mode from the distancing superiority of the conventional (also male) reporter, Medora Perkerson understood, even if she did not argue so, a womanly basis of her friend's gifts. Margaret Mitchell acknowledged the same truths. Thus it was that she had written about ingratiating herself with "the lady axe murderess" who was unwilling or unable to unburden herself to "crude male ears." Superior masculine egos and "crude male ears" did not need to listen, much less to appreciate and then describe the killer's dowdy dress, but that very dress of dotted-swiss fabric shines as a vital little detail that makes the story live.

As a function of a female vision or not, the young reporter wrote very well. Her prose, however, also suffered from a slew of faults; some her own, some connected with newspaper writing in general. Journalism is evanescent by its nature. Aiming for an immediate, not long-term effect, it must seize the reader's attention quickly; staying power has little relevance. Papers are discarded even more rapidly than they are taken up. Also the amount and variety of copy required of professional journalists—especially in the age of Mencken—fostered shallowness. Deadlines proved more critical than quality, although the nature of Sunday feature writing mitigated the worst effects of this for Angus Perkerson's staff. More personally, Mitchell's prose tended often to wordiness. Her usage was sometimes inept, inappropriate, or even wrong. As if striving for effect, her language sometimes lost its way. Writing as much as she did, however, perhaps the wonder lies not in the scarcity of good writing but that in her three and a half years' tenure on the paper she created genuinely memorable prose. It still reads well.

Mitchell's prose for the *Journal* stands on its own merits. The young reporter turned a vivid phrase. She invented striking figures of speech. She cut her language to fit her themes. She possessed the strongest narrative sense. If she had problems with her endings, she had a special talent for imaginative leads. She had the keenest ear for dialogue and the spoken word, and her interviews' quotations capture the widest variations in tone and character. She excelled at characterization. She isolated critical details to make a scene or character spring to life. She seldom wrote with classical restraint, but the welter of her facts, details, and other data all evoked a vivid picture of her subjects. Her successful journalism anticipates the craft that went into her novel. It also showed the skills that she had cultivated since she first picked up a pencil. She wrote well.

Gold lay often even in the dross. In the summer of 1923, for example, she wrote an imminently disposable article on summer camps. She stuffed it with the trite, heavily modified images of mountain air, cool breezes, quiet water, and all the other obvious references; this familiar litany, however, culminated in the most striking image, not of cool but of heat. The mountain scene, Mitchell concluded, was "a pleasing change from the steaming Atlanta streets where even the asphalt softens underfoot."[9] The figure of a street-melting summer is as fresh and original as it is natural and unstrained. It has the mark of good writing, both subtle and appropriate. Such striking images and telling juxtapositions appear often in her prose. In one of her several articles on circuses, sideshows, and freaks, she made a quasi-anthropological study of the peculiar customs and rituals of the circus world, and she introduces the idea with the expression, "the thin canvas is as redoubtable as The Great Wall of China."[10]

Mitchell varied her usage to fit the occasion, and her command of language appeared particularly powerful in her essay on the wretched old Atlanta jail.[11] The essay is notable for various reasons. While Mitchell generally worked her essays around dialogue and quotations, thereby reducing her own most obvious voice in the proceedings, this feature contains almost none. Very competent as straight reporting, it also contains passages that inspire the imagination, not least because of their very restraint. She suggests the horror of incarceration here by artful understatement. She had toured the building in the hottest part of summer, and the essay captured the desperation of the ghastly heat—and the desperation of the inmates just as well especially in her depiction of the quarter for black females, where the unfortunate women

> lay on the floor or sprawled across chairs, trying to find a little coolness. The air was close and choky enough in the corridor, but when the matron opened one of the iron-barred doors and displayed three small cells opening onto a tiny hall, the atmosphere was sickening.
>
> The day was hot. The window to this small partition onto which the cells opened was high from the floor and narrow. The cells themselves were low and dark as fox dens. From the stifling gloom of two cells came the unceasing moans of inmates who lay on their narrow cots.
>
> "Crazy," said the matron, an efficient and intelligent-looking colored woman. The other prisoners lay on the floor too limp with heat and the close proximity of fellow inmates to notice anything. Had they the energy or the strength of the men prisoners they might have climbed up to the window to breathe at least one cool breath. But they only sprawled miserably in the heat.

This essay lacks embellishment, and the prison, the heat, the hopelessness, especially of the women, speaks for itself. The one quotation, "Crazy," uttered by the matron, fits this mode perfectly. The essay works very well indeed.

Mitchell adopted flat, reportorial objectivity for the prison essay, but she used another tone entirely for an interview with a forty-two-year-old drifter who made a profession of attending notable sporting events without ever paying admission. She introduces her character as flesh and blood:

Connelly is a thick-set, short man, with a bullet head set on a short, thick neck. His eagle beak nose is criss-crossed with scars, his face full and placid, his one green eye shines with the quiet confidence acquired only by one who is convinced in his own soul of the laudability of his life work. . . . Across his front is draped a gold watch chain of cable proportions, holding a nickle with a hole in it that John D. Rockefeller gave him for a newspaper sixteen years ago, when newspapers sold for two cents.

"He's still got three cents coming to him," said the wanderer proudly. "But he ain't never going to get them."

After this great opening, the young reporter then retells in mock-epic fashion how Connelly came by his life's calling. In the process, of course, she reveals some other of her talents, like the gift of narrative and an ear for the spoken word:

"I never paid for admission but once in my life," Connelly added, in explaining his "conscientious objection" [to buying tickets]. "And that was to a prize fight. I paid for a reserved seat and when I got in there was another bird in my seat." He paused in pained memory and then drew the veil over the scarring recollection. "That started me. I've never paid nobody nothing since then, and I don't intend to. Fr'instance, I got put out of the Dempsey–Carpenter fight thirteen times, but I always got back in and finally they give up and let me stay . . . ."

At the Canadian national rodeo in Calgary, he hoodwinked two sets of people. He convinced the reporters he was an official of the Canadian Pacific Railroad, while the Canadian Pacific officials believed he was an American journalist. He gave up the ruse, finally, because it bored him. "'It was right after that,' continued One-Eyed Connelly, 'that I found out that the Canadian jails was the easiest gates to crash that I ever come up against.'"[12]

The piece on One-Eyed Connelly demonstrates Mitchell's strongest talents as a writer. A surpassing story-teller since her childhood, she brought this gift to bear in much of her journalism. Some articles, of course, lent themselves much more than others to plot and narrative line, but she made the most of the potential whenever it appeared. As a function of her narrative talent, she possessed a great sense of good leads. One has only to recall "The Little Pioneers" of her childhood to apprehend her gift. That story opens in the middle of the action with a shouted remonstrance from one character to the protagonist, "Hold on, Margaret, hold on," a cry that establishes the heroine's character and the story's theme.

As in her juvenile story, she often began her newspaper articles with quotations, an unconventional practice that she used very effectively. She demonstrated the device classically in a book review when she began the review itself with the lines that actually opened the novel: "'The guiding impulses of Marigold Trent's life were politeness and a feeling for the dramatic' is the first line . . . and it is on this sentence that the entire book hangs. Marigold poses always and never fails to do the dramatic thing at the correct time."[13] The remainder of the review simply elaborates these ideas, which, not incidentally, come close to matching the young reporter's own attitudes. The essay "Girls Used as 'Blinds' by Rum-runners" also began with a vivid quotation from the woman warder condemning male justice. The warder's anger set the essay's temper.[14]

The one news article she wrote and saved from her *Journal* days also began with a quotation. This, in her hyperbole, was the story of the "lady axe murderess." The point of the quotation was to emphasize the dramatic reversal; the murderer, a victim of her husband's brutality, herself being a counselor for female offenders and now finding herself needing counsel: "I have been through tragedies like this so often with so many other poor girls when I was a policewoman," she began, "but I never thought that I would ever have to go through it myself."[15]

Opening with quotations was only one means of grabbing readers' attention. She often used a short, punchy, mostly monosyllabic opening, sometimes not even a complete sentence, which she isolated as a separate structure. "Last straws," she began the essay on divorce;[16] "Alas for romance!" she commenced the article on elopements;[17] and "Charles Clements played in hard luck,"[18] introduced the essay on an amnesiac who came to to find himself a criminal in his "prior life." "Subdebs Pass up Tutankhamen," the sparkling article that chronicled the Grand Tour of five giddy Atlanta teenagers, opened nicely with the lead, "It's all a matter of viewpoint." Thereby Mitchell established at the outset the broader implications she wanted the essay to advance.[19]

She provided a zippy lead for a long article on faith healing. "Is the day of miracles over?" she inquired. Although such an entry provided ample oportunity for her to ply her wit and skepticism, this article surprises by playing it straight. She attended the healing services, filled her article with the "Praise Gods!" of the afflicted cured, interviewed the preacher, and quoted the recipients of his healing ministry. She also spoke to more mainstream Protestant divines, like the Methodist minister who waffled on modern miracles. In all this she had ample opportunity to do a Mencken turn, but she forbore. Indeed, she turned to other sources that confirmed the healings. The day of miracles had not passed. "Dr. Blanche Loveridge, woman psychologist who had degrees from the University of Chicago, the Sorbonne in France, and the University of Berlin," proved the case. By 1923, the young reporter had discovered psychology herself and read passionately in the field. Dr. Loveridge's answers pleased her. "There is no ailment, either organic or functional, that cannot be cured by faith, providing the super-conscious mind can be reached. . . . By the super-conscious mind," she elaborated, "I mean that which most people call the sub-conscious mind with God."[20] Rather than for sneering and debunking, then, as one might have expected of this devotee of H. L. Mencken, Mitchell used this lively, catchy lead to consider the relationship of faith healing to psychology.

The reporter frequently launched articles with questions of one kind or another, and her answers often came up as fresh as the one about the day of miracles. "Why does the modern woman stay young longer than her mother did? Why is this generation, as a whole, a younger seeming one than the last?" she pondered. In this case, too, she found the proper answer from a professional psychologist.

> "Women of today have plenty to occupy their minds," said the psychological expert. "Formerly, they were required and allowed to do only things that, at best, took little constructive thought. Nursing babies, keeping house, cooking, gossiping were their chief occupations, and they avoided new ideas and intellectual things for fear of being considered 'forward' or a 'blue stocking' . . . .
>
> "As a result, their minds virtually atrophied and a stodginess of body reflected their stodginess of mind. A mind that has no new ideas inevitably shows itself on the face."[21]

For all her various talents for turning a phrase, creating a compelling narrative, and seizing readers' attention, Mitchell also possessed the greatest talent for delineating individual character. She made her subjects live. Her One-Eyed Connelly proved the case. She did the same with far less vivid people. The warder at the old Atlanta jail, the circus people, silly subdebs on their European tour—she allows each some distinguishing mark or trait of character even in the briefest appearance. The famous, of course, came with ready-made public images, and discovering something fresh and new within those images defined Mitchell's task when writing about these folk. For the notables she wrote about—the millionaire, murderer, ex-convict Harry K. Thaw; the operatic Ponselle sisters; the inventor Hudson Maxim; the movie idol Rudolph Valentino—she found some "angle" that allowed her to present each one fresh despite his or her fame. Her treatment of Maxim represents the norm. Featuring the inventor's wife (Mitchell actually began the essay with Mrs. Maxim) provided the "something extra" for the essay. Although Maxim's fame arose from his invention of the tools of war, Mitchell chose to emphasize a softer, feminine, domestic aspect of his character. The presentation of his busy wife at the outset, then, establishes the theme that dominates the entire piece.[22]

The introduction of Mrs. Hudson Maxim as the star of the essay on her famous husband is more than a journalistic ploy. It also suggests a more fundamental orientation in Mitchell's articles towards women's themes, issues, and concerns. Mitchell wrote as a woman, with women, and for women, and women dominated the content of her essays, too.

Her first month's labor offers a nice introduction to the subjects she treated during her entire tenure on the paper. In this period she wrote seven major pieces. She inaugurated her career with a long interview with an Atlanta woman just back from Italy; it centers around the latest European modes in women's fashion but treats Mussolini and the Fascists, too. Her second essay interviews a Peachtree Road horticulturist who was developing new strains in fruits and vegetables. The same Sunday she did a second, un-bylined piece as well, on the introduction of the spring line of fashion to the city. On January 14, she wrote a long (also anonymous) article on an exclusive, all-male Atlanta fishing club. The next week saw her account of a spelunking adventure, "Through the Cave of the Lost Indians," an essay of special interest because it marked her rejection of her married name as a byline and her adoption of Peggy Mitchell as her *nom de plume*. Also notable, while she generally shied away from the first-person singular, she wrote this essay as a personal adventure. On the last Sunday of the month, she contributed two essays. The first chronicled the record of an Atlanta member of the American Graves Registration Bureau, a committee for identifying American soldiers lost in the Great War. The second, altogether different, was the first of many interviews with Atlanta society girls. "'No Dumb-bells Wanted,' Say Atlanta Debs" introduced her own friends into her writing; in this case, the insouciant Julia Drayton Memminger and the companion of her childhood, one of the Sewing Circlers, Elizabeth Buchanan. Of these seven articles, two deal exclusively with males; three with females; and in two Mitchell gives ostensibly gender-free themes a woman's slant. And so it was increasingly over the next three and a half years. Mitchell's essays tended powerfully towards gender-focused themes and the particular concerns and interests of women.

In part, the nature of the Sunday Magazine determined the subject matter of Mitchell's articles. With its food and cooking columns, advice to the lovelorn, fashion tips, and other domestic-oriented writing, Sunday Features aimed for a primarily, although not exclusively, female readership. Given her own engagement with many of these same issues in her personal life, Mitchell fell easily and naturally into this subject matter. Despite her professional employment, for example, her family still expected her to mind the house, shop for food, and oversee the servants; then, too, fashion had always intrigued her and she had actually considered taking up design as a profession. Articles on such topics came naturally. The largely female staff encouraged this general bias, too. At the same time, however, Mitchell brought her own specific

values and feminist orientation to bear even within this general framework, and her own peculiar feminist vision distinguished much of what
she wrote.

Two articles in the spring of 1923 nicely summarize her particular
concerns with women. They explore women's history. Specifically, they
aim to redeem women's role in the traditional—and otherwise masculine—past, but they also strive to redefine a peculiarly female tradition beside or within patriarchal mores. They offer a fitting introduction to the way Mitchell used women in her journalism.[23]

The first essay, on May 13, "Georgia Romances That Live in History," set out to distinguish women's history from men's. The public
roles of men filled the pages of the recorded past with exploits in war
and politics; women's parts are more ephemeral and obscure, the writer
maintained. She associated the female tradition with evanescent and
transcient sense, sensibility, and sentiment. In this regard, she employed both the formal and the popular conceptions of "romance" as
she recounted five love affairs set in a timeless, heroic Georgia tradition. The first involved General William Tecumseh Sherman; the second, John Howard Paine (the author of the ballad "Home, Sweet
Home"); the third, John Wesley; and the fourth, Fanny Kemble and
her American husband, Pierce Butler. The final episode chronicled the
tragic affair of a Cherokee Chief Elias Boudinot, and his white wife,
Harriet Gould, during the Indian removal under Andrew Jackson.

As befits the form, Mitchell uses lush, evocative, and sentimental
language to match the content; still, she fills the essay with surprises.
If the essay sets out to "humanize" great men, its males actually suffer
at the author's pen as well as from their sweethearts' affections. "Mr.
Fanny Kemble" (Pierce Butler) hardly appears at all, while all the others develop as a rather pathetic lot: they sigh; they mope; they grieve.
Their ladies do them in. The ladies themselves, however, play much
more varied parts. Harriet Gould Boudinot personifies the angel who
wastes away in good works and selfless affection for the world; but
Mary Harden, the object of the balladeer's affection, at least survived;
so did the otherwise invisible Cecilia Stovall of the Sherman tale.
Sherman did not burn her house. Sophia Hopkey of the grossly mis-
named "Wesley's Sad Romance" feels no sense of loss at all as the
Methodist divine abandons her; indeed, she shouts something like "Good
riddance!" as he goes, and she wreaks her vengeance against her pious
lover. Fanny Kemble offers a still more insouciant and militant model.
Little of romance or even love surrounds her life or marriage, the essay's theme notwithstanding. She completely overshadows her husband, wins a divorce, and celebrates her victory by writing *Journal of
a Residence on a Georgia Plantation in 1838–1839*. Mitchell interpreted
the "Journal" as a most successful act of revenge, but the publication
also guaranteed Kemble's place even in formal, recorded history, the

reporter maintained, as it "had more influence in arousing anti-slavery sentiments than any other book published at the time." Told through a series of the most engaging letters, Kemble's journal offers a compelling record of slavery, but it is even richer in chronicling the oppression of women in the nineteenth century and the response of one very vivid rebel to these restrictions. Fanny Kemble appealed very powerfully to the young Atlanta woman, and over the years, she returned repeatedly to reread the journal.

Mitchell's inclusion of Kemble—this most aggressive and willful heroine—in her foray into romance suggests very unromantic subthemes in the essay. For all the sentiment of the essay, Mitchell's own tone confirms rather more the style of the dashing Fanny Kemble than the self-effacing Harriet Boudinot. The piece moves along very forcefully. It uses language aggressively. Even while evoking simpering romance, then, the essay bristles and suggests a forceful mode even for private womanhood.

If Mitchell implied positive roles for women in "Georgia Romances," her second venture into women's history went much farther. While the first reserved a place for ladies, senses, and emotion alongside the masculine world of documented history, war, and politics, "Georgia's Empress and Women Soldiers" of May 20 preempted even these bastions of masculinity for Georgia womanhood. Not incidentally perhaps, she signed her name to this piece, where the other in the series had no byline.[24] From the beginning of the essay, Mitchell claimed the public tradition for women in her state. "From the earliest pioneer days until the present, Georgia women have made this tradition a glorious reality," she began.

> Born and bred in a Southern civilization where womanhood is exalted and knightly regard for the protection of women is the first mark of a gentleman, Georgia women have not been merely beautiful chatelaines, but have been gifted with brilliant ability and a capacity for assuming difficult responsibilities when the need arose.

Mitchell explored this tradition through the biographies of four different women. She began with the most contemporary, Rebecca Latimer Felton, the first woman in the U.S. Senate. In 1922, the governor of Georgia appointed the eighty-seven-year-old matron to the Congress to fill the unexpired term of the old populist radical, Thomas Watson. Although Mitchell failed to mention it, she was Governor Hardwick's second choice and served only seven weeks. Mitchell took this service, however, to be the final crown of a lifetime of accomplishment. Felton "was a 'new woman' long before the 'new woman' had arrived," the future novelist proclaimed. If Felton had led a fairly typical private life of a Southern woman before the Civil War and Reconstruction,

Mitchell made the case that, even then, she was "laying the foundation for the public life that was to be hers in later years" through her omnivorous reading. Although Felton's career began as an adjunct to her husband's, she soon overshadowed him, the journalist exulted. She made her own name and established her own reputation through her writing; specifically, through her personal correspondence.

> Night and day the indefatigable wife wrote letters to fourteen counties and towards the end of the campaign she kept a man on horseback at the door to catch every mail train. She made appoints for speeches, answered vitriolic newspaper attacks and kept a brave face to friend and foe.

Although Senator Felton introduced the essay, this old lady did not really interest the reporter-historian very much, and Mitchell moved quickly from Felton's political feminism to the women who really trespassed onto male turf. She found in the more distant past a crop of women to meet the most demanding criteria for rebellion—Nancy Hart, Lucy Kenny, and, most of all, Mary Musgrove.

An American patriot in the Revolution, Nancy Hart looked like a man and acted worse. Six feet tall, muscular, and broad-shouldered, she was cross-eyed and cross-grained to boot. She had red hair and a temper to match, according to Peggy Mitchell. Lacking all traditional female "sweetness," she "vociferously voiced her hatred" of all her enemies and "feared neither Tories nor devil." When her "unheroic husband and the neighbors fled to the swamps" in a British raid, she stood her ground, bamboozled the Tories, and then challenged them to call her bluff:

> One of them not knowing Nancy's reputation for sharpshooting, tried to rush her, but she coolly shot him down.
> Whether the others were unnerved by her suddenness or by the certainty of death at the hands of the Whigs or the incongruity of her cross-eyes that seemed to make each one the object of her ferocious gaze, suffice to say that they made no further resistance.

When the males slunk back, this Giant-Argus-Medusa went back to her appointed chore of making pies and fixing dinner.

Nancy Hart looked and acted like a man. So did Lucy Kenny, but this character also dressed like one. "She was large, masculine in appearance, a fine rifle shot, and absolutely fearless," the young reporter enthused. "It was only necessary for her to cut off her hair and put on a suit of her husband's clothes to complete her transformation from a very proper wife to a very good soldier of the Confederacy." Under her *nom de guerre*, "Private Bill Thompson," she fought beside her husband in the Confederate Army for the first half of the war. Severely wounded at Sharpsburg and hospitalized for months, she still managed to preserve her secret identity. Not until her husband died in battle did she reveal her true self: she requested leave to return home and bury her man.

Mitchell boasted of Lucy Kenny as an unsung Joan of Arc, but her last subject, Mary Musgrove, overshadowed even this Confederate paladin. A young Indian woman in eighteenth-century Georgia, Musgrove, in Mitchell's description, had no interest in politics or even patriotism, much less in baking pies. She lusted after power, pure and simple. Mitchell stressed her intelligence and charisma. She was bilingual and multitalented. General Oglethorpe courted her authority and three European males her person. She affected her own people no less powerfully than the foreigners: "Mary was a woman of great personal magnetism and the idol of the Creek nation, but despite her years of life among the civilizing influences of the colony and her three successive white husbands, she remained an untamed savage until she died."

Her husbands were mere appendages; the first two lacked even names. The third won fame only as a muse of power. "Be queen," he whispered in her ear. "Naturally," the young reporter answered for her subject, "the idea appealed to the untamed soul of Mary." Thus inspired, Mary Musgrove summoned the Creek leadership, and made them an "impassioned address. She set forth the justice of her pretensions and the injustice of the colonists' treatment of the Indians, and, firebrand that she was, so inflamed the warriors that they pledged themselves to stand by her to the last drop of their blood." Borne up with this "surge of power," Musgrove "swaggered into the town" and dictated her terms to the terrified Europeans. She professed "not the slightest scruples about torturing and scalping." She especially terrified Savannah's women and children. "Drunk with power," she faced a wily antagonist in Oglethorpe. He outfoxed her: he persuaded her "fickle warriors" to betray her. They scalped her evil-genius husband instead of him. The "empress" spent her last years like Napoleon, exiled to a remote island "in distinctly unregal circumstances and the little colony that she threatened with annihilation grew into a great state."[25]

This second foray into women's history began with the goal of asserting women's legitimate place within the ostensibly male preserves of politics, war, and traditional history. As shown by her cursory treatment of Senator Felton, however, statecraft held few charms for her. With her depiction of Nancy Hart and Lucy Kenny, even patriotism provided mostly a pretext for celebrating women's aggressive will and energy. With Mary Musgrove, she abandons the pretext. From this figure, Mitchell created a new model. Musgrove stood outside the traditional order of war and politics with its idealization of discipline and the common good. Ethnic marginality confirms the image. This virago existed for the exercise of power alone.

In salvaging Mary Musgrove for the historical record, what is the lesson Peggy Mitchell intended? Actually she was of two minds about her heroine. On one level, she validated ambition and female leadership: women possessed the same talents as men and the same drives for power, Mary Musgrove's life instructs. In the same way, as Oglethorpe and the Indian warriors betray her, her life affirms males' untrustworthiness. On another level, however, demonstrating those otherwise male sins like gross ambition, overweening pride, unlicensed will, and lust for dominion, Mary Musgrove fails and falls appropriately, punished for her hubris. In the context of gender values, however, Mitchell's treatment of Mary Musgrove's career is still more complex. She is not just violent, savage and untamed, she is these things and a woman, too. The error, then, is double. She violates the social order but she also violates her nature, effectively, as a woman. Mary did not like women and children. When these dependents appear in the narrative, Mitchell introduces them only as objects of her empress's terrorism. Her victory, Mitchell assumes, would have perverted the course of history and precluded the rule of law and order in the state. By this measure, even her literary exponent almost sighs relief when Oglethorpe regains the upper hand and banishes the Fury.

Mitchell presented the Indian woman as an ideal, but ultimately she rejects the model. Actually, this ambivalence defined her larger sense of women's history in these two essays—the dreaminess of one versus the aggression of the other. Mitchell celebrated the Nancy Harts, the Mary Musgroves, and the Fanny Kembles as worthy models; without contradiction she also praised the self-effacing Harriet Boudinot and vaguer objects of masculine affection. She was keen to these poles and the degrees of variance in between. Her newspaper stories reflect the fascination with its diversity. Yet rebellious maids fascinated her most of all.

The rebel belle fascinated the young reporter wherever she found her, anywhere in the world. A tourist from South Africa allowed her the chance to discover the curiosity of a land where "Flappers Wear Pigtails Until 21"; with her references to such writers as Cynthia Stockley and Rider Haggard, it also provided the opportunity to demonstrate her familiarity with a variety of African authors.[26] She also featured English rebel women in a most unlikely interview with Sir James McKechnie, one of the great British munition makers. The essay focused exclusively on the impact of the Great War on women, and the changes that the new women then wrought in sexual relations, the home, domesticity, and English civilization in general. While the essay consisted of over 80 percent direct quotations, Mitchell zeroed in on the critical issues again and again. It is a particularly telling essay and stands, ultimately, as a penetrating summary of the impact of war on any society. War liberated women; they refused to return to the old ways with the return of peace, Sir James grieved. Meanwhile, the men had not changed at all:

> "The boys want the old type of English home, a solid place that they can count on, a wife and children ready and waiting when they come at night. The girls want to be forever gadding, they want work, money, excitement, politics. So there is a grim deadlock. Perhaps the next generation of men will approve of the girls—or the next generation of girls will conform to the wishes of the men.
>
> "However," said Sir James, as a gloomy afterthought, "I don't think the women will change."[27]

Whether in Manchester, Johannesburg, or New Delhi, but especially in Atlanta and the South, the lives, adventures, and aspirations of young women attracted Mitchell's most persistent interest. She wrote up frivolous debs and silly belles the same as she did the female professionals and pioneers. She allowed them equal shares of merit. Detailing their adventures and careers constituted the largest single subject of Mitchell's journalism. She wrote with wit and verve about their taste in men, their definitions of beauty, their notions of household management, and their ideas of civic responsibility: as in "No Dumbbells Wanted," "Pep, Brains and Clothes Win in Beauty Contest," "What Makes the Pretty Girl Pretty?" "Debs Keep House While Mothers Are Away," and "Debs Give Up Bridge for Civics."[28] She had her own problems with the Junior League, of course, and doings of these young women might have been wonderful targets for her bracing wit; still, she chronicled their yearly theatricals with all seriousness for four seasons, too.[29]

While she wrote many such pieces, her review of the escapades of the five "subdebs" just returned from a five-month tour of Europe and the Mediterranean suggests her general approach. The monuments of the Old World made these "Georgia peaches" yawn. " 'Oxford isn't a bit like Tech or Georgia'," the ringleader complained. And while the world went mad over Tutankhamen, the girls were mooning over their sheik-guide. "Although he was a little too dark to be romantic," one of them burbled, "he had wonderful manners and was splendidly educated. We rode on camels out to the pyramids and saw the sphinx with Elsie Janis in our party. She is so adorable. No, we didn't waste any time on Tutankhamen. We couldn't be bothered." If the girls scorned London, Oxford, archeology, and culture in general in their stream-of-conscious babble, they dismissed the Fascists with the same contempt. These bumptious, unpretentious provincial belles actually represented something close to the models that the author herself admired. " 'I had the thrill that comes once in a lifetime when I drove a Buick at top speed through the streets of Jerusalem with my hat off and my red hair flying,' " Mitchell quoted Peggy Davis, one of the girls. " 'The Eastern women are so subservient, they are always veiled and silent and afraid to call their souls their own,' " she continued. " 'We could see them peeking out at us in horrified awe as we tore around in the car, without hats or veils, honking the horn and being generally noisy. They came to the windows and stared and whispered till I felt sorry for them.' " The reporter concluded her interview with the quotation: " 'We certainly had the right of way in the Holy Land!' " [30]

The sympathy between the writer and the subject shone through in the most unlikely ways; even in her usage. Mitchell gave this article to John Marsh to criticize, and in the margin he noted that no subdeb knew the word "subservient." He was right, of course; it was a word that grown rebels used, not juvenile females. The error, however, is revealing: Marsh missed the authenticity of his beloved's own voice in the expression and her sympathy and kinship with this other red-haired Peggy as she seized the right of way in the Holy Land.

Mitchell's interest in her young women's liberation centered especially around financial independence and careers outside the home. "Could a girl be virtuous and bob her hair? Could she have a home and husband and children and a job too? Should she roll her stockings, park her corsets, be allowed a latch key?" This was how Mitchell later summarized the burning issues of her journalism.[31] Over and over, the reporter returned to the subject of careers and professions for women. It dominated her writing long before one of her subjects, Willa Roberts, fiction editor of *Home Companion*, had instructed her about the fictional demand "for independent girls, preferably those who earn their own living."[32]

The enthusiasm for financial independence for young women formed the centerpiece of one essay in particular, as Mitchell interviewed high school students about working before marriage. When they agreed unanimously on this course, Mitchell pressed them. " 'But,' stammered the interviewer, 'Joseph Hergesheimer, the novelist,' " she wrote, " 'says that women shouldn't work—that it spoils their charm. He says that women should stay at home and cultivate charm. What about it?' " "Old stuff!" they shot back. She pressed them further:

> "Don't any of you want to stay at home and be a comfort to your families?" questioned the interviewer, somewhat taken aback by the vast array of ambitions spread out before her eyes. . . .
> "Hasn't anybody here a Hope Chest? Doesn't any one of you want to get married?"

When she queried finally, "Then it is independence that makes all of you want jobs?" the response was overwhelming. "At that a tumult arose in which the words, 'Self expression!' 'Independence!' 'Pay check!' were loudest. . . ."[33]

Even amidst this consensus, the young reporter still chronicled the hindrances to women's independence. Actually, she devoted entire essays exclusively to the problems of marriage versus careers. In a conflict between the two, none of her subjects went with work. Indeed, all of them agreed that a primary benefit of working was to make a woman more sympathetic and understanding of her man—"she isn't so likely to nag her husband," they agreed. Even among the most independent-minded girls, Mitchell found no support for working mothers. The subject never even reached the point of discussion. Then, too, some of the working women themselves insisted that careers, even temporary jobs, were not completely natural for women, and that working unfitted a woman for a family. "She gets so accustomed to having her own money and things her own way that she keeps putting off getting married till she doesn't have any desire to."[34]

Regardless of her particular subject or the specific role women played, however, Mitchell always emphasized female integrity. This rule did not always hold true with men. Sometimes she let her subjects attack patriarchal prerogatives directly, as in her subdeb's pity for Arab women's imprisonment or in another's outrage over the suttee, which, she raged, constituted only the grossest symbol of the oppression of women in the Orient.[35] Other times she let her men condemn themselves out of their own mouths. This governed her response to the British patriarchal reactionary Sir James McKechnie, where her auctorial voice is nonexistent except for the original (and fitting) usage of the words "iron" and "gloomy" to describe the subject. More lightly, she let the dopey students at Georgia Tech display their foolishness for the whole world to see. She had interviewed them collectivly on "Why Girls Are Rushed." They snort and chortle about their affection for "modern girls," which they define mostly as women easy with their favors. One character, however, "Sugarfoot" Gaffney, adds a "serious note," in the author's phrase. He prefers modern girls only "if sincere about their modernism." " 'It's my belief,' " he added ponderously, " 'that most modern girls who smoke wouldn't do so if they were alone. Of course,' he admitted seriously, 'I have never been with a girl when she was alone with herself, and so I can't speak with absolute authority on the subject.' "[36]

Another collective interview with male students about *their* career goals could hardly have differed more from the ones with young women. If the reporter interposes her own voice, it is to mock the boys' ambitions, in a manner worthy of her idols H. L. Mencken and Ring Lardner. "There is a glorious certainty about boys at the age when they are graduating from high school," she began.

> Life is such a simple, open-and-shut proposition to them. One does certain things and when those things are done, fame, wealth and a Packard automobile will be waiting. One goes to college, is industrious, and honest, learns a few simple rules for selling things or for building bridges or writing books and success follows as logically as dinner follows lunch.[37]

Given her own and the girls' struggles for these same goals, Mitchell's ironic tone is especially rich; so, too, the metaphor of lunch and dinner: the young reporter knew exactly who was putting the biscuits on the table for the lads.

Occasionally, Mitchell's tone suggested personal resentment against male prejudices. She wrote in the neutral third person when she criticized "Latin Lovers" in an essay of March 1924; she herself, however, had just returned from an abortive trip to Cuba, and she had firsthand experience with those males who take advantage of a woman's desire for liberty and independence.[38] "Just Like a Woman; Ditto for Men" described an even broader area for complaint. This piece was a little theoretical critique of the way men do almost everything. Their habits are as strange, eccentric, and bizzare as "some African aborigine" to their long-suffering women. Thus, she concludes: "Wherefore and because of these things it is unquestionably evident that in the matters of peculiarities and inconsistencies, man yields the palm to none. Man can never yield the palm to woman." This was as close to anger as her articles ever came.[39]

Peggy Mitchell knew all the patriarchal restrictions against women. As in the prohibition against using the dictionary in the newsroom, she felt the burden daily. She had, however, internalized them, too. Despite her skill, energy, and productivity as a journalist, and despite, too, the plaudits of her peers and bosses, she continued to reflect an almost pathological despair about her own efforts. Medora Perkerson remarked upon her "unhappiness" with something she wrote. Usually she used stronger language. "This here is mine—and it's rotten," she scrawled across her essay on Mrs. Bell's boardinghouse. Her response puzzled her faithful copy editor, John Marsh, as much as it did Medora Perkerson: "I can't see what makes this story eat on you. . . . It shows good reporting in the historical data collected and the number of prominent men interviewed. I also like it because it does not rave, but gives the facts and lets them sell themselves."[40] He disputed her judgment in the margins of other articles. "You have an ability to make your people lifelike which is seldom an accomplishment of newspaper reporters," he wrote her, and *"This is very well done."*[41] The Mitchellian negativism did not disappear with time.

On the eve of her own great fame, she looked back at her *Journal* days and completely dismissed her efforts. "The articles I have are so dreadful that my toes curl in my shoes when I look at them," she said. "I keep them around to mortify my spirit every time I get puffed up." She could tolerate only the historical ones, and only these because of their accuracy and the research she applied to them, she said. Their art had no appeal to her.[42] It was curious: she drove herself heedlessly towards some ideal that guaranteed her own sense of inadequacy. Her difficulty lay, in part at least, in the most fundamental contradictions that drew her into the trade in the first place. Where did women belong? What was their proper role? The subject of so many of her essays, it plagued her in these years, and her society and culture offered no satisfying answers. On the contrary, they exaggerated the dilemmas she felt as an individual woman.

PART III

STRUGGLE

IX

St. John

Only a few men on the campus know John's real worth. He has
worked silently and calmly regardless of any immediate reward.
We who know him know only that when John promises you to do
anything, you can just as well forget it, knowing it will be *done.*

The Kentuckian, 1916 [1]

The handwriting is fastidious. The sentiment is precise. "I hope
my pleasure over your ability to write so much more smoothly
than you used to won't have the effect of making you 'flowery.'
That would be too bad. Oh my yes!" [2] In the margins of article after
article, the copperplate script reminds the writer of the rules. It points
out when she changed verb forms, when she mixed singular and plural
pronouns, when she used wrong words, or when she violated Victorian
rules—"like," for example, instead of "as if." This was the proofreader's staple fare, but this particular copy editor really liked this work,
and his emendations went beyond strict usage and grammar. In the
process, he revealed as much about himself as what he deemed his
subject's literary weaknesses. He called for transitional sentences, for
example, when dramatic power lay in the sudden, unexpected shift. In
trying to clarify an idea or expression, he cumbered the prose with
excessive, bog-slow words and clauses. Sometimes he called for a more
formal word, like "crucial," where the original choice—say, "ticklish,"
even if colloquial and inexact—added a whip and crackle to the sentence and served the purpose of a paragraph. She wrote like she talked,
and her essays vibrate with living voices. Margaret Mitchell's work, in

short, brimmed with her own virtues: vitality, exuberance, enthusiasm, and curiosity. Her devoted copy editor lacked them all himself, and he required them in all he loved. In his stability, patience, perseverance, and absolute devotion, he served her needs just as critically. Except for May Belle Mitchell, no one played a more important role in her life. Marrying him proved the single most important decision of her life. Their odd union—and it was curious indeed—completed her as much as that was possible.

John Marsh and his relationship to Margaret Mitchell baffled most of the former debutante's high-class friends. The kindest, like dear Julia Memminger, struggled for praise: "John hardly talked at all, but he was very polite, a gentleman, a real gentle man. And he was devoted to her, too, waited on her hand and foot."[3] Willie Snow Ethridge spoke more frankly. She and her husband Mark knew the Marshes well through the Georgia Press Association when he edited Sue Myrick's old paper in Macon, the *Telegraph*. Even when the family relocated to Kentucky as Mark Ethridge assumed the nationally important editorship of the *Louisville Courier-Journal*, the Ethridges kept up relations with the Marshes. John and Willie Snow actually fancied each other; her liveliness attracted him to her particularly. Still, Ethridge joked about the blandness of her friend's personality. "He was just about the slowest, most methodical man who ever lived." Her rich Southern-lady voice laughed after forty years:

> John was a very close husband, extremely protective, and he doted on her. He was not really jealous of her, but something sort of like that. Where she was real quick and lively, just the center of everything going on all the time, especially at those meetings [of the Georgia Press Association], John was just the opposite. He talked so slow, just drawled out everything he ever said, that we all about died waiting for the next word! She was very gay and easy to know, and at those press conventions she was always the center of attention. She just about held court in her bedroom, perched in the center of a big hotel bed telling all those ribald stories. But John was really a very colorless character and very proper.[4]

Other old friends sat in harsher judgment. "We all thought she married beneath herself," her former fellow debutante Caroline Tye averred. "I never understood what she saw in him. John Marsh just wasn't very interesting, and we moved apart after the marriage."[5] The acerbic Harvey Smith minced fewer terms: "That slug!" he quipped, when queried about the husband. Mitchell's celebration of her husband's virtues made Smith wince. It was "embarrassing to others for it seemed incredible that either she or he could tolerate such digressions from the obvious," he judged.[6]

Mitchell's defensiveness about her husband became notorious, especially after she achieved worldwide fame, but before that she conceded much the same characteristics her friends acknowledged. "John can use more sleep than any white boy I ever saw," she told her sister-in-law. "As I try to turn him in by eleven every night, we don't go many places and all that Sunday means is a chance [for him] to sleep till three o'clock in the afternoon and eat breakfast at four."[7] Just so she noted his aversion to any sort of physical exertion. "When summer comes around I'll have to drag him off to swim every day as he's too lazy to go unless pushed," Mitchell groaned in the winter of 1925. "The doctor says he doesn't exercise enough."[8]

Marsh looked the type. Little distinguished him. He was tall, just over six feet, but he possessed no notable grace of carriage and nothing of the sharp angularity of his much younger competitor, friend, and roommate, Berrien Upshaw. In contrast to the sharp features of the other swain, he had something of a lantern jaw, while his nose and lips were fleshy, his eyes puffy. Too many years of too much fried chicken, too many biscuits, far too many cigarettes, and much, much too little physical exercise blurred his features even more. His eyesight was poor, and thick glasses obscured his eyes. A childhood bout with scarlet fever impaired his hearing, recalled his sister, and this exaggerated his natural reticence.

No one ever called John Marsh handsome; still, he had his charm. When he was genuinely amused, he glowed. His face lit up when he smiled, and he looked a different man. Photographs capture the mood occasionally. In his doughboy uniform he grins appealingly from beneath his pulled-down cap—he captioned the picture "Smiling Jack," appropriately enough; or, svelte in his three-piece suit, he leans back against some outdoors rail, jacket flapping in the breeze, and beams radiantly. Mostly, however, he looked preoccupied, as if he had a slightly sour stomach. This was understandable. He was dyspeptic; strange digestive problems plagued him constantly. Nameless ailments sapped his strength all his life, but some of them bore terrifying names, like "myocardial infarction." Long before his massive heart attack, however, he regularly spent vacations in the hospital between bouts of sickroom care at home. In no way did his life resonate more with his beloved's than in their fears and failings in physical health. It proved an extraordinary bond, critical to their union.

For himself, John Marsh simply thought decrepitude and old age even in his youth. He was not yet twenty-seven when he described himself to his mother as "your middle aged son."[9] In other letters he repeated the phrase but elaborated by muttering about having become "set in my ways since growing old" and having attained "a fairly ripe old age with the idea that I would never marry." He had turned twenty-nine three months before.[10]

Even with all the pair's "neuroticisms," as Marsh's brother-in-law termed their illnesses,[11] their marriage proved very nearly perfect; the stars, however, could hardly have foretold the union itself. John Robert Marsh shared no more with Margaret Mitchell in class, origins, and heritage than he did in personality, character, and social interests. His hometown, Mayesville, Kentucky, lay on the other side of the world from Ansley Park and Atlanta's posh North Peachtree. If his native state boasted cavaliers aplenty, Mayesville bred few gentlemen. Strung out along the river just across the state line from Ohio, it won its reputation as a bustling commercial center. Well before Marsh's birth the town had beaten out the older, neighboring, planter-run village of Washington for county seat of Mason County. The planter families in the older center cultivated genteel arrogance towards the hustling upstarts, but aristocrats did not stir John Marsh's imagination. He did not know who his ancestors were, much less worship them. Where from oral and written tradition Margaret Mitchell and almost any of her cousins could regale an audience with stories of ancestors from two hundred years before,[12] John Marsh's knowledge of his family ended with his grandparents. It blurred even there.[13] His grandfathers, for example, lived in the Civil War generation, but he never mentioned if they had seen any military service, nor even if they were Confederates. Given Mason County's location, it was likely that they were Unionists, not seceders. His forefathers left faint evidence in the written record. The oral tradition spoke little more.

Nothing distinguished the Marshes from the thousands of anonymous small farmers who drifted south and west from Pennsylvania after the American Revolution. In the disruption that followed the Civil War, however, John Marsh's father won some local eminence. An exponent—and product—of the New South creed, Millard Fillmore Marsh abandoned the rural Kentucky hinterland of his birth, made his way to Mayesville, practiced law, and edited *The Mayesville Bulletin* where he sang the village's bright commercial future. In that classic pattern of regional culture, "the Squire," as his neighbors came to call him, also married up. In 1889, at thirty-four, he wed the twenty-three-year-old Mary Toup, daughter of one of Mayesville's "good families."[14] The Toups lived in a big Victorian house on the main residential street, and Millard Marsh built his own house next door where the couple produced five children in rapid-fire order. The eldest was only fourteen when the Squire dropped dead just after Christmas in 1904. He was forty-nine. John had just turned eight two months before. If the boy remembered his parent, as surely he must have, he betrayed nothing of the memory in any of his letters and correspondence afterward. Other than indirect references to continuing the family tradition of journalism, John Marsh never mentioned his father. His mother was a different case entirely.

A model of matriarchal authority, Mary Toup Marsh, with assistance from her own mother and maiden aunt, held her brood together in the crisis of her widowhood. Although sole breadwinner for her family, she never slacked her social and religious commitments in the process.[15] A warm and compassionate parent to all her children, she had a special relationship with her second son. She named him after a favorite, if eccentric and completely dependent, sibling; but more than anything, sickness bonded them. Two long, serious illnesses before he was three almost killed him, and family lore perpetuated the legend that the mother's love alone saved his life. His younger sister believed that the intimacy between parent and child in their distress stamped his entire personality and "helped to make him the man he was—sensitive, always giving to others some of that life-giving love he had received from her.[16]

A singular woman produced notable children. All five put themselves through school; all won academic honors and social distinction. After college, they went on to graduate school and achieved success in the most far-flung corners of the Republic, from California to Delaware, Connecticut to Georgia. The eldest, Henry, even won national fame, as a scientist for the War, then Defense Department.[17] Their successes bespeak the parent's achievement, but other truths emerge from the story of the Marshes' accomplishments. None of the children stayed in Mayesville, population 8,000. Only one, Gordon, even remained in their native state.

That is a small story in itself that also helps illuminate the life of not just the Marshes but a generation of Southerners. If nearby Washington, Kentucky, seemed old and slow beside the Marsh hometown, Mayesville itself was little more than a sped-up village in 1915. It offered few rewards to Mary and Millard Marsh's bright, progressive offspring. Mayesville shared this problem with Kentucky; Kentucky shared it with most of Dixie. Since the Civil War, especially since the terrible depression of 1893, unseen market forces squeezed the countryside and constricted opportunities in the regional hinterland. At the same time, Southern population soared as the regional birthrate far outpaced that of the United States. The land could not absorb the excess. The Marshes of Mayesville fell into the center of this demographic flood of Southerners born around the turn of the century—the "Generation of 1900."

This, of course, was Margaret Mitchell's generation—and Sue Myrick's and Nell Lewis's—and also William Faulkner's and Allen Tate's and Caroline Gordon's and W. J. Cash's and Erskine Caldwell's—and all the rest. The forces that unsettled and shaped their histories lived powerfully in John Marsh's life. If this was "the Lost Generation" in modern culture, as Gertrude Stein and Ernest Hemingway had called it, these young Southerners had been displaced well before the Great War disrupted Western civilization. No one was more displaced than this Generation of 1900 in the old Confederate states. Where was John Marsh's home? Where indeed? In 1912, when the skinny blond teenager packed his bags for the big trip to Lexington to begin college, no one anticipated such precipitous, region-wide dislocations. He discovered them soon enough.

John Marsh passed four uneventful years at the University of Kentucky. He graduated in 1916 with a degree in English and accepted a job at the *Lexington Herald*, where he worked for about a year. In September 1917 he moved back across the street again to the university when he accepted a teaching fellowship in the Department of English. Six months later, halfway through the academic year, he enlisted in the army.[18]

To cheering crowds, John Marsh and company departed Lexington for Europe in March 1918. That marked about the last excitement the war provided him. Assigned to a medical unit, he passed the remainder of the war as an aide in a military hospital in England near Southampton.[19] After the Armistice, he finally crossed the Channel, where he attended the AEF University at Beaune, France.[20] There, finally, Marsh received his own war wounds. The trouble with his stomach first appeared in France. "The food was lousy," his wife judged later, "and, like many another soldier, it was bad on his digestion." Unlike most of the other victims of "lousy food," however, Sergeant Marsh never recovered. He spent weeks in military hospitals in France, but seven years after the Armistice, the problem still haunted him.[21] Nor did it vanish after 1925. Throughout the twenties and early thirties, he spent weeks in veterans' hospitals. He applied for permanent partial disability from the Department of the Army. Although he received a small monthly compensation check until 1933, at least, when Franklin D. Roosevelt slashed benefits, the government granted him the compensation reluctantly. The obscurity of his illness hardly convinced the Veterans' Administration. His wife summarized his "compensation fights" with equal measures of pride and rancor. "John has been trying to gouge the Government for some compensation and has been held up, because he couldn't locate any of the three boys who were detached with him and sent to the American University at Beaune . . . [where he] was fed on ground glass and iron filings," she groused in 1926.[22]

No one knew what to make of Marsh's strange malady. The digestive problem somehow became translated into gallstones and kidney stones, according to some doctors. This at least was operable—and the surgeons had their fun with him. Then, however, these ailments transmogrified with greater mysteriousness into epilepsy, supposedly. This is what he told his sister; Stephens Mitchell heard the same report. His brother-in-law Roland Zane never believed it.[23] It was all very mysterious. While his wife admitted that any nervous strain caused his stomach to explode again, stories that his condition was "only nervous" sent her into tantrums. In 1936, that story circulated in the national press. Mitchell determined its source—or so she thought, and she descended like a hungry hawk on the hapless chickens she thought responsible. "To be sure he was ill, had two operations which were directly connected with his war experience," she raged, "but I cannot find it possible to think that a gall bladder operation can be classed as 'shell shock.' "[24] The angry novelist, however, did not even try to explain the connection between her husband's "war wounds" in 1919 and a gall bladder operation twenty years later.

Sick or not, Marsh was mustered out of the army in July 1919. He had no clear plans for himself. Although he returned to Mayesville, he hardly unpacked his bags. Within six or eight months, he moved again. If Mayesville now seemed insignificant, so did even Lexington, the place that had served him as home between 1912 and 1918. "How ya gonna keep 'em down on the farm after they've seen Paree," his generation hummed. In the most momentous decision of his life, he drifted south and east. By the beginning of 1920 (perhaps late 1919), he had taken up lodgings in Atlanta.[25] He returned to journalism. By June 1920, he was reading proof at the Hearst paper in Atlanta, *The Georgian.* A year later, he graduated to the newsroom. In the winter of 1921–1922, he left journalism for a brief stint as assistant manager of the public relations department of the Georgia Railway and Power Company, but he also gave up that shortly to join his then-roommate Legare Davis in freelance advertising. The fall and summer found him in Tuscaloosa, where the University of Alabama hired him to direct its million-dollar fund-raising campaign.[26]

The late winter of 1923 brought more changes. It found him back in Atlanta reading proof again. This time, however, he drew his pay, not from the *Georgian,* but the *Journal.* He did not stay long there, either. By the late fall or early winter of 1923–1924, he moved to Washington, D.C., where he worked for the Associated Press.

In September 1924, he returned once more, and this time finally, to the Georgia capital. Just shy of twenty-nine (his birthday was in October), he became assistant director of the publicity department at the Georgia Power Company. In the previous five years he had worked perhaps ten jobs or more in four different cities. Now he settled in. He kept the same job for nearly a quarter century. He liked the work, but of course other reasons drew him back to the Gate City. The courts dissolved the Mitchell-Upshaw marriage just as he relocated. And, once again, he began to hover around the big house on Peachtree Street. Actually, he had hardly left Eugene Mitchell's stuffy parlors, in his mind at least, from the first time he knocked on that big Palladian door almost three years before.

John Marsh had first met Peggy Mitchell in January 1922. He was immediately smitten. His courtship, however, completely matched his personality. As a man of steady habits, long hours, low energy, and almost narcoleptic need of sleep, the Kentuckian spent his time with his beloved mostly talking and listening. Marsh was very intelligent; he loved literature, and Mitchell liked swapping literary ideas and criticism with him. They shared a passion for James Branch Cabell, and Don Marquis provided them endless hours of delight. They plunged into other favorites in these years, Sherwood Anderson and D. H. Lawrence, among others.[27] Actually, sitting at the other end of Mitchell's legendary "squashy sofa" suited him fine. He liked the "liberal platonism" of their relationship, as he called it. In truth, he felt anxious about matrimony, perhaps even more than Mitchell herself. Coupled with his ambivalence about marriage, his general passivity precluded his making a more aggressive courtship.

And he lost out to his own roommate.

In the summer of 1922, he informed his sister of his defeat in a letter that conveys much about his character. She had just written him of her plan to leave home and make a career in New York. He glowed. "Bravo! Viva! New York, ho! And to hell with the commonplace! Adventur-r-re, R-r-romance!" he crowed, but he concluded with a Hamlet-inspired contrast with himself: "I always wanted to do that sort of thing but never had the courage to make the plunge. It will make me proud if a Sister of mine has the courage to do something I thought over too long." Even as he wrote, his failure of nerve was costing him the woman he loved. Indeed, this same letter included a copy of the newspaper announcement of the Mitchell-Upshaw engagement. Sandwiched between his celebration of his sister's courage and successes, then, he announced his roommate's victory and offered Frances advice about how to handle the matter of the Mitchell-Upshaw nuptials. Write her, he instructed, "but don't bear down *too* heavily on the congrats. Tell her you hate her for not marrying me but wish her good luck anyhow. Ask for some inside dope on how a girl tosses a lover into the ash can, so that the lover still remains her devoted slave. That's what I am."[28]

The letter appalled the sister. She told him so. He absorbed the criticism without any obvious effect except to take still more secondhand pleasure in her courage, even in criticizing him. "After your lecture I shall continue to hold on to my Third Person Impersonal attitude and may you do the same," he told her. "I admire the success of people who are of the 'Red' type (well characterized by you, by the way), but I prefer myself. I have found my attitude brings a certain amount of success also."[29]

Liberal platonism? Third Person Impersonal? If these ideas characterized his courtship, nothing changed with the announcement of the Upshaw-Mitchell wedding. He continued as if nothing at all was different. His response after the engagement puzzled his sister still more. Only three weeks before the wedding, he wrote Frances from Tuscaloosa about his ongoing affair with his old flame. "Peggy and I are quite romantic these days," he started:

> Friends though divided and all that. Write to each other frequently and interestingly. While I write this letter I am waiting on a long distance call to her. She has been sick again and I have decided she has lived long enough without me. I am going to run over to Atlanta Sunday and be the Kind Doctor if she will let me. We are a funny couple. Sometime within the next five years I may tell you the full account of the affair. It is intriguing and in spots dramatic. . . . She and I have no secrets from each other. . . .[30]

Slave, indeed. At the time of the wedding, Marsh's business had kept him in Alabama almost six weeks. Two and a half days before the ceremony, he returned to Georgia for the festivities. Mitchell pressed both him and poor Winston Withers—another groomsman and former suitor—into hauling and toting. "As per usual, Peggy put me to work within half an hour after I arrived in Atlanta," he informed his mother, "and I did the labor of several sweating negroes, moving furniture here and there, shining up floors and woodwork and other such little tasks, arranged the presents in the display room, and wrote the stuff for the newspapers." On the morning of the wedding, he also checked out the groom and found him woefully unprepared. "Red was as wild and nervous as a bridegroom is expected to be. . . . He didn't have a thing but his dress suit!" Marsh exclaimed. With the ceremony only hours away, the best man wrote, "I stuck him into his car and we spent a hectic two hours shopping before I turned him loose, and then I had to dress him, and push him up into line at the altar when it came time for him to say 'I do.' "[31]

In describing it all to his parent, he anticipated her disapproval. "Don't think the two were imposing on me," he protested. "It was a pleasure for me to have even that sort of part in the wedding and an abundance of energetic hard work prevents thinking." He had a lot to think about, and every thought pained him, his even tone notwithstanding. "I said I hadn't had time to write to you," he scribbled on the very night after those awful nuptials. It was not altogether true, he confessed: he hadn't the heart:

> Dearest Mother, there were many times when I wanted you terribly. No one else could have taken your place. But I am the sort that doesn't like to put out much in the way of admitting things I feel, and since *you* weren't here and no one else could take your place I went through it with my head up and barrels of cheerio for the entertainment of the mob.

> We're all children even when we grow up, I suppose, and we don't want
> nobody else but our mothers some times.[32]

So it was then, "head up and cheerio." And back in Alabama he threw
himself still more furiously into his publicity work.

Things got worse before they got better, both for John Marsh and for
his two friends. Even had he wanted to avoid the pair, his return to
Atlanta in March 1923 pulled him into the middle of the Mitchell-
Upshaw chaos. For one thing, he now worked in the same building
with the troubled bride. Less than three months after Peggy Mitchell
drew her first *Journal* paycheck, John Marsh signed on with Major
Cohen, too. Moreover, as a copyreader, he established a new sort of
relationship with Mrs. B. K. Upshaw. In terror of her job, the cub reporter had sought help from every available source; now she had a real
friend at court. For the following six to eight months or so—during his
tenure at the *Journal*—Peggy Mitchell gave him much of what she wrote,
and he sent it back emended. She saved at least ten examples of his
corrected copy, and these tell their own story. His corrections underline how really well, and quickly, the young woman had mastered her
craft—and how little confidence she felt about her talent. Not least,
however, the literary exchanges illustrated another aspect of the "liberal platonism" that characterized their relationship.

Playing professional advisor to Peggy Upshaw was the only pleasurable part of John Marsh's relations with the bridal couple in the spring
of 1923. Separately and together, both bride and groom appealed to
him as father confessor, confidant, and advocate. Six months of the
agitation wore him to a frazzle, and only a rigid sense of duty prohibited him from cutting loose entirely "as I wanted to do many times,"
he protested in a singular show of self-assertion. "The position of an
outsider in any family quarrel is always an unpleasant one, especially
if he cares as much as I do for both parties." He then described the
couple's last day together for his sister:

> On the night they actually broke, they argued the thing over for hours
> and called me up after midnight to come out. Just why I never found
> out, for I wasn't asked to arbitrate or decide their difference. They seemed
> to think my presence might be good for shattered nerves and I talked
> about the weather with them for half an hour and left.

Although he felt like a fifth wheel, he still judged his "soothing influence" may have prevented something worse:

> I feel sorry as the devil for both of them. It is as true an instance as I
> ever saw where two people are more to be pitied than blamed. They
> attempted the impossible and they failed after an honest effort simply

because it was impossible. Naturally it busted them both up badly for a while but they both seem to be coming out of it all right now. Both of them have brilliant possibilities for the future if they leave each other alone. If they had tried to stick it out together it would have been ruinous for both of them, the ruin possibly taking a tragic form.

He concluded this summary of his role in the affair by asserting one more time a version of his Third Person Impersonal: "It is most gratifying to me that our trio remained a trio and didn't turn into a triangle."[33]

In this letter to his sister, John Marsh gave one version of the rupture of the Mitchell-Upshaw union; the Fulton County Court preserved another. The dates correspond. July 10 marked the separation. In their suit, however, Mitchell's lawyers added to the record in naming "sufficient cause." Upshaw, they maintained, smashed his fist against his wife's arm "and raised a bruise of large size and caused the said left arm to swell and be very painful to her for over a week's time." In addition, "he also jerked her against a bed, causing her to be bruised all over her body." Although John Marsh had hinted about the threat of "tragedy" and some violent parting, he referred to nothing violent in his retelling of the story, so the episode seems rather more a shoving match than any full-fledged abuse.[34] A second confrontation led to real violence.

After Peggy kicked Red out in mid-July, Marsh himself took Upshaw in. The husband planned to clear his head with a trip west. In October, Berrien Upshaw returned to Atlanta from "the wide open spaces" where he had fled in July. He returned to the house on Peachtree Street, according to court records, and he did genuine damage to his wife. Lawyers recorded the affair in the suit for divorce they filed one month later.

The defendant struck the plaintiff in the left eye with his fist, caused said eye to swell up and be closed for a space of several days' duration. As a result the plaintiff has been confined to her bed for over a month and is still so confined. She has been obliged to give up the work that she had taken up to support herself, and has incurred a very large doctor's bill in an endeavor to regain her health.[35]

The record of her writing confirms the lawyers' brief about her injuries. In the summer and early fall of 1923, Mitchell had been working like a dervish. She had seldom produced more or better copy. On August 30, she had completed the article on "the lady axe murderess," to the plaudits of the newsroom. From then until the end of October, she produced at least seventeen features in a nine-week period. Her star ascended. After October 28, the pattern changed drastically. Red had come a-calling just before. In the next three weeks, she wrote only four small articles and one review. After this, she contributed almost nothing to the paper for nearly three months. She wrote one short feature on December 30, a smaller one on January 13, and another the next week, plus one review. After writing nothing for February and only a short fashion piece on March 2, she was at least working again on a regular basis by March, but she did not really hit her stride again until April 1924.

If Upshaw's visit had wrecked her life, she also prepared for his return. She bought a pistol for her bedside table, and, according to her brother, she would have delighted in the opportunity to demonstrate her marksmanship against her former husband.[36] Her private secretary, Margaret Baugh, remembered the pistol, asked her about it, and later recorded her own opinion about its presence by her bed:

> All I know is there was a pistol on her bedside table for years. She never explained why. Once when I asked her if she could shoot it, she said of course, her mother had taught her or had seen to it that she learned to shoot. In January 1949 Red's stepmother wrote that he had died. I didn't notice at first, but a while afterward I realized that the pistol was no longer there and it never reappeared. . . . I took the pistol for more than a gesture. I expect she had reason for it. You know Red was an alcoholic and was in and out of mental institutions for years. . . .[37]

Eccentric, erratic, and violent, Red Upshaw was not right. In a very different way, however, neither was his wife. The violent, erratic husband represented only one part of her problem. The separation and then the divorce reopened all the old questions about her future, her professional career, marriage, and family. Between 1919 and 1922 in her correspondence with Allen Edee, the young woman had expressed her skepticism of marriage many times. The dilemma tortured her: "I realize that my happiness lies in a husband and children. I don't believe much in happiness. I know I can never be really happy, but my best chances lie in love. And I can't love." She twisted against her fate in 1921. Her separation and divorce reopened the awful problem in 1924.

She fought these devils at least as fiercely as she had fended off Red Upshaw. Soon after her twenty-third birthday, in the winter of 1923–1924, she decided to make a new life. She left her father and brother to mend their own socks and watch their own diets. She chucked her job. She abandoned Atlanta. Now or never, she determined. She hit the road.

A few years later, she reconstructed the affair for Harvey Smith, then himself on a *wanderjahr* in Europe. "My traveling has been scant, God knows," she started,

> but once before I married John, I was driven with an urge most violent
> to escape from something—which as you remarked in your letter, I do
> not recall the nature of. But I was sure I'd lose my mind if I did not take
> my foot in my hand and "visit the ends of the earth and judge them," as
> J. B. Cabell's "Don Manuel" expressed it, for he too had that same urge.[38]

Had she really forgotten the source of her violent urge to escape? She
betrayed her reasons in prefacing her remarks with the reference to
marrying John and in avoiding reference to Upshaw and separation
altogether. To marry or not: leaving everything obviated the dilemma.

In Mitchell's recollection of her decision to travel, her identification
with John Branch Cabell's Don Manuel offers nice clues to her thinking. Cabell's work celebrated the adventurous knight-errant, who, unlike the Arthurian prototypes, demonstrates his mobility not only in
space but in time as well. To assume such kinship was to claim the
freedom of movement for herself that is the aristocratic and free man's
most fundamental right and privilege. By the same token, it defines
the very antithesis of women's roles: stability, home, immobility, even
sequestration. For Mitchell, of course, it necessarily recalled both the
form and content of her own female paladin, her parental St. Joan.
Female knighthood involves significant contradictions, too. If knightly
adventure verily personifies merit for men, what is the meaning of
"adventuress" and female adventure? It is the reverse of virtue for the
woman. All of these issues (and more, of course) flit around the edges
of Mitchell's assumption of a Jurgenesque identity. Most of all, however, her identification with Jurgen and the knightly quest underlined
her desire for freedom and the assertion of her own will as represented
in movement. Mobility was freedom. Off she went:

> I wanted to see what the world was like, and what I was like, when adrift
> in the world. I had a little money and urged on by John, who is the most
> understanding of humans, I set out first to Florida, then Cuba, the
> Canal Zone, Honolulu and Tahiti. My craft was not as rusty then as now
> and I figured there were enough English newspapers to keep me in jobs
> and food.

Alas, alas, everything worked against the venture. The wonder is less
its failure than Mitchell's having conceived of and actually launched it
against all the odds. First of all, of course, the idea utterly appalled
her father. She later referred to it as the "wild eyed Cuban expedition
which so horrified the family."[39] More devasting problems undermined her ambition. Like the Judith Shakespeare whom Virginia Woolf
created in *A Room of One's Own*, Margaret Mitchell soon discovered
the vicissitudes that beset a woman who traveled by herself. Woolf
framed the issue as art; the young Southern woman lived it.

Perhaps it's different with a man. A man on the loose can take up with anyone and a woman can't. Or if she does she's several kinds of a fool or just doesn't give a damn. And I wasn't that kind of a fool and I gave several damns. And I can conjure up now, all too vividly the mad longing I had after supper for some one easy going to talk to—some one who didn't think I was a tramp and who wouldn't try to make me and who loved to talk and I found out that most women drifting alone thru the Tropics wanted to be made and it was neither my own peculiar charms nor the overweening lust of all males that interposed a curtain between me and most of the men I met and kept us from congenial conversation.[40]

She got as far as Cuba, and she discovered the full import of life for a woman on the lam. Soon after her return, she summarized her adventure in a feature for the *Journal*. She wrote in acid. Latin gentlemen, she sneered, "have as much chivalry in their souls as hungry sharks." In the heart of Havana, she found no protection from the lascivious young bucks who hung about the plazas. The police? ". . . they are no comfort to an enraged young American woman who has run the gauntlet of smirking dandies—twisting their tiny black moustaches and insolently murmuring remarks as the lady passes by with head in the air." If the white-clad, malacca-caned dandies shamed her, the gossip-mongering women burdened her in other ways. Latin America, she wrote, "is full of half-whispered stories of foolish American women who 'picked up' strangers to do small service for them and came to grief over it."[41] Yes, Judith Shakespeare's friend Nick Greene was very much alive and well in Margaret Mitchell's time, and he asked very little in return for his "small service." But the devil, the very devil was to pay for poor Judith, and for the young American girl as well, even had she been inclined to accept some gentleman's protection.

The young woman had charted an impossible course. In Havana, she said, she looked ahead and saw "that my life was going to be lonelier in Panama, Honolulu, etc., than I really wanted it to be. . . ." At that very moment, as so often happened, her body compromised her will: the flu got her, and illness dictated a new course. "A good case of Flu—pneumonia stopped me in Cuba and sent me home but not before I learned a lot about traveling alone."[42]

In Virginia Woolf's reconstruction of the plight of women on the road, Judith was got with child, hanged herself, and found a nameless grave. She never wrote Shakespeare's plays. In *A Room of One's Own*, however, Woolf also argues that even successfully resisting the threats and blandishments requires such effort that it cripples the muse for women. Even had her Judith not succumbed to Nick's pity and affection, her future was fated just the same. Mitchell acknowledged Woolf's truth four years before the English novelist-critic made her elegant discourse on the plight of women in the arts.[43]

In Cuba, Mitchell determined her fate. Unlike Judith Shakespeare, she returned chastened to her Atlanta/Stratford and to her kindly copy editor/wool stapler who wanted nothing more in life than to bask in her glow and make her happy. She returned as chaste as chastened. So much for the female picaro. She took up her new load of self-knowledge; if not happily, at least willingly. "So having learned a lot of things about myself," she concluded,

> chiefly that I had been born a chaste woman and would probably die uninterestingly chaste, I wasn't too sorry to come home. And after all, I'd gotten my perspective and knew what I had left home to find and knew that, like the Princess in the fairy tale, it wasn't at the ends of the earth but at home, at my door step. So I came home and took it.[44]

Beginning as the knight-errant, she concluded as the virgin princess of the fairy tale.

She did not actually settle into hearth and home quite so easily as she declared. Her letter recounting her adventure suggested that she returned immediately to accept John's patient company after surrendering her ambitions for independence and world travel. That was not the case. John, for one thing, no longer lived in the city. Simultaneously with her decision for world adventure, he had abandoned Atlanta for the new job in Washington. Circumstances link their divergent travel plans and suggest Mitchell was the agent of both moves. For one thing, John's conservatism would have worked against such a relocation on his own; he was, moreover, never happy apart from her, and he loathed his job in Washington, even though it put him near his mother, who had moved to Delaware.[45] In any case, while his beloved took wing for Havana and parts unknown, John Marsh had trudged dutifully off to the night shift at a new job and a narrow bed in a strange city. When flu and Cuban dandies did her in, he remained stuck in the sweltering Washington summer.

Six months after she returned, he finally made it back to the city he now considered home as well. The courts finalized the Mitchell-Upshaw divorce two months later, and two months after that, John Marsh finally asked Peggy Mitchell to marry him.

If Peggy Mitchell kicked against her fate as wife and bride, John Marsh also harbored the deepest reservations about marriage, despite his adoration of the woman. Occasionally he admitted some of them. "I allowed myself to reach a fairly ripe old age with the idea that I would probably never marry," he wrote his mother just past his twenty-ninth birthday. He continued rather less than half in jest:

> After that, certain aspects of the relationship impressed me as being very distasteful. There aren't many women in the world that fit my ideas of what a girl ought to be. You put certain ideals in my mind that not many

can come up to. And, on top of that, I am naturally a very selfish person and I have become set in my ways since growing "old." The idea of having to conform my ways to suit the convenience of some other person, and giving up having my own way about things, and surrendering certain things I enjoy, didn't seem worth while. I enjoyed the companionship and friendship of women, but being married to one of them seemed going a little too far, overdoing the thing. I couldn't imagine not becoming bored with *any* woman after a certain length of time of close confinement. Peggy gave me the feminine friendship I wanted, she's the finest and most loyal friend a man ever had, and I thought I could depend on her to stay that way, because her experiences with matrimony had convinced her it was a fine thing theoretically but impossible practically.

Such hindrances notwithstanding, they decided to marry anyway, "We have decided to toss our several distastes for matrimony into the lake, and give the ancient and honorable institution a try," John wrote his mother in mid-January of 1925.[46] They decided on a Valentine's Day wedding, "the only date on the calendar for which I unashamedly cherish a sentimental weakness," the fiancée told her prospective sister-in-law.[47]

Finalizing the divorce had taken a great load off Mitchell. In the fall, she was working hard and thriving physically. If poor health had burdened her for years, Marsh told his mother, "she began to improve just as soon as the courts took the worry of Red off her mind, and is now in better health than any time since I have known her."[48] John Marsh could not say the same about himself. Indeed, for all his apparent satisfaction at securing the object of his affections, *his* body now rebelled. By mere hours, an extraordinary physical breakdown followed his decision to wed. It is certainly one of the most curious affairs in the bizarre health records compiled by the ever-sickly pair.

On Sunday night, January 18, 1925, Marsh asked and won Mitchell's favor. The following evening, he gained Eugene Mitchell's reluctant consent for the match. On the twentieth, he wrote the long letter to his mother, asking effectively for her blessing. The following day, he fell curiously ill. His fiancée described it to her prospective in-laws two weeks later:

> He had no sooner obtained Dad's consent for the nuptials than he got sick. It wasn't his appendix, this time. It was Flu—a brand new type, the "hiccoughing flu." He has hiccoughed about every other breath he drew for thirteen days now. He hasn't been seriously or painfully ill—I don't want you to be worried—but as it interfered with his eating and sleeping he has become very weak.[49]

All of the circumstances of the odd malady were extraordinary. Not the least striking, four weeks before the seizure's onset, Mitchell had written a long article about chronic hiccoughs. She has researched the essay thoroughly, medicine being her hobby, and the *Journal* had published the essay on December 28. Three weeks later, that very illness struck Mitchell's beloved. As he hicked away, then, he found in her, miraculously, a resident expert on the mysterious condition.[50]

On January 31, concerned about her inability to nurse him during the day while she was working, Marsh's bride-to-be finally checked him into St. Joseph's Infirmary. He grew progressively weaker. The seizures destroyed their plans for the wedding. Mitchell still hoped for a Valentine's Day ceremony. "If he gets well in time I suppose we will still use that date," she wrote on February 2.[51] He did not. His condition deteriorated so that his elder brother was summoned, and the doctors gave up hope. He reached his lowest ebb on February 14. He survived his would-be wedding day, however, and his condition improved a little. His otherwise prospective bride then allowed herself to think of weddings—but only barely: "we won't get married till God knows when but I shouldn't worry because he's alive and that's the main thing. It was a pretty stiff 24 hours when I thought I might lose him."[52] And while John still languished in the hospital, she produced another *Journal* article, one that also suggests her own sense of the future: on March 15, the Magazine ran her essay, "Marriage Licenses That Are Never Used."[53]

The illness baffled the hospital staff. Besides ordering special diets, the doctors pumped his stomach and finally resorted to surgery. The patient invented remedies of his own. Nothing worked. When the physicians offered a psychosomatic explanation, however, the fiancée hit the ceiling. Here she first recorded what was to become a standard practice in all her family's bouts with illness. When a physician offered some disagreeable diagnosis or remedy, she was ever ready to reject that expert as a quack and find a doctor more amenable to her own version of the ailment. This was especially true when the diagnosis even hinted at psychological causes. Even though she might draw such conclusions on her own, she disallowed the privilege utterly for others. This prejudice informed her initial skepticism of John's attendant. Not "worth a hoot in Hades," she described the man to John's sister.

> I suppose I took a dislike to him when after poor John had been sick as a dog for a week and unable to sleep or digest any thing this poor ass of a medico remarked to Kelly Starr [John's boss] that there really wasn't anything wrong with John except "A touch of nerves." I yearned to swat him for his diagnosis.[54]

The explanation of neurosis haunted Mitchell, and she found validation of physiological sources of the illness where she could. As sleep improved John's condition, she determined, that seemed to support her thesis of somatic origins. "If he can just grab off ten hours' sleep he looks as if nothing had ever happened to him and if he misses it, he looks like a fatal accident looking for an unhealthy place to happen. How ever this proves that beyond a doubt his trouble is stomach and not nervous in origin and that's a comfort," she concluded.[55]

For all these experiments, John Marsh hung at death's edge for months. No one, according to his expert fiancée, had ever hicked so long and lived. His hospital stay stretched from deep winter into spring. Mitchell hovered at his bedside constantly when not at her office. He required her presence. In mid-February, when the doctors thought he was dying and prohibited her visits, her absence drove him to hysterics.[56] Meanwhile, Mitchell flirted with nervous prostration herself. While she passed her afternoons and evenings in the sickening ether-iodine atmosphere of St. Joseph's corridors, she still worked full-time, putting in fifty-hours weeks or more. As the sixth week of his hospitalization approached, however, the hiccoughing returned. She despaired.[57]

He did not die, and by the end of March, the hospital finally discharged him. He had been abed two months. He remained unwell; he looked worse, "like a famine victim," Mitchell said.[58] Nor could he return to work. He had incurred large medical bills as well. He was not a "catch" at all, as the debutantes might say. As he slowly recuperated, however, with his fiancée tending him every step of the way, they determined to carry through with their wedding plans. The illness sealed their union. Playing nurse fulfilled some of the young woman's deepest instincts. Her natural prospensity to succor the sick bound her to Marsh in a way that nothing else could have done.[59] His condition elicited all her maternal instincts, even as her nursing evoked for him the bonding with his own mother in illness. Mitchell, meanwhile, displayed the same needs for nurturing, and they easily reversed roles. As their friend Augusta Dearborn observed, John was "protective of Margaret Mitchell as well as of 'Red' Upshaw and me."[60] Illness made them perfectly compatible, and they set a new date.

If Mitchell liked the idea of a Valentine's Day wedding, her alternative choice, July the Fourth, pleased her for other reasons. She later proclaimed the ceremony "a queer way to celebrate Independence Day,"[61] but the date amused her. It provided the equivalent of the red-rose bouquet at her first wedding. It suited her fancy in other ways as well: it suggests an ambition for her new life: independence coexisting with dependence. The wedding itself and the newspaper announcements carried through the themes of the unconventional union. The notice in the *Atlanta Constitution*, for example, could hardly have differed more from the false and stuffy chronicle of her first wedding. "Mrs. Marsh is a brilliant young woman and has done some creditable writing, especially of short stories," ran the article.[62]

The ceremony itself differed completely from the Mitchell-Upshaw nuptials. Mitchell asked Medora Perkerson to be matron of honor instead of any of her old girlhood friends or debutante associates. The bride did not want a "slow-drag" wedding, she informed her matron of honor, "and we stepped lively down the aisle to a speeded-up Lohengrin," Medora laughed.[63] The "rowdy Frank Stanton" attended John. Actually Stanton's service as best man cast a shadow from the past. Like John Marsh in the Upshaw wedding, Stanton had courted Mitchell earlier, and at least one friend, Aggie Dearborn, was puzzled why Marsh instead of Stanton stood before the altar at the Unitarian-Universalist Church on West Peachtree that hot afternoon.[64] While the bride had dressed at her father's house, the couple hosted their own reception at the quarters they would call their new home on Crescent Court in midtown.

This apartment posed problems initially for the pair. Eugene Mitchell had little more enthusiasm for this match than for the first, and while he consented to the marriage, he hated John's announcement "that I intended to take Peggy away from him." He insisted they live with him after the ceremony. The bridegroom refused. "It would be nice to live at the Mitchell house, but I would rather live in a one room apartment with Peggy than in a big house on Peachtree Street with in-laws," he told his mother.[65] Instead of moving in with Steve and Mr. Mitchell, then, the couple returned from their honeymoon in the mountains of north Georgia to take up residence in the small rooms of a home converted to an apartment house. This was "The Dump on Tight Squeeze" where the couple lived for the next seven years. They occupied what had originally been the basement in the back of the house as the main entrance had faced Peachtree originally. The place was dark and cramped and a little seedy even then, but they fixed the place up themselves before moving in by painting and making other improvements. The bride also made it livable by filling it, according to Medora, "with shiny old mahogany, old silver and china handed down in Peggy's family," and, most of all, "so many books they hardly left room for the wedding presents."[66]

The dwelling had little to recommend it other than the cost and convenience. It was cheap and allowed easy access to public transportation. Crescent ran parallel to Peachtree one block west in midtown, near Tenth Street which then stopped at Peachtree on the east. It was not far from her father's house and the other haunts of her adolescence. The apartment house itself boasted a rather bohemian clientele: artists, writers, and reporters among others. The sculptor upstairs asked Mitchell to pose for him, and he did a bust, now lost, which the subject joked "keeps looking more and more like an exhibit in a Racial Types museum, with a label entitled "Pure keltic pioneer woman'."[67] Friends also lived all around; and as it was hard by the Georgia Tech campus, the location provided a collegiate atmosphere, too. The trolley ride to the Journal Building remained a nightmare, especially at rush hour when she had to stand, but at least she had cut off a few blocks from her old route. Worst of all, the Marsh apartment was small and cramped. The bride had come from an enormous house, with bedrooms, closets, and space to spare. This place, at least, she could heat to her own pleasure, however. Almost pathologically cold-natured, she ran the thermostat to stifling degrees. John's sister laughed about it: "At least when she married John, he said, if she wants tropical heat in the apartment at all times, she shall have it."[68] Without her father's icy looks, she could warm it, too, with the bawdy laughter of her friends. Was it tiny and bland? She paid little attention to her physical environment in any case, and she never regretted the swap.

This place was hers, in a way she could never claim for the Peachtree house. It was hers and she claimed it—appropriately enough—in her own name. She tacked two cards to the door. One read "John R. Marsh"; the other, "Margaret Munnerlyn Mitchell." The action provoked a minor scandal. It amused her friends. It was a joke, and she was deadly serious. She had fought for her own name and she kept it. Likewise, she kept her own byline, her own desk, and her own job at the *Atlanta Journal*, too. Especially given the debts of her husband's illness, she provided a major portion of the Marsh family income. Not for nothing did she choose Independence Day for her wedding. As for John Marsh, he approved of anything she said or did. She could do no wrong for him. His wife in turn, found in the kindly copy editor an endless source of tenderness, attention, nurture, and encouragement. He was the self-effacing, selfless mother whom May Belle Mitchell could never completely be, at least to her only daughter. He provided her, in turn, endless opportunity to nurse, to pet, to baby.

Marriage and John Marsh: this was what she wanted, she determined. At the same time, doubts remained. The muse still beckoned. She still harbored old ambitions. She tried to explain it to a soul mate, Harvey Smith:

> I do not believe that people like you and I and a few others I could mention ever utterly find what we are hunting for—it doesn't exist except in our minds, it's "Music from behind the Moon" and while it's maddening to hear, God knows we are better off than those who've never heard it.[69]

The mysterious music did not stop on July 4, 1925.

X

Hell in Narrow Quarters

Nancy doesn't mind working, in fact, she would rather keep her job. Her pay check would help out on the expense, and besides she thinks it would be more fun working than keeping house in their little apartment. Her best friends are the other girls in the office and she doesn't want to give them up. . . . . She'd feel like an exile if she had to leave it.

PEGGY MITCHELL, "MATRIMONIAL BONDS"[1]

A failing marriage launched her career; a successful one ended it. In July 1925, marriage looked good to Peggy Mitchell. She could anticipate a general improvement in all her circumstances. She would keep her job and her own income, and she would bear responsibility now for only one man in a tiny apartment instead of two in a barnlike house. And unlike her father and brother, this one man blessed everything she did. Did she want to run the temperature up to the subtropical? He nodded agreeably. Did she keep the oddest hours? He never blinked. Did she fill the apartment with handsome young men and bawdy flappers? He actually encouraged her. Married life proved more difficult than she had planned, however; the commitment to John, marriage, and family forced her to deal with issues she had not fully considered before. Children, job, ambition, finances, and health—always health, which summarized and subsumed the others. By the spring of 1926 and for the remainder of the decade, she wrestled fiercely with a new set of devils attendant upon her successful marriage to John Marsh.

To have babies or not: this proved a primary dilemma. In 1925, having children hardly seemed an option. Couples wed in order to produce offspring. People did not go childless who had the physical capability of reproducing. The issue was not even "if," but rather "how many." Margaret Mitchell, however, did not want children. With her intense need for privacy, she had no disposition to share her biases with friends or even family;[2] at the same time, her life manifested the logic of her determination. She remained very skeptical of sex; pregnancy and childbirth horrified her; she had no inclination towards biological motherhood and considered her lack of maternal instincts a genetic trait; children made her wince.

If Mitchell failed to own her decision completely even to herself, she littered her correspondence in the first years of her marriage with evidence of her biases. In the spring of 1926, a critical nine months after her marriage, the young matron issued an initial jeremiad against conventional families. Frances Marsh had sent her a novel by the English writer Storm Jameson, and *Three Kingdoms* provided Mitchell the occasion for a long dissertation on literature, men, marriage, sex, birth control, and independent women, all sandwiched together with asides about her own failing flesh and her financial disabilities. Although she began with thanks for the gift, she launched immediately into a diatribe against what she expected to find—a sappy story by another damned scribbling Englishwoman. She loathed such novels. Their gloomy notions of household arrangements depressed her; the arrogance of their men offended her; the passivity of their women drove her crazy. Launched, then, onto gender characterizations and family arrangements, she hurtled on to the related themes of sex, children—and birth control.

> And evidently birth control hasn't penetrated to England because the little garments always appear in the chapter directly following the wedding. I'm sure any manufacturer of well known birth control contrivances could start on a shoe string in England and clean up more than a realtor in Florida. And English heroines seem to put up with so much from their hubbies with out any back chat what so ever. An English husband says severely, "My dear, your conduct isn't cricket" and wifie crawls off and dies instead of gulping a whiskey neat and roaring "Who gives a dam if it isn't, you S.O.B.?"

At this point, she meandered back to literature again, but she could not leave the baby-pregnancy issue alone. Relating how she had just completed the highly praised *Hounds of Spring* by Silvia Thompson, she announced that, as usual, the baby ruined it for her. "English births are depressing, too, in novels, at least," she continued. "They seem to be unattended by such refinements as scopolamine or ether and the husbands stand around the delivery room and mutter about cricket. Yes," she added at this point, "I've said 'depressing' six times so far and that's nearly as good an average as 'Lorelei.' " She closed with one more shot against conventional domesticity: "I'll reserve my thanks to you for likening me to Laurence Storm until I read it and if she is an ass who has no hot water in her house and a lot of children I'll make a special trip to Wilmington to brain you—."[3]

While literature triggered her outburst about birth and babies on this occasion, she found plenty of other opportunities in the months that followed to continue the discourse. In 1928, "Mother Marsh" had come calling with her granddaughter, Henry's child, Mary, and they had hardly left when the youngest Marsh sibling, Gordon, and his pregnant wife, Francesca—"Frank," to family—appeared at the tiny apartment in Atlanta. All these Marshes and all this fecundity provided more occasion for her skeptical observations about sex, motherhood, and children in another letter to Frances Marsh Zane, who was, in any case, eight months into her own first pregnancy by this time.

In detailing her mother-in-law's visit, she began with references to John's little niece, Mary Marsh. She liked the child very much, she said, but in the course of her praise she also intimated what she considered the norm for children. "Mary seems to have none of the more heinous sins of childhood," she declared, "—interrupting, begging, whining, tattling and lying." Despite her admiration of the child, she also expressed mock horror over the child's taste in reading. She was "heartbroken and disillusioned," she told her sister-in-law,

> over the impassioned way in which Mary took to a dog eared copy of "Elsie Dinsmore" which, for appearances, I keep shelved between copies of "Jurgen" and "How Kate Lost Her Maiden Head" (a most informative volume). There seems to be a perpetual charm about the Sadistic Mr. Dinsmore and his Masochistic Elsie. What a completely congenial pair.

Not for nothing did Mitchell link sadomasochism and children.

Soon after the two Mary Marshes departed, Gordon Marsh and his chipper spouse Frank decamped. Then in the (secret) throes of novel-writing, Mitchell had also endured three weeks of menstrual pains when the couple appeared. Feeling out of sorts and vaguely put-upon, the young writer found more cause for cynical irritation in the effulgence of the new bride's enthusiasm for motherhood. "I couldn't quite subscribe to Frank's outspoken desire for seven children and fourteen dogs," she mused ruefully. "I've never owned more than seven dogs at once and can't help but feel that the line should be drawn some where— and the same applies to the seven little ones." The thought of all these infants set her off on still another Freudian string of associations about motherhood and maternal instincts, and their notable absence from

her own family. Without a break, other than her own pregnant ellipses, she continued gloriously into the heart of the matter of mothering for herself, suggesting in the process evidence of the kind of
mothering she had received as well.

> It was a shock to me when I read in a delightful book on the ductless
> glands, last week, that lack of secretion from the posterior pituitary gland
> causes a total absence of the maternal instinct. I thought that the lack of
> mat and pat instincts in this family were due to mental and not glandu-
> lar processes.

And there it was: the delightful discovery that she could blame glands
and genes for shortcomings otherwise defined.

Mitchell closed this eight-page treatise on motherhood and children
with one last shot at childbirth. A friend recently had experienced a
painless method. Have you heard of it? she inquired. An ether enema?
It sounded strange, she admitted. "Maybe she got it mixed up with
some thing else—but she says she didn't . . . and that it was as painless as having a baby can be. . . . Didn't paralyze any muscular or
nervous reactions as scopalomine some times does."[4]

Besides her own family, friends were producing babies in these same
years, and these births prompted still more pronouncements on pregnancy and horrors of childbirth. The lying-in of her old newspaper pal
Evelyn Lovette Kling, in August 1930, provoked an especially revealing discourse on obstetrics. Mitchell attended the labor, and she described it to Elinor Hillyer in New York.

> I was over at her house the afternoon the pains began and Mrs. Lovette
> and I were doing our level best to divert her mind between pains, know-
> ing that as they were so far apart it would be hours before the actual
> labor began and so we wanted to keep her mind off it as much as pos-
> sible. Well, you know how persistently contrary a mind can be. It seemed
> to me that dreadful afternoon, while I was trying to be airy and talkative
> that my mind would produce no conversational material that was less
> gruesome than the last chapters of "A Farewell to Arms." I almost talked
> about Caesarian sections. I strangled remarks about eclamptic convul-
> sions. I felt myself grow purple restraining remarks about high forcep
> cases and the broken necks of babies. I thought of babies who had been
> blinded by forceps. In fact, I was in a perfect agony for fear I'd say some
> little some thing that would cause her worry and add to her pain. She
> was such a trooper about it all. I think women have a kind of bravery
> men can't possibly have. I don't believe men could sit through an after-
> noon of intermittent pain and crack jokes and be so calm and glad it was
> nearly all over—when they knew that in a few hours they were going to
> be into some thing no morphia could help.[5]

The passing reference to Hemingway bears special note. Mitchell admired *A Farewell to Arms* more than any other novel, and those terrible last chapters in Frederick Henry's life as Katherine Barkely and her child die a-borning spoke profoundly to the young Atlanta woman.[6] The same theme dominated another of her favorite novels, Michael Arlen's *The Green Hat*. This classic of twenties culture, which she read and reread throughout the decade, culminates in the secret pregnancy, aborted birth, and jaunty suicide of its gallant heroine, Iris Storm, and replicates the horror of Hemingway's last scenes.

This letter bears other significance for Mitchell's notions about motherhood, childbirth, and babies. Coming to assist her friend, Mitchell presents herself as a kind of midwife. But the birth assistant bears another face: she practices a perverted midwifery. "You know how persistently contrary a mind can be," she wrote; she then described the strangling, convulsions, and other tortures of childbirth that dominated her own mind. With all her emphasis on death, pain, and destruction, the birth assistant makes herself out as something closer to an abortionist.[7] Finally, her description hides a third identity. The image of herself—purple-faced and strangled—likens her less to the mother or the midwife than to the desperately struggling infant itself in some botched birth.

No, with the images of dying mothers, aborted births, and whining children in her mind, and the literary models of Katherine Barkeley, Iris Storm, and *The Hounds of Spring* ever before her—she would not be a mother. The choice, however, raised all sorts of other problems. For one thing, she could hardly ignore the social and familial pressure against this eccentric, anomalous, and heretical choice. Society in general and her Catholic heritage in particular scorned the idea of free will in pregnancy and motherhood. The conflict between personal inclination and social imperatives created the fiercest contradictions. Cultural values, indeed, virtually prohibited the free choice of childlessness. That sort of autonomy for a woman bespoke the most radical form of revolution and even anarchy, especially in the South, and Mitchell, for one, was hardly willing to alienate herself so completely from her culture. Unwilling to own the decision as a matter of personal choice, then, Mitchell needed the most compelling justification to avoid childbearing. The overlapping categories of health and money— of physical debility and financial woe—bridged the gap between personal choice and social mandate. They created, in effect, her inability to bear children, even as they provided the rationale for such a decision. These two issues had their own causes, of course, and they produced their own consequences quite apart from the matters of birth and children. Health and sickness; wealth and poverty; autonomy and selflessness: she jumbled the contradictions almost hopelessly together in these years.

Financial insecurity terrified Margaret Mitchell. She came by the fear honestly, of course. If her mother offered the example of generosity—profligacy, even—Eugene Mitchell illustrated the most antithetical values. She followed his model. She always fretted about money. It constituted a theme of her short story "The Kiss," as the protagonist surrendered her true love for a guaranteed income. The young reporter made it the subject of numerous articles and essays in the *Journal*. She isolate the theme of financial security in many of the books she reviewed. In college, she wanted to know about her dates' economic standing, and Red Upshaw's financial instability provoked her decision to take a job in 1922. She worried the matter constantly.

Mitchell's constant "po' mouthin'" (poor-mouthing), as the regional term went, became something of a joke among her friends. The repeated stories of debts and losses? "None of us took it very seriously and always said we were sorry in much the same way one would commiserate with a friend about the loss of a Confederate bond," joked Harvey Smith.

> We may have been mistaken in each detail but we were certainly disbelievers in any reference made to loss. The impression I always had of Peggy as related to her own finances was that she never under any circumstance let her right hand know how much change her left hand held. Certainly none of her friends ever asked any questions but we all had the distinct realization that successive facts didn't gibe with one another. Certainly the fear of poverty was one of the motivating characteristics of her life just as some strange compulsion to have people (or was it herself) believe her to be ill and suffering, was also. As regarded money she was so scrupulously careful to pay each cent she owed that it was sometimes embarrassing, and just as determined that each cent owed her should be paid.[8]

"Tight as Dixie's hatband," quipped another family friend.[9]

Illness and fear of illness spilled over constantly into Mitchell's terrors about cash. She continually groaned that she and John had entered marriage with numerous debts; those debts, however, had arisen from John's months-long hospitalization in the winter before they wed. Even when they were both well, the fear of catastrophic illness, and equally catastrophic expenses, never left the writer's mind. She thought and wrote about these illnesses constantly. The pattern that she exhibited on first returning to Atlanta after her mother's death persisted throughout the twenties. Her personal correspondence overflows with innumerable references to the most diverse aches, ailments, illnesses, conditions, seizures, and syndromes. There were always "little" infirmities: colds, flu, allergies, hives, and the old condition of "abdominal adhesions." At another time she reported she had come down with malaria. Nine months after her marriage, however, she developed a new, chronic complaint that changed her life permanently: a mysterious and science-baffling arthritic or rheumatoid condition that settled disastrously in her ankle.

Although in the spring of 1926 she related that her ankle had bothered her for two years, she had never mentioned it before in any of her correspondence. Not until April, exactly nine months after her wedding to John Marsh, did she refer to the condition. Even had she experienced ankle problems before, from this time on, they took a new turn. She could no longer walk, or she could walk only with the aid of crutches and special footwear—clunky orthopedic shoes that became, incidentally, the talk of all her friends and a kind of hallmark even among her peripheral acquaintances—the outward sign of inward pain.[10]

For all the dysfunction in her foot, she insisted, the ankle condition actually constituted only the most obvious manifestation of a larger, deeper problem. A mysterious spring of corruption, she quoted her doctors, poisoned her whole body, and this toxic fountain became the source of all the other ailments of one sort of another that plagued her in these years. If the doctors could only determine the source of this corruption, all her problems would be cured, she believed. In the search for this primary infection, then, she subjected herself to all manner of operations and experiments after her marriage. Dentists pulled her teeth, and surgeons extracted her tonsils, all in the effort to stanch the toxic flow. These produced their own train of new afflictions. The tonsilectomy in the late winter or early spring of 1926 offers a perfect example. "My tonsils were dreadful," she groaned to Frances Marsh. "No, I'm not going to speak of operations, but don't let any one ever tell you that its 'a slight operation, no pain at all and you're up in three days.' It's been ten days now and I am just getting to where I can eat and still can't swallow with out pain. Appendicitis was nothing compared with it." Was this the source of the greater poison? "I'm waiting patiently to see if it will have any effect on my foot. Seems that I have to watch diet, teeth, tonsils, sinuses etc. to make sure there's no poison being put out by any of them and if I still don't improve, I guess they'll have to operate on my foot." Then she launched full-steam into the foot condition:

> I'm on crutches and haven't touched the floor in three weeks except on the one glorious day that the doc told me he *might* have to fuse two ankle joints together and make it solid for life. I felt somewhat depressed, came home, bought a quart of rye, and took three drinks, threw away my crutches and getting a taxi went calling on all my friends. I had a lovely five hours. I didn't even know I had a bad foot until I sobered up when John came home and he, poor angel, kindly sat up all night rubbing the blamed thing.[11]

Here the writer also demonstrates the other side of her marriage to John Marsh. Actually, his health obsessed her as much as her own physical condition, and she played ministering angel to him no less than he to her. "I have to feed him as if he were a prize Persian, put him to bed around nine thirty except on the one night a week when we go out and hardly see him any other time," she told his sister. "But if I didn't," she continued, "I guess I wouldn't have any husband at all, for John is far from strong and his digestion has a decided tendency to blow up under emotional strain of any type.[12] This routine described her life when her "prize Persian" was actually hale and hearty. God help her when he developed a temperature. And, indeed, he seemed constantly down with some complaint or another, and his devoted wife always expected even small maladies to explode into another long-term visit to St. Joseph's.

"I can't imagine anything more distasteful than living with a man who became bored every time you had a pain," Peggy Mitchell told her sister-in-law.[13] John and Peggy Marsh's aches and illnesses united them in the most extraordinary way. It helped define the very nature of their marriage. Not least, it virtually precluded having children. She hardly needed infants to cultivate any latent maternal, nursing instincts. John provided quite enough scope for that. While illness—hers and his—provided both direct and indirect reasons for avoiding motherhood, her deteriorating health reflected still other crises in her life in the first year after her wedding. Even in the absence of children, her marriage to John Marsh compelled her to reconsider her professional employment. Health and illness again proved to be both cause and effect of her choices.

The year after their marriage, John Marsh's health improved notably; his wife's deteriorated drastically. This disparity provoked and buttressed the argument of her husband that she should quit work. Her father and brother had never approved her employment, and her new debilities added weight to their arguments. Her bum ankle, however, also caused problems in the workplace. Angus Perkerson lacked sympathy for her ailments, and his attitude chivvied her in the same direction as her menfolk's counsel. Her "labor pains" peaked in mid-spring of 1926. She described the circumstances in the same rancorously jolly letter to her sister-in-law that repudiated orthodox families.

"I am of the opinion that I am through with my job at the Journal," she informed Frances Marsh in the spring.

I have no business doing it. . . , but I considered that Mr. Perk did me a dirty deal, while I was on sick and not being able to walk. I sent John down to tell him to shove my job up his—well, the place reserved for such things. Perk is a lousy little beast and I've gotten so tired working for him. However, he sent his wife Medora out to patch up things and ask me to do Elizabeth Bennet while I was here at home. I don't know if I will. Lizzie is due tomorrow and I haven't written a line. I may keep up Lizzie for a while and then let it go but I don't think I'll go back on the mag. Unless the economic pressure becomes too hard to stand. For one thing, if I quit the dam job then I won't have anything pulling me back to work and I'll stay home long enough to get my ankle well— instead of going back, half cured, because we need the money so dam bad. When I do get well, if I ever do, then I suppose there'll be time enough to look for another job. I suppose I'll land one on the "Georgian" tho' I don't care for a Hearst paper. . . . However, John wants me to stop work (until I'm well) [an emendation she scribbled in in pencil after she had typed the letter], even if we starve and Steve and Father do, too. So I guess I will.[14]

Still, the decision gave her pause. She waffled. If work was awful, the prospect of staying home pleased her little more. How would life be outside the paper? It made her apprehensive:

I rather shiver to think what it will be like for me for while, on bad days, when work piled up and Perk cursed like an inspired fiend, I used to listen to the press grumbling in the basement and think grimly—"Yes you damned animal, I work nine hours a day feeding you and each day it's the same thing over and over and over and you are never full. And I am feeding you youth and verve along with my copy." But on good days, it rumbled just like a good natured and so comforting giant and gave me an at-home feeling I've never had any where else.[15]

While everything conspired against her professional employment— her boss, her family, her husband, her flesh itself—other motives inspired her to quit work. If journalism frustrated her, it did so in part because of the higher hopes she nurtured secretly for her talent and the near impossibility of finding time to write creatively in her manic workdays. John Marsh recognized the problem, too, and it added fuel to his arguments that she quit. "John has such beautiful hopes about my eventually proving a genius," she mused to his sister Frances; "how such hopes persist after we've been married so long [nine months!] is beyond my comprehension."[16] Free of the daily grind, she could devote herself to fiction, he told her.

Despite job pressure and ill-health, however, Mitchell did still write on her own. In mid-spring, describing her frantic schedule to her sister-in-law, she also detailed her non-journalistic writing. After grousing about the time required to instruct young cubs and do her weekly features, she continued:

And so my days are taken up with teaching and with trying to find a moment to write my own stories and my nights with trying to gut out the line of chatter that pays enough to cover the rent. (I once told John that the Elizabeth Bennet Colyum was going to keep the wolf away from the door and he brutally asked if I was going to read it to the wolf.) Then, ever and anon, I get a chance to earn a dishonest penny by writing articles for poor woiking girls' magazines at ten bucks a throw which buys suppers on Sunday night, at horsey hostelries which we could not otherwise afford. But, after all this is done there ain't much time for nothing else. . . .

Among other literary things we've been trying to do is a one act skit, to be used by New Wayburn, who is producing the Junior League Follies (April 4, 1926). Even if he buys it and gives us $500 apiece in hot or cold cash, it won't be worth the agony I've gone thru on the matter.[17]

The author left no record of the "poor woiking girls' " journals that paid for the rare ritzy dinners on the town, but one of these stories survives. "Matrimonial Bonds" appeared in the March 1926 edition of *Open Door*, the house organ of the Hurt Building in downtown Atlanta. It contains little of literary interest, far less so than either of Mitchell's high-school short stories, and less indeed than most of her newspaper writing; at the same time, the story offers insights into Mitchell's own state in the dismal spring of 1926.[18]

Short, only about 1,700 words, "Matrimonial Bonds" describes, on one level, a typical romance: Nancy Charlestons by, Bill falls in love, and the story chronicles the couples' engagement. On another level, however, it is a feminist tract disguised as a short story. It treats "Bill" and "Nancy" as types—generic males and females—and like so many of the articles and interviews she had produced over the preceding three years, the story defends young women's having their own labor, independence, and integrity. In the same way, if more subtly, it vouches for women's intelligence, knowledge, and self-awareness, in particular contrast to masculine illusions, delusions, and innocence.

Nancy works. She likes her job. It has given her friends and comrades, both male and female; it has instructed her in human relations; it has schooled her in patience, perseverance, and even sympathy; it has taught her financial responsibility; it has allowed her to acknowledge her own integrity and her ability to stand alone in the most difficult circumstances. "Labor" equals "wholeness and vitality" by all these measures, but the alternative makes it all the more attractive. What happens when "an up and coming young person" remains alone all day in a "two by four apartment?" She mopes in depression: "For though mother's work was never done when it came to house cleaning, Nancy's work is done in an hour with the aid of carpet sweepers, dumbwaiters, furnaces and electric appliances that make the apartment shining and new looking in less than no time." She has nothing to do otherwise, "unless she joins a bridge club and learns a lot of gossip or spends all Bill's money at movies."

Bill sees none of this. First of all, he insists that his own mother did not work. "Being a normal boy," the author chides, "it has never occurred to Bill how hard his mother did work—at home." She had no choice except to perform the most arduous, diverse—and unpaid—labor: "whether she liked it or not, she had to cook and sweep and make clothes and swab out little sore throats—and frequently carry in coal and wood and make fires. Oh, no, mother never worked!" Then, too, he believes that working women lead to all sorts of other social dislocations because he vaguely recalls seeing some magazine article about how "so many girls working has broken up the Great American Home and lowered the birth rate alarmingly. Of course all this is high grade applesauce, but Bill, being an innocent boy, doesn't know it." He is innocent, too, of the connection between the vitality of his beloved and her career. "Of course, Nance is the sweetest thing in the world—but Bill believes that he would have preferred to have found her, a little-stay-at-home girl seated with folded hands, hopefully waiting for some one to take her off pap's payroll." In contrast, then, to the girl's intelligence and self-awareness, Bill has no idea of the reality about his fiancée or himself. He cannot acknowledge the truth of things. When the golden wedding anniversary is approaching, maybe: "Yes, when Bill is ninety, he may admit that Nancy's job certainly taught her how to be a good wife—but not till then will he admit it."

While Bill knows none of this, Nancy knows it all: she possesses complete self-knowledge, but recognizes her boyfriend's ignorance as well. That notwithstanding, she prepares to truckle. Leaving her work would make her an exile in her own home, "but, as Bill has the habit of climbing onto a high horse and riding it to a lather every time she mentions the idea, she is willing to give it up." This, then, defines the story's latent theme: the woman's silent knowledge that has no object other than its own satisfaction. If a kind of rational fatalism pervades the tale, the author does allow one (remote) alternative. However much she sets up the wedding and all that surely follows, within the story itself, the author does not bind Nancy and Bill in matrimony.

Bill was no double for John Marsh, and Peggy Mitchell was not Nancy, but the story glitters with biographical data, not least the otherwise odd inclusion of Nancy's conflicts with her mother. Given the resonance of the narrator's voice with the heroine's, "Matrimonial Bonds" also suggests the tensions that Mitchell herself felt as she wrestled with her own destiny as 1926 moved towards summer.

Mitchell was also writing other things in this period, and they illuminate still other of her values in these years. After her death, John Marsh testified that his wife also began a "jazz age novel" while at the *Journal*. "That book was never more than a rough draft," he related. "It was never completely developed, never put into finished form."[19] These remarks take on special significance in the light of a surviving fragment of this or a related story from this time. It consisted of about thirty pages and chronicled "flaming youth" in post-Armistice Atlanta. Although this manuscript survived both Mitchell's and her husband's death, Stephens Mitchell ordered it destroyed in the early sixties. Margaret Baugh, Mitchell's faithful private secretary, read the work before burning it, and it remained fresh in her memory when she wrote a synopsis in 1963:

> The heroine is Pansy Hamilton, daughter of Judge Hamilton, of an old Georgia family. Pansy's mother is an unsympathetic Northern woman. The other characters are Pansy's young friends in Atlanta, and the opening scene gets them into trouble when Pansy and several boys go for an automobile ride. One of the boys is drunk, there is an accident, and he is hurt. They go to a drugstore for help, and find it closed at the late hour. Pansy climbs the side of the building and gets through a small window. There is a description of the store's interior, dark and full of mysterious smells. Pansy finds bandages and antiseptics, manages to get out the window with them, and the young people are talking about how to get the injured boy home without waking his mother when the author abandons the story.[20]

Even in bare plot outline, this tale goes much farther even than "Matrimonial Bonds" in suggesting the author's values. It approaches the autobiographical. If Nancy of the *Open Door* story is hardly Peggy Mitchell's double, Pansy Hamilton is.

Mitchell and her heroine are contemporaries. Both live in postwar Atlanta. Both are scions of legal fathers of old Georgia families through whom they possess inherited wealth and status. Both indulge in wild scrapes and escapades. Even the disparities are revealing.

The most glaring difference between the fictional and real-life flappers involves their mothers. The otherwise nameless Judge Hamilton's wife is a Yankee. Eugene Mitchell's lady, May Belle Stephens, was the daughter of a Confederate captain, the offspring of slave plantations and the planter South, and a loyal Southerner withal, who insisted that her children attend Confederate Memorial Day parades and who sang them to sleep (even if off-key) to songs from Dixie's past. The characterization of "an unsympathetic Northern woman," however, has double reality for Mrs. Eugene Mitchell—and also for Peggy Mitchell's notions of her parent.

If May Belle Mitchell was no Yankee, much about her made her just as foreign in provincial Georgia society. Her religion, her religious politics, her public life, her foreign education, her intense, self-conscious intelligence, all these set her apart. If "Northern" might be read as "different," the characterization of Judge Hamilton's wife begins to fit, and of course, "Yankee" or "Northern" has traditionally been applied to outsiders, not just people of New England birth *per se*. At the same time, "unsympathetic" might as easily be read as "cool," "detached," "objective," and "rationalistic." May Belle Stephens was certainly all those things.

On a more important level, however, the characterization of unsympathetic Northern woman suggests a breach between this character and the flapper protagonist. Other references to women in the story confirm the same idea. A second mother appears in Margaret Baugh's retelling. The tale breaks off with the group's effort to avoid still another vigilant matriarch. Is this other mother an Argus? a sleeping dog? If there is room for a kinder interpretation, the youths are anxious, nonetheless. In any case, mothers in this story are not nurturing figures to whom the children flee for comfort but characters to fear and avoid. In this way, the story recasts essential elements in the author's relationship with her own parent.

If the narrative rejects mothers as unsympathetic, hostile, and foreign to the story line itself, the author presents traditional motherhood in disguise. In Margaret Baugh's retelling, the otherwise wild flapper heroine replicates the nurturing, self-sacrificing figure associated with the classic iconography of mothers. In a crisis, Pansy Hamilton turns nurse and healer. In the process, she also assumes the responsibility of violating the law and of course risking her own safety in entering the drugstore. The attributes of traditional womanhood do not end here. The drugstore episode resonates with all manner of female imagery: the closed door, the small, obscure opening, the emphasis on the description of the interior, "the dark and mysterious smells." More notable still, all these classic womb-related images are also connected with healing. The feminine redeems doubly: the drugstore itself is feminine, and it is the young girl who makes her way in and then reemerges with the healing "secrets" from this mysterious inner sanctum.

The young writer never completed the narrative of "Pansy Hamilton, Flapper Heroine." She did, however, finish another story. Although radically different, it also speaks profoundly of other values that fired the young writer's imagination in 1926. " 'Ropa Carmagin" was that story, and it has its own convoluted history.

As they did the flapper fiction, Mitchell's heirs destroyed " 'Ropa Carmagin," but, far more than with the other story, controversy swirls around this novella. In 1963, Margaret Baugh recalled that she had read it many years before. "It must have been early 1937 (not the early 1940's) that Peggy told me to read the story 'Ropa Carmagin'," the secretary reminisced.

> She knew I was interested. She did not say not to read it "because I have a feeling you will anyway, and I don't want you to have a guilty conscience." She was pretty tactful about handling people. She just said for me to read it and then put it away. It was I who thought that in her understanding of human nature she knew that I would be consumed by

curiosity in it. I was relieved that she did tell me, for it would have been a sore temptation not to have read it.[21]

Baugh then dredged up her own memory of the plot. "All I remember was its Faulkneresque quality and its decayed aristocratic girl in a crumbling old big house and a hint of miscegenation."[22]

Time and carelessness transformed these sketchy memories into something new and strange. The distortion began with Mitchell's first biographer, Finis Farr. He took Baugh's vague memory of twenty-five years before and mixed it with his own invention. "Miss Baugh found the novella of somewhere between 12 and 15,000 words a fascinating story," he began.

> The heroine was Europa Carmagin, a girl whose once good family had come down in the world. Margaret depicted the grim and haunted atmosphere in which the Carmagins lived, the old house, the weed-choked garden, the rotting fences around the worn-out fields. The heroine had character which might have surmounted all this, but her story could not have a happy ending: she was in love with a handsome mulatto. Europa was to remain a shadowy figure. . . .[23]

By such literary sleight of hand, Baugh's vague recollection of "a touch of miscegenation" became the central element of the story—the tragic ending of the heroine's love affair "with a handsome mulatto." This was a touchy area for a biographer to interject his own interpretations, and even worse to present them as fact. Mitchell's later biographer, Anne Edwards, spun her own version of the tale, giving it fanciful dates and facts and a specific Georgia locale, while confirming the interracial theme.[24] However ill-founded this interpretation, others picked up these sad, romantic themes, and standard elements in the imagery of the South, and turned them into an entire thesis about Mitchell's latent fascination with black men.[25] Mitchell had her obsessions, but they did not include this category of folk. Such fancied racial interpretations utterly obscure the real story of " 'Ropa Carmagin" and its significance for Margaret Mitchell's biography.

What was the story really about? Both contemporary and modern evidence answer the question. At least three people read the novella in 1935; two recorded their opinions about the story; one described the plot.

In April 1935, when the distracted young writer slammed all the scattered chapters of her then-unnamed epic into a giant pile and carted them off furiously to the hotel room of the Macmillan editor Harold Latham, she had included, willy-nilly, the sixty-page novella she had written ten years before. Soon after, Latham read it and waxed as enthusiastic as he had about the epic. "It seems to me a splendid piece of work, expertly done," he told her. "It confirms my very high opinion of you as a writer—if that needed confirmation—and shows you can handle more than one type of material and character."[26] Mitchell's friend at Macmillan, Lois Cole, discovered the manuscript on her own and praised it even more fully. "This is one of the most effective pieces of writing I have ever read, and I would be proud of you for that if for nothing else," she told the author. "You have done a beautiful job on it and some day it should come out. . . . The story is too fine to go to any but the best." In the process of praising the tale and discussing its future, Cole also revealed the content. "Why don't you enter your ghost story in the Little Brown novelette contest?" she had written.[27]

Lois Cole left still other evidence about the story. When Finis Farr raised the subject in 1963, he jogged her memory, and she recalled having heard the story the first time in the Mitchell-Marsh apartment. They were all sitting around The Dump telling ghost stories, she related, and their young friend from Alabama, Harvey Smith, first shared the tale with them. Mitchell took his story and reworked it into " 'Ropa Carmagin."[28] While Mitchell's version of the tale is lost, Harvey Smith's original survives in manuscript, and it confirms Lois Cole's recollection of Mitchell's narrative.[29] Without anything to do with race or miscegenation, it contained other elements that beguiled the writer. The tale was Southern gothic. It hinged on regional eccentrics, Dixie decadence, and not least, superannuated virgins in crumbling mansions.

In Harvey Smith's version of the story, 'Ropa Carmagin was India Finch, a real-life person out in the countryside near Opelika, Alabama, where his family had lived for generations. The Finches were trashy locals who had fallen low in the world. Miss India lived with her brothers, but she had locked herself in her upstairs room and never left for any reason. She showed herself only at the upstairs window, where she indulged herself in "the brushing of her long snow white hair while leaning on the window above the porch every night except in the rain." India Finch died in great agony and wretched filth, and the nature of her passing added horror to her story. The abandonment of the old Finch place exaggerated her legend and turned the old woman into a supernatural spirit and the ruined dwelling into a haunted house. This was the substance of Harvey Smith's story: his boyhood discovery in an evening thunderstorm of India Finch's ghost.

The narrative of the Finches possessed all the earmarks of a great story—mystery, horror, awe, and pity. The specific elements of the narrative, however, struck the strongest chords in Margaret Mitchell's life.

First, the crumbling mansions. Even at the twentieth century's closing, abandoned houses still dot the Southern landscape. They were far more common four generations ago. Rich Yankees might have bought up some and restored their elegance; some few others might have survived, even been retained by the original family. These were excep-

tions. Every rural district, most villages, and even towns had their hulks
with doors flapping against the wind, shutters hanging loose from rusty
hinges, rooms filled with refuse, fireplaces heaped with droppings from
chimney swifts, and even tall columns lying burst like overripe melons
in the yard amid straggled boxwood hedges. And if the house was lucky,
some snaggle-toothed, coveralled tenant might have witched off fire-
wielding vandals.[30] For generations of Southerners, such places were
the very essence of the South and constant reminders of a thwarted
past. Ancient houses gone to wrack and ruin—the theme obsessed the
movement. Faulkner made them art: the abandoned mansion of *Sanctuary* now the hangout for bootleggers, bandits and perverts; Sutpen's
Hundred of his *Absalom, Absalom!* whose ghosts finally sent it up in
flames; or the otherwise haunted and perverted estate in *Light in August* with its mad once-virgin.

These physical relics of the past fascinated Margaret Mitchell no less
than William Faulkner. She was, wrote Harvey Smith, "intensely interested in such old places and derived a strong nostalgic and romantic pleasure out of the abandoned and half ruined old hulks." Their art
or architecture failed to interest her; rather, she concentrated on their
"derelict state" and "the implied commentary it bore on the civilization that meant so much to her."[31] It also exerted a perverse attraction, akin to her delicious excitement over the obscene graffitti in the
trash-strewn home of the late U.S. Senator Rebecca Felton. Trooping
about the Georgia countryside, Mitchell and Harvey Smith had discovered Mrs. Felton's house in Rockdale County. Its walls boasted a spectacular graffitto: a man as plow, his colossal erection turning the fur-
row. She derived endless pleasure from the juxtaposition of the mythic
obsenity and the lady senator's parlor.[32] Such literal decadence appalled and thrilled her simultaneously.

The stuff of Sutpen's Hundred and all the rest, ancient mansions
gone to ruin provided the same commentary on Southern history to
Margaret Mitchell as to William Faulkner; still, as a woman, she found
other meanings in ruined homes and faltering family lines. Who, she
might have queried, was responsible for domestic order? Was there
any question? Was it even necessary to ask? In her old newspaper article "Just Like a Woman," she had reflected on disorder in the home
and acknowledged ruefully the guilt and shame. If she considered mess
on a cosmic scale, the rule still applied. Society held women accountable for the home's disorder, she judged, whether justly so or not. Patriarchal values affirmed the grander version of women's responsibilities: women were the sacred vessels that carried the order of tradition.
If that vessel cracked, then order and tradition failed. And if tradition
failed and if families faltered, the fault, perforce, had to lie with womankind. The congruence, then, between the images of decaying houses,
domestic disorder, regional declension, and the girl gone bad is no co-

incidence at all, whether Caddy Compson, Temple Drake, or 'Ropa Carmagin, or the girls of Peggy Mitchell's own generation. Were such young women the cause or the effect of the decline? The distinction between cause and effect collapsed. For Peggy Mitchell, Harvey's story forcefully delineated the mysterious dilemma about women, history, and the social order in the old Confederacy.

Harvey's tale had another appeal. As much as crumbling mansions, superannuated virgins also fascinated the Generation of 1900. Faulkner depicted the standard gallery in Emily, Miss Jennie, Miss Rosa, Judith, and Clytie. Even so, the image of the ancient virgin in a crumbling dwelling possessed the most intensely personal meaning for Margaret Mitchell, and the most specific reference to her mother. This was the very stuff of the most memorable single episode of her life, the affair when her mother took her out the Jonesboro road to hector her about women's fate and women's hope. On the road that sweltering day, May Belle Mitchell had pointed out the desecrated gardens and ruined homes of once-great families. She had scorned the aging, china-painting virgins whose lives these crumbling hulks imprisoned. 'Ropa Carmagin was no more than these ancient belles *in extremis*. By the same measure, however, this ancient hag represented the child herself, grown old, dependent, and helpless, her mother's and her own nightmare now materialized. In this old madwoman in the attic—this transformed once-belle—Margaret Mitchell could see herself as projected in her mother's somber mirror. Prophesying this awful future and dreadful fate for her own child, however, May Belle Mitchell had become a witch herself, with all her threats and dire warnings. In reflecting on this episode, Mitchell might well have chanted, "Maid, Mother, Witch. Which was which? Which was which?"

Margaret Munnerlyn Mitchell's own caldron brimmed and boiled as winter gave way to spring and summer in 1926. She was conjuring her own images. Meanwhile, her fictions fought for place with John, with Angus Perkerson, with her sense of wifely duty, and with her own flesh. But the flesh returned the favor. Life was terrible. Citing her bad foot, she quit work officially in May, but she kept a small income of her own by freelance writing. For most of the summer, she continued to produce the *Journal* Magazine's gossip column, "Elizabeth Bennet," which her old nemesis Frances Newman had initiated four years or so before. It entailed spending hours on the telephone picking up tidbits of society news from the Driving Club set. She loathed it. By August her life staggered towards a turning point. In August she gave up her professional work entirely. Then the real horrors began.

XI

Labor Pains

❖❖❖❖

> I can hardly tell for I began it at least ten years ago and have forgotten my reasons. . . . I vaguely recall that I just sat down and began to write a book to occupy my time. And after I finished it and was able to walk again, I put the book away and forgot about it for years.[1]
>
> MARGARET MITCHELL

*T*he last half of 1926 made the dreadful first half seem almost idyllic. The next three years were no better.

Mitchell's story "Matrimonial Bonds" had dealt with the issue of how a "woman of leisure" occupied her time—or not. Mitchell anticipated her own situation. Her "two by four apartment" required little care. Then, too, she had servants (Loula Tolbert, and then later Bessie Berry) to cook and clean. Another (Carrie) did the wash. How did the mistress of this establishment pass her days with nothing else to occupy her time after she left off all employment in August 1926? She read, for one thing.

The author's confinement in the summer of 1926 only exacerbated her old obsession with reading. "As a reader, Peggy was omnivorous and all through the years I knew her went to the library from one to three times a week and never came away with less books than she could carry. Of these she skimmed through many and read many," her friend Harvey Smith recalled.[2] Queried about her friend's favorite things, Lethea Turman replied immediately, "Books—Books—Books."[3] Long afterward, old co-workers at the *Journal* remember her lost in some volume or other while she waited for her husband after work. She filled her valise with numerous volumes whenever she went away on vacation, and she haunted hotel libraries and local bookstores once she began her holidays. She read in transit, too. She made funny stories, for example, about riding the trolley line with her nose buried in one tome or another. She related one such tale to the old Atlanta newspaperwoman Julia Collier Harris. "I used to ride the car to town with your husband quite frequently, and I always had about ten books in my arms," she began.

> I was dreadfully anxious to impress him with my erudition but it never failed that when he sat down beside me and took a peek at my arm load the titles of my books were "The Corpse in Cold Storage," "A Scream in the Night," "The Clutching Claw." Sometimes I ardently wished I could have swallowed them. Not that I am ashamed of my passion for low murder stories, but I did so want to impress him! On the days when I was lugging "Excavations in Ur of the Chaldees" did he get on the car? Never. When I was laden down with "Records of the War of the Rebellion" (each book weighs three pounds) did he come and sit by me? Never. But just let me have a cargo of mystery murder stories and he popped up and grinned and said "Aha! Ruining your mind again with cheap mysteries!"[4]

If she read feverishly when well, her sickness encouraged her escape to literature. Her husband left his own picture of his life with an invalid bibliomaniacal insomniac that fall. When the foot gave out, he said,

> one of my jobs was keeping her supplied with reading matter. Which was quite a job—first, because she had already read so many books, and second because she reads so rapidly. Picture me if you can—as we used to say in the Kentucky legislature—digging through the library shelves, trying to find something she hadn't read, lugging home ten or a dozen books at night and lugging them back the next morning—because half of them she had previously read and the other half she devoured during the night.[5]

Her innumerable letters overflow with literary references, no more so than in this dreadful season of 1926. "As you gather, I do little else but read," she summarized her life to Frances Marsh that summer:

> By this time I've gotten fed up on fiction. John brings home large armfuls of books from the library and recently we've had everything from Lombroso's "Female Offenders" to the "Casting Away of Mrs. Lecks and Mrs. Aleshine." Also the "Tertium Organum" and Frank Harris' "Confessions of Oscar Wilde." Did you ever read the "Organum"? You must, if you haven't. I must be ignorant, not to have read it long e'er this. Next to Ring Lardner's "I Gaspari" (The Upholsters") it is the most humorous thing I've read in years. And did you read "Microbe Hunters"? We both

liked it so much. And I know, being an ex-young intellectual, that I shouldn't have liked "Show Boat" but I read it in the magazine install-ments with my tongue hanging out. . . . Last night after reading Cabell's latest story in the Mercury, John read me Revelations (not one of the MacFadden publications, but the Bible). . . . I was fascinated by it all because it was so much like the hallucinations of acute alcoholism and paresis. . . .[6]

As here, discussing one book or literary subject triggered her recol-lection of another author or volume—and off she went. In 1928 she related how a novel about witches prompted her to check out an an-thropological study of witchcraft; and with the gates of her reading open, she pressed on to describe the other books she had been poring through: Stephen Benét's *John Brown's Body*, which she had read twice herself and listened to twice being read aloud; Louis Bromfield's *Annie Spragg*, which she described as"Norman Douglas out of Thornton Wil-der"; and finally Donn Brynn's *Destiny Bay*.[7] When someone asked her about *Tobacco Road*, she shot back with another string of references: "When I read it I thought it was intended for a grand parody on the gloomy Russian novelists and I laughed almost as much as I did over *Gentlemen Prefer Blondes*." So here they are: her old co-worker Red Caldwell cheek-by-jowl with Anita Loos and Dostoyevsky; Frank Har-ris and Oscar Wilde embracing Ring Lardner and St. John on Patmos; anthropological treatises on witches colliding with poetic fictions of the Civil War, the plays of Thornton Wilder careering through the night with mannered novels of British café society, running smack up against the White Russian P. D. Ouspensky's bizarre ruminations on "the third canon of thought: a key to the enigmas of the world."

As 1926 ran its course, however, her temper soon ruined even liter-ature for her. Fiction failed to sate her appetite by summer. Even the nonfiction soon palled. And with that she nearly went insane. It was a godawful time. "Just at present I'm about as pleasant to live with as a porcupine or a snapping turtle," she exploded to her sister-in-law in August just as she floundered into her new leisured status. She wanted Frances to stay with them awhile, she professed, but the prospect seemed impossible. Neither she nor John altogether trusted her ability to han-dle visitors just then. The furiously frustrated writer made it only half a joke:

My disposition wears so thin that I even quarrelled with Aggie Deerborn and Peggy Porter—unheard of happenings and then John would become frightened lest I lure you South just when you were in your most loving and helpful mood, sink my fangs in the fleshy part of your leg. And then you'd butt me over the head with a portable typewriter and go North to inform the family that I had an ingrowing disposition.[8]

It was less than half a joke. She was raging. It was about this time that she had a terrible explosion with her oldest friend, Courtenay Ross McFedyen. Court had heard about Mitchell's illness and stopped by with flowers. She found the apartment door ajar, walked in, and proffered her roses. "Peggy slammed them on the floor, stamped her foot and shouted at me to get out and never come back." The completely astonished friend retreated sheepishly and did not return for years.[9]

Furious at the world, bitterly unsatisfied, and consumed by pain, the young matron stewed in her own bile as fall turned cold and winter loomed. At some point in this gloomy season, she turned once again to her own fiction. She began to write a novel about the Civil War.

Why did she write? When did she first put words to paper? What was her inspiration? What ambition did she hold for the manuscript? How did she conceive of plot and characters? At the time, she revealed nothing to anyone about any of this. She commenced in complete secrecy. Secrecy, indeed, is the very first, even primal characteristic of her writing. If the story of *Gone with the Wind* is now a part of the common heritage of English speakers everywhere on the planet, its contemporary popularity is matched only by the obscurity in which the author herself conceived and executed the novel and the mystery with which she later surrounded its origins. The story of the novel, then, begins with understanding the author's pervasive desire for concealment.

She had a fetish about privacy. Even as a child, her brother testified, "Margaret always fiercely resented being asked what she was doing, had done or was about to do."[10] For the child grown up, novel-writing elicited the trait's extremest forms. "I not only did not ask anyone to assist me but I fought violently against letting even close friends read as much as a line," she told her special friend Herschel Brickell in 1936.[11] She spoke truly. Medora Perkerson had no inkling of the novel's existence. Nor did Augusta Dearborn. News of the epic flabbergasted her old newspaper friend Frank Daniel, who had been in and out of her apartment during the entire time.[12] Her faithful housekeeper Bessie Berry saw her constantly at her typewriter. She never asked what her employer was doing, and Mitchell never volunteered. "I was with Miss Mitchell at the time this wonderful book was started," Bessie Berry related afterward, "but she made such little noise I thought she was only writing a letter to a friend."[13] The author never corrected the impression. She could not, however, hide her labor completely from others. She liked to work best in the mornings, her brother testified, and her madcap flapper girlfriends—without jobs, families, or domestic responsibilities—often barged in to discover her pecking away at her manuscript. Julia Memminger often surprised her at her work. Mitchell gave her nothing to satisfy her curiosity:

She'd be typing and we'd all barge in—unannounced, as always! She would get up, but then we'd say, "We'll pull out because you are writing the Great American Novel and we don't want to be around to get in your way." If she talked a lot about the war and history and all, she wouldn't talk about her writing ever.[14]

Harvey Smith, another intimate, learned of the novel late and even then knew nothing of the plot. She held her tongue around other intimates as well. Lois Cole's experience was typical. A fellow Smith alumna, this Yankee girl had come south to work for the local office of the Macmillan Publishing Company. She met Mitchell through Medora Perkerson, but the two soon became friends on their own. Although they spent much time together, Cole had only the vaguest idea of her companion's labors. Like Julia Memminger, only by coming over completely unannounced one morning did Cole discover her friend aspired to writing fiction.

Once when I came in with a friend, Peggy, in shorts, blouse, and eyeshade, was at the typewriter. She got up and threw a bath towel over the table. "Well, Peggy," said the friend, "how's the great American novel coming along?" "It stinks," Peggy said with a half laugh, "and I don't know why I bother with it, but I've got to do something with my time."[15]

From other evidence, Cole inferred the subject concerned Atlanta and the Civil War. Mitchell barely confirmed even this information.

The bath towel hid the writing. The careless laugh did so even more effectively. Indeed, laughter became the most critical means by which Mitchell obscured her work, especially after news of its existence seeped out among her intimates. If anyone ever asked specific questions between 1926 and 1935, she always brushed them off with a joke or smile as she had Lois Cole. Her mysterious work, indeed, became a minor joke within her circle. It was "the Great American Novel" to them, and, like her constant ailments and anxieties about money, it served as a subject of affectionate mockery. Elinor Hillyer captured some spirit of the jest. "Anytime you met Peggy downtown or on the street car she was always just coming from or just going to the Carnegie Library to 'do research on the Great American Novel.' The phrase was good for a laugh any time. Lots of people were doing the Great American Novel. We once took a poll at a party to see how many."[16] Yes, the joke proved far more effective than a closet full of towels in disguising the writer's epic labors.

In his recollections of his aunt, Jane Austen's nephew related how his famous relative worked under much the same circumstances more than a century before. Without a study of her own, Austen used the family common room to write. Interrupted regularly, she forbade her nephew to oil the door into the chamber. She wanted warning. She hid her work whenever anyone approached. The sound of squeaking hinges signaled her to thrust her "small pieces of ivory" on which she wrote beneath her sewing or to secure them in some other safe place. The Atlanta writer hid her work even more insistently.

Mitchell's obsessive secrecy was all the more notable, given the physical and social circumstances of her life as she began to write. The Dump as she had christened her apartment on Crescent Court, did not lend itself to privacy. The building had been a private home and later owners had divided it into ten small units. It was not an attractive place to live; the turnover was high, and apartments were often vacant. The Marshes occupied Number One, perhaps the largest, with a total area of rather less than eighty feet by twenty, counting partitions and dead space. The Marshes' front door opened from a semi-public hallway directly into the living room. With its sofa, two easy chairs, and shelves of books, this roughly fifteen-by-fifteen space abutted a hallway with bath and closets on each side to the rear. The bedroom lay just behind, and in shotgun fashion the kitchen and service area lay behind that. These tight quarters had no extra room, and Mitchell could claim no special area for her own. Harvey Smith remembered that in all the years he visited in the apartment between 1925 and 1932 the writer maintained no regular location for her typewriter at all. She made do. She created one unlikely office in the living room. At the front, beneath minuscule windows, the Dump possessed a tiny alcove made by ranks of shelves on each side. She set up her original "study" here. Her workshop consisted of her portable Remington typewriter on an old-fashioned sewing table. But even this small corner proved both temporary and inadequate. As her reams of copy grew, this altogether public area could not hold it all, and she abandoned it for another, somewhat remoter, space when she set up her work table right by the kitchen, or alternately in the tiny hallway between the living room in the front and the bedroom. At one time, she even lugged her typewriter and sewing table into the bedroom itself.[17]

Even in the remotest corner, a thousand distractions broke her concentration. The jangling telephone regularly brought news of some fresh pains and problems among her family or friends, and she considered herself on call for every fainting heart and wounded spirit. Beginning in 1925, her father ventured regularly in and out of the hospital and his sickbed at home. She attended every rise in his temperature or fall in his spirits. Steve married in 1927, and those nuptial festivities played merry havoc with her schedules. Within a year of the festivities, Carrie Lou Mitchell began a difficult pregnancy that culminated in a miscarriage and severe depression. The writer dropped her work to attend her sister-in-law. Strings of visitors broke into her work time, too. The two sets of Marshes called at length in 1928; so did John's old girlfriend, Kitty Mitchell Hill. This former flame came with her family, and before she left, the novelist admitted, she had played nurse even to one of this woman's sickly offspring. But even without guests from out of town, she rarely worked without interruption. Her myriad friends never hesitated to pop by when they needed company. Harvey often dropped in on his way home from his Tech classes. Sometimes she could hear Annie Couper's voice all the way out in the street. Julia Memminger and Peggy Porter gave no more warning of a visit than their rapping on the door or the sound of merry laughter at the entrance. Her servants—first the rough and hearty Loula Tolbert, and then later the very refined "black jewel" of her household, Bessie Berry (later Jordan)—admitted them all with an exchange of pleasantries. Those small conversations usually allowed Mitchell time to hide her work or disguise her concentration at her makeshift office.

In the most extreme manifestation of the writer's obsessive secrecy, Mitchell revealed little of what she was doing even to her faithful spouse. In 1936, the rumor circulated that John had actually co-authored the novel. The allegation deeply offended her. "My husband had nothing whatever to do with it. . . . In fact, he never even read the whole of the manuscript until after the Macmillan Company had bought it," she protested. In explaining how he could not possibly have helped her, she also described the way she worked. "It was not that I didn't want him to read it," she explained.

> It was because the book was not written with the second chapter following the first, and the third following the second. It was written last chapter first and so on until the first chapter was written last—written in fact several months after the book was sold. My husband could not be expected to catch the continuity of the story when I could only give him scattered chapters to read, which to him, did not connect up.[18]

Mitchell herself allowed John Marsh one role in the creation of her book. In 1936 she initiated the story that she had begun her novel only at her husband's badgering. After "three years" (her chronology) of "lying there thinking I'd never walk again," she had exhausted the potential of the city library—not to mention her husband's physical strength in lugging books home for her to read. "Finally," she related, "he brought home a pound or so of copy paper and said, 'Write a book. I can't find anything at the Carnegie that you haven't read, except books on the exact sciences.' "[19] Perhaps unaware that his own beloved had first circulated this story, John Marsh himself disallowed even this part for himself. It was simply one more instance of his wife's "embroidering." He encouraged her, but only in the most general way. He met his wife's ambitions and anxieties, indeed, with no specifics at all, but with his general and persistent encouragement in the face of her near-debilitating fears.

When she finished the book, he participated in its polishing; until 1930, however, beyond his moral support, John Marsh played no role in his wife's writing. Besides the author's own compulsions, the nature of their marriage and of both their personalities militated against any such activity. In the first place, John Marsh lacked curiosity, and he had no disposition to plunge into her affairs. Indeed, his wife considered this one of his greatest merits. She bragged about his willingness to let her mind her own business. He involved himself only when she asked. She seldom did; certainly not before 1930 when she was essentially done.

For her part, various circumstances guaranteed her reluctance to request his aid or share her "burdens" with him. He held a difficult job with a rough and long work schedule; it often demanded his presence out of town at conventions, tours, and other business. With the most abysmal energy level and his constant, nagging aches and pains, he flirted constantly with physical collapse. With any stress his old bad stomach revolted, and the late twenties marked a particularly difficult time for him under his difficult and heavy-drinking supervisor, Kelly Starr. In the best of times, he trudged home from the Georgia Power and Light Company only to eat and then collapse in bed. In bad times, he called in sick and never left the apartment. To give him more responsibilities would have violated his wife's fundamental sense of him, of herself, and of their peculiar partnership. Asking or requiring him to read or oversee her work, or sharing her burdens of writing with him went completely against her nature. "I have always hoped that J would be able to help me but it seems no less than brutal to shove a job of copy reading and criticism on him at night when he is always so exhausted so I guess I'll have to go it alone till it's all finished—if ever—and then let him do a wholesale butchering," she wrote in 1928, in one of the exceedingly rare references to her work while she was actually creating it.[20]

The reference to "wholesale butchery" introduces another reason for her reluctance to share her manuscript with John Marsh: she dreaded the prospect of his red pencil. Later, in a letter to her publisher, she joked about the "mortification" his expert criticisms entailed.

> My husband is not only a boss advertisement writer but he was formerly that rare creature, a newspaper reporter who knew the difference between 'a shambles' and a 'holocaust.' He also had a feeling for words and a feeling that there was an exact word for an exact meaning. And before that, he was a professor of English at the University of Kentucky. I fear that nothing you or your advisers could say would be quite as hard boiled as what he has already said to me.[21]

The author fabricated the picture of "John the Butcher." It contained far less of the benign John Marsh than of the wife herself and the anxieties that she projected onto the husband-critic. The husband himself recognized her predisposition, and felt helpless before her fears. "Long ago I discovered that anything uncomplimentary I might say was accepted 100%," Marsh himself remarked, "but just let me be complimentary, especially about the book and it was discounted as affectionate flattery. ('Just the old fashioned wife who laughed with delight and trembled with fear at his frown')," he added half-ironically.[22]

If Mitchell hid her work as she created it from her closest friends and kin, she obscured its origins just as insistently after its success. She did so then less by refusing to reveal anything about the novel than by circulating the most divergent tales about the work. The welter of publicity that accompanied her book's success elicited from her the most contradictory statements about the fundamental details of her novel's origins.

For a person who took great pride in her memory and who possessed truly phenomenal powers of recall, Mitchell provided the fuzziest and most conflicting recollections of the chronology of her novel-writing when she reconstructed that time afterward. Her earliest letters about her novel reveal an almost whimsical disregard for facts behind her decision to write. She offered various chronologies, even to the same correspondent. "I began the book about eight years ago, I think," she ruminated in April 1936. That dated the beginning as 1928; but she strained to think: "It was after I left the Journal and after I married John in 1925 but I can't quite place the date." On she rambled in the first version of the story for this particular correspondent:

> It was while I had a bad ankle and was on crutches. I couldn't walk for a couple of years so I put in my time writing this book. When my foot got well, I stopped writing because walking seemed far more interesting. I didn't finish the book and it just lay around the house. I never sent it to any publishers because, to be quite frank, I didn't think much of it.[23]

If one reference dates the beginning of her writing to roughly 1928, the second puts it closer to 1929. Within two months of mailing these epistles, she provided different chronologies to other correspondents. As the dates changed, the motives shifted, too. When and why did she begin? "I can hardly tell for I began it at least ten years ago and have forgotten my reasons," she explained to an admirer early in the summer of 1936. "I vaguely recall that I just sat down and began to write a book to occupy my time. And after I finished it and was able to walk again, I put the book away and forgot about it for years."[25] "To save explanations, I usually say, 'Oh, ten years,' " she told another inquirer. "But that's really not true. I began it in 1926 and except for three chapters it was completed by 1929." She summarized various delays she encountered in her writing and concluded that, had she been able to square off and write full-time, "I could have done the book in a year." "It's hard to explain all of this to the casual questioner so I usually say 'Oh, ten years,' and let it go at that," she concluded.[26]

Three years? Ten years? One year? 1926? 1928? 1929? She left a tangle of evidence. By 1942, the impression of Mitchell as a Ouija-board writer had taken permanent hold on the popular imagination, and she told a different story entirely. She now presented the decade-long labor as a fact, and she groaned about readers' failure to believe the arduousness of crafting her epic. Writing another newsman-friend in Tennessee at that time, she complained, "I had a hard time convincing people that I worked about ten years on *Gone with the Wind*."[27] With right good cause she had such difficulty: she had by then spent a decade and a half obscuring the true story of her novel-writing.

Besides secrecy and concealment, a second theme dominated the creation of her book. At the time and afterward, she never failed to associate her fiction with disease and suffering. While physical disability, of course, was an inseparable part of her existence, at least after 1919, writing evoked the strongest associations of all with physical torment. Even more than secrecy, pain is critical to understanding the nature of her decision to write, her attitude towards her craft, how she wrote, what she finally produced, and finally, even when she began. Her aliments hid the work; her work covered the disease.

First of all, it was only physical disability, she insisted, that had driven her to write in the first place: that "broken ankle that would not heal," disabilities that prohibited her riding to work downtown or even holding a telephone receiver with comfort. Here, then, emerges the sequence of events. Her ankle went bad in the spring of 1926. She quit her regular job in May. She freelanced three additional months for Angus Perkerson. For two or three more months she read like a maniac; and then, just about the time of her birthday, bored and anxious beyond endurance, she put her first words to paper. Although she protested to the world that she was twenty-four, on November 8 she began her twenty-seventh year. And what she wrote first was the conclusion. If the author circulated the most various tales about the chronologies and origins of her novel, she never varied her testimony of having begun her epic with the composition of the last chapter, and the content of that chapter confirms the special anguish and torment—physical as well as mental—that racked her in those glowering days of late November 1926.

That chapter begins, and ends, with virtually unrelieved disaster: a fitting measure of her mood when she commenced. It opens with news of Melanie Wilkes's death. A deflated and miserable Rhett Butler receives the solemn tidings. "She is dead?" he asks. Scarlett nods speechless affirmation. "A very great lady," he reflects. "She was the only

completely kind person I ever knew."[28] The quintessential good mother
has died, and she has died specifically *as* a mother—from a miscarriage. Rhett grieves; but so does Scarlett, as she acknowledges (for the
first time, as it turns out) her profound attachment to the deceased.
This first disaster in the chapter anticipates a second. With Melanie's
death, Scarlett recognizes her love for Ashley Wilkes has died as well.
As her old obsession with Ashley disintegrates, Scarlett discovers she
has loved Rhett all along. A third fatal revelation follows. As Scarlett
flies to Rhett and reveals her heart, he renounces his devotion. His love
has withered as completely as her affection for Ashley. In the course of
explaining why he cannot love her anymore, Rhett also recaps and
chronicles the disasters of their relationship—the tragedies, of course,
of the yet-unwritten book to come. The list is long: It includes still
another death, of their child Bonnie, but also the smaller pains—Scarlett's cruelty, his own thwarted affection, the perpetual "cross purposes" of their existence, and finally his inability to sustain his wife's
insatiable needs any longer. In this dire chronicle, Rhett retains no
passion from their old relationship and no feelings at all except pity,
kindness, and perhaps contempt. He is already detached from her
completely, then, by the time he abandons their marriage and leaves
her physically. This is the chapter's natural ending on page 1,035, Rhett
Butler's quiet, sad, and factual response to his wife's longing: "My dear,
I don't give a damn."

The book "opens," then, with a chronicle of horrors—death, abandonment, rejection, alienation, smashed hopes, and fatal misunderstanding. And this was the last for which the first was made. A reporter described Mitchell's objective with a telling metaphor:

> Anyone practiced in the drudgery of reading newspapers must under-
> stand by now that the ritual of a reporter is to announce first, with mar-
> velous effect, that someone was killed and then, as a sort of afterthought
> to go along and describe the events leading up to that tragic first para-
> graph. . . . So Margaret Mitchell, with all those hundreds of pages of
> "Gone with the Wind" marshalled in platoons in her orderly mind, sat
> down and wrote her climax first. Then she started her process of describ-
> ing the events leading up to the tragedy.
> . . . She understood thoroughly just what the book was to be from the
> beginning to end. Then she wrote the various chapters as she felt in the
> mood.[29]

"That someone was killed": from the outset, the author conceived of
the ending as both final and unhappy. That "beginning," marked by
its famous losses and bereavement—of husband, child, companion, lover,
and even surrogate mother in Melanie Wilkes—reflected the author's
grim passions in that horror-shrouded season of the fall of 1926. It was
little wonder she desired concealment and disguise.

She began in pain, and her literary production absorbed her hurt, but disease persisted through the entire course of her writing. Even when the ankle healed or seemed to heal, other ailments appeared to take its place, or the new hurts simply coexisted with the old. And almost invariably, the author connected them one way or another, in some primary or secondary relationship, to her writing. One letter to her sister-in-law, Frances Marsh Zane, illustrates the relationship in her own mind between her writing and her illnesses over the two-year span of some of her most intense endeavors, between the fall of 1926 and 1928.

Towards the end of 1928, Frances Zane had sent John and Peggy a warm letter than included an essay she had written about her childhood in Mayesville, Kentucky. The letter triggered a powerful train of associations for the novelist, then in the middle of her most concentrated period of writing. Mitchell took her sister-in-law's literary recollections of small-town Kentucky, related it to her own childhood experiences in a similar small town, Jonesboro, and then transposed Jonesboro to the Fitzgerald plantation nearby. She did not mention that these places were at the heart of her own story. Skipping this logical item in the sequence, she moved on instead to a fresh chronicle of new physical disabilities. Only after this intervening catalogue of illnesses did she turn to the subject of her own literary labors. Underlining the psychological implications (and sources) of this progression, she began by saying she was digging into her own past as "a child digs . . . in such things."

Once started, then, on she rushed. "Speaking of writing," she began, "I'm expecting to be able to write again shortly. I can't write in long hand and for nearly two years the type writer has been out of the question due to the injury to my breast, received when I caromed against the sharp point of the bed one evening." That injury in that ghastly fall of 1926, she feared, had given her breast cancer, and only after two years did she feel some release of anxiety. "The none too attractive spectre of cancer and operation which has been hanging over 979 Crescent Ave. has been about dispelled," she bubbled finally in 1928. Some of the original disability, however, still remained, she insisted: "the breast has a way of getting sore if I use my left arm and shoulder to any great extent (painting walls, waxing floors, even dancing, etc.) but I guess another six months will see me absolutely okay (knock on wood)." From this discussion of breast cancer she hurtled forward without a break, not even of a comma or a period, to her book—"I'm throwing away the two former MSS of my novel and starting fresh, as after two years the errors seem so numerous, the style so crude and the characterization so unmotivated and childish."[30]

Here it was then: She had given herself breast cancer, she had determined, in the middle of the broken-ankle time of 1926; for two years afterward, she had lived in constant dread of a malignancy, and this supposed malignancy, of course, had affected her ability to write. Her breast pained her too severely to use the typewriter, so she had composed laboriously by hand. But what she produced proved inalterably "childish." The child was digging, but she shoveled up fresh pain. Pain: childhood: writing: memory; childhood: memory: writing: pain—the sequence might have changed, but the associations never failed.

If her body intervened to stop her writing, she fought back to continue the project anyway. Her flesh swore vengeance against her will. This struggle lay at the very heart of the creation of her fiction: the imperative to write clashing perpetually with the rejection of her creation. The battle never subsided.

The terror of self-induced malignancy lifted in the fall of 1928, but still other ailments crowded into the breach. In the late spring or early summer of 1929, she had been at novel-writing for two and a half years. Her nerves tormented her even more furiously as she approached the completion of the manuscript. More pain, more anxiety oppressed her flesh and spirit. Her raw nerves had cost her the companionship of Peggy Porter, Augusta Dearborn, and Court McFedyen in 1926; she feared the same results in the summer of 1929 with her friend Harvey Smith. He had embarked for Europe at this time, and as he had departed without a word, she feared she had offended him. She considered her agitation cause enough for a friend's pique, "for my state of mind about the time you left town was nothing short of manic. I never hope to have jitters quite so badly again," she informed him. "I had seen so much sickness that I felt sick myself and couldn't think or talk of much else, even though those thoughts were the ones I most wanted to avoid. I'm sure I was a care and a bore to every one and, thank Heaven, I'm about over them."

Her "manic depression," as she described it, however, shaded once more into somatic dysfunction, once again with direct consequences for her art. "My writing," she continued immediately, "goes so slowly as to be almost imperceptible. After the jitters came a spell of pleurisy which made writing impossible and now that I'm trying again, it seems sillier and siller."[31]

She never thought of writing without pain. In addition to her own agonies, however, she associated the disease of others with her book as well. As in her letter to Harvey Smith in 1929, her physical ailments, her mental anguish, her friends' needs, and the tortures of writing all flowed together into one ghastly river in her mind. In fame she explained it all to a curious reader.

> I labored under considerable difficulties with my writing. For one thing I have a large number of friends and kin to whom I am devoted and for five years there wasn't a day that some one of them wasn't in the hospital

with babies, gall stones, automobile accidents, etc. Once I counted up that for eight months I spent every day in a hospital by a sick bed. You can imagine how little work I did during that time. Then I was crippled for four years with arthritis with no expectation of ever walking again— but I walk nicely now, thank you! And for months my hands were too stiff and swollen to touch a typewriter. So there were months between the writing of one chapter and another—years between the writing of some of them. I suppose if I could have squared off and had days without hospitals calling me that my friends were dying, I could have done the book in a year.[32]

If Mitchell ached constantly while she wrote and if she projected her anguish into the text itself, pain came into play in still another aspect of her writing. The actual processes and techniques she followed tormented her, even as they mirrored and extended the pain that had driven her to write in the first place.

Mitchell wrote with tremendous intensity and commitment, both in terms of getting masses of words on paper in a given period, and in striving constantly for the exact word, phrase, expression, or effect she wanted. "Writing is a hard job for me. . . . Night after night I have labored and labored and have wound up with no more than two pages," she told an early interviewer-friend. "After reading those efforts on the morning after, I have whittled and whittled until I had no more than six lines salvaged. Then I had to start all over again."[33] She would reel in a page of copy paper, type a sentence, and then more likely than not tear it out again, ball it up, and toss it in her wastepaper basket. At least two fragments survive to confirm the manner of composition. Not every reject hit her wastebasket. In writing letters to friends, she grabbed up whatever paper lay at hand, and on one occasion she typed on the back of one of these discards. Both came from the oft-rewritten and much despised first chapter: "And the civilization of which she was a part would have been unbelieving too, for at no time had so little premium been placed on feminine naturalness," reads the one, with bold cross-hatching over it. "How detestable it was that all the men at the picnic could talk about was Fort Sumter. The day was perfect the scene perfect" reads the other, with the bolder scribble across it addressed to her friend Elinor Hillyer, "Think nothing of these notes. I didn't realize that this was 'used' paper.[34]

She described the excruciating process in much more vivid language and detail to Stark Young, a writer whom she particularly admired. The novelist and drama critic for *The New Republic* had commended her work in 1936, but in the course of his letter he had mentioned his own difficulty in getting words on paper. She considered this admission both comforting and disillusioning. "You see," she explained,

I had believed that established writers, writers who really knew how to write, had no difficulty at all in writing. I had thought that only luckless beginners like myself had to rewrite endlessly, tear up and throw away whole chapters, start afresh, rewrite and throw away again. I knew nothing about other writers and their working habits, and I thought I was the only writer in the world who went through such goings-on. After I had rewritten a chapter ten or twelve times and had what I thought was a workable "first draft," I'd put it away for a month. When I dug it out again I'd beat my breast and snatch out my hair because it was so lousy. Then the chapter would be thrown away, because the content of it had not been reduced to the complete simplicity I wanted. Simplicity of ideas, of construction, of words. Then there would be another awful month of substituting Anglo-Saxon derivatives for Latin ones, simple sentence constructions for the more cumbersome Latin constructions.[35]

The exaggerated form of her expression here prompts disbelief. After her book appeared, she often prattled about her motives and work habits. She left, in the process, a picture of a giddy, scribbling amateur who hit the jackpot quite by accident. This was one more means of masking her labor and denying her efforts. The letter to Stark Young, for example, stresses the idea of the unbridgeable gap between what *she* was doing and what "real authors" do. She possessed, in truth, almost a morbid sense of her writing. "I am oppressed by the knowledge of the lousiness of what I write," she groaned,

for even though I may not write well, I do know good writing and my knowledge was intensified by my years of manuscript reading and rewriting for the Journal. I have felt that there was some thing lacking in me that other authors, real and fancied, possessed, that passionate belief in the good quality of their work, a belief so passionate that they have no qualms about gathering in groups and reading each other's stuff.[36]

Here it was again, the combination of pain and secrecy—of "something lacking," of the oppressiveness of her own inadequacy, and an inability to reveal her deficiency, disease, and lacks to others, which of course was one more evidence of those very inadequacies. She used the same terms repeatedly to dismiss all the effort: "lousy"—small, eminently disposable, and less than worthless. Just as she labored fastidiously over her essentially disposable news articles, however, she worked even more intensely on novel-writing. The more intensely she labored and the closer to her work she grew, however, the more useless, silly, and childish it all seemed. She was producing an abortion, a false pregnancy, or a deformed brainchild.

Despite her despair of achieving excellence and all her covering blather about her weaknesses, Mitchell knew precisely what she wanted to do, the impression she wanted to leave, the kind of book and perspective she sought, and how she planned to achieve all this. She left irrefutable evidence of her purposes. Her use of quotation marks, for example:

although she varied her usage, she employed them consistently to distinguish her heroine's thoughts. When a Macmillan copy editor later regularized the usage and eliminated them from the protagonist's conversations with herself, Mitchell insisted on their replacement and offered an elaborate justification of her practice. The result was a livelier appearance on the printed page, she insisted; it therefore made the book more attractive and easier to read. Similarly, she argued, the strategy made the reader more likely to "hear" the heroine's thoughts. The quotation marks had other ramifications. "Eliminating the quotation marks . . . tends to create the effect on the reader that Scarlet is a thinker, rather than an actor. And Scarlett is *no thinker*," Mitchell insisted. Her husband summarized her position. Scarlett, he asserted,

> prattles away to herself throughout the book, and prattling *ought* to be in quotation marks. Eliminating all the quotation marks tends to make the thing look like a stream-of-consciousness book, and that is definitely something Peggy doesn't want. Even though the story is told from Scarlett's viewpoint—and Peggy has worked like the devil to retain that viewpoint, while at the same time getting in the needed information about things not happening in Scarlett's mind or right under her nose—this is not a stream-of-consciousness book. And Peggy doesn't want it to *look* like one.[37]

A greater reflection of her literary vision is seen in her sense of the book's narrative structure. Later, when critics regularly singled out the novel's architecture, structure, pace, or tempo for special praise, she usually responded to such high-flown commendations, as was her wont, with self-mocking incredulity. She responded to the high-falutin' literary judgments with mockery; with herself, as always, the goat. "In particular was I charmed by your remark about my 'tempo,' " she later wrote one critic.

> I was completely dumbfounded as I was no more conscious of having tempo than I was of having a gall bladder. I nursed your remark to me in silence until one day when my husband was reading the manuscript which had just been returned. . . . He was reading along and suddenly rushed out onto the porch with a double handful of dangling participial clauses and dubious subjunctives, crying "In the name of God, what are these?" I said with as much dignity as I could muster that they were tempo and let no dog bark. From then on, I heard about my tempo from all members of the family, including the colored cook. When she made her first, and only, failure on a lemon pie and I asked her what had happened she said gloomily that she guessed something had went wrong with her tempo.[38]

Her boffo humor disguised her real commitments and clear intentions. In the first place, the story of her writing the ending first supports (at least anecdotally) the idea that she had the whole story of the novel clearly in her mind from the beginning. As her reporter friend Lamar Ball summarized: "So Margaret Mitchell, with all those hundreds of pages of 'Gone with the Wind' marshalled in platoons in her orderly mind, sat down and wrote her climax first." So, too, with individual actors: with a clear sense of the whole character in mind, she had only to illustrate that figure in actions and behavior. She explained "that she decided first what she wants a character to do and then she decides how to have it done gracefully."[39] In each instance, reality lay in the idea of the book, the chapter, the actor. Her role as writer was merely to reify the perfect forms that had an independent life in her imagination.

She always knew where she was going and roughly how she intended to get there. At one point, for example, two-thirds of the way through the manuscript, she decided that the narrative pace bogged down completely. Especially after the excitement of the war itself, the first phases of Reconstruction failed to hold her imagined readers' attention. "There was a very definite sag of interest over a range of six chapters," she related. "As 'Alice' would have said, 'There was no conversation and absolutely no pictures in that part.' " The difficulty (as she perceived it) demanded major changes. In order to brighten the narrative, she created a new chapter. The "sagging" section had originally dispatched the hapless Frank Kennedy by way of pneumonia. An alternate version dismissed him more dramatically by way of a Ku Klux Klan raid. She put no emphasis at all on the political implications of the second version of Frank Kennedy's death. Her object was esthetic: to bolster a limp narrative. Nor, in this respect, did even this alternative dispel her doubts. "God knows I don't love that second version for its own sake," she grumbled. "I was trying to build up that section in strength—" she explained, "and by 'strength' I don't mean a lot of melodramatic incident."[40]

Margaret Mitchell had very clear notions about style and its relationship to characterization. She imagined the book in its totality, and she had equally clear ideas of how she wanted her book to look and be. The pain she associated with writing reflected accurately her relentless struggle for words, usage, and structure to match her ambitions for the book, even as her despair at ever doing so produced its own agonies. The ambition was too vaulting, the standards too exacting, and the hurts too painful, and so she shrouded everything—including her ambition—in mystery and secrecy. Thus she wrote: "I have felt that there was some thing lacking in me that other authors, real and fancied, possessed, that passionate belief in the good quality of their work, a belief so passionate that they have no qualms about gathering in groups and reading each other's stuff."[41] The author lacked the fundamental ability to appreciate her work; still, if finished very far from her satisfaction, by 1929 all the major pieces were in place. She owed it polishing and honing, and the manuscript had no first chapter even then; but the narrative was done, the plot finished. And what she had completed just as the Great Depression hit that fall was by and large what the world would get seven years later. Its plot, its history, and its characters tell their own stories about her life.

XII

History Riddled
卍卍卍卍

The Great American Novel was one of the things to talk about. . . .
We all agreed that whether the Great American Novel had been
written or not, the Great Southern Novel had never been. The story
had just never been told. It was agreed one of us ought to write it,
and Peggy said she was going to write a book about Atlanta, the
War and the Reconstruction. She was going to get into it all the
stuff she had picked up doing historical features for the paper, all
the lore, the sixty-year-old gossip and scandals, the people and how
they felt.

ELINOR HILLYER[1]

*I*s there anyone in the United States now innocent of the plot of
Margaret Mitchell's fiction? Actually, she spun two great narratives. First, she told of the rise and fall of Southern independence
in the American Civil War, the social changes wrought by the conflict,
and the collapse of the plantation order in Reconstruction. With regular flashbacks back to earlier times, the chronology begins with the
Fort Sumter crisis in 1861 and ends in 1874 with the end of Radical
Reconstruction and the restoration of the Bourbon order. These epic
events are witnessed through the eyes of a clever but ignorant young
planter's daughter who divides her time between her father's plantation in minor, frontier Clayton County in Georgia and the bustling railroad town, Atlanta, a few miles up the tracks. These places define the
physical setting of the novel.
    Interwoven with this story of the ill-fated Confederacy, the author

created a second narrative of equally ill-fated individuals and their hopeless relations with one another—Scarlett O'Hara, Ashley Wilkes, Melanie Hamilton, and Rhett Butler (in order of their appearance). On the very eve of the war's outbreak, the rich, willful, and lusty sixteen-year-old belle, Scarlett, falls in love. The object of her affection, however, Ashley Wilkes, rejects her to wed his own very conventional cousin, Melanie Hamilton. Consumed with rage and lust for vengeance, the girl then marries the new bride's brother, Charles, to spite the other man. Amid these disorderly affairs of hearth and nation, the fourth central character, Rhett Butler, appears. At thirty-three, this swarthy, mysterious aristocrat is nearly twice the protagonist's age, actually the same generation as the heroine's mother, but he is hopelessly smitten by the fiery Scarlett. As the two new husbands go off to war (Charles to die), Rhett remains behind to pursue the unlikely teenage widow as relentlessly as she herself schemes for Ashley. Each plots vainly, and the course of their thwarted romantic ambitions weaves in and out of the military and political story of the doomed Confederacy.

If less obvious or dramatic then these romantic configurations, the relationship between Melanie and Scarlett constitutes an important subplot. Scarlett's marriage to Melanie's brother makes the two women sisters-in-law: "dearer," as Melanie says, "than any blood sister could ever be." Indeed, Charles Hamilton serves no other purpose in the plot but to unite these two, and, doing so, he vanishes with a fatal case of measles and pneumonia soon after getting his bride with child. The two women survive the deprivations of the home front and then the horrors of war, invasion, and siege alone together. Indeed, their relationship reaches its dramatic climax during the Battle of Atlanta as Melanie gives birth to her baby with Scarlett in terrified attendance. The post-war world continues their connection in both town and country. While close, however, their bond echoes the motif of frustrated love and spurned affection of the other relationships in the novel: Scarlett despises Ashley's sickly wife, but Melanie adores the vital heroine.

Peace brings as many difficulties as war. As the military conflict concludes and Southern economic woes mount, the Widow Hamilton plots her own reconstruction. First, to pay the staggering taxes on Tara, she proposes to become Rhett Butler's mistress. Rebuffed, she then steals her sister's rich beau and establishes a more conventional liaison with this middle-aged Atlanta merchant, Frank Kennedy. Using his money and name to establish herself in business, she succeeds grandly. She does so, however, at the cost of honor, morality, and the approval of all her old friends, save Melanie. Frank Kennedy also gives her a second child, and, like Charles Hamilton, he, too, dies soon after. Only after she enters widowhood for a second time does she allow Rhett Butler's enormous wealth to persuade her to be his bride. A third child, her second daughter, appears within a year. Despite her fecundity, Scarlett dislikes children, and she determines that Wade Hampton, Ella, and Bonnie Blue are quite family enough. She is also taken by the romantic, schoolgirl notion of being "true" to Ashley. Soon after, then, she practices her own version of birth control by taking a separate bedroom and locking the door against her husband.

Through all three husbands and the three progeny they provide her, the heroine never surrenders her twin ambitions for material security and Ashley Wilkes. Just so, her scorn for Melanie Wilkes and Rhett Butler seldom wavers, either. Melanie's death then removes the critical hurdle to having Ashley all to herself. At that ostensible moment of triumph, however, she realizes her passion has been an illusion. To her own amazement, she discovers she has really loved both Melanie and Rhett all along. She pours out her revelation to Rhett; but he has changed, too. Indeed, he has come to similar conclusions about *his* old attachments. He loses his passion and desire for her just as she abandons Ashley and just, of course, as Melanie bids them all a rather more permanent farewell. And so the story closes, the personal fates of the characters just as doomed and final as the lost Cause of the Confederacy.

Margaret Mitchell drew neither her history nor her characters from a vacuum. On the contrary, she built on both oral tradition and literary conventions. Likewise, she spun her narratives from both formal historical scholarship and lore from her own family history. At the same time, she infused her history and her characters with some of the most contemporary values of her time and age. Those values illuminate *Gone with the Wind* itself, and the place of Mitchell's novel in American and Southern culture.

Although *Gone with the Wind* has come to be identified with the most conventional romances of the antebellum South—indeed, it has come to be taken as the very embodiment of that tradition—Margaret Mitchell herself conceived of her history as radical, revisionary, and rebellious. No less than her insouciant behavior as a debutante, her unconventional life as journalist, and her defiant decision to leave the church, get a divorce, and remarry, she intended her fiction to challenge the accepted literary image of the South and to repudiate the traditional definitions of Southern history.

If her history seems less radical in the last half of the twentieth century than she considered it in 1926, it is because the standard interpretation of the regional past has changed so radically since then. When she began writing, however, one school of thought had dominated both Southern and national notions of the regional past for forty years; it had virtually eliminated competing views. Characterized chiefly in the popular fictions of Thomas Nelson Page and Thomas Dixon, the Lost Cause Romance had celebrated the halcyon days of the prewar plantation South, the tragedy of a brothers' war, the horrors of Reconstruction, and the sacred cause of the redeemers who restored the white South by 1876. The plantation romance of Page *et al.* had chronicled the lives of aristocrats identified with vast estates, slavery, and the knightly order of *noblesse oblige*, and the romancers had set their stories chiefly or exclusively in the geographical centers of planter culture—Tidewater Virginia, the Georgia, South Carolina Low Country, and the Mississippi Delta. Its heroes were gentlemen, its women ladies, its blacks loyal and faithful (if innocent and childlike) servants. Margaret Mitchell's contemporary, W. J. Cash, began his monumental analysis of Southern culture, *Mind of the South*, by ridiculing this image. All fantasy, he hooted. "It was," he mocked,

> a sort of stage piece out of the eighteenth century, wherein gesturing gentlemen moved soft-spokenly against a background of rose gardens and dueling grounds, through always gallant deeds, and lovely ladies, in farthingales, never for a moment lost that exquisite remoteness which has been the dream of all men and the possession of none. Its social pattern was manorial, its civilization that of the Cavalier, its ruling class an aristocracy coextensive with the planter group—men entitled to quarter the royal arms of St. George and St. Andrew on their shields, and in every case descended from old gentlefolk who for many generations had made up the ruling classes of Europe.
>
> They dwelt in large and stately mansions, preferably white and with columns and Grecian entablature. The writers of the Lost Cause Romance sketched a world of social harmony and ease devoid of inward strife and conflict. Their estates were feudal baronies, their slaves quite too numerous ever to be counted and their social life a thing of Old World splendor and delicacy.[2]

As suggested in Cash's caricature, Page's vision had no room for poor or middling sorts: no Crackers, yeomen, rednecks, lintheads, businessmen, or merchants jangled its harmony. This world "devoid of strife and conflict" collapsed through no internal dynamic but fell from external forces: Yankees destroyed this gentle cosmos with their hireling armies and industrial war machine. Afterward, these mercenary and misguided outsiders heaped revenge and dishonor on the region, chiefly through their determination to impose black rule on the poor defeated Confederates. The Lost Cause romancers never questioned the complete error of black and Carpetbagger rule, but they scorned equally the Scallawag collaborationists of these black and Yankee villains. Just so, they defended the Ku Klux Klan and assumed the righteousness of the redeemers who restored white rule after Reconstruction.

The young rebels of the Generation of 1900 scorned almost everything associated with this nostalgic, sentimental image of Dixie's past. H. L. Mencken, the demigod of the Young South renegades, instructed the insurgents to toss dead cats into the stuffy parlors of regional tradition.[3] They did: Famous, infamous, and unknown, members of the generation of 1900 mocked and ridiculed the Southern past. No generation in regional history set out so consciously to outrage their elders, customs, and taboos. Few succeeded so successfully in doing so. They drank themselves into oblivion, spilling booze and throwing up without much dignity (like Faulkner); they danced on tables at the Piedmont Driving Club (like Margaret Mitchell); they slept with one another before getting married and had children out of wedlock (like Allen Tate and Caroline Gordon). Some of them, like the Pulitzer Prize-winning Paul Green, the novelist Lillian Smith, the Raleigh journalist Nell Battle Lewis, and the genteel Georgia social worker Katharine Lumpkin even questioned the region's racial shibboleths.

If they violated all the rules of conduct laid on young ladies and gentlemen of the region, the rebels repudiated tradition in other ways as well. They ignored history altogether by emphasizing sociology, reform, and contemporary arts, letters, and politics. In her column for the *Raleigh News and Observer*, Nell Lewis gave one of the nicest versions of the bias when she challenged even her friend Paul Green's democratic, egalitarian version of the past. As in "damnyankee," she conflated the terms "hoopskirt" and "history," and dismissed even plain folks' tradition. Continuing the clothing figure of speech, she insisted that "the 1924 calico wrapper of the mill hand in her hours of ease (?) frankly interests us more. . . . Give us the masters and slaves of the present," she demanded, "before you reproduce the plantation owners and the black bondsmen of the [1850s]."[4] She declared that regional mythology of the idealized planter romance corrupted all history in the South, however realistically rendered. This prompted her to deemphasize the past altogether and encouraged her burning interest in contemporary social conditions, especially among poor whites. This bias informed the values of a generation. The development of the great program in regionalist sociology at the University of North Carolina embodies the same motives. Although Howard Odum, its founder, had concerned himself with black folklore initially, the program itself emphasized the investigation of small white proprietors, tenant farmers, sandlappers, Crackers and hillbillies. Thus defined, sociology provided an alternative to history, while the objects of sociological inquiry reconfirmed the repudiation of a specific past associated with the plantation, slavery, and the gentry.

When the young rebels dealt with the past at all, the same biases governed their response. In New Orleans, youthful heretics launched their "little magazine," *The Double Dealer*, in 1921 with broadsides against "the storied realm of dreams, lassitude, pleasure, chivalry and the Nigger." The following year, the Fugitive poets in Nashville initiated their own rebellion with proclamations against "the high-caste

Brahmins of the Old South" and the "treacly lamentations of the old school."[5] One has only to reverse these characterizations of the mythic tradition to find the rebels' paradigm of regional history: Instead of dreams and fantasy, they called for realism and sociology; instead of lassitude, for hard work; instead of pleasure, for diligence and self-advancement; instead of chivalry, for the values of the bourgeoisie and middling sorts. And instead of slavery and the Nigger? They focused on the culture of the White Folk. And where the romancers had invariably set their scenes in Virginia or on the coast, the Generation of 1900 looked to the interior, the backcountry, the mountains, the Southern frontier for their settings, or cast their dramas in towns and cities.

These values permeated all their work. Cash's *Mind of the South* touched all of them. History, for example, actually concerned him very little, and the bulk of his great work detailed contemporary society and sociological values of the region. In the brief section that dealt with the antebellum social order, however, he created an archetypal character to debunk the traditional planter of Southern mythology. Although it was a fabrication quite as mythical as the one he criticized, he presented this figure as a "concrete example" of the real and true "aristocrat." He began appropriately with the man's inflated obituary in a pompous Charleston paper. Mourned as " 'a gentleman of the old school' and 'a noble specimen of the chivalry at its best,' " this mythic planter, he smirked, was really only "a stout young Irishman" without family, breeding, or gentility at all. He has only a horny-handed wife who is just as aggressive, ambitious, and materialistic as he, and the rare good fortune to hit fertile soil at the beginning of the cotton boom.[6] His "typical planter" should sound familiar to any reader of Southern letters after World War I: his figure resembles the character of Augustus Baldwin Longstreet as sketched in 1925 by John Donald Wade; it is Thomas Sutpen's tale in Faulkner's *Absalom, Absalom!;* and it is, of course, the story of still another "stout young Irishman"—the Gerald O'Hara of Mitchell's fiction. It is the same story, more or less, that the historians Frank Owsley and Irvin Bell Wiley told in their monographs, *Plain Folks of the Old South* and *Johnny Reb*. The revisionary impulse clung to the Generation of 1900 like ticks to dogs. It was, even so, a peculiar response of a peculiar generation in a peculiar time to a peculiar circumstance. The "realism" this generation demanded involved as much bias and ulterior cultural motives as the creation of the plantation romance had in the two generations preceding.

Peggy Mitchell shared all these biases. She mocked the "gentle Confederate novel." She poked fun at the "moonlight-on-the-magnolias" legend. "Professional Southerners" made her choke. She scorned the aristocratic pretensions of her own family and ridiculed even the genuinely aristocratic lineages of her friends and cohorts. She intended praise for none of these traditions in her book. Especially after the release of the movie version of her novel, she wearied of protesting her intentions, but in 1942 one particularly sympathetic notice won a full explanation of her social and historical vision in her epic. A fellow rebel of the Generation of 1900, the very aristocratic Virginius Dabney, editor of the *Richmond Times-Dispatch*, had dismissed the mythic Old South in his 1942 survey of the region, *Below the Potomac*. In the process, he had praised the historical realism of Mitchell's fiction. The Atlantan basked in the commendation. "I certainly had no intention of writing about cavaliers," she agreed. "Practically all my characters, except the Virginia Wilkes, were of sturdy yeoman stock." She despaired, however, of ever being read correctly.

> I believed that we Southerners could write the truth about the antebellum South, its few slaveholders, its yeomen farmers, its rambling, comfortable houses just fifty years away from log cabins, until Gabriel blows his trump—and everyone would go on believing in the Hollywood version. The sad part is that many Southerners believe this myth even more ardently than Northerners. . . .
>
> Since my novel was published, I have been embarrassed on many occasions by finding myself included among writers who pictured the South as a land of white-columned mansions whose wealthy owners had thousands of slaves and drank thousands of juleps. I have been surprised, too, for North Georgia certainly was no such country—if it ever existed anywhere—and I took great pains to describe North Georgia as it was. But people believe what they like to believe and the mythical Old South has too strong a hold on their imaginations to be altered by the mere reading of a 1,037-page book. So I have made no effort to defend myself against the accusation but it was a great satisfaction to me that a man of your perceptiveness knew that my South was not "The South That Never Was."[7]

Mitchell's fiction revised Lost Cause history both directly and indirectly. Like so many of her fellow rebels, she recast the old images by setting her fiction in Georgia, not Virginia, and in the interior, hundreds of miles from the turf of the coastal aristocracy. In contrast to the plantation romance, too, Crackers and small farmers abound in her fictional world. One of these, Will Benteen, occupied an important place in the story line. Critically, the narrator credits him with redeeming the O'Hara homestead after the war: "Tara's bloom was not the work of a planter aristocrat, but of the plodding, tireless 'small farmer' who loved his land."[8] Another countryman with another active verb-like name, Abel Wynder, plays the same part. In the notorious wife-killing, black-baiting, Yankee-hating ex-convict Archie, Scarlett's and Melanie's "mountain man" driver in Reconstruction Atlanta, Mitchell offers another example of her sense of the white South's diversity. As a class, such people also figured significantly in the book. The county cavalry unit overflows with them. Containing only a handful of rich planters, the Troop consists mostly of hunters from the backwoods, swamp trappers, Crackers, small farmers, and even " 'po' whites," although Mitchell adds with some irony that they would have been few "and above the average of their class." Insofar as the cavalry represented the Southern cavalier tradition in truth, denying aristocratic virtue to the mounted men struck at the heart of the region's aristocratic pretense. She intended the swipe.

If significant in themselves for defining Mitchell's larger social vision, these characters serve a still more important function in the novel, the same as W. J. Cash's people do: they define the fundamental character even of her ostensible aristocrats. Her planters as a general category are farmers, with only the veneer (if that) of mythic Old South culture. Possessing none of the grace, virtue, or breeding of the traditional aristocracy, her typical planter is only a farmer writ large. She sets up the idea on the book's first page as she introduces Scarlett in the company of the Tarleton twins:

> Although born to the ease of plantation life, waited on hand and foot since infancy, the faces of the three on the porch were neither slack nor soft. They had the vigor and alertness of country people who have spent all their lives in the open and troubled their heads very little with dull things in books.[9]

Mitchell makes the Cracker–gentry connection genealogical as well as cultural. Chapter I elaborates the theme. When the Troop elects Abel Wynder, the illiterate son of a swamp trapper, as one of its three officers, she notes that the gentlemen could afford no pretense about their own bloodlines: "Too many of their fathers and grandfathers had come up to wealth from the small farmer class for that."[10] Indeed, the "small farmer made good" describes Mitchell's essential planter no less than it did the "aristocrat" of W. J. Cash's vision. Gerald O'Hara typifies the breed. He is a cultural illiterate. Even Beatrice Tarleton, hardly a scholar, catches him in his comic confusion of "stentor" and "centaur." His ignorance does not faze him: " 'Stentor or centaur, 'tis no matter,' " he snorts.[11]

> While he entertained the liveliest respect for those who had more book learning than he, he never felt his own lack. And what need had he of these things in a new country where the most ignorant of bogtrotters had made great fortunes? in this country which asked only that a man be strong and unafraid of work?[12]

An immigrant, alien, and a foreigner, Gerald makes his way in commerce in his brothers' stores before striking it rich in the cotton boom.

A self-made man, he makes his fortune by grit and wit. "He had done it all, little, hard-headed, blustering Gerald," Mitchell writes. "He cleared the fields and planted cotton and borrowed more money from James and Andrew to buy more slaves."[13]

With Gerald as a typical Southerner, Mitchell's Dixie is no stable aristocratic order at all, but a dynamic cultural melting pot that rewards energy and ambition as does any capitalist order. As such, it attracted all sorts of people from all over: Frenchmen and Irishmen, Catholics and Ulster Presbyterians, members of old families and newcomers with no families at all. Repeatedly, she describes her South as a brawling, democratic, egalitarian frontier. Eschewing the stable, aristocratic order of the plantation romance, Mitchell opened society at the bottom as well as the top. If anyone could rise, no claims to birth or manners could prevent even the most aristocratic from collapsing back into the white trash-dom from whence they might have risen. While the theme of social Darwinism underlies the whole text, Mitchell illustrates this vision most insistently in the section that chronicles Gerald's funeral, Chapter XL. At the outset, the narrative affirms that Gerald had fallen just as he had risen. "Couldn't nothing stop him when his mind was made up and he warn't scared of nothin' in shoe leather," Will intoned from the graveside. "There warn't nothing that come to him *from the outside* that could lick him."[14] If Gerald's rise and fall illustrates a general principle for Mitchell's South, the reintroduction of Cathleen Calvert into the narrative at this juncture underlines the same themes still more forcefully. Once second in popularity only to Scarlett as the belle of the County, Cathleen slides down a steep and slippery slope. At the funeral, she stands apart from both the stolid country folk and her former planter friends,

> her faded sunbonnet hiding her bowed face. Scarlett saw with amazement that her percale dress had grease spots on it and her hands were freckled and unclean. There were even black crescents under her fingernails. There was nothing of quality folks about Cathleen now. She looked Cracker, even worse. She looked poor white, shiftless, slovenly, trifling.
>
> "She'll be dipping snuff soon, if she isn't doing it already," thought Scarlett in horror. "Good Lord! What a comedown!"
>
> She shuddered, turning her eyes from Cathleen as she realized how narrow was the chasm between quality folk and poor whites.
>
> "There but for a lot of gumption am I," she thought, and pride surged through her as she realized that she and Cathleen had started with the same equipment after the surrender—empty hands and what they had in their heads.[15]

Lest the reader miss the point of all this, old Grandma Fontaine enunciates the theory that lies behind the picture. In the most ruthless terms, she defines the sources of her family's survival and success; in the process, she validates the very course that Scarlett is pursuing:

> "When trouble comes we bow to the inevitable without any mouthing, and we work and we smile and we bide our time. And we play along with lesser folks and we take what we can get from them. And when we're strong enough, we kick the folks whose necks we've climbed over. That, my child, is the secret of survival." And after a pause, she added: "I pass it on to you."

Most of the County's families, she continued, were sliding towards history's dustbin. "There never was anything to those folks but money and darkies," she cackled, "and now that the money and the darkies are gone, those folks will be Cracker in another generation."[16] This old witch specifically numbers the Wilkes among those destined for destruction. Ashley Wilkes lacked "gumption"; Cathleen Calvert presaged his future.

Margaret Mitchell had told Virginius Dabney that she "had no intention of writing about cavaliers." While she did not intend her fiction to focus on them, however, she did include the most conventional aristocrats in her social order, but her treatment affirms the same generational prejudices that prompted her celebration of the frontier, egalitarian, small-farmer South.

In the Southern tradition, Virginia and South Carolina (with coastal Georgia as an adjunct) represent the twin peaks of the region's aristocratic conceit. In *Gone with the Wind*, the Wilkes and Hamilton clan represents the one; Ellen Robillard (chiefly), the other. With fair consistency, Mitchell depicted these folk as queer, anomalous, exceptional, and literally out of order in this frontier world. The Wilkeses characterize the misfit: "The Wilkes are different from any of our neighbors—different from any family I ever knew," Gerald testifies in Chapter I. "They are queer folk. . . . The whole family's that way, and they've always been that way. And probably always will. I tell you they're born queer."[17] The Tarleton twins muse on the same characteristics and use the same adjective to describe their neighbors. Why was Ashley queer? they puzzled. Their mother had the answer: "it's because their grandfather came from Virginia."[18]

If Mitchell's aristocrats are relatively odd in North Georgia, she also describes them in absolutely negative terms. She defines the Wilkes clan both culturally and physically as overbred, inbred, over-refined, attenuated, and bloodless. She compares them to such passive creatures as does, rabbits, and lapdogs. Unable and unwilling to adapt to changing circumstances, they are doomed as both individuals and a family. Fulfilling prophesies about their extinction, they have trouble reproducing: Melanie, of course, barely survives one childbirth and a second actually carries her off; in the same way, the "queer" Ashley Wilkes is socially if not sexually impotent. He characterizes himself "as much less than a man—much less, indeed, than a woman."[19] While he rides, hunts, drinks, and gambles with the other planters, he is still, in Gerald's terms, not a "proper man." "He can do all those things, but his heart's not in it. That's why I say he's queer," Gerald concludes.[20] Ashley in the postwar world confirms the picture. He cannot run a business, balance accounts, or even perform odd jobs around the farm like splitting wood.

Mitchell elaborates these qualities when she considers the rice-country nabobs of Charleston and Savannah. While Mitchell's depiction, especially of Ashley Wilkes, mirrors not a little of the fainting quality of Sir Walter Scott's Edward Waverley, H. B. Stowe's St. Leger, and even Faulkner's Compson men (excepting Jason, of course), her descriptions are rather more negative. The rice-country nabobs have no redeeming features at all. Like the spavined, pallid, and anemic Wilkes, the planters of the coast's malarial marshes are also linked with morbidity, disease, and death. Bloated with family pride, Mitchell's Charleston aristocrats are pompous, stilted reactionaries who stifle life. Scarlett compares her stay there to living in a prison. The same forces drive Rhett Butler from his native city, too.

Low Country aristocrats are as ill-fated as the Wilkeses. If, however, the passing of the rabbity Virginians causes sadness and nostalgia, no one regrets the extinction of the "lumbering dinosaurs" of the Carolina tidal marshes. On the contrary, Rhett actually celebrates the death of his "old school gentleman" father who typified the rigidity, brittleness, and hidebound qualities of Charleston aristocracy. Much of this bias extends even to Mitchell's treatment of Ellen Robillard, a classic version of the Old School Lady. For all her good works and rustling crinolines, the Savannah-born Ellen Robillard lacks color, passion, and life itself, as do her Charleston sisters. She is distant and aloof, restrained and repressed. She virtually never speaks in the text, and when she does, she seldom speaks directly; rather, her voice filters indirectly through her vital daughter's vivid imagination. With a kind of ghost-like quality while she lives, she attains her real power in the narrative after her death.

Mitchell describes the traditional aristocrats as useless and impractical ornaments in the social order. Her treatment of slavery supports and sharpens this view. Slavery as a social or economic system hardly exists in the novel. Slaves, in Mitchell's treatment, are chiefly social decorations for upwardly mobile white farmers. Symbolic of this idea, Gerald O'Hara's first slave, Pork (won in a poker game) was a valet. Indeed, he seeks a Low Country wife from the exact same motive. Although Pork helps the family survive by foraging after Sherman passes through, he is incapable of sustained hard labor, unable even to mend a shirt. And while Mammy busies herself with all the affairs of the O'Hara establishment, her labors are essentially ephemeral, too. Mitchell affirms this quality in all her black characters, with one exception—Dilcey, of course, who is doubly exceptional in being bronze, not black; more Indian than African. If individual slaves are materially or economically ineffectual, this merely echoes the explicit attributes of the traditional aristocrats. The author cuts Pork and Ashley from precisely the same cloth. Underlining further the relationship between the white aristocrats and the slaves, the black characters are all associated with tradition, the old ways, and the codes of the past. The new world order unhinges them quite as much as it does Gerald and Ashley.

As Rhett Butler and Grandma Fontaine insist, the traditionalists all go under, and they should go under because they lack courage, vigor, and vision. Repressing life in others, they do not deserve to live themselves. When aristocrats survive and prosper, it is only to the extent that they abandon the virtues of the old way. In such ways Mitchell's values once more reflect her generation's skepticism of the "treacly lamentations of the old school," even as her emphasis on yeomen, the small-farmer origins of her planters, and an open and fluid social order creates an alternative version of Southern social history.

In the course of revising Southern history, Margaret Mitchell also revised her own genealogy, with much the same rebellious spirit. She took her own ancestors, roughed them up considerably, and projected them, thus transformed, into her epic. The genealogical aspects of the text introduce the nature of her characters and critical biographical elements in *Gone with the Wind*.

The author herself always and consistently rejected any connection between her family and her fiction. She did so with good reason. The popular search for prototypes among her own kin, living as well as dead, produced absurdities. The absurdity reached a peak when Mitchell's old friend from Smith College, Virginia (Morris) Nixon, wrote an essay that identified Gerald O'Hara with the austere, puritanical Eugene Mitchell. They were both very short; other than that the comparison boggles the imagination. If this bizarre connection could be advanced, Mitchell rightly thought, sense had fled the universe. The novelist so argued to the editor of *Photoplay*, where her friend (now former friend) had submitted the piece. "If you publish that Bela Lugosi is like Shirley Temple or that Deanna Durbin is like Jimmy Cagney, your error would be no greater than hers [Nixon's] in saying that Gerald O'Hara is like my father."[21]

Despite the author's protests, the parallels between her family and her fictions shine through. The kinship begins with the Gerald/Fitzgerald name. Similarly, it was hardly incidental that her Gerald O'Hara and her mother's people were both Irish Catholic, large slaveholding planter families. How many Irish Catholics of the planter class really did reside in antebellum Clayton County, Georgia? One set was in fiction, one set was in fact. Actually, of course, the real-life Fitzgeralds and Stephenses bore little resemblance to the fictional O'Haras except in religion, place of birth, and economic status. Where she depicted Gerald as rough, semi-literate, and uncultured, Phillip Fitzgerald and his son-in-law were actually members of the Irish gentry and fit naturally into the planter order. Her forebears' knowledge and intelligence set them apart, and even Protestant locals valued their learning and subsidized the schools these immigrant gentlemen founded. Her own ancestors possessed good connections and cultivated better ones in the antebellum South. Unlike the O'Haras, they turned political activity and Democratic party loyalties to good account. They also tied up with local communities of well-established, non-Irish Catholics in the back country and married among them. By such methods outsiders had traditionally won entry into the Southern ruling class since its seventeenth-century origins. Just so, the Fitzgerald/Stephens men won a clear jump even on many natives who sought entry to the planter class.

Still further, Mitchell's maternal kin had far more in common with other planters than with most Irishmen in the South. While numerous Irish lived in the South, few resided in the interior, fewer planted cotton, and fewer still owned slaves or qualified as planters. They remained mostly in the large coastal cities like Charleston and Savannah; they lived mostly as single men rather than with families; and they came as close to representing a regional underclass as any category in the entire population. Before the Civil War, for example, they were the majority of those charged and convicted of crime in the state of Georgia. Despite their small representation in the entire population, they made up an absolute majority of the state's prison population.[22]

Mitchell effectively took elements of the real Irish in Georgia and tacked them onto her own ancestors to produce Gerald O'Hara. At the same time, she made her fictional Gerald something like a standard for her own genealogy, too. In unmasking the plantation South, she debunked her own family. She downplayed her own ancestors' power and influence. Rural Home, she insisted, was no great plantation, but an ordinary farm. Phillip Fitzgerald and John Stephens were just as ordinary. "They were both Irishmen born and proud of it and prouder still of being southerners and would have withered any relative who tried to put on dog," she continued. "I'm afraid they were so proud of what they were that they'd have thought any putting on the dog was gilding the lily and any way, they left that to the post war nouveaux riche who had to carry a lot of dog because they had nothing else to carry."[23]

This down-to-earth portrait of her own ancestors resonates nicely with her depiction of the fictional Gerald O'Hara. She offered this revisionary critique of her own genealogy, however, in a specific context that reveals her larger intentions. She aimed at *women's* pretensions, the Ladies' pretentiousness. In *Gone with the Wind*, women were the font of aristocratic snobbishness. They were the ones who raised their eyebrows at the rough-and-ready democracy of "the Troop" at the beginning of the book. It was the ladies who haughtily scorned cross-class marriages and who looked down their noses at "barbarians" from Alabama.

Mitchell condemned the women in her own family for the same sins. She delighted in deflating what she deemed the Stephens women's inflated notions of their past. When she had visited her rich Aunt Edythe in Connecticut, her snobby relative had trembled, the niece wrote, lest "I'd say her father was born in Ireland and even her husband didn't know that—. Or that I'd let out that the farm at Jonesboro was just a plain Georgia farm and not a plantation home with white columns, gravelled walks and magnolias such as she had described." She despised her aunt as hypocritical and false, but she found the greater source of evil in her own grandmother:

> By the time the younger girls were coming along, Great Grandpa and his wife were dead and Grandma had gotten all Grandpa's money tied up and spent it as she pleased. She always wanted to splurge and swagger and the younger girls . . . got a different education from the older ones. They were sent north to finishing schools where they were taught that it was shameful to be the daughters of an Irishman born in the Old Country.[24]

Margaret Mitchell loathed these women, and their aspirations to social grandeur provided merely another excuse to vent her fury. Her passion, in turn, brings her fiction closer, literally, to home.

Tyrannical and false: that was how the author described the women of her mother's family. Vulgar and mercenary; full of splurge and swagger. She specifically spared her immigrant patriarchs from this characterization and isolated the evil completely in the women. And here Mitchell drops another clue about the relation of history to her fiction. Money, splurge, and swagger: the terms she applied to Annie Fitzgerald Stephens have the most powerful resonance in her novel. They underline the central characteristics of none other than the central figure of her fiction: the vulgar, mindless character of Scarlett O'Hara herself.

While general parallels exist between the fictional O'Haras and her mother's people, those between the historical harridan Annie Elizabeth Fitzgerald Stephens and the fictional Scarlett O'Hara are more remarkable still, and they present a mother lode of biographical significance.

   The two characters are essentially the same age. Scarlett was born in 1845 and Annie in 1844. Both had Irish immigrants for fathers, native American Catholic women for mothers. Both were girls amid a raft of exclusively female children. Indeed, Scarlett's all-girl family echoed the folklore in Mitchell family history: the Fitzgeralds explained their exclusively female progeny as the result of a curse by the small farmer whom they dispossessed, while the novel details the slew of boys' graves in the family plot at Tara. Both Scarlett and Annie were born and bred in rural Clayton County and both made their careers in Atlanta, but neither surrendered her obsession with country real estate.
   Not to defame Annie Stephens, their characters bore notable parallels as well. If Mitchell's grandmother remained fiercely within the bosom of the church, kept one husband all her life, and avoided the sexual and social peccadillos of the fictional heroine, still, family lore depicted her as grasping, possessive, and materialistic; a kind of natural capitalist; devoid of sympathy as a mother, friend, or landlord. As was the fictional character, too, she was furiously headstrong, willful, stubborn, aggressive, and determined. Also like Scarlett, Annie Stephens cared little for books and culture. In the same way, if for different reasons, she was estranged from the polite Atlanta of her day. She, too, like Scarlett, prided herself inordinately on her huge Victorian house, and she relished the presence of her own name on all the property maps that listed this grand place. In the same way, she was the one most "cursed" by the desire for having land. She collected odd lots in Atlanta, but she was willing to dispossess her own family and her poor relations and pervert her father's will to claim a share in the property at Rural Home in Clayton County. Once having asserted her claim, she drove her tenants as fiercely as Scarlett ever dominated her sawmill workers. Without the most determined resistance, everyone around both figures succumbed to their willful domination. The granddaughter resisted; and therein lies another tale.
   In general, Mitchell despised all the old Confederate battle-axes—like Mrs. Peel—who pried into her business, censured her behavior, and gossiped about her doings. Her grandmother was a caricature of the type. Violent, opinionated, and dogmatic, Annie Stephens tested the patience of saints. Peggy Mitchell was not a saint; indeed, the granddaughter had enough of these same traits to guarantee explosions with the old lady. After May Belle Mitchell's death, the two scrapped constantly. Their guerrilla warfare, however, escalated into a full-fledged battle in the mid-twenties. The old lady had objected violently to her granddaughter's social relations, but she had participated in the Upshaw wedding in 1922. The young woman's employment irritated her as much as it did Berrien Upshaw, in all likelihood, but the civility between them did not survive Mitchell's divorce and

remarriage. The old lady had lived with the Mitchells for years, but after a huge battle, the matriarch stormed out of the household and removed her lodgings permanently to the Georgian Terrace Hotel.[25] The explosion echoed for years. It had more immediate implications. Mrs. Stephens's wealthy sons and daughters, for example, contributed money each month to the Mitchell establishment as long as the old lady resided there. When she moved out, that income ceased, and the family now asked the Mitchells to begin contributing a share to the grande dame's maintenance.[26] For the inhabitants at 1149 Peachtree Street, this heaped injury on insult.

The situation worsened in the late twenties and early thirties, with legal harassment, threats, and diatribes flying back and forth; and finally, graveyard disinterments. In any case, after the mid-twenties, Mitchell never spoke of the old woman or any of her mother's kin except in the most violent, antagonistic terms. Only two years before the old lady died at almost ninety, the author still sneered at the mention of her name. In 1932, Mitchell took John out to Jonesboro and Fayetteville to show him the old Fitzgerald place. She discovered, to her complete surprise, that her very wealthy Jacksonville aunt, Alix Stephens Gress, had bought the farm, fixed it up, and installed the octogenarian Annie Stephens in the house. "She is eighty-six now and she was born there," the writer reflected afterward.

> She's done a lot of travelling since that day and managed, among other things, to split a large, loving and closely knit family into so many antagonistic parts that hardly any brother speaks to brother or sister to sister. Well, she's made the round of the circle and come back there to die. I hope when I do that, I won't have for company some of the memories she has—if she has any, now.[27]

The Widow Stephens returned the feeling. Alone among the numerous Stephens progeny, May Belle's family received nothing from the old woman's estate after her death in 1934.

Mitchell's relationship with her grandmother raises a puzzle. If she hated Anne Fitzgerald Stephens—and she surely did—that character still exerted the most potent appeal for her, for at the very time their estrangement had become irrevocable, Mitchell was creating the vital, violent, and compelling figure based on this character. This powerful disjunction extended itself into the author's extraliterary response to her fiction, too, as she expressed the most radically divided mind about her protagonist. Thus, despite the character's power and popularity and the energy with which she was created, the author herself repudiated the character, or otherwise evinced the most consistent ambivalence about her creation.

In the storm of enthusiasm that followed the publication of the novel,

Mitchell took pains to distance herself from Scarlett O'Hara. Most often, she insisted that she had not intended to praise or blame her heroine but that she desired only to create a consistent figure driven by the logic of her character. By the same measure, she lauded those who took the same neutral stance towards the protagonist. "You were good to Scarlett, understanding her so well and crediting her with what she had instead of what she didn't have," Mitchell praised Henry Steele Commager's laudatory review in the *New York Herald Tribune*. This extremely perceptive reviewer had hit upon some of the most critical underlying issues in the novel, including the potential source of all the heroine's problems, when he had assayed that Scarlett "wanted to be her mother's child but was inescapably her father's." This insight, indeed, elicited Mitchell's special commendation. "I think your paragraph of summation beginning that she wanted to be her mother's child but wasn't is perfectly marvelous. . . ! I thanked God as I read along that you accepted characters for what they were and not what they should be," she told the historian.[28]

She took a different but related tack with a friend-to-be, Edwin Granberry, who praised the novel even more passionately and applauded the protagonist more enthusiastically. Without endorsing his judgment of her heroine, she offered some justification for his position. "Thank you for your kind words about poor Scarlett," she replied. "It never occurred to me while writing her that such a storm of hard words would descend upon the poor creature's head. She just seemed to me to be a normal person thrown into abnormal circumstances and doing the best she could, doing what seemed to her the practical thing. The normal human being in a jam thinks, primarily, of saving his own hide, and she valued her hide in a thoroughly normal way."[29] When another reader wrote to ask her plaintively whether she had intended to depict a character without "a single honorable intention," Mitchell insisted that she had not wished "to pass any judgment on any character but only to tell what they did and said and let the readers draw their own inferences." She went on, however, to list her protagonist's virtues. "Surely courage is commendable, and she had it," she began.

> The sense of responsibility for the weak and helpless is a rare trait, and she had this, for she took care of her own even at great cost to herself. She was able to appreciate what was beautiful in her mother, even if she could not emulate her. . . . She had perseverance in the face of defeat.

Yet what she gave with one hand, she retracted with the other. The author completed this catalogue of merits by negating all of them. "Of course," she finished, "those qualities are balanced by her bad qualities."[30] Trying her damnedest, Mitchell could hardly get her heroine past Purgatory.

To still others, the author conceded all Scarlett's sins and folly but explained she had depicted her heroine's offenses only as a means of advancing virtue. When a Catholic prelate, Monsignor James Murphy, worried about her apparent glorification of a wicked woman and its effect on youth, she quoted a local nun, Sister Mary Loyola of St. Joseph's Infirmary, to support her case. *Gone with the Wind* "was basically a moral book," the author repeated, "in that it showed that people pay inevitably for the wrong they do, and that certainly there was nothing in Scarlett's character that would induce any young girl to copy her." She had not written the book for children in any case, she reassured the prelate, "but for mature people who realize the truth of 'as ye sow—.' " At this point the ghost of her mother flutters once again past her imagination: "I must confess a sense of shock at finding that any number of children were reading my book and seemingly enjoying it," she continued. "My mother would not have permitted me to read that book until I was eighteen. She did not permit me to read 'Tom Jones,' 'Moll Flanders' and other books of that type until I reached that age."[31]

By the same measure, the author insisted, she had not intended Scarlett as the heroine at all. Mitchell used the concerns of this same anxious Catholic prelate to explain her real intentions:

> A number of times the character of Scarlett O'Hara has been attacked and I have been accused of portraying a "bad woman" who by her wickedness cast into disrepute virtuous Southern ladies of a bygone day. I am not one to rise up in defense of my book, but I frequently feel downhearted at such remarks for this reason. I had tried so hard to portray the wonderful women of the old South. I had striven to show that Ellen O'Hara was indeed a woman whose children rose up and called her blessed, a woman whose ideals prodded the hardening conscience of Scarlett, even thought Scarlett did not obey the prods. I had tried to show Melanie as a Christian character so honorable that she could not conceive of dishonor in others. Mammy was as uncompromising about right and wrong as was possible. The stout-hearted matrons who knew right from wrong refused to tolerate Scarlett. Having put a great deal of work upon these ladies, I naturally felt a sense of disappointment that the eyes of many of my readers focused entirely upon the bad woman and paid no heed to the many good women.[32]

With her praise of motherhood and tradition and paraphrasing of scripture and otherwise anomalous references to Christianity, this letter oozes with disingenuousness. Here, as is obvious throughout her epistolary oeuvre, Mitchell is willing to flatter almost any correspondent's argument or position. She quotes nuns and Scripture to a Catholic priest to carry her point. It was not all folderol, however. She had made similar assertions in the fall by 1935 when she had no special ax

to grind or audience to flatter. "I would rather like you didn't eliminate any references to 'Melanie,' " she told Lois Cole in the fall of 1935,
as her publisher was preparing advertising copy for the book. "After
all, she's the heroine of the book, although I'm afraid I'm the only one
who knows it." [33] With no more than four people having read the book
at that time, Mitchell's comment is particularly odd.

What is going on? In one context, Mitchell's ambivalence about the
book's heroines relates to a tradition of the Catholic morality tale.
Regularly she fell back on the idea of depicting immorality as a means
of promoting virtue. Her desire to see and publish old Blanche Betterous's journal of Atlanta's high-class whorehouse days elicited the same
unselfconscious justification more than a decade earlier. Vice, pornography, and wickedness titillated her, but Puritan morality exerted its
own independent pull on her imagination too.

For all her ambivalence about the character, however, Scarlett O'Hara
completely dominates Mitchell's literary imagination. Like Becky Sharpe
in *Vanity Fair*, Scarlett might be no "heroine," strictly defined, but she
completely overshadows the other characters in the book. For all Me-
laine's virtues and Scarlett's sins, the story belongs to Scarlett O'Hara,
not Melanie, not Ellen, not Mammy, despite Mitchell's spirited defense
of these characters. The author, moreover, intended just this; and
nothing, indeed, compromised more thoroughly her claims for the good
heroine than the literary centrality of the bad one. Scarlett's career
shaped the very form and fabric of the narrative. From the outset
Mitchell had intended the novel as a revelation of Scarlett's mind, as
she herself admitted. The heroine issue then rotates perpetually back
to Mitchell's conception of this character; and of all her references to
Scarlett, none are more significant than her revelations to an Augusta
psychiatrist, Dr. Hervey Cleckley.

Although Mitchell offered many different judgments of her protagonist to different readers, at no time did she ever praise Scarlett out-
right as a model of behavior. While she might have rationalized or
justified her heroine in certain contexts, as with Monsignor Murphy,
she also left evidence that she had intended to create a psychological
deviant whose actions flowed naturally out of the necessities of her
delusions. This intention actually resonates with some of the deepest
interests of her own life. She harbored a secret wish to practice neurology and psychology, and she boasted often of her skill in psychoanalyzing her companions. She read psychology and psychoanalytic theory as avidly as some people read novels and romances, and her own
library boasted a wide range of titles, from Krafft-Ebbing and Havelock Ellis, to Brill, Karen Horney, and Theodor Reik. In this context,
her correspondence with Dr. Hervey Cleckley acquires a special significance, and to no one did she reveal more of Scarlett O'Hara's flaws as
a personality.

One of the few psychiatrists (and certainly the most notable) south of Washington, D.C., Cleckley appealed to Mitchell in various ways. A native Georgian, he sprang from a distinguished Augusta family, matriculated at the University of Georgia, and won a Rhodes scholarship while in Athens. After leaving Oxford, he returned to Georgia to complete his medical degree with specialties in neurology and psychology. He remained in his native state to chair the Department of Neurology and Psychiatry at the Veteran's Hospital in Augusta and teach at the Georgia School of Medicine. He had an extensive private practice and published widely. From his college days as editor of the student newspaper and yearbook, Cleckley had also cultivated literary ambitions. He knew belles lettres, read widely, wrote fiction himself, and even in his psychoanalytic studies aimed for nonspecialists and a general audience as well as other physicians. He won an international reputation in the mid-fifties with his phenomenally successful examination of split personality, *The Three Faces of Eve*, in its time the only psychoanalytic study ever translated into a very successful, Oscar-winning, Hollywood movie. Although the Atlanta author did not live to see Cleckley to his worldwide notoriety, she acknowledged his genius long before. She hailed him from the publication of his first book in 1941, *The Mask of Sanity*. Describing "a type of insanity which heretofore has not been called insanity," this text examined the psychopathic, sociopathic, or antisocial personality, variously so-called.

Mitchell loved the study. "His case histories were interesting and well done, and it was obvious that the writer had a sense of humor," she wrote. The book moved gracefully, too, and she related having read most of it aloud with her husband. It also won a special commendation, "that this was the first psychiatric work we had ever seen which dealt with the mental problems of Southern people." She turned the pages with "genuine enthusiasm," but nothing pleased her quite as much as her discovery of her own creation in Cleckley's pages.[34] *Mask of Sanity* had included a very wide-ranging discussion of "fictional characters of psychiatric interest," and this section chronicled none other than Scarlett among its categories of notable psychopaths in literature.

The Augusta psychiatrist considered Mitchell's characterization of Scarlett true-to-life and "very convincing." He thought her picture captured the same "emotional impoverishment" that his own book described in a category of people he called "partial psychopaths." The character, he wrote, "fails regularly to respond to sincere emotion in her lovers and pursues above all else aims that are fundamentally egocentric and trivial." He elaborated:

Her incapacity for true commitment in love is apparently unmodifiable; her egocentricity is basic. She seems to be without means of understand-

ing the strong emotions in those about her or of having adequate awareness of what makes them act when they act in accord with principles
they value. Unlike the complete psychopath, she successfully pursues ends
that lead to her material well-being and she avoids putting herself in
positions of obvious folly and shame. In her, however, we sense an inward hollowness and serious lack of insight.[35]

Mitchell cherished the analysis. She thought that it summed up her
heroine "very shrewdly," as she informed her editor at the Macmillan
Company.[36] Writing Cleckley himself, she praised the judgment even
more lavishly; she added, in the process, her own most remarkable
arabesque to his analysis:

> Perhaps most authors would not take it kindly that a psychiatrist spoke
> of one of their characters as a "partial psychopath," but I feel distinctly
> pleased. Of course, I did not set out to delineate a psychopathic person-
> ality nor to do a psychoanalytical study. The novelist who consciously
> ventures into the realm of psychiatry does so at her peril and generally
> to the detriment of story and character. I set out to depict a far-from-
> admirable woman about whom little that was good could be said, and I
> attempted to keep her in character. I have found it wryly amusing when
> Miss O'Hara became somewhat of a national heroine and I have thought
> it looked bad for the moral and mental attitude of a nation that the na-
> tion could applaud and take to its heart a woman who conducted herself
> in such a manner. I have been bewildered and amused, too, when my
> book as been attacked because I pictured in detail a "passionate and
> wanton woman." I thought it would be obvious to anyone that Scarlett
> was a frigid woman, loving attention and adulation for their own sake
> but having little or no comprehension of actual deep feelings and no re-
> actions to the love and attention of others. I suppose it takes a psychia-
> trist to realize this, so perhaps you can understand my appreciation of
> your remarks.[37]

In the author's elaboration of Cleckley's themes, the reference to
frigidity leaps in from nowhere. She did not use the term casually.
While Mitchell had followed the field of psychoanalytical theory as a
favorite pastime for years, the reference to frigidity must have had the
most explicit meaning for her, as she left evidence of having studied
the expert in the field. One of the earliest members of Freud's circle,
Wilhelm Stekel had built his reputation on the examination of "dis-
pareunia." His major study on the subject had appeared much earlier
in German, but the two-volume English translation, *Frigidity in Woman
in Relation to Her Love Life*, went to press in 1926, published by Boni
and Liveright, that notable purveyor of the forbidden that had made
notorious, such authors as Hemingway, Joyce, and the local hero Frances
Newman of Atlanta. Mitchell read the work. Indeed, she was poring
through Stekel's text just as she commenced her novel.[38]

Stekel's work attracted Margaret Mitchell's interest for many reasons. Although scientific and analytical, Stekel and his translator wrote in a graceful literary mode that completely eschewed psychological jargon. The text also brimmed with all the sexual, scatological, half-pornographic kind of material that always excited the young Atlantan. Besides the case studies by Stekel himself, Freud, Havelock Ellis, and others, it also contained very long, apparently unexpurgated, firsthand "confessions" of women who had gone to Stekel for assistance. It was Blanche Betterous all over again. Finally, a book about women interested her beyond all else, and Stekel wrote not just about deviance but women's condition—their relations with men, with children, and not least with their own mothers and fathers. Like Freud, Stekel discovered the root of distortion in the victim's family circle, and he defined his task as tracing all the manifestations of the perversion as a means of discovering their sources in her childhood. His object was to discover the secrets of a woman's life that produced the ailment. He drew out, effectively, the whole woman, who was his real interest.[39]

When Margaret Mitchell referred to her heroine as "loving attention and adulation for their own sake but having little or no comprehension of actual deep feelings and no reactions to the love and attention of others," she might have paraphrased the Austrian psychiatrist's ideas of frigidity. Indeed, Stekel's formulations fill out the sketch of the heroine's egocentricity that Cleckley made. Category after category in Stekel's lexicon applies to Mitchell's heroine. In his terms, she "anesthetized feeling"; she could neither give nor respond to love and affection. With a shriveled capacity for the affective, she lacked integrity on her own terms. Something was the matter with the heroine: something was missing. She was only half a person by the good physician's analysis—but by the author's evaluation, too, and indeed, by the logic of the character's development in the text.

Scarlett O'Hara was perverted. She was not a happy girl, nor a contented woman. Mitchell captured the truth of that perversion, and her own ambivalence about the figure echoes the protagonist's divided mind. The author's conflict reflects more fundamental discordances within the text. These reveal, in turn, deeper levels of biographical significance in the novel and deeper levels of the author's personal engagement with Scarlett's infirmities.

XIII

The Strange Disappearance
of Pansy Hamilton
🏵🏵🏵🏵

As to where I "fit in" in the book, I do not know. I tried to write as completely an objective book with nothing of myself in it. I am sure I am not Scarlett, and I could not hope to be Melanie! However, I know that the personality of an author will creep into a book no matter how hard the author struggles, but I do not know what part of me is in it. All I know is that a number of years of my life and a lot of sweat went into that book.

MARGARET MITCHELL TO MR. A. W. WOOTTON [1]

*A*s every aficionado of *Gone with the Wind* knows, Margaret Mitchell did not christen her lusty heroine "Katie Scarlett"; she conceived her first as "Pansy." Indeed, she identified the name so thoroughly with the character and the character so thoroughly with the book that she used it to refer to the manuscript, too. "By all means keep 'Pansy' longer if you feel it necessary," she had instructed the Macmillan Company in July 1935.[2] Not until mid-fall of 1935, with publication scheduled for only six months away, did she propose the other name by which her heroine lives in the popular imagination. As late as November 7, 1935, she still worried about the new choice and toyed with alternatives.[3] For almost ten years, then, from the novel's inception in the fall of 1926 right up to finished draft in 1935, the author addressed her protagonist as Pansy.

The name, of course, has its own history. Her earlier fiction about the Atlanta Jazz Age flapper introduced the figure. Mitchell had begun her story of contemporary Atlanta only to lay it aside for the Civil War epic, but it had described many of her most interior concerns.[4] Those concerns did not evaporate when she abandoned the first story. They lived in part through the reuse and extension of the old heroine's name in the new novel.

In the Jazz Age story, the names "Pansy" and "Hamilton" have their own meaning, both separately and together. As noted earlier, Mitchell identified the surname "Hamilton" with stability, tradition, and the Old South. "Pansy," conversely, suggests alternative values. In *Gone with the Wind*, Mitchell took the name and split it into its component parts. Scarlett, most obviously, represents all the Pansy values of rebellion, insouciance, and change; Melanie embodies the Hamilton virtues. While Mitchell separated her old heroine into two, she also recombined them twice over. In the first place, Pansy, born O'Hara, was actually Pansy Hamilton through almost half the original text. Pansy/Scarlett as Hamilton introduces the richness of Mitchell's intentions. In the first place, Pansy is only a nominal Hamilton. Appropriately, Rhett always sneers at and ridicules her title of "Mrs. Hamilton," reminiscent of Lord Nelson's mistress. "Did you ever really have a husband, my dear?" he jeers.[5] Like the original Pansy Hamilton in the flapper story, Pansy O'Hara is also the product of a *mésalliance*, and her marriage to Charles Hamilton is another. She assumes the aristocratic surname, but she remains an illegitimate Hamilton.

In the second place, the name binds Melanie and Scarlett together. For all the artificiality of "Mrs. Hamilton" for Scarlett/Pansy, the name seals her sisterhood with Melanie. The marriage to Charles Hamilton provides the means by which Mitchell reunites the halves of her old heroine, but the union is ragged and incomplete. If the two belong together, they also belong apart. Mitchell's further play with names suggests as much. The author deprives Melanie of her surname just as Pansy/Scarlett acquires it, and the change confirms the tension of the new sisterhood. While Melanie clings to her old name now through her new "sister" whom she adores, Pansy/Scarlett bitterly resents the sisterhood, despises Melanie even more, takes no pleasure in her surname, and looks to change it at the earliest opportunity. Melanie acknowledges and honors their sisterhood; Scarlett repudiates and hates it. Nevertheless, the two remain inextricably tied throughout the novel through the putative family/name relationship.

Mitchell took her narrative of her own times, borrowed its protagonist, separated her into her component parts, transposed the fragments back in time, recombined them, and separated them again. Her naming illustrates the meaning of her one-in-two heroine/heroines bound fitfully together and then separated again. But the play with names, of course, spilled beyond the writing itself, for in the manuscript's last hours before becoming a book, Mitchell obscured the original identity almost completely when she jettisoned "Pansy" for "Scarlett." She denied her heroine her nominal identity as decisively as Pansy's husbands did. With all this confusion and obscuring of identity, Mitchell might well have appreciated and understood her old friend Hervey Cleckley's "Eve."

For the author of *Gone with the Wind*—a.k.a. Margaret Munnerlyn Mitchell, Margaret MacKenzie Mitchell, Peggy Mitchell, Mrs. B. K. Upshaw, Peggy Mitchell Upshaw, P.M.M., Peggy Mitchell Marsh, Mrs. John R. Marsh, and M.M.M.M.—names and naming constituted a fundamental aspect of her identity. She also used names as dress, costume, or disguise to suggest a different persona or variation on her identity. For all her playing with different names, she did not use them casually. She did not name her fictional characters casually. Certainly she did not use "Scarlett" casually.

In the flapper story, Mitchell made Pansy Hamilton her double. Her peculiar reuse of the name in the novel suggests the heroines together represent the halves of her own ego and alter ego. By this measure, if she is neither Pansy/Scarlett nor Melanie alone, she is both together, and they represent the fragmented impulses of her own character. Even this biographical fact, however, disguises other issues. Pansy/Scarlett and Melanie represent both much more and rather less than the author's own divided sense of self. They define the circumstances of women's lives. And this leads to the larger purpose of her novel. She wanted to write *women's* history. Even before she knew what her friend was planning, much less that she was actually writing a long novel, Elinor Hillyer received Mitchell's confidence about these other intentions. "Elinor, I want to write a book about women," Mitchell told her. "Every one has always told the men's stories; I want to tell the women's and what it was like for them during the War."[6] According to her friend, her revelation implied a plan to redeem women's place in history and in Southern history. She stated the same motive explicitly in the series of articles she wrote on women's history for the *Atlanta Journal* in the spring of 1923: to restore women to their proper role in history.

Telling women's stories, however, engaged far more complicated aspects of Mitchell's own personal story than she suggested to her friend Hillyer. Hidden within the concept of women's history, for Mitchell, lay a whole series of other issues about the nature of womanhood. Do Pansy and Hamilton together equal Peggy Mitchell? Pansy versus Hamilton also equal the divisive unity between Peggy Mitchell and May Belle Mitchell. This is the final and most critical set of identities, and they provide both form and content for Mitchell's epic: the story of parents and children, mothers and daughters, daughters and mothers, birth and death, autonomy and dependence. And behind all this lay the specific paradoxes that governed the author's own life and the relationship with her own mother, feared and sainted, May Belle Stephens Mitchell. In this issue is the beginning of *Gone with the Wind*, as the author herself admitted, and the great, if often hidden, content of the story.

The romance in *Gone with the Wind* between Rhett Butler and Scarlett O'Hara has tended to obscure other relationships in the novel. With justice, readers have focused on the dark, handsome, dashing hero. On the surface at least, Rhett represents a classic masculine type in fiction, and Mitchell herself confessed she drew him out of Victorian women's fiction. Stephen Vincent Benét made the connection in his notice of the novel in *The Saturday Review*, and Mitchell responded enthusiastically. "And I yelled with delight at your mentioning St. Elmo. I had a bet up that either St. Elmo or Mr. Rochester would be Rhett's comparisons," she told the poet. These characters had power, she insisted, and they bespoke the fundamental values of the age. "They are pretty hackneyed now but, as far as I could see, there was nothing for me to do but take Victorian types and put them into my Victorian background," she explained.[7]

Rhett Butler, indeed, bears more than a passing resemblance to St. Elmo Murray of Augusta Jane Evans Wilson's *St. Elmo* and Edward Fairfax Rochester of Charlotte Brontë's *Jane Eyre*. He differs just as significantly. He shares with them their dark, handsome looks, mysterious hurts, haunted history, and masculine authority; like them, too, he is finally broken by a woman. The course and meaning of that break, however, underline the vast differences between the characters. Mr. Rochester and St. Elmo Murray are broken for a higher purpose; women are the agents of their effective conversions to both domesticity and Christianity. Women save the men of the Victorian model; they release them to their better selves. That is not the case with Rhett Butler. On the contrary, he effectively reverses this pattern. For all his roguery, he plays the better part to Scarlett. All along, he seeks to encourage her true self and elicit the tender, compassionate side in her nature. He finally succeeds, but he wins a Pyrrhic victory: his own will breaks in the process. Scarlett has worn him down, and he cannot enjoy the fruits of his triumph. The end of pride, then, produces not the natural contentment, union, and romantic resolution of *St. Elmo* and *Jane Eyre*, but despair.

By much the same token, the women in *St. Elmo* and *Jane Eyre* help the men acknowledge the gentle or feminine traits in their own natures: tenderness, compassion, human sympathy, and self-abnegation. In contrast, Rhett possesses those virtues without need of tutoring. Indeed, without being effete like Ashley or feminine in any way, Rhett displays many of the positive virtues associated with women and mothers. He is sympathetic and intuitive. He is compassionate and tender. He nurtures not only his own child, Bonnie, but also his step-children. Indeed, he is far superior in this regard to their biological mother, who lacks any "pat and mat instincts" whatsoever. Rhett demonstrates, effectively, the best of trans-gender virtue, being at once intensely male but equally capable of otherwise feminine responses. He resembles in this way a kind of ideal type that Mitchell first sketched in her high school story, "Sergeant Terry," in his personal integrity and his ability to maintain coherence—until the very end at least—despite divergent trends in his own character. In contrast to the heroes of the Victorian novel, then, Rhett nurtures and—literally—mothers Scarlett. "I wanted to take care of you, to pet you, to give you every-thing you wanted," he confessed:

> No one knew better than I what you'd gone through and I wanted you to stop fighting and let me fight for you. I wanted you to play, like a child—for you were a child, a brave, frightened, bullheaded child. I think you are still a child. No one but a child could be so headstrong and so insen-sitive.[8]

Rhett plays, in short, the part of ideal mother. Just so, Margaret Mitchell also linked Rhett specifically with her own mother.

With general consistency, Margaret Mitchell disassociated real peo-ple from her fictional characters. In a notable exception, however, Mitchell identified Rhett Butler with May Belle Mitchell's voice and vision. In that seminal episode in 1907 when the child refused to go to school, May Belle Mitchell had taken the little girl out the Jonesboro road and hectored her about survival for a woman in a ruthless world. The daughter wrote her parent's sermon, she said, into the text almost verbatim. In Chapter XLIII, Scarlett has just given birth to Frank Ken-nedy's child. Rhett had disappeared upon her confinement, and he has just returned to Atlanta. He visits Scarlett. In the course of discussing his own survival after his own father disinherited him, Rhett turns the conversation to Ashley Wilkes. Rhett mocks him. Scarlett defends him, although in her heart, she acknowledges the validity of all Rhett says. Rhett knows this, and he wants her only to own up to what she knows. Don't be stupid, he challenges her. She rises to the bait, and resists him by trying to annoy and distract him. Rhett presses on. He points out the real heroes, people with spunk and determination—like Scar-lett herself. There follows his diatribe against Ashley and all those who, "in an upside-down world," "have neither cunning nor strength or, having them, scruple to use them. And so they go under and they should go under. It's a natural law and the world is better off without them. But there are always a hardy few who come through and, given time, they are right back where they were before the world turned over."[9]

With the addition of a feminist context, this was the lesson that May Belle Mitchell had delivered almost twenty years before.

The association of Rhett Butler and May Belle Mitchell possesses the most potent implications for the novel and its latent biographical content. Most popular readings of *Gone with the Wind* search for models for the novel's men in Mitchell's husbands and lovers—Rhett is Red Upshaw; Clifford Henry becomes Ashley Wilkes; John Marsh, Frank Kennedy.[10] Those masculine comparisons, however, hide this more critical identity. Making Rhett a surrogate for May Belle Mitchell offers the most compelling insights into Mitchell's relationship with her own parent; it illuminates the fatal conflict between the two fictional characters as well. Mitchell characterizes the fictional relation as racked by cross-purposes and misunderstandings that vitiate and pervert a basic harmony of interests between the two. When Scarlett finally in that last chapter does realize the truth of things and acknowledges that fundamental unity, her awareness comes too late. The "good mother" Rhett has expired, effectively, by then. Rhett's love has died as surely as Melanie Wilkes, and he resigns his charge now permanently (sequels notwithstanding). Scarlett, of course, has brought this fate down on her own head through her stubborn willfulness and blind obstinacy. This revelation in the last chapter, of course, was where Mitchell actually commenced writing; she began and ended the book with Rhett's rejection and the death of that other "good mother," Melanie. In defining the fatal cross-purposes of Rhett's and Scarlett's lives, then, Mitchell hints that the same forces governed her relations with her own parent.

Beyond this general Rhett–May Belle identity, Mitchell left still other evidence of her mother's powerful influence on her novel. That affair on the Jonesboro road provides the key to understanding central conflicts in the writer's life, how she worked them through in *Gone with the Wind*, and how, finally, they provided the overarching themes of the novel itself: the fundamental conflicts between parents and children—specifically, mothers and daughters—and the conflicted nature of womanhood itself.

In the first place, Mitchell never varied her testimony that the confrontation with her mother on the Jonesboro road provided her the most obvious theme of her novel: survival. On the simplest level, her mother's fierce homily inspired her interest in the social problem of who rose, who fell, and who merely hung on in the shattered South after the Civil War. Survival, however, also had much more personal implications for Margaret Mitchell and for her attitudes about her parent. May Belle Mitchell had used a lesson in social history chiefly as a means of forestalling failure and encouraging her child to take "the high road of success." While the child returned to school, of course, the mother never convinced herself she had won the battle. Late in her life, she admitted to Mrs. Paisley that she did not know whether her Margaret was headed towards success or failure. The same ambivalence characterized the daughter's response and helped shape her later attitudes about herself and her accomplishments. While *Gone with the Wind*'s triumph might have proved the mother wrong and the child right, Mitchell never could fully savor her attainments: something, as she wrote earlier, was missing. The compromised successes and half-won failures of the Jonesboro Road affair, then, provide a paradigm for the larger issues at stake in Mitchell's relations with her mother. They also introduce the conflicts over women, mothers, and motherhood that pervade the novel itself.

Underlining the importance of the 1907 confrontation with her mother in the creation of her novel, Mitchell also included the Jonesboro road itself in her fiction. It provides the setting for some of the most critical literary episodes in the book, but these passages also replay many of the same elements that characterized the real-life struggle between the mother and the daughter.

The road makes its first appearance in Chapter XXIII as Scarlett's little crew flees the burning Atlanta. Melanie has just survived, if barely, her dreadful labor; the city has surrendered to the Yankees; the invaders are entering the town; and the Confederates are torching what had survived the siege guns. Panic rules. Scarlett calls frantically for Rhett; he commandeers a priceless horse and wagon; and the six—Rhett, Scarlett, Melanie, Prissy, Wade Hampton, and the newborn infant— flee the invaders through the conflagration and chaos deep in the night between September 1 and 2. The little party survives the holocaust, and as the chapter ends, they reach the point at which the city straggles off into the countryside. And just there, as they set the first foot on "the Jonesboro road, 'the road to Tara,'" Rhett abandons Scarlett. His gesture outrages and baffles her; and well it might. Ostensibly the sight of the broken soldiers goads Rhett's conscience, and stirs the "betraying sentimentality that lurks in all of us Southerners,"[11] yet little or nothing in his character up to that point anticipates this turn to Confederate patriotism. If the transformation dumbfounded Scarlett, it also plagued other audiences. In translating the novel into film, the scriptwriters labored long over this section and complained bitterly about Rhett's unanticipated transformation.

On the one hand, Rhett's gesture "betrays" (his own term) his real nature—his sentimentality, his kinship with the soldiers, his human capacity for shame, and his desire for exculpation. The reader learns Rhett's secret, and this scene allows a full measure of sympathy, then, for the misunderstood, noble, self-sacrificing, and grandly quixotic Rhett. His now-selfless behavior contrasts sharply with Scarlett's dense egoism. She, of course, is stupid, and cannot understand Rhett's real virtue. Or so it seems. In another sense, Rhett's leaving Scarlett, regardless of the reasons, serves its own purposes.

As in the death of Frank Kennedy, how or why Rhett leaves matters far less than the mere fact of his departure. Two critical issues follow. From one perspective, his leaving clears the way for what follows to be Scarlett's show alone—her awful Mother Courage journey back to Tara in Chapter XXIV. The author herself equated Rhett's voice and her mother's on the Jonesboro road, and Rhett's departure here duplicates the good mother's hard counsel—the hard mother's good counsel. He forces her to stand on her own. If his leaving provokes her antipathy, that is even better for her, if not for him. While he suffers in silence, her courage rises with her gorge. His apparent rejection pricks her pride and thereby bolsters her determination. While he prompts or aggravates her problem, then, his leaving also multiplies the chances of her success. Scarlett, of course, sees none of this. Thus, from another perspective, while his leaving liberates her heroism, she herself sees only rejection and abandonment. From her immediate perspective on the road to Tara, her real source of strength has vanished. His departure isolates, alienates, and terrifies her. In stark terror, she attacks her protector who is failing her through motives of his own. The future without his strength dismays her. She does not like living with him, but living without him terrifies her more. She is, however, now on her own on the Jonesboro road.

These underlying emotions and reactions at Rhett's departure on the road to Tara suggest the dynamics between the mother and the daughter in 1907. And lest Mitchell leave any doubt about the meaning and origins of Rhett's rejection as a replay of her own biography, she manages even to slip a six-year-old girl into the scene. As Rhett announces his decision to abandon her, Scarlett panics, and her mind flies helplessly back to a childhood accident. "Once, when she was six years old, she had fallen from a tree, flat on her stomach," she remembers. "Now, as she looked at Rhett, she felt the same way she had felt then, breathless, stunned, nauseated."[12]

William Faulkner declared that the only thing in his literature that ever moved him very much was "Caddy climbing the pear tree to look in the window at her grandmother's funeral while Quentin and Jason and Benjy and the negroes looked up at the muddy seat of her drawers": an affair that grew out of his own childhood experience at his own grandmother's death in 1907 when he was ten, the same age as Quentin in the story.[13] This memory inspired not merely a scene but a vision of the book's great purpose. So it was with Margaret Mitchell. While she re-created that seminal episode with her mother, complete with bruised six-year-old, she, like Faulkner, charged the affair with a meaning that inspired her whole novel. This larger purpose of her book centered on what Mitchell herself elsewhere declared the central, defining characteristic of women's lives—the birth experience. Giving birth and being born evokes natural connections to life and death, to women and children, to motherhood, to womanhood, and to a legion of contradictory issues related to autonomy, independence, and self for womankind. Mitchell clearly establishes this context for the conflict on the "road to Tara" in the chapters immediately preceding that event.

Among the most memorable and dramatic of the entire book, Chapters XXI, XXII, and XXIII tell the story of Melanie's awful labor, Prissy's lying midwifery, Scarlett's more successful (if hardly less ignorant) efforts, and little Beau's dreadful entrance into the world; all this played out against the final battle of Atlanta and the raging destruction of the town itself. David Selznick made these scenes some of the most memorable and spectacular of his movie, but the author had already burned them into the popular imagination by 1939. The author commanded her material completely here. And she knew precisely what she wanted to accomplish. Frequently in her private correspondence Mitchell linked or associated battle and childbirth: the one was to men as the other was to women. She does so richly here, playing the one off against the other to heighten the dramatic impact of both.

Amid these literally epic scenes of life and death, birth and destruction, the character Prissy also holds a special place. Chapters XXI through XXIV belong to this figure like no other section of the book. These are Prissy's chapters; she has no other real place outside them. Her depiction illustrates the most potent themes in this section and illuminates the significance of these episodes for Mitchell's own life. The end of Chapter XXI reveals the little black maid as a worthless, irresponsible child and, worse yet, a false and lying midwife. Not the least of Prissy's characteristics, however, is that she is also a bad daughter. Although David Selznick omitted Prissy's mother, Dilcey, from his film, the "pickaninny's" foolishness and errors, played so nicely by Butterfly McQueen, assume their full meaning only in contrast with the dignity, nobility, and success of her mother. Mitchell contrasts the two characters throughout the novel, and the comparison always underlines the declension from mother to child. Indeed, that contrast is nowhere stronger than in this very section of the text. If Chapters XXI, XXII, and XXIII feature Prissy's idiocy and foolishness, particularly as a midwife, this section concludes with an almost iconographic rendering of Dilcey as the complete woman and natural mother in Chapter XXIV. The two contrast completely: the responsible adult and ideal mother versus the prevaricating child and foolish daughter. Actually, not the least element of Dilcey's nobility is her loyalty to her stupid daughter. Gerald O'Hara's willingness to keep mother and daughter together lays the foundation of Dilcey's unswerving sense of obligation to the white family. Yet despite her filial devotion, Dilcey herself acknowledges and even condemns her child. "She all nigger lak her Pa," she says. Dilcey is, of course, more Indian than African, but the epithet has much more to do with a tense mother–daughter relationship than with racial slurs. If an ideal mother, then, Dilcey is a most exacting parent. As the plantation midwife, for example, she refused to share her art with her own child. "Ah jes' see one baby birthed, an' Maw she lak ter wo' me out fer watchin'," the girl moans to the enraged and terrified Scarlett.[14] Prissy can never live up to Dilcey's model. The mother's successes are the measure of the daughter's failures.

If Scarlett plays something of the punishing mother to Prissy's foolish child, the two characters are sisters beneath the skin as well. A curious artifact of regional culture confirms it. Southern girls often played with rag dolls of a black pickaninny in calico, which, when turned upside down, flipped its skirts to show a blue-eyed, blonde, pigtailed doll beneath.[15] And so it was in Mitchell's fiction. Flip Pansy over, and there is Prissy. Mitchell depicts them both and centrally, as irresponsible, foolish children. Prissy does no more than caricature this element in Scarlett's own nature. This, indeed, represents one source of Scarlett's violent and unrestrained antagonism to her: Prissy embodies all the features she fears within herself. The mothers of the two girls also resemble each other in general outline, so that the two girls share the common burden of daughterhood to ideal, iconic matriarchs. And finally, they share the common role of midwife who very nearly doubles as abortionist. If Prissy's ignorance leads in this direction, Scarlett actually wishes Melanie dead in labor.

Prissy occupied a crucial role in the critical central section of the book, but she also held a unique place in Mitchell's imagination. This character provided a rare occasion for the author to project herself into her fiction. Mitchell made claims for this character that she did for none other in the whole book. "I have been especially interested in who would play the little varmint possibly because this is the only part I myself would like to play," she told her friend Kay Brown in 1937. "For this reason, whoever plays Prissy will be up against a dreadful handicap as far as I am concerned, for I will watch their actions with a jealous eye."[16] Mitchell joked, of course, but she left other, otherwise odd clues that this character truly occupied a special place in her imagination. She confided to still another correspondent that "the little black maid Prissy" was the only character in the entire novel to be based on a real person.[17] She volunteered to still another reader that Prissy was one of her favorite characters, but she included a significant qualifier when she added, "She aggravated me unendurably while I was writing her and, when Scarlett slapped her, it was really Margaret Mitchell yielding to an overwhelming urge. . . ."[18] Pansy, Prissy, Peggy: the similarity in names underlines the union.

While Chapters XXI through XXIII introduce the horrors of childbed and the fatality of motherhood, Chapter XXIV deals even more intensely, if not always so directly, with death and loss. The closing lines establish the tone as Rhett leaves Scarlett: "He had set his varnished boots upon a bitter road where hunger tramped with tireless stride and wounds and weariness and heartbreak ran like yelping wolves. And the end of the road was death."[19] The language anticipates the course of Scarlett's journey, too, as she makes her way home.

At the beginning of Chapter XXIV, then, the author begins again with the Jonesboro road—the road to Tara. This is where the novel had begun in September 1907; this was where she finished it in the fall of 1929. It is also, effectively, where she began writing in the fall of 1926. That first/last chapter had ended with Rhett's final first abandonment. In both XXIV and LXIII, the themes are all the same and echo all the motifs of the real road episode in 1907. It was a blistering day on September 2, 1864, when Scarlett hit the road—it had been "the hottest day I ever saw" for the six-year-old in that other September of 1907. The big battle? the two armies? the desolation of the field? It had been the battle of Margaret and her mother no less than of Generals Hood and Sherman. May Belle Mitchell, like her own heroine, Joan of Arc, thought in military terms. They came easily for her daughter, too. Scarlett materialized through the mist of both battles. If the novel was born in a battle royal between a mother and a daughter, themes of mothers and daughters dominate the chapter, too. In 1907 the subject of the conflict had been dependence versus independence, the role of women in the world, the ways that women might survive upheaval. But what is independence for a woman? While May Belle Mitchell had demanded her daughter's autonomy in 1907, she had blurred the question in her deathbed letter. That blurring certainly existed long before, and the tangled skein of dependence/independence, mothers as daughters, daughters as mothers, lay at the core of female identity for Margaret Mitchell, for May Belle Mitchell, and for the heroines in Chapter XXIV. No less than the chapters that precede it, this one chronicles the burdens of birth and the paradoxes of motherhood. Scarlett herself is reborn on the road to Tara.

Mitchell left no doubt that Chapter XXIV chronicled her heroine's complete transformation, and that the Jonesboro road equaled birth for her quite as terrible as little Beau's had been. The heroine does not wish to be reborn. She resists all the way. In this regard she hits the road to Tara initially as a regression and an escape from womanhood and adult responsibility. If in the birthing chapters she exercised skills and authority she did not know she had, the very activity repulsed her. She longs to reverse the course of her own development. She seeks to lose herself in the old, matriarchal shelter her mother, Mammy, Tara, and the very idea of home:

"Mother! Mother!" she whispered. If she could only win to Ellen! If only, by a miracle of God, Tara were still standing and she could drive up the long avenue of trees and go into the house and see her mother's kind, tender face, could feel once more the soft capable hands that drove out fear, could clutch Ellen's skirts and bury her face in them. Mother would know what to do. She wouldn't let Melanie and her baby die. She would drive away all ghosts and fears with her quiet "Hush, hush."[20]

Scarlett would make herself a little girl again, subject to her mother's authority.

If she could only lie down and sleep and wake to feel Ellen gently shaking her and saying: "It is late, Scarlett. You must not be so lazy." . . . If there were only Ellen, someone older than she, wiser and unweary, to whom she could go! Someone in whose lap she could lay her head, someone on whose shoulders she could rest her burdens![21]

Mammy's bosom was even broader than her mother's, her lap more copious, and Ellen's death pushed the heroine more frantically towards this other matriarch. "Soon Mammy would be with her—Ellen's Mammy, her Mammy." She comforted herself with the thought as she watched Dilcey suckling Melanie's baby:

She sat silent, intent on nothing, while the baby, already glutted with milk, whimpered because he had lost the friendly nipple. Dilcey, silent too, guided the child's mouth back, quieted him in her arms as Scarlett listened to the slow scuffing of Mammy's feet across the back yard. . . . Scarlett ran to her, laying her head on the broad sagging breasts which had held so many heads, black and white. Here was something of stability, thought Scarlett, something of the old life that was unchanging.[22]

Scarlett would be to Mammy as the tiny, helpless newborn was to Dilcey. Mitchell's juxtaposition here of Dilcey, the nursing infant, and Scarlett and Mammy's breast underlines the heroine's elemental desires. Scarlett's passivity, as she "sat silent, intent on nothing," mirrors the infant's utter dependency and anticipates her own desire to lose herself at Mammy's "friendly nipple."

Yet, however much against her own will and desire, Scarlett is reborn anyway. The chapter ends with an explicit statement of the change. "She was seeing things with new eyes for, somewhere along the long road to Tara, she had left her girlhood behind her. . . . Tonight was the last time she would ever be ministered to as a child. She was a woman now and youth was gone. . . . Tomorrow she would fit the yoke about her neck."[23] In Chapter XXV, Mitchell restates the transformation one more time. She does so, significantly, in renewed images of roads. The heroine has gone to Twelve Oaks. Maddened by hunger, she claws those famous radishes from the dirt, devours them, vomits them back up, and collapses behind a slave cabin. "For a timeless time, she lay still, her face in the dirt, the sun beating hotly upon her, remembering things and people who were dead, remembering a way of living that was gone forever—and looking upon the harsh vista of the dark future." Things would never be the same again.

> When she arose at last and saw again the black ruins of Twelve Oaks, her head was raised high and something that was youth and beauty and potential tenderness had gone out of her face forever. What was past was past. Those who were dead were dead. . . . And as Scarlett settled the heavy basket across her arm, she had settled her own mind and her own life. . . .
>
> She gazed at the blackened stones and, for the last time, she saw Twelve Oaks rise before her eyes as it had once stood, rich and proud. . . . Then she started down the road towards Tara, the heavy basket cutting into her flesh.[24]

Scarlett's transformation involved tremendous loss, pain, and, ultimately, anger. It meant the loss, first, of affection, sentiment, and feeling. In this sense, this passage from *Gone with the Wind* echoes the sentiments and even the language of Mitchell's first published story, "Little Sister" of 1917. After the rape, murder, mayhem, and general destruction of that earlier tale, the Little Sister changed in much the same way Scarlett did: "the little freckled face was tear-streaked and dirty, but set in stone, and grim lines, so alien to the childish mouth, had been drawn there by unrelaxed vigilance. But the blue eyes were not wet now. She had cried—in the night—a million years before." Both stories evoke images of birth and labor. In both, mothers die. So does innocence. So, effectively, do innocents: if the virgin Big Sister went to be with the angels, courtesy of the bandits, Scarlett and little Peggy die just as effectively as girls and children and emerge into a hard, ruthless world as dry-eyed stony-visaged women. In *A Room of One's Own*, Virginia Woolf insisted that a woman must slay "the angel in the house"—the self-constricting order of feminine domesticity—before she can create her own world. Mitchell does this. In the process, however, tenderness, affection, sympathy, and the sense of human community—values linked with nurturing motherhood—also wane. With their mothers dead, Scarlett and the Little Sister are reborn into a ruthless world of violence, force, and aggression. Are these values stereotypically male? Mitchell assumes so, and both characters assume explicitly male attributes. Scarlett actually moves towards an almost pathological masculine desire for power. The author denies them middle ground. Forbidden feeling and sensitivity, the characters are cut off from other women and even themselves. This affirms an elemental feature of Scarlett's personality: that she is only half a person. The Pansy longs for the Hamilton, its genuinely "better half." The halves belong to one; they also belong apart. This paradox defines the fundamental tension in the chapter that reveals the daughter's birth and the mother's death.

Scarlett's rebirth also involved a conscious repudiation of her mother. If Rhett's abandonment enraged her, her mother's death provoked related feelings. In her new self, she discovers "that everything her mother had told her about life was wrong. Nothing her mother had taught her was of any value whatsoever now." Her mother had instructed her that life treated women well when they were gentle and gracious, honorable and kind, modest and truthful. Absurd! Scarlett sneers. " 'Nothing, no, nothing she taught me is of any help to me! What good will kindness do me now? What value is gentleness? Better that I'd learned to plow or chop cotton like a darky. Oh, Mother, you were wrong!' "[25]

If a reader might second-guess the character here and judge her anger misguided, the author otherwise paints the sorriest picture of mothers. Over and over in these central chapters, Mitchell illustrates how home and mothers fail their offspring. All of Chapter XXIV underlines the fatality of domesticity and motherhood and equates death and mothering. With the exception of Dilcey and the pregnant cow the refugees discover, all the mothers betray or fail their offspring in one way or another. Although Scarlett flees to Tara for the "friendly nipple," all the other characterizations promise a withered tit and the taste of ashes.

The association of motherhood, birth, and death permeates the entire chapter from its beginning. The actual depiction of the road to Tara grins with chattering skulls. An early passage sets the tone.

> There was death in the air. In the rays of the late afternoon sun, every well-remembered field and forest grove was green and still, with an unearthly quiet that struck terror to Scarlett's heart. Every empty, shell-pitted house they passed that day, every gaunt chimney standing sentinel over smoke-blackened ruins, had frightened her more. They had not seen a living human being or animal since the night before. Dead men and dead horses, yes, and dead mules, lying by the road, swollen, covered with flies, but nothing alive. No far-off cattle lowed, no birds sang, no wind waved the trees. Only the tired plop-plop of the horse's feet and the weak wailing of Melanie's baby broke the stillness.

Mitchell continued immediately with a curious and compelling passage, one of the most vivid in the book, that equates this scene of fatal desolation with an almost mythic image of dead mothers. It evokes the impression of the sleeping princesses of fairy tales, of haunted groves of legends—of Medusas and Gorgons and vengeful Furies, too. And beneath it all, the mother's death agonies suggest, again, death in child-birth:

> The countryside lay as under some dread enchantment. Or worse still, thought Scarlett with a chill, like the familiar and dear face of a mother, beautiful and quiet at last, after death agonies. Thousands had died in the fighting near Jonesboro. They were here in these haunted woods and where the slanting afternoon sun gleamed eerily through unmoving leaves, friends and foes, peering at her in her rickety wagon, through eyes blinded with blood and red dust—glazed, horrible eyes.[26]

Mothers fail. The chapter opens with Melanie's inability to provide for her baby. She has no milk. Moreover, giving birth has wrecked her health; her ruined condition, in turn, endangers the lives of those around her as she proves to be deadweight to Scarlett, who tries to save her. Ellen, of course, is dead, but Mammy fails Scarlett just as thoroughly. On seeing her former charge, the black matriarch offers no strength and comfort. Instead, she blurts out her own dependency. Her first words dispel Scarlett's hopes, but the author had already foreshadowed the failure. Mammy has changed. Time has sagged her old bosom. Mitchell presages the failure in other ways in referring to the old woman's "ponderous weight" and "shoulders dragged down by two heavy wooden buckets." The reference to Mammy's "kind black face sad with the uncomprehending sadness of a monkey's face" has less to do, in this context, with negrophobic prejudice than with setting up this alternative matriarchal figure as the frailest of barriers against Scarlett's terrors.

While mothers fail their children, motherhood is also fatal to the mothers themselves. Melanie's birth-induced morbidity is only the initial example. This chapter also reveals that Ellen died because of her mothering. "Miss Ellen had mo'n she could tote anyways," Mammy grumbled, but she "wuz so sot in her ways an her heart so sof' she couldn' never say no ter nobody whut needed her." After nursing "dem trashy, no-good, low-down po'-w'ite Slatteries," and running herself down, she cared selflessly for her own sick family, wore herself out, and died without a fight. Mammy also noted, in passing, Ellen's almost suicidal disregard for her own health. Her mistress always "eat lak a bird anyways," she grieved.[27] The Yankee physician who tried to help repeated the observation. "He said she had undermined her own strength," Gerald recounted.[28]

If mothering is fatal, children are the agents of death. Chapter XXIV dwells on this theme: Children kill mothers. Beau almost killed Melanie; nursing the ill-begotten Slattery infant destroyed Ellen's health, while ministering to her own daughters Suellen and Carreen finally killed Ellen. Scarlett lives, in part, by repudiating the nurturing function. Motherhood for her is only biological. She lacks real affection for her children Wade and Ella and considers them nuisances and distractions at best. While this characterization is true throughout the novel, Chapter XXIV contains the most powerful language in all the book against babies and children:

> Why had God invented children, she thought savagely as she turned her ankle cruelly on the dark road—useless, crying nuisances they were, always demanding care, always in the way. In her exhaustion, there was no room for compassion for the frightened child, trotting by Prissy's side, dragging at her hand and sniffling—only a weariness that she had borne him, only a tired wonder that she had ever married Charles Hamilton.[29]

"Why did women have babies?" she had fulminated during Melanie's lying-in.[30] Infants made her shudder: white ones, black ones, the differences were inconsequential. "Babies, babies, babies," she thought to herself when Pork informed her he was a father again. "Why did God make so many babies? But no, God didn't make them. Stupid people made them."[31]

Scarlett is an awful mother, but she is, if anything, a worse daughter. She represents a kind of moral equivalent to the murderous physical burden that Ellen assumed in nursing Emmy Slattery's brat and her own children. She lived her life in persistent repudiation of her own mother's values. This provides a central paradox of this chapter and of the book itself: however much she longs to lose herself at Mammy's breast and in her mother's spreading skirts, Scarlett, from the outset, is a bad girl and a worse daughter who lives all her life in constant revolt against her mother's precepts. Unconsciously, for all her devotion to the Lady icon, she repudiates feminine virtue and her mother's and Mammy's code of self-abnegation, devotion, and family. However much the daughter admires Ellen Robillard O'Hara, however much she compares her mother to the Virgin Mary, however much she thinks of her as Holy Mother, her own career honors such standards only in the breach. Long before the transformation on the road, Scarlett failed to honor any of her parent's lessons. It took the crisis on the road to Tara to acknowledge the failure—and to blame it on her mother. Like Prissy's, Scarlett's character assumes its full meaning only in the rebellion against and rejection of matriarchal authority. This conception dominated Mitchell's imagination. She conceived of Scarlett first as a bad girl *qua* bad daughter. She had explained this to Monsignor Murphy in celebrating the virtuous Ellen O'Hara, "a woman whose children rose up and called her blessed, a woman whose ideals prodded the hardening conscience of Scarlett, even though Scarlett did not obey the prods." She had repeated the sentiment to that other correspondent in trying to defend Scarlett herself. Her heroine, she wrote, "was able to appreciate what was beautiful in her mother, even if she could not emulate her."

Yet another element enters here, too. Scarlett was a faithless daughter, true, but her mother's model betrays a powerful negative element as well. For all the Holy Mother images of Ellen Robillard, her character reflects the austerity of the ritualized "tower of ivory" in the Hail Marys her daughters chant. Despite all Scarlett's adulation of her mother, Ellen Robillard nurses out of duty, not affection. She is cool, aloof, and untouchable. She lacks life and color. The actual space allowed this character indicates her ambiguous place within the novel, too. She fades into the novel's shadows and shrinks beside her husband's and her daughter's ebullience and energy. Still more notable, she almost never speaks. The text provides almost no examples of her dialogue, and when she voices her opinion, she does so monosyllabically. She rides herd on her own will, thought, and tongue. Violently repressed, she vents her passion only when her flesh itself is broken. Only then, as life flees flesh, does she speak her love. Scarlett hopes against hope for acknowledgement. "Did she—did she ever mention me—call for me?" the daughter stammers on hearing of the deathbed scene. The mother, however, had cried for neither husband nor children, but for her old, juvenile love. Scarlett does not know the name "Philippe! Philippe!" but she hears the mysterious answer with fitting despair and deprivation.[32]

A perverted child, Scarlett is the logical spawn of Ellen Robillard O'Hara's mothering. If Ellen O'Hara represses her own will, in the same way, her idea of motherhood is to break her daughters' wills and impose her own rigid model on them. This is what her mother did; this is what she would do. This is Mammy's function, too. The model is of mothers as dutiful soldiers or even martinets. If they failed in their objective, it was not for want of effort. Scarlett survived as a person only by rejecting traditional motherhood, and she survived as a daughter only by repudiating her mother and her mother's counsel. Although Ellen failed to break Scarlett's spirit, however, her constant prods and pricks still ensured the daughter's fundamental misery. When alive, Ellen Robillard was an abstract principle of virtue. A kind of ghost when living, her power actually grows once she shuffles off her mortal coil. She haunts her daughter. Even before Scarlett knows her mother is dead, in that luminous passage near the beginning of Chapter XXIV, Ellen is imagined dead and associated with the haunts and terrors of the road to Tara. In her own way, then, she is an ominous, deadly figure.

While Scarlett survives by rejecting her mother and her own motherhood, however, she suffers other consequences of her stubborn integrity. She survives at the expense of almost her entire repertory of emotions. Her whole characterization hinges on unfulfilled longing, unmet desire, and thwarted needs. That is a part of her mother's legacy, too.

Scarlett remains the compulsively needy, eternally hungry child. The deprivations of the war provide a logic for her hunger and give her appetite a name, but the emptiness had deeper roots—as Dr. Hervey Cleckley, for one, detected. She is literally starving in Chapters XXIV and XXV, but her physical deprivation echoes the greater needs in her character, as is demonstrated early on in the connection between eating and matriarchal constraint in the famous corset-lacing scene and at the Wilkeses' barbecue. She wants to stuff herself. She is forbidden to do so. What she misses from Ellen's lap and Mammy's breast, she later tries to find in eating in particular, and greedy acquisitiveness in general. Her ravenous appetite amuses Rhett on their honeymoon, but it speaks of the deprivation that began before Fort Sumter. Mitchell links the deprivation of love and food in the second generation, too, as Scarlett cannot satisfy the demands of little Wade Hampton's heart or stomach. Indeed, she despises Wade's cries for food in part because they remind her too sharply of her own hunger.

Starved for affection, Scarlett cannot recognize love when offered. Rhett adores her; Melanie worships her. So do Charles and Frank and even Ashley. She has no sense of their regard. She takes their devotion as a sign of their inadequacy, and punishes them for their failing. "She could not love anyone who was weak," she says to herself.[33] " 'You're so brutal to those who love you, Scarlett,' " Rhett accused her, accurately. "You take their love and hold it over their heads like a whip."[34] Others' weakness reminds her of her own, and she tries to beat anxiety out of others even as she fights it inside herself. The contradiction makes her a bully and a tyrant. Scarlett herself acknowledges the disparty between her bold appearances and her inward terror. No one knew her aright, she thought. Everyone looked to her for strength and guidance, but they all misread "in her straight back courage she did not possess and strength which had long since failed."[35]

On the road home, Wade's and Prissy's helplessness and anxiety is her own, so she terrorizes them. When Wade sobbed and shrank from her touch, she responded automatically: " 'Make him hush,' " she instructed Prissy. " 'I can't stand it.' " In one of those desperate evocations of male nightmares, she turned on her son: " 'Be a little man, Wade, and stop crying or I will come over there and slap you.' "[36] She responded just the same to Prissy's terror. After hitting the maid with a broken tree limb, she justifies the violence to herself: "She was too exhausted and weak from fright to tolerate weakness in anyone else."[37]

If these forces surged to the fore as she struggled home, they multiplied on her settling in at Tara. Her son ceased to be a person to her. She barked at him incessantly, and each reprimand revived the nightmare of his own road home.

> Whenever Scarlett raised her voice in reproof, he went weak with fright as his vague childish memory brought up the horrors of the first time

she had ever done it. Now Yankees and a cross voice were linked forever in his mind and he was afraid of his mother.[38]

And she still admonishes him to stop sniffling and be a little man; otherwise, she promises again, " 'I'll wear you out.' "[39]

Scarlett gave full vent to her newfound authority and bullied everybody: her sisters, her father, the servants. She gloried in the power.

> Like others suddenly elevated to authority, all the bullying instincts in her nature rose to the surface. . . . It was because she was so frightened and unsure of herself she was harsh lest others learn of her inadequacies and refuse her authority. Besides, there was some pleasure in shouting at people and knowing they were afraid. Scarlett found that it relieved her overwrought nerves.[40]

There was another cause of her behavior. Those around her substituted for the real object of her wrath. She could get at them; she could not attack her sainted mother. She bullied everyone, "not only because she was too worried and strained and tired to do otherwise but because it helped her forget her own bitterness that everything her mother had told her about life was wrong."[41]

And so it went: the tangled relationship between birth and death, being and nothingness, success and failure, autonomy and dependence, girls and women, mothers and children, mothers and daughters. The themes hold Chapter XXIV together. And lest the biographical meaning of these paradoxical relationships be lost, Margaret Mitchell left other evidence of the uniqueness of this chapter. She singled out this part of the book from the entire text: It was the hardest to write; it was the last part she wrote; it was the only section she considered genuinely inspired; and it was the only part she never rewrote. It was, moreover, the chapter in which she named the novel—not only the title it bears to posterity, but the name she thought fit it best from the beginning.

"I do not write with ease, nor am I ever pleased with anything I write. And so, I re-write," she informed one correspondent. "There are, however a few chapters which were never altered from the first way in which they were set down. If you are interested, I made no change in the text from page 398, when Scarlett is struggling home to Tara, to page 421, when she decided to take up her load and carry it."[42] These pages define Chapter XXIV. The year before, she had described the same unretouched part, she allowed it contained three rather than one chapter. In the fall of 1936, she had granted an interview to Lamar Q. Ball of the *Atlanta Constitution*. The paper printed the results in a very long, very important, five-part installment in November 1936. Ball's query about her literary work habits evoked her reference to the central, unchanged section of her manuscript, and her general description confirmed what she told her other correspondent. The unchanged section began, she said, at "that spot in the book where Scarlett leaves Atlanta and goes back home to find her mother dead, the plantation looted and Tara in a desolate shape."

Her interview with Lamar Ball provides still additional evidence of this section's distinction. If she wrote this part with complete confidence once she actually started, no chapter had "worried" her more initially, she told the reporter, and she constantly delayed its composition. She could not get it in her head as she knew it was. "I struggled with it in my mind," she told Ball.

> I prowled around it mentally for a long time, looking at it from all angles and not getting anywhere. I could never write a line of it and never made a try at it on paper. I didn't seem able to capture the smell of the cedars; the smell of the swamp; the barnyard odors, and pack them into those chapters.

Once she conceived the images, however, she knew immediately it was right, and she executed the section without another thought. She wrote with pure inspiration and never looked back.

The Ball interview reveals still other peculiarities about this section. This was the last part of the narrative she composed. She had completed the entire story before she undertook this portion. Once she finished it, the final elements of the structure fell into place. While she had much left to do, checking, polishing, and honing, the completion of this section ended her great creative surge. Finally, the Ball interview revealed the most curious origins of this chapter. She wrote it quickly and effortlessly because it came to her like a revelation, without any warning or expectation. Like an epiphany, it materialized completely in her imagination.

The circumstances of her epiphany are as curious as she thought they were. In late 1929, soon after the stock market crash in October, she was approaching, or had just passed, her own twenty-ninth birthday; she had been writing three years, almost exactly. She was attending a convention with her husband in Atlantic City, New Jersey. "I was in the Ritz hotel at Atlantic City when it all came to me. I can't explain why. The Ritz is nothing like Tara," she laughed.

> I can only tell you this. I was not even thinking about the story when all this came to me very simply and very clearly. It was cold, wet winter when we were at Atlantic City, and yet I could see clearly how dusty and stifling a red clay road in Georgia looks and feels in September, how the leaves on the trees are dry and there isn't any wind to move them and how utterly still the deep country woods are. And there is the queerest smell in the swampy bottom lands at twilight. And I suddenly saw how

very haunted such a section would look the day after a big battle, after two armies had moved on. So, I came home and wrote it.

. . . We had intended, while we were in the east, to go to New York where we were to see some shows and I was to buy some clothes. I gave that up. John agreed that if I had the atmosphere that had been eluding me for two years it would be best for me to get home as quickly as possible. . . . Those three chapters that I wrote as soon as I returned home from Atlantic City are about the only ones in the book that I did not rewrite at least twenty times. As they appear in the book, they are substantially as they were first written.[43]

If these revelations confirm the significance of this section, one more exists as well. She dispelled all doubts about its importance by setting the title of her book here. "Was Tara still standing?" Scarlett pondered as she plodded along the homeward road. "Or was Tara also gone with the wind which had swept through Georgia?"[44] Mitchell might, of course, have written this sentence virtually anywhere in the text. It bears no inevitable, organic relationship to the chapter. That she chose to put it here, however, is important in itself. Far more significant is that Mitchell placed her original title here as well, and this one bears a direct relation to the chapter, to the book, and, ultimately, to Mitchell's experience as a woman, a writer, a person, and the daughter of a peculiar woman.

Gone with the Wind, of course, was only one of several titles Mitchell considered for her novel. She preferred "Tote the Weary Load," and, far more than the name she actually chose, this other dominates the section: Mitchell repeats the phrase or some variation on three different occasions in XXIV. The words, their source, and their meaning in the text define and reinforce the meaning of the road experience in the novel.

As Scarlett toils desperately to get home after the destruction of Atlanta, the phrase returns again and again to her, a catch from a song she can't remember:

Through her mind ran a few words the song she had once sung with Rhett—she could not recall the rest:
> *"Just a few more days for to tote the weary load—"*
"Just a few more steps," hummed her weary brain, over and over, "just a few more steps for to tote the weary load."[45]

The doleful words and melody step off the journey home without any immediate meaning for the protagonist. Soon enough, however, meaning breaks through to Scarlett's consciousness, and she realizes the full pessimistic import of the lines. Scarlett has made it home to discover her mother dead, her father unhinged, and disaster everywhere, but she remains hopeful of consolation. "Soon Mammy would be with her—Ellen's Mammy, her Mammy," she comforted herself. The old black matriarch appears but at this dramatic moment, however, the very moment of ostensible comfort, Mammy repeated the phrase, "weery loads," to the most awful effect. It jogged Scarlett's memory, and hope evaporated with knowledge.

As Scarlett lay with her head hugged close to Mammy's breast, two words caught her attention, "weery loads." Those were the words which had hummed in her brain that afternoon so monotonously they had sickened her. Now she remembered the rest of the song, remembered with a sinking heart:
> *"Just a few more days for to tote the weary load!*
> *No matter, 'twill never be light!*
> *Just a few more days till we totter in the road—"*
"No matter, 'twill never be light"—she took the words to her tired mind. Would her load never be light? Was coming home to Tara to mean, not blessed surcease, but only more loads to carry? She slipped from Mammy's arms and, reaching up, patted the wrinkled black face.[46]

The lines that thread through Scarlett's mind are verses from Stephen Foster's "Old Kentucky Home." The verse and song underline the whole motif of the chapter.

> The head must bow and the back will have to bend,
> Wherever the darkey may go:
> A few more days and the trouble all will end
> In the field where the sugar canes grow.
> A few more days for to tote the weary load
> No matter, 'twill never be light,
> A few more days 'till we totter in the road,
> Then my old Kentucky home, good night![47]

Foster's melody laments an irretrievable past and a hopeless future in a fatal present. The song in general, and these stanzas in particular, chronicle fatal journeys, failing flesh, lost homes, and doom preordained. The road begins in loss and nostalgia and terminates in exile and death.

In its most straightforward meaning, the ballad anticipates what Scarlett will find when she finally trudges up that long avenue of cedars before the whitewashed brick house itself; namely, ruin, death, pain, and woe. It presages what her life will be thereafter. But doubling back and restating the particular image of roads, the verses underline the original power of that seminal episode between Mitchell and her mother. A song about roads in a chapter about roads speaks once again of the power of Mitchell's own road experience with her parent. The image has still greater power for Mitchell, as Mitchell's mother used it as a standard reference.

In the author's reconstruction of that hot September day in 1907, the Rhett–May Belle diatribe equated roads with paths to success or failure. In one of the few surviving records of her own voice, Mrs. Mitchell used the same figure of speech in her deathbed letter. Refuting what she assumed would be her daughter's charge of failure, she justified her life as having given her children "what will put them on the high road to mental, moral, and perhaps financial success." This helps define at least a measure of the burden that the daughter felt her mother had laid on her, not only to succeed, but to measure up to her mother's desire that she succeed. The weary load in Stephen Foster's ballad, for Margaret Mitchell, was fulfilling her mother's wishes. Her mother became a measure of the burden.

But the song evoked still other aspects of the mother–daughter relation for the author. Mitchell had specifically associated her parent with just such melodies. Her mother, she said, had sung her to sleep with "doleful songs of the Civil War," to which habit, only half-coincidentally, the novelist attributed her plaguing insomnia. Finally, the minor-key lament for a lost home evokes still other images critical to Mitchell and her mother. Metaphorically, Tara is the same as the Old Kentucky Home. Tom Moore's ballad "Where Once Through Tara's Halls" makes the same point as Foster's song. So did Magin's "St. Patrick's Hymn before Tara," another favorite she learned from her mother. Tara was, of course, the ancient seat of Irish kings, the stuff of legend. It represented all old—and vanished—glory. The sad, mythic evocation of the dead Tara was close to the heart of Gaelic culture and Irish identity. And all this circles back again to May Belle Stephens Mitchell. In its mythic purity, its representation of an ideal, and all the rest, Tara personifies all those forces that Mitchell associated with her own mother. One has only to recall May Belle Mitchell's own references to the image of Tara in her girlhood letters to her father, if nothing else, to sense the ease with which her daughter made the identification.[48] Tara is the mythic mother. Tara is also May Belle Mitchell. It is also ruin, and, in its own way, ruining. That is understood throughout Mitchell's critical Chapter XXIV. She makes the connections clear in the recognition scene when Scarlett, at Mammy's bosom, remembers the lost part of the song she has hummed all day along the road. The juxtaposition of "weary loads" and Mammy's breast anticipates the deeper meaning of the phrase for Scarlett—and its significance for the novel, too: womanhood is the burden. Sex, reproduction, pregnancy, motherhood, babies, children, domesticity—that whole set of values associated with home and the woman's sphere become the load to carry. " 'Twill never be light": the phrase has special meaning, "light" being another term for parturition, meaning "delivered of."

By these means, the author clarified the meaning of the entire critical section of the text that she claimed to have written in a white heat of inspiration and never touched again. In the same way, it illuminated the motifs in her own life. Birth represented both loss and gain; childhood was despised and craved; motherhood was threat and hope; a woman's life was a burden of contradictions. Sex and gender was the heavy load. This was where the author began the novel, in her own struggle for automony and integrity, and she projected the struggle into the very substance of the fiction itself. This was Margaret Mitchell's sense about her mother whom she celebrated and repudiated and honored and mocked. That was one lesson she learned on the road to Jonesboro in 1907; it inspired the dreadful forces at work in Chapter XXIV. These themes underlay the more obvious gender identities of the narrative. They governed how and when she wrote, the content of the fiction, and the structure of her work. Nor did they disappear when she typed the last line of the section on the road to Tara in the early winter of 1929.

PART IV

FAME

XIV

Lamed Ambition

❦❦❦❦

. . . and her friends asked, "Wasn't Peggy writing a book? What happened to it?"[1]

*T*he door slammed. The sound echoed through empty rooms. John and Peggy Marsh were gone. In the little alcove where she had worked in the morning gloom, the afternoon sun streamed in and lit the motes suspended in the air. The rickety table in the hallway had vanished, and with it the stacks of manila folders that she had stored beneath it. John and Peggy Marsh had packed up and moved. While most other tenants had arrived at the Crescent Court apartments only to flee within a year or less, the Marshes had remained at the same address for seven years after their marriage in 1925.[2] Peggy Marsh had agonized about moving for years, but terror about money had constantly deterred her. Her husband's promotion to head of his division in May of 1930 had eased her fears, but it hardly eliminated them. While she scoured the north side for improved quarters in the early thirties, her letters groaned ceaselessly about the price of new apartments. Despite the Depression, owners had not dropped their rents a penny, she groused. She still hesitated, even after she discovered the ideal place in 1931, the Russell Apartments on Seventeenth Street.

The Russell had special appeal. With an extra bedroom and greater space, the unit she liked boasted a sun porch, light, and air—unlike the dark basement rooms on Crescent. The location suit her perfectly as well. The building stood on the west end of Seventeenth Street, which

ran between Peachtree and West Peachtree. It lay only a short, pleasant, uphill walk around the corner from Eugene Mitchell's house. Other
familiar names and faces graced the neighborhood as well. The side
windows looked out on the back of Peggy Porter's house, and her rowdy
friend Ann Couper lived at the Peachtree intersection. It was perfect.
Although she fretted for another year, in 1932 she took the plunge. The
Marshes signed a lease, and the couple began to pack.

As they crated up their worldly goods in the spring of 1932, no small
measure of their packing involved the manuscript of Mitchell's epic.
At this time (so the story runs), the author contemplated discarding
the manuscript of her novel along with the other rubbish collected
over the years. She thought so little of her labor, she related later, that
she considered tossing it into the garbage or simply leaving it behind
in the narrow rooms of its conception.[3] It was, in any case, a lot to
pack. She had generated a great deal of paper and her storage system
hardly helped. After completing a chapter, she would file it in its own
manila envelope along with various additions, notes, and memoranda.
By 1932, these lay in every nook and cranny of the apartment. The
folders showed coffee stains and probably the marks of Mitchell's cigarettes as well. She had also used the files for jotting notes to herself,
including grocery lists. She had tucked them in closets, shoved them
under chairs and sofas, and used them to balance legs of uneven furniture. Later, friends made jokes about the ubiquitous files. "Once, when
two were serving to prop up her back as she lay on the couch, a friend
asked, 'Why don't you use a pillow and show someone your manuscript?' She only smiled and said, 'This suits me just fine.' "[4] She cultivated the impression of complete uninterest in her work. In later years,
she insisted that she lost all interest in the book and paid it very little
attention after 1929. "And after picking it up now and then during
1930 and 1931," one interviewer paraphrased her in 1936, "she decided finally that she had nothing more to give it."[5]

Like so much Mitchell lore—regularly generated by the author herself—these tales have metaphorical truth but lack actual veracity. For
all her casual blathering about her work, her few surviving letters from
the period between 1929 and 1935 leave a different impression of her
attitude.

If her great creative surge had ended before the close of 1929, her
commitment to the manuscript persisted long afterward. In the six
years after 1929, she spent her days revising, rewriting, and polishing.
The penciled emendations and changes multiplied on all the pages in
all those folders that she carried to the new apartment. She also continued to compose new material. As she reviewed the manuscript in
this period (probably 1933), she decided that the plot and drama sagged
in midtext. She therefore composed an entirely new chapter, the one

that dispatched poor Frank Kennedy by way of the Ku Klux Klan raid rather than by pneumonia as in the less dramatic first version.[6]

Other tasks absorbed her energy. She spent a vast amount of time verifying historical facts. The fear of missing something or getting something wrong drove her to distraction. She felt an overwhelming burden to avoid factual error, and having composed completely from her memory, without recourse to any other sources, she began an obsessive check for factual accuracy. She used the archives of the *Journal*, she told Elinor Hillyer in October 1930, "to help me with my own opus, which, alas, is rapidly nearing the siege of Atlanta, a period in history concerning which I know as much as I do about the Sanskrit dative."[7] She spent hours on end checking data in the collated files of both ancient and contemporary newspapers, volumes that seemed almost as big as she was, she joked. She also continued to check her sources in the great published (and sometimes unpublished) memoirs of the time, and she still searched for the "old inhabitants who were in Atlanta the day it fell and see if I can get anything out of them," she wrote at the close of 1930.[8]

All these labors entailed familiar pains. Before 1929, in the most intense throes of creation, she had always associated mental agitation with her physical disability and connected both, in turn, with her difficulties in writing. The litany continued in the new decade. "If my eyes just get better I can use this dullness and lack of friends to get some writing done," she wrote in the summer of 1930.[9] Nothing had changed by the year's end. "I've been trying to work hard as long as my eyes will let me and have accomplished a little tho it all goes so slowly," she grieved to her friend Elinor in December over a year after she completed the final chapter, number twenty-four.[10]

Other aspects of her labors proved more attractive. She loved to travel, and in her effort to re-create the spirit of place in her work, she covered the turf where her action had taken place. In 1931 the Georgia Press Association met in Dalton in the northwest corner of the state, and the author used this occasion to troop over the battlefields where Sherman had launched his great offensive almost seventy years before. She also dragged John off to the nearby points of Chattanooga, Chickamauga, and Lookout Mountain for the same purpose. "Neither of us had ever been there and that tour, and the entire trip was especially interesting because it was the scene of big events in the Civil War— and in Peggy's novel," John Marsh related afterward to his sister. He went on to elaborate on both the campaign itself and his wife's dramatic retelling of that story.[11] This was nearly two years after she supposedly put the manuscript out of her mind.

This reference is John Marsh's first recorded notice of his wife's novel. In all his detailed correspondence to his sister and mother throughout the twenties, he had never mentioned it before. This supports the impression that only now was Mitchell sharing her writing, even with her husband. Whether or not she had allowed him to read her work prior to 1931, however, her ideas and attitudes about her manuscript shifted subtly after this time in other ways. As she drew towards some inevitable rounding-out of her work after 1932, she became freer about discussing both the existence and the content of her fiction. Sometime after the move to Seventeenth Street, Helen Turman Markey was visiting, and in the course of the conversation, her old debutante friend recalled Mitchell "reaching under the mattress and bringing up the manuscript of her book . . . Getting out the manuscript was in answer to a question of mine—what are you doing with your time these days?"[12] She discussed her work with Elinor Hillyer,[13] and she revealed still more about the characters and content to her faithful correspondent Harvey Smith. Indeed, her revelations to Smith are a special case.

Prior to 1932, Mitchell had disclosed nothing about her book to her younger friend. He knew that she was working on a literary project of some sort because he often appeared at her apartment in the middle of her labors, and he saw with his own eyes all those manila envelopes. She told him nothing. This changed after 1932. In the twenties, she had persuaded him to drive her all over rural Georgia; now she revealed the purpose of those trips—to fill in the landscape and background of her novel. "I know as well as you do that it's pretty hard to write with any degree of conviction about things you don't really feel," she explained. "So I thought it over a lot and looked around a lot, and you unwittingly contributed some by riding me about the countryside." Once into the discussion of her novel, she went on to discuss both the form and the content of her fiction—the first time she had ever done so in any letter to anyone. She introduced Pansy O'Hara, for example, and explained her protagonist's character. "I remember so well, saying when I was twenty that God being willing, the curse of the Mitchells and Fitzgeralds would never fall on me," she began. She proceeded, then, to define this "family curse" and connect it to her novel:

> The curse I refer to is loving land enough to give every thing you've got to get it. Never would I own a foot of it, city or country land. If I had spare money it would stay in the bank or the stock market but never in red clay. Then about two years ago when I set out to write the great American novel I was confronted by the fact that whether I liked it or not, it was a story of land, love of land and a woman who was determined not to part with it.[14]

This reference to her work merits other notice. What of her reference to "two years ago" as the time she "set out to write the great American novel"? She had not begun to write in 1930; on the contrary, she had by then effectively completed her fiction. Why did she falsify the record even informally to a friend in a private letter? Like the mystery writers she adored, she gave clues to the truth even amidst her fabrications. As a lowly drudge in Angus Perkerson's domain, she admitted long after, she had fantasized about her literary future. In 1930, her book was no longer a formless hope: it existed as a real manuscript. She could see the mass and shape of her own creation. How did all those pages piled up so furiously over the years pique her ambition or her imagination? Perhaps by 1930, with the work essentially concluded, she first allowed herself the outrageous notion of her book as a real entry in the literary sweepstakes for the great American novel. "I mean that as a joke, of course," she said, "but I mean it seriously too."[15] If she used the term to belittle her own ambition, half-mocking like her friends, her references to the great American novel also illuminate the Furies that drove her almost frantic in writing, writing, and rewriting for five years after 1929.

By 1933, she owned a mostly finished manuscript. She had polished and polished. She had created new episodes to perk up a sagging narrative. She had checked her facts. And there it sat in all those envelopes on her sun porch and in her living room at her pleasant apartment on Seventeenth Street. Did ambition beckon? If done, why not send it into the world? One thing, obviously, prohibited her: formally, it remained incomplete. It still lacked a first chapter. She could not finish the introduction, and so the book remained, for her, unfinished. This final and emblematic difficulty—capping off the novel—reveals much about her circumstances in these years.

For all the other difficulties with her manuscript, this one moved increasingly to the fore after 1932. She fought the first-chapter battle as fiercely as any skirmish she ever launched. She herself expressed mystification about her inability to conclude. "I never knew so silly a situation," she wondered in the late spring of 1933. "Here I have a book practically finished except for a few here and theres and no first chapter!" She wrote version after version after version. Bessie's trashbin ate them all. Her groans finally aroused her husband's attention. He considered it only a technical difficulty, and he offered his own solutions. Working from her drafts, he preempted her Remington in 1933 to make his own version of Chapter I. His assistance hardly touched the problem's root. He failed to appreciate the real issues at stake in his wife's inability to finish off the volume. She herself suggested as much. She liked his version less than her own. Indeed, his intervention on her behalf irritated her. His effort "charmed" her, she wrote Harvey Smith, but her condescending appreciation barely cloaked her resentment. She had had her own plans for her Remington that day, even if they did not include finishing her book. She had wanted to write letters, but John had preempted her machine. "John went to work on the many times damned first chapter of that many times damned book of mine, and so charmed was I at having help that I did not tell him that I had counted on the typewriter to write to you . . ," she wrote Harvey in mid-spring.[16] This was perfect Mitchell subterfuge: she knew what she was doing, one way or another, even if her husband failed to perceive it.

Mitchell's inability to cap off her work is neither accidental nor incidental to her life and the history of the manuscript itself. It relates, indeed, to some of the same forces that prompted her to write in the first place. In the mid-twenties, her ambitions for a career in journalism clashed with her commitment to ladyhood. Illness resolved the difficulty. The ankle that would not heal forced her to quit her job, retire from public life, and sequester herself in her tiny apartment. Once more, however, ambition broke through the limits of ladyhood. A massive manuscript resulted. If the house-arrest of wifehood had culminated in her novel, however, then the circumstances of its creation also exaggerated the private, domestic, and intimate aspects of her labor. This logic dictated that she minimize her work and her achievement, and it increased her inclination to explain her efforts as something only for her private amusement. Publication threatened the very basis of this well-wrought scheme. As long as the work remained officially unfinished, this justifying fabric held together, and she could avoid the consequences of her unladylike activity, including unladylike ambition.

If fiercely repressed, however, her thirst for success and fame still lived. In the past, crises of one kind or another—illness and accidents—had allowed resolution of the divergent impulses within her character. And so it happened again in 1934. An automobile accident initiated the train of events that led eventually to her decision to submit her yet-unfinished manuscript to a publisher.

At the outset, Mitchell and her husband both had an odd thing about cars. "I never saw anybody with such a phobia about automobiles, driving, and accidents as John and Peggy," a relative observed.[17] John never drove at all, and the fear of wrecks and accidents obsessed his wife; indeed, she used car wrecks and traffic accidents as a favorite metaphor for disaster. In 1933, however, the couple finally broke down and bought an automobile. At that time, Mitchell related, she had not "handled the wheel" in ten years. She relearned to drive—after a fashion. She was truly eccentric as a motorist. "Once we would get into the car, she would take hours to get going," Harvey Smith remembered.

> She had this whole ritual that she went through that just drove us all to distraction. She'd get in the car and then spend hours it seemed adjust-

ing pillows and cushions behind her back. Then out came her glasses which she adjusted. Then she put on an eyeshade, one of those old green ones that newspaper people wore. Next came this routine of checking all the gauges and peering into every mirror. When she finally pulled away from the curb and drove off down the street, she never went over about 2 miles an hour. And she took every corner like she was driving a big moving van or bus or some such vehicle: If she were turning left, she would swerve 'way out into the opposite lane, scaring all of us out of our wits. You just wouldn't believe it.[18]

Margaret Mitchell was, according to her old friend, an accident looking for a place to happen. She found the place in the fall of 1934.

On the evening of November 22 that year, the Marshes had invited two venerable friends to dine with them—John Cohen, the owner and publisher of the *Atlanta Journal,* and John Marion Graham, an ancient, beloved cousin and a distinguished figure in Georgia legal history.[19] At about midnight, Mitchell and her husband volunteered to take Cohen home; Graham had left earlier. She drove. Traveling south on West Peachtree, she prepared to turn left on Eighth. Seeing a car approaching in her rearview mirror, according to her husband, she responded by pulling all the way into the right lane where she stopped dead in the street for the vehicle to pass. It didn't. The driver of the other car was drinking, alleged the Marshes, and his Terraplane roadster plowed into their rear.

Five months later, John Marsh described the injuries they sustained. "All three of us had our necks snapped very badly and could scarcely move our heads for a day or two on account of stiff necks. Mr. Cohen and I, however, suffered no injuries except the shock and muscular strains." Not so his wife. She went to bed and remained there three months. She could not move her head for ten days or more; she suffered severe pain for two months; and after five months her neck remained sore. Nausea accompanied all these aches as well. Her physicians rejected any somatic relationship between the injury and the stomach problem and explained the strange symptom "as the result of a nervous reaction caused by the pain of her injuries," wrote her husband, but the nausea persisted. All winter she moved around even the apartment only with the use of a therapeutic girdle. When she removed it, even briefly, all the old pain returned afresh, as if it had never gone away. With the pain, the nausea returned as well, even after nearly half a year.[20]

In addition to a sore neck and nausea, she also now developed another and still more horrible pain, and one that more than any other corroded her peace of mind for the remainder of her life. In the spring of 1926, Mitchell had joked about a broken back: "Two years more slavery and John's out of debt and if I have not fractured my spinal column or something by then, I'll be free too," she had written her sister-in-law, "and if I can just keep John fascinated by my brightly colored beauty, my brilliant wit and my otherwise charming personality, all will be well."[21] As Mitchell typed this letter originally, she had omitted the "not" before the reference to the broken back, and she added it only with a caret when proofing. Now it actually happened. She got her long-dreaded, long-anticipated fractured spinal column. This produced, in turn, still weirder symptoms. The pain manifested itself in renewed outbreaks of agony in her feet and legs—the same symptoms that had prompted her to quit her career in journalism and take to novel-writing nearly a decade earlier. The physical horrors of 1926 loomed like old ghosts.

She went from doctor to doctor for help. One administered "electro-therapeutic treatments." Nothing improved. She returned to the physician who first treated her arthritis a decade earlier. This same practitioner had yanked her tonsils ten years before, looking for the mysterious root of arthritic infection. While he had not cured her arthritis, he comforted her, and she liked him. He now diagnosed the new problem as a manifestation of the old condition, and he prescribed injections "to counteract the arthritic infection" and advised extracting teeth "in the hope that this might remove the focus of infection." Out came the teeth; a bridge went in. Nothing happened. Another fitted her for the therapeutic corset. It worked after a fashion, but take off the girdle and she was hanging over the toilet again. Nothing changed. Time brought no relief. In April, five months after the wreck, she still suffered, tired easily, and was "greatly handicapped in all her activities," her husband related.[22]

Although not basically peaceful, Mitchell believed in controlling her violence and anger in the same way she disciplined her willfulness and ambition. After the wreck, however, she raged and stormed. She was determined to give pain as well as receive it. The other driver provided a focus for her fury. She decided to sue. The move astonished her friends. "It was the middle of the Depression and Peggy sued him. It all seemed mean and petty. It showed a side I hadn't noticed before, and I think it was the beginning of the end of the old Peggy that we had had such fun with," Harvey Smith judged long afterward.[23] In April 1935, John Marsh laid out all the evidence for his father- and brother-in-law in preparation for legal proceedings. The Mitchells and the Marshes prepared for court.[24]

Everything was awful. It could not have been much worse. And it was precisely in the middle of this legal and physical crisis that Harold Latham dropped unwittingly into the snakepit of the author's life. On April 9, and again on the tenth, Mitchell instructed her father and brother to begin legal proceedings against the other driver; two days after she dispatched the second letter, the kindly, sympathetic editor from the Macmillan Company appeared in Atlanta. Margaret Mitchell's life changed forever.

The Macmillan Publishing Company had an old and justified reputation as one of the great publishing houses in the United States. Although no longer a part of the British company of the same name, the American company still had strong ties with England. For years, Harold Latham had visited Great Britain annually to find fresh manuscripts. In late 1934, he and the company determined to try the same ploy in the United States. Latham planned a great swing around the country. With much advance fanfare, he scheduled his first stop in Atlanta, from which he anticipated going on to Charleston, New Orleans, and, from there, traveling through Texas and to California before returning to New York. Presaging David Selznick's cinematic amateur hour of 1937 and 1938, Latham's literary journey generated a great deal of excitement among writers everywhere he went. This was "one of the first such scouting trips to be made by an officer of a big publishing house," he related. "My coming to a city was heralded in the newspapers and announced at libraries and in schools. The result was that many appointments were made with men and women who desired conferences with a publisher's representative about works in progress."[25] His visit created precisely this response in the Georgia capital. "Atlanta authors and would-be authors were in a flutter Thursday when the news got around that Harold S. Latham . . . was in Atlanta looking for manuscripts to be published. Desks were ransacked and papers dusted," the press reported, for anything that the editor might be willing to examine.[26]

Latham planned his Atlanta trip to coincide with the highlight of the literary year in Georgia, the annual meeting of the Georgia Writers' Conference. Sponsored by Rich's Department Store, the Atlanta Writers' Club, and the city's literary magazine, *Bozart* (named in homage to H. L. Mencken), the convention showcased Georgia talent in general, Atlanta writers in particular. The main event included a luncheon on April 12 and a keynote address by Emily Woodward of the Georgia Press Institute, one of the leading journalists of the state. Latham occupied a place of honor at the luncheon, and Medora Perkerson, the doyenne of the Atlanta Writers' Club, had placed him next to Peggy Mitchell Marsh, herself a still-active member of the local writers' guild. Although the editor had never met his diminutive table companion before, her reputation had preceded her. Mitchell's old friend Lois Cole had worked in Macmillan's New York office since June 1932, and before Latham packed his bags, she had told him to look up her old pal when he hit Georgia. Cole knew, if only vaguely, of Mitchell's novel, and she advised her boss in a formal memo to check it out. No one knew much about the book, she informed him, and she thought

Mitchell would never finish it; the manuscript remained a possibility he should explore, however.[27] Later, Cole recalled a little more enthusiasm in her references: "No one has read it but her husband, but if she can write the way she talks, it should be a honey of a book."[28]

Cole had written another note to her friend herself. She made no reference to Mitchell's manuscript, but she asked her old companion to show the editor around. The social responsibility could hardly have come at a worse time. To ask, however, was to see the hospitality extended, despite Mitchell's physical pains and the mental turmoil of the pending lawsuit. Local obligations reinforced Lois Cole's request. As a friend of Medora Perkerson and a member of the formal association of Atlanta newspaperwomen, Mitchell was helping to plan and execute the luncheon, tea, and other functions of the writers' conference and the editor's visit in any case. In addition to her formal responsibilities, she also volunteered to drive visitors to and from the train station and chauffeur them to scenic spots around the city. She played the charming, untroubled hostess, despite her own pain and anxiety. She could hardly have felt more rotten and still been ambulatory. Yet she appeared all smiles and graciousness. No one, she insisted, should be allowed to miss Atlanta's dogwoods, then in full bloom; so she also conducted the editor on a guided tour of the city's beauty spots. Drizzly and overcast, the weather matched her mood. The temperature never rose above 62°, as they drove about Druid Hills and its environs. Pain racked her the whole time. If walking distracted her, driving was excruciating, even with her therapeutic girdle. But she never let on.

At various occasions during the day, the issue of her manuscript arose. At the luncheon, someone spoke across the table about her novel. Latham later repeated the dialogue that followed:

> "You have a novel?" I asked.
> She looked at me in a startled sort of way. "No," she answered, "I have nothing." There was a pause in the table conversation, and I could sense the feeling of surprise that ran through the group. No one, however, took issue with the reply.[29]

Afterward, two or three more people pressed Mitchell's case, and Latham raised the matter a second time. " 'There is no novel,' she replied evenly," he quoted her. The dogwood tour followed, and with it more inquiries.

> During the ride, at what seemed to me an appropriate moment, I ventured once more to broach the subject. "Is your novel historical in nature?"
> She stopped the car, faced me, and said emphatically: "I wish you'd stop talking about that. I have told you that I have no manuscript to show you."

"Very well, but will you agree that if you ever should have a manuscript to submit to a publisher, you will let me see it first?"

"Oh, yes," she answered in tones indicating that this was the most remote possibility in all the world, "if I should ever have a book manuscript, I'll let you see it first."[30]

At this point in Latham's recollection, the two then began discussing contemporary Southern literature in general, focusing on Caldwell and Faulkner. "I made some uncomplimentary remarks about the novels that were then coming from the South which I characterized as 'sordid,' " Latham recalled. Mitchell remembered his speaking of "degenerates" in Southern fiction.[31] The conversation ended; she returned him to his hotel; and that was that.

The author, however, had one more task. She had agreed—or been pressed—to do one more service. Within an hour of returning Latham to his hotel, she was still chauffeuring other guests home from the festivities. When she had hardly been outdoors for five months, and out of bed less than two, such strenuous activity was draining. Her nerves were stretched to the breaking point as well. All day she had heard about writers, old and young. All day she had listened to people less qualified than she touted as the wave of Georgia's literary future. She was on the edge. This last chore tipped her over the brink.

A year after the episode, Mitchell retold the story of the affair to Lois Cole. The context of the retelling reveals almost as much as the story itself. After the novel had been accepted for publication, Mitchell had insisted on keeping the contract secret. Indeed, she had even asked for a stipulation in her contract to this effect. The publisher refused, of course, but the issue concerned her no less for that. In spite of her most definite wishes, word of her novel leaked back to Atlanta. Lois Cole turned out to be the culprit. Found out, the editor wrote an embarrassed apology. In the course of her apologetic note, Cole also recounted the occasion when she had blabbed. A mutual Atlanta friend had been visiting in New York, Cole explained, and the subject of Peggy Mitchell arose. Unaware that Mitchell had already signed a contract, the visitor pooh-poohed the supposed manuscript and ridiculed Peggy's "never finished novel." Cole bridled. To put the woman in her place, the editor then revealed the contract to the catty friend. From thence, the news of the contract spread as a very tasty tidbit of almost incredible gossip back in Georgia.

Unknowingly, the editor had blundered onto a most sensitive subject for the author. Cole's references to supercilious women, Mitchell's lack of seriousness, and the themes of achievement and success triggered some of the author's deepest passions. It was this note and sequence of events that prompted Mitchell to retell her version of surrendering her manuscript to Harold Latham in the spring of the year before.

At the beginning of her response to Cole's apology, Mitchell protested insistently that she cared not a whit for the opinions of the catty friend or her equally catty sisters. Such viciousness was really typical of her acquaintances, she declared, and she had toughened over the years to such snide asides. Oh yes, she continued, her friends were vicious and rapacious. " 'Isn't it a shame that somebody with a mind like Peggy's hasn't any ambition?' " the novelist imagined their dialogue. They all misunderstood her completely, she maintained. She did not lack seriousness, but social obligations demanded her time and energy. None appreciated her commitment to such thankless chores of charity as visiting the sick, boosting the spirit of the depressed, or instructing the naïve. Most, she argued, took her nursing, sympathy, compassion, and hospitality as a given, or even as their right; they assumed, she snarled, that she performed such acts of charity for witless want of better things to do, for want, she said, of purpose and ambition. How little they knew! Think what she had sacrificed to such churls!

Who was speaking here? Mitchell was quoting, ostensibly, her catty friends, but May Belle Mitchell's shade was stirring, too. The writer protested that the issue did not bother her, but no question struck her deeper as a woman, a writer, or her mother's daughter than this challenge to her own accomplishments. If she dealt with others' misunderstanding, ingratitude, and mindlessness in this affair, the issue also raised the specter of the most elemental divisions within her own character. Her protests and her countervailing passion carried her into the vortex of her interior life. And on she went.

Others' misapprehension of her motives had never bothered her, she protested one more time.

> It never made me especially mad until the last straw came. After all, when you give your friends something, be it money, love, time, encouragement, work, you either give it as a free gift, with no after remarks, or you don't give it at all. And, having given, I had no particular regrets. But this very same situation was what really made me turn over the manuscript to Mr. Latham.

There followed, then, the most critical incident of her career. And in contrast to her protests of regretting nothing, the tale turns upon her fury and outraged sense of justice. The very day that Latham visited, she began,

> I'd called up various and sundry hopeful young authors and would-be authors and jackassed them (that is a friend's phrase) about in the car and gotten them to the tea where they could actually meet a live publisher in the flesh. One of them was a child who had nearly driven me

Her Grandfather Mitchell (ca. 1880) personified the nineteenth-century patriarch. Great muttonchop whiskers added to his domineering mein, while the scars across his pate bore mute testimony to his Civil War heroics. *Atlanta Historical Society*

She derived her name and excellent memory, she said, from her Mitchell grandmother, Deborah Ann Margaret Sweet (ca. 1880), who died long before her birth. *Atlanta Historical Society*

Her Ireland-born maternal grandfather, John Stephens (ca. 1865) earned his wife's description as "the 'hardest-headed man she ever saw.'" *Atlanta Historical Society*

Annie Fitzgerald Stephens (ca. 1890), Margaret Mitchell's maternal grandmother, lived to influence three generations of her progeny, not always to the good. She also helped inspire the creation of Scarlett O'Hara. *Courtesy of Fountaine LeMaistre*

A demanding if devoted parent, May Belle Stephens Mitchell set her children "an impossibly high standard," according to her daughter. *University of Georgia*

A leader of the Georgia bar, an eminent amateur historian, a most dutiful citizen, and scion of one of Atlanta's first families, Eugene Mitchell (ca. 1925) proved a proper and humorless parent. *University of Georgia*

Though small and exquisitely made, she delighted in energetic and competitive play, as here with her two first cousins, David and Stephens Crockett, around 1910. *University of Georgia*

The girl loved physical exertion of every sort, and she especially loved to swim. Here she cavorts with an unidentified friend on her right, Courtenay Ross, and Erkie Jarnegin on her left. *University of Georgia*

Miss Margaret Mitchell, daughter of Mr. and Mrs. Eugene Mitchell, who is one of the attractive young girls in the college set, and who has marked literary talents. (Photo by Stephenson.)

Her reputation as a writer had become a matter of public record by the time she was fifteen, and the local newspapers featured her more than once in the role of budding literary talent. *Courtesy of Courtenay Ross McFedyen*

Males buzzed around Peachtree like bees on summer flowers, but Lieut. Clifford Henry (center) won her heart in the lovely spring of 1918. *Atlanta Public Library*

Her year at Smith College (1918–1919) entailed far more woes than pleasures, but it did bring the lasting friendship of a few young women; among them Red Baxter, standing immediately to Mitchell's left. *Courtesy of Courtenay Ross McFedyen*

Dark, suave, and wryly self-possessed, Allen Edee proved a refuge in her desperate second semester in Northampton and a faithful correspondent for three years afterwards. *University of Georgia*

At the debutantes' "Macrame Ball," Mitchell and her partner delivered a sensational performance. Not everyone applauded. "I thought this was supposed to be an Indian dance," wailed one horrified matron; "did you see how he kissed her?" *Atlanta Public Library*

Debuting in the 1920–1921 season, she set polite Atlanta on its ear. In an elegant (and also very low-cut) gown, she struck poses even more provocative than the dress. *Atlanta Historical Society*

After her mother's death, she struggled desperately with her own divided sense of self, and even wrote about "two Margarets" competing for her spirit. A trick photograph taken in these years represents the murderous conflict. *University of Georgia*

"When a girl is making a social career, clothes are a uniform to be worn like a soldier's . . . ," she said, and she varied her costume to suit the conflict even when it required dressing for the part of storm trooper or motorcycle moll. *University of Georgia*

"I always weep at weddings—weep from the sheer horror of imagining that it might be mine!" Shortly after she penned these lines, she took her own wedding vows in a ceremony distinguished by the presence of three former suitors in the wedding party: John Marsh (in glasses with Augusta Dearborn), Berrien Upshaw (the groom), and Winston Withers. Stephens Mitchell (far right) also served as groomsman. *Atlanta Historical Society*

When the staff of the *Atlanta Journal Magazine* posed, Medora Perkerson took her husband's place and dominated the picture with her ready smile. To her left, Peggy Mitchell ignores the camera, but with vermilioned lips and pencil poised loftily in her right hand, she injects herself into the center of the image with the mock heroics of a journalistic Irene Castle. *University of Georgia*

A collective interview with male students about *their* career goals could hardly have differed more from the ones with young women, and the young reporter mocked the boys' ambitions in a manner worthy of her idols H. L. Mencken and Ring Lardner. *University of Georgia*

While working on her book, Mitchell kept up her social relations with friends; even the most intimate, however, knew little of her project. Here she posed with some of her bohemian circle, including Harvey Smith (foreground), at Smith's country place in Alabama. *University of Georgia*

She wrote compulsively on her novel, only to be interrupted constantly by her bohemian friends. "She would get up, but then we'd say, 'We'll pull out because you are writing the Great American Novel and we don't want to be around to get in your way.'" *Courtesy of Herb Bridges*

Mitchell, Harold Latham, and Medora Perkerson appeared together in the spring of 1937 to celebrate the announcement of *Gone with the Wind*'s Pulitzer prize, looking much the same as two years before when the Macmillan editor first uncovered the famous manuscript. *University of Georgia*

In her first fame, she had written warm letters to a variety of reviewers, including Herschel Brickell (here on her right), and Edwin Granberry (on her left); they, in turn, offered the hassled author the refuge of a writers' conference at Blowing Rock, North Carolina. *University of Georgia*

Amidst the hubbub of the premiere festivities in 1939, she laughed and chatted amiably with the megastars. *University of Georgia*

At the Junior League's charity ball, the choir of Ebenezer Church sang in slave costume, and young Martin Luther King, Jr. (in front) made his first appearance in the national media. *Atlanta Historical Society*

Atlanta's display of provincial vulgarity distressed even the Hollywooders, but Atlanta did not care. On the evening of December 15, 1939, the new capital of Dixie lay at the entrance to Loew's Grand. *Atlanta Historical Society*

During the screening, Gable, according to legend, went to sleep. Mitchell, with her theater companions Olivia de Havilland, Jock Whitney, and John Marsh, stayed wide awake throughout. *Atlanta Historical Society*

Nothing about the film distressed the author so much as Selznick's glorification of the plantation South. "I had feared, of course, that [Twelve Oaks] would end up looking like Grand Central Station," she wrote Sue Myrick, "and your description confirms my worst apprehensions." *Turner Entertainment Company*

True to Mitchell's feelings about the restrictions put on antebellum Southern women, Selznick appropriately repeated both of Mitchell's corset lacing scenes, each to great effect. *Turner Entertainment Company*

The two abortive midwives of this birthing scene, Scarlett and Prissy (played by Butterfly McQueen), also conveyed essential themes of Mitchell's novel. *Turner Entertainment Company*

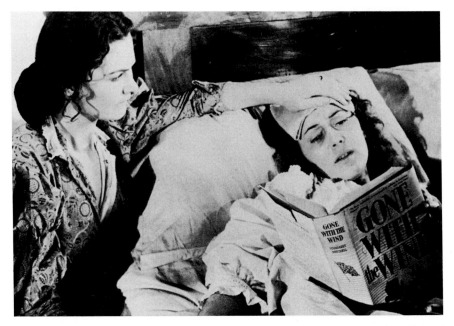

The film captured nicely Mitchell's emphasis on the convergence of birth and death in Melanie's dreadful lying in; set photographers made a joke of it. John Marsh insisted that Olivia de Havilland's look here duplicates perfectly his wife's appearance as she labored over her epic. *Turner Entertainment Company*

Her friend on the set, the ever-jovial Sue Myrick, kept her posted on the Hollywooders' doings, including Clark Gable and (to his left) Victor Fleming, the director, who, immediately after completing *The Wizard of Oz*, replaced George Cukor on Selznick's backlot. *Turner Entertainment Company*

American entry into the war multiplied Mitchell's patriotic activities. She participated in the launching and commissioning of both Navy cruisers named after her hometown. *Atlanta Historical Society*

In the postwar world, she continued her charitable enterprises. Here, with her servant and companion, Bessie Berry, she makes up care packages for Europe. *University of Georgia*

Although little caused her so many headaches as managing her foreign rights, she posed peacefully before a display of foreign editions of her book two years before her death. *University of Georgia*

crazy about her book. I'd no more than settled at my own work than here she was, bellowing that she couldn't write love scenes and couldn't I write them for her? Or she was on the phone picking my brains for historical facts that had taken me weeks to run down. As twilight eve was drawing on and I was riding her and some of her adoring girl friends home from the tea, somebody asked me when I expected to get my book finished and why hadn't I given it to Mr. Latham.

Then this child cried, "Why, are you writing a book, Peggy? How strange you've never said anything about it. Why didn't you give it to Mr. Latham?" I said I hadn't because it was so lousy I was ashamed of it. To which she remarked—and did not mean it cattily—"Well, I daresay. Really, I wouldn't take you for the type who would write a successful book. You know you don't take life seriously enough to be a novelist. And you've never even had it refused by a publisher? How strange. *I've* been refused by the very best publishers. But my book is grand. Everybody says it'll win the Pulitzer Prize. But, Peggy, I think you are wasting your time trying. You really aren't the type."

Well, suddenly, I got so mad that I began to laugh, and had to stop the car because I laughed so hard. And that confirmed their opinion of my lack of seriousness. And when I got home I was so mad still that I grabbed up what manuscript I could lay hands on, forgetting entirely that I hadn't included the envelopes that were under the bed or the ones in the pot-and-pan closet, and I posted down to the hotel and caught Mr. Latham just as he was about to catch the train. My idea was that at least I could brag that I had been refused by the very best publisher. And no sooner had I done this and Mr. L was out of town than I was appalled both by my temper and by my acting on impulse and by my giving him the stuff when it was in such sloppy shape and minus so many chapters.[32]

It is difficult to overestimate the importance of this narrative. Considering her tremendous resistance to going public with her manuscript, the story describes a reversal of the first order. This is where the continental plates of her life collided. Echoing and repeating the other crises and the critical values of her life, this tale's very language affirms its value as fundamental revelation. In this regard, finally, the actual truth of what Mitchell recounted is less compelling than the tale as metaphor.

What is actually happening in the story? What are its dynamics? It chronicles, first, a confrontation between women. More specifically, however, the drama hinges on the differences between irresponsible girls and burdened women. The language defines the oldest mother–daughter conflict that filled the author's imagination. Mitchell associated her antagonists with the most negative aspects of childhood. "This child," she sneered, "cries," "bellows," and "babbles" in the company of "her adoring girl friends." This witless creature dominates the conversation with her silly questions; she fails to listen; she answers her own queries with the grossest, most insensitive judgments. She has insatiable needs and tugs perpetually at Mitchell's literary skirts. The characterization summarizes a familiar attitude towards children: *Gone with the Wind*'s heroine reflects the same attitude. Completing the configuration, however, Mitchell depicts herself as the "good mother," muse, and self-effacing patroness of these irksome, graceless, and unappreciative children. The story begins with her selfless service to the belles. She set them up with Latham and Medora in the first place. She is chauffeuring them home from the gathering. She has rendered the same sort of self-abnegating service literarily to these innocents as well, and her role in the story embodies these selfless virtues. In contrast to most of her stories, Mitchell does not quote herself directly here. She hangs at the story's edge. They babble; she holds her tongue. Even when she paraphrases herself, the end is self-effacement: she dismisses her work as lousy; it embarrasses her; it does not merit Mr. Latham's attention and flattery. Mitchell in the narrative performs the role of bounteous, selfless, Great Lady and Mother to the cruelly self-absorbed Daughters.

The narrative does not end here, of course. It contains a dramatic transformation that shapes the dramatic ending. When Margaret Mitchell was twelve, she recalled that she had goaded her mother into a violent outburst: the child forced the mother to drop her guard and respond like another child. That is the result of this story, too. Irritated beyond endurance by these children, she exploded. The narrative culminates with Mitchell responding, as she defined it, like a juvenile herself, hardly better than the undisciplined girls she shepherded. The dynamics of the protagonist's transformation are critical. First, an external force—the wickedly stupid children—prompts the change. They drive even the kindly mother to madness. Rage turned into manic laughter. She responds like one possessed. Power external to her will dominates her action: fury, passion, and irrationality dictate her course. Careless and crazy, she begins throwing all those envelopes together almost randomly. And here, too, the first real hint of the old self-deprecating humor appears in the story. Its introduction here serves the impression she wanted to convey as well, that she really was a "silly old thing." As in the seminal first story, "Little Sister," the protagonist is driven by force of circumstance to become the unlikely heroine of the story, even against her own will or her physical capacities. Achievement thus becomes a kind of miracle disassociated from the actor.

After submitting her manuscript, Mitchell soon recovers her senses, and, after coming to, she feels the horror of her impulsive, thoughtless, bad-tempered action. She admits then that she had acted against her own interests and certainly out of character. Denying rationality had been bad enough; surrendering the manuscript only compounded the sin, for she concluded the tale by reasserting how really bad she thought her work was all along.

Of the various lessons of this narrative, one is most profound. She could absolve herself of formal responsibility for offering her manuscript to the world. It allowed her to maintain the ancient fiction of her life, of a will-lessness and innocence that co-existed with a terrific ego and determined ambition. Mitchell did not struggle merely with the silly aspiring writers in her car that April afternoon. In them she heard her own voice and echoes of her mother's hectoring. Were there really such awful characters in the Marshes' Chevrolet that drizzly April evening? No matter; she read challenge into their babble, and their chatter touched her fears about herself. Even so, the raging fury that prompted her to gather up those scores of envelopes—that anger, ambition, and determination—they really were her own as well. If lamed, her ambition remained as much her own as her self-abnegation and self-effacement.

On the evening of his arrival in Atlanta, Harold Latham was preparing to catch his train when the telephone rang. He recognized the pleasant voice from that afternoon. "I'm downstairs," Peggy Marsh told him. "Could I see you for a moment?" Latham got himself together and went down to the lobby. What he saw surprised him. His former luncheon companion sat on a divan and beside her towered two enormous stacks of brown envelopes, almost seventy of them, reaching almost to her shoulders. This was the woman he had entreated steadily all day for a novel, and this huge pile was the manuscript whose existence she had steadily denied at every query. On seeing him, she rose, told him, "Take the damn thing before I change my mind," and promptly fled.[33]

She did change her mind almost immediately. She "came to her senses," as she called it, almost at once. She had hit Latham just before his departure on the train, and the steel tracks were still singing when the author panicked. The next day he received a telegram, which he quoted thirty years later: "Send it back, I've changed my mind."[34] By that time Latham had already scanned the manuscript, and even his cursory reading convinced him of its excellence. He replied with a very positive note. It arrived on the evening of April 15, and the author responded the first thing the next morning. The letter was classic Mitchell. It began with a most characteristic expression of self-denial and her desire to serve Latham's cause and assume his burdens. Had the editor come South to look up new authors? Why she would beat the bushes for him. Did he know of Emmett Snellgrove down in Macon who wrote mysteries and whodunnits? She guaranteed she could turn up others. She would scour the countryside for him for works of genius. "I intend to spend the coming week at Louisville, Ga., . . . and I think I may be able to dig up something for you there. At any rate, I'll try. I fear you must resign yourself to being pursued by letters from me across the continent because my blood is up on the subject of tracking down manuscripts." Here she was again, the good little Peggy doing other people's scullery work. Only after a page of this diversion did she get around to her real subject, her own manuscript. "Now, about your very nice letter that arrived on last evening's mail," she began.

> I cannot tell you how pleased your words of commendation made me and how glad I am if the extracts you read interested you. If I had not met you and realized that yours is an honest face, I'd be sure you were joking with me. I know the following confession sounds strange, coming from a would-be writer but you must take it at face value. I am oppressed with the knowledge of the lousiness of what I write for even though I may not write well, I do know good writing and my knowledge was intensified by my years of manuscript reading and rewriting for the Journal. I have felt that there was some thing lacking in me that other authors, real and fancied, possessed, that passionate belief in the good quality of their work, a belief so passionate that they have no qualms about gathering in groups and reading each other's stuff. . . . I am more than a little frightened when you write of taking it to New York for "careful reading." . . . I fear that your manuscript readers may have a dreadfully difficult time making heads or tails of the stuff. What do you think? If, after you have read more you find that *you* can get some continuity out of the story, then take it on to New York with my appreciation and thanks. But if on further reading you find it too scrambled to be intelligible, send it back to me and I will remove the extra versions and where chapters are missing put in a brief summary of what is contained in those missing chapters.

Her letter underlines her skepticism about her own work and her supposed foolishness in surrendering it. Part of her response was typical belle-ish self-deprecation, but her self-criticism went very much beyond conventional modesty. She closed with still more self-effacement. What she really wanted, she insisted, was the chance to see the editor again and lavish more hospitality on him. May your tour turn up a Pulitzer Prize winner for sure, "so it will be necessary for you to come back to Atlanta and stay awhile."[35]

Before the novelist posted this letter, she received a second from the peripatetic editor. It glowed with still warmer praise. To affirm his complete seriousness, Latham also suggested that he return to the Georgia capital to talk about her novel. His train to New Orleans passed through the city in any case, and he had played with the idea of a quick revisit even before he received her tome. The Atlantan took the note as warmest flattery. She responded in kind. His "kindness," as she called it, overwhelmed her. "I hope you do make a 'special trip' to Atlanta, even if it's just to say 'your stuff won't do!' " she gushed. And she closed: "I thank you again for your encouraging words. I'm sure they'll have more healing affect on my back than all the braces, electrical treatments and operations the doctors devise."[36]

The editor kept the manuscript, but Mitchell's sense of the novel's "lousiness," as she termed it, persisted. Over the next three months her anxiety increased and, with it, her horror at having let anyone read the thing at all. In early July, she wrote Latham again, confessing all her sins, real and imagined, against the craft of novel-writing: "When I look back on giving it to you I shudder at what I unloaded on you and marvel at my own gall—or thoughtlessness. In the shape it was in I don't see how you made heads or tails of it. Perhaps you didn't!" Then again, most characteristically, she invited his objections. "If you have any suggestions and criticisms, I would be most humbly grateful for them if you have the time to write me about it. . . . I don't believe you can see as many things wrong with it as I do or can think it as rotten as I think it." Once more, then, she asked him to return the manuscript. She insisted. She pled. She apologized:

> I know that when a would-be author is lucky enough to have an editor looking over her stuff, she is a fool to write and ask to have her manuscript back. But that is just what I'm doing because I am very anxious to finish the thing and begin rewriting it. . . . At present, I am out of my spinal brace and can sit up at the typewriter for an hour or so at a time for the first time in seven months. I am one of those clumsy or unlucky people who are always being run into by drunken autoists, sat on by horses, struck playfully with bottles by guests. Or I get influenza or a return of arthritis. Or some of my friends have babies and demand my presence at birth. This last is far worse than the catastrophes listed before. At present, I am able to work and very anxious to work. However, knowing my past record, I realize that it is only a matter of time before I have an arm in a sling or my skull fractured again. With me, writing is sandwiched in between broken bones and x-rays and, as I am all in one piece at present it looks like flying in the face of Providence not to take advantage of it. So could I have my manuscript back, please?[37]

Latham never complied with the author's panicky requests. Not in April; not in July. He kept all those folders. But what exactly did he have? Mitchell's heirs destroyed this manuscript, but a fair record of its form and content remains to suggest how it differed from the final publication. As published, the book contained sixty-three chapters, but the number of files she dumped on Harold Latham hardly matched this number. Nor did the chapter numbers correspond to those of the final printing. All the early section differed significantly in the earliest draft. While it still contained no Chapter I, the material in the first five chapters was not in its published order, either. Latham's stack also included both versions of Frank Kennedy's death midway through the book and two entire chapters that vanished before galley stage.[38]

The final sections of the manuscript differed even more significantly from the published version. Originally, Mitchell had summarized all the material on Reconstruction in two long chapters towards the novel's conclusion. These also vanished in the final version.[39] Finally, this mess included material completely extraneous to the novel. In her haste to deliver the book to Harold Latham, she had gathered up envelopes that contain the long story "Ropa Carmagin," which she had completed before beginning her epic. This is how Harold Latham and Lois Cole came to read that novella. It had its own envelopes; the author had stashed them indiscriminately with the others. In her frenzy, she threw him in with the rest.

Mitchell's haste in getting the manuscript together also made her miss other chapters. The batch that Harold Latham received omitted the envelopes that covered the birth of the heroine's second child, Ella, and the first appearance of the mountain man driver, Archie (in published form, Chapter XLII). The company had already extended her a contract before she even realized this material was missing. The discovery caused new panic. "I can't find them in my files and really lack the courage to dig in the three foot pile of revisions and discards in the closet to see if they are mislaid there," she fretted. "However, I have rescued a draft of those chapters, an incomplete one, from the top of the pile, and, at the risk of further confusing you and your readers, I am sending it by this mail," she wrote Latham in July.[40]

Individual chapters also differed in the manuscript and the book. She rearranged material from one chapter to another. As with the opening section and the treatment of Reconstruction, she broke up the Dalton-to-Atlanta military campaign and scattered it through several chapters. Individual chapters bulked larger; many scenes and episodes wound up in her trash. She changed much. At the same time, she altered nothing of the fundamental narrative. And even in its physical disarray, her tale completely transported everyone who plunged into those dirty envelopes.

XV

Bloody Work Done

. . . before I went to press I snatched out double hands full of copy, whole chapters. Snatched them out under such pressure that I didn't have time to tie up the severed arteries. In my eyes the book will bleed endlessly and reproachfully.[1]

*I*n Atlanta, Harold Latham had collected six or seven manuscripts in addition to the one Peggy Marsh had given him. The lot required its own luggage, and when he boarded the train that night for South Carolina, a porter carried another bag into his compartment for manuscripts alone. As the train pulled out of Atlanta's Union Station on the cold, drizzly evening of April 12, the editor opened his new valise and perused the folders that Lois Cole's friend had dropped on him so unexpectedly that afternoon. He had never seen anything like this before. Physically, it was the sloppiest manuscript he had handled in thirty years of editorial work. The fastidious New Englander reached gingerly for the first envelope, but he turned the pages with increasing fascination as the train cut through the foggy night towards South Carolina. Twenty years of reading manuscripts told him immediately what he had. While the terror-stricken author wailed about the inadequacy of her work, bit her fingernails about her own effrontery, and pledged herself to find Latham a Pulitzer-winner in the provinces of Georgia, the Macmillan editor recognized instantly that he possessed a prize already. His enthusiasm grew as he plowed deeper into the manuscript in the azalea-blessed spring of colonial Charleston; it multiplied as he whistled through the greening countryside towards New Orleans.

Rather like John Marsh (whom he resembled), Harold Latham was not given to enthusiasm, and he shied from making commitments he could not guarantee; his delight, however, overcame his reserve. On April 14 or 15, he had written Mitchell about his pleasure in her novel. Within twenty-four hours, he wrote again; and on April 18, he dispatched still a third commendation from New Orleans. This novel is something very special, he insisted. "I see in it the making of a really important and significant book. . . . we are going to keep at this project until a novel is issued that is going to be regarded as a very significant publication."[2] Time diminished neither Mitchell's fears nor Latham's enthusiasm. When she wrote again in July asking that the editor return her manuscript, the editor came as close as he was able, given the circumstances, to committing himself to the book. "You have created in Pansy a character who is vital and unforgettable," he told her. "A number of your scenes were made firmly fastened in my mind. As you may have gathered, I am taking a very keen interest in your book and I hope you will not insist on its return before our advisors are through with it."[3]

For all his praise to the author herself, Latham waxed still more enthusiastic to his company. "It is a book of tremendous importance and significance," he told his bosses. "We shall make a serious mistake if we do not immediately take it." Mitchell's pleas for her novel's return actually increased the urgency of Latham's arguments. He assumed her pleas meant "other people are after her," and he pressed the company for a quick decision lest it lose the prize.[4]

Every early reader shared this same response.

With the author's reluctant consent, Latham had dispatched her manuscript back to New York from New Orleans in April. There, Mitchell's old friend Cole read through the batch of envelopes, and her pleasure matched Latham's. Cautiously, however, the company officers had determined to check these judgments against an outside evaluation, and in the late spring or early summer, Macmillan asked Professor Charles W. Everett of Columbia Unviersity to assay the work. With an M.A. and Ph.D. in English literature, Everett had taught courses in the English novel, English romantic poetry, and American literature at Columbia since 1923, and Latham deemed him "a critic of no mean ability."[5] The Columbia professor submitted his report July 15. If Latham and Cole had ever had doubts about their judgment, Everett's evaluation vanquished them completely.

Everett began with the highest praise of the novel's polish and literary finish. He isolated one episode in particular to illustrate his sense of the author's literary taste and sophistication. Consider, he offered, the ridiculous appearance made by the aristocratic Mrs. Elsing in the morning as she drives furiously out of town with her carriage bulging with flour and beans and bacon. Then see Pansy leaving that night—with a worn out horse and broken down wagon, and those literally beyond price so that only a strong man like Rhett could have secured them. And at Tara Pansy faces starvation. Yet there is no reference made by the author to the previous scene; it simply marks an increase in the tempo. It is perhaps in this control of tempo that the book is most impressive. When the writer wants things to seem slow, timeless, eternal, that is the way they move. But her prestissimo is prestissimo and her fortissimo is FFF. For like King Lear, Pansy learns that "There is no worst, as long as we can say, 'This is the worst.' "[6]

He continued: "There really are surprisingly few loose ends, and the number of times one's emotions are stirred one way or another is surprising." "I am sure that it is not only a good book but a best seller," he said enthusiastically. Comparing the book very favorably to Stark Young's Civil War romance, *So Red the Rose*, which had appeared the year before, he followed with four pages of plot summary and suggestions. He concluded with more encomiums like "breathtaking" and "magnificent." "By all means take the book. It can't possibly turn out badly," he instructed. "With a clean copy made of what we have, a dozen lines could bridge the existing gaps. . . . Take the book at once," he repeated.[7]

Macmillan acted immediately upon receiving Everett's recommendation. On July 17 the company wired the author that a contract would be forthcoming. Mitchell responded with a classic hand-to-the-bosom, pass-me-the-smelling-salts pose. "Today's telegram put me into a happiness that can best be described as a 'state'—a 'state' which necessitated a luminal tablet, a cold towel on the forehead and a nice, quiet nap. I emerge this evening to write you my grateful thanks and to try to be businesslike." She specifically refused, however, to fire off an immediate acceptance. "Coming of a legal family, I do not like to accept any contract, no matter how nice without seeing it," she explained. There followed a long series of questions and queries about the terms of the agreement. The company might have been forewarned.[8]

By the time the actual contract arrived a week later, the author had packed away her swoon bottle long before. After consulting with her attorneys, Mitchell and Mitchell, she replied to the contract with a six-page, six-point request for information, clarification, and change. She raised matters ranging from control over dust jacket design and requests for secrecy to clarification of wording in the Clause 14 relating to dramatic and motion-picture rights, serialization, and issues of "spin-off" productions from the novel. The publisher, however, disregarded her objections to this, and indeed all her other anxieties as well. "My dear child," Lois Cole shot back,

> may I take the liberty of pointing out that you are not dealing with a fifth rate Jewish publisher? If your contract had come from Greenberg or even A. A. Knopf your suspicions, in fact all suspicions, might be easily understood. However, the contract came from us and it was the regular printed form which some twelve thousand Macmillan authors have signed without a qualm—In fact, I signed one myself.[9]

Cole and Latham failed to understand. Had not she been breathless and aflutter all along? Had she not been so apologetic about her own work? And did she not now possess a contract from one of the great publishing houses in the world? Her reservations and niggling hardly seemed to fit the picture. For all her old friendship with the author, Cole in particular failed to appreciate the steely quality that lay behind the frills and furbelows of Mitchell's manner.

Mitchell finally signed a contract essentially unchanged from the one she had received, but she remained skeptical of both Macmillan's explanations and the document itself, particularly the obscure Clause 14. In the fall of 1935, however, she had little time to fret about the legal issues, because she entered a period of near-crazy labor in creating an acceptable manuscript: for "acceptable," by her standard, entailed the most strenuous, mind-breaking, eye-straining, and back-breaking efforts.

By September 3, the author received her manuscript back, and she set to work in high spirits. The old problems appeared immediately. Like the Ghost of Christmas Past, the specter of Chapter I soon turned her to jelly. Later she insisted that she had never really written a proper first chapter at all, and that what passed for Chapter I she had actually thrown together on the day she gave the manuscript to Latham. "I decided also that none of the many first chapters I had written were worth showing, yet I wanted Mr. Latham to have some notion of what the first chapter was about so I hastily knocked out a synopsis of the first chapter," she told her friend Norman Berg. "This synopsis included practically all the conversation between the Tarleton twins after they left Scarlett. As it stands in the book it is pretty much as I wrote it that afternoon."[10] At the time, however, she nearly worried the issue to death. She proved no more capable of producing something to her own satisfaction after she had signed a contract than she had two, three, four, or even five years before. In October, she broke out in boils all over her head. Anxiety was the cause. "It is the first chapter of my book, the first two or three pages of the first chapter, to be exact," she groaned to Harold Latham.

I think they are pretty dreadful. I think they are amateurish, clumsy and, worse of all, selfconscious. What ever may be wrong with the rest of the book, at least, it isn't selfconscious. . . . I've covered the opening of the story from every possible angle I could think of and in every style and in every way my husband could suggest, too. Each one looks worse than the last.

Sometimes I think that the version I sent to you can't possibly be as dreadful as I think it. Nothing could. Other times, I reflect gloomily that probably only conceit prevents me from seeing how really bad it is. My dissatisfaction with the opening of the book keeps me from getting on with the rest of the work which should be easy. I cannot work on anything else but keep coming back to the first chapter, pouncing on it, worrying it and then leaving it. Each time I hope that by creeping up on it I will catch it off guard and find it more pliable but I have no luck, so far.[11]

As with Chapter I, she poked and probed all the first six chapters like an old scab. She moved the second chapter of the original manuscript, with Scarlett waiting for her father to return home, into the third slot. The Wilkes barbecue, originally number three, moved to sixth place. Meanwhile, she took snatches from all of these, among other elements, and collapsed them into what she now called Chapter I.[12]

Like it or not, she finally finished what passed for Chapter I and sent it off about October 10. Whenever and however she produced it, and despite her own agonies, Latham genuinely liked it:

Reading this chapter now stirs again in me the emotions which your entire book arouses: admiration for your style of writing, for the excellence of your characterization, and the very human note which predominates in it. I am exceedingly gratified that we are to have the privilege of publishing this novel.

He closed prophetically: "I know we are going to do well with it."[13]

With the rapids of Chapter I behind her, she now navigated other shoals. Grammar, punctuation, and spelling demanded her attention. "And there's an awful lot of loose ends to be hitched up and repetitions to be eliminated," she continued. "And I'm trying to condense and to—" She dared not complete the sentence.[14] Condensing came to mean ruthless chopping and whacking for her, and hence the metaphors afterward of wholesale butchery, severed arteries, and endless bleeding. She excised two complete chapters. John Marsh summarized their content: "A chapter more than 30 pages long where Rhett lends Hetty Tarleton some money to buy her mother some horses" and "A long chapter going into detail about what happened after Sherman entered Atlanta."[15] Numerous individual episodes disappeared now, too. John Marsh outlined some of them:

A 7 or 8 page section in Part V where Mammy finally leaves Scarlett and goes back to Tara. Condensed into 2 or 3 paragraphs;

Several pages in which Miss Pitty talks at length about how the Carpetbagger gentleman got her property away from her. Condensed into a few sentences because it seemed to get in the way of the action;

Several pages eliminated from the description of the education, etc., of a young lady in the Old South in the early part of the book because it seemed to be tediously overwritten;

Two rather long sections on what happened to various minor characters after the war. These were greatly condensed and sprinkled here and there where items could be brought in in conversation, etc.

As the author treated those first five chapters, so she cut and pasted others. Sherman's Dalton-to-Atlanta campaign originally had its own chapters. Now she scattered it through the first half of the book; in the process she heightened the dramatic tension of the novel by integrating the military part with home-front affairs. She did the same with Reconstruction, to somewhat less felicitous effect. Two chapters chronicled it originally. In the fall, Bessie Berry lumped them with the chicken bones from dinner and dropped them down the garbage chute. This section involved greater difficulties than mere recasting, and the author soon discovered her historical errors as she plunged into her work. She had composed this section originally, as her husband explained, "under the impression, as most people are, that Reconstruction arrived with a bang right after the war ended. Her further investigation showed that conditions were relatively pleasant in 1866, by comparison with the worse horror that developed over a period of years."[16] Her historical discoveries demanded a complete revision.

Mitchell had begun her initial section on the postwar world with D. W. Griffith's striking images of Reconstruction from his film *Birth of a Nation* uppermost in her mind: Appomattox came; the North and South prepared to work out their differences; Lincoln died; evil politicians took his place; they created a wicked coalition that immediately captured the governments of the Confederate states; their alliance consisted of spiteful, narrowminded politicians in Washington, ignorant former slaves, self-serving white collaborationists, and the nefarious Yankee mercenaries, the Carpetbaggers; while their wicked rule lasted for over a decade, finally, the local forces of righteousness, pressed beyond endurance, expelled the aliens; only then did peace, as Lincoln had desired it, return to Dixie and to the nation.

Even at the close of the twentieth century, historical reality has hardly eclipsed this mythic chronology. In Mitchell's day, it completely dominated the popular imagination. It left a powerful impression even on formal, professional history. Indeed, under the aegis of science and scientific history, scholars like Walter Fleming at Columbia confirmed the profoundest prejudices of this popular interpretation. However deeply she read in academic history, Mitchell could meet almost nothing to challenge his dominant view. Although *Black Reconstruction* by W. E. B. DuBois offered an alternative, this notable black scholar had only a narrow following in 1935. His insights made no headway at all in the popular mind. Actually, American historiography was on the brink of a monumental shift in its approach to Reconstruction, black history, slavery, and the South just as *Gone with the Wind* was going to press. Circumstances caught Mitchell's novel in a historiographical vise. The radical revision of scholarship in the forties, fifties, and much more afterward, made Mitchell's work appear especially reactionary, and this shift helps account for the academic revulsion against her novel after World War II. Mitchell herself, however, had conceived of her novel as a revisionist history of the planter class before and after Appomattox. If she confirmed most of the racial stereotypes of Reconstruction, her emphasis on economic motives, in particular, challenged the old pieties and put her work in the vanguard of new interpretation of the Southern experience, advocated especially by Charles Beard. As matters stood with Mitchell in the fall of 1935, the wonder is less that the old racial biases pervaded her book than that she challenged the prevailing mythology at all. She did. In the fall of 1935, she plunged innocently into the primary and secondary sources to make her work as historically accurate as she knew how.

Mitchell's research affected various aspects of her historical vision. The old school of thought had emphasized the innocence and hegemony of the white South after Appomattox. Mitchell discovered shades of gray, even in otherwise slanted history. Such former Confederates and loyal Georgians as Governor Joseph E. Brown, General John B. Gordon, and General A. B. Longstreet, Mitchell emphasized, had "gone over to the enemy." "Good families" collaborated. The Solid South lost some of its solidity as Mitchell read more history. It also lost much of its innocence and idealism. Academic history might have confirmed racial biases about the past, but by stressing economic motives and capitalistic drives, it undercut one of the classic tenets of the romance, and economic motives dominated her work. The placing of rapacious and self-conscious capitalists at the novel's heart confirms her debts to the economic revisionists like Charles and Mary Beard and the early U. B. Phillips. To have glorified Scallawags like Scarlett and even considered the merits of war profiteers like Rhett would have been a contradiction in terms for any Civil War fiction before World War I.[17]

As she rewrote and redrafted in the fall of 1935, the author also turned to the concerns that Professor Charles Everett had raised in his evaluation the summer before.[18] While his praise far outweighed his criticisms, she emphasized—as was her wont—his objections. Some of these overlapped the larger problems she confronted in her treatment of Reconstruction. "The author should keep out her own feelings in one or two places where she talks about negro rule," Everett had recommended. "And to refer to Mammy's 'ape face' and her 'black paws' seems unnecessary." "I 'meant no disrespect,'" Mitchell responded. "But I had not realized how differently this sounded in type. . . . I have tried to keep out all the venom, bias, bitterness as much as possible. All the V, B & B were to come through the eyes and head and tongues of the characters, as reactions from what they heard and felt."

With much the same cause for concern, Everett also objected to the Ku Klux Klan episode in the book. She had included the two versions of Frank Kennedy's death with her manuscript, and Everett did not like the Klan death. "I prefer the version where Kennedy dies of illness to the Ku Klux one, exciting though that is," he offered, "because the K.K.K. material has been worked pretty hard by others." Mitchell had her own reservations about the chapter. "God knows, I don't love that second version for its own sake. . . ," she grumbled. She had included it only from dramatic necessity, she explained; she professed no ideological commitment to the Klan version. "Let me complete the book with the second version (the KKK one) and send it to you and if you do not like it and your advisers do not like it," she responded, "I will be most happy to change it back to the first version."

Everett also raised a final issue that had nothing to do with race, Reconstruction, or Mitchell's history, but with style, form, and, indeed, the basic meaning of the narrative. The ending disappointed him. This was the only place where he recommended specific and discreet changes in the novel. "Tell the author not to do anything to it but bridge the few obvious gaps and strengthen the last page," he had instructed Harold Latham. "As it is, there may be a bit too much finality in Rhett's refusal to go on. . . . I think she gets him in the end. . . . and it might not hurt to hint as much a little more strongly than the last lines." This objection gave her pause. "It's been a long time since I even looked at it and I hardly recall what's in it," she apologized.

> But he's probably right. My own intention when I wrote it was to leave the ending open to the reader. . . . My idea was that, through several million chapters, the reader will have learned that both Pansy and Rhett are tough characters, both accustomed to having their own way. And at the last, both are determined to have their own ways and those ways are very far apart. And the reader can either decide that she got him or she didn't. Could I ask you to withhold final criticism on this part until I have rewritten that and sent you the whole book to look over again? . . . If you don't like the way it looks when you get the final copy, tell me so and I'll change it. I'll change it any way you want, except to make a happy ending.

No happy ending: that confirmed the basic object of the story. Her response, however, reveals two levels of ambiguity about the conclusion. In the first place, her own language and motives here are ambiguous. She takes with one hand what she gives with the other. While declaring that she really intended all along an "open ending," she undercuts that assertation with her own suggestion that the weight of the narrative was completely against reconciliation. In the second place, while she rejects a happy ending, she offers to make any changes short of that. She declares the willingness, in effect, to make the clearly unhappy ending not happier, but at least less clear.

While she refused to write a hopeful, much less happy, resolution, stylistic and internal evidence, coupled with Everett's recommendations, suggest she did indeed alter the text here along the lines that the reader suggested. In its published form, the novel ends naturally on page 1,035, when Rhett leaves. "He drew a short breath and said lightly but softly: 'My dear, I don't give a damn.' "[19] It is no accident, of course, that Rhett's parting shot has become a part of American lingo. It has high verbal appeal. The intimacy of "my dear" couples neatly with the "damn," and the monosyllabic burst rounds out the phrase perfectly. The language matches the drama of the sentiment and of the moment itself. From her newspaper days, if not before, Mitchell loved just such dramatic moments and vivid expressions, and the phrase is perfect in this regard. It marks the perfect end. In its published form, however, the novel does not end here. It runs on an additional page and a half. This coda (marked off in the text by asterisks) undermines the power of this natural ending even as it opens up the possibility that Scarlett might indeed redeem her marriage. It fits ill. Most critically, it undermines the otherwise powerful and dominant impression in the last chapter, that the heroine has finally grown, developed, and changed positively in the ultimate crisis. Thus, in the confrontation with Rhett just preceding, she has resisted her old childish impulse to stamp her foot, rage, and manipulate. She accepts Rhett, Melanie, Ashley, and herself in an honest and open way for the first time in the novel. She sees clearly for the first time. In doing so, she establishes her own humanity and dignity; these allow her to accept her losses and limitations, even Rhett's leaving, with an awful grace:

> For a moment she was on the verge of an outburst of childish wild tears. She could have thrown herself on the floor, cursed and screamed and drummed her heels. But some remnant of pride, of common sense stiffened her. She thought, if I did, he'd only laugh, or just look at me. I mustn't bawl; I mustn't beg. I mustn't do anything to risk his contempt. He must respect me even—even if he doesn't love me.
> She lifted her chin and managed to ask quietly: "Where will you go?"[20]

Scarlett changed. The coda denies the growth. In the last two pages, Scarlett reverts to the old, failed tactics. She "summons up her old

charm," now unnaturally, and avoids the present pain in her traditional way, by escaping to the future: "Tomorrow is another day," she
says—and the past: "I'll—why, I'll go home to Tara tomorrow," she
mutters faintly. There, she will plot as of old to catch her man, just as
in yesteryear she schemed for Ashley. She has already acknowledged
her alienation from history and her exile from home, but this ending
asserts their escapist, romantic validity after all. If this ending still has
credibility within the whole sweep of the novel and within the definitions of the heroine's character, it smacks rather more of Charles W.
Everett's concern than of Peggy Mitchell Marsh's.

Whether or not the author recast the final pages in these months,
she faced still other problems in the text. As she wrote, she had not
thought to make sure that marriage dates, death dates, birthdays,
pregnancies, and so forth all jibed properly with one another. Nor had
she confirmed the details of other references. Now all the incidents,
data, and trivia rose up and demanded verification. Did little Beau
Wilkes's birth correspond properly with Sherman's siege and Ashley's
furlough? Did dresses use buttons and loops or hooks and eyes? What
was the weather like on September 17, 1864? How much did a bale of
cotton weigh? How did women wear their hair in 1867? What was
buckwheat, and was it really different from regular wheat? Almost every
page of her manuscript contained some such data. She wanted to confirm everything. She created elaborate chronologies and genealogies to
check against the text. She haunted the research facilities of the Carnegie Library. She hit the road looking for primary evidence. She
quizzed experts. Repeatedly, for example, she called on Dr. H. P. Stuckey
of the Georgia Department of Agriculture to fill the gaps in her knowledge of nineteenth-century agriculture. Her letters also illustrate her
obsession with historical reality. "I worry if I don't have ten references
for each fact," she explained. "Even if I made an error, I suppose few
people would realize it. No one outside of north Georgia would know.
But I would know and would probably wake up screaming in the night
about it." [21] "And what ever else may be wrong with my book, I do
want it to be accurate," she testified still later. [22]

She played with other changes in these months. She had contemplated a name change for her heroine as early as July 1935. "When I
began this book and called the central character 'Pansy,' the unpleasant connotation of the word had barely reached the South," she explained. "However," she continued, "if you think the name of Pansy
should be changed please let me know and I will try to think of another name, equally inappropriate," she told her publisher. [23] In September, she had found her alternative to Pansy. When she mailed away
her new first chapter in October, Scarlett appeared for the first time
in type. Mitchell herself left no record of her choice for renaming, but

by October 29 she had confirmed the name with her publishers and secured their approval.²⁴ When Harold Latham read the new first chapter with the heroine renamed, he shot off his immediate approval. "I like Scarlett as the name very much, indeed. It seems just right as I read these pages."²⁵ Although the change troubled Lois Cole, Mitchell fortunately stuck with the change.

After fifty years of living with "Scarlett" O'Hara, one can hardly image the character bearing any other name. It seems complete, natural and organic, a perfect evocation of the heroine herself. But how did the author come by the name, so different in tone and feeling from the one that she had lived with for a decade by then? If Mitchell never said, some evidence offers clues. Hawthorne's *Scarlet Letter* with its deviate, adulterous heroine illuminates the choice most obviously; so, too, does the theme of the scarlet woman of Hawthorne's own allusion. If Mitchell's "frigid" heroine did not sin like Hester Prynne, she was, however, certainly a sinner and certainly deviant. Perhaps the name evoked another connotation for the author—something of "scar." That defines the protagonist's perversions in a somewhat different but equally illuminating way: the heroine was scarred. Beyond such conjecture, the name fit in other ways. It was an Irish surname, and reflected the character's genealogy. At the same time, it was not a mere abstraction that Mitchell seized from nowhere. Mitchell knew at least one minor literary Scarlett who embodied much the same spirit that her character did.

In the two decades before *Gone with the Wind* appeared, Southern letters languished, but the Savannah-born, Irish-heritage Marie Conway Oemler made a small reputation for herself in the nation and a much larger one in Georgia. In the twenties, only one other Georgia woman, Corra Harris, had a more extensive literary reputation. Mitchell knew Oelmer personally. If *Slippy McGee* proved Oelmer's most famous book, *A Woman Named Smith*, published just after in 1919, became nearly as well-known. The plot and characters of *A Woman Named Smith* appealed to the Atlantan: it was a mystery story set in the contemporary South of an ancient old town, Hyndsville (a fictionalized Bluffton, South Carolina) in a great old antebellum mansion, Hynds House, and "starring" a youngish, very modern heroine. The heroine came by her name and legacy through her great-aunt, Sophronisba Scarlett. Oelmer deliberately graced this figure with an Irish name. While she dies before the book opens, her spirit hangs over the whole fiction. She is a vengeful old virago, not incidentally, who had all those traits of greed, possessiveness, and furious will that dominated the renamed Pansy—and indeed, old Annie Fitzgerald. Oelmer introduced her vividly in her first chapter, aptly named "The Scarlet Witch Departs":

> If it had been humanly possible for Great-Aunt Sophronisba Scarlett to
> lug her place in Hyndsville, South Carolina, along with her into the next
> world, plump it squarely in the middle of the Elysian Fields, plaster it
> over with "No Trespassing" signs, and then settle herself down to a bliss-
> ful eternity of serving writs upon the angels for flying over her fences
> without permission, and setting the saved by the ears in general, she
> would have done so and felt that heaven was almost as desirable a place
> as South Carolina.[26]

Oemler's name fit perfectly.

The author also changed other names during this time. The reader's
report confirmed that Mitchell had originally called Pansy's mother
Eleanor D'Antignac. If she pulled the French surname from the air, it
bears noting that Phillip Fitzgerald, Mitchell's great-grandfather, had
married an Eleanor, too.

Mitchell also wrestled with the name of the book itself in the fall.
She submitted a whole list to her publishers. If "Tote the Weary Load"
spoke best of the novel's theme, it smacked of excessive regionalism,
she thought. Although Lois Cole preferred "Tomorrow Is Another Day,"
it had its liabilities, too. Another book bore the exact same title, and
fifteen other books began with "tomorrow." Then too, she added, it
seemed awfully long. "I hate to seem a chopper and a changer," she
apologized to her editor,

> but the more I think of it, the more I incline to "Gone with the Wind."
> Taken completely away from its context, it has movement, it could either
> refer to times that are gone with the snows of yesteryear, to the things
> that passed with the wind of the war or to a person who went with the
> wind rather than standing against it. What do you think of it?[27]

Mitchell cited no source for the felicitous phrase at the time, although later she attributed it to the lines from Ernest Dowson's poem
"Non sum qualis Eram bonae sub regno Cynarae." She professed ignorance of the Irish writer James C. Mangan's use of the line in another poem; it would have fit even better. She never referred to still
another source that used the lines in specific reference to the Confederate past. Again, the Savannah novelist Mrs. Oemler used it first in
the most famous novel she wrote, *Slippy McGee*. In the opening pages
of the book, she describes the provincial charm of the town of Apple-
boro, and uses the local monument to the Confederate soldier to characterize both the charm and the provincialism of the place.

> I hate to think that any Confederate living or dead ever even remotely
> resembled the gray granite one on our monument. . . . as a work of art
> he is almost as bad as the statues cluttering New York City. But in Ap-
> pleboro folks are not critical; they see him not with the eyes of art but

with the deeper vision of the heart. He stands for something that is gone on the wind. . . .[28]

And so the fall and early winter passed as the frantic author cut and altered, honed and polished, checked and verified, named and re-named her characters, and searched for the perfect title. Meanwhile, a score of non-literary issues sapped her time. She corrected advertising blurbs. She posed for publicity photographs. She checked illustrations. She oversaw dust jacket designs. Taking none of these matters lightly, she kept the mails and wires hot between New York and Atlanta with her queries and comments. And in the middle of ten-, twelve-, and fifteen-hour work days, she still fired off long, engaging, often hilarious letters about these activities to Latham, Cole, *et al.*

> Lois asked me for a picture and I will do what I can for you but I fear it will be no credit to Macmillan. I've had no pictures taken in ten years, not since the Journal used me so frequently to pose by dead bodies, two-headed calves, the first cotton bales of the season and the largest water-melon at the county fair. At present I am seventeen pounds underweight and could not afford to lose one pound so I look pretty bad. And on top of that, during a recent epidemic of boils, in my head, worse luck, the enthusiastic doctor shaved round spots on my skull varying from the size of a silver dollar to a penny. It gives me a curious piebald look. If I can find one of those postage stamp sized hats that will cover all the shaved spots, I will get you a picture. If not, I suppose my only hope is to be photographed like T. E. Lawrence in a turban.[29]

Her humor helped her survive the rigors of her labors in the fall and winter. In January, however, she was done—with one campaign at least. The next two months had a very different objective: correcting galley proofs and fighting with proofreaders about her usages. Her old com-pulsiveness for accuracy now found a new object, but she faced new problems that had her literally pulling out her hair. With elaborate fastidiousness, for example, she had individualized her characters, in particular, the ways they spoke. She did this with her whites as well as with her blacks, but the latter proved a special difficulty. The proof-readers standardized all of Mitchell's carefully worked colloquialisms. "Unacceptable!" she raged, and she demanded a return to her original usage. They had also standardized punctuation, and worse, from the author's perspective, the use of quotations. This fundamentally dis-torted what she intended, she howled, and demanded a reversion to her original forms. Her letters grew fractious. She was not happy.[30]

Other friction arose in this same season between the author and her publisher. When Mitchell's final revised manuscript arrived in New York at the end of January, suddenly the business managers of the company intervened in the Mitchell-Macmillan story, and there was the devil to pay. The accountants tallied the pages, weighed the bulk, recalculated the publication cost—and fell into a swoon. On February 6, the company responded officially to their dire warnings. Lois Cole took the task of asking the author for a contract revision. "When the contract was drawn we visualized something between 250,000 and 300,000 words which could be made to sell for $2.50 . . . but the book has more than 400,000 words!" Cole exclaimed. With more exclamations about losing four cents per copy, Cole then asked, "Would you agree to accept 10% on all copies?"[31] The original contract had allowed for 15 percent royalties on all sales above 10,000. The request distressed the author. In the first place, she insisted that the Macmillan Company knew what it was buying—or should have. She herself, she fumed, had told them so repeatedly. "If you are astounded at the length of the book," her husband-amanuensis replied,

> it is only the same feeling Peggy has had about it for several years. For a long time before you ever saw it, she had been saying that it would never be printed unless she found a publisher who was willing to bring it out in two volumes. And she has been in a state of continuous mystification ever since you bought it, because of Macmillan's insistence that she should do nothing to it but link it together and deliver it back to you. She expected at the beginning to be told that it would have to be cut. But beginning with your "reader's" report on it and on down until this past week, Macmillan's attitude has been that the MS you saw last summer was just right—and never a word about cutting.

The episode sat very, very ill with her. The idea of changing the contract after the fact aroused her deepest suspicions. She operated on the basis of duty and obligation, but formal contracts and agreements she considered more than semi-sacred. And now her publishers were reneging. Worse yet, from her perspective, they placed the entire burden on her. They had made the error, but she bore the responsibility. Not only did she surrender the potential of extra profit, she also felt the company blamed her for having increased the book's length. The company gave her no alternative. Finally, but not least, she resented the money loss. She agreed to the change, but as she dictated her approval, her husband wrote, "she says she is sure all her Scotch ancestors must be turning over in their graves tonight while this letter is being written."[32]

Still other matters tainted good relations between Mitchell and her publisher in the new year. Anxious about the expense of alterations in the galley proofs, Cole had casually warned her about her "contractual" commitment to pay for changes. The author went into orbit.[33] She also bridled at the company's equally casual assumption that she would come to New York at Macmillan's bidding. She would go only if and when she decided to, her husband wrote testily.[34]

Despite such caveats, Macmillan did not take warning. The author simmered. Her physical condition exaggerated her impatience. "Techy," as they say in regional parlance, Mitchell had worn herself out in her labors. The work of preparing the manuscript between September and February took its toll. Within a year of the first, she had a second car wreck in the middle of all her heaviest work. Manuscript revision complicated those aches and pains and added others. Her scalp had broken out in those boils. Her fingers developed painful calluses, which physicians removed surgically. The last two weeks of manuscript revision finally sent her to bed. The old ailment of "abdominal lesions" was cutting up again, and the doctor wanted to operate. Her back agonized her. "Sitting up for hours at a time, day after day, over a period of weeks, typing, editing the MS, handling heavy reference books, etc., was about the worst possible thing she could have done," John explained. "It was a marvel to me that she held out as long as she did."[35] She did hold out, however, both finishing the manuscript itself and correcting the galley proofs.

When she slid the last galleys through the airmail slot at the local post office on March 16, she breathed easier and relaxed more thoroughly than she had in years.[36] While other issues still bothered her—like the possibility of more contract negotiations about the movie rights, issues with agents about that contract, and the hurly-burly that grew with the Book-of-the-Month Club selection in late April—still, mid-March to mid-May proved to be the last, even relatively quiet, interlude of her pre-fame life. As the dogwoods and Judas trees exploded into bloom, she had never felt more self-confident. Her euphoria prompted the most uncharacteristic behavior. She agreed to give, not one, but two public speeches in this period.

Above almost all else, Mitchell hated speaking in public. A high school student interviewed her and captured her feeling nicely: "She says that people think if you can paint, write, or toe dance that you can make a speech, but this isn't true with her because it terrifies her to make a speech."[37] Invariably she associated public speaking with physical trauma:

> I cannot make talks and when forced into it become ill. . . . Moreover, I get sick every time I think of it, so greatly do I *not* want to talk. . . . I do not see why people want to make me sick and miserable in this matter . . . the fact remains that it takes days and weeks for me to struggle with writing something to say, days and weeks of being sick and wishing an auto would run over me before the fatal moment and days afterwards, generally in bed, getting over it.[38]

"I was not cut out to make speeches or public appearances; I get the jitters just being in crowds. . . . I have made three public appearances and it made [me] so ill that I was sick in bed," she observed to still another correspondent.[39] At the same time, however, she spoke very, very well, and as her brother insisted, once on her feet, she could no more avoid entertaining people than she could stop breathing.

Public speaking, of course, did not exist in a vacuum for Margaret Mitchell: it possessed direct associations with her mother. By all accounts, May Belle Mitchell was an especially accomplished speaker. She spoke as well as often, as easily as passionately. The intensely reticent child, conversely, did not like to speak at all, publicly or even privately, according to her brother. She hid behind her mother's skirts, and only Mrs. Mitchell's application of her hairbrush or slipper forced her from her shell. Just so, the "last beating" she ever got arose over a declamation: the time in school when she said she plagiarized, delivering someone else's work as her own in a public speech, and won the inevitable punishment at home when her mother found out. Her earliest memory, of the suffragette rally, rotated around the axis of her mother's oratory and the inevitable punishment that followed the child's upstaging. Public speaking evoked numerous old ghosts. All this makes her decision to deliver two talks within a month-long period all the more remarkable.

The first speech she delivered to the Macon Writers' Club on Friday, April 3, 1936. Accepting ran especially against her grain. It required making a major presentation of close to an hour. She also knew very few people in the audience. This group, however, as she well knew, possessed considerable discrimination. Although a local organization, the club had sponsored such notable speakers in the past as Sherwood Anderson, Richard Halliburton, Irving Batchelor, Ben Ames Williams, and Caroline Miller. Macon was special, too. The city prided itself (with justice) on being an oasis of culture amidst the provincialism of the Georgia countryside. With its law school and thriving college, Mercer University was a light to the Gentiles in Baptist-Prohibitionist Bibb County. The town possessed an old and established Catholic community and even boasted a convent at Mount De Salles on the highest hill in the town. A thriving Jewish congregation called Macon home, too; one of their number, Aaron Bernd, being one of the intellectual lights at the *Macon-News* before his untimely death in 1937.[40] Its newspapers also had a reputation for liberalism, polish, and sophistication. Mark Ethridge had edited the *Telegraph* and went on to the *Louisville Courier Journal* from Macon. Speaking before the assembly of Macon's intelligentsia, then, challenged the hardiest souls, but Peggy Mitchell Marsh hardly considered herself among such heroes. All her anxieties notwithstanding, however, she accepted.

She screwed her courage to the sticking-place, in part to sell some books. "Practically every paper picked up the Macon speech—as I hoped and thought they would," she gloated afterward.[41] Quite aside from marketing her wares, her confidence had never been higher, her anxieties never more submerged, than in early April. As she elaborated the story of her invitation to speak and her acceptance, however, she remained the helpless young thing unable to withstand the wiley Maconites—chief among them the energetic Susan Myrick and the local genius, Aaron Bernd himself. She made the story a ribald narrative as she repeated it to Lois Cole.

The club had scheduled another speaker, Edison Marshall, and when he backed out late, the officers, having heard rumors of Mitchell's book, called long-distance to tender an invitation. She refused. Thirty minutes later, the Atlantan related, Myrick and Bernd were on the line:

> Sue, in her hoarse baritone, told me that the Literary ladies had learned that she knew me and they had brought pressure on her to bring pressure on me to come. I repeated that I hadn't been published, that I loathed meeting strangers, that I had never made a speech, and God Willing, never intended to and, moreover, that I had glands.
>
> "You and your goddam glands," said Sue. "If your glands would hold up under writing such a long book they will hold up as far as Macon. The UDC as well as the Literary ladies are on my neck so get yourself over here." I refused and heard a muffled argument with Aaron: "Appeal to her better nature." "Bah," said Sue. "Try bribery, then." Sue said, "We've got Sherwood Anderson hid out at Aaron's country place and if you'll come, we'll let you associate with him." I said that not even James Branch Cabell would be bribe enough for making a speech. "Try intimidation," said Aaron. "If you don't come," said Sue in a sinister voice, "I will review you in the Telegraph and compare you favorably with Ethel M. Dell and Temple Bailey and Aaron will review you in the News and compare you with Diddie, Dumps and Tot and moreover he will use the word poignant seven times and the word nostalgic eight times and he will refer to your opus as "Adequate."[42]

She allowed her friends to twist her arm. At this point in her narrative, she laid out all her comic woes about her inability to prepare properly for the ordeal. After her acceptance, she related, she wasted the next thirty-six hours searching Atlanta stores for proper clothes. Finding nothing adequate outside of children's departments, she finally settled on "a green affair that was unendurably juvenile." The color actually was apple-green, according to the reporter who covered the event—surely one of the last times the novelist could ever allow herself to be so garbed after the scene of Scarlett at the Wilkeses' barbecue became common property. Choosing clothes, however, green or not, took time away from lecture preparation. When she might have been getting things together, she spent the train ride to Macon chatting with old friends. Once in town, she stayed up all night gabbing with Sherwood Anderson at Aaron Bernd's place "Teeter-on-the-

Jitters." The next morning, she said, she overslept. She had done nothing, nothing at all in preparation. And so she approached the podium that Friday morning, in her reconstruction, blank as a baby:

> And when I got to my feet and saw that enormous room jammed with something over two hundred people, I ardently wished I was dead for by that time I was incapable of connected thought as far as a speech was concerned. While the president was introducing me I sat like a newly gigged frog and tried to think of what I would say and I couldn't think of a thing. Life will never hold as dreadful a moment as that. . . .
>
> When I rose trembling I had a vague memory of how horses "lock" their knee joints when they go to sleep standing up and fearing that I'd fall on the floor, I locked my knee joints and took a good grip on the table and also on some whipped cream on the table cloth. Don't ask me what I said. I haven't much idea. I only know that I hadn't said five words when the crowd began to bellow which so disconcerted me that I couldn't get a word out for a moment. And from then on it was a riot. I don't know what was funny but they laughed till they wept and two UDC ladies fell off their chairs and were replaced with great difficulty.

When she suddenly "came to herself" from this comic trauma, she remembered that she was describing her conversation with Harold Latham about her book. She remembered trying to put him off with the comment that her book would not sell because it contained only "four Goddams . . . and one dirty word." At this, disorder erupted anew:

> Some kind of friend in the back of the hall yelled, "Come on! What was the dirty word?" and cornered, I refused to tell and hastened on with my saga that I didn't think the book would sell because the heroine was in love with another woman's husband for years and they never did anything about it. This was where the UDC's fell on the floor.

Her version of her conclusion was full of the same outrageous humor. Halfway through the talk, she said, she forgot herself one more time, and never recovered her senses until the thing was done.

> I had only flashes of consciousness. I recall sitting down and rising with violent abruptness because the waiter had brought some corsages for me and put them in my chair and I sat down on them and the pins were right up. This seemed to complete the disorganization of the meeting. . . . I asked afterward how long I talked and they said forty minutes and at that they had to bear me off and revive me with Bibb County corn. So help me I'll never get cornered again, come what may or make another speech. I never went through such a horrible experience in my life (except when I dropped my drawers in the church aisle when I was six or seven).[43]

Whether or not Mitchell thought out all she planned to say, the speech, as reported by disinterested third parties, proved a model lecture. She began not by speaking but with a gesture that intrigued and captured everyone's attention—and it was not seizing a fistful of whipped cream: she carefully removed her corsage and placed it in her water glass. After a witty, self-effacing introduction that set the audience chuckling, she launched into her main theme: why authors write the books they do, and how they sell their manuscripts. This hit the aspiring writers in the audience where they were most vulnerable. In elaborating the first part, she told, for the first time, the story of her inspiration with her mother on the "road to Tara." She spun other narratives of her book as well—all soon slated to be the stuff of legend; as, for example, rushing madly about her apartment just a year before, trying to round up all the scattered envelopes of her manuscript. The audience howled as she depicted herself crawling under the bed to retrieve one batch that substituted for a broken caster.

She concluded the talk on a serious note with a patriotic appeal to regional feeling as she admonished her auditors to write about the South as it really was. Actually, this little conclusion provided the author's one serious reservation about the talk. In the course of the speech she had repeated snatches of conversation with her editor about refusing to write about "Southern degenerates." In trying to disassociate her characters from the likes of Popeye and Jeter Lester, she worried that she had left a very wrong impression of her own fiction. As other papers picked up the story around the state, she discovered, to her dismay, that what they emphasized was the appeal to regional pride and literary chauvinism at the talk's conclusion. Within the context of the Southern mind, that could only mean one thing. She shuddered:

> I found to my distress that everyone had gotten the impression that Gone with the Wind was a sweet lavender and old lace, Thomas Nelson Pagish story of the old South as it never was. The newspapers all over the state picked up the story, commending me for writing a book that put the South in its true light. Alas, what shall I do about Rhett the speculator and Scarlett the Scallawag? I can never visit Macon after publication. . . . I'm sure they got this impression from the juvenile dress and hat and not what I said. . . .[44]

She had delighted her hearers, informed them, and inspired them. She had also won their hearts. She had two hundred people eating from her hands before she resumed her chair. If she sprang to her feet again on sitting down, it had less to do with corsage pins than with acknowledging the enthusiastic applause and cheers.[45] A very different talk, delivered to Atlanta librarians about six weeks later, replicated the grace, humor, and intelligence of the first. The second audience responded with the same enthusiasm.

Aside from the curiosity of her speaking publicly at all, the two talks were classic Mitchell: lively, sympathetic, humane, unpretentious, saucy, and very funny. They also underline aspects of her life that were critical to appreciating her literary gifts and the impact of her work. Beneath her apparent and self-professed artlessness, naïveté, innocence, and even ignorance lay the clearest sense of structure, motive, intent, and form. The ovation at Macon was no more an accident than her novel's wild success would be. At the same time, Mitchell's anxieties, self-effacement, and raw terror—however wreathed in humor—were just as real as these gifts. She trembled to stand up in public. She did believe herself inadequate to the tasks before her. She could not accept the praise and plaudits of her audience. Even with such obvious speaking successes behind her, the prospect of additional commitments of this kind did drive her to physical distraction. Her constant references to losing herself, losing consciousness, forgetting herself, and all the rest are also important in this regard. When the muse seized her, she could tell her "dirty stories" with impunity. She was not responsible. But when the audience roared approval, she could not claim full credit, either.

Here were the old basic motives of her life: one goaded her forward, feeding her ambition, driving her relentlessly down the "high road of success," as May Belle Mitchell called it; the other impulse denied these claims, repudiating her genius, and disdaining rewards of all her efforts. In the spring of 1936, Mitchell needed new strategies for harnessing the disparate forces in her life. Her circumstances were changing more rapidly than she could even imagine. By the time she addressed the librarians in May, her novel was already hurtling down the tracks like a locomotive stoked by a frenzied fireman, and she, like some real-life version of Buster Keaton in *The General*, clambered heroically and often comically across the speeding train.

In April, the Book-of-the-Month Club accepted her novel as its July selection. This required the official delay of publication from May 31 to June 30. It also guaranteed a minimum additional printing of 40,000 copies. As significant, it further fueled the growing public speculation that Harold Latham had (as he knew all along) hit on something very hot indeed. In anticipation of a very wide readership, the Macmillan Company had begun circulating galley-proof editions of the novel as soon as they were done. These had their own stories. Airplanes took them to Great Britain, where readers at major publishing houses waxed as enthusiastic as Latham and Everett had in the United States, and these houses fought angrily for the English publication rights.[46] Seven thousand miles west of London, Hollywood moguls sniffed success and money just like Harold Macmillan at Macmillan London.

Yes, word was out: hot property. Katharine (Kay) Brown, David Selznick's New York agent, had procured a copy of the proofs in May.

She read it long-distance over the telephone to Ronald Colman. It moved the actor as deeply as it affected Brown, Harold Macmillan, Harold Latham, and the ever-lengthening list of other readers. On May 20, Brown sent her boss a synopsis and appended the advice: "DROP EVERYTHING AND BUY IT."[47] The escalating interest on the West Coast accelerated the excitement back in New York. Well before the formal release date, then, rumors and scuttlebutt had already pushed the novel over the top. "The forthcoming Civil War Novel, *Gone with the Wind*, will undoubtedly be leading the best seller lists as soon as it appears."[48] *Publisher's Weekly* made grander assertations: *"Gone with the Wind* is very possibly the greatest American novel."[49]

The delay in publication created odd problems. In addition to the galley-proof editions, the publisher had released hundreds and hundreds of review copies in the spring. By May 5, for example, the author had received her own copy, read it laboriously for errors, and returned her list of typos to the publisher. Once more, the anguish of revising gripped her imagination. "I can't even endure to look at the book because I nearly throw up at the sight of it," she informed Lois Cole. "One shouldn't feel that way about one's first and only child and I hope I'll recover but the sight of it reminds me of the nightmare of getting it ready."[50]

Despite all these copies in circulation, the official publication date bound reviewers to silence. Few could contain themselves in the hiatus. The national literary maven Constance Lindsay Skinner got her copy early on, read it, and chafed wildly at the reviewing restrictions. "Now I seem not to be able to contain myself!" she exploded to friends in the literary world. Lois Cole got the overflow of Skinner's emotions. "GONE WITH THE WIND is one of the greatest man-&-woman stories ever written. It is grand and gorgeous Romance with a capital R. The character-drawing is penetrative, consistent. Scarlett & Rhett are magnificent and the minor characters excellent. And there is *thought* in the book." With the enthusiasm that would soon set highbrow teeth most vengefully on edge, on she raved:

> Every other known and proved device to stir sentiment and sobs is there and I can hear the women weeping from coast to coast. It'll mow 'em down. The author has something of the splendid theatre-sense in her progressing and pitching of scenes which make THE THREE MUSKETEERS the thrilling, vivid and startling reading it is. She stems from that school which saw life as drama and never tried to "rationalize" passion, thank God.
>
> But the real stroke of genius is in the story of Scarlett's struggles to survive—it is the story of thousands of young (& older) women during the depression. It is so very *modern*—and yet it is set in the most romantic period of America's past. . . . *It is a very modern story.* Thousands of women have lived it since the crash in October, 1929.[51]

Success slammed through the Mitchell-Marsh apartment on Seventeenth Street like Huns and Tartars. On May 21, Macmillan sent Mitchell a check for $5,000. Simultaneously, she signed the contract with the British Macmillan for the publication of the novel in England. At the same time, in anticipation of upped sales, the company backed away from the contract's royalty revision of February and returned to something closer to the original royalties. The author was incredulous. She also faced a harsher reality: the perpetually ringing telephone, endless waves of visitors, inundating loads of mail, and multiplying demands upon her time—and still the book's official publication date lay six weeks in the future! She tried to fulfill every claim on her time.

One caller in these hectic days of May warrants special notice. Lillian Smith had no particular reputation in 1936, but history fated her for a special role in the next three decades as one of the most notable and even notorious, if late-blooming, members of the Young South movement. She won a special place in Southern history for making an aggressive case for eliminating Dixie's racial barriers after World War II. She came late to fame, however. Although born three years before Mitchell, she was middle-aged when her darkly Freudian novel of race and sex, *Strange Fruit*, thrust a national audience upon her in 1944. For more than a decade before, she had run a girls' summer camp and published a reformist "little magazine," *Pseudopodia*, at her home in northwest Georgia. Keenly alert to everything in Southern letters, Smith caught wind of the Atlantan's fame in the spring of 1936. In early May, she and her companion, Paula Snelling, came calling on the novelist. When her own novels brought her notoriety, Smith would soon enough be mourning and groaning about fame's drain on her time and psyche; no such worries hindered her in the spring of 1936.[52] Smith and Snelling stayed an afternoon at Mitchell's apartment. The North Georgian basked in Mitchell's hospitality, attentiveness, and good talk. Although she had intended the visit as an interview, when Smith returned to her North Georgia home, she could not write the article, and she laid her burden on the harried novelist in Atlanta. "And here I sit," Smith began disingenuously,

writing up that interview with a thousand unanswered questions in my mind which you would have answered I know had I possessed the sense to insert them in the proper places in that delightful three-cornered conversation. You were very generous with your time and I think it's a damned shame to bother you again but I'll have to do it or else the interview in my column won't be half as much fun as the real one was. But wouldn't you prefer really to write us 300 words (or more) about the writing of the book . . . rather than trust it to come out right at second-hand?[53]

The novelist declined. In a second letter, Smith persisted:

I would like to suggest that you crawl up on your divan, drink another cup of that delicious black coffee you gave me, and just let it write itself, as you talked. What we want (although we shall be delighted and charmed with whatever you give us) is how you happened to write the book, how you gathered your materials for it, and please include that description of the irate old Confederate whose white moustaches blew out at you as he indignantly asked "Sister" what she meant by saying so and so. I felt it was too good for me to spoil by trying to quote you. You tell such things perfectly.[54]

For a second time, Mitchell asked to be relieved of Smith's request.[55] She never wrote Smith's essay. Smith never wrote up the interview either. The editor of *Pseudopodia* did, however, review Mitchell's book. Indeed, she gave it the nastiest notice the novel got in Dixie.[56] Lillian Smith, not unlike Mitchell herself, proved capable of vengefulness, resentment, and fierce jealousy, however veiled in gauzy flattery and ideological earnestness. If it was often obscured by her racial liberalism, Smith was still the Southern lady, and even "fine ladies" practiced bitchiness and cattiness as a refined, if intuitive and unselfconscious art. Indeed, Mitchell was doing something analogous at this very time with Smith herself. While the Atlantan presented herself to the North Georgian as the perfect hostess, for example, and wrote those long, personal letters to the editor in Clayton, she was also writing letters to other friends about Smith's and Snelling's lazy self-indulgence. In them, indeed, was something of the artiste and her "adoring girlfriends" that prompted her to give her book to Latham in the first place. The same day she wrote Smith so charmingly, she vented her spleen to Harold Latham:

I am appalled at the inability of the average person to get an interview. Having gotten them myself in taxi cabs, through bars of jails and in the cabs of locomotives, it would have seemed like heaven to me to catch a victim in the home, and have hours with her. People who interview me come and practically spend the day, talk my ear off, go home and write me nice letters telling me how much they enjoyed themselves and finish by saying "And Mrs. Marsh, will you please write me 5000 words about yourself and your book and its aims. I really didn't get an interview with you while calling on you." . . And then I moan, "Godalmighty.[57]

For all their dissimilarities, Smith and Mitchell sprang from the same cultural background. The Atlantan, however, was even more contradictory. Here she effectively volunteered her time, her energy, and her house to a stranger, and then blamed that other party for the violation of a trust. After May of 1936, such interruptions became the violent norm of her life. Her world truly went crazy then. And the two halves of her life became public property as well.

XVI

Ground Exceeding Fine

"According to Dr. George Gallup, director of the American Institute of Public Opinion, 'Gone with the Wind' is a close second to the Bible in the esteem of the American reading public." (news item)

> Is this the land of Emerson,
>   of Whitman and Thoreau,
> Of Melville, Hawthorne, Holmes,
>   Mark Twain,
>   Longfellow, Lowell, Poe,
> Where currently we are revealed
>   In doubt regarding which'll
> Stand first upon our reading list,
>   The Scriptures or Miss Mitchell?
>   RICHARD W. ARMOUR (from *The New Yorker*)[1]

*R*adiators clanked unholy welcome to the predawn November chill. By 4:30, if not before, she had rolled over one last time. She crept from bed, feet on the cold floor, and quietly dressed herself. She fastidiously avoided waking John. Finally in the kitchen, she flicked on the light and brewed her introduction to the morning. With her first cup of black coffee, she stole into the living room and surveyed the chaos she had quit barely hours before. She picked up a letter and then another from the piles, or she scanned another review. She adjusted her octagonal glasses on her nose and considered the great stack of neatly addressed envelopes, the product of last night's work. All the while, she listened intently for the visitor. At the sound of steps in the hallway, she hurried to the door to anticipate the buzzer. John needed his rest.

It was 5:00 A.M. The postman had been up much longer by then. He made the special deliveries and trekked irregularly all over town, but he might have walked Seventeenth Street and this quiet corridor in his sleep, he made the trip so often. As he approached Apartment 4, the door swung open, and the diminutive resident greeted him sunnily, the hour notwithstanding. Albeit in muted voice, she offered conversation, some small joke, sometimes a cup of coffee, or other pleasantries. He in turn rewarded her with the great pack of telegrams, special deliveries, and night letters that had accumulated since the last delivery at sundown the night before. The tiny figure signed for the bundle. The two faces smiled. The postman returned to his rounds.[2]

As the author eased the door shut, her smile evaporated. Elation fought with horror as she contemplated the letters in her hand. One more day; the volume had not slackened. She fanned the envelopes; her eyes raced through the return addresses. Was Macmillan writing again? Her stomach turned slightly at the hassles she endured over that damned Clause 14. Was the "DOS" return address postmarked from Hollywood? Night letters from David Selznick never boded well. She shuddered. She allowed herself to be distracted by the thick packet from the clipping service, an airogram from Wisconsin, a stamp from England.

Slowly she settled in to review the letters in more orderly fashion, pulling those with the familiar names, working from her own system. Soon she was lost in the clicking of her typewriter as she tried to get a jump on the other postmen with their greater volume. They came as faithfully as the dawn, and at about the same time. She picked up speed. Soon John would be up, and she would mediate between him and the morning. Soon after that, she knew, the telephone would start to jangle. Bessie should be in by then. Sometimes it started before she came. She typed faster. Would Bessie beat the first batch of visitors? Her index fingers flew across the keyboard. The typist would come in at nine. Another coffee would help now. Caffeine-charged, on she raced.

She beat out Herschel's letter, but what about that damned Englishman! What the hell does that SOB know about iodine in Atlanta fifty years before he drew his first breath in Liverpool? she grumbled to herself. But where did that damned reference to iodine come from in the first place? Perhaps Miss Jessie can get one of the girls to check it out at the library. She paused. But what if it means a trip to the library herself? She contemplated her last jaunt downtown. Who would be lying in wait today if she ventured out? Swedish tourists, like the other day, lurking in the hedges? Photographers? Neighbors? Or just the gawkers who gathered across the street? What else? Who was coming to the Tech game? When, for heaven's sake, *was* the Tech game?

Check the calendar. Is the company due today or tomorrow? When are Katharine Brown and those crazy Selznick people scheduled to arrive? "Call the club," she noted on a paper scrap; "reserve two tables," surely that would be sufficient. She typed faster.[3]

Margaret Mitchell's day had dawned. All this, two hours before she heard John's alarm, two hours before her indispensable Bessie Jordan had arrived. She roared full throttle while most of Atlanta still slept. She only slowed when others woke, but midmorning found her at the same manic pace again. She seldom slacked off before dinner, but at seven she was *au point* again. While the first-shift secretary took dictation and typed her fingers raw from nine to five, the second girl came in at seven and worked through till midnight. Sometimes when this other secretary left, the author collapsed hopelessly in bed. More often than not, however, she was wound too tight to relax. As she closed the door behind the last typist, then, she returned to the letters, scanned reviews again, and then often squeezed in other small chores that the day's rush had prevented—like washing her hair. And sometimes, despite aching eyes, she refugeed to a detective story or a murder mystery. This was the way things were in November 1936. The craziness had already lasted six months. And little changed over the next three years. It had been like this ever since the first reviews.

For over fifty years, the characters, plots, subplots, scenes, and episodes of Margaret Mitchell's novel have been an integral part of American lore and legend. Tara, Twelve Oaks, the Wilkeses' barbecue, the armory dance, the flight to the country, the murdered Yankee "bummer": everything from Mitchell's epic is so familiar now that it is difficult to imagine the time when her creation was all new. There was such as time, but barely. The *Gone with the Wind* phenomenon started early.

Even among the earliest reviewers, many, if not most, had already heard something about Mitchell's epic before they wrote their notices. By the time of *Gone with the Wind*'s formal release on June 30, 1936, more people had read the galleys than ever read most novels. Hundreds of advance copies had floated from hand to hand across the country since April. Despite the publisher's strictures, reviews had appeared a full seven weeks before the official release date. By early May, *Gone with the Wind* had been the liveliest topic of literary conversation for weeks. Long before readers ever saw the Confederate-gray dust jacket for the first time, the publishing rumors led them to anticipate the novel as a major work and a literary blockbuster of the first magnitude. Most reviewers, then, came to the book prepared for something grand indeed.

They found what they were looking for.

The novel's reception in New York fairly typified (and set the pace for) the national trend. The *New York Times*' initial notice boded ill.

Ralph Thompson did not like the book when he reviewed it on Tuesday, June 30, but the notice was otherwise ragged and eccentric. The nationally syndicated reviewer Isabel Paterson liked it better, although she mixed praise with criticism. "Miss Mitchell has inexhaustible invention, and her people are always credible, even in their melodramatic moments," she wrote. The details and background carry conviction, she continued, and the narrative never flagged. "And if depth and literary distinction are wanting—well, it is the lesson of Scarlett's career that one can't have everything. The style," she concluded, "is commonplace."[4] Paterson actually celebrated the novel grudgingly, and in the fall when the charts could not keep pace with the novel's sales, she recanted her praise. Fortunately for the novel, neither Thompson nor Paterson were typical of the first reviews in Gotham on that Tuesday morning.

In contrast with this mixed assessment in the *Times* and the *New York Herald Tribune*, two other New York reviewers—Herschel Brickell in the *Post* and Edwin Granberry in the *Sun*—had far fewer criticisms and made much greater claims for the epic novel. The more famous of the two, the Mississippi-born Brickell, began with a personal testimonial. Of the thousands of volumes he had read as a professional reviewer, none had affected him like this one. Unlike this book, few "left me feeling I'd much rather just go on thinking about them, savoring their truth and treasuring the emotional experience that reading them was, than to try to set down my impressions of them," he wrote. Like Paterson, he acknowledged problems in the fiction—melodrama and undistinguished writing among them—they were nothing, however, "considered against the merits of the book, and the most profound merit of all is the simple and elemental truthfulness of the picture." Throughout his very long review, he returned again and again to the vitality, reality, and raw power of Mitchell's fiction. While he demurred at a friend's assessment that *Gone with the Wind* was "the greatest novel ever written in the United States," he closed this first of his several notices of the epic with the firm assessment that Margaret Mitchell had certainly produced the finest Civil War novel ever written.[5] The *New York Sun* reviewer made still grander claims for Mitchell's epic. Edwin Granberry bracketed the author of *Gone with the Wind* with the great novelists of the nineteenth-century tradition—Tolstoy, Hardy, Dickens, and Undset (an early twentieth-century Norwegian novelist). He also insisted that Mitchell's epic marked a turning point in the modern novel. The power of her storytelling and brilliance of her characterization, he declared, challenged the modernists who had abandoned plot for mood, ambience, and angst. Here, he trumpeted, lay the alternative to the pessimism, obscurity, and fatal complexity of most contemporary novelists.[6]

The Sunday reviews five days afterward echoed and amplified all

Granberry's and Brickell's encomiums. In a front-page notice in the literary supplement of the *New York Times*, J. Donald Adams, the book editor, completely reversed the opinion of the "harried daily reviewer," Ralph Thompson, of the week preceding. Meanwhile, the young Columbia University professor Henry Steele Commager challenged Isabel Paterson's guarded praise, in an equally prominent notice in the *Herald Tribune*. These two extremely important reviews in the two most important newspapers in New York guaranteed *Gone with the Wind*'s critical and financial success, had it ever been in doubt. In addition, Commager and Adams confirmed the final contours of opinion that governed attitudes towards Mitchell's work.

Like Herschel Brickell, Adams conceded the novel's literary and stylistic limitations; nevertheless, he considered the shortcomings insignificant beside the book's merits—its structural clarity, dramatic vigor, and vivid characterization. In narrative power and "sheer readability," he wrote, nothing in American fiction surpassed it. *"Gone with the Wind* is by no means a great novel, in the sense that *War and Peace* is, or even *Henry Esmond*, to name only novels which dealt like this one with past periods of time," he judged. "But it is a long while since the American reading public has been offered such a bounteous feast of excellent story telling." He also concurred with Brickell's assessment that *Gone with the Wind* surpassed all other novels of the Civil War.[7] For all Adams's praise, his *Times* review actually failed to reveal the depths of his enthusiasm. He had acquired a copy by the end of April and called Macmillan very early to share his excitement.[8] He also returned to the novel year after year, and as late as 1961 confessed that his original notice actually underestimated the work's power, strength, and—not least of all—its staying power. It grew rather than diminished over time, he insisted.[9]

Professor Commager in the *New York Herald Tribune* outpraised even Adams in the *New York Times*. "It is dramatic, even melodramatic," he conceded; "it is romantic and occasionally sentimental; it brazenly employs all the trappings of the old-fashioned historical novel, and all of the stock characters of the old-fashioned Southern romance, but it rises triumphantly over this material and becomes if not a work of art, a dramatic reaction of life itself." He lauded the novel as the prose equivalent to *John Brown's Body*, Stephen Vincent Benét's epic, which had appeared to universal praise ten years before.[10]

If the New York papers fixed the grounds of debate, literary magazines and journals of opinion repeated and expanded the discussion over the summer, fall, and even later.

If Henry Steele Commager had called *Gone with the Wind* the prose equivalent of *John Brown's Body*, Stephen Vincent Benet himself celebrated the novel in the *Saturday Review*. Not so passionate as Granberry, Brickell, Commager, or Adams, Benet judged it "a good novel rather than a great one," but he also considered it "as readable, full-bodied, and consistent a historical novel as we have had in some time—a novel which, in certain passages, as in the flight from burning Atlanta, rises to genuine heights." He isolated key elements of the novel for praise, including both the "woman's angle" and Mitchell's realism. Indeed, everything seemed so authentic and familiar that it seemed impossible that Mitchell could have conjured it all from her imagination. It possessed, Benet asserted, "the convincing ring of folklore."[11]

While Harry Hansen's review in *Harper's Weekly* added little to the discussion of the novel itself, he addressed one issue that would haunt the novel for fifty years. One of the most significant reviewers in the United States, Hansen wrote a syndicated column whose audience extended from Main Street to the ivory tower. He liked the book enormously and praised it lavishly, but he also used it, as did Edwin Granberry, as a means of challenging contemporary fiction and critiquing the tenets of modernism. "Primarily, the object of a story-teller is to tell a story," he began.

> There has been so much talk in reviews about social criticism, biological evidence, and psychological quirks that we have forgotten that the novelist is not a scientist. He may castigate his age and expose the foibles of his contemporaries, but if he is a real story-teller he wants to create his world by narrative, and let the critics, pedants, and self-styled intellectuals go hang.[12]

Gone with the Wind's defenders asserted that Mitchell's epic would reverse the currents of modernism. They erred. Mitchell's novel marked a watershed, but the current flowed in the opposite direction. Modernism triumphed. The victors soon took their revenge. Hansen's loathesome "critics, pedants, and self-styled intellectuals," then, told Mitchell, Granberry, Hansen, and company to go hang, instead of the other way around. While the modernists' triumph came chiefly after World War II, reviews in *The Nation* and the *New Republic* anticipated the countercharge. They deserve special notice for the identity of their authors as well as for their content.

Evelyn Scott wrote *The Nation*'s notice. One of the notorious if second-rank members of the Lost Generation, Scott had achieved a significant though limited fame with her experimental Civil War novel, *The Wave*, published in 1929. An important, innovative, and almost unreadable exercise, Scott's fiction provided a regular reference, both positive and negative, for many *Gone with the Wind* reviewers. A bellwether, if now almost forgotten, modernist within the Generation of 1900, this transplanted Southerner reflected a commitment to the most contemporary values on the one hand, while she struggled with regional tradition and history on the other.[13] Her review offers singular insights into Mitchell's work.[14]

As did most other reviewers, Scott commended the author's vigor, "dramatic buoyancy," and vivid characterization. It is especially notable that, as a Southern lady herself, Scott deemed Scarlett particularly convincing. Rhett, too. Indeed, she argued, "the whole-heartedness with which [Mitchell's] imagination yields itself to the interpretation of these two favorites makes the reader's absorption in a narrative sprinkled with clichés and verbal ineptitudes a contagious growth." As a militant proponent of modernism, Scott also recognized the trait where she found it, and almost alone among contemporary reviewers she connected Mitchell's epic with literary currents of the twenties. She acknowledged Mitchell as something of a fellow-traveling modernist, in her identification of Scarlett as "a petty Nietzchean" and her criticism that Mitchell's literary vision was governed by that "undigested literature of pessimism" that dominated the 1920s. For all its merits, however, Mitchell's epic, finally, was simply not modern enough for Scott. She faulted the Atlantan for the absence of sociological truth and her failure to employ what Scott considered new developments in personality analysis. The review is singular in other ways. It was one of two or three that genuinely irritated the author. Given the author's passion for psychology, Scott's criticism concerning personality development was bound to irritate, but the author also steamed for years over Scott's objection to "her temperamental limitations as a critic both of mass movements and personal behavior [which] are such that she often gives a shallow effect."[15]

While Evelyn Scott actually found much to admire in *Gone with the Wind*, the *New Republic* disdained Mitchell's work. This important left-liberal journal ran, not one, but two notices of Mitchell's epic in the summer of 1936. The first dismissed the novel out of hand; the second damned with faint praise. John Peale Bishop—still one more displaced Southerner—found almost nothing worthwhile in the novel in his July notice. This former Vanderbilt Fugitive approved of Mitchell's historical accuracy, but that was all. He dismissed her novel as "one more of those 1,000 page novels, competent but neither very good nor very sound." The lack of "soundness" distressed him most. The author told two contradictory tales, Bishop argued, and the moral ambiguity repelled him.[16]

Bishop's review did not distress the author. Indeed, she professed actually to have admired the piece. "In view of the fact that The New Republic and I have such different viewpoints, my opinion, when I read Mr. Bishop's review, was that the magazine had done rather well by me . . . ," she told Stark Young, another former Fugitive, the journal's drama critic, and a devoted Mitchell fan.[17] If Mitchell took no offense at the first notice in the *New Republic*, however, the second deeply offended her.[18] In September, Malcolm Cowley, one of the bright young men of the New York literary left, reviewed the book one more time for *New Republic* readers. He began, not with the book itself, but with sales and readership. Cowley was the first of the major reviewers to consider Mitchell's epic as a phenomenon. He was not the last. Indeed, the extraordinary sales and the still more general public acclaim came eventually to obscure the text itself for most critics. Cowley related the book's success to publisher's hype and an appeal to the lowest common denominator in the American reading public. He went on to identify this market with women, and this female readership with social pretentiousness, intellectual vacuity, false sentiment, and intellectual self-deception. With more or less witty, flip misogyny, Cowley managed even to condemn women in class terms by identifying these characteristics with the "amiable weakness" of the bourgeoisie. He then read all this back into the novel itself. After casually pairing *Gone with the Wind* with exotic romances like *The Sheik* and the tear-jerking *If Winter Comes*—romances that Mitchell had ridiculed herself as a young reporter—he smirked at the prospect of one more scribbling woman soon driving the current heroine from the scene.[19]

Cowley, of course, was not the first to link Mitchell's novel with women. He, however, first introduced invidiousness into the discussion. Others quickly drew similar conclusions. Although a radical antimodernist—unlike the leftist maven at the *New Republic*—Bernard De Voto followed Cowley's lead on this one question. *Gone with the Wind* offended the Pulitzer Prize–winning editor of the *Saturday Review*. If Stephen Vincent Benét had used the *Saturday Review* to celebrate the woman's angle as the source of the volume's merit, the female connection sparked De Voto's violent opposition. Over the next two years he found various occasions to attack Mitchell's work in much the same language as Malcolm Cowley—which, increasingly, became the norm among the literati after 1937. Equating *Gone with the Wind* with decadence, mass culture, and the "feminization" of literature, he lambasted the social values that spawned such novels. "The slick writers of the highest bracket (they are practically all women), believe firmly in the moral overtones of their stuff, which are what give it cash value," he snarled. "In all ages these simplicities are what the popular audience has most wanted from literature and what it has most rewarded. The women's magazines, and the slicks in general, merely canalized the popular taste."[20]

Unlike De Voto, Cowley, for all his snide condescension, actually liked Mitchell's novel; it moved him, he admitted, however reluctantly. In contrast to Bishop, too, he recommended it and concluded his notice with the affirmation of Mitchell's power as a writer. Even against his will and better judgment, he conceded, her characters engaged his imagination. They lived for this snappy New York intellectual no less than for the lady readers he dismissed. Mitchell, he concluded,

> writes with a splendid recklessness, blundering into big scenes that a
> more experienced novelist would hesitate to handle for fear of being

compared unfavorably with Dickens or Dostoevsky. Miss Mitchell is afraid of no comparison and no emotion—she makes us weep at a deathbed (and really weep), exult at a sudden rescue and grit our teeth at the crimes of our relatives the damnyankees. I would never, never say that she has written a great novel, but in the midst of triteness and sentimentality her book has a simple-minded courage that suggests the great novelists of the past.

Such virtue, he judged, finally justified the sales: "No wonder it is going like the wind," he closed.[21]

Malcolm Cowley's sincere, if belated, concession of the power of Mitchell's characters only confirmed what most reviewers had been commending for four months, and Mitchell's editors had celebrated for much longer. From the very beginning, critics had affirmed the power of Mitchell's people. If the likes of Malcolm Cowley admitted it reluctantly, the book's proponents were thunderstruck by Mitchell's ability to charge their passions. If Scarlett, Rhett, and all the rest sprang to life in the imaginations of these exponents of high culture, how much more spontaneously and immediately did the mass of readers respond!

Most obviously, the volumes sold represented one measure of the popular enthusiasm. The publishing world had never experienced anything like this. The week after publication, Herschel Brickell had predicted publicly that the volume would reach 400,000 sales by January 1, 1937, and 600,000 by June 30, 1937. No book sold longer than a year; so he presumed that this would equal total sales. By August, the urbane Mississippi writer had become a confidant of the Mitchell-Marshes, and privately he revised these estimates steadily upward. "Up here we hear of nothing except the book," he wrote the Marshes from New York in midsummer; "everybody is reading it and talking about and liking it, so my guess of at least 600,000 copies in total sales will have to be revised, I suppose. I think now at least 750,000, and I'm an old hand at such guessings."[22] The occupants at Apartment 4 at the Russell snickered. And you didn't offer to bet on it, the author added in her glee.[23] His honor impugned, Brickell then wagered a case of burgundy. Mitchell accepted with alacrity. In astonishing time, the Atlantan was placing an order for a case of Beaune: by January 1937, sales had topped one million copies in the United States alone. They rose inexorably through the new year. In the spring of 1937, the American Booksellers Association awarded *Gone with the Wind* its annual prize for the best fiction of the preceding year, and on May 4, the Pulitzer Committee announced Mitchell's capture of that crown, too. On the anniversary of publication, total sales swelled beyond 1,700,000, over a million beyond Brickell's original estimate. Even in 1938, the printers still labored to supply the demand of booksellers for over 1,000 copies every month. And by now, too, foreign presses were milling out their translations by the thousands and the tens of thousands.[24]

Even these astonishing figures fail to show the depth of the popular passion for the book. Malcolm Cowley had conjured up a glib readership that had taken up the book like a fad and would abandon it just as quickly for something new. This did not happen. People read it over and over. They passed treasured copies from hand to hand and back again. And the reviewer for the *New Republic* notwithstanding, people did check out the novel from the lending libraries: indeed, libraries could not keep copies on the shelves; patrons regularly wore them out; and these institutions proved an important source of sales.

The variety and ubiquity of the readership startled even the most blasé critics. Mitchell's new friend Edwin Granberry provided one glimpse of this vast, heterogeneous audience. "Word of it has seeped into the farthest out-of-the-way hamlets and into strata of society where one supposes there was little time for the reading of novels," he related. He then repeated an odd encounter to demonstrate his point.

> Standing recently under the steel girders of a railroad shed, discussing Miss Mitchell's book with a friend while waiting for a midnight Pullman to start, I suddenly realized that standing near us in the dim light were two men, their faces blackened with coal smoke, tools swinging in their hands. They were trainmen of some sort, and they were listening to what we had to say. I asked one of them if he had read the book. He grinned in the affirmative, adding: "And I hope she never gets him back. . . ."[25]

Mitchell made her people live, and readers threw themselves wholeheartedly into her fiction. In 1936, Mitchell's now-friend Herschel Brickell sent the author excerpts from a letter he had received about the novel. His friend could not contain herself; "I'm half-way through *Gone with the Wind*," she exploded, but she had to stop and catch her breath before continuing.

> My God, I can't stand it! I read a chapter or two and then I have to stop and walk [up] and down in a perfect torrent of feeling. How can a book be that good. My God. When Scarlett came home to Tara from Atlanta with her desperate wagonload—I can't remember anything in fiction taking me off my feet like that. . . .

She added a postscript upon actually completing the novel: "simply incredibly good," she wrote. "I am depressed now that it's all over. But I think there will be a new pleasure in reading it again a little later."[26]

Brickell's enthusiastic friend actually was no ordinary reader. Marjorie Kinnan Rawlings had already achieved critical acclaim herself with *South Moon Under* in 1933. She was capable of still better. the Pulitzer Committee thought so, too, and awarded her its highest accolade in 1939 for *The Yearling*. Still, Rawlings's excitement differed little from that of the masses of readers. An example of the latter was Gordon Ray Young. Although he professed to know Paul Jordan-Smith, the notable reviewer for the *Los Angeles Times*, nothing else distinguished him, but his outpouring to "My dear Mrs. Morse" of July 24 has the same spontaneous passion of Marjorie Kinnan Rawlings's reaction. "For the first time in so many years I can't say, I was anxious about what happened to the characters. I cared," he wrote.

> A few times I choked up, had to wipe my glasses; and anybody who moistens my glasses has to have something very unlike what most people who write have. Your characters are beautiful as works of art, even the minor ones, like Frank; so authentic, so consistent and casually splendid. I do not know how much awareness you have about your "technique" and do not care, for technique is a mechanical thing, admirable only in so far as it secures the effects aimed at; but you succeed in a way that no experienced writer could even have attempted—I guess as the oak does. It grew from feeling and brooding rather than thinking and plotting, and you mothered it with a creative love; and *Gone with the Wind* is a permanently great novel and will endure.[27]

Here it stands, then, in some raw state: the passionate affinity readers felt for Mitchell's characters and her creation. If the arch-critic Malcolm Cowley suggested that he wept, "really wept," at deathbed scenes, so did millions. Could Marjorie Kinnan Rawlings hardly wait to finish but then grieve when she was done, finding consolation only in the prospect of plowing through the whole thing again? Thousands and thousands duplicated her reaction. Popular ardor had no limits. Folks bought the book, they read it, they reread it, they discussed it with their friends, they debated it in newspapers, they welcomed sermons on the subject, they used it as a metaphor for politics and a theme for poetry. And so, like *Uncle Tom's Cabin* three generations before, the novel burst upon American culture and provided a whole new set of images, metaphors, and ways of seeing the world.

Popular passion for the novel had one other especially notable expression: the letters readers wrote to the epic's author. As Mitchell's friend Edwin Granberry noted, the novel " 'does something' to people and they turn instinctively to the one person who can lift the spell she has put on them—Margaret Mitchell herself."[28] Like Gordon Ray Young, readers dried their glasses one moment and typed letters to the author the next. They closed the book in the evening; the dawn found them composing tributes to the author. From the very first, this reaction was a general phenomenon.

In the 1920s and 1930s, the outpouring of letters to public figures was characteristic of the age. The most famous Georgia novelist before Mitchell, for example, Corra Harris, author of the now sadly forgotten

The Circuit Rider's Wife, received innumerable letters from readers emotionally involved in her work. Eleanor Roosevelt's secretaries could hardly keep up with the bags of mail delivered to the White House, either.[29] Mitchell's correspondence stands out even in this context. The volume was astonishing. Mitchell would crawl from bed to catch the first batch at 5:00 A.M., but this would be no more than a tenth of the daily deliveries to her apartment. In the summer and fall of 1936, the author never left home for more than three or four days at a time, but after one of these brief trips, she returned to find over 1,200 pieces of mail. This preposterous figure declined in 1937, but every delivery, even then, brought still more scores of letters from people whom her fiction had ensnared, and this persisted for years.

The curiosity of the content matched the volume of these missives. As did Corra Harris and Eleanor Roosevelt, Mitchell received numerous requests for loans and cash from hard-luck cases in the Great Depression. Others asked other favors: speak to our club; tell me how to write a best-seller; share the secret of success; will you contribute an article to our journal? More correspondents longed to state their curiosity about the personal life of a celebrity. How old are you? they inquired. Are you married? Are you a Catholic? Why don't you have children? Still hundreds more poured in with such queries about the proper pronunciation of the heroines' names or "Tara" ("first 'a' as in 'at,' " she politely informed them).

Another category of readers demanded to know the sources of her inspiration. Everything seemed too real to them to be fiction, and they assumed she had based everything on real people. Who were they? they demanded; where did they live? they wanted to know. The same motive prompted more mailbags of letters that begged for information about how to get to Tara driving up from Valdosta or coming over towards Atlanta from Augusta. And where exactly, Mrs. Marsh, was Aunt Pitty's house? I know it must surely be torn down by now, the letters ran, but the wife and I would just like to see the site. It was all too real. She could not have made it up. One more huge category of correspondents grieved about that notorious ending and demanded she tell them how it really worked out. Surely she got him back! they insisted. They could not stay apart; say it ain't so, Miss Mitchell! Readers' passions simply defied Mitchell's finality.

The Atlantan had produced something close to scripture in the minds of thousands, and many of their letters, according to her husband, had "the tone of the confessional about them"—or the analyst's couch, he might have added. Women wrote that the estrangement of Rhett and Scarlett opened their eyes to difficulties in their own marriages, while "husbands write that Rhett's separation from Scarlett after he had loved her so many years has kept them awake at night, fearful that they might also lose beloved wives."[30] In the same mode, according to Edwin Granberry, men broken by the Depression poured out their hearts in understanding for Ashley, and wives wrote long letters full of bitter sympathy with Scarlett because "no woman knows the degradation she will stoop to until she needs to defend her home and those she loves."[31]

These letters reconfirmed what reviewers had testified from the earliest: that Mitchell beguiled readers to believe her world. She spoke to people's hearts, and the letters she received measure her ability to pierce the boundaries of art and life. They are, in this regard, significant in themselves. Her replies, however, are still more astonishing.

In her fame, Mitchell's correspondence became an extraordinary aspect of her life and character. In the thirteen years before her death in 1949, Mitchell wrote at least ten thousand letters; perhaps twice that number. If many of these were one-page notes, an astonishing number ran pages and pages. Little absorbed more of her time, energy, and imagination. Her post-1936 letters, however, only confirmed a pattern that she established even as a little girl. She wrote letters all her life. Almost all of her pre-fame efforts have been lost, but those surviving— to Allen Edee, Elinor Hillyer, Harvey Smith, Frances Marsh, and some to Eugene Mitchell—underline her extraordinary commitment to the form. A seventeen-page typed letter to Harvey Smith in 1932 was fairly normal. A run of nineteen long letters between 1919 and 1921 to former boyfriend Edee was not exceptional. All this suggests the energy this writing absorbed. Mitchell's correspondence is one of the most extraordinary aspects of a singular life. In form and content no less than in volume, her letter-writing suggests very much about her sense of self and also her identity as a woman and a Southerner.

Margaret Mitchell did not write letters in a vacuum. Although a bastard, only semi-public, art, letter-writing has its own standards and criteria of merit. Regional culture exaggerated self-conscious epistolarity and encouraged the development of public or at least consensual definitions of good letters. When Southerners wrote letters, they generally (or often) assumed an audience beyond the addressee. Southern emphasis on family and tradition dictated the sharing of letters in both time and space. Even when ostensibly personal, letters passed from hand to hand, sometimes as an enclosure of still another letter. They were read aloud at family gatherings. By such means, public or at least consensual definitions developed about good letters. Indeed, the Good Letter became a regular, common, and generally accepted compliment among Southerners: "He writes a good letter." The commendation still echoes through Southern conversations as the twentieth century closes. Recipients saved good letters. These became a part of the common store of culture, too; both regional and familial. Any Southern family that made any obeisance to tradition or that saved anything at all usually preserved packets of old letters. Just so, letter-writers wrote with an unselfconscious eye cocked towards future generations and larger audiences. This helps account, for example, for the common postscripts to "destroy this letter"—the norm being, of course, that the recipient would save and circulate the missive. They were saved; they were circulated.[32]

Not infrequently, personal letters found still more obviously public audiences. Thus, for example, if a recipient especially liked a letter, it might be submitted to a local newspaper. Few considered this unseemly. To cite one example already treated in this book, when John Marsh was stationed in Europe during World War I, one of his correspondents gave at least one of his letters to the Lexington newspaper, where it was published in its extensive length of perhaps twenty-five column inches.[33] Issues of the private and personal did not seem to influence the decision to submit letters to this genuinely public forum. What did determine such decisions was the quality and the topicality of the letters themselves—that is, basically, their literary merit.

These various motives and implied epistolary standards encouraged correspondents to mind their letters in a particular way. People wrote with these broader standards and broader audiences virtually understood. These considerations apply with special force to Margaret Mitchell.

The earliest long, surviving letter she ever wrote—that notable epistle to her father and grandmother written from her aunt's home in Greenwich, Connecticut, in September 1918—introduces her ideas about the form. At its end, she added the postscript, "save this letter." Everything about the missive validates the request. She was writing with her eye on the future. With its histrionics about patriotism, its judgments of her mother's family, and its anticipation of her coming academic experiment, the content of the letter affirms that she approached its writing as an historical act; she created or re-created historical time; she related her own experience within that time.[34] And finally, she need not even have made the request to have the postscript honored. She knew her father's sense of documentary history and his propensity to save everything; she knew of his appreciation of stylish letters in particular (his own reflected the mode most clearly); she knew he loved letters quite as much as he adored his daughter; she knew that he thought she wrote a good letter—that was common family knowledge. He had also saved her most childishly scribbled letters. Her postscript, then, simply flags the letter's self-consciousness in the boldest way.

Other aspects of Mitchell's correspondence confirm her use of letter-writing as a self-conscious—or at least semi-selfconscious—art. Although she wrote the liveliest and most vigorous, engaging, and otherwise spontaneous letters, she recognized and employed regular conventions of the form and often referred to the conventions within the letter itself. Regularly, for example, she apologized for some deviation from the norm: This letter is too long, this note too abrupt, she might say; another missive, she might scribble, is too disconnected or too impersonal. In one especially "lettery" epistle to Harvey Smith, she apologized for violating still another, rather more delicate, convention—of replying too quickly to his previous letter. Her apology relieved him of the necessity of responding in kind and manner, but having violated the convention, she considered it necessary to explain why she wrote at all. "I know you think that I answer your letters so quickly because I have absolutely nothing else to do but t'aint so," she explained. After recounting all the chores she faced, she concluded, "I guess I just write to you because I like to."[35] Letters were, in short, her literary form of choice.

As the "form of choice," letter-writing filled her needs well. Insofar as domestic duties and social obligations fragmented her days, the epistolary form was well adapted to her circumstances. She could squeeze in pages here and there between her rounds of chores and duties. She could write in bursts and snatches when she had neither time, energy, nor imagination to conceive other literature. One has only to recall her scribbling letters while she commanded her servants, or jotting pages while she waited for an escort to arrive, or finding time only for postscripts between the time that her date returned her home and she fell asleep, to gain a sense of the importance of the mode for her. When actually engaged with other writing—journalism, short stories, novellas, novels, and then finally her epic—letter-writing provided a relieving variation and a means, often, of objectifying and clarifying that other project; as for example, in her mulling over the literary difficulties of "The Kiss" with Allen Edee in 1920. Similarly, letters allowed her the opportunity to hone her style and usage, to experiment with plot and even dialogue.

In another way, letters gave her a means of objectifying herself literarily. Through letters, she shaped and molded her own experiences and her own life and imposed art and order on otherwise random events. In this sense, of course, Mitchell had far more in mind in composing letters than the dissemination of simple facts and discreet information to friends and kin. Just so, her missives were not necessarily "true" in a strictly factual sense. If based on actual experience, they were constructions and artifices rather than the mere detailing of actual events themselves. In the most extraordinary and compelling way, they allowed her, effectively, to experiment with personae for herself. If the images she projected of herself were not true in a "scientific" sense, they were true from another perspective: that of the truth in any art.

Epistolary literature filled still other needs in Mitchell's life. It fit her particular needs as a woman. Being a bastard art, neither fully public nor completely private, letter-writing lent itself particularly to women's circumstances and to the paradoxes of female lives in a patriarchy. This was, first, completely acceptable writing for a woman because it was ostensibly private or domestic writing. Two of Mitchell's heroines had done just this. In Mitchell's notable *Journal* articles, "Georgia Romances" and "Empress and Women Soldiers," Fanny Kemble in the first and Rebecca Felton in the second had established reputations through their correspondence. Fanny Kemble's *Journal*, which the writer so admired, actually took the form of a series of private letters to a friend; while Mitchell argued that Felton's public fame and power rested on the letters she wrote while a completely private person. The exact same themes apply to another Mitchell heroine, the Duchesse d'Orleans, sister-in-law of Louis XIVe, the wonderful and witty "Madame," whole letters first saw print in English in 1924. Indeed, in their published form, as *Letters of Madame*, they were one of her favorite reading subjects as a young woman. All these women established their reputations through their epistles. Mitchell sympathized.

Gender came into play another way. The nature of the form disguised its art. Indeed, women could explain and justify writing letters as a necessity within patriarchal definitions of their role. It followed from their obligation to maintain harmony, community, intimacy, and good relations within the family circle and the social order. Just so, it allowed for literary expression within, ostensibly, an accepting, nonrestricting community. The intimacy of the form also allowed enormous liberty, invention, and experimentation—in short, individual expressiveness—without the full burden of literary responsibility. Mitchell's servant Bessie Jordan suggested something of this liberty when a reporter inquired whether or not she had seen the novelist laboring over her tome. "I was with Miss Mitchell at the time this wonderful book was started," Jordan related afterward, "but she made such little noise I thought she was only writing a letter to a friend."[36]

One other gender-related issue arises out of Mitchell's commitment to her correspondence and illuminates, one more time, the writer's fierce legacy from her mother and the fiercer obligations of ladyhood.

For all the ways letter-writing gratified the author and satisfied the needs and imperatives of her life, she often complained bitterly about writing, particularly about how it stole time from fiction writing. Whether she liked corresponding or not, however, she always insisted she had no alternative. She considered it an obligation of womanhood, a test of her heritage as a Southern lady, and a social and cultural responsibility that she could not avoid, whatever its negative consequences. "She is often distressed that she must decline the invitations, turn away the callers and refuse the autographs," her husband wrote, but she feared this self-assertion made her seem unwomanly—tough and hardbodied, unfeeling and unappreciative. Such an action stirred her oldest guilts: "She has the feeling that she is not holding true to her Southern upbringing."[37] In one matter, however, she refused to spare herself, "and that is in answering the stream of letters," her husband related: "she answers all the letters she receives and she answers them herself. She has a secretary—sometimes two . . . but every letter receives Miss Mitchell's personal attention. No form-letter replies are sent."[38] The fear of failing her heritage of Southern ladyhood—her mother's legacy—dictated her response. Correspondence presented an "obligation she could not evade." Unlike Corra Harris, who simply ignored most of the letters she received from strangers, or Eleanor Roosevelt, who delegated secretaries to draft responses, Margaret Mitchell took each correspondent as a personal challenge.

With the prodigal generosity of ladyhood, Mitchell turned away no one except the most obvious cranks. This commitment accounts for some of the odder incidents of the novelist's career. Lillian Smith asked her to write a 300-word essay for *Pseudopodia*. The author replied with an elaborate 900-word explanation of her inability to do so. Similarly, although she decided against autographing any more books, she apologized with long, personal holograph letters to the perfect strangers who requested her signature. She set out to answer all the myriad pleas, requests, advice, admonitions, and confessions that filled the postal sacks that she could not even lift. And as John Marsh testified, she never sent form letters, either. Furthermore, her missives were generally much more than one-page notes and acknowledgements, even to strangers. Even more remarkable, she calculated each letter, as near as she could tell, for the specific recipient. Sometimes she repeated the same stories and the same figures of speech when she fired off ten letters almost simultaneously, for example; even so, she still altered details and added special effects for each correspondent. Her letters duplicated her strategies with people face-to-face: she stroked and flattered others while playing down her own efforts and successes. She almost never disputed or contradicted an opinion; on the contrary, she always sought some common ground between herself and those to whom she wrote. The correspondents were beguiled. Who could resist this world-famous novelist scribbling as if the universe contained no one but the two of them?

One batch of letters she wrote just after the appearance of *Gone with the Wind* reveals all these characteristics. After those extraordinary New York reviews on Sunday, July 5, the pressure in Atlanta became unbearable and on the Tuesday after, the author hit the road, trying to find some respite. In the space of just over twenty-four hours—counting driving time to Gainesville, Georgia, where she holed up in a hotel under an assumed name—she wrote at least ten letters. They averaged five or six pages each. She favored Herschel Brickell, Edwin Granberry, and Stephen Vincent Benét for their New York reviews. George Brett, president of the Macmillan Company, got his letter, too. She also whipped off long notes to a clutch of admirers in East Tennessee, who had reviewed her book earlier and with whom she had already established a correspondence: Gilbert Govan, Julia Collier Harris, Julian Harris, and her old friend from the *Journal* days, Hunt Clement.

Another remarkable lot followed in the hours after her return on July 9; especially significant among these were her letters to J. Donald Adams, Henry Steele Commager, and Fanny Butcher of the *Chicago Tribune.* Charming individually, they lose none of their shine taken together. They sparkle with wit, intelligence, information, and, as always, her self-deprecating humor. Notably, too, they all establish a well-defined relationship with the correspondent. She is the innocent and suppliant maiden who begs their indulgence. Edwin Granberry's review had been the first she read, she told him, and her elation prompted her to write immediately:

> As soon as I read what you said, I had what I thought was a perfectly marvelous letter to write you, a letter which would tell you exactly how much I appreciated your kindness. But that letter has gone, disappearing somewhere along the road of this last nightmare week and I find myself tonight here in a hotel in Gainesville, incoherent from exhaustion and from gratitude to you. So forgive this letter its inadequacies. . . .

She then surveyed the chaos of the week preceding to justify her epistolary shortcomings. This chronicle offered still more reasons for apology. "I did not mean to fling all my troubles upon you, a stranger, who has been so kind to me," she wrote. "But I'm trying to explain my seeming discourtesy in not writing to you sooner; explain, too, why this letter is such a hash."[39]

However experienced, senior, or jaded the reviewer, few failed to melt with such treatment. Thus she favored everyone she wrote. She aimed to make everyone feel good or better. In its literary manifestation, here was her old role of nurse or bedpan-toter. It spawned, however, a batch of problems. While this attitude flattered individual correspondents, it also established difficulties and contradictions from letter to letter and from correspondent to correspondent. Someone might write about Scarlett as a pervert: Yes, she would agree, Scarlett was a "partial psychopath." Doesn't the heroine have any redeeming features? another pled. Yes, she replied, Scarlett was really perfectly normal; only the times were out of joint. Did one reviewer commend one passage? Her reply raved, that this is indeed *my* very favorite passage in the whole book! But another reader might commend another, and that would elicit a similar response.

All these responses confused the record of what she really intended in her novel; biographically, however, they confuse the record even more. Ariadne in the labyrinth, she left scores of strings for those who followed. She fired off literally thousands of letters with almost as many conflicting stories about herself. These letters or their summaries often floated to the press—she wrote to many journalists—and her public image became hopelessly tangled with her own legendary, epistolary self. The situation became all the more confused when her correspondents elaborated or filled in the blanks of her hyperbole; then, too, the press itself often garbled fact and legend. She herself had referred in her letters to "being crippled," "breaking her ankle," and "going blind." She had also claimed her husband as the inspiration for her writing. Afterward, she spent countless hours writing *more* letters trying to undo these very impressions when they circulated in the press as facts. Generosity had its price.

And other problems arose from her letter-writing. If reading her correspondence now absorbed three-quarters of her waking hours, her responses aggravated the problem. The very warmth of her missives guaranteed response in kind, and more. She effectively invited more correspondence by her openness, friendliness, and accessibility. High and low alike answered the invitation, and she established still more "obligations she could not refuse" to people she now deemed "friends." Her correspondence with Herschel Brickell was completely characteristic of this pattern.

After his very generous review of June 30, Mitchell had written him warmly in those hectic days when she had first fled Atlanta. The transplanted Mississippian took the bait. Within a fortnight their letters flowed freely back and forth between New York and Atlanta. In her original letter of July, Mitchell had also written him about the rumor that he wanted to meet her. She gushed with flattery. Y'all come! she insisted. "I'll give you a party if you want a party or I'll feed you at home and listen to your talk. My cook's a good old fashioned kind, strong on turnip greens and real fried chicken and rolls that melt in your mouth."[40] No Mississippi-bred boy could resist this culinary siren. Brickell did show up, and the two sealed their friendship. Brickell returned her favors, too, almost immediately in helping her escape the Atlanta crazies by abetting her flight to Blowing Rock, North Carolina, in early July after the publication of her novel.

Even amidst the insanity of the summer, they made other visits back and forth; more followed in the fall. The exchanges between them grew in frequency, length, and intimacy, too. Although Mitchell did not particularly like Norma Brickell, her primary correspondence with the husband also spawned separate letters to the wife. This correspondence finally slowed after about four years and perhaps 100 letters. The fault lay with the reviewer not the novelist. Years before his suicide in 1952 at the age of sixty-three, Brickell's creative energies had atrophied. Although Mitchell sensed this early and filled her letters with encouragement and praise, his epistolary commitments fell early victim to his black moods. He could not match Mitchell's energy level. But that was not unusual either: few kept up.[41]

Her correspondence with Brickell led to still more objects of her epistolary attention. The Mississippian had inspired her friendship with Edwin Granberry; he also encouraged her relationship with another budding young Southern novelist, Clifford Dowdey. At thirty-four, Dowdey had published his first novel in 1937, *Bugles Blow No More,* a fiction set in Civil War Richmond. Among reviewers, naturally enough, his story found immediate comparison with Mitchell's work. Actually, it makes a very nice fit, and both represent the literary changes that the Generation of 1900 was ringing on Southern culture. Although both dealt with the antebellum South, both novels had an urban setting. While both dealt with the planter class, they also treated the types who hardly figured in the plantation romance, making the petty bourgeoisie their primary focus. At the initial comparison, however, Dowdey bridled. In what Mitchell herself called a "why-the-hell" rejoinder, Dowdey fired off an angry letter to the offending reviewer, making the most invidious comments about Mitchell's book. Mitchell saw his angry missive. Despite his references to her own work, the Atlantan took no offense. On the contrary, she was full of sympathy. She had read *Bugles,* liked it, and prompted by Brickell, wrote the fiery young man a letter of the highest praise. Indeed, she initiated the correspondence as if she had no other purpose in life than to bolster young artists' egos—even at the expense of her own. Although three years Dowdey's senior and possessing the most extraordinary national and international reputation, Mitchell began her letter with a classic girlish gush. She had already written a couple of letters before, she groaned, but she had torn them up. "I wanted the author of *Bugles* to have some faint respect for me and he couldn't have had had he read that incoherent letter of praise."[42] She continued in this mode for pages. Dowdey responded immediately. His boyish abjection sounded the perfect note, and Mitchell wrote a second letter even more devoid of obvious pride or ego. And, as usual, she added that they must, simply must, get together. They did. Blowing Rock in the summer of 1937 again provided the occasion, with Granberry and Brickell also in attendance, on a particularly joyful occasion.

Even more than Brickell, whom Mitchell especially liked and respected, Dowdey delighted her. This summer saw the first of many visits back and forth, and the richest correspondence flowered in the intervals. With Dowdey she seemed particularly at ease. They exchanged views on the widest range of literary subjects, but also laughed and joked almost endlessly. They spent great energy, for example, inventing fractured epigrams, each trying to outdo the other. The Atlantan won the palm with, "Those whom the gods love they grind exceeding fine." On the same track, however, she also invented names for new Civil War fictions. When Dowdey came up with "Green Grows the Lamb in Her Bosom," the Atlantan got it much better with her own version, " Wind in Her Bosom."

Mitchell carried on very much the same kind of correspondence with a host of other major and minor literary notables, among them Stark Young, Julia Peterkin, and Marjorie Kinnan Rawlings. Her correspondence with lesser folk, however, was hardly less remarkable: the Catholic priest from Kentucky, Father Lelen; the reviewer from Los Angeles, Paul Jordan-Smith; a fan from New York. Sometimes a decade lapsed between letters, but Mitchell had the most remarkable recall, which allowed her to remember the original letter received in the flush of fame, and, as in the case of the otherwise anonymous Gordon Ray Young, to cite the original back to him after ten years' time.

Margaret Mitchell never wrote another book or novel after *Gone with the Wind* appeared. Her correspondence proved both cause and effect of this "failure." Nothing consumed more of her time and energy in the crazy times between 1936 and the outbreak of the European War, especially. Even had she chosen or tried to avoid all this letter-writing, however, these first years after the publication of her book were crazy.

Fame seeped into the privacy of her apartment to disrupt her most sacrosanct routines.

> I can't put cold cream on my face during the day. As sure as I do, Bessie, the maid, goes out to the store and a delegation of women call to interview me. I go to the door with the cream all over my face and my head wrapped up in a towel and they come in and there I am.[43]

The stream of the curious blundering down her hallway at the Russell Apartments never ceased, except in the deadest hours of early morning. Fame had boiled with the Southern summer in the middle of 1936. In the fall, nothing cooled off except the weather. "The cook is off, the secretary isn't here, the phone is going every minute, the door bell ringing and the door belching strangers who want autographs and want to see what I look like and want me to make speeches and go to parties and tell what I like for breakfast and if I wear lace on my panties and why I haven't any children," she groaned in November. "It's only eleven a.m. and I've been going since dawn and feel as thought it were midnight."[44]

Everybody wanted something. Invitations poured in for teas, parties, receptions, department-store autographing sessions, and requests to give speeches all over the country. They offered any price. She professed horror. "No literature even of permanent value is worth what they offer and they don't even want literature of permanent worth," she grumbled. "I don't believe if Matthew, Mark, Luke and John offered to write some more Gospels, they'd be worth the prices that have been offered me."[45] She went slack-jawed at *Vogue Magazine*'s request. "They wanted [an article] about anything about 'Gone with the Wind,' especially the 'modernity' of Scarlett. Good God, do they think hardheaded women only came to life in the 1930s? Why don't they read the Old Testament?"[46]

She hesitated long before going out. What if her dress rode up in public? Aha! the reputation of a slattern loomed: ". . . if I go down the street now with my petticoat accidentally hanging a fraction of an inch below my skirt, it becomes a city-wide scandal. They ask one another: 'Isn't she careless? Isn't it too bad?'"[47] Did she forget her garters? Did her stockings sag? "If the hose of this author fell down in the street it *would* make a story! . . . I guess they'd write me up as going nudist!"[48] Every actual downtown foray had its terrors. She related the story of sneaking out to a local department store to buy a dress, making her selection, and slipping into a changing room to try it on. Just then the curtains of the fitting both parted like the Red Sea to reveal, not the fleeing Israelites, but a gaggle of bugeyed locals. There she stood in her petticoat. The gawkers persisted. Look how tiny she is, chortled one. "And a second voice: *I* don't believe she wrote it—she's too little!"[49] "They wanted to know the size of my intimate wearing apparel. They screamed to one another about me as I stood there like an animal in a cage, one asking another: 'Ain't she skinny?' while still another observed: 'I expected her to look more middle-aged around the hips.' "[50]

She reeled beneath the assault. She explained it to Julia Collier Harris, who had grown up with the Stephens sisters on Jackson Hill.

> I have led, by choice, so quiet and cloistered a life for many years. John likes that sort of life and so do I. Being in the public eye is something neither of us care about but what good does it do to say it? No one believes a word of it or if they do they get indignant. I have been caught between two equally distasteful positions, that of the girlishly shy creature who keeps protesting her lack of desire for the limelight but who only wants to be urged. And that of a graceless, ungracious, blunt spoken ingrate who refuses to let people do her honor. It has all been very distressing to me. I was brought up to consider it better to commit murder than be rude and it is hard to depart from Mother's teachings. Yet I find no other way, short of rudeness, in meeting the situation.[51]

Actually, of course, Mitchell found it almost impossible to be rude, which in the Southern lady's lexicon basically meant saying no. So she answered the telephone and chatted politely to the people she considered idiots. She greeted strangers at her door with a grace that belied her anger, and most of all she answered all those letters. "Being true to her Southern heritage," as John Marsh wrote, demanded this response. The tension remained. Her letter to Julia Harris, her mother's old friend, made it explicit. Here is the old conflicting duality again. The belle is on the one side; on the other, the hardbitten, sexless "ingrate"—like the Mitchell kinsman with whom her mother had angrily compared her once so long before. But even the ingenue's spirit is divided: she wants and does not want attention. It is altogether appropriate, too, that in conceptualizing such conflicts, Mitchell places murder, disobedience, and her mother in the intersection of her divided loyalties. She was playing the theme song of her life now to an audience of millions.

XVII

Hollywood Follies

My innocent chickadees, do not lull yourselves into any sense of
false security or think that you will emerge from any slight contact
with the movies with all your sanity still with you . . . as you know,
I was in the trenches for four years, from Fort Sumter to Appomattox, fighting them off every day. They are very fine and charming
people, but it is my belief that they originated on the planet Mars
where atmospheric conditions are different and customs strange to
us. They are attractive and incredible, and with no trouble at all,
can drive normal people to frenzies.

MARGARET MITCHELL TO CLIFFORD AND HELEN DOWDEY[1]

*T*he doorbell rang, and the visitor burst into Margaret Mitchell's
living room. She had heard about Hollywood and the filming of
the Atlantan's epic. She knew, just *knew*, Mitchell could help
her. She had talent; all her friends confirmed it. All she needed was
her break. She *was* "Mammy." That she was white, she thought, would
be only a minor problem. She had her burnt cork in her purse. Watch
this, she demanded! Thereupon this brazen lady proceeded to offer her
interpretation of Mitchell's sable heroine for the dumbfounded author.
The novelist managed to salvage some small dignity for the witless
stranger by denying her visitor the opportunity of playing the role actually in blackface. "I wish to God you could have seen [her]," the
novelist sputtered to Katharine Brown. "I sat on the blackening so she
couldn't put it on her face, and for forty minutes watched her play
Mammy up and down the rug."[2]

Hooray for Hollywood!

With the completion of the film version of *Gone with the Wind* in 1939, the public mind tangled David Selznick's production almost inseparably with Margaret Mitchell's very different vision of the Civil War, and that tangle produced its own difficulties for the Atlanta writer. Long before that time, however, as demonstrated in the appearance of the fair-skinned aspirant for Mammy's part, Hollywood and the movies proved a major source of the joys and torments of Mitchell's fame. For the harried author, the movie business ran together with the novel business, literally from the very day she mailed away the corrected galley proofs of her novel in March.

By the late winter of 1935–1936, long before the novel's publication, the Macmillan people knew they owned a very successful commodity; they sniffed the air, and smelled equally successful movie rights as well. While they communicated their hunch to the author, she did not take it very seriously. "I can't imagine the movies buying it anyway," she scoffed. "I don't see how it could possibly be made into a movie unless the entire book was scrapped and Shirley Temple cast as 'Bonnie,' Mae West as 'Belle,' and Step'n Fetchit as 'Uncle Peter.' "[3] Her insouciance failed to dampen the movie mania, and the riot swelled with the buds of spring. Dealing with the issue one way or another became increasingly difficult to avoid.

According to her contract of 1935 the author retained the dramatic rights to her book, but Mitchell had no notion whatsoever about what she possessed or how to go about selling movie rights, even if Hollywood wanted to buy. She lacked all knowledge and experience about how to hire an agent, too. In her innocence, Mitchell relied completely on the advice of her publishers. Macmillan, however, provided the most confused and contradictory advice about agents. "The movie agents are pursuing me with their tongues hanging out, just as the movie companies are pursuing us. But don't do anything yet—" Lois Cole warned her friend, "and if anybody writes you direct keep on stalling."[4] The author stalled and stalled, but time and circumstances wore her down in the mad spring of 1936. Even in the best of times, however, her patience would have met its match in the chief contender to broker her manuscript to Hollywood. The business of the broker was Mitchell's first (and ominous) introduction to the idea that the movie people first drew breath on Mars.

A Texas country girl who made good in Hollywood and New York, Annie Laurie Williams had marketed all the Macmillan Company's cinematic rights to the West Coast studios before 1936. Well before she secured an actual copy of the manuscript in the late spring, this wheeler-dealer Texas hustler presumed to do the same with this hottest of all hot Macmillan properties. She pressed her case furiously with Lois Cole in the late winter of 1936. Meanwhile, she opened a campaign against

Mitchell herself. In April she came to Atlanta and laid her case directly before the author.[5] When Mitchell stalled, as per instructions, the wily Texan proceeded to play the author against the publisher. Thus she informed Cole that the novelist would soon "be ready to talk business with her, and give her at least an option for a few months. . . ."[6]

Mitchell had no idea how to proceed, but sensing a hidden agenda in Williams's relationship with Macmillan, she actually volunteered to sign a contract with the Texan early on if that might solve her publisher's problems. Cole demurred. In May, then, pestered beyond endurance, the author, with Cole's encouragement, formally disclaimed Williams's having any authority as her agent whatsoever.[7] Mitchell believed she had rid herself of the aggressive cowgirl once and for all; other events encouraged this conviction. Within a fortnight after Mitchell dismissed Annie Laurie Williams's claims, her publishers suggested she make Macmillan itself her broker. She agreed enthusiastically, and on May 21 she signed a contract designating the Macmillan Company her legal agent. Harold Latham would handle the matter. The author sighed audibly: "I feel very relieved about having it in your hands instead of an agent's," she told her editor. "That's not disparaging agents but then, I don't know agents and I do know you. . . . I know you can do far more about movie people than any agent could."[8]

Harold Latham had told Margaret Mitchell much less than half the story when he requested agent's rights for the Macmillan Company. Although Williams had failed to win Cole's or Mitchell's trust, she had hornswoggled the senior editor. Williams managed to convince Latham that she had compromised the company's initiative in the movie sale. "I believe that if we should conclude a contract with a motion picture publisher, she might claim part of the returns from having talked about the book to this or that producer, and perhaps having introduced the book to the very producer who finally took it," the laconic editor said in a memo to his boss. Less than a week after Mitchell assigned the sale to Macmillan, the company signed over the brokering to Williams. For the favor, the Texan claimed only 5 percent of the agent's fee. She allowed Macmillan to keep the other half.[9] The author herself knew none of this. The fat was in the fire; it soon began to sputter.

By the time Annie Laurie Williams assented to "help" Macmillan sell the movie rights on May 27, she was, as Harold Latham had anticipated, up to her armpits in the project. Operating on chutzpah and the expectation of an enormous commission, she had already narrowed the field of buyers down to three studios weeks before she actually signed a contract with Macmillan: Warner Brothers wanted the film for Bette Davis, R.K.O. for Katharine Hepburn, and warmest of all, David O. Selznick wanted it for himself.[10] Williams's negotiations with Hollywood coincided with the great furor over the novel between mid-June and mid-July, and while the agent used the excitement about the novel to increase her bargaining power, her negotiations fed the frenzy all the more.

In June, Harold Latham had suggested a selling price of $50,000 for the film rights. The author nodded dumbly. No one had ever asked for, much less received, such a phenomenal sum from a producer, and the figure created an uproar when Williams leaked it to the press soon after. The world descended on Atlanta for confirmation of the news. Help! the harassed author cried to Lois Cole amid the chaos:

> feebly I take my typewriter in hand to ask just what the hell Annie Laurie means by jumping on me about rumors that Fox Films had bought the book. At present I am hunting for some one to jump on about all the damn movie rumors which are driving me nuts. . . . People are driving me crazy, folks on the relief rolls asking for a hundred because I won't miss it out of my many millions etc. Friends wondering why in hell I persist in driving a 1929 model car and wearing four year old cotton dresses and fifty cent stockings and calling me an old Hetty Green to my face.[11]

These stories coincided with the first rave notices about the book between June 30 and July 5. Now, on top of this, Williams was leaking news about "the sale of the century." The uproar became intolerable. Aiming for the mountains of North Georgia, the beleaguered author fled Atlanta. She never arrived. Again she had Annie Laurie Williams and her publisher to thank.

On July 8, she had holed up under an assumed name in a hotel in Gainesville, Georgia. Almost simultaneously, Williams sealed the movie deal with Selznick International. Cole wired the news at once. URGENT! URGENT! her telegraph screamed.[12] John Marsh received Cole's dispatch on July 9 and called his harried wife home posthaste. Only two days out, then, she wearily drove back to the city. And she waited. No contract arrived. Cole did not even send the contract until the fourteenth—the day she had urged Mitchell to send it back to her. While the author waited for the document that never came, the excitement in Atlanta swirled ever higher.

If the rumors of the contract had set the world on its ear, the completion of the negotiations multiplied the insanity. Milking all the publicity possible from the hoopla, David Selznick had called Louella Parsons, the widely syndicated, more widely read Hollywood gossip columnist, and given her the inside dope. The next day, she bannered Selznick's story (the Triple Crown of every West Coast mogul, a Parsons headline) of how the courageous independent producer had battled and outbid all the major studios and finally won the prize for $65,000.[13] Selznick gloried in the idea of the greatest, biggest, highest, and most expensive anything, and even if the $50,000 selling price actually set a new record in the industry, that was still inadequate to his fancy. Parsons treated his exaggeration as fact. Miss Mitchell, Georgian, meet David Selznick, Martian. And soon enough, the flabbergasted author discovered that Selznick was hardly the worst of the lot. Russell Birdwell had far less shame than his boss. Miss Mitchell, meet Hollywood.

Hollywood papers picked up the item and publicized the agreement on July 10. New York journalists jumped on the story at once, and the Macmillan Company issued a formal news release soon after—still without any consultation with the author. At this point, the author still had seen no contract and knew no more than what she read in the newspapers. The American public knew as much about the agreement as she did, but the world now beat a path to her door to get more information. Once again she fled.

During her aborted retreat the week before, the hassled author had written warm and urgent letters to a variety of reviewers, including both Herschel Brickell and Edwin Granberry. Her epistles had prompted them to offer the refuge of a writers' conference that weekend at Blowing Rock, North Carolina. Encouraged by her husband, she soon entrained for Hickory, and thence to the cloud-topped peaks of the Blue Ridge. The uproar, however, echoed even through the remote blue valleys of the Appalachian Mountains. She now found herself reading about her most private affairs even in the Boone, North Carolina, weekly. She gnashed her teeth. Williams was a monster; David Selznick was a beast; Louella Parsons was the devil; and Macmillan had broken a trust. She did not bear such transgressions lightly. John Marsh anticipated her fury at this sequence of events. "Please don't be angry with Macmillan for putting out their story," he pled. "Personally, I don't see that there was much else they could do, in view of the fact that the item had ready been widely published."[14] His advice did nothing to ameliorate her rage.

Other irritations set her off. Everyone considered her signature on the contract a *fait accompli.* Indeed, two days before Macmillan even mailed the contract, Cole and Williams were fussing "because nothing has been heard from you or John in regard to this sale of the motion picture rights and [Williams] is afraid you may not be available to sign this contract and get it back in our hands by Friday."[15] They gravely miscalculated their correspondent. They had been forewarned. John Marsh now reminded Lois Cole of the initial contract negotiations the year before and insisted anew that his wife would not be hurried. "The Mitchell family just doesn't work that way, as you all may have discovered last summer. With their legal training and legal habits, they wouldn't sign *any* contract without careful consideration and due deliberation."[16]

The business of the actual contract put all Mitchell's other anxieties in the shade. A consuming horror in the summer, it worsened in the fall, and for the rest of Mitchell's life it remained a plague.

From the beginning, Mitchell had clear ideas of what she wanted in a contract. While she never mentioned cash, she insisted on authority over the screenplay and sought a hand in the casting, too. She had read Faulkner's *Sanctuary*, and she had guffawed through Hollywood's *Story of Temple Drake*. She set her face against any such perversion of her work. On May 25, when she first signed over agent rights to Macmillan, she clarified her position: "I should like to have something in any contract you may make with a movie producer that I can have some say so about the final scenario. I won't be tough-mouthed about changes—at least some changes," she added.

> I know that the book will be a difficult one to make into a movie, if, indeed, it can be made into a movie. And I know too that many things are easy in a novel and difficult, even impossible to reproduce on the screen. I know that some changes are necessary in transferring any book to the screen, characters have to be completely eliminated, incidents collapsed into each other, etc. But there are a few changes I wouldn't put up with. I wouldn't put it beyond Hollywood to have General Hood win the Battle of Jonesboro, Scarlett seduce General Sherman, and a set of negroes with Harlem accents play the backwoods darkies. . . .[17]

Harold Latham had little interest in her request. Annie Laurie Williams had none. No one even suggested it to David Selznick. Mitchell was undeterred. She had signed nothing, she insisted, and she asserted her prerogatives. But amidst the uproar, she made her voice heard only with the greatest difficulty. To complicate matters, she remained in Blowing Rock and communicated with the Selznickers through the most complicated chain. She channeled her demands through John, who relayed them to Lois Cole, who passed them on to Williams—and then the chain reversed itself that frantic week of July 12 through 18. Throughout all these negotiations, the author did not yet even know the terms of the contract itself. She would soon enough, and the new problems in that agreement made her anxiety over script and casting diminish and then finally disappear.

The actual contract finally arrived on July 14. Mitchell remained in Blowing Rock. In her absence, Stephens Mitchell and his father, as her legal counsel, debated the contract's clauses late into the night. John Marsh sat as silent partner in these debates and conveyed their substance to his wife.[18] More than contract hassles worried him. He knew the toll all this was taking on his high-strung lady; over and over, he encouraged her to relax and let others assume the burdens for a time. "My affectionate and husbandly advice is that you enjoy your vacation and let us bother about these preliminary legal technicalities," he counseled.[19] Those "legal technicalities," however, grew bigger and bigger in her imagination, and the troubles finally led her screaming back down the mountain to Atlanta by July 23.

As Mitchell and Mitchell had pored over the contract, issues of copyright disturbed them most of all. The contract erred, for example, in referring to her as the holder of the copyright, instead of the publisher, as stipulated in the original contract with Macmillan of 1935, they decided. They discovered other anomalies. While the agreement signed away dramatic rights to Selznick International, it also required the author to defend against infringements of those rights. The Mitchells protested. They found sympathy nowhere. For nearly two weeks, the frazzled author was worried to distraction. The letters, wires, and long-distance calls to New York availed nothing. When a long, formal letter of July 27 brought no results, she decided to negotiate directly. If she dreaded and hated the prospect of a trip to New York, the alternatives seemed worse. "I will lose my mind certainly if this thing isn't settled soon," she told Brickell in late July. "Just now I don't care which way it is settled."[20]

On Tuesday evening, then, July 28, Mitchell and her brother boarded a night train for New York. They went immediately from Penn Station to the Macmillan offices upon their arrival the next morning. The negotiations began at once. If the long-distance calls and letters had fouled their lives, the direct conversations offered no improvement. She had boarded the train "in a lather of rage," she wrote, but everything got much worse. The two Mitchells endured two days of marathon meetings with the Selznick people, the publishers, and the publishers' lawyers, Cadwallader, Wickersham & Taft, one of the great corporate law firms in the United States. What did the long, involved contract mean? What was she signing away? What responsibilities was she accepting? Nothing seemed very clear. Did the contract obviate her television, radio, and other dramatic rights? Her friends Allan Taylor and Lois Cole thought so and warned her over dinner that evening. The next day, the lawyers dismissed the claim. She was chewing nails and spitting tacks. Long-distance, John urged them to leave the document unsigned and come back home. Having invested so much energy thus far, the pair resisted. The matter of copyright still baffled them, but they determined finally to trust the word of the experts present. George Brett, president of the company, and J. A. Swords, the company's lawyer, assured them that the contract was standard and satisfactory. Mitchell accepted their verbal assurances about the company's responsibility in matters of copyright, and she demanded no written agreements before she signed.[21]

She signed; but still she seethed.[22] She decided at least to make a virtue of Hollywood's refusal to honor her hopes of affecting the film.

She decided to shake the West Coast's dust forever from her feet. Beyond the cash, this proved to be her only victory. Her brother summarized her attitude:

> She said that she had sold the motion picture rights because she was worried by a great many things. The sale would get rid of one worry. She did not want another to take its place. She was happy to hear Hollywood did not want her and she was certain she did not want the worries which Hollywood could bring to her. She would not bother them, and they should not bother her. They had the movie rights; she had the $50,000 less commission; and we were all happy. With that, she went off to visit friends and I came home.[23]

Despite Stephens Mitchell's bland summary, the negotiations and the trip had exhausted her. The effects showed almost immediately. After the signing, Mitchell accepted Herschel and Norma Brickell's invitation to stay with them in Connecticut. As she unwound, however, she fell apart. She had arrived on the thirtieth, spent the entire night talking, and when she awoke the next morning, she discovered herself as blind as St. Paul on the Damascus road. Once again, she fled home. Her physician prescribed absolute rest in a darkened room. Shortly after she returned, her husband wrote the Brickells to explain her condition and its consequences. "The doctor told her that she would have to give [her eyes] a complete rest for 21 days, and this is the 12th day," he wrote on August 14.[24]

A month later, she had recovered enough to write Norma Brickell a note of apology and thanks herself. At this time, she gave a rather different summary of her ailment and her physician's prognosis. The two versions make a nice contrast. In distinction from John's assessment, Mitchell described her condition in the darkest, most dramatic terms. In her version, the twenty-one days' rest swelled to three months or more. "I have a period of inactivity before me," she groaned on September 1, a week after the doctor had allowed her to be up and about.

> At the end of three months they may spring another three months on me. Of course, I had it coming to me. I have overworked my eyes for two years and the bill has come in. Lest you get the idea that I am ready for a dog and tin cup, I had better be more detailed. I can see pretty well but lights of any kind give me a headache. I can read headlines but if I read more than three lines of small type, words run together, a hand grenade explodes inside my skull and I see Roman candles going off for hours. On such occasions I retire to the bedroom, pull down the shades, turn on the radio and spend the day pulling feathers through the ticking of the pillows.[25]

Almost congenitally unable to sit still, Mitchell flunked her recovery program almost before it began. She had no time for rest. In the middle of her recuperation, anxieties about the contract flared anew. The copyright clause issue provoked a whole new slew of troubles.

During the negotiations in New York, Brett and Swords had convinced the author and her brother that the copyright issue should be no hindrance to signing. Although the contract stipulated that the author must still defend the copyright even after she no longer owned it, Brett had assured her that this fell within the the company's responsibility. Though reluctantly, the pair had accepted this guarantee. After Mitchell returned to Atlanta, however, John Marsh took up the issue. On August 5, he wrote the president of the company, George Brett, for clarification one more time. Brett took a month to reply, and his answer of September 3 sent them all into a frenzy. He failed to assuage their misgivings about the copyright issue; indeed, he even complicated the question. He dropped a second bombshell when he informed them blandly that the company had not been her agent at all in any of the proceedings. He therefore disavowed any responsibility whatsoever for any problems in the contract. He and his lawyers attended, he declared, only to protect the company's interest. "I am sorry that there should have been any misunderstanding as to our function in this transaction," he informed the flabbergasted author. "We originally undertook to act as Mrs. Marsh's broker in the contemplated negotiations but you will remember that shortly thereafter Miss Annie Laurie Williams was substituted for us in that capacity. At the meeting when the final terms of the contract were agreed upon, Mrs. Marsh was represented by her own attorney and our attorneys there took no part in the negotiations other than to protect the Macmillan company's interests."[26]

For Mitchell, incredulity fought with fury on reading this announcement. Brett had given her his word. To her bitter wrath, he now renounced all his assurances. The matter of the agent grossly compounded the author's sense of having been betrayed. True, the contract had formally named Annie Laurie Williams as her agent, but Lois Cole had insisted all along that this was a mere formality. No problem, she had insisted; Macmillan is still your agent. Mitchell took her word. In the late summer, however, when Mitchell turned to Macmillan in that capacity as agent, the publisher denied any responsibility. With some logic, Mitchell had assumed that the Macmillan people and the representatives of Cadwallader, Wickersham & Taft had appeared at the sessions with Selznick International to defend her interests. No wonder, she now raged, that the company had done no more to clarify the 'godalmighty clause," the pet name she gave the contractual stipulation that she defend copyright infringements.

In the very middle of her summer crazies, then, in September 1936, the author mounted her Pegasus to battle her publisher. Throughout the fall, increasingly angry letters heated the mails between Atlanta and New York. Steve and John lept into the fray. Stephens Mitchell tended towards the brusque in any case, and when he detected breaches in contractual obligations, he felt even less need for grace. His letters infuriated George Brett, who fired off cannister and shells of his own. Cadwallader, Wickersham & Taft's big guns lumbered out, too. By October, the situation had grown very nasty indeed. It waxed so ominous that even the otherwise neutral observer, Allan Taylor, Cole's husband, intervened to try to smooth the situation over. Without his spouse's knowledge, he said, he wrote the novelist, his old flame, a long letter describing how the situation had distressed his wife. She was all "broken up," he grieved, and he pleaded for reconciliation. The author replied coolly. Brett's response had been "a slap in the face," she informed her old beau, but she told him how circumstances had deteriorated since then, too. Brett, for example, had invited Steve to New York to discuss the matter in full and agreed to pay his attorney's fees for the labor. He then disinvited the lawyer and renounced the commitment to pay the fees.[27]

Harold Latham alone retained the author's trust, and the situation threatened even this charmed relationship. The matter of the agent rankled especially. "As you know, I was besieged with requests from people wanting to be my agent, Miss Williams among others," she reminded him. "I refused them all and would never have had any agent had you not offered the services of Macmillan."[28] Two days later, she dispatched a still cooler letter. "As you can see, I am still writing you frankly and freely about things on my mind, in spite of my disagreement with The Macmillan Company about which I wrote you a few days ago," she postscripted a letter to the editor on September 25. "I certainly hope that difficulty can be cleared up promptly, for I want to regain the feeling of confidence in The Macmillan Company which I have had all along until that trouble arose."[29] Latham ducked. He discussed the matter with Brett and the company lawyers drafted a response that simply restated the company's position in kindly terms. "Although we were your agent in effecting the sale of the motion picture rights," he explained, "you were represented in the negotiations of the sale by your own attorney, and apparently it was your own attorney who approved the contract that you signed." He showed the letter to the head of Cadwallader *et al.*, but Henry W. Taft gave only grudging approval of Latham's "generosity."[30] Cadwallader, Wickersham & Taft hankered for a fight. The Mitchell and Mitchell firm was ready, too.

The author blinked first.

While Macmillan never accepted responsibility for the final shape of the Selznick contract—including the godalmighty clause—the company tried to make amends in other ways. They compensated in part by returning the foreign copyrights to the author. The Marshes puzzled over the gift, and remained unmollified. Finally, however, she caved in, but the issue smoldered for the rest of her life, and periodically over the next decade it erupted to mar the superficially good relations with her publisher.[31] Even had she chosen to fight the copyright-agent controversy through, other matters militated against such a crusade at this time. In the fall of 1936, the furor over the book itself had not waned, and now the Hollywooders launched their full offensive. The hullabaloo over the film broke in full fury in October. Margaret Mitchell had her hands full without wrangling with her publisher.

By the fall of 1936, probably a million Americans had read *Gone with the Wind*. After David Selznick bought the movie rights, the frenzy over the novel merged with the Depression-era love affair with Hollywood to produce what was certainly one of the most extraordinary epiphenomena in American cultural history. The negotiations over the book excited passions coast to coast. Selznick's phenomenal purchase price made front-page news. The producer and his minions (like "Bird" Birdwell) kept the flap going for over two years, even before filming started. They hardly had to work to cultivate publicity: the United State was a gargantuan petri dish ready to culture any rumor they dropped on its rich surface.

Most readers of Mitchell's novel had visualized her characters so clearly that they knew beyond any doubt who should play the various parts, and how. These ideas seldom converged, except possibly in the consensus that Clark Gable deserved the role of Rhett. Demonstrating some weird form of Democracy in Action, thousands, tens of thousands of citizens wrote and wired David Selznick their advice. If the publicity boded well for marketing the picture ultimately, the intensity of fans' passions worried the producer. Extremely cautious and sensitive to public opinion, Selznick pressed his ear to the ground, and the distant thunder vaguely unnerved him. "Never in my experience in the moving picture business has there been such a deluge of letters on the casting of a picture, not even in advance of the casting of David Copperfield," he testified:

> Some of the letter writers makes the suggestions mildly; some state frankly that they will not go to see the picture unless it is cast as they suggest; and some inform us formally we have no right to make the picture unless it is cast as the writer suggests. These letter have us frightened because their authors are far from agreeing as to who should or should not play the roles. Every rumor is met with written outbursts of commendation or disapproval; and it is clear that there is simply no casting possible that will please everyone.[32]

Quickly, the casting had become something of a national pastime, if not an actual plebescite; it threatened, indeed, to eject real politics and the national presidential election of 1936 from the frontal lobes of the American citizenry. In the fall, Selznick hit upon the scheme of formalizing this plebescite while opening the contest to all comers. "At the moment," the press quoted him in November, "we feel that the safest thing to do would be to find unknown players—at least for the roles of Scarlett and Rhett for a large part of the screen public has an unfortunate tendency to associate actors with roles they have formerly played and to refuse to concede the possibility of versatility." This was just an idea, he cautioned, and he covered his bets: "However, I do not want this to be taken as a promise to cast the picture with 'unknowns,' as there are two or three players . . . who would be more than acceptable to all but a carping few."[33] In addition to solving this problem of typecasting, a nationwide search would resolve subtler issues for the producer. He could not begin shooting soon anyway: he wanted Gable for the lead, but contractual obligations prohibited the star's early release. The casting contest, then, filled the time while keeping the film in the public mind. And did it keep it in the public mind!

The search also quieted the popular clamor about what established players should act the principals. Did the small but powerful Katharine Hepburn claque exert the most potent machinations on behalf of its candidate? Did diehard Bette Davis fans threaten boycotts on behalf of theirs? Did Norma Shearer's violent gang roar for its angel? And what to do with the Joan Crawfordites glowering ominously on the sidelines? Or the Southern fans muttering darkly for their fellow Confederates Tallulah Bankhead or Miriam Hopkins? And what of the thundering indignation generated by even the hint that Charlie Chaplin's ravishing, witty mistress, Paulette Goddard, might take the part? Selznick ignored these opinions only at his peril. Like the Reds and the Blues in Roman gladiatorial contests, these factions exerted tremendous, if bizarre, influence over Hollywood decisions. The plebescite did not solve the problem, but it avoided immediate battle while maintaining public excitement before filming started. Selznick had had experience, in any case, in such a campaign. Three years before, he had opened the casting of *David Copperfield* to unknowns. Like a Hollywood Major Bowes (who hosted the famous amateur hour on radio), he had conducted a nationwide, million-dollar search for an unknown boy to play the lead. This had proved to be an extremely successful ploy for generating publicity for the film that followed. It appealed to some of the era's most fundamental anxieties and hopes. Amidst the angst and deprivation of the Great Depression, some anonymous character from the hinterland might win fame, wealth, and glory in the Hollywood lottery. The same motives applied with even greater force to *Gone with the Wind:* this time the lottery winner eyed the biggest stakes of all.

Selznick did launch his search, of course. For two years, he and his cohorts barnstormed the country in a publicity caper that competed, sometimes successfully, with Hitler, Mussolini, the Japanese, and the recession of 1937 for the front pages. In the process, he created a legendary episode in American social history. If Clare Boothe's Broadway comedy, *Kiss the Boys Goodbye,* mocked Selznick's prodigious talent search, the affair did make sense in a general framework of American values. As do other chapters in the national legend—of the Cowboy, the Frontier, or the Self-Made Man—Selznick's talent search revealed some of the most peculiar dimensions of the American character. Margaret Mitchell's novel had appealed to very basic human passions, impulses, and motives in her vast readership. She had dealt darkly with survival; she had appealed to courage, energy, and dignity in the face of inevitability, defeat, and fate. Selznick's search reversed those values. His lottery began, not in ruin and death, but in hope and faith. By opening up the parts to everyone, he underlined the most positive themes of egalitarian individualism in the United States. His talent search encouraged the emulation of Scarlett's virtues—willfulness, ruthlessness, and determination—and the exclusion of her fatal liabilities; specifically, her inescapable burdens. He affirmed the possibility of fame and fortune for those even at the very bottom of the economic and racial heap. If they could not aspire to Rhett's and Scarlett's parts, even blacks still had most important roles to play in the making of the movie. And in this respect, the film was a milestone even among the otherwise most obscure and disenfranchised in American life.

If the talent search appealed to the desire for gain and fame among the masses, the affair electrified the American élite hardly less. Two such well-known scions of old money and power as Eleanor Roosevelt and Mrs. Ogden Reid trumpeted their candidates for film roles with the same enthusiasm the common folks displayed. That Mrs. Reid advanced the cause of the aristocratic Katharine Hepburn for Scarlett while Mrs. Roosevelt made the case for her maid to play the part of Mammy has less significance than the power of the cinematic plebescite to galvanize their energy and attention at all.

While an extraordinary affair in American cultural history, the casting episode had the most immediate effect on an astonished Margaret Mitchell. As the casting question heated up in 1937 and boiled furiously into 1938, the author found her kitchen impossibly hot, but she had nowhere to hide. For three years, she mopped her brow and sweated like a charwoman.

Long before David Selznick ever bought her book, the casting had fascinated the author, and early on she had shared her feelings about it with her intimates. "Dear God, Lois. NOT Janet Gaynor!" she had wailed in the summer of 1936. "Spare me this last ignominy or else tell Bonnie Annie to hold her up for a million. May I ask which part she intends to play—Belle Watling?" She proffered her ideas about who should play what roles, not last for the most coveted part in cinematic history:

> Miriam Hopkins has been my choice from the beginning but I know what I had to say wouldn't matter so said nothing. She has the voice, the looks, the personality and the sharp look. And I wish that lovely creature (I think her name is Elizabeth Allen) who played David Copperfield's mother could do Melanie. And I wish Charles Boyer didn't have a French accent for he's my choice for Rhett. Next to him, Jack Holt is the only person I can think of.[34]

Such confidences became impossible for the writer as the campaign for the roles expanded. "Life has been awful since I sold the movie rights!" she cried in early October. "I am deluged with letters demanding that I do not put Clark Gable in as Rhett. Strangers phone me or grab me on the street, insisting that Katharine Hepburn will never do."[35] "I get letters from all over the country about the moving picture; people call me up on the telephone to advise me on it; they stop me on the streets to offer suggestions," she was groaning the next month. "I am dragged into argument after argument as to whether I believe Clark Gable should play Rhett or Joan Crawford should play Scarlett or do I believe this actress should play Scarlett and that actor should play Rhett."[36]

Once Selznick's Million-Dollar Major Bowes Movie Sweepstakes went into full swing, the folks assumed (with considerable encouragement from Hollywood) that every part was up for grabs. Now the author faced the popular expectation not only of thumbing up (or down) contenders for the major roles, but of using her influence for *every* part. "Little Minnie would make a great Scarlett, but she would settle for Carreen. And you, Miss Mitchell, can help her out." Such requests ran her ragged, even if she often found occasion for humor in the furor, as with the Anglo-Saxon madame who with her tin of blacking showed up at Mitchell's door to demonstrate her mastery of the part of Mammy.

> Then there are fond mothers all over the country whose daughters are natural born tap dancers. They have read a movie is to be made of the book and the insist I find some spot for their tap-dancing daughters. I am quite sure they have never read the book. I can't remember a single character in it who was a child tap dancer. Many of them become indignant when I tell them this and seem to feel it would be the easiest thing in the world for me to work a tap dancer into the story, but the trouble with me, according to them, is that, "I just don't care, so there!"[37]

For Mitchell the movie-buff, the vision of *Gone with the Wind* cast a la Busby Berkley, *42nd Street, Their Dancing Daughters*, Shirley Temple and all the rest elicited guffaws that resounded late into the evenings. But the absurdity did not end there. How she now thanked her stars that Selznick and Annie Laurie Williams had resisted her desire to oversee the script! Even so, she got grief enough on that score, too. As you write the scenario, many begged her, change nothing! The ether soundlessly absorbed her protests that she was writing nothing for David Selznick. Others demanded that she hold the line for Dixie in the film. You must intervene to forestall any character from saying "you all" while addressing one person, others pleaded. Allow only Southerners to produce the script! the unreconstructeds hollered.[38]

While she fended off the masses, the author also faced the onslaught of the moviemakers themselves. From the fall of 1936, they massed on her front and her flanks and sallied forth with whoops and yells worthy of her own ancestors who served with Lee or Hood. Some of the Selznick people—like Kay Brown, Sidney Howard, George Cukor, and, in his own way, even Selznick himself—she admired and genuinely liked. Others sent her into frothing rages. All regularly tested the outer limits of her gentle rearing. With none of them, however, did she shirk what she considered her social obligations. She offered herself to them with the same generosity she volunteered to all the others passing through her life. "Count on me for any help you need," she told Kay Brown on first hearing of Brown's desire for a swing across the South.[39] She committed herself to make "contacts with them for finding new talent, for rounding up research workers and local historians," she later told Sidney Howard.[40] She offered the same service to the mogul-in-chief. "I hope you will not think me selfish if I ask you to please let us—my husband and I—have you out to our apartment for supper on at least one night," she wrote Selznick. "I know very well that everyone in Georgia will descend upon you as soon as you arrive, but we do want to see you and hope you will save us at least one evening."[41] Peggy the Good offered her all.

She did as she had promised. Selznick and his crew did come South, although in typical Selznick fashion, he filled the air with the great noise of these impending visits for six months before the trip actually materialized in April 1937. When the Selznickers finally arrived, she dined them, squired them about Atlanta, and introduced them to a variety of locals who she considered might offer them assistance. This was not the full extent of her unsparing hostessing of the entourage. She knew the importance of the Hollywooders' visit to Atlanta for the city itself, and she put herself out no less for the town. She assumed responsibility for mediating between the studio people and the city, especially the local newspapers. As the Selznick people swept into the city, she fretted lest outside journalists scoop the locals on their own turf. So she asked Kay Brown as a "special favor" to allow the Atlanta papers the news break on the Southern trip. "Your trip may not be a

big story up north but it *is* a big story in this section. The very idea
that a movie company thinks enough of a story to send a talent scout
and a director and an adaptor down here will go over big. . . . Oh,
yes, it will be a big story." But like a good mother moderating between
greedy offspring, Mitchell wanted to be completely fair to all the Atlanta papers, too. It would not do, she insisted, to show favoritism
even to the *Journal*, her old paper, when the others "have been kinder
than anyone can imagine to me since the book came out." As a consequence, she interposed herself between the visitors and the press, but
also between the fiercely competing newspapers themselves.[42] She became a kind of larger-than-life Mrs. Dalloway, Virginia Woolf's heroine who lived for planning and executing social occasions. Generosity,
as always exacted its price.

If in such ways Mitchell created some of her own burdens with the
Hollywooders, they complicated her life in ways completely beyond
her own reckoning.

None of the movie people could appreciate that Mitchell, or anyone
else, for that matter, might resist California fame and fortune. David
Selznick in particular was simply incapable of believing that Margaret
Mitchell did not really want to join his enterprise. He assumed that he
had only missed the proper inducement or reward for enticing her,
and for three years he challenged, begged, and even threatened her in
a storm of letters, telegrams, and telephone conversations. His publicity director Russell Birdwell was worse yet. When he heard (apparently from Kay Brown) of Mitchell's volunteering to host the Hollywood dog-and-pony show in Atlanta, this son of an itinerant Texas
revival preacher immediately issued a press release about the author's
involvement. She exploded. "My contract specifically provides that I
have nothing to do with the movie and I have stated personally and
by letter to various Selznick people that I will have nothing to do with
the talent search, casting, adaptation of story or filming," she wired
him angrily.[43] A still more furious letter followed.[44] Every publicity
release like Birdwell's provoked a new spate of letters and visitors, all
of which demanded more of her precious time and energy, she complained. And so it went.

The situation calmed down in 1938. Although *Gone with the Wind*
finally eased off the best-seller list and the popular excitement waned
in the year's last half, the final selection of the cast and the commencement of the filming itself aroused all the old devils to something close
to their original fury. The cameras began to roll in late December when
Selznick torched his entire back lot for the burning-of-Atlanta scene.
Even when the filming had actually begun, Selznick still lacked a heroine, and it was at the shooting of that conflagration, of course, that
the producer first met the India-born British actress Vivien Leigh, who
became his Scarlett. The announcement of all the other principals fol-

lowed shortly in mid-January. Vivien Leigh's name provoked a special burst of public excitement. Carping and backbiting now focused on Selznick's choosing foreigners when good, homegrown Americans might have played the parts. Old Confederates seethed especially. Mrs. Dolly Lamar Lunceford, the weighty president of the United Daughters of the Confederacy, voiced outrage to Selznick and the press, and she demanded that the author undo the sacrilege. The author clucked in sympathy; beneath her breath she murmured, "Goda'mighty!"

Despite the burst of excitement in December and January of 1939, the worst seemed past by February. With the players chosen and cameras rolling, Mitchell felt a tremendous burden was lifted from her shoulders. Then, too, the actual production engaged her interest and curiosity almost as much as it did the American public in general. She relaxed and sat back to enjoy the show, and she had a direct line to the most intimate workings of the Selznick International lot through her pal Sue Myrick. While Mitchell had resisted exercising any of her "influence" with Hollywood, she had recommended two people who could assist with the historical aspects of the filming: Wilbur Kurtz of Atlanta and Sue Myrick of Macon. She respected Kurtz, but she treasured her friend from the *Macon Telegraph*—with due cause. During her stint on the West Coast, Myrick wrote a regular series of features for Georgia papers back home,[45] but these pale beside the ribald letters she dispatched to the author herself about the extraterrestrials who were turning *Gone with the Wind* into a movie. This was better than Louella, said the Atlanta writer.

All along, Mitchell had been eager to know what actors were contracted to play which parts. "If you have any news about the casting of even minor characters, such as Miss Pittypat or Mrs. Merriwether, of course, I'd love to know about them," she wrote Kay Brown.[46] Myrick fed the author just such information. She shared her pleasure in Laura Hope Crews as Aunt Pittypat—"a darling," Myrick judged. "She is SO thrilled over doing the part and has read the book nine times." She filled the author in on the struggle between Thomas Mitchell and William Farum for the role of Gerald. The black roles particularly interested both women. Myrick dissented from the choice for Pork—Oscar Polk, who had played Gabriel in the film *Green Pastures*. "His accent is rotten but maybe I can teach him," she averred. She also disliked the selection of Hattie McDaniel as Mammy: "she lacks dignity, age, nobility and so on and . . . she just hasn't the right face for it." She was enthusiastic, however, about Eddie Anderson (Noah of *Green Pastures*) for Uncle Peter.[47] She also knew a star when she saw one in Butterfly McQueen. Myrick took special pleasure in chronicling the on-set set-tos between the director and this actress. Long afterward, McQueen related how she had played the film's director with all the wiles at her disposal, acting Prissy off-camera as well as on. Myrick missed both the wit and strategy of this role-within-a-role. McQueen, Myrick gloated, "is 'nigger' through and through and when George [Cukor] tells her three things to do she can't remember them. I sit off and laugh to myself and know that I could manage her by telling her one thing, letting her do that, then telling her another."[48] George Cukor also put Myrick in charge of a talent search for black actors, and she related how she had attended an all-black Federal Theater WPA production of *Run Little Chillun* in this capacity. She also negotiated with Hall Johnson, the black choral director, on the issue of background music for the film.[49]

Of course Myrick kept Mitchell well informed on all the principals. She had been very skeptical of the Britishers at first, especially Olivia De Havilland as Melanie, but she came to like her best of all, with Gable and Leigh close behind. The players delighted in this horsey Southern belle as much as she in them. She enjoyed entertaining them, even as she liked retelling the stories of the set to Mitchell:

> Vivian [*sic*] and Clark were reading the new script—delivered hot off the press at three for rehearsal at three fifteen—and it was the morning-after-the-rape scene. Rhett comes into the room where Scarlett is lying in bed and the script says she is humming a song of the period—obviously very happy. Clark grinned at her and said what was she going to sing and she said I would have to suggest some Southern song of the period. Where upon I, with my usual quickwittedness and my fine acquaintance with [the] South and [the] period suggested, "It ain't what you do, it's the way that you do it." They yelled so loud people came in from the next stage where Intermezzo is being shot to see what was the matter.[50]

Myrick delighted Mitchell with still another bedroom story of a rather different order:

> We all nearly died laughing when we were reshooting the birthin' scene. While the cameramen were fixing the million things they have to fix, Olivia lay in bed and read GWTW, once more. George saw her and ordered the "still man" to make a picture of it for you.[51]

Cukor guessed right. The photograph convulsed the author. It also prompted John Marsh to reflect that Miss De Havilland's expression resembled nothing so much as the look on his wife's face as she labored on draft after draft of her manuscript for all those years.[52]

Of the other figures on the set, Myrick liked Selznick, but this ball of fire overawed her, too, especially his imperial whimsey. He changed his mind with every breath, she said, and with every change, the cameras stalled. "I'd be wetting my pants if I had four principals hired at seven, four-fifty and such thousands apiece a week. Clark gets $4500 and Leslie [Howard] $7000. . . . And the four principals are just sitting around loafing and drawing their pay."[53] Like De Havilland, Leigh (and indeed, Mitchell herself), she liked and respected George Cukor very much, but when "Pappy" Selznick fired him in February, she made her peace with Victor Fleming, whom she also admired.[54] Among the Selznick intimates, she discovered the notorious Bird Birdwell on her own. He was, she declared "a revolving bastard if there ever was one (the Revolving Bastard in case you don't know," she elaborated, "is a bastard any way you turn him)."[55]

Folks lower on the cinematic totem pole delighted Myrick as much as the high and mighty did. They fascinated Mitchell equally. Of all the wardrobe people, the hairdressers, the script girls, and all the rest, no one pleased the Maconite quite as much as Monte Westmore, the head makeup man. She especially treasured his knowledge of the sexual peccadillos of the stars. Westmore "adores talking about their private lives and washing their dirty linen for us while we roll on the floor with laughter," she related. She knew Mitchell would appreciate the story of his visiting the apartment of Mae West. "Mae's bed, he told us is wide enough for six men to sleep in—then without a change of countenance he added 'no doubt six men had slept in it' and cont'd the tale."[56] Myrick herself got into the swing of things with her casual references to the sexual proclivities of the various production figures. One, she sighed, "is a love even if he is a pansy"; while another, she added with special emphasis, "is a love (even if he ain't no pansy)."[57]

Besides keeping her friend back home abreast of all the gossip, she also conscientiously performed her job as Southern Expert. This had its difficulties, and she shared these with Mitchell, too. She battled movie fantasy for the duration. She denied Selznick his horticultural novelty of having dogwoods blooming in the same frame with cotton being chopped. She fought his desire to plant cotton in Tara's front yard. And she protested all manner of ideas for costumes. She prided herself on getting Pork out of livery and Gerald out of English riding britches. Slave headdress proved to be a major conflict, too. Selznick liked the idea of Prissy and company with "ten or twenty pink bows on their hair!" she gasped. "They think plain 'wrapped hair' is not pictorial." At this she raged again: "If I hear that word 'pictorial' again I'm likely to scream." She won on this count.[58] On other issues, neither logic nor fury weighed in the scales against Selznick's demand for the "pictorial." Myrick even formed a committee to appeal to the producer on the matter of removing Scarlett's widow's veil and bonnet from the scene at the bazaar. No luck. "Pappy wanted the effect like that and it continues to be," Myrick groaned. "Scarlett still wears the veil and bonnet."[59]

The matter of architecture became an entirely separate field of battle. Selznick insisted on the grandest sets for Tara, Twelve Oaks, and Scarlett's postwar Atlanta mansion. Sue Myrick had little interest in this contest, but the other Southern Expert in Hollywood, Wilbur Kurtz, did yeoman's service on behalf of Mitchell's original vision. He won small concessions only with greatest difficulty. The producer would not compromise on his grandiose image of the plantation South.[60]

In Atlanta, the recipient of all this delicious information haunted the postbox for new letters from her friend in California. "I know you'll have a crown in heaven for the great joy your letters have given us," she exulted.[61] *Re* the Mae West story: "What a pity you are not writing such tidbits as this for the local press," she guffawed.[62] Mitchell also vigorously nodded assent to Myrick's characterization of the redoubtable Russell Birdwell as a Revolving Bastard; she purred over Laura Crews as Pittypat, and plugged William Farum for Gerald's role—"He was once my very ideal," she said. Hattie McDaniel's name rang no bells for her, and she pleaded for more information. Send more material on Eddie Anderson and Oscar Polk as well, she also asked.[63] Myrick could never satisfy the author's insatiable curiosity.

Mitchell also gloried in Myrick's victories as the film's historical consultant. She congratulated her friend on her triumphs with horticulture, hairdos, and costumes, and she shared Myrick's grief over the defeat about Scarlett's mourning clothes. When newspapers had published the first stills from the movie in mid-February, including shots from the Armory ball, the author went through the ceiling. "I have had to endure so much conversation about that bonnet that I do not want to get out of the house," she moaned.[64] "I cannot imagine even Scarlett having such bad taste as to wear a hat at an evening party, and my heart sank at the sight of it."[65]

Myrick's information about the sets, however, agitated her still more thoroughly. "I grieve to hear that Tara has columns," she groaned. "Of course, it didn't and looked nice and ugly like Alex Stephens' Liberty Hall."[66] News about the Twelve Oaks set sent her into spasms:

> I had feared, of course, that it would end up looking like Grand Central Station, and your description confirms my worst apprehensions. I did not know whether to laugh or to throw up at the *two* staircases. Probably the Twelve Oaks hall will be worse than the one in *So Red the Rose*. . . . When I think of the healthy, hearty, country and somewhat crude civilization I depicted and then of the elegance that is to be presented, I cannot help yelping with laughter.[67]

The issue touched her fundamental conception of the book. Architecture symbolized much for her. It was the dress her society wore. Her emphasis on the plain and country style of dwellings, in explicit contrast with classical grandeur, defined her vision of the Southern social order. She frequently mentioned it in discussing both the film and the novel. Early on, for example, she had exulted when Stephen Vincent Benét had noted her architectural realism:

I'm glad . . . that you noticed and mentioned that Tara wasn't a movie set but a working plantation. It's hard to make people understand that North Georgia wasn't all white columns and singing darkies and magnolias, that it was so new, so raw. Even people in other sections for the state, older sections, still don't get the distinction and ask me why I didn't make Tara a Greek Revival house. I had to ride Clayton County pretty thoroughly before I found even one white columned house in which to put the Wilkes family. And I found that its life had been brief, built in the mid-fifties, burning in 1864.[68]

Mitchell had, moreover, pressed the matter with the studio people from the very beginning. When Cukor and the scene designer, Hobe Erwin, had visited her in that flying trip in April 1937, she had driven them abut the countryside to exhibit what upcountry antebellum houses were really like. "While they were polite, I am sure they were dreadfully disappointed, for they had been expecting architecture such as appeared in the screen version of *So Red the Rose*," she related to her friend Brickell.

I had tried to prepare them by reiterating that this section of North Georgia was new and crude compared with other sections of the South, and white columns were the exception rather than the rule. I besought them to please leave Tara ugly, sprawling, columnless, and they agreed. I imagine, however, that when it comes to Twelve Oaks they will put columns all around the house and make it as large as our new city auditorium.[69]

The author actually came close to threatening the producer on this issue. Mitchell knew about Selznick's regard for public opinion and his sensitivity to her wishes. Perhaps she knew, too, about his dislike and skepticism of the cinematic adaptation of Stark Young's *So Red the Rose* that appeared earlier in the decade. Knowing that the information would find its way to the mogul's ear, she wrote about how patrons had stormed indignantly from the theater after seeing the "ghastly" grandeur of that film. "And I will never forget," she added for emphasis, "the pungent remarks about the level of Hollywood brains" as the offended moviegoers fled their seats. She warmed to the subject:

God help me when the reporters get me after I've seen the picture. I will have to tell the truth, and if Tara has columns and Twelve Oaks is such an elaborate affair I will have to say that nothing like that was ever seen in Clayton County, or for that matter, on land or sea. This would be somewhat embarrassing to me and perhaps to the Selznick company, but I am not going on record as telling a lie just to be polite.[70]

She, Sue Myrick, and Wilbur Kurtz all fought a losing battle. "Sauve qui peut," she began to mutter. Thus when the Georgia Committee for the 1939 World's Fair wanted to erect a columned replica of Tara on the fairgrounds, she was adamant: "I implore you, if they wish to put up a Southern Colonial house of the Greek Revival type such as the beautiful ones in Milledgeville, please use your influence to prevent it. Or if they insist on building that type of house, please don't let them call it 'Tara'," she wrote the committee chairman.

> I am mortally afraid the movies will depict it as a combination of Grand Central Station, the old Capitol at Milledgeville and the Natchez houses of So Red the Rose. I fear they will have columns not only on the front of "Tara" but on the sides and back as well, and probably on the smoke-house, too. But I can't do anything about that, as I have no connection with the picture. I do hope, however that the "Tara" that goes to the World's Fair will be a North Georgia house in keeping with its times and not a Middle Georgia or a Coast Georgia house. . . .[71]

Mitchell lost this critical battle of the columns, and it had the widest repercussions for the impression of her fiction in the popular mind. Long before the film was done, many readers had confused *Gone with the Wind* with the traditional plantation romance. For every reader like Stephen Vincent Benét or Virginius Dabney who congratulated Mitchell on her realism, another like Malcolm Cowley credited the Atlantan with creating "an encyclopedia of the plantation legend." The author seethed at the description; for her own health and sanity, however, she retreated from the battle. "People believe what they want to believe," the author chanted as a consoling mantra. Retreat was the better part of valor, for after David Selznick had completed his film, she could not have won. After the premiere, people forgot even the vestiges of Mitchell's literary realism in the flood of Selznick's visual fantasy. The distinction between Hollywood and Atlanta remains, however, and the movie and book still make a vivid contrast. Indeed, that contrast illuminates the values of Atlanta and the South as well as of Hollywood and America. The movie's premiere, in any case won a whole new audience for Mitchell's work and dictated still more alterations in the author's already harried life.

XVIII

Pee Soup

Producers and what they do with scripts is like a chef making soup.
The chef gets an idea from a soup he ate. He spends days making a
stock that is just right. He tastes, adds seasonings, tastes again,
adds again. Perfect. Then he does more things to it until he has the
finest soup in the universe. Whereupon, he calls in the other chefs
and they all stand around and pee in it! And this, the treasonable
ones of us seem to agree is what has happened about GWTW.

SUE MYRICK TO MARGARET MITCHELL[1]

*T*he four old men dozed in empty rooms. Where once scores of
them tottered through the halls, these alone remained. And they
had but poorly withstood time's ravages. Their eyes were rheumy,
their hearing failed, their memory ebbed and flowed. Their voices were
cracked, but, lost in their own worlds, they hardly spoke anyway. Hidden away in the city's last Confederate veteran's home, these four alone
survived of those thousands who had once marched with Lee and Jackson, ridden with Nathan Bedford Forrest, and primed the cannon of
the gallant Lt. Pegram. Even in their dotage, however, they might have
been expected to occupy a place of honor in the festivities. The premier
of *Gone with the Wind* was, after all, a great celebration of the Confederate past, or so it certainly would have seemed. But nothing happened with the four old veterans. December 14 came and went—still
nothing. Finally, late in the afternoon of December 15, 1939, the day
of the grand affair itself, someone remembered. The four were bundled
up against the cold, put into a car, and shepherded to Loew's Grand

Theatre downtown. They made their way with difficulty through the hordes of bodies straining against the police barriers. The crowd "greeted the bowed remnants of the proud, tattered armies of the Confederacy with spontaneous applause, but the applause was light in comparison with that given Hollywood's glamorous boys and girls," a reporter noted acidly. In their freshly pressed, bemedalled gray uniforms, the four shuffled to their places. The noisy theater swallowed them completely.[2]

These figures were daguerrotypes in the talking, color, moving picture world of 1939. How different it had been before! Generations of Southern children had watched the companies of these old men with their tattered banners limp down Peachtree Street in the annual Confederate Memorial Day parade on April 26. Eyes watered and voices hushed at their approach. Such men had awed two generations of Southern youth. No more. They had little relevance to the aspirations of the Georgians who stamped their feet against the December cold outside Loew's Grand in 1939. The engines of modernity had roared past these last Confederates long before; they were stranded outside of time. Margaret Mitchell had not forgotten, and her novel honored the raw power of collective memory, but after December 15, even her vision of the past would be subsumed by Hollywood, just as these four old relics disappeared in the shadows of the West Coast stars and luminaries.

The Atlanta premiere of David Selznick's *Gone with the Wind* crowned the madness that had begun almost four years before. While public fascination with the film had known no regional boundaries, Southerners, Georgians, and most of all Atlantans looked forward to the affair with an interest bordering on craziness. "The ink was hardly dry on my movie contract before various Atlanta organizations, civil and social, began angling with Hollywood for an Atlanta premiere," Mitchell told Kay Brown soon after the shooting had commenced in 1939. Without any sanction from the producer, even otherwise staid and conservative Atlanta organizations proceeded with all their plans for premiere parties and fêtes.[3] With the commencement of the filming itself, the city basked in its own prospective glory. Never known for reticence about their town, Atlantans now swelled with pride to bursting.[4]

As 1939 wore on, Selznick began discouraging the idea of a local opening. In the early summer, he circulated the rumor that the local premiere was off. At this news, the citizenry, led by Atlanta matrons, went berserk. James Pope, Mitchell's old friend at the *Journal*, kept the author well informed about these bizarre goings-on, and Mitchell, in turn, retold the zany tale for Lois Cole.

> Jimmy said the ladies . . . descended on Mayor Hartsfield's office like a pack of well dressed Eumenides. His Honor, a passionate Confederate

and a stout defender of Atlanta's civic rights and honors, leapt eight feet into the air. . . . Jimmy said the reporter at City Hall phoned in excitedly that it sounded like a WPA riot and he, for one, wanted a police reserve called out. Mayor Hartsfield announced to the press that this was the worst outrage since Sherman burned the town. Of course Atlanta was going to have the premiere. "Why," said the Mayor, "in a large way the book belongs to all of us." Various members of City Council were assembled and, for all I know, the Governor, too, and they all began bombarding poor Mr. Selznick, who is now in the last stages of the picture (and of nervous prostration, no doubt) with telegrams telling him he must quiet the unrest in Atlanta occasioned by the rumor.[5]

This furious campaign had its effect. Although David Selznick still protested his right to premier his movie wherever he wished, Atlanta ignored the protest. Now the local lunacy began in earnest.

Between Selznick's qualified concession on July 18, 1939, and the actual event five months later, the excitement intensified with every passing week. By late November, the society sections of the *Journal*, the *Constitution*, and the *Georgian* overflowed with photographs and notices of out-of-town guests. The uproar in November paled beside December's agitation. The governors of the old Confederate states arrived with their entourages. Regional literati swept into town. Yokels poured in from the countryside. Confederate bunting decked public and private buildings alike. Waitresses doffed uniforms for hoopskirts. Zealots likewise transformed the façade of Loew's into, sure enough, Mitchell's nightmare of a Greek Revival mansion, with fake columns soaring three stories above the street. After ten months of planning (no wonder they screamed at Selznick's rejection!) the young matrons of the Atlanta Junior League lived out their historical fantasies in a similar fashion. They preempted the City Auditorium, draped gargantuan festoons of ivy and smilax from the ceiling to the floor, and filled the stage with a colossal be-columned reproduction of what they called Tara Hall as decorations for the great ball they planned for December 14.

Atlanta's display of provincial vulgarity distressed even the Hollywooders: no small feat. The "idiotic festivities" embarrassed David Selznick.[6] Even the Revolving Bastard, Bird Birdwell, blushed (supposedly). Clark Gable could hardly stand it. "He is still squawking about the ball, claiming that going to the opening is bad enough, but that selling thousands of tickets because of a personal appearance by him is a little thick," clucked the producer in sympathy with the star. The war had just erupted in Europe, and "the idea of a town receiving us as though we had just licked the Germans," the producer fumed, "is something that I for one will not go through with."[7] He did anyway.

Atlanta no longer cared what anyone thought. Mayor Willie Hartsfield declared a city-wide holiday for the hullabaloo: for everyone, that is, except the cops. For them, he cancelled leaves. Newspaper reporters, Movietone cameramen, and photographers were all doing double shifts as well, locals as well as out-of-town journalists. And the Ford executives, who supplied limousines for all the stars, fought with each other for the privilege of chauffeuring them around town. From all over the world, people swelled the city's population. The city partied. "We really did have a grand affair," the author recounted afterward. "Everybody gave a big party and the traffic jam was so terrible no one could get to the party he was invited to, so when anyone passed by where a party was being given he stopped in. It really was open house for three grand days."[8] The political and artistic notables had already swarmed into their suites at the Biltmore and the Georgian Terrace—indeed, in every available hostelry in the city—when the first Hollywooders appeared on December 13. By the fourteenth, everything was set when the secretly resentful but outwardly charming Clark Gable and his spectacular wife, Carole Lombard, stepped off their plane just before sundown.

The city had gone entirely mad, and with it, the state of Georgia and the region itself. This triumph blotted out the stigma of Appomattox. Indeed, this victory rendered politics and the larger world itself irrelevant. Had FDR just declared the South the nation's number-one problem the year before, to the furious insult of Southern honor? Hollywood's attention rebutted the charge. Was the world itself going mad? The horrors of the European war seemed fantasy beside the new reality of Hollywood in the provinces. Hitler's blitzkrieg had reduced Poland to ashes less than three months before. France and Great Britain were preparing for a repetition of the Great War. Few in Dixie gave a fig the week before Christmas of 1939, and breathless bulletins from the Georgia capital pushed the European news to inside pages all over the former Confederacy.

Amid it all, Margaret Mitchell carried on like a keeper in a lunatic asylum. Early on, she decided to turn down all invitations and to abandon Atlanta itself until just before the opening and then leave again just after. She adhered closely if not exactly to this scheme.

She had no qualms or reservations whatsoever about the regrets she sent to the Junior League. The young matrons had planned the greatest event of all, next to the actual screening itself. They had commandeered the City Auditorium and issued several thousand invitations for their great charity ball on December 14, the night before the actual premiere. Even this number failed to satisfy the demand. Even had the ladies stipulated that guests could attend only in ancient dress, they still probably could have filled the hall. Invitees actually did arrive in eighty-year-old costumes and most others came in some facsimile of antebellum dress. Margaret Mitchell was shyer than Clark Gable and

still more reluctant to market herself or display herself for the delectation of the hoi polloi. Then, too, of course, old feuds even gave her
some pleasure in scribbling her regrets. Although most of the membership in 1939 was too young to have played a role in blackballing Mitchell
eighteen years before, she appreciated the chance to even old scores.
As it turned out, though, few missed her presence. The ladies had snared
everyone else who mattered anyway. If guests from New York and Hollywood puzzled over her absence, Atlanta gentry paid little heed. This
was just Peggy Marsh acting up again. The novelist kept her cool.

She had no problem in squashing George Brett's grand party in her
honor, either. Brett, the villain of the contract affair three years before,
wanted a big reception; Mitchell summarily rejected the proposal.
Towards the local Macmillan people, however, like the Book Department at Rich's Department Store, and Norman Berg, the company's
chief Atlanta agent, Mitchell felt much greater loyalty, and she acceded
to their entreaties to honor her at a luncheon on December 14. She
accepted one other invitation; she could hardly have refused:

> The only organization I have joined in the last three years is the Atlanta
> Women's Press Club. The members are all active newspaper women. I
> am the only non-working member, and I am very proud of my member-
> ship, for most of the girls are old friends of mine and I am happy that
> they are still willing to accept me as one of them—as Peggy Mitchell,
> newspaper woman, rather than Margaret Mitchell, author. . . . I am un-
> der obligations to them that I can never repay.[9]

These women had planned a simple do and presented the scheme to
the writer as an accomplished fact. She accepted for the afternoon of
the premiere itself.

The Rich's luncheon occupied the writer on the afternoon of the Junior League's grand fête. Although the author had flatly rejected a party
by the corporate office, Brett and company had wedged themselves into the luncheon early on. Poor Norman Berg could hardly refuse the order of his employers to participate, and Harold Latham had
gone to work on Mitchell, too, to let the company honor her. No one
claimed more of her loyalty than he. She crumbled, and the affair proved
much grander and more elaborate than she had hoped. Actually, the
luncheon turned out to be a notable gathering of the regional literati.
Besides big names in the publishing world, guests included her staunch
admirers Julia Peterkin of South Carolina and Marjorie Kinnan Rawlings of Florida. The three Southern Pulitzer Prize winners graced the
head table. The celebration went well but not without a hitch. Mitchell
managed to wrench her ever-ailing back when she missed her chair
and landed on the floor. The day of the premiere itself, then, found her
in considerable pain, but she soldiered on.

The fifteenth, the big day itself, she fulfilled her other obligation, the reception hosted by the Women's Press Club. It turned out to be much, much larger and far, far grander than she had expected. It was held at the Piedmont Driving Club, which possessed the sole merit of physical convenience. Earlier in the year, the Marshes had vacated the Seventeenth Street address for a new apartment directly across Piedmont Avenue from the Driving Club's hallowed halls. The author had only to dash across the street to make the luncheon. And she did dash to make the affair. "The movie stars came 40 minutes early because of one of those mix-ups that can happen in official schedules," recounted Medora Perkerson afterward. No one else was there to greet the celebrities. Perkerson panicked. She screamed for Peggy. " 'We've tried to quiet Clark Gable with a mint julep,' " she telephoned her friend, " 'but he seems to doubt you'll really appear.' " The phantom author, after all, had not been visible so far. Mitchell leapt—dashed—into the breach: "Everybody connected with the picture had arrived at the Piedmont Driving Club in a fanfare of motor escort sirens. The author came panting up on foot, unattended, her orchids dangling in her hand. She had not even taken time to pin them on." [10]

Beginning in error, the party continued in terror. Mitchell's special demons, rather than her friends, might have planned it. Selznick, Gable, Vivien Leigh, and all the other idols of the screen were there. So was the press. Photographers demanded shots, and she had to pose with all the stars. She feared and loathed such situations. She barely reached Gable's and Selznick's shoulders, and her simple, dark, lace-trimmed dress faded beside Leigh's and De Havilland's elegant, furred finery. Still, as the flashbulbs exploded in her face, she laughed and chatted with the megastars as amiably as she had with the anonymous postmen who delivered her night letters. She betrayed no turmoil or awkwardness, but she neither looked nor acted as the rich and famous should. This unprepossessing figure actually fooled a few. As she had rushed across the street to this very party, a *Life* magazine photographer had blocked her path to plead for admittance. He wanted a photograph of Margaret Mitchell. She admitted her identity. He laughed: big joke. He missed the photo opportunity of a lifetime. Later, the persistent photographer actually fought his way into the inner sanctum, and as the sturdy doormen ejected him, Mitchell heard the ruckus, pitied the fellow, invited him back in, and posed now for his flash camera. It was all thoroughly and perfectly in character.

The reception that afternoon had hardly ended before she rushed back home and dressed for the premiere itself. She had laid out her clothes that day even before the Press Club tea: the long kid gloves, the white velvet, embroidered evening coat, the silver slippers and purse, the floor-length pink tulle gown with its bouffant skirt and tight-fitting bodice. If it seemed a little innocent, it fit at least John Marsh's image of his spouse: he had picked it out and made the purchase. This costume concealed the corsetlike bandages she wore beneath to support her back against the pain of the fall the day before. She had little time to think about that pain in all the rush of preparation and making her way through the crowds to Loew's Grand.

When Clark Gable appeared at the theater just before the author, the master of ceremonies asked him for a few words for the crowd. "This night should belong to Margaret Mitchell," he said.[11] Beside the familiar faces of Gable, Lombard, Claudette Colbert, and the other stars, however, the diminutive author provoked no spontaneous stir of recognition and aroused little more enthusiasm than the aged Confederate veterans had. When she was announced—as with them—a cheer arose, but this mob did not brave the cold to see the tiny figure dressed in little-girl pink with her hair held back with tiny pink bows. Nor did they care about the tall, bland man onto whose arm she clung. This fellow wore only a tuxedo, while even Mayor Willie shone in white tie and tails! The crowd did not detain them long. Mitchell read three sentences she had written on a scrap of paper; then the couple swept through the minked and ermined audience in the crowded lobby to their seats near the front. The Marshes sat with the movie's crème de la crème. Jock Whitney, the film's financier, sat on Mitchell's right, and John Marsh made small talk with Clark Gable on his left. The other stars filled out the row, while the Selznicks and other notables, such as media personality Herbert Bayard Swope, occupied the row in front.

As the houselights dimmed, Clark Gable dozed; or so the legend runs. Did the hisses wake him as Sherman began his march to the sea? Did he start at the cheers when Vivien Leigh blasted the Yankee bummer? He stirred, of course, at the intermission, and was wide awake at least when the audience leapt yelping to its feet as the film ended over four hours after it first began. Mayor Hartsfield now took the stage. After naming all the principals in the production, he called on the author to come forward. Gable escorted her to the microphone. They made their way forward to a wild ovation, cheers, and late approximations of the Rebel yell. If she had trembled at addressing the Atlanta lady librarians' professional club, this frantic audience really filled her with the fear of God. She carried it off the way she always did. She began, as ever, with an apology for her inadequacy at public speaking and continued immediately to render thanks to all those people who had made the evening successful. Most of the hardest workers, she insisted, were not present: "the taxi drivers, the librarians, the bankers, the Junior League, the girls behind the counters, the boys in the filling stations. What could I have done—and my Scarlett—without their kindness and their helpfulness!" It was classic Mitchell generosity.

> You know everybody thinks it's just when you are dead broke and you are out of luck that you need friends. But really, when you've had as

incredible success as I have had, that's really when you need friends. And, thank Heaven, I've had them. And I've appreciated everything people have done for me, to be kind and to me and my Scarlett.

Having begun by focusing her attention on others, she now turned from herself completely to praise David Selznick. She did so with typical humor: "He's the man that every one of you cracked that joke about, 'Oh well, we'll wait till Shirley Temple grows up and *she'll* play Scarlett.' "[12] The audience loved it, and roared its approval of her commendation of the production and the players that followed.

And so it ended: everyone went home, and tomorrow was another day. But it had also just begun. David Selznick's vision of *Gone with the Wind* became the standard by which the folks came to judge Margaret Mitchell's intentions in the novel itself. The two were not the same at all. Their plots and emphases differed notably; their histories contrasted just as much. The genesis of the final script had its own zany story.

After buying the film rights in the summer of 1936, Selznick International commissioned Sidney Howard to write the scenario in October. WASPily aloof and cool, this New England dramatist had won a Pulitzer Prize and established a reputation as both a dramatist and screenwriter. He had produced a successful version of Sinclair Lewis's *Dodsworth* for the stage, and later he transferred this work, as well as *Arrowsmith*, to equally successful screenplays.

For all his literary skill, Howard found adapting *Gone with the Wind* especially difficult. He thought Mitchell prodigal; *Gone with the Wind* did everything "at least twice," he complained. He chopped and cut ruthlessly. He also particularly scorned her characterization of the male lead. He protested a "lack both of variety and invention in what Rhett does," and objected to inconsistencies in Rhett's character. He thought this renegade's decision to join Hood's retreating army was completely unconvincing; nothing, he thought, prepared the reader for this turnabout from Rhett's cynical disregard for Southern patriotism. He also disapproved of the imbalance in Mitchell's presentation of her characters, with Scarlett dominating the first two-thirds of the novel, he thought, and Rhett the last third. His script attempted to even out what he perceived as these literary flaws; as, for example, when he expanded Rhett's part and revealed the hero "doing his stuff" as a blockade runner.

By early January, Howard had completed a first draft. He dispatched it to Hollywood soon after New Year's. David Selznick's direct intervention began now. If the script had given Howard fits, David Selznick now complicated his labors immeasurably. But the script plagued Selznick just as thoroughly in turn.

David Selznick had already established a significant reputation for translating literary works into film. His *David Copperfield* and *Tom Sawyer* had won both popular and critical acclaim. He considered those screenplays his own, and he laid claim to Howard's work, too. Even before Kay Brown had finally secured Sidney Howard's services, the producer had staked out his sovereignty over writers and scenarios in general. "I have never had much success with leaving a writer alone to do a script without almost daily collaboration with myself and usually also the director," he had told Brown in October 1936.[13] The New Englander might have been warned. Finally, of course, this was no ordinary script, even for this extraordinary producer. "I find myself as a producer charged with re-creating the best-beloved book of our time, and I don't think any of us have ever tackled anything that is really comparable in the love that people have for it," Selznick noted truthfully. The novel lived in readers' imaginations; but more, he added, "people seem to be simply passionate about the details of the book." Then, too, the producer wanted to tap the enormous readership of *Gone with the Wind* for his film, and he was anxious about what he called "trying to improve on success." He elaborated these ideas for the screenwriter in his initial responses to Howard's first draft.

> One never knows what chemicals have gone to make up something that has appealed to millions of people, and how many seeming faults of construction have been part of the whole, and how much the balance would be offset by making changes that we in our innocence, or even in our ability, consider wrong. . . . I urge that we abide by Miss Mitchell's failures as well as her successes, because I am frankly nervous about anybody's ability—even Miss Mitchell's—to figure out which is which. I think that she herself might well rewrite the book into a failure.[14]

Actually, the producer concurred with many of Howard's criticisms; he also anticipated the cinematic problems these would create. He agreed with Howard, for example, that Mitchell *did* do everything twice. Some of these repetitions he found especially difficult—such as what he felicitously described as "nights of love." "Certainly," he objected, "I think one scene of husbandly rape is enough. How the hell we can even use one is going to be a problem. . . ." For much the same reason, he agreed (initially) to jettison Scarlett's late miscarriage. "These infallible pregnancies at single contacts are a bit thick," he reflected. What to do with Frank Kennedy and Frank's child, Ella, bothered him as much as Howard, but he had no solution except dropping both characters. He also agreed to kill off little Wade Hampton from the script. Howard wanted to drop Bonnie Blue Butler as well; but here Selznick protested. "I feel she is absolutely vital to the heartrending quality of the portrayal of Rhett in this section of the book," he objected.[15]

Selznick sympathized less with other issues Howard raised.

Rhett's inconsistencies did not distress Selznick. "I think his boorishness and bad manners, if that's what they are, are as much a part of Rhett as his charm," the producer declared "and I don't think we should attempt to white-wash him in the least. The balance of Rhett's behavior and Scarlett's behavior has come off brilliantly and I am afraid to tamper with it. . . . ." The hero's conversion to Southern patriotism was nothing, he insisted: "this can be made completely believable if what we see of the plight of his fellow Southerners immediately before this is sufficiently heart-wringing to make everyone in your audience want to get out and fight with them." Like Charles Everett, the novel's first outside reader, Selznick also disliked the Klan episode. He asked Howard to eliminate it. "Of course, we might have shown a couple of Catholic Klansmen, but it would be rather comic to have a Jewish Kleagle," he mused; "I for one, have no desire to produce any anti-Negro film either. In our picture I think we have to be awfully careful that the Negroes come out decidedly on the right side of the ledger. . . . I do hope," he concluded, "that you will agree with me on this omission of what might come out as an unintentional advertisement for intolerant societies in these fascist-ridden times. . . . "[16]

This long letter of January 6, 1937, merely scratched the surface of Selznick's concerns with the script. His worries escalated as the fame of Margaret Mitchell's novel grew. If the novel's success multiplied the chances of a successful film, it also multiplied the possibilities of missteps and error: People simply knew the novel too well. He grew increasingly anxious about compromising anything substantive in the novel, but the length and excesses of the epic did not permit literal and exact translation to film. The producer's anxiety and agitation rose with every tide. A difficult man in any circumstance, the producer became quite daft on the matter of the film and script. His obsession threatened to drive everyone around him to drink, dope, or madness.

In the spring of 1937, he decided the difficulties called for closer cooperation between the writer, director, and producer, so he summoned Sidney Howard to the West Coast. The dramatist dropped his own work to answer Selznick's bidding. He arrived in Hollywood, however, only to sit around for five weeks doing nothing but drawing a fat paycheck.[17] In the fall of the same year, "some spirit of madness," as Howard called it, prompted Selznick to rent a railroad car and pack his whole entourage off to New England to hammer out the script with the scenarist in Connecticut.[18] The transcontinental joy-ride in October 1937 produced no more results than Howard's journey west six months before, but Selznick was soon screaming for Howard to come to California again. In January 1938, Howard wearily repacked his bags. He went, as he explained to the author, "not only because I should hate like the devil to turn the job over to some other writer but also because I am interested to see how much money a picture producer is willing to spend to pay men for not being allowed to earn their pay."[19]

This time he earned his keep. The producer drove him like a galley slave. In a memo to his director, George Cukor, Selznick described a fairly typical session with the scenarist that January. "Sidney and I have a terrific job on our hands," he wrote ominously, "as is apparent from our work today when we spent the whole morning up to one-thirty on nine pages of the script."[20] No sitting in the pleasant California sun sipping gin-and-tonics by the pool this time. Still, none of this brought them any closer to a satisfactory script than they had been the year before. Nothing changed in the rest of 1938 either. Indeed, all this tinkering with the original Howard scenario actually moved the production farther from a decent screenplay, not closer.

One problem in particular came increasingly to the fore as the end of the work on the scenario grew closer and closer: what Hollywood called "continuity." This difficulty actually reveals as much about Mitchell's novel and literary style as it does about writing movie scripts.

From her earliest juvenile fiction (as in "Little Sister"), Mitchell regularly employed a distinctive style of beginning in the middle of things and then cutting back to fill in the narrative blanks through dialogue, snippets of description, and other devices. From the first chapter, *Gone with the Wind* employed the technique repeatedly. After introducing Scarlett and the Tarleton twins, Mitchell abandons them for a leisurely meander through the O'Hara-Robillard genealogy and a subtle exploration of the parental influences on Scarlett's life, a theme Mitchell had actually adumbrated in the novel's opening lines. The death of Bonnie Blue provides another example of this technique towards the novel's end. Mitchell does not tell that affair in normal sequence, but allows Mammy to recount the episode after the event. In rather the same way, Mitchell also made the sharpest cuts from scene to scene and time to time to create or heighten dramatic tension. Charles Everett had praised the method early on. Incongruous juxtaposition, he argued, helped give the novel its power.

This created the problem of "continuity." If episodic artfulness contributed to the novel's literary appeal, it drove Hollywood to distraction. The technique adapted poorly to film. David Selznick's blood pressure soared every time he thought about the difficulty.

The studio demanded the most obvious visual continuity and the most linear story line. The novel's sharp shifts in time, space, and setting would not do. Everyone connected with the script felt the necessity, then, of evening out the narrative. But how? Howard had suggested "the series of dissolves technique." Selznick objected. "It becomes obvious and is a distraction to audiences, who immediately become aware of movie tricks instead of being immersed in the story and forgetting that they are watching a picture," he argued.[21] Adding scenes—

"bridgeovers," they were called—would be another answer. This entailed its own train of difficulties. New scenes added to the script's length—and even Howard's first draft looked oppressively thick to the producer. Selznick also feared the public reaction to added episodes, especially when scenes, characters, and episodes original to the text itself were dropped. "We will be forgiven for cuts if we do not invent sequences," he warned.[22]

The longer the producer reflected on the problem, the more he worried. He reached a kind of compromise with himself. If cut he must, at least what remained, he determined, would be pure Mitchell. He described the ideal script: "one that did not contain a single word of original dialogue, and that was one hundred per cent Margaret Mitchell, however much we juxtaposed it. With this idea in mind," he enjoined his staff, "call to my attention even individual lines that might be substituted for original lines that we have created."[23] His obsession took obsessive forms. His "script girls," like Barbara "Bobby" Keon, indexed the entire novel as a means of isolating the best dialogue for a given character in a particular circumstance. "As an example, Rhett's attitude towards the war is dealt with in many dialogue passages in the book. . . ." Find them all, he ordered.

> I would be anxious to examine all such passages in the book to make sure that we have used the best. . . . The same is, of course, true of all subjects with which we deal and all scenes between important characters. . . . I want to examine all the dialogue between Rhett and Scarlett in the book and make sure that we have done the best possible editing job, and have retained the best of it. . . .

Selznick's passion wore down all but his most faithful or servile minions. It finally drove the frazzled Howard from the studio in despair. In February 1938, he abandoned Hollywood, this time permanently. Margaret Mitchell's Atlanta friend Wilbur Kurtz recorded Howard's departure. As the dramatist vacated the set, "he wheeled, threw back his large shoulders and, with incisive speech somewhat on the sardonic side orated, 'Yes, I'm through. It's not a movie script. It's a transcription from the book. But what else could I do. I just used Miss Mitchell's words and scenes.' "[24]

Selznick's *idée fixe* also drove him back to the author herself. If the text were sacred, if the masses would allow no tampering with the narrative, he could solve his problem, perhaps, by persuading Mitchell to legitimize the changes, bridgeovers, additions, or whatever. Hugh Walpole had written Dickensian lines for *David Copperfield;* Mitchell could write Mitchellian ones! Having conceived of this solution, he heated the transcontinental telegraph wires to Atlanta, begging, pleading, and cajoling. We must work this out, he railed. We could do it on a trip to Sweden, he offered. Or Bermuda. Yes, Bermuda! In the fall of 1938, this, like the train ride the year before, offered hope. He shared his plans in a wire to Jock Whitney and Kay Brown:

> CONCERNING THE WRITER, IT WOULD, OF COURSE, BE JUST WONDERFUL IF YOU COULD TALK MARGARET MITCHELL INTO A BRIEF BERMUDA JAUNT AT OUR EXPENSE. PERHAPS IF HER HUSBAND COULD GET A WEEK OR TWO OFF AND COULD GO ALONG IT WOULD BE HELPFUL. IF I COULD HAVE MITCHELL FOR SO MUCH AS EVEN A WEEK TOWARDS LATTER PART OF MY TRIP I FEEL CONFIDENT I COULD DO WHAT REMAINS TO BE DONE ON THE SCRIPT BY MYSELF. . . . AND I THINK THE MOST WONDERFUL THING WE COULD POSSIBLY ACCOMPLISH FOR "GWTW" WOULD BE AN ANNOUNCEMENT THAT THERE WILL NOT BE A SINGLE ORIGINAL WORD IN THE SCRIPT THAT IS NOT WRITTEN BY MARGARET MITCHELL.[25]

Born on Mars, Mitchell might have muttered.

Selznick also demanded Howard's presence on this cruise to the Devil's Triangle. The Yankee writer refused. "I have a cow with calf," the gentleman farmer replied. Selznick fired him.[26] Selznick could not fire Margaret Mitchell, so he persisted. If not Bermuda, where? You name the place, he wired. Charleston perhaps? This was not the producer's last frenzied plea for help from the Atlantan, but her answer never changed.

Almost daily, new disorders shook the studio. Selznick's sacking of Howard caused new upheavals. It necessitated more chaotic searches to find a new screenwriter and also dialogue writers.

> WISH YOU AND NEW YORK OFFICE WOULD HAVE LIST AVAILABLE ON MY ARRIVAL. . . . PARTICULARLY INTERESTED ROBERT SHERWOOD, STARK YOUNG. NOT INTERESTED SIDNEY HOWARD. UNDERSTAND [OLIVER H. P.] GARRETT'S PLAY TERRIBLE FLOP, SO SHOULD BE ABLE TO BUY HIM CHEAPLY.[27]

The list swelled daily. "I am interested in Robert Sherwood, Stark Young, James Boyd, Rachel Field, Evelyn Scott, MacKinlay Kantor," the producer fired off after sailing from Bermuda.[28] He even considered taking Howard back. "WITH BIG EFFORT I HAVE BECOME BROAD-MINDED AND FORGIVING AND AM WILLING TO HAVE SIDNEY TO DO DIALOGUE WORK. . . . I SHOULD THINK SIDNEY WOULD HAVE THE GRACE TO HUMBLY ASK TO DO THIS JOB ON ANY TERMS IN VIEW OF THE WAY HE LET ME DOWN," the producer wired Kay Brown in December 1938.[29]

Of these notables, Selznick finally "bought" the hapless Garrett—he of the Broadway flop. Meanwhile, Bobby Keon continued to take Selznick's own dictation for the script. Selznick raged; Keon and Garrett jumped. One notable screenwriter got the scene in perfect perspective: "Half the sum paid to me for writing a movie script was in payment for listening to the producer and obeying him. The movies pay as much for obedience as for creative work."[30]

The disorder increased daily throughout 1938. The length of Howard's script had distressed the producer in January 1937, but under Garrett's hand, the bridgeovers multiplied, transitions spawned new scenes, and the script ballooned. Surveying the mess, Selznick then hired *new* hands to undo what he had ordered Garrett and Keon—and Howard—to create. Sometime in the early winter of 1938–1939, he brought in Donald Ogden Stewart and F. Scott Fitzgerald to take dictation. One of the brilliant figures of his generation, a humorist, radical, and preeminent WASP gentlemen, Stewart disappeared from the script almost as soon as he appeared—sacked, according to his friend Fitzgerald, over a fight with the producer about how to make Aunt Pittypat "bustle quaintly across the room." While a comparable problem eventually cost Fitzgerald his job, the author of *The Great Gatsby* served a longer, more tortured tenure.

Joining the writing crew by January 7, 1939, Fitzgerald had been charged primarily with cutting and tightening the bloated script. He labored over the massive tome with the actual novel before him. He had not read *Gone with the Wind* before he signed on with Selznick, and he liked it. "I read it—I mean I really read it—," he wrote his daughter Scottie at this time, and it surprised him. It was "a good novel," he thought.

> —not very original, in fact leaning heavily on *The Old Wives' Tale, Vanity Fair*, and all that has been written on the Civil War. There are no new characters, new techniques, new observations—none of the elements that make literature—especially no new examination into human emotions. But on the other hand it is interesting, surprisingly honest, consistent and workmanlike throughout, and I felt no contempt for it but only a certain pity for those who consider it the supreme achievement of the human mind.[31]

Fitzgerald had far fewer problems with Mitchell's prose than with Garrett's or even Howard's. "Book restored," he scribbled in the script's margin. "Why must this good dialogue be made trite and stagey," he jotted over Garrett's additions. And then again, "Book restored. It is infinitely more moving."[32]

Working for the manic producer weighed on Fitzgerald even as it had burdened Howard. Like his predecessor, he marveled at Selznick's obsessive commitment to the actual language in the novel. "Do you know in the *Gone with the Wind* job I was absolutely forbidden to use any words except those of Margaret Mitchell," he wrote his old friend, the editor Maxwell Perkins. "That is, when new phrases had to be invented one had to thumb through as if it were Scripture and check out phrases of hers which would cover the situation!"[33] The tyranny also

helped erode his appreciation of the novel itself. By 1941 he compared
it unfavorably to *A Portrait of Dorian Gray*. Wilde's work, he argued,
"is in the lower ragged edge of 'literature,' just as *Gone with the Wind*
is in the higher brackets of crowd entertainment," he reflected two
years after his abortive stint on the screenplay.[34]

If the producer's tyranny failed to break Fitzgerald's ego, the mogul
managed it another way. On or about January 24, 1939, Selznick simply fired the novelist.[35] Two days later, the regular filming schedule
started. Selznick still lacked a shooting script.

The filming had actually begun on the evening of December 9 with
the shooting of the burning of Atlanta. At this time, the producer not
only lacked a script, he had officially contracted with only one of his
principals. Although he had signed Clark Gable on August 25, 1938, he
had no final commitments for the other major parts. The dramatic
conflagration on his back lot on the ninth actually brought him together with his movie Scarlett.

On January 13, he sprang the news of Vivien Leigh's contract on the
world, less than two weeks after she had first appeared before his cameras for a screen test. Simultaneously, the studio announced Olivia De
Havilland and Leslie Howard for the parts of Melanie and Ashley. The
lover and later wife of the great British actor Laurence Olivier, Leigh
had virtually no name recognition in the United States beyond her
part in *A Yank at Oxford* with Robert Taylor. The public knew De Havilland best as Errol Flynn's leading lady in *The Adventures of Robin
Hood*, while the forty-six-year-old Howard, playing the much younger
Ashley, had been a leading man in films and stage productions for twenty
years.

With the cast in place, the absence of a script became more ominous
still. And new problems cropped up, too. The director, George Cukor,
now demanded authority over the scenario. Selznick refused; a new
impasse loomed. Sue Myrick described the deadlock to her friend back
home in Georgia. The director, she related, had decided the script was
the problem.

> David himself thinks HE is writing the script and he tells poor Bobby
> Keon and Stinko Garrett what to write. And they do the best they can
> with it, in their limited way. Garrett is just a professional scenario writer
> while Howard knows dramatic values and—oh hell, you know what
> Howard is. And George has continuously taken script from day to day,
> compared the Garrett-Selznick version with the Howard, groaned and
> tried to change some parts back to the Howard script.
>
> So George just told David he would not work any longer if the script
> was not better and he wanted the Howard script back. David told George
> he was a director, not an author, and he (David) was the producer and
> judge of what is a good script. . . .[36]

The issue was more complicated than Myrick suspected. It involved set politics as well as shooting scripts, scenarios, and conflicts with the producer. Regardless, Selznick terminated Cukor's contract. Now production stopped altogether. Within a week, however, Selznick had a replacement: Victor Fleming, who had just completed *The Wizard of Oz*. Indeed, as a special friend of Clark Gable, Fleming would probably have signed a Selznick contract sooner except for the other film. In any case, he left the sound stage of *Oz* and entered the Land of Oz in real life. Part Indian (supposedly), Fleming lacked Cukor's refined sensibilities, but he shared completely his predecessor's estimation of the screenplay. He expressed it rather more bluntly. "David," he informed the producer, "your fucking script is no fucking good."[37]

With everything else in place now except a working scenario, panic mounted hourly in the front office. Selznick called in still more chefs to taste his soup. Ben Hecht of *Front Page* fame appeared on the scene at this time, and he left a comic tale of his contribution. The producer was outraged that Hecht had not read *Gone with the Wind* but decided that an overhead of fifty thousand dollars a day prohibited the writer's leisurely perusal of the epic. Anyway, Hecht continued,

> David announced that he knew the book by heart and that he would brief me on it. For the next hour I listened to David recite its story. I had seldom heard a more involved plot. My verdict was that nobody could make a remotely successful movie out of it. . . . I suggested that we make up a new story, to which David replied with violence that every literate human in the United States except me had read Miss Mitchell's book and we would have to stick to it. I argued that surely in two years of preparation someone must have wangled a workable plot out of Mitchell's Ouidalike flight into the Civil War.

At that point in the encounter, Selznick supposedly hunted down Howard's original script, and the producer and director then acted out the scenes for Hecht—"David specializing in the parts of Scarlett and her drunken father and Vic playing Rhett Butler and a curious fellow I could never understand called Ashley." After each such scene, Hecht declared, he "sat down at the typewriter and wrote it out." They worked like this for a week until Hecht fulfilled his contract. "Thus," he concluded, "on the seventh day I had completed, unscathed, the first nine reels of the Civil War epic."[38]

Hecht exaggerated his part in producing a script. No more of his contribution survived than Scott Fitzgerald's, except for the notable introduction to the film:

> *There was a land of Cavaliers and*
> *cotton fields called the Old South. . . .*
> *Here in this patrician world*

the Age of Chivalry took its last bow. . . .
Here was the last ever to be seen
of Knights and their Ladies Fair,
of Master and of Slave. . . .
Look for it only in books, for it
is no more than a dream remembered,
a Civilization gone with the wind. . . .[39]

Pure Hecht. Pure Selznick. Pure schmaltz. And a pure violation of Margaret Mitchell's vision. The indignity of these grand phrases, however, still lay in the the future for the author, and back in Atlanta she could still watch all the Hollywood nuttiness with a mixture of horror and delight. In late winter, she heard the most astonishing and hilarious rumor of all: that her beloved Robert Benchley was heading for California to work on the screenplay. "I was overtaken by unseemly merriment and laughed until I cried," she wrote Wilbur Kurtz and his wife in Hollywood. "I was thinking that Groucho Marx, William Faulkner and Erskine Caldwell would probably be on the script before this business was over."[40]

The Atlantan did not miss the mark by much. At final count, no fewer than seventeen men and women contributed more or (mostly) less to the writing.[41] In April 1939, the producer even managed to lure the original scenarist back to the West Coast. "I suppose Mr. Howard discovered that there was practically nothing left of his original script," Mitchell replied to the news of Howard's return. "I would not be surprised to learn that the script of the other sixteen had been junked and Mr. Howard's original script put into production."[42] Mitchell came close to truth. The final version consisted very largely of Howard's original work.

For all the disorder in the script and all the furor on the set, Selznick finally concluded the regular shooting on June 27, 1939. For the next two months, the producer edited the 225,000 feet of film down to a "rough cut" about five hours long. As he cut, the script problem arose one last time. The shooting script proved impossible because of the incalculable number of annotations, revisions, and addenda. The producer then instructed one of the "continuity girls" to make a new scenario based, not on this mess of "the rainbow script," but on the five-hour rough cut. She spent a week glued to a film viewer to produce what was now, at last, the "official shooting script," according to Roland Flamini. "Bound in leather, it was presented to members of the cast who had never received a complete script during the filming of the picture!"[43]

So, finally, it was done. But what had David Selznick produced? The producer had sworn allegiance to Margaret Mitchell's text, and to a remarkable degree, he proved true to his commitment. For all his fidelity to Mitchell's words, however, he layered his own vision of the world on Mitchell's text. The opening lines of Mitchell's epic could apply to the relationship between Selznick and the book. "Scarlett's true self was poorly concealed," the author had written. "The green eyes in the carefully sweet face were turbulent, willful, lusty with life, distinctly at variance with her decorous demeanor." In just that way, the words in the film were Mitchell's, but its look and spirit belonged to Hollywood.

What was the film's look? How was it "distinctly at variance" with the text? Those much-fought columns at Twelve Oaks and Tara offer clues. Selznick, Cukor, and all the rest simply could not resist the impulse to aggrandize and ennoble Mitchell's South. Ben Hecht's rolling introduction spelled out the vision: "There was a land of Cavaliers," he had begun, "of Knights and their Ladies Fair. . . ." Did Margaret Mitchell choke? The language revealed the informing sentiment of David Selznick's vision of the book and of his film. Hecht's introduction and the triumphant columns are only the most obvious hallmarks of Selznick's vision of a romantic plantation South. His treatment of blacks and slavery is another. The producer expanded their roles both relatively and absolutely in the film. In one of those rare "original" scenes, as he called them, Selznick invented a sequence at the film's beginning showing field hands at work in the cotton fields. Nowhere does Mitchell depict slaves at labor. Indeed, she illustrates no "field hand" blacks at all under the antebellum regime until the Reconstruction scenes, late in the book. Although Big Sam figures in two important episodes in the novel—as Sherman approaches Atlanta and, of course, the Shantytown affair—Selznick created an initial cameo for this character in the comic "Quittin' time!" exchange at the film's beginning.[44]

While Selznick retained and elaborated the roles of most of Mitchell's blacks, his one major omission actually underlines the look and feel he sought. The film omitted Dilcey. As with Faulkner's character of the same name in *The Sound and the Fury*, this figure was exceptional among both blacks and whites in Mitchell's book. Except for Scarlett, she is the only figure in the novel depicted at sustained and disciplined manual labor. No other character exceeded her stoicism, endurance, loyalty, and nobility. Also, Mitchell twice described her as being part Indian. She was light-skinned. Selznick uniformly ebonized his slaves: more pictorial, he might have judged. The omission of this character affected still other aspects of Mitchell's vision. Quite aside from issues of race and slavery, Dilcey underlined the theme of mothers' relations with their daughters in the novel. Mitchell considered Prissy an important role in the book and film, but all Prissy's lying, whining, and cowardly, evasive childishness, famous in both mediums, acquires its full significance only when juxtaposed against the noble mother's character. In the film's absence of the good mother Dilcey,

Prissy becomes a caricature, a racial stereotype, "all nigger lak her pa."

Selznick's other omissions determined the look of the movie even more strongly. While he spared and even expanded the roles of virtually all Mitchell's blacks, he dropped many of her white characters. More significantly, he eliminated a whole category of her people: her lower class and middling sorts. Only the "porch cotton," po'-w'ite Slatterys survived the cut. Their presence actually exaggerates their eccentricity in the film's social world and establishes the mythic planters as the norm. If Selznick dropped all Mitchell's Crackers and middling sorts, he erased even more thoroughly the lower-class origins of her gentry that the author worked so assiduously to establish. This omission transformed the fundamental values of the novel. In Selznick's treatment, Thomas Mitchell's Irish brogue has no social significance at all. The author attached to it the profoundest meaning. The presence of such a character challenged almost every tenet of the Southern tradition. This Irish immigrant's outlandish speech signified the fundamental nature of the regional social order for the author. In case the lesson lacked clarity in the text itself, Old Miss Fontaine enunciated the principles of social Darwinism in the clearest terms. Selznick eliminated this old witch, too.

The net effect of Selznick's omissions confirms the themes he chose to celebrate—nostalgia for the innocent, lost world of the plantation South. How very far from the author's intentions! Conflict and inner disorder dominate Mitchell's literary vision in the novel. Mitchell's prewar South, in short, is a place waiting for a disaster to happen. Selznick's version misses that point. For him, the conflict is external. By implication, the force of circumstances therefore defines Scarlett's actions rather than the inward dynamic as in the novel. If Scarlett is courageous and indomitable, she is also coarse, vulgar, violent, mean-spirited, vengeful, and uncultured. She is also truly and genuinely stupid about folks, as Rhett and Old Miss confirm on various occasions in the text. Vivien Leigh was just too beautiful, and she played the role with too much intelligence and too little repulsive snarl. The less-beautiful Bette Davis of *Jezebel* might have captured more of the book's heroine.

In evening out the narrative, Selznick also clouded the author's paradoxes, ironies, and even incongruities, which were essential to her vision of the past and to her own biographical motives. Finally, insofar as all these conflicts in the text itself rotate on one fundamental axis, David Selznick's film utterly obscured that most potent of all the novel's conflicts and the source of the fiction itself: that repulsion-attraction between mothers and their daughters; women and their children; women and other women. Selznick had no inkling of the hopeless affection that drove the author and fired her fiction.

For all its alteration of Mitchell's themes, however, David Selznick's version of *Gone with the Wind* stands on its own merits as both a social document and an artwork. The film underlines the fascination with history, the South, regionalism, and local culture that characterized the thirties.[45] His fantasy vision of the South evokes a particular fantasy of the past but, hardly less, a bright hope for the future. More specifically, Selznick's Scarlett spoke to the generation of the Great Depression with the most powerful voice. In both justifying (effectively) her actions and softening her character, Selznick created a very model of the Depression heroine, not a figure who challenges the order from the left, but who girds her loins to work within the system. The movie failed utterly to confirm or advance a leftist model of social or political activity, and its reputation has suffered accordingly; but it remains, if anything, a classic representation of the values that dominated the age itself. In this sense, Selznick's film pairs nicely even with such otherwise incongruous contemporary movies as John Ford's *Grapes of Wrath*.[46]

Selznick's *Gone with the Wind* has suffered critically as much as it has politically. As the small, black and white European film came to dominate the cinematic aesthetic after World War II—just as film criticism became a serious enterprise—*Gone with the Wind* began to look something like a dinosaur to the avant garde. Unlike *film noir*—and the book, too, for that matter—Selznick created a very bright movie in both technique and content. This worked against its critical appreciation. If no one had exploited Technicolor like Selznick, his story line matched the visual art: things *will* work out for Scarlett in the movie, Margaret Mitchell's objections not withstanding. This accorded poorly with the existential pessimism that surged through the American intelligentsia with the collapse of Europe in war. As an exemplary product of the American studio system—huge, vulgar, and star-studded—it also came to represent reaction. Not least, of course, its apparent glorification of the South, slavery, and nostalgic history militated against its canonical inclusion, just as these elements affected the book's critical reception amid the growing skepticism about Southern mores and the swelling tide of racial liberalism between World War II and the civil rights movement of the sixties.

While ordinary folks have never questioned the power of the movie, even its popularity worked against it in the American ambivalence about "popular" taste and values. Therefore citations of its honors—ten nominations, seven Academy Awards in the Oscar ceremonies of 1940—confirm rather than refute the prejudice. The phenomenal ticket sales do the same. Although the film now ranks a mere twenty-fifth in profits, those figures, when converted into modern dollars, put it near the top of moneymakers in cinematic history. For decades it was the top-grossing picture of all time. The *New York Times* estimates the converted figure at $800 million.[47]

Film scholars, by and large, have simply rejected the work as a legitimate subject for inquiry. At the same time, the movie remains a benchmark in its own terms, not unlike the novel itself. It remains one of those standards, like it or not, against which most other films are measured, more or less consciously. If the sources of its power remain essentially unstudied, it has insinuated itself into the very heart of what a film might be. Judith Crist conveyed the spirit well. In a discussion of "getting one's money's worth" out of films, she conjures Selznick's epic from nowhere: "It's the quality and not the quantity that clocks out the hours," she began. *"Gone with the Wind,"* she continued,

> that greatest of spectacles, runs three hours and forty minutes, plus intermission. We last had a chance to re-view it six years ago—happily, we will again next October, on its next release. We know that at fade-out time we will linger, wishing for "and then what happened." It holds us with classic force, the sweeping background of the ante- and post-bellum South, the war spectacle itself, the power of the four movie stars involved in triangles epitomizing eternal romance. And there is not—I say this retrospectively, with a promise to recheck in eleven months—a frame of film I would surrender.[48]

PART V

REACTION

Hawk and Buzzard Time

It appears to me now that Merciful Providence long ago decided I
should spend my life with my hands on a bedpan rather than a
typewriter. . . .

MARGARET MITCHELL TO HAROLD LATHAM[1]

*I*n September 1939, Hitler's panzer divisions roared across Poland.
Simultaneously, the Soviet Union moved from the other direc-
tion to consolidate its empire in Eastern Europe. France and Great
Britain declared war. The "sitzkrieg" or "phony war" that followed
fooled no one, and the Battle of Britain in the late spring of 1940 removed the last hopes there would be no cataclysmic conflict. The Great
War, Phase Two, had started. Inexorably, the conflict sucked the United
States towards its vortex. Washington prepared for battle. With Pearl
Harbor and the German declaration of war in 1941, the United States
joined for the duration. The world grew grievously sick. Margaret
Mitchell had always deemed herself a nurse and bedpan-toter, and now
these international calamities gave her the whole earth as a field for
these activities. Her sense of obligation rose with every fresh disaster.
The conflict affected every aspect of her life. At the same time, the war
provides an apt metaphor for her own circumstances after 1939. Illness, death, and disruption at her own hearth mirrored the international strife and forestalled the enjoyment of her fame and fortune,
even had she desired to glory in her celebrity and wealth. It was indeed "a hawk and buzzard time," as she said.

Mitchell's sympathies lay completely with England and the Allies, but what with the premiere and other difficulties that followed in the new year, she had no time or opportunity to manifest that sympathy. With the Battle of Britain, however, the author plunged into the middle of the American Allied war effort. She collected clothes and money for English relief. She rolled bandages and made surgical dressings. In some version of Rosie the Riveter's labors, she also learned how to operate a factory-type machine with a six-inch rotary blade capable of cutting through twenty-five thicknesses of cotton. She alone of the volunteers seemed genuinely to relish this labor. She took perverse pleasure in this linthead patriotism.[2]

From the summer of 1940, Mitchell also assumed American involvement in the war was unavoidable, and she encouraged preparedness and national defense. She agreed to participate in what she termed "Mayor La Guardia's national-defense-for-the-home-folks-plan," adding the only half-jesting proviso, "I'd be glad to join if they'd teach me how to operate a machine gun. I always did want to know how those things work. This seemed to upset them somewhat, for I think they had knitting on their minds."[3] She also began her first war-bond drives about this time.[4] For the first time, she volunteered freely—and even with some enthusiasm—for public speaking engagements. "I found myself making from three to five speeches a day in Atlanta schools, in an effort to get lunch and movie money from the pockets of the little ones," she explained to Harold Latham. "You know how I am about public speaking, and the queerest thing of all this war to me is that I manage to get through without screaming or fainting or having the children burst into uproarious laughter."[5]

Her commitment to bond sales rose still higher in the spring of 1941 when she agreed to sponsor the new Navy cruiser *Atlanta*. Her sponsorship also involved her participation in the ship's launching and commissioning, a separate category of her patriotic activities in these years. The ship slid down the runway on September 6, 1941, at the Kearney, New Jersey, shipyards, and the Atlantan was there to smash the bottle of champagne against the prow. As sponsor of the ship, she also appeared at the commissioning three months later. The Japanese had attacked the United States only three weeks before, and Pearl Harbor cast a dark shadow over this event. The Navy allowed only three days' notice of the commissioning, and scheduled the ceremony inauspiciously for Christmas Eve. What with transportation delays and problems in finding a train berth, Mitchell barely made it to the grand and somber event, but she managed just the same.[6] As a part of her participation, she went beyond the call of duty. She presented the ship's officers with a rare set of Wedgwood china as a personal gift. Nor did she forget the enlisted men in whose name she contributed to the seaman's fund.[7] She made another completely characteristic gesture towards the sailors, too. At the conclusion of the formal commissioning ceremonies, she asked the captain to call up all the crew from Georgia. Outfitted smartly in her khaki Red Cross uniform and looking neat and trim, she chatted amiably with every sailor, asked about their homes, and made all the connections that Southerners always make. The men loved it. Her participation in this affair, she wrote afterward, gave her as much pride and pleasure as any human being might aspire to.[8]

The American declaration of war in December multiplied Mitchell's patriotic activities. Three weeks after the U.S.S. *Atlanta* was commissioned, John Marsh accepted the responsibility of neighborhood air-raid warden, and Mrs. Marsh signed on as his deputy.[9] She took the work very seriously and performed civil defense duties faithfully throughout the war. Manpower shortages complicated her job, and the most "bewildering confusion of contradictory orders and the most complacent amount of ignorance" in the government bureaucrats drove her crazy.[10] Then, too, for one who delighted in heavy machinery and dreamed of operating a machine gun, the tedious civilian labor made even routine military service look exciting. "I am convinced," she grumbled, "that worry about getting killed is a minor matter compared with having to make a hundred telephone calls an evening and finding no one at home or receiving a hundred telephone calls an evening and having to remember all the diverse messages."[11]

The American declaration of war also intensified Mitchell's commitment to bond sales. Traveling all over the city to receive funds and offer thank-you talks, she spoke everywhere to the most diverse groups of people. She hit the wealthy matrons of the Northside—"Paces Ferry Roaders," as she called them—but she appealed to their po'-white sisters in the Southend, too. This campaign also drew her within the walls of Atlanta's grim federal penitentiary for the first time. Facing "2,401 prisoners in convention assembled," she could think of only one convict story: the time the state liberated all Georgia convicts to fight Sherman in 1864—the story of her beloved wife-killing Archie from *Gone with the Wind*. The prisoners ate it up. The warden told her later that "almost all the men were r'aring to get out and get in the army," she boasted.[12]

On November 13, 1942, the Japanese sank the *Atlanta* at Guadalcanal, and Mitchell's involvement in the bond drive took a quantum leap. She led the campaign to replace the ship. The new bond drive lasted all winter; she rushed everywhere. "I am up to my neck and scarcely able to swim," she exploded in mid-January of 1943. The year's coldest day found her hawking bonds outdoors at Five Points downtown. "We had all the Atlanta marines with us and they fired off a cannon every time anybody bought a thousand-dollar bond," she laughed afterward. "We were deafened and frozen but we had a wonderful time." That noisy, frigid day generated $500,000 for the new ship.[13] The bond

drive finally concluded in mid-March of 1943 with a great "to do" at
the City Auditorium that featured Secretary of the Navy Frank Knox,
"sloughs of admirals, slathers of gold braid, so many flashlights we
were blind for hours, and lots of flags," the novelist wrote.[14] The campaign had raised 63 million dollars. Fewer than eleven months after
the festivities in the City Auditorium, the Navy christened the new
Atlanta. Once again the author swung the champagne bottle. The commissioning took much longer, but on December 3, 1944, she attended
that ceremony, too. She repeated her performance of two years before,
complete with the personal gifts and the kindnesses to the Georgia
crewmen.[15] This was Mitchell at her best.

Between the launching of the first *Atlanta* in September 1941 and
the commissioning of the second in the closing days of 1944, Mitchell
drove herself relentlessly. "There are seventeen kinds of volunteer work
I am fitted to do and volunteers are as short as professionals now, so
many people are upon my neck to get me to work," she had written.
"Nothing would please me better than to be doing seventeen things at
once, for such a course of action would seem only natural to me."[16]
The pace and excitement took its toll. If new physical infirmities limited her scope after 1943, she maintained a presence, at least, at all
her old activities up through the war's end—the bond sales, the bandage-
rolling, the clothes drives, and civilian defense. She even took on new
commitments. While working double-duty shifts of volunteer service
in the war's last winter, for example, she also volunteered to work on
the Red Cross Prisoner of War Committee, devoted to assisting men
held captive by the Japanese and Germans. It entailed more speechi-
fying and public relations, but it also involved something like social-
worker assistance to the captives' families.[17]

Besides all these public commitments, one activity exemplified her
patriotic impulses and natural inclinations better still—her personal
attentiveness to individual servicemen. For all the author's concern
with bandage-rolling, civilian defense, bond drives, launching ships,
and all the rest, much of her most passionate engagement during World
War II lay outside these public activities. Like her mother before her,
she assumed an immediate and personal responsibility for the welfare
of those in uniform. She might see single men downtown or hitchhik-
ing, and she would volunteer a lift. Often she invited them home, and
when John returned from work, he found strange men in uniform in
his living room—like the two Royal Air Force cadets whom the author
put up for a weekend in the middle of August 1942.[18] Throughout the
war, her servant grew accustomed to the words, "Bessie, set two more
places at the table tonight." Or, "Bessie, make the sheets on the sofa
before you leave."

Nothing, however, absorbed more of this personal attention than
writing letters to men in uniform. Her letters to soldiers, sailors, and

marines put her in a category of a one-woman epistolary USO. She
wrote officers and fellow members of the Piedmont Driving Club no
more often than enlisted men whom she met through the Georgia Press
Association. She established correspondence with people she had met
but momentarily as they passed through her city and her life. She wrote
to perfect strangers the same way. While she calculated her letters to
appeal to every individual, they all have this much in common: her
sympathy, encouragement, humor, and down-home news of every sort
to men very far away from home.

A fellow member of the Atlanta gentry, Cary Wilmer, had been her
friend forever. Was he feeling old at thirty-eight, and infirm with his
bad leg as he faced the rigors of the front with boys literally half his
age? She cheered him with stories of her own ailments and the Driving
Club's Vanity Fair.[19] Leodel Colemen had little in common with Cary
Wilmer. She knew him through the Georgia Press Association, and this
country reporter from rural Statesville and the *Bulloch County Herald*
won his own distinctive missives after he joined the Marines in 1942.
Between 1943 and 1945, Mitchell wrote him about forty long, typically
rich Mitchellian letters. She kept him posted on every turn of Georgia
social life, and these letters form a remarkable survey of domestic history during the war years. At the same time, she calculated her correspondence to challenge and inspire the young journalist. After the Navy
made him a combat reporter in 1943, she offered him generous advice
about style and writing and goaded his ambition by comparing him
with journalist Ernie Pyle. She sandwiched all this between humorous
narratives and delicious anecdotes about their doings before the war.[20]

The author's letters to the much-younger Jay McGahee of Augusta
reveal still another facet of her nurturing. They also show more of the
variety of her own personality. Here, no talk of high society or debutante to-dos ripples through the correspondence; here, no queries about
battle fatigue or advice about journalistic style. Instead, the author
offered her ideas on literature and art. She aired her views on Gertrude Stein, James Joyce, and the modern novel; she shared her opinions of Wordsworth, Coleridge, and Byron. She talked politics and reform, sometimes combining all of these topics in a way certainly
calculated to appeal to her earnest young correspondent. At one point,
the youthful soldier blushed about "receiving so much from you when
I have as yet never returned any of these favors." Her response reveals
much about the author's character, the roots of her interest in so many
different folk, and her own sense of obligation to such a variety of people. Reciprocity actually did exist between them, she insisted. His letters were his gifts. "I enjoy them, first, because they are from you; I
enjoy them, secondly, because they are well written, interesting and
they give me information about what is going on in a part of the world
I shall never see. . . ." If their correspondence involved no one-to-one

exchange, that was a matter of no consequence. "In this world we do not repay in kind. Generally it is not possible," she told the soldier:

> Socially many a poor person more than repays the hospitality of a rich person by their charm and their amusing qualities. Children repay the generosity of grownups with treasured garter snakes, damaged spiders and beautiful pieces of quartz that might be gold. The old repay the young with enthusiasm. My colored friends are always returning more to me than I ever give them. . . . They repay me with what they can do but who knows what may happen in this post-war world. I've seen better fixed people hungry on the streets. So, some day you may be buying things for me instead of writing me very entertaining letters. The foregoing is just to make you see that we are even and the account is balanced.

And so she described the web of obligations and reciprocal relations that shaped her life.

Mitchell's attentions to McGahee did not stop with words on paper. He got his books and dictionary from her, his subscriptions to the *New Yorker* and the *New York Herald's* Sunday book review.[21] Her fellow Driving Clubber Wilmer received a package of "that dreadful stuff you smoke," while, after many delays in transit, Leodel Coleman's thesaurus arrived safely. And so it went.

World War II made Margaret Mitchell a Sister of Charity to half the world, but the war years also imposed still more arduous nursing duties much closer to home. Circumstances in her own domestic circle mirrored the dislocations of the war. Besides her own notorious ill-health, which took still odder and more calamitous turns in these years, she played nurse to her disastrously ailing father, a crew of sickly servants, and her perpetually frail husband.

Her father proved the weariest load of all. He suffered from chronic ill-health, especially kidney problems. In the five-year period prior to 1930, surgeons had operated on Eugene Mitchell three times, and his health worsened every year of the Great Depression. As he approached seventy, about the time of the publication of *Gone with the Wind*, he deteriorated disastrously. The crises came in regular waves thereafter, and the physicians expected every new bout to take him off. Against all odds, he survived for eight grisly years. His only daughter seldom left his side.

In the fall of 1938, Eugene Mitchell had his first apparently fatal seizure. The family mounted a death watch. He survived, but less than a year later he was down again. The doctors had been insisting on a kidney removal for nearly a decade, and now, finally, the Mitchells concurred. It brought no sustained improvement. Despite "two operations and many weary months in bed with trained nurses and attendants," her father still showed no improvement, she wrote on the fearsome eve of the Battle of Britain. "The physical discomforts of such an illness are obvious, the mental ones, I believe, are worse, although not so apparent. It is hell for an active man who has led a busy life to lie in bed month after month, bored, depressed and almost hopeless."[22] She was just out of the hospital herself; so was John, and her observation suggests something of her own mood.

The summer of 1940 brought new crises.[23] Everyone, including Eugene Mitchell, expected him to die, and he made his peace with God. In tribute to his still-adored wife, he formally abandoned his ancestral faith for his wife's Catholicism. His acceptance of the inevitable, however, was temporary. He fought death four more years.

Nineteen forty-one brought no relief to anyone. While rolling bandages at the Red Cross, participating in British relief efforts, speaking out for war-bond sales, and preparing for the imminent launching of the *Atlanta*, the harried novelist also tended her once-more hopelessly ill father. For two weeks in the late spring, the family expected his death from hour to hour, but he outlasted pneumonia and other infections. Later, she related the horror of still another abortive death-watch, with "all the strains and worry and sitting up all night in the hospital and jumping when the phone rings."[24] The actual outbreak of war multiplied the difficulties of her father's illnesses. Nurses, orderlies, and aides now vanished. Searching for competent (or even half-competent) assistance now consumed still more of her time. With such scarcity of labor, Mitchell so gave even more time and energy to keep the best ones working. When one of the most reliable orderlies fell sick himself, she found herself tending *him*. "He would not go to the hospital unless I accompanied him to 'speak for him,' " Mitchell groaned. "So I went and spoke for him and have been back to the hospital every day to 'speak' for him again." This particular routine lasted two full weeks. When, finally, no amount of beating the bushes flushed out help, Mitchell herself assumed still more primary care-giving responsibilities for her father. Besides the gentler care of bathing him and feeding him, she also heaved him about physically. This, in turn, exacerbated her own physical problems, especially her ailing back. During the final eighteen months of Eugene Mitchell's life, his daughter hauled herself out of her own sickbed on innumerable occasions to oversee his sickroom. He refused to die.

In the best of circumstances, such illness would have burdened any family, but Eugene Mitchell's character complicated his nursing. The old man's testiness kept pace with his physical deterioration. He was dour in the best of times; illness made him impossible. "He does not sleep more than an hour or two in the twenty-four and this makes him very nervous," his daughter related.

> He has no idea as to how to occupy his time because he has spent all his
> life working and he does not know how to relax or play when he is not

working. He is very easily depressed and it takes the efforts of the entire family amusing and diverting him.[25]

If often delirious at his sickest, he improved only to become fiercely cross and irritable. "Father came home from the hospital yesterday," his daughter wrote after one of his earlier crises, "and, despite the fact that he is as cross as a bear after hibernation season, he is doing fine."[26]

Aged seventy-eight and now literally (and finally) at death's door in May 1944, he still demonstrated the general cantankerousness that had complicated his personal relations since boyhood. "Life goes on with all its fits and starts," his daughter sighed the month before his death.

> I am beginning to think that our situation in regard to Father's medical attendants is like the fable of the man trying to get the fox, the goose and the cabbage across the river. When we have three able bodied orderlies, the line of battle draws up, with two orderlies and father against the third; when one orderly is sick or missing and we are getting by on two, the lines re-form with Father and one orderly against the other.[27]

June 17, 1944, ended Eugene Mitchell's protracted death agony. During the dreadful eight years preceding, his daughter had ministered to him virtually without surcease. She had spent her own energies heedlessly on the old man. While Mrs. Mitchell had warned the child against this aspect of her character, the mother herself had demonstrated something very much akin to it. Eugene Mitchell, for one, saw the relationship between the two. He worshipped the selflessness of both. Only two years before he died, he reviewed his own state and counted himself especially fortunate in his wife and daughter. "I am blessed now and have been for many years blessed with everything a man's heart should desire except the companionship of May Belle who died twenty-two years ago," he wrote his cousin in 1942. He still mourned that loss after a score of years, but he found his consolation: "But Margaret is so much like her that it lightens the loss."[28] A father's benediction; a woman's curse.

In the middle of one of her father's crises in January 1943, the Atlanta novelist summarized her life for her friends Clifford and Helen Dowdey: "we've been having what my grandmother used to call 'a hawk and buzzard time,' " she wrote.[29] If the war's catastrophe and her father's health prompted this assessment, a new round of physical woes of her own confirmed it finally and irrevocably.

She had opened the new decade with major surgery. What she called "abdominal adhesions" had troubled her chronically for twenty years. She had first undergone corrective surgery for the condition in 1921. The symptoms flared regularly afterwards, and her physicians recommended operating once again after the publication of the novel. She agreed, but the always imminent premiere delayed the procedure week after week, month after month. In mid-January of 1940, as the film fever finally broke, she signed into St. Joseph's one more time. She had planned to spend a year recovering, but the pressure of the war hounded her from bed much sooner. The "bellyaches," as she called it, did not improve. Moreover, other still more mysterious, ailments now made their appearance. Inexplicable fevers and the oddest symptoms sapped her strength in the early war years. She described them to a specialist after one of her sieges:

> I began running a temperature again. Diarrhea was bad at that time and I had the usual accompanying skin eruptions on the chest and some in the scalp. Sometimes these bumps in the scalp remain so long that I have to have them burnt off. Those on the chest persist, too, and generally leave small scars. . . . The fever is accompanied by sweating, which is also usual . . . the usual headaches which accompany the temperature lasted only about a week. Ordinarily they are the worst features of this.

Debilitating unpleasantness characterized these bouts, "bad headaches, fatigue, depression, and aching muscles."[30] Although she said the condition had plagued her for many years, in the fall of 1942 it grew so bad that she checked herself into the research hospital at Johns Hopkins University to allow medical experts to have a go at her agonies.

After every battery of tests known to the most advanced medical team in the country, the physicians found no organic condition to account for all the myriad fevers, sweats, skin eruptions, and stomach pains that the author suffered. She rejected their diagnosis. They rechecked. Still nothing appeared. While in the course of their examinations they did discover a ruptured vertebrate disc, they said there was no connection between this condition and the other ailments. They repeated this assessment in both oral and written diagnoses. "To follow up our conversation of earlier today," her internist reiterated in December, "I want to stress the fact that we did not find any organic disease with the exception of the ruptured intervertebrate disc."[31] While the physicians insisted that the disc had no bearing whatsoever on her other complaints, however, they maintained that her back should be plaguing her, and they recommended an operation to cure that problem. Despite the doctors' repeated denials, the author decided on her own that the ruptured disc was indeed the culprit in her other pain. All this produced the oddest predicament: with physicians recommending an operation to cure one problem that she did not acknowledge, the patient consented to surgery to correct another set of woes for which they found no organic cause. The situation portended very ill. Her relations with her chief physician grossly complicated the difficulties, too.

Mitchell's surgeon, Walter Dandy, was the most important neurologist in the United States.[32] He left an indelible mark in the field. Fifty years after his death, medical journals still cite his practices and discoveries. In his prime, the great and famous flew to him from all over the world. The family of George Gershwin had consulted him before the musician's death, and he had tried to save Thomas Wolfe in that writer's last illness. A pioneer of vertebra fusion, he had performed the operation over 500 times by the spring of 1943. All evidence supported the idea that Dandy was a virtual miracle worker. He was "the great man" to his residents, and these assistants early on had encouraged Mitchell to let "Dr. Dandy wave his magic wand over you."[33]

For all his medical genius, however, Dandy completely lacked the human touch. As the complete scientist, he had no sympathy with sympathy. Blunt, outspoken, bullish, and devoid of personal grace himself, he utterly discounted "bedside manner." As a part of his rise to national and international fame, he also possessed the most vaulting ego—which, not coincidentally, provoked hatred as well as devotion among fellow neurologists. He treated his assistants like servants and condescended to all his patients. He remembered them, according to his biographer, not as names or individuals but as physiological disabilities. Beneath her constant self-effacement, of course, Margaret Munnerlyn Mitchell Marsh had her own ego. Moreover, she took special pride in her reading in neuroscience. The failure of her knowledge to win so much as a blink from the Great Man might have almost been calculated to set her off; but worse yet, she determined early on that Dandy considered her complaints psychosomatic. From this point, the two set on a collision course of classic and almost epic proportions. Their conflict reveals very much about the author; it also suggests some of the inherent problems in the practice of medicine as pure science as exemplified in Walter Dandy's career.

Mitchell boarded the train for Baltimore on March 20, 1943. She straggled back home on April 19. She considered these four weeks among the most horrible of her life. The trouble began immediately. First off, the operation failed to alleviate the old pains. "My spine, which should have bothered me enormously, has always been a minor discomfort," she told the Dowdeys; "my hip and knee and foot, which the doctors say I should never know I had, keep singing like larks."[34] Worse, the pain both spread and intensified after the operation. Her right foot and leg had never bothered her before; they now ached and burned constantly. The old villain, her left foot, now drove her nearly crazy. "Where I formerly had only spots of pain in the left leg, I now have what appears to be a complete sciatic nerve involvement." As for her back, it "is worse than before and involves a larger area," she groaned.[35] Four months after she returned to Atlanta she estimated that she was only three-quarters recovered from these new aches, not to mention to the problems she went in for. "I will be happy just to make a complete recovery from the surgery, even if I never get any relief from the original problem," she complained.[36]

Beyond the physical distress, very early on, other difficulties appeared. Increasingly they came to be the focus of Mitchell's growing antagonism towards her physicians. Mitchell was hardly out of the recovery room when she detected a problem in her doctor's attitude to her. Her agitation increased daily during her month-long sojourn in Baltimore. John Marsh summarized his wife's agitation when they returned to Atlanta: "When she did not make a prompt recovery at the hospital," he charged, "Doctor Dandy seemed annoyed with her for disappointing his expectations."[37] The regimen ordered by the doctors offended her all the more and seemed to be additional evidence of the doctor's impatience with her suffering. "She told me that she would have gone home if she had had to walk every step of the way," the husband fumed, "for she was so anxious to be in a quiet and restful place where, if she was suffering, she would not be hauled out of bed, forced to walk and then told that all her pain was 'nervous.' "[38] The Marshes indicted the whole staff. They saw plots everywhere. The outraged husband believed that everyone had agreed that his wife was "neurotic and therefore anything she said was to be discounted or disbelieved. . . . Her pains were assumed to be imaginary and she was treated on that basis. Anything she said about being in pain was used against her, to support the diagnosis of neurosis. . . ." The physicians were prejudiced against her "from the fact that my wife is not only Mrs. John Marsh but 'Margaret Mitchell.' . . . it was assumed in advance that she *must* be 'temperamental,' " he declared. "She was not judged on the basis of herself but on a preconceived notion that if she was 'Margaret Mitchell' she must be nervous, queer, neurotic."

If John Marsh insisted that his wife was perfectly normal except for her physical condition when she entered the hospital, he also proclaimed that the doctors' prejudices produced the very "nervous" reaction they were looking for. Being "made to feel that she was being a great trouble and annoyance to busy people because her pains and discomforts were considered neurotic imaginings and not real," he wrote Dandy afterward, "she became hesitant about saying anything when she was in pain and, in fact, began to worry whether she had really turned neurotic." He described her as mystified, embarrassed, mortified, and bewildered. "She wondered if you all did not consider her crazy or a liar when she was even refused simple relief for discomforts. . . ." If she had been completely sane before, the hospital made her crazy.[39]

While she vociferously rejected the charge of "nerves" as the cause of her illnesses, the author herself conceded the connection in another way. Thus she declared that Dandy's lack of understanding gave her a "case of the nerves," even where she had none before. If "nerves" did not cause her problems then, she insisted, they now intervened, through no fault of her own, to foul up her recovery. "When I first left the hospital I found it bad enough to be painfully disabled without being told that I had no physical reason for any disability," she wrote Dandy. "When I know how and why I feel bad, I don't worry about it and I try to do the things which are within my reach."[40] "I had a bad time at the hospital," she explained to friends, "not only because I had a bad time but because the doctor insisted that the reason I was in pain was because I was 'nervous.' "[41]

After the operation, the case—and, not least, the Marshes' fury—quite thoroughly mystified the surgeon. "I must say it is beyond my comprehension," he replied to John Marsh's first angry indictment in May. "I just cannot see how there can be pain there now and I have had experience with over five hundred cases." He continued, then, with the overweening egoistical innocence that helped make him a Great Man, to raise one more time that most delicate and forbidden subject of "nerves":

> I have never had any one who has gone this long with the pain; some of them have gone a few weeks but always it has stopped. It was for that reason that I felt all along that it must be a nervous state. The operation went as it always does and nothing could go wrong. . . . I should like to see her get interested in her literary work and do a little more each day to divert her mind.
>
> Frankly, I know you do not like to hear that it is nerves, and I do not like to say it, but I just cannot explain it on any other basis.[42]

This response failed utterly to palliate the Marshes' ire. On the contrary, of course, it set them boiling, confirming all their dark suspicions about the great man's prejudice. John Marsh replied angrily again, but the neurologist remained as perplexed as ever. Perhaps a second disc was involved, he speculated. He then recommended a second operation to fix the other disc. Meanwhile, he expressed unalloyed astonishment about the supposed prejudice against the famous patient. "I never said that she was neurotic, and if I had believed it I would not have operated upon her," he protested, "and if I believed it now I would not suggest the second operation, so that cannot be." Perhaps, he volunteered, the Marshes were creating the issue themselves unwittingly. "I wonder if you and she have not really become obsessed with the neurotic attitude. Of course, one always thinks of it, but it is always the last resort."[43] Had Walter Dandy calculated the response most likely to enrage Margaret Mitchell, he could have done no better.

In January 1945, Mitchell summarized her outrage in a long letter that she finally thought the better of sending. After describing her physical condition and suffering in the most minute detail to the physician, she then dealt with the issue of her own psyche. Attentiveness and kindness, she testified, helped make her well; their absence hindered her recovery.

> I have had other doctors make errors of judgement and treatment which turned out to be painful for me. I have never held this against any of them and they all remained my doctors and my good friends. They shouldered the blame and the whole responsibility for treatments that worked badly. . . . It never occured to them, as it did to you, to cast all the blame for their mistakes on me. Because of my doctors' genuine regrets at their mistakes, I was made to work all the harder to get well, if for no other reason, to show them my abiding confidence. The worst part about this whole affair with you was that I was not only badly disabled but had to bear the added mental discomfort of your putting the blame on me.[44]

Walter Dandy's rigidly scientific mode was not without fault in this disastrous episode, and the conflict between Mitchell and her physician typifies perhaps irresolvable conflicts about the nature of healing and medicine: Dandy on the one side representing an aggressively technological approach, with the patient on the other desiring something more personal, humane, and holistic. Otherwise, however, the affair was a virtual caricature of Mitchell's old pattern of sickness and her relations with physicians. When Dandy refused to accept Mitchell's symptoms after the operation, she fled back to her old Atlanta doctors. From them she got much of what she wanted. They told her her pain had somatic origins. She found that triply comforting. Her illness was not her fault; she was relieved of that guilt; and they blamed the trouble on Dandy. They found "operative trauma," Mitchell related, in addition to "ten years' compression" on the sciatic nerve. These doctors "comforted" her, too, in contrast to Dandy's scientific counsel.[45] "Thanks to the Atlanta doctors who tried the 'palliatives' you said would be of no value," she stormed to Dandy, her health had improved. "The assistance given me by these doctors was almost invaluable for it gave me back some part of a normal life at a time when I seemed doomed to invalidism."[46]

If the dreadful encounter with the experts at John's Hopkins confirms old patterns in Margaret Mitchell's life, it also radically altered her last years. Both sitting and standing agonized her. She required all sorts of paraphernalia to reduce her pain, like footstools and cushions of various designs. Actually she had relied on such devices for twenty years or more, but after 1943 she considered them indispensible for even minimum comfort. Furthermore, because of her reluctance to lug all these props about with her, not to mention the new pain itself, she felt constrained to curtail her social engagements and public work. She had gone under Dandy's knife in order to *expand* her activities, she declared, but the opposite had resulted: "While in discomfort constantly, I had been able to sustain a program of work in handling my personal business and helping in war activities that would have fazed a commando," she summarized her condition before the operation. "I was handicapped and in discomfort, but I was able to do a man-sized job."[47] Now her very flesh rejected her weary load. She struggled on, but about the time of the launching of the second *Atlanta*, she decided she had to cut her activities from the width of the cloth she had, "not the one I'd like to own," she said. "I have hardly seen anyone. I am unable to get about very much or stay up very long. . . . When night comes, I am too done in to have company."[48]

Her life changed. The author never became a recluse, but this state of affairs did force her to rely increasingly on herself and John. The operation wrought mental changes, too. Early on she could still jest about her condition. "I got home the day before yesterday and stood the trip very well," she wrote on April 21. "I've been able to sit up half of the day, strapped up in a brace which improves my figure below the waist but does nothing for me above, as thirty pounds below the waist have been displaced to the north. John says with the addition of a few medals I'd be a dead ringer for General Goering."[49] The wit and grace and charm never left her, but another Margaret asserted herself increasingly with the pain and anxiety after 1943. Generosity leached from her life. Her bitter reaction to the operation spread across her existence. And just as she might have been improving, John Marsh fell apart. His near-fatal illness confirmed, finally and irrevocably, his wife's primary role as toter of bedpans.

John Marsh, of course, was ailing as perpetually as his wife and father-in-law, if seldom so disastrously. *Gone with the Wind* undermined his strength further. In the fall and winter of 1935–1936, he had spent as much time and energy on the manuscript as the author herself, and the labor drained him as thoroughly as his wife. As his wife's front man, too, he wrote the long, protesting letters to the Macmillan Company over the movie contract and took her part in the violent and tedious negotiations that followed. As a professional public relations expert, he worked assiduously to control her image in the press and public media as her reputation spiraled to Lindbergh-like heights after 1936.[50] He acted as her shield, too, against ravenous publicity hounds.

One typical incident occurred in 1938 when Mitchell was entertaining a Danish tourist as a part of her Copenhagen publisher's sales promotion. The *Atlanta Constitution* wanted photographs. She refused. She even hid herself in one of the dining rooms in the Athletic Club behind locked doors to avoid the flashbulbs. Marsh intervened to sweet-talk the journalists. "Spare the little girl Lindbergh's fate," he pled. His appeals won no friends. The resulting story mocked his efforts. Running an old photograph of the author, the newsman wrote a caption that summarized the ill will of the press: "Margaret Mitchell, author of 'Gone with the Wind,' photographed at a time when her husband John Marsh, a 'public relations' agent, permitted photographers full swing in picturing his talented wife."[51]

He also acted as his wife's informal business agent. In addition, after Macmillan returned the foreign copyrights to the author in the fall of 1936, she deeded them to her husband, and he managed the foreign rights exclusively. He continued to hold his full-time job as director of the publicity department at the Georgia Power and Light Company. It was a responsible position at any time, but the antimonopoly, antibusiness tendencies of the 1930s magnified the burdens of his office.

John Marsh seldom complained, but all this wore heavily on him. In 1937, his "bad digestion" went haywire, and surgeons called for the removal of his gallbladder. The doctors recommended three weeks' rest before he returned to work. A month afterward he lacked the strength to do more than trudge laboriously around the block at Seventeenth Street. Although he finally returned to work, his condition hardly improved. He struggled through the movie doings, but just barely. He took to bed immediately after with more strange symptoms. His ailment had its own pattern. Whenever he left the bed, the fever returned. He missed work as often as he appeared.[52] His wife grew frantic about his health.

In January 1940, Mitchell herself had checked into St. Joseph's for her long-deferred operation for her "intestinal adhesions"; the husband signed in almost simultaneously. Tests proved nothing. His illness baffled the doctors as thoroughly as his hiccoughing had thirteen years before. On April 1 he returned to work. The fever came back, too. Finally, later in the spring, his spouse insisted he take a leave of absence. The two of them decided to recuperate together: she from the operation of January 13, he from his mysterious fevers, both of them from the horror of tending the cranky, debilitated Eugene Mitchell and the chaos of *Gone with the Wind* affairs. They took off for the West, winding up with Clifford and Helen Dowdey in Arizona. By June, the couple had returned home, but John was still officially on leave. If better, he remained sickly.[53]

Between 1940 and 1942, John Marsh plugged along with no significant improvement in his health, but the war added immeasurably to his load. Within a month of Pearl Harbor, his hours at the office had already lengthened appreciably. His work escalated with the fighting. With increasing regularity, he did not even return home at night; home, he seldom slept in the bed but napped on a sofa in the living room. At the same time, in addition to all his other responsibilities, his civil defense duties demanded still more time and energy. With 130 people working under him and a raft of bureaucrats above, this job entailed the most strenuous and tedious negotiations. Meanwhile, he took almost equal turns with the Mitchells around his father-in-law's bedside between 1940 and 1944, and acted as nurse to his ever-ailing wife in her numerous bouts with illness. All the while, he still worked in partnership with her on all her business dealings. Overworked, overweight, underexercized, and a heavy smoker, John Marsh had a health profile that spelled disaster.

As the war ran down, so did his resistance. Soon after V-E Day, his old, strange, intermittent fever returned full blast. He laid off work, but his conscience drove him back. While the war's end decreased some of the family's obligations, it increased others, especially those to the book. The year's end brought little cheer. The author described their exhaustion as the couple struggled to take their annual vacation in December:

> John is just barely getting by at the office by working like hell on the days when his fever is down and crawling along on the days when it is high. This has not been a good six months for us, but then it has not been good for anyone. We are made happy very frequently by the return of our friends from all those strange far off places that used to be just spots on a map. Maybe by another year all of us will have gotten over the war fatigue.[54]

The couple finally straggled off to St. Simons Island on Christmas Eve, 1945. Their arrival boded ill: they stepped off the train in a cold drizzle and found no porters to carry their bags. John proceeded to lug their suitcases to their quarters. They finally settled in their rooms, but soon after, John collapsed with incapacitating chest pains. He suffered a massive heart attack. Eighteen months after her father's funeral, the author faced the likelihood of burying her husband, too. He had just turned forty-nine two months before. He credited her afterward with having saved his life. While she remembered some old first-aid techniques from something she had read long before, she also managed, more remarkably, to find a physician and get him there at that inauspicious hour of midnight on Christmas Eve.[55] The ambulance rushed him to the hospital in Brunswick, Georgia, and for weeks no one could predict whether he would survive or not. Mitchell registered at a hotel and lived at the hospital. It was the worst time of her life.

In mid-January of 1946, the doctors allowed his wife to return the invalid to Atlanta. He spent two more months in the hospital there, and the distressingly familiar routines of Eugene Mitchell's illnesses began all over again: the endless visitations, the sleepless nights, the numbing worry, the hopeless disruption of domestic schedules, and the perpetual search for nurses and orderlies. There was more, too. The Marshes' angry confrontation with doctors played a second performance.

After the attack, Mitchell had sought out "one of the best known doctors in the United States," she said, to help her husband. The cardiologist had prescribed a steady and increasing tempo of exercise to restore the husband's damaged heart. He advised that the patient could return to work around the first of May. Even in the best health the sedentary patient had avoided physical exertion. He overate and showed it, and he chain-smoked up to sixty cigarettes a day. The cardiologist's prescription, then, entailed a radical change in his life. Neither Marsh could make that adjustment. As he tried the new routine, his body rebelled. His condition deteriorated. The repudiation of the expert followed quickly. "Next time we will hire a veterinarian if one is available, for this doctor was full of the new idea of getting sick folks out of bed as soon as possible and setting them to exercising," the wife sneered.[56] "When I think of John's other doctor," she railed, "I feel that John and I should collaborate on a book, 'The Marshes and Their Mad Medicos.' "[57] They returned to their family doctor, who prescribed six months of bed rest. "I hope rest will accomplish more than exertion and badgering," she exclaimed soon after firing the cardiologist.[58] Their old physician gave them what they wanted; not least, according to the author, "sympathy and understanding."[59]

The family practitioner prescribed a regimen (if it could be termed as such) exactly in line with Mitchell's own conventional wisdom of how to deal with the sick. It called for total bed rest. John Marsh hardly put his feet to the floor—or even sat up in bed—for over a year after his coronary occlusion.[60] Mitchell had always equated weight with health, so a part of her prescription for his recovery included stuffing her husband with food. Snacking all day on chocolate bars and candy, he also managed to pack away "spoonbread for breakfast, apple pie for lunch, caramel pie and peppermint ice cream for supper." He gained an enormous amount of weight, so much that even his wife voiced concern. While the doctor took no steps to reduce his tremendous intake (nor to up his expenditure of calories), Mitchell herself put him on a mild diet. Characteristic of her, only after she began did she ask the physician if it were allowed. She did not stick to the routine, and after almost two years she joked about the rolls of fat that billowed behind his neck. He was the one, she chortled now, who resembled Goering, the Nazi air marshal.[61]

After two years of this treatment, John Marsh's condition remained unchanged, and the couple decided the disability was permanent. The physicians concluded he should never attempt hard work or subject himself to strain or deadlines again. In keeping with this judgment, on September 5, 1947, Marsh resigned his job at the Georgia Power Company. He was home for good now. Nursing him became the primary object of his wife's life and future. If he fretted of indigestion (naturally enough), she would hover over his bedside till dawn, watching every breath. She monitored his pulse and other vital signs like a true professional. She installed a buzzer by his bed, and its ring brought her racing through the apartment. With the continuing shortage of help, trained or otherwise, she also levered his bloated body about the bed and to the bathroom—this, despite her own ailing back.[62] Had she spent hours trying to divert her father? Entertaining her husband absorbed even greater numbers of her hours. She tried to get him interested in plants. She encouraged him to take up bird-watching. She rigged up bird-feeders outside his window and trekked regularly to the library and bookstores to find bird books for him to read. She set up a movie house at home for him. Renting a projector, she dispatched the building's ancient janitor downtown for films each day. Sometimes old friends joined them for the screenings, and these times provided virtually the only social life she had during all these years. "We had old Chaplins and some wonders like 'The Last Mile,' 'Scarface,' 'Hell's Angels,' *et cetera*" she told Helen Dowdey. "Machine guns rattle everynight here or the roar of the motors of 1918 Curtis Jennys deafen the neighbors or the tom-toms of 'South of Pago Pago' wake the echoes."[63]

As the author had not confronted enough with her own disabilities, her father's health, and her husband's near-fatal heart attack, she took on the burdens of still others in these hawk and buzzard times as she played sister-saint to her sick and dying employees, too. Near the war's end, physicians diagnosed her washerwoman of twenty years with terminal cancer, and the author spent weeks visiting her and trying to find space in the crowded charity wards of Grady Hospital for the dying woman. Mitchell attended her faithfully through her death in the late winter of 1947. Still closer to her heart, the faithful Bessie Jordan was quite as "poorly" as her employers. She had struggled through major illnesses in the mid-thirties with Mitchell in attendance. Only weeks after Mr. Mitchell died, she collapsed again. The author had a new nursing job on her hands. The doctors suspected meningitis, Mitchell wrote, and she spent weeks "savaging interns" on behalf of her servant.[64]

After major surgery, Jordan had limped back to the Mitchell-Marsh apartment, but the novelist spent as much time attending her servant as Jordan did tending the apartment itself. "I try to make her sit down in the middle of the morning and the middle of the afternoon and lie back and get a nap. Sometimes she does and sometimes she does not, but she does not appear tired whether she gets her nap or not," Mitchell wrote Jordan's daughter, Deon Ward, in the late summer of 1947:

> You know I am not going to let your mother wear herself out and I try to get Carr [the janitor who went for movies] up here to do any heavy lifting or mopping. Of course your mother gets around me sometimes

when I am busy about other things, but on the whole I keep her from straining herself.[65]

Only a little less than Jordan herself, the daughter Deon also had her troubles, and she became an additional object of the writer's solicitude. In the summer of 1946, when John was desperately ill, the washerwoman Carrie dying, and Jordan hospitalized, Deon Ward had appeared almost by magic in the Mitchell-Marsh apartment. She cooked, washed, hauled, and lifted. In the middle of all this, however, the young woman herself took sick. "Because I was so harrassed with many things, Deon did not mention to me that she was ill. . . ." Cancer, or so the doctors said, had struck again. At the height of all the other woes, in that dreadful summer of 1946, Mitchell nursed Bessie Jordan's daughter through the trauma of a mastectomy.[66] Nor did the novelist's caretaking end even here. When Ward moved from Atlanta to New York after the war, Mitchell, and her husband, too, kept in close contact. They wrote her long, chatty letters that described Bessie Jordan's health; they counseled her about things to do and see and how to take advantage of the city; and they kept themselves informed about the daughter's, and even granddaughter's, health and well-being.

Special bonds existed between these two families, black and white. The bonding worked two ways. If Mitchell felt the deepest obligation to Bessie Jordan and her kin, Jordan reciprocated fully. In 1936, she had published a tribute to her employer in the *Atlanta Journal*. In 1951, on the second anniversary of Mitchell's death, she repeated the gesture. The tribute began with a reference to Mitchell's estate. Besides a cash legacy, the novelist had lent Jordan money to buy a home, and by her will, she freed her servant of the obligation. By that time, these terms were common knowledge. Jordan began with recalling this bequest, but this assistance, she added quickly, shrank beside her employer's other generosities.

> She nursed us when we were sick. She gave clothes, she gave us trips North and South, she gave my granddaughter a trip to N. Y. in 1948 and had given her school clothes in July of 1949.
> I have not spent one week in her service that I did not receive a gift of some kind. She was a friend to everybody.

Jordan found analogies for describing Mitchell's life in religion. Her employer, she testified, personified the good Christian—she was a "person who always thought of herself last," she testified. "If there ever was a Home Missionary, she was one," Jordan continued:

> She Fed the Hungry.
> She gave drink to the Thirsty.

She clothed the Naked.
Sheltered the out of doors.
Ministered to the Sick and in Prison.[67]

    Bessie Jordan's essay would certainly have embarrassed the novelist, but for very different reasons that it might make the modern reader blush. The author cringed at publishing her private or domestic benevolence. She also did not consider these acts as benevolence *per se*, but rather a necessary function of the social role she played. She assumed virtually inviolable responsibilities towards the members of her wider family circle, her servants included. Jordan's memorial did no more than return the favor in the special reciprocity of an archaic relationship. Since the end of the war, events were undermining the social basis of the Jordan–Mitchell bonding. Deon Ward's move to New York City was only one tiny reflection of the radical changes going on within the Southern social order and regional race relations. The Mitchell–Jordan bonding may or may not have survived Dixie's racial turmoil, but the resolution of that crisis in favor of blacks' civil rights makes both the form and style of Bessie Jordan's praise seem all the more archaic or reactionary. The bond, however, was real and powerful for both parties during Mitchell's lifetime. It not only defined truth about Bessie Jordan and her relationship with her "dear employer," but also underlines an inexorable reality in Mitchell's life. "Grace, bounty, and generosity" fail to describe the complete Mitchell; still, her life must be understood in part at least within the traditional discipline of the Great Lady. That icon existed in regional mythology—which the author herself embodied in her fictional characters of Melanie Wilkes and Ellen Robillard. It also lived in her own history in her personal recollection of May Belle Mitchell. And as the author worked diligently at this role herself, her largesse took still other notable forms in these years. Her nursing, nurturing sense of being a great lady did not begin with medical crises, nor did it end there.
    Bessie Jordan's tribute in 1951 followed ritualistic formulae of Christian commendation. The novelist did, however, actually practice such virtues. Basically, the saucy Margaret Mitchell, even in her forties, was simply too irreverent to have set out purposefully to obey the admonitions of the Sermon on the Mount, yet "ministering to those in prison," for one thing, became a genuinely significant part of her life in these years. From early in her newspaper days, she had expressed the keenest concern for prisoners and convicts, and she seldom wrote better than when describing conditions in the ancient, intolerable Atlanta city jail, or when chronicling the adventures and misadventures of convicts and the accused in her articles for the *Journal*. From the time she first spoke to the prisoners in her war-bond drive, however, she made Atlanta's federal penitentiary and its inmates one of her cen-

tral concerns. She encouraged the prison magazine, *The Atlantan*. She organized and sponsored writing contests among the prisoners. She appeared regularly within this gray keep to honor the winners. Characteristically, too, she kept up with these fellows even after parole and liberation. One of these, by the name of Red Rudensky, typified the lot. Prison authorities described him as one of the most unreconciled and rebellious felons in the prison, but he also possessed considerable talent as a writer. Mitchell encouraged his gifts. Released from jail, he appeared at odd hours at the Marshes' door. She always took him in. She also answered all his letters, however odd and distant the return addresses. She went another mile beyond this. On one of his visits, Rudensky had sung the praises of a Minneapolis man; Charles Ward, who ran special programs for former offenders. The author then took it upon herself, in that ghastly summer of 1946, to write the Midwesterner and endorse Rudensky's tribute. She added her own commendation. "So often in these hurried days we only speak up when something has irritated us to the point of explosion," she began. "So seldom do we speak when we see something good. So forgive a stranger for speaking up and saying with Red Rudensky that if there were more people like Charles Ward there'd be fewer repeaters in the Federal Penitentiaries of this country."[68]

Her bounty overflowed to people she had never met and never expected to know in person. The list of such people Mitchell favored is almost endless.

In the darkening times of World War II, the "sister of charity" was on call like no other time in her life. Turning herself inside-out for the world, she suffered accordingly. Indeed, given the expanding fame and notoriety of her novel abroad, the whole world now literally beat a path to her apartment door. At the end of that pathway, many people discovered the same great lady that Red Rudensky and others honored. Many others discovered someone who might have been another character entirely. "Another Margaret," as Mitchell herself referred to her, still cohabited with the kindly nurse. The foreign business allowed both free rein.

XX

Wildcats of the World, Unite!

...a four-cornered dogfight of a piracy in Yugoslavia; the piracy in Belgium; the misappropriation of funds by my Spanish publisher and agent and my subsequent recapture of the funds; the mad rush to get money out of France before the devaluation of the franc, et cetera. Oh yes, and Miss Baugh reminds me of the three new contracts we signed . . . Slovakian, Yugoslavian, Palestinian. . . .

MARGARET MITCHELL TO GEORGE BRETT IN 1946[1]

W. A. R. Collins headed one of the venerable publishing houses of Britain—William Collins and Sons of Glasgow. In the spring of 1936, he received one of the galley proof copies of *Gone with the Wind*. He poured over every word of the manuscript and shared his enthusiasm with his wife. Her excitement matched his own. "Tremendously keen on it," he was determined to publish the English version. Unfortunately for Collins, other houses had the same idea. Although formal ties no longer existed between the British and American houses of the same name, Harold Macmillan, the firm's head, used every device at his disposal to finagle the contract. Collins would not concede. Crying foul, he pleaded his case to both Harold Latham and Harold Macmillan. In the process, he illuminated the book's universal appeal. "As you know," he innocently told them, "there are some books in which one gets interested personally and is very keen to publish

418

whether one thinks they will have a big sale or not, and I feel this way about *'GONE WITH THE WIND'*, although I think it should have a good sale."[2] Except for the pleasure of being one of the first Europeans to read the novel, poor Collins got nothing for his pains, while the future Prime Minister considered the publication of this novel one of the great coups of his career.

The enthusiasm of Macmillan, Collins, and Collins's wife matched the excitement that the first proofs had generated in the United States. Their affection also anticipated a public reception in England that very nearly matched the popular fervor for the book on the western side of the Atlantic. And all this presaged a more general passion on the Continent, throughout the European empires, and ultimately in every corner of the earth where the denizens read novels. Within a decade of the novel's first appearance, readers from Tokyo to Djakarta, Shanghai to Bombay, Capetown to Cairo, Oslo to Palermo, Minsk to Glasgow, and Mexico City to Valparaiso were as familiar with rural Clayton County, Peachtree Street, and the American Civil War as the most devoted aficionados of the novel in the States. This vast international readership brought joy, satisfaction, and cash to the author. It also added the most extraordinary complications to her life.

The English edition appeared four months after the American, and British reviewers already knew about the popular mania the novel had generated across the ocean. The furor made them skeptical. The book's great length also predisposed them against the epic. As Wilfrid Gibson of the *Manchester Guardian* wrote, "I could not help approaching a story told at such extravagant length, if not with active prejudice, at least with a passive misgiving." The reviewer for the *The Times of London* shared these biases. The actual reading dispelled their reservations. Turning the last page, Gibson wanted more, not less. "1,036 pages!" *The Times'* Ralph Strauss exclaimed. "Were they all necessary?" Yes! he concluded roundly. This was no ordinary, sentimental story of the American Civil War and the romantic Old South, he explained. It did something altogether new and created altogether fresh characters. If, like many American reviewers, *The Times'* Strauss dismissed the writing as "undistinguished," he proclaimed the novel's general structure "astonishingly" good. Throughout the book's massive length, he wrote, the narrative never flagged. As for the characters, while no author ever sketched a less lovely heroine, he conceded, the protagonist never failed to command the reader's absolute attention. "I do not wonder that so good a story is enjoying a huge success," he concluded enthusiastically. The *Guardian*'s review was just as lavish. "Strikingly original," Gibson had termed the conception of the two central characters; while the relations between them "are revealed with a sure touch, as subtle as it is ruthless," he continued. "And the innumerable characters black and white, morally or physically, in whose company these two work out their destiny, are drawn with an easy certainty." And he fell back on the same terms as the *Times* reviewer: astonishingly vital, he concluded. Again, as did many American journals, the *Guardian* gave the book a second notice, which, if anything, was still move lavish with praise: "Long as it is, the chronicle never becomes tedious; its style is smooth and it has unforgettable moments." It "can hardly be overpraised," the second notice said enthusiastically. Even after concluding the book, "the reader continues to be fascinated by the gradual and skillful development of the central character, with her strength and weakness, her generosities and meanesses. . . . GONE WITH THE WIND never falters."[3]

Thus the two most important newspapers in the British Isles simply confirmed the enthusiasm of reviewers in the United States. The British reception established the pattern for the book in Europe, and ultimately the rest of the world.

Like Harold Macmillan and William Collins, bookmen all over the Continent fell over themselves to gain publication rights. Editors liked the book for itself, as had Harold Macmillan and Collins, but now the likelihood of runaway sales and profits excited them even more. Furthermore, as in the United States, the excitement fueled itself. *Gone with the Wind* was a hot news item, not just copy for the literary pages. Taken altogether, all this guaranteed a market wherever the book was sold and in whatever language it was published. Whether counting in rupees, pounds, francs, or yen, booksellers and publishers smiled blissfully at the prospects. And they roared and pled and cajoled and promised, and finally lied and cheated, to publish this most extraordinary novel in their own countries. The beleaguered author watched the scramble with the dumbfounded expression (to use her term) of a gigged frog.

Through mid-fall of 1936, foreign publication inquiries came directly to the Macmillan offices in New York. Although a large, old firm, the publisher was ill prepared for such business. Without a regular department to handle such inquiries, the company lacked even regular procedures for farming out foreign contracts. Actually, the selling of the foreign publication rights repeated exactly the bargaining with Hollywood. The matter of agents arose again, and it produced, ultimately, the same difficulties as in the brokering of the film rights. Annie Laurie Williams had finagled her prize in the spring of 1936 to bargain with Hollywood; Marion Saunders repeated the pattern to broker the book abroad.

Marion Saunders had actually competed with Annie Laurie Williams to sell the dramatic rights, and while she lost on that count, she used her foreign contacts to appropriate the international field in the same way Williams did with Hollywood. Saunders never had any prior agreement with Macmillan, but when she appeared with contracts from foreign publishers, Macmillan signed. Saunders, George Brett explained much later, "was just one of a lot of literary agents but she seemed to be at the time the one literary agent who was working hardest in placing American books in the foreign markets in foreign languages."[4] Technically, Brett was right; the reality was rather different. Saunders pushed herself on the publishers, and simply crowded all competitors off the field. Macmillan accepted her *de facto* control. "It is understood that all offers from foreign publishers might be first submitted by me to the Macmillan Company and then, if they waive their rights in any particular country in favor of the Author, I will submit such offer to the Author," she informed Mitchell in the later summer of 1936. "This is my understanding with the Macmillan Company who have authorized me to proceed with the sale anywhere in the world except in England."[5] In the fall of 1936, when Macmillan returned all the foreign copyrights to the author herself, the agent had entrenched herself so deeply in the foreign business that Mitchell felt no alternative but to continue with her. Moreover, Saunders wangled a formal contract with Mitchell, where she had none with Macmillan. *De facto* control became *de jure*. She hornswoggled her adversaries even more effectively than the Texas roper Annie Laurie Williams.[6]

Although *Gone with the Wind* effectively sold itself, Saunders worked her end aggressively; too aggressively for some tastes. George Brett, for one, rued the day this person joined the Mitchell entourage. In the spring of 1940, for example, she hectored him to allow the Chilean publisher to sell his Spanish edition in Puerto Rico. Brett refused. This was U.S. territory, he replied, and for that reason, Macmillan turf, regardless of what language the inhabitants spoke. Moreover, he elaborated later, allowing any foreign edition legally into the United States compromised the American copyright, which, of course, Macmillan held. Saunders had no sympathy for this argument. "Dog in a manger," she complained to the company president. She accused him, too, he related, of "cheating the author out of royalties, that there was a market in Puerto Rico for a Spanish translation, and why couldn't I be gracious about it?" The case reached the author's ear, and ever vigilant about his wife's privileges, John Marsh took up the matter with the Macmillan president himself. Brett was piqued, not the least because, Iago-like, Saunders had now added new poison to the often-troubled author–publisher relationship. Brett fulminated to Marsh against this "agent who is trying to earn a very small commission and in the earning of it perhaps giving us a peck of trouble."[7] Worse lay in store.

Brett's rancor notwithstanding, Sanders's performance did not displease her employer. As if by magic, she generated foreign contracts all over the world. A contract for a Brazilian edition in Portuguese had just arrived, and a Latvian one was forthcoming, the author informed George Brett in the fall of 1938. Saunders "has been in Europe for six weeks and has visited every foreign publisher. I don't know how she gets about so fast, even with the aid of air transport. Doubtless, before she has returned she will have incited Icelanders, the Lithuanians and the Zionists of Palestine into issuing editions."[8] Icelandic? Lithuanian? Hebrew? Yiddish? The author considered these examples comically farfetched. She joked too soon. *Gone with the Wind* eventually found its way into more obscure tongues than these.

By 1941, Saunders had negotiated with innumerable publishers, and secured contracts with nearly a score of foreign presses. She did not win everywhere. In 1939, Mitchell discovered a Japanese publisher had produced a translation without her permission. By the time she received a letter from the translator, the book had already sold 150,000 copies. The Japanese, by treaty, were not bound to honor American copyrights, but Mitchell sicced Saunders on the pirates just the same. While no yen were ever forthcoming, Mitchell received instead "a very pretty silk kimono from the publishers and, shortly afterwards, a Japanese doll nearly three feet high in a red lacquer glass case about four feet high. . . . I was somewhat puzzled why I received these gifts," she related afterward. She found out shortly. "They wanted a picture of me standing by the Japanese doll so that they could use it for publicity purposes. A nation with so much gall certainly should go far," she reflected.[9] Mitchell kept her porcelain geisha as a reminder of the indignity. She christened her "Miss Oh So Solly," and after Pearl Harbor, she gave her to a Red Cross auction to raise money for one of her war-bond drives. She considered this a witty and fitting dénouement to the irritating affair.

The tremendous impact of her novel (pirated or not) in Japan always interested her. In 1940, she heard the rumor of a cinematic piracy of her novel in Japan, and while she deplored the theft, she also decided that she would really like to see such a movie. It would make a great theater, she insisted. "If they placed it back in the sixties, the Japanese Confederates would doubtless be marching forth to defend Atlanta in Samurai armor and Scarlett would be dashing about in a rickshaw instead of a buggy."[10] Mitchell had a great eye, and it would have made a perfect Kurasawa film. Actually, the great theater very nearly came to be, and after the war, the Japanese settled on a bizarre musical version with an all-female cast. The author was long dead by then; it would have amused her.

The Japanese, at least, kept her well informed of their nefarious doings. Not so the Chinese. She discovered a Mandarin piracy accidentally, upon receiving Chinese advertising pamphlets for the book. She secured a copy of the abomination later through her contact at the State Department, Dr. Wallace McClure.[11] After the war, a returned missionary in Augusta translated its effusive introduction. "I am sure you understand why my family has never let me forget the following part of the introduction: 'Miss Mitchell is pure, benevolent, filial and obedient to her husband,' " she laughed.[12] "I am interested to see that the Chinese have presented me with those traits which the Chinese consider attractive in a woman, and also that they have credited me with another highly thought of Chinese characteristic—that I am a perfect housekeeper."[13] This particularly inefficient housewife might well have been amused at the description.

Fighting multiple piracies in China and inadequate international copyright protection in Japan hardly defined the limit of the author's international business. Each year before the war brought some new hassles, as with the Bulgarian case.

> Not in my wildest imaginings did I think the Bulgarians would be interested in my book, especially when the threat of war hangs over their heads. But some months ago I heard that a publisher was bringing out an unauthorized edition. I believe it was translated into Bulgarian from the French translation, and I am appalled to think what a sea change my book has suffered!

Leaping into battle, Saunders won a contract out of the company in Sofia, but immediately the publisher wrote privately asking to be relieved of royalty payments to Mitchell. "It appeared from his letter that it was not the custom of 'great authors' to charge Bulgarian publishers money for translations."[14] The Atlantan groaned anew. Then problems arose in Estonia. The grapevine carried word that an edition was appearing; Saunders got on the case; but the Russians invaded in the meantime. "We do not even know if the edition *was* published. Moreover, the matter is complicated by the Russians, for we do not know what, if any, rights we have or can enforce in the face of Russian domination." In the same letter to her helpful correspondent McClure, Mitchell also catalogued a series of other foreign difficulties. A Greek newspaper serialized the novel without release; Saunders went into action with the Greek consul in New York; and the Athenians gave in, except to disagree about the royalties that the author wanted.[15] Mitchell once described her battles with international copyrights as fighting fire and killing snakes. Just as she extinguished the flames in Athens, she heard hissing in the Caribbean. A Cuban newspaper, *Diario de la Marina*, was also publishing the novel in regular installments: into the breach again. Then a Chilean piracy case proved to be both fire and snakes.[16]

Fighting fire and killing snakes—still, it was not all horror. Even the pirated editions brought some pleasure. She installed all of them, authorized and otherwise, in one bookcase in her apartment, and before the war, few months passed that she did not add a new one. In 1939, she added the French edition[17] and discussed its relative merits with

Harold Latham, to whom, in gratitude, she also sent copies of all her translations. "I have not had the chance to read much of it, but a few phrases here and there have delighted me," she told her friend:

> Gerald saying "oo, la la!" was especially amusing; when the "Clayton County Wildcats" became "les chats sauvages de Clayton" I felt some consternation; I especially liked the way Aunt Pittypat's "swoon bottle" became "la bouteille aux vapeurs." I understand the feelings of Clarence Day when he was reading a French Bible and discovered that when the Lord waxed wroth he merely became "irrité."[18]

As a matter of business, Mitchell followed closely the sales and publication of her book abroad, but the epiphenomena of foreign publication fascinated her for itself. Her response to the Danish edition was typical of her interest. Published initially in the fall of 1937, the first Danish edition numbered 10,000 copies; it sold out in eleven days and went into a second printing immediately. In a country of fewer than one million, the publisher anticipated eventual sales of 40,000 copies.[19] Mitchell quoted her Danish publisher with mingled pleasure and incredulity. No book had sold anything near these figures before in Denmark, he told her. He added: "We are glad to note daily that your book's fame penetrates every social stratum and that its title also in Danish 'Borte med Blaesten' has been used everywhere for every possible occasion even in our churches f. inst. in the inaugurating solemnities when our parliament commenced its sessions this fall."[20]

As her novel penetrated obscure provinces of the world, so did the legends about the author. They, too, fascinated and amused her. The Chinese tales of her domestic felicity were neither the first nor last of these. She had often discussed the folk myths of her relationship with Harold Latham, and now those stories took on incredible new life abroad. "Harold, our literary legend has crossed the ocean and has suffered a sea change into something very rich and something exceptionally strange, especially in the French papers," she told her old friend. She shared with him the variety of the tales. One version, she related,

> is that I had creeping paralysis and it crept and crept but somehow I managed to stay two jumps ahead of the creeps and finished the book. Miraculously I recovered on its completion. My faithful husband and my faithful old black Bessie (This is a literal translation) cried, "Voilà, a masterpiece!" My husband felt that this book was more than a symptom of the disease. (You figure that one out. I can't.) He stole it from me and went to New York. In practically no time une auto puissante drew up in front of a beautiful home my husband had bought for me, and a dashing gentleman said to the old and faithful and black Bessie, "Announce to madame the presence of monsieur Harold S. Latham, Vice President and Editor of the Macmillan Publishing Company." This well prepared editor

also whipped a contract out of his pants pocket. I cannot get the next idiom, but it appears that I went into lady-like vapours, but my husband spoke to me with kindness and firmness and, like an obedient wife, I signed a contract just prior to a long swoon.[21]

She could laugh about all these matters before the war; that conflict changed everything after 1939. The period after 1940 was worse still. The disruptions of the fighting cut deeply into the manufacture and sales of the book almost everywhere abroad. To the author's dismay, editors and publishers disappeared in coups and purges and in the seizure of Jews for the concentration camps. Her Polish publisher was Jewish; he disappeared, she grieved, without a trace. Around 1941, the Nazis also banned *Gone with the Wind* from all the territories under their control. The proscription only ended the book's legal sales; underground it circulated as merrily as ever. She exercised even less control than the Nazis over the clandestine printings of her novel, its black market sales, and its secret circulation.

American entry into the war further disrupted her foreign business. By the end of 1942 and the beginning of 1943, however, Mitchell's foreign accounts began to trouble her for other reasons. Her foreign income slowed more than she deemed reasonable even in wartime. Something did not seem right. Marion Saunders fell under a cloud. Mitchell's suspicions peaked in the summer of 1943. She hired an independent auditor. More trouble. The agent had been keeping double books. The war had disrupted Saunder's foreign business, and to keep her agency afloat, she had skimmed Mitchell's royalties.[22] The discovery could have come at no worse time. In April of 1943, Mitchell had just returned from her disastrous experience at Johns Hopkins. Grievously ill and bitterly hostile to her physicians, she also carried the burden of caring for her (perpetually) dying father in his last, disastrous year of life. All this notwithstanding, she now entered the arena with her agent. She weighed legal proceedings. She longed to slug it out with the perfidious Saunders. Her husband dissuaded her. "If we had brought any legal action against her, it would have brought down on Peggy the whirlwind of publicity that always follows anything that puts her into the newspapers. That," he declared, "would have been too much to bear. The added harassment of letters, telegrams, newspaper interviews, phone calls, and other inevitable complications of such a situation, would have been an unbearable burden on top of many other very heavy burdens."[23]

Even without redress in the courts, resolving the Saunders matter demanded time and energy enough from the hard-pressed novelist. Through lawyers and accountants, the contending parties worked out an official agreement, which eliminated Saunders completely from the novelist's affairs. With the resolution of one difficulty, however, others took its place. Mitchell entered still another phase of woe. Completely turned off by agents, she now decided to manage her own affairs directly and assumed primary responsibility for negotiating all foreign contracts or delegated it to John, to whom she had legally granted the foreign rights. Checking into a lunatic asylum might have made more sense. Also, just as she assumed the responsibility of being her own agent, her foreign business accelerated. New tides of interest in her novel accompanied every liberation of territory from the retreating armies of the Third Reich, and each surge posed new problems for the author.

Not all of Mitchell's new problems waited for V-E Day. In the fall of 1944, she heard reports that her French publisher, Gaston Gallimard of Nouvelle Revue Française, had collaborated with the Germans. Was it true, she needed to know first of all; and if it were, she wondered, how would it affect her French contracts, her legal rights in France and its empire, and even her novel's reputation in the French-speaking world?[24]

As with the affair in France, German defeat revealed the full extent of the chaos in her affairs in nation after nation. "The fiends of hell" might have dreamed up the difficulties, the author groaned in November 1945.[25] Then, with John's heart attack the next month, she assumed full responsibility for all her business affairs. "Like trying to swim where a dyke has been dynamited,"[26] she moaned. The problems had no end. Some of her publishers had become refugees; others had gone underground with the Resistance; others had simply disappeared, and she needed to find their legal heirs. Sifting through all this rubble of European civilization required the patience of Job and the inventiveness of a multilingual Sherlock Holmes.[27] Sometimes publishers sought her out, but they wrote to the disgraced Marion Saunders or to Macmillan. Letters got waylaid when in the best of circumstances international mail was slow. Besides clearing up old business, she also faced a welter of new inquiries and entreaties for publication rights.

One can hardly calculate the complexities of these affairs. Consider the German case. Before the war, *Gone with the Wind* had sold very, very well in the edition printed in Hamburg by H. Goverts Verlag. Before proscription, sales reached probably over 250,000. Only Great Britain exceeded this figure. The market for German editions, of course, included far more than Germany proper. It extended to Austria, Switzerland, and indeed throughout much of Eastern Europe. As soon as the war ended, her publisher, Dr. Henry Goverts, had written her from Liechtenstein confirming that he was alive, acknowledging his debts for royalties, and naming the bank that held Mitchell's funds. International law held the prewar contract was still binding, and Mitchell liked Goverts in any case. He had dealt honorably with her; his mother was English; and he had supposedly opposed Hitler "—but then I understand, oddly enough, that there is not a Nazi in all of German today," she added sardonically.[28]

However eager to resolve her German problem, Mitchell was stymied. Federal law circumscribed her ability to trade with the Germans before a formal peace was concluded; meanwhile, both military and civilian bureaucracy created a nearly impossible maze of regulations. The State Department had one set of rules. The United States Office of Military Government (USOMG) had another. Then, too, as her publisher had operated out of Hamburg (which lay in the British Zone of Occupation) she felt constrained to run through a comparable set of English officialdom. The rules changed with fair regularity and different individuals in all this bureaucratic maze offered their own counsel, often in the craziest contradiction of official regulations—and one another. "I understand from the best advice I can get that I must not discuss business with a former enemy until a peace treaty is signed; then I am informed, by supposedly competent authorities, that I may discuss business but must not discuss money," she groaned. Also, as individuals moved in and out of the system with maddening frequency, the advice she got zigged and zagged with every shift in personnel. When she found one especially helpful military bureaucrat, she assumed he had probably resigned his commission and returned Stateside as soon as he signed her letter, "and that a cretin has been assigned to take his place—and I do not mean a native of Crete either."[29] The tangle had no end. One agency of the government recommended making a contract with a new publisher. She wrote the State Department to make sure. State did not object, but recommended she confirm with Simpson at the War Department. If the Pentagon concurred, she had her connection in the USOMG; he, then, could intercede between Goverts, the British, and her. But even this arrangement, she feared, was probably optimistically simple-minded:

> I note that the War Department is giving up this sort of business July 1st. It is very likely I will *not* get permission by July 1st for my correspondent Major Peebles will have come home, Mr. Simpson will have disappeared, and I will have to start all over again, doubtless with the United States Department of Wildlife.[30]

She might have cut through all the maze and simply written directly to Goverts, but her old legalism and commitment to propriety prohibited this move. She sanctioned no course that knowingly violated the legal injunction against trading with the enemy. Unknowingly, she reminded George Brett, she and he had already violated such regulations. "For a few brief minutes I saw you and me standing against a brick wall bravely waving away the eye bandages. Then I cheered up as I recalled that after all I am a Democrat and my type of Democrats are beginning to be stylish again," she joshed the arch-Republican president of Macmillan, "and maybe I would get life imprisonment and so have the time to write another book. But, George, I couldn't see much hope for you, and I am afraid a firing squad is just around the corner."[31] Given Mitchell's old ill-feeling against the company president, she might well have smiled at imagining Brett against this wall.

By the spring of 1947, she had waded through the Teutonic swamp for almost two years. She had nothing to show for her labors. But these problems did not exhaust the difficulties even of her German business. At one point, she learned that the USOMG itself planned to republish her novel in Germany—without so much as a fare-thee-well to Goverts or herself. When she first heard about the idea, she had no information on whether these excerpts were to be in German or in English. If the possibility of a new translation raised problems, the presence of an English version printed in Berlin promised nightmares. She had no idea who owned the English rights outside of England and the United States. Was it Macmillan-U.S.A. or Macmillan-Britain? Or were they still her property? She dreaded new legal tangles. But such an edition piled still more obligations on the novelist, for she demanded that everything in the excerpted edition conform exactly to the original in spelling, punctuation, sequence, and all the rest.

> I must explain that sentences and paragraphs cannot be taken from their context and placed in paragraphs in another chapter to give an entirely new meaning. I must insist that when deletions and omissions are made they must be indicated. I must be firm that they cannot take an idea from "Gone with the Wind" and quote it to prove something which it was never intended to prove. I must go into detail about why they cannot be permitted to quote enormously long segments, as The Macmillan Company and I are not in business for our health. . . .[32]

She foresaw other difficulties with this project. The USOMG presented the re-publication as a means of advancing constitutional government in Germany. If she refused, she wondered, only half in jest, would she be culpable of obstructing American policy? This set her on another tack. "I think 'Gone with the Wind' is not exactly the best book for the re-education of the Germans," she noted:

> One of the reasons it was so amazingly popular [before the war] was, as a number of Germans told me, because it gave a picture of the defeat of a people whose cause was just (the Confederates) and how those people eventually and by their own efforts fought their way back to their rightful place in the sun. Some of the Germans identified themselves with the Confederates to a degree which made my blood run cold. The psychology of proud and beaten people is probably the same anywhere in the world.[33]

The prospect of a U.S. government–sanctioned edition was, all in all, simply too painful to contemplate. She had, however, a Confederate ace in the hole if worse came to worst. Thank God, she sighed, General Lucius Clay was a Georgia boy—from Marietta, no less! If she did not know the commander of the American occupying forces personally, she was friendly with his Atlanta family. "I somehow feel that General Clay, whose home was in the path of Sherman's troops and who had a battle practically in his front yard, would look kindly upon any request I might make for assistance in protecting my German language rights."[34]

Resolution of the problem could not wait indefinitely. The constant and growing threat of piracies added urgency to all these deliberations and negotiations. As 1946 slid into 1947, every other mail seemed to bring new requests for new editions in German: from Germany itself, Austria, Switzerland, and even Sweden. The demand for the book was outrunning her control. Experience had taught her what to expect. "I have developed a sort of sixth sense about piracies, unauthorized dramatizations, swiped serializations et cetera," she noted in the spring of the new year:

> I know when I refuse permission for publication or dramatization to a certain number of people and over a certain length of time, the steam in the boiler inevitably rises and busts the top off, and I have a pirated edition to fight. During the past few months I have become more and more nervous about this situation, for the German language rights do not apply only to Germany but to almost all of Middle Europe, where German is the second language.[35]

Such problems pestered her up through the last year of her life. Three years after the German surrender, she still wrestled with the difficulties. Her publishers could not publish in the American Zone because of the critical paper shortage. They requested then the privilege of completing the work in Switzerland. This meant, however, going through an entirely new set of copyright procedures and all the rest. Worse still, the American authorities considered it a "new contractual agreement" that demanded she pursue the matter all the way up through the impossible channels of the USOMG again. Were it not for the pleas of her German publisher and the constant threat of piracies, she groaned, she would toss in the towel. Still, for all this, by the fall of 1948, her German publisher registered twelve-year sales of 368,629 copies.[36]

Fighting fire and killing snakes. Something new appeared perpetually to challenge her reserves of strength and energy, and even her imagination. The request for a Bengali edition failed to faze her. Routine stuff for the postwar world, the Indian letter hardly merited a second thought.[37] It was routine, at least, compared to the mindboggling Ukrainian episode, which she described to George Brett:

A publisher in Innsbruck, Austria, British Zone (nationality unknown) requested Ukrainian translation rights many months ago and I sent him a contract. . . . I was unable to understand what this Austrian publisher intended to do with a Ukrainian translation when the Russians would not permit the book within the Soviet boundaries. While the publisher has not answered me yet or signed the contract, we have about figured out that this book is probably to be sold in Western Canada, where there is a large Ukrainian population.[38]

If Europe was a publishing nightmare, it hardly exhausted her problems, for the whole world wanted her book. As early as 1936, she had fought a Chilean piracy of the novel. She thought the problem licked, only to see it rise again like Lazarus just after the war. By 1948, her Chilean publisher, Empressa Ercilla, was writing anguished and indignant letters about the importation of editions printed in Spain itself. The author intervened at once.[39] Not long after she had straightened out the Spain–Chile issue, she discovered another representative problem. Perusing *Time Magazine* in December 1948, she discovered a review of a new Macmillan book, *Literary History of the United States.* The notice made passing reference to "how 'Gone with the Wind' was garbled in Japanese." It set her on her ear. She hated the idea of poor translations; also, she was just then negotiating a Japanese contract. Was the rumor true? Was her novel really garbled in Japanese? Which version of her work was garbled? Was this one of the pirated versions of a decade ago? Was this pirate the publisher of her authorized version? Would her authorized edition be garbled just the same? Each question demanded her attention.

Then there was the issue of serialization. Newspaper serialization, even abroad, had the most far-reaching ramifications. Importation of the serializing journal into the United States, for example, challenged the American copyright held by the Macmillan Company. For this reason, Macmillan vigorously resisted Mitchell's exercising her rights abroad to sanction reprinting the novel in the popular press. It happened anyway. In Argentina, Greece, Cuba, and elsewhere, newspapers simply printed it. These constituted piracies, and Mitchell sent out her minions to defend her rights, usually by negotiating a contract after the fact. In France, however, *France-Soir* pestered her almost endlessly after the war for serialization rights. She hated the idea, largely because of more copyright difficulties. While the politics of the matter softened her refusal and she finally acceded, still, she insisted on a contract so difficult that she anticipated no one would be willing to sign.[40] She guessed wrong one more time, and soon thousands and thousands of the French were following her beaux and belles in weekly installments from Marseilles to Calais.

Only about ten months before she died, *Harper's* planned a story on her epic and its equally epic sales abroad. The reporter asked Mitchell for a rundown. She had never totted up the figures, she related, and when she did, she did not feign amazement. "When I read them, it does take my breath away and makes me feel humbler than you can imagine," she wrote. She then summarized the totals for the magazine.

Brazil (last report through June 1948)	25,785
Chile	61,171
Belgium (French language); through December 1947)	20,000
Belgium (Flemish; 1945)	7,000
Bulgaria (through March 1945)	8,000
Czechoslovakia (Czech language; 1948)	84,000
Czechoslovakia (Slovak; Aug.–Nov. 1947)	5,000
Denmark (through 1948)	90,000
Finland (through April 1948)	50,000
France (through February 1948)	172,641

(In March my French publisher put on sale an edition of 80,000 copies, to be followed by another edition of 50,000. He wrote that he already had a guaranteed sale of three-fourths of the 80,000 edition. I will not have a report on this for four months or so, so I hardly know whether to include these figures in the total or not. My agent in France informs me that the book is having an excellent sale, helped along by the current serialization in a French newspaper.)

Germany (through 1948)	368,629
Holland (through June 1948)	48,549
Hungary (through February 1947)	56,902
Italy (through June 1948)	81,132
Latvia (through June 1948)	2,453
Norway (through 1939)	47,356
Rumania (through March 1947)	20,000
Spain (through 1947)	25,047
Sweden (through 1947)	67,363
Yugoslavia (through March 1948)	4,665
Poland (through March 1948)	5,500

The Polish sales, she noted, covered only the period after the war. She had no report on the prewar edition, she added, "because my publisher was liquidated." For China and Japan, she had no proper figures because of the piracies, but with numerous editions in each nation, informal reports suggested hundreds of thousands of copies were circulating in both Asian countries. A Palestinian edition existed, too, but the outbreak of the war in the Middle East had prevented reports from this edition. Although she kept no reports on English sales, her published noted the British had manufactured 716,048 books by December 1948.[41]

The simple sales figures for each country were extraordinary, but for Mitchell herself, these figures gave only the tiniest hint of her foreign labor and engagements. Take the Yugoslavian number. What stories lay behind the 4,000 copies sold! Four publishers had fought for the rights to publish her in that country. While they fought one another, they all assumed the novel lay in the public domain, so they fought the author, too. She had negotiated with all of them and mediated between them while defending her own rights. These negotiations opened another front with all manner of officialdom. "It was a merry affair while it lasted, with the embattled Yugoslavs, the United States Embassy, OWI [Office of War Information] in Belgrade and Rome, and me, at home," she wrote afterward.[42] But there were other stories. She had found it necessary to rustle up translators for her letters to and from the Yugoslavs as well, and she won a new set of acquaintances in Atlanta among native speakers of Serbo-Croatian (among other alien tongues). The problems did not end here, of course, even with the contract finalized. In 1947, she did not even know if the book had been printed, and she feared to ask after Marshall Tito's victories and the Communists' success soon after the agreement had been settled. With the Communists' antipathy to her work, she feared for the safety of her Yugoslavian contacts. "If the project was abandoned out of deference to Russia's dislike for 'Gone with the Wind,' I wouldn't want the matter brought up for fear that it would bring my publisher to the attention of the authorities and perhaps get him into trouble."[43] Amidst all this hassling, Mitchell also discovered her publisher was a woman, which pleased her all the more. The book was printed; it did sell; and though Mitchell never asked, the publisher sent her the figures of those sales. All this lay behind the simple number, "4,665 copies sold."

A thousand other issues also engaged the author's greatest interest and attention; the printing, sales, and reception of her book abroad in the uproar of postwar days. She puzzled over the book's popularity abroad only slightly less than she wondered at its appeal to domestic audiences. Foreigners wrapped themselves up in the novel the same way Americans did. "I am sure I will never get a cent out of the Balkans, and nothing except a headache," Mitchell noted in 1946. "However, I do get the information that Roumanians and Bulgarians are not very different from Mississippians and New Englanders."[44] Readers abroad liked the book, it seemed, for most of the same reasons they adored it in the United States. "It is the sense of character and the art of presenting personality that give her tale its astonishing vitality," The *Manchester Guardian* reviewer had proclaimed; "her people are really alive; they are . . . living people. . . ." Mitchell's characters engaged readers in translation quite as much as in the original English.

If devotees abroad loved the novel for the same reasons as Americans, they also manifested their affection in much the same ways: longing, for example, for a happy ending just as passionately as folks did on the western shores of the Atlantic. And this, of course, produced its own train of events, not all of which delighted the beleaguered author.

> All the maddening rumors I had to undergo in the United States some years ago simply went underground and, as soon as peace came, burst forth in Poland, Roumania, Bulgaria, Czechoslovakia et cetera. I keep getting letters from publishers and agents wanting the "rest of 'Gone with the Wind'" or the "end of 'Gone with the Wind.'" . . . They will not believe me when I write that the book was ended where it ended. Then, simultaneously several people in Roumania got to me through the OWI with the news that they were dramatizing "Gone with the Wind." All were full of enthusiasm and violent emotions. One of them was making Abraham Lincoln the hero of his version of "Gone with the Wind." Franklin Roosevelt was the hero of a lady dramatist, and for all I know President Truman is hero of a third. . . .[45]

It was the same in France two years later, where, she wrote in 1948, "it has come to my attention that a magazine, as a publicity stunt, has opened a competition with prizes for the four or five 'best last chapters to *Gone with the Wind.*'" She continued:

> Sometimes John and I are forced to laugh, though with little mirth, at how the same reaction to "Gone with the Wind" appears in widely separated countries, shows that people are not too different after all. Each person who turns up with the bright idea of writing a "last chapter" to bring two loving hearts together thinks he or she is the only person in the world who ever thought of a "last chapter."[46]

The reception of the work abroad also prompted her wonderment at her novel's ability to absorb various political meanings. From the outset of her fame, the author had steadfastly and even adamantly scorned political, ideological, or similar "hidden meanings" for her novel. It was just a story, she insisted. She repudiated any larger themes except for the fairly neutral one of "survival," which she defined as the record of who goes under in a time of crisis, who hangs on, and who sails through with colors flying. She never completely abandoned this view, but the exigencies of war helped alter her conception.

A decade before, during the Spanish Civil War, she noted, "Americans fighting on *both* sides wrote that English editions had been read aloud at night in the camps and each side, feeling their cause was just, identified themselves with the Confederates." She told another correspondent that, while American reviewers had concentrated upon the narrative or the love interest, European critics focused on its element of " 'universal historical significance.' " Her correspondent in this case was none other than the loathed Malcolm Cowley, and she certainly wanted to prove the larger significance of her work. Still, she argued soundly:

> Each nation applied to its own past history the story of the Confederate rise and fall and reconstruction. French critics spoke of 1870, Poles of the partitioning of their country, Germans of 1918 and the bitterness which followed, Czechs wrote not only of their troubled past but of their fears of the future, and I had letters from that country just before it went under, saying that if the people of the South had risen again to freedom the people of Czechoslovakia could do likewise. The Brazilian reviews and letters were especially interesting, as the Brazilians discovered for almost the first time that they had something in common with North America. Brazil has its "North and South," one agricultural and the other industrial. They also had slavery and emancipation with economic chaos following the freeing of the slaves.[47]

During the war and increasingly afterward, Mitchell also came to attach distinct political meaning to what she had written. It was a book about freedom, she declared. When she heard the story of Hitler's having seized the only copy of Selznick's film in Europe, she wondered what he thought of it at his rumored private showing. Her story "about a conquered people who became free again" was hardly good propaganda, she judged, for Germany and Nazi-held territories.[48] For the same reasons, the novel's popularity with the Resistance also made perfect sense to her. In Poland, she had heard, the novel was especially appreciated by the underground, who used *Gone with the Wind* for " 'morale-building purposes.' "[49] She got the same stories about to the French Resistance. "I have found that the French people read 'Gone with the Wind' during the German occupation, and liked it above all other books," she reported. She gloried in the story from another correspondent, a Southerner living in France at the time. "They all ask me about the book and the author, Margaret Mitchell," he reported; "they published it secretly, distributed it through the underground, and passed it on to one another—many people reading a single copy." Mitchell later came into possession of one of these tattered editions. She treasured it and the idea, too. "It made me proud and happy," she wrote the original owner, "to know that something I wrote could give pleasure and comfort to French people during the occupation."[50] "It was anti-Fascist during the occupation of European countries by the Germans, and now it is being anti-communist,"[51] she mused in 1948. Skeptical initially, she was increasingly pleased with these political identities after the war. Indeed, the war expanded Mitchell's own ideological consciousness and encouraged her to accept the politicization of her work. After V-E Day, her patriotism flowered into a virulent anti-Communism, but even this violent Americanism fit the other patterns of her life after 1944. Sometimes the alterations were subtle, sometimes gross, but with the war, her operation, the Marion Saunders affair, her father's death, and John's heart attack, the bias of her character shifted. In the last five years of her life, she snarled as often as she smiled.

XXI

A Strange, Dark Country

> I suppose they don't know that I never have been frightened by
> people being large or rich and have never ducked out of a fight
> either. It's a pity I never had the opportunity to give wide publicity
> to the very long legal fight I undertook in Holland and the way I
> wiped out the old lady who sued me for plagiarism and how I took
> Billy Rose through the cleaner and various other people who dam-
> aged me or tried to damage me.
>
> MARGARET MITCHELL TO HAROLD LATHAM [1]

*I*n September 1941 when she christened the first *Atlanta*, she had
appeared neat and trim in the smart khaki of a Red Cross worker's uniform. She smiled broadly and waved jauntily as she
boarded the train for the launching. Three years later at the launching
of the second *Atlanta*, a full-length mink coat did nothing to obscure
the nearly forty additional pounds that now encumbered her small
frame. She glowered at the camera from behind an armful of roses
almost as big as she.

She had changed.

The alteration in her physical appearance was nothing compared with
the changes in her attitude in the forties. In *Gone with the Wind* Mitchell described how Gerald's character came increasingly to dominate
the heroine's as Scarlett drifted farther and farther from her mother's
model. This process was reflected in Mitchell's own last years. Conservative and punctilious, suspicious and resentful, narrow and legal-
istic, Eugene Mitchell displayed these traits more as he aged and ailed.

So did his daughter. Although her altruism, grace, and wit hardly disappeared, other smaller, meaner emotions crowded the writer's life. Skepticism and distrust bloomed like malignant flowers in her character. Rigidity and dogmatism assumed new places in her life and letters. Even her humor waned. She still reacted in the old generous way, but bitterness and resentment scurried beneath the rock of her bounty. When she had written Charles Ward, Red Rudensky's friend, for example, to commend his work with ex-convicts, she had opened her letter to this stranger with the justification, "So often in these hurried days we only speak up when something has irritated us to the point of explosion." She herself now exploded often. For all her genuine and compelling kindness and altruism, Margaret Mitchell was capable of towering fury and determined vengefulness when she felt wronged or trodden on. "I have always felt that people who would not fight for what they had deserved to lose it. So, I intend to keep fighting," she maintained.[2] She retrained herself effectively as a lawyer, and litigation became a favorite sport.

Increasingly after 1941 and still more militantly after 1943, combat dominated her life. The times were grim; her mood matched. With her father's fatal sickness, her own debility, John's heart attack, and the new world rigors of the war, her world constricted. So did her spirit.

Her turn to politics demonstrates one aspect of the change. Throughout much of her life, Mitchell took no obvious interest in politics. In this she mirrored her father's values rather than her mother's. May Belle Mitchell had relished the limelight, but the victory of the suffrage movement eliminated the chief inspiration of her political engagement. Eugene Mitchell took no pleasure in the public hurly-burly at all. He had accepted public office, but as a duty and without enthusiasm—a function of his family heritage, social standing, and civic obligation. Moreover, insofar as Eugene Mitchell reflected any political concerns at all, they tended towards the right. Although he and his children fought the Ku Klux Klan, decried white-rabble lawlessness, and supported blacks as individuals and a group, they did so without any suggestion of commitment to leftist causes, much less to furthering racial equality. They assumed the patrician's position. In later recollections, Stephens Mitchell described his family, including his sister, as "extremely reactionary." "Now by that," he elaborated, "I don't mean a conservative. We are not conservative. She believed that there are certain principles we've always got to go back to. In any era, until the second coming of the Lord, there will be things that are bad. So you'd better go back and look for the things that were good in the past."[3] Stephens Mitchell might have overstated the case, but only a little. If this was generally true, the New Deal sealed their reaction.

Mitchell herself had welcomed aggressive leadership in Washington in 1933, as had her family. By the mid-thirties and increasingly more thereafter, all of them repudiated their initial response to Franklin D. Roosevelt. John Marsh inspired a part of this opposition. His job as chief publicist for the Georgia Power and Light Company, the greatest private monopoly in the state, alienated him naturally from New Deal policies, but his wife shared and even exceeded his biases. John and Peggy Marsh reinforced each other's conservatism in the mid-thirties. Roosevelt's intervention in Georgia affairs in the senatorial campaign of 1938 against Senator Walter George solidified their opposition. In that critical election, John and Peggy Marsh actually supported the demagogic former governor, Herman Talmadge, against both the patrician incumbant, Walter George, and his New Deal opponent, Lawrence Camp. They maintained that beneath the galluses and tub-thumping rhetoric, "the wild man from Sugar Creek" came closer to their values than even the conservative Walter George.

Few of their old newspaper associates and no more of their newer literary friends sympathized with the Mitchell-Marsh politics. "I practiced silence during Margaret's vituperative denunciations of FDR and all his works," Clifford Dowdey wrote afterward.[4] Mitchell actually practiced some of the same restraint. She did not give full vent to her opinions around most of her liberal friends, but she indulged in gentle mockery in private. Mark and Willie Ethridge came in for their particular share. As early as the 1920s, the Ethridges had established themselves in the vanguard of Southern progressivism. Along with such other regional notables of Southern journalism as Virginius Dabney of the *Richmond Times-Dispatch*, Jonathan Daniels of the *Raleigh News and Observer*, and Ralph McGill of the *Atlanta Constitution*, the Ethridges, now of the *Louisville Courier-Journal*, occupied a critical place among the regional apologists for the New Deal. Mitchell used the publication of Willie Ethridge's 1938 novel, *Mingled Yarn*, to register her general complaints against their ideology. The novel chronicled a love affair between a crusading journalist and the daughter of the textile-mill president (according to Mitchell, Mark and Willie themselves, thinly disguised) as a means of exploring social issues in a Southern textile town, in this case, Macon, Georgia. "She wanted to be completely fair to both sides in her book and to give that ole davvle, Capitalism, its due," Mitchell laughed. "We wouldn't want to tell Willie this because we don't want to hurt her feelings, but we finished the book with a much higher opinion of mill owners than we had before and a far greater approval of their paternalism."[5]

In 1938, she could still joke. Her political humor soured yearly thereafter. Her correspondence with Dr. Henry C. Link revealed the drift of her thinking. This exponent of American conservative individualism had published in the *Saturday Evening Post*, and Mitchell read his books still more avidly: such as *The Rediscovery of Man* and *The Rediscovery of Morals*. By 1941, she was writing enthusiastic encomiums of his individualist philosophy. Betraying her own reaction, her letters also suggest a new, dark tone as well. He was a voice crying in the wilderness, she wrote, "for in these days it is rare to find in print anyone who says uncompromisingly that the individual is responsible for himself and that the potentialities of the individual are limitless." "This is a strange world when an article such as yours can be almost revolutionary," she told him in the summer before the American entry into the war.

> I am old enough to recall the time when little children were taught to recite "Invictus" and to believe in it. But when I grew up it was fashionable for the intellectuals and sophisticates to cry down this poem and its implications and to point the finger of laughing scorn at Kipling's "If." We are in a period now when no man is expected to be the master of his fate and the captain of his soul but as you expressed it, a mere helpless pawn of circumstance. I hope I live long enough to see us come out on the other side of this strange country in which we have been wandering.[6]

American engagement in World War II expanded these concerns and exaggerated the passion with which she held them. She became increasingly strident. In the fall of 1942, the Cox newspaper interests (which owned the *Journal*) invited her to write a regular column for the chain. No time, she demurred. Anyway, Cox could not really want her articles even if she chose to write them. She was so conservative and opposed to the New Deal, she explained, "that I make Westbrook Pegler look like a Communist with a torch in each hand."[7]

As the war wound down, her urgency intensified, her rhetoric grew more virulent, and the objects of her scorn multiplied. The circumstances of her denunciations changed, too. Now she looked for occasions to issue diatribes. Typically, in the late spring of 1944, she volunteered the most militant advice to Georgia's genuinely conservative senior senator, Walter George. The nation was sacrificing its blood and treasure to fight European tyrants, but the United States itself was moving along the same road to totalitarianism, she exclaimed. "Somewhere along the line of our retreat from our earlier standards of democratic government, we will have to halt and dig in and fight to defend them," she counseled her senator. "The longer we wait to fight, the harder the battle will be. This is a good time to start the fight."[8]

Her virulence washed over into personal relations. In the winter of 1945, her old friend Mark Ethridge had used a forum in Atlanta to defended Henry Wallace in the flap over the Secretaryship of Commerce and the Vice-Presidency. The novelist saw red. If she had joked about Willie and Mark as "Liberals or Radicals" being "strange bedfellows for such Tory Conservatives as John and me" in 1938,[9] her old wry smile now twisted to a snarl. She castigated her old friend in the bitterest terms. Ethridge and his ilk represented no one, she sputtered. If there was a real problem in the South, she insisted, it lay in a general worry about the absence of a Southerner in Roosevelt's Cabinet, not the absence of Midwestern pinko like Henry Wallace among the President's advisors.[10] Willie Ethridge came in for even nastier, if more private, scorn. Mitchell had poked quiet fun in 1938 at the politics of *Mingled Yarn*. Six years later, the jest withered. She ridiculed her old friend's pretensions to being a serious writer; she mocked Willie's craftmanship and castigated her as a "gushing Southern authoress."

The progress of Communist tyranny abroad confirmed her in these biases. Indeed, after 1944, the focus of Mitchell's bitter and strengthening ideology narrowed increasingly on the dangers of international Communism. She did not, however, hold anti-Communism merely as an abstract ideal. She found real and material sources for her indictment. The history of her book both at home and abroad helped shape her ferocious and growing political antipathies.

The American left had attacked her book from its first appearance. Among non-Communists, Heywood Broun and Malcolm Cowley represented the norm. Although Cowley's *New Republic* notice had ultimately allowed the novel's merit, the body of his review had mocked and ridiculed the epic. It had also relied, not on literary values, strictly speaking, to judge Mitchell's failure, but rather social and economic standards. Mitchell had elaborated a myth, he declared, that was "false in part, silly in part, and vicious in its general effect on Southern life today." Broun's notice echoed the same values. "Am I wholly alone in thinking that the book is just a shade too sweetly Southern?" he asked rhetorically. "Economically the South was wrong, and that is vital. It is more vital than charm or the fragrance of the flowers."[11] Communist reviewers and reviewers in Communist journals eschewed Broun's and Cowley's jaunty and somewhat cynical style for a harder, more earnest righteousness, but their grounds for dismissing the novel were the same as the fundamental concerns of these two. Generally, they attacked Mitchell for romance and nostalgia; more critically, for her lack of realism, which they defined in terms of laboring-class consciousness and progressive social movements.

Other issues sealed the left's opposition to Mitchell's work. By the time *Gone with the Wind* appeared, Communists had isolated race and American blacks as a chief focus of party interest. They identified this stance with the larger one of social realism, so that Mitchell's failure to deal with blacks and slavery represented, by definition, her romanticism; and by extension, her fiction's failure. While this thinking influenced the non-Communist left and American liberals, the official position on the matter guaranteed a united front within the party itself. The CP-USA disallowed dissent. One party regular, Howard Rushmore, a writer at *The Daily Worker*, lost his party standing—his job, too—over his refusal to condemn *Gone with the Wind*.[12] The American Writers' Congress, a literary front organization, showed the same spirit. The month after the Pulitzer Committee awarded Mitchell its prize, this left organization voted almost unanimously to honor *The Big Money* by John Dos Passos, who was then in his most radical phase. Margaret Mitchell received one lone vote to Dos Passos's 350.[13] Communist journals kept the issue alive not only in the thirties but throughout the war. Mitchell's fiction became, indeed, the left's touchstone of capitalism, Anglo-Saxon racism, and the malignant influence of the reactionary South on American life and letters. Between 1936 and 1944, no journals in the United States paid as much consistent attention to Mitchell's novel and its cinematic avatar as *New Masses* and the *Daily Worker*.[14]

The author tracked every expression of such opinions, and each reconfirmed her ideological commitments. From the first reviews, she told George Brett in 1948, "the Communists, the Left Wingers, the Pinks and the Liberals loathed me and my works, and, even after ten years, a Mr. David Platt on the Daily Worker scarcely lets a week go by without writing an anti–"Gone with the Wind" editorial," she fumed in 1948.[15] She delighted to return the favor to Platt *et al.*

Privately, she kept a "Red" file on Southern fellow travelers. It included such characters as the kindly, aristocratic, social-working Southerner Katherine DuPre Lumpkin. It also contained information (as might be expected) on the more genuinely radical Lillian Smith, who eventually came in for her own grief from the American Communists.[16] While she never went public with her anti-Communist campaign, Mitchell also lent her voice to some of the most vociferous leaders of the movement in the United States after the second world war. In 1941, she had proclaimed she might outdo the virulent Westbrook Pegler in his uncovering of domestic Communists. Though she never eclipsed Pegler, she struck up a warm correspondence with the ill-tempered newsman, welcomed him into her home, and assisted him in at least one of his anti-Roosevelt, anti–New Deal campaigns when he tried to link FDR with the radical Reconstruction governor of Georgia, Rufus Bullock. While Mitchell admitted that none of his history made any sense, her faith in Pegler's crusade never wavered.[17]

While urging Pegler on, she also took up with others of his hue, like Eugene Lyons, the author of *The Red Decade* and other exposés of leftist infiltration of American life. She concurred heartily with his ideas. "It interests me to observe that ultra radical statements about 'Gone with the Wind' and the South which appeared in publications such as the Daily Worker in 1936 traveled towards the Right and by 1946 were appearing as newly hatched ideas in the Saturday Review of Literature, Harper's and magazines heretofore considered conservative," she wrote.

I know it's the style to low-rate "Gone with the Wind" and even to state, as Time did some while back, that when it appeared the first-string critics dropped it as though it were a hot potato. The facts, however, are different.

The sudden skyrocketing sale of "Gone with the Wind" and the good words of the big critics caught our Left Wing friends off their balance and it was several weeks before The Nation and the New Republic and the Daily Worker et cetera could unlimber and get into action about this Fascist anti-Negro book, this false picture of the South, this distorted retelling of the "plantation myth" et cetera.[18]

To still another militant rightist, Isaac Don Levine, editor of the hard-line *Plain Talk,* she described an anti-Communist exposé she wanted to write: a full-length article to "explain why the communists attack the South and attempt to inflame the Negro press and public against the South." She never wrote the piece; in part, at least, because of what she deemed might be the consequence. Such an exposé, she fulminated, "will mean that I am going to sacrifice much of my peace and quiet, my security, perhaps my health and my good reputation, for I know very well the type of character assassination these people deal in."[19]

The reception of her book in Communist-dominated countries confirmed her sense of the Communist menace and conspiracy. The Yugoslavian case offered clear evidence for her of the connections of local and European denunciations of her novel. "I have just received some more book reviews from Yugoslavia where my embattled female publisher is still publishing the book," she noted in the spring of 1948.

The reviews are from Communist-controlled newspapers, of course, and they sound very much like the anti–"Gone with the Wind" reviews and editorials in the New York Daily Worker et cetera. They are less subtle than the Daily Worker but the content is the same. It appears that I am trying to reintroduce Negro slavery into the United States. Just what point there can be in their writing about this in Yugoslavia I don't know, for I cannot imagine their Negro population is very large. But there, as well as here in the United States, the Communists are bending all efforts to smearing the South and Southerners, because they know that we are one of the strongholds of Conservatism and are likely to resist Communism more fiercely than the large industrial sections of the North and the Middlewest.[20]

Though the government press attacked the book in Yugoslavia, the novel seldom made it even to the reviewing stage in other Communist countries. The Soviet Union proscribed the book within its own borders, and the prohibition moved with the Red Army. The blackout hit Hungary in 1947. For years she had grumbled and griped about her publishers in Budapest, but the Soviet resolution dismayed her: "As the Russians moved into Hungary, I felt that another one of my problems was settled—alas, not in the fashion I would have preferred," she grieved that summer.

> Whenever the Russians move into a country where "Gone with the Wind" is published, I am so fearful for the lives of my publishers that I am generally afraid to write them lest I get them in trouble. The Communists in this country and abroad have fought "Gone with the Wind" ever since its publication, and I never know whether something I might write in the friendliest manner might make a Soviet censor decide to liquidate my publishers.[21]

She repeated the fearful refrain the next year when the Czech government tottered. And with still another year, she reflected sadly on "the publishers, agents, newspaper critics, and just plain letter-writing friends who have suddenly become silent and disappeared as Russia rolled over their countries—Bulgaria, Roumania, Hungary, Poland, Yugoslavia, and now Czechoslovakia." In the late spring of 1949, the new Czech government nationalized her publisher's firm. She held her breath. "He is still alive and at liberty," she continued, "but I do not know for how long."[22]

She fought back. In spite of her own and her publisher's anxieties about copyrights, for example, she sanctioned the serialization of *Gone with the Wind* in France for political purposes. Organizing a conservative opposition in late 1947 and early 1948, the Gaullists decided that serializing *Gone with the Wind* would increase their readership, their following, and their cause. "A number of people high up in government in conservative circles added their requests to those of various publishers of newspapers, and among others was André Maurois," the Atlantan noted.[23] Her copyright anxieties yielded to her ideology. She then asked George Brett to accede as well. He fretted, but her justification convinced him. Fiercely conservative himself, he signed his permission with the cry, "Yours for the death of Communism."[24]

If part of her opposition to Communism, liberalism, and the American left arose from ideological commitments and her sense of real interests being violated, another part, just as surely, sprang from more obscure and inward motives. She hankered for a fight. Her world was out of joint, and she looked for objects for her wrath. The left gave her a notable opportunity, but she found less obvious occasions to leap into the ring in these years as well.

She took out a considerable portion of her festering resentment in the mid-forties and later against her publisher. Small provocations set off her fury, and she descended like a virago on the hapless George Brett in particular. The mess with her foreign agent, Marion Saunders, in 1943, provided the occasion for one such explosion. Mitchell had discovered Saunders's embezzlement in the summer of that year. She had not pressed criminal charges or brought a civil suit but had handled the matter informally and privately through her attorneys. By the winter, the difficult problem was resolved, but it embittered the author and increased her skepticism of anyone outside her circle. In February 1944, just as the affair wound down, the president of the Macmillan Company heard about the problem through Harold Latham. Immediately he fired off a sympathetic letter to the harried author. In the course of his epistle, however, he suggested the Atlantan might go public with Saunders's knavery as a means of defending others from similar problems.[25] This otherwise benign aside put Mitchell in a rage. She read the remark as a moral judgment—Brett condemning her for failing in a public responsibility—and she countercharged. You were the one who saddled us with Marion Saunders in the first place, John Marsh replied for his wife, and, he continued, "from that day on, she was a constant source of trouble and expense. . . . You are in no position to be critical of us."[26]

Still rankling over Brett's letter, Mitchell found more cause for fury in the fall of 1944. This still-odder circumstance involved another bestseller, *Forever Amber*, which had just appeared in the Macmillan list. Kathleen Winsor was barely out of adolescence when Macmillan published her notorious novel that year. The story had more than a passing kinship with *Gone with the Wind*, particularly in the historical settings for the adventures of the most willful heroines with literally colorful first names. If this relationship was obvious, a notice in the *New York Times Book Review* of October 8 dealt with other similarities. Both writers, the reviewer related, professsed a certain casualness about their material. The books, he said, had effectively "written themselves." Although Mitchell herself had cultivated this very impression in the days before and after her novel had appeared, she now objected violently to this judgment. At the same time, she found the villainy not in the *Times* reviewer but within the Macmillan Company. She determined her own publisher had to be responsible for this canard. Immediately, she dictated a fire-and-brimstone letter to Macmillan's publicity department for perpetrating a scurrilous rumor about her writing.[27] The horrified head of the division disclaimed any responsibility for the reference and dropped the issue in George Brett's lap. Brett replied at once. Although guiltless, the company president offered a profusion of apologies; insisting, for example, that he forbad the use of Mitchell's name in any advertising for any Macmillan title other than *Gone with the Wind* itself.

Unmollified, Mitchell now shifted the grounds of her objections. Brett had failed to address himself specifically to Mitchell's charge that the company believed she wrote "carelessly." It was not really the use of her name that offended her, but rather that Macmillan made her out to be "a dope," she raged:

> for no one but a dope would go on record that they did no planning on their book but just sat down and wrote. If Miss Winsor does not mind appearing to be a dope and The MacMillan Company is willing to cooperate with her in making her appear a dope, I am sure that is none of my business. . . . There was nothing in my letter to Miss Grinnell that would in any way give the impression that I was resentful or jealous or upset at Miss Winsor's success and at the coupling of "Gone with the Wind" and "Forever Amber."[28]

She added a familiar qualifier at this point, too. She minded this error less for herself, she insisted, than as a violation of principle. It inspired carelessness and irresponsibility in the young, she protested. It would convince every "would-be" author in America that writing involved only magic—as opposed to the decade of sweat she poured into her novel.

Nothing in Brett's letter suggested his disregard of Mitchell's talent, energy, and discipline. He knew better. Also, he never even hinted at the motive of jealousy. Mitchell read it into his letter; the reference reveals far less about Brett than about Margaret Mitchell herself. This was a dreadful season in her life, and now she confronted the possibility of the Amber tart's replacing her own Scarlett woman in the affections of her publishers and the reading public. Her explosive reaction to Winsor's novel fits this logic. Her response also underlines her waxing touchiness, her growing sense of being unappreciated for her hard work, and her willingness to believe the worst of others—conniving publishers and careless, irresponsible "would-be authors" among them. Brett absorbed her spleen. It was not the last time.

In the fall of 1947, John Marsh was reviewing his wife's account, and he found an item that made no sense to him: "1,093 copies @ .30— $327.90." He inquired about the matter, and George Brett explained that hardback sales that year had fallen below 5,000 copies and triggered a clause in the contract calling for reduced percentages of profits to the author.[29] *Gone with the Wind* had actually sold almost 45,000 copies that year, and his wife's contract made no distinction of sales between hard and "cheap" copies, the invalid husband replied tersely. He then took the opening of this misreading of the company's obligations and reviewed the entire business of contracts dating back to February 1936 and before. He dredged eleven years of bitter sludge and ill-concealed resentment. "In our family, when we make a contract, we go through with it if that is within our power—even when it is a bad and unfair contract such as the one Macmillan, acting as Peggy's agent, made for her with Selznick International Pictures, Inc.," he scolded the company president:

Macmillan made its original contract with Peggy with its eyes open and with her manuscript in front of you. You had all the knowledge of publishing matters and she had none. She did not demand a certain royalty rate; you suggested what it should be and she accepted. But several times you have asked Peggy to accept modifications in the contract, making reductions in her royalty rate. So far as I can recall, Peggy has never asked you for any modifications of her contract in her favor.[30]

Once more, Brett responded immediately—and abjectly. He apologized over and over, sent a check for the additional funds, and also hinted that he had sacked the person in the accounting office responsible for the error. His reply, however, failed to mollify the Marshes. On the contrary, he stirred an even angrier hornet's nest: the infamous negotiations with David Selznick in the summer of 1936. John Marsh, of course, had raised the matter initially in his passing reference to "a bad and unfair contract such as the one Macmillan, acting as Peggy's agent, made for her with Selznick International Pictures, Inc." George Brett took the wrong cue altogether from the reference. "I am sorry that you feel that Mr. Latham let you and Peggy down on the movie contract with Selznick," he had begun cheerily. Impugning Mitchell's beloved Harold Latham was sin enough, but his casual aspersions on his senior editor also ignored what the novelist considered Brett's own primary responsibility for her betrayal. She had not forgotten, but his failure to own up to his guilt she counted an even greater error. But Brett blundered still more. After casting the blame for the Marshes' unhappiness onto Latham, he then consoled the irritated novelist by arguing that the contract was not so bad after all. Innocently ignoring her appeal to principle, he couched his consolation completely in monetary terms. Yes, he remarked benevolently, she might have held out for more money had she waited a year to sign, but no book was selling for over $50,000 at the time. All in all, she made out just fine, he concluded: "I still think that Mr. Latham did as well as could have been done at the time the sale was made and under the circumstances."[31]

The dollars-and-cents mistakes about royalties had irritated the author; Brett's version of the original contract negotiations simply enraged her. Here was something analogous to Dr. Walter Dandy's casual references to "nerves." His innocent remarks fired a decade of smoldering hostility. Once more, John Marsh argued his wife's case. "At their mildest [your remarks] were slurring," he began. The money? You distort the situation, he wrote bitterly. Money did not interest them. The question was one of principle. Neither publicly nor privately, Marsh told the company president, had Mitchell ever complained in any way about the money she received. "Everybody else seems to think she ought to be dissatisfied and unhappy about the $50,000. It all carries the suggestion that she would wish to welsh out of a trade which she had made," he declared, "and we don't like it. Now you have joined your voice to that chorus." You above everyone, he said, know the real objections to that deal: "Macmillan put a blindfold over Peggy's eyes and tied her hands behind her back and delivered her over to Selznick." He then chronicled anew Macmillan's betrayal of its responsibility to protect her interests and all the harm that had arisen from that perfidy. "We relied upon Macmillan, as Peggy's agent, and Macmillan failed us," he closed.[32]

George Brett never mastered the management of this prize filly in his literary stable. He never completely understood her. Harold Latham did. In this very episode, Brett had passed the hot epistles on to his vice-president; Latham replied with some version of "loose lips sink ships." The editor first defended himself from Brett's very careless rendering of the Selznick story; he also drafted a letter for Brett's signature; and finally, he admonished his president to steer clear of any specifics altogether, in any response to the furious Atlantans. Stay general, he advised.[33] Of all the Macmillan people, Latham alone never lost Mitchell's confidence. While she never forgot her debt to him, he also nurtured and cultivated his advantage, and his own voluminous correspondence with the author suggests still other guides for good relations: Never challenge her. Keep a certain distance. Don't take literally everything she says. Take her part. Agree. Sympathize. Follow her lead. Be attentive, but seek no obvious gain.

The Macmillan president never got the role down pat; his egotism showed through even his efforts at self-effacement. At the same time, however, there was little Brett could have done to redeem himself completely in the author's eyes, once she determined he had failed her back in 1936. It took only the strains and changes of the war and postwar years to prompt the author to renew the old accusations. She never forgot what she deemed his betrayal when she signed the Selznick contract. That contract, indeed, provided still more evidence of the changes of her life after World War II.

In both the Macmillan and the Selznick contracts, the author had objected especially to the covenant about copyrights. Her reservations very nearly prevented her from signing the movie contract. Although she herself no longer held the copyright to her book, what did Clause 3 mean in requiring the author "to prevent the Property . . . from vesting in the public domain"? No one took her objections very seriously. This was a standard, form contract, everyone repeated, and no one expected anything special from this clause. Her anxiety puzzled the other parties, then and afterward as well. Neither Brett, Macmillan, the Macmillan legal retainers, Selznick, nor the Selznick-International lawyers held her strictly to the clause, and all of them effectively allowed and even encouraged her to forget the matter. Her publisher's very conservative legal counsel, Cadwallader, Wickersham

& Taft, allowed her to ignore it when the attorneys argued the unlikelihood of any court's holding her negligible for inaction.[34] Selznick's New York attorney told Macmillan he took no particular interest in pressing her, and he assumed his principals shared his opinion. George Brett agreed and urged the author to disregard this "goda'mighty" business.[35]

None of this mattered to the author herself. When Brett, for example, urged moderation, she rejoined immediately: "having put my name to a contract, there was nothing to do but abide by it even it was a bad contract and even if I had agreed to do an impossible thing."[36] Couching her efforts in terms of abstract principles, Mitchell made copyright infringement a crusade, and she tried to enlist Macmillan, George Brett, Selznick, and still others to join her. No one did. Unwilling to hold her strictly to this clause, they found even less reason to adhere to it themselves. George Brett, for one, thought the author simply daft on the subject. The willingness of "the Mitchell tribe," as he called them, to hit the warpath at the most obscure provocation and to entangle the company in their crusades, Brett found tedious, trying, and offensive.

Besides a ferocious determination to fulfill the letter of the law—against all this formal legal advice, and in consultation with her family alone (who knew nothing about copyright law)—Mitchell also imposed the broadest conceivable reading on the clause. She allowed that it governed any use whatsoever, including any reference at all to any plot element, narrative circumstance, or character from her novel, without prior written consent. She drew no distinction between great infringements, moderate ones, and the most obscure. Moreover, she extended this interpretation to cover the entire planet. Was Billy Rose mounting a silly musical parody in Las Vegas? Was a great Dutch publishing house pirating her novel? Did a rural Georgia women's co-op want to make "Mammy dolls" for charity? Had she heard of an amateur theater group in Bucharest staging a *Gone with the Wind* skit? Did someone else inform her about a French magazine's holding a contest to write a new ending to the novel? They all became the same to the author. She hovered hawklike over the packets her clipping service dispatched to her apartment, scanning each for signs of violation of her rights. Nothing escaped her attention, and every infringement prompted letters and threats of legal action. In no way did the daughter come more to resemble her father.

Mitchell pressed this issue not only against virtually all counsel but against practicality, cost, and even common sense. Although her response cost her most dearly in time, energy, and cash, the burdens actually seemed to spur her on. Her expenses effectively proved the purity of her fight. Her misery vouched for her rectitude. It was not for self-interest that she campaigned, but for the principle, she repeated.

While she complained perpetually about the woes involved in defending her copyright, and they were legion, she also derived enormous satisfaction from exacting penalties from those who crossed and challenged her. One case in particular represents the form and spirit of her commitment to defend herself and punish her enemies: a ten-year battle she fought over her copyright in Holland. While it actually began well before the war, the case illuminates her growing contentiousness, in the forties especially, and her unwillingness to forgive or forget any foe. It also revealed her swelling list of adversaries and her tendency to find opponents among any who differed with her view of things. Before the affair concluded (more or less bitterly) by 1947, she had unleashed her wrath against virtually everybody involved, including her publisher, her publisher's lawyers, her Dutch lawyers, the Dutch publishers, and the whole Dutch people.

Although the Berne Union agreement provided authors international copyright protection, the United States had never ratified that agreement, and only simultaneous publication in Canada, a member nation, allowed American writers international protection for their work. In 1937 a Dutch publisher, Zuid-Hollandsche Uitgevers Mij—ZHUM, for short—produced an unauthorized version of Mitchell's epic, justifying the piracy on the technical grounds that the American edition, unprotected by the Berne convention, had appeared before the Canadian. Immediately upon hearing of the Dutch edition, Mitchell ordered a legal challenge. She anticipated no problem. She lost, and the pirated edition went legally on sale in Holland in the late fall.[37] She picked up her shillelagh. "Ordinarily I am a mild individual," she protested, "but my blood is up on this matter and I intend to take it through every court in Holland."[38] She did.

She had retained the Macmillan lawyers to help her with the foreign business, and on the advice of Cadwallader, Wickersham & Taft she hired a new Dutch attorney, Dr. J. A. Fruin, to appeal. For four years the case wound tediously through the Dutch courts. The Germans invaded on May 1, 1940, but neither the destruction nor the occupation stopped the process. Finally, on February 14, 1941, the High Court of Justice in The Hague judged in Mitchell's favor on all the principle issues and called for a retrial. At this point, in the fall of 1941, Cadwallader, Wickersham (the intermediary between Fruin and Mitchell) recommended a settlement that included $1,000 cash restitution. The Atlantan agreed, not for the money involved, she insisted, but as a warning to other pirates.[39] Just as Fruin began these final negotiations, however, Pearl Harbor and the American entry into the European war interrupted all communications between the Dutch and American litigants.

The negotiations between ZHUM and Mitchell's Dutch lawyer continued despite the war. By the summer of 1944, Fruin reached an informal agreement with ZHUM that made the pirate now the official Dutch publisher. It also provided for royalties on the pirated prewar editions. Finally, it significantly increased the old cash settlement. Because this money was liable to German seizure as long as the Nazi occupation continued, however, the contending parties signed nothing formal. The final settlement came on September 17, 1945. ZHUM allowed the author 28,000 florins for royalties and 500 florins on account of costs.

At another time, this agreement might have pleased the author. Not now. With her father's illness and death, the infirmity of her husband and servants, her botched back operation and the conflict with her surgeon, the embezzlement by her foreign agent, and the alienation that most of these episodes entailed, this was a terrible time in her life. She smelled rats everywhere. The Dutch case focused her general dissatisfaction with the world. Nothing about the agreement pleased her. She complained bitterly that as late as six months after the official settlement, she herself had received no formal notification of the agreement.[40] Then, too, without her permission or even her formal knowledge, ZHUM had sold its rights to a Flemish publisher for a Belgian edition. That imprint had appeared in December 1945; but to complicate the situation further, none of these books bore, by her lights, the proper copyright information on the flyleaf. At the same time, she discovered that both of the Dutch editions themselves failed her minimum copyright test as well. She scented plots and conspiracies in all these facts.[41]

When she finally received a copy of the actual agreement that Fruin negotiated with ZHUM, she found more cause for indignation. "There's nothing to keep them from putting out the usual cheap European glued or bradded type of book and not paying me," she protested. Nor, she added, was she informed where the settlement money was on deposit. Fruin's deduction of his fees from this fund set her foaming, too. Her counsel, she raged, "is not going to be permitted to deduct whatever he pleases from my money and then be gracious enough to send me the rest, after he has been so dilatory. Moreover, I advanced him a large sum of money before the war for expenses. . . ."[42]

Such references to "the money due me," "the deduction of fees," and "not paying me" introduced a new element in her discussion of the Dutch case. Mitchell's stinginess had been a joke among her bohemian friends; it now became oppressive. While she had insisted that she began and fought the fight on the principle of defending international copyrights and honoring her contractual obligations, money matters steadily pushed these other questions from the picture in this round of negotiations after 1943. As her resentments multiplied, her animosity focused on chiselers depriving her of her rightful income. Just as Scarlett had dealt with Frank Kennedy's poor customers in post–Civil War

Atlanta, Mitchell refused to acknowledge any excuses for the settlement of her accounts in Holland, even if Holland was a catastrophe zone with the Third Reich's collapse. Fruin was ill, his files were destroyed, he had refugeed from Holland itself, and international relations were in a shambles. None of this mattered. She honored her obligations to the letter; she demanded the same of others.

Her fury with Fruin, ZHUM, and the whole Dutch business also now slopped over onto Cadwallader Wickersham & Taft. Soon the old Wall Street firm actually replaced Fruin (not to mention the actual Dutch pirates!) as the chief demons in the affair for her. At best, she declared, the firm failed to pursue her interests aggressively enough. At worst, they intrigued with her Dutch enemies to deny her her rights and profits.[43] When she complained to her New York lawyers about Fruin's deducting his fees from her account, Walbridge Taft, to her fury, took the Dutch attorney's part; this, she decided, offered *prima facie* evidence of a conspiracy. Convinced now of economic malfeasance, as with the Marion Saunders episode, she hired an external audit in the spring of 1946 that convinced her of her rightness.[44]

Truly on the warpath now, she wanted Wall Street scalps. On October 4, 1946, her brother, acting on her behalf, formally terminated his sister's relationship with the New York firm. His very long, angry letter catalogued Fruin's and Cadwallader's sins against his sister's rights. Although Walbridge Taft rejoined with a recital of the facts of the case, the distinguished senior partner could barely restrain his anger over what he considered Stephens Mitchell's "really scurrilous letter." He took special pleasure, too, in ridiculing Stephens Mitchell's opinion that the case was only a small collections claim. His reply also charged the Mitchells with hypocrisy when he underlined the contradictions between the author's claims of rectitude and principle against what had become claims for cash: petty cash, too, he sneered.[45]

But the Mitchell tribe got its scalps. Exacting vengeance against the New York lawyers pleased the author, and she felt that it opened the bottleneck of her Dutch affairs as well. It was like sacking her medical experts and returning to the local practitioner: Good old Louis for the arrogant Dr. Dandy; trustworthy Steve for Cadwallader's lordly ineptitude. She got her money; soon afterward, too, she gloated. Towards the end of 1948, she summarized the resolution of the conflict for George Brett. "Though I know it is not a nice thing to say, our Dutch matters went very well after Cadwallader, Wickersham & Taft got out of the picture," she exulted.

The contract went forward better, adjustments and concessions were made between me and the former pirate, the settlement money made over to me has been paid, and I've even gotten almost all the royalty money due me up to the present paid to me too. Of course, I'll never collect one

fiftieth of the amount of money I spent on this lawsuit, but still it's encouraging to get what I have gotten, which is considerable.[46]

The Dutch case was important. It did help guarantee Mitchell's foreign rights. It also secured her royalties and profits, which *were* considerable both in Holland and more generally wherever her novel was
published. But the affair has other significance. It reveals how furiously the author was willing to fight for what she deemed her rights
and privileges, not least the monetary ones. Indeed, the case also suggests the ways she focused her claims to principle increasingly on issues of cash and gain, especially after 1944. It revealed and exaggerated the pettiness and the spirit of revenge in her character. It convinced
her all the more of a world of plots and conspiracies as well, and deepened her distrust of everyone except her family. She circled her wag-
ons tighter and tighter, and as her circle constricted, she found more
enemies in the world, less reason for tolerance and grace, and more
cause for suspicion, anger, and irritation. She found still other objects
and excuses for her wrath in the last six rancorous years of her life.

As she had behaved with the Dutch, her New York lawyers, her publisher, and politics, so she behaved, increasingly, with the world. Her
clipping service forwarded every published reference to her, her book,
or her characters from everywhere in the United States and all over
the world, and within this mass of material she found ample occasion
to vent her anger. In late 1945, publisher Bennett Cerf had referred
incidentally to the author's "allergy to roses" in the *Saturday Review*.
She used this error as the occasion to attack "neo-journalists who have
broken away from the old tradition that writers are supposed to write,
and publications to publish, true facts." She failed to call on Cerf when
he visited Atlanta: "On any occasion when Mr. Cerf is to be present, I
will always wish to be absent. One reason is that I do not care to associate with a professional South-hater," she fumed. "Another is that
I despise cheapness."[47]

Granville Hicks got the same fury. Her clipping service sent her a
reference from the Framingham, Massachusetts, *News* of a speech the
critic had delivered weeks or months before. Incidentally to his address, according to the report, he had referred to Macmillan's having
gambled on buying *Gone with the Wind* after seeing only one chapter.
The factual error enraged her, but she found a still stranger reason to
lambaste the critic—the supposed effect of such a statement on young
writers:

> They read that I sold "Gone with the Wind" on the strength of one chap-
> ter, and they wish to do likewise. . . . Such statements as yours make
> young writers think that writing is a very easy type of work. They refuse
> to give ear to the truth, that it is the hardest work in the world and one

serves a longer apprenticeship than at any other trade. I have so many writers and would-be writers on my neck, and practically none of them want to do any work because they believe erroneous statements that I wrote a bestseller with no previous experience and sold it on the strength of one chapter.[48]

Nothing seemed small enough to miss. When she heard the rumor of an imposter from an article with a San Antonio dateline, she "plastered the big papers of Texas, New Mexico, Arizona, Mexico and Southern California with letters that I had not been in those towns and that there was an imposter abroad," she related.[49] She sent copies to everyone. Virginia Patterson, the new director of the publicity department at Macmillan, got one and had no earthly idea what to make of it. "I have written her a polite letter, a copy of which is attached," she memoed Harold Latham. "The Margaret Mitchell business is pre-Patterson and slightly over my head."[50]

And then there was the flap over the *Readers' Digest*.

In the July 1949 edition of the popular journal, Mitchell discovered a tiny reference in one of the humorous filler items the journal ran in every issue. The anecdote referred to Ashley Wilkes being killed at the battle of Gettysburg fourteen months before little Beau was born during the siege of Atlanta. Complete nonsense to any reader of the novel, the story's stupidity reflected on the *Digest*, not the author. The joke was actually a garbled version of a story she had told against herself when she had addressed a meeting of Atlanta librarians back in May 1936. Making births coincide with conjugal visits had proved a tedious aspect of checking galleys, she had related. Tired of correcting, she joked about making a footnote correction: that gestation took longer back then.[51] Thirteen years later, the appearance of the anecdote in print provoked the most furious pyrotechnics from her Piedmont Avenue apartment. She demanded a retraction and apology. The magazine failed to understand the ruckus and paid little attention: "The Margaret Mitchell business is slightly over our heads," the editors might have quoted Virginia Patterson. But such abuse was not to be borne, Mitchell might have quoted Tony Fontaine in reply. One more time she pulled down her legal squirrel gun from above the mantel. "They must want to be sued," she seethed. "This could not have come at a worse time." And then commenced the old, familiar litany.

I developed a bronchial infection in New York and it is still with me; the Japanese business took an enormous amount of cabling and writing; so did the French sequel; the Communists are closing one of my best publishers; a rush contract for a movie edition had to go to Spain; we've been trying to buy a house for we may have to move whether or not we wish to do so—etc. etc.

On top of all this to have this stupid thing happen through no fault of my own and have the Reader's Digest hang back on an honest reparation had almost made me ill from fatigue, over work and indignation.[52]

What was the issue? The apology she demanded spelled it out. "The anecdote as published might give the impression that Miss Mitchell was careless with historical facts in her novel." It was a similar issue that ignited her rage in the affair of *Forever Amber* five years before or with Granville Hicks earlier in 1949. It was, indeed, something of the same impulse that prompted her to surrender her manuscript to Harold Latham in the bitter dogwood spring of 1935. In any case, she could not let the issue go. However small it seemed, she was determined to ride it just as thoroughly as she had the Dutch piracy, or any one of the other scores of infringements, libels, and all the rest that she had detected. "I do not intend to let them get away with it. I cannot afford to do so, what they did to me was so inexcusable and reprehensible that I do not intend to take it lying down," she snarled. "They appeared to have no comprehension of any damage they had done me, nor did they appear to care. In fact, they have acted like a hit-and-run driver that had damaged an innocent pedestrian, and have been trying to get away from the scene as fast as possible," she concluded on July 12, 1949.[53] On August 4, she won her apology, and the magazine agreed to publish a "correction" in the September issue.[54] She gloated in bitter triumph. Her victory lasted eleven days.

Epilogue
A Story Told

*T*he fifty years after 1936 have witnessed curious tides in the reputation of *Gone with the Wind,* and, by extension, of its creator.
While the popular enthusiasm for the novel has never waned,
critical opinion turned sharply away from the work in wake of World
War II, as the author herself had noted in 1947. She attributed the
shift to the influence of Communism and the political left in the United
States. If not as insidious as her criticism suggested, new political ideas
in the nation did influence the novel's reputation, especially insofar as
critics linked the novel with the South. As Dixie's national image
changed, Margaret Mitchell's Confederate epic suffered accordingly.

Between 1941 and 1945, the nation fought a hot war against Nazis
and Fascists, and afterward, a cold one against Communists. In this
setting, the conservative and even reactionary South, particularly its
racial mores, proved an international embarrassment at best, a critical
liability at worst. James Loeb, Jr., one of the founders of Americans
for Democratic Action, had rallied wartime progressives in 1945 with
just this connection: "On the one hand, America fights to wipe out
park benches in Berlin marked 'Jude,' on the other, America below the
Mason-Dixon line marks trolley cars seats 'for colored only.' "[2]

Shifting demographic patterns within the country hastened the changes. War-related industry and business drew black workers out of the South towards major urban centers in the North, Midwest, and West, and local politicians in these areas responded to the alteration in their constituencies. Even in the South itself, the war and returning black soldiers had encouraged black citizens to claim their equal share of liberty. Then, too, the New Deal had nurtured old progressive, egalitarian ideals in the nation, which had the deepest roots in American ideology. All these forces challenged regional values and undermined the idealization of Southern "peculiarism."

At this very time, however, many of the forces that cultivated change elsewhere actually spawned anti-liberalism in Dixie. Paradoxically, the very popularity of the reforming FDR and the New Deal had increased conservative power in both the region and the nation. The dominance of the Democratic Party in national politics, the one-party system in the South, and the powerful role of conservatives within the Southern wing of the party all exaggerated the influence of conservative Southern Democrats, especially in the Congress. With very few exceptions, race remained the common denominator of Southern politics: right, left, and center, but especially right. Occupying key positions in Congressional committees, then, Southern politicians imposed their will on national legislation and prohibited racial change through legislative channels. In such positions of power, they came to be virtual caricatures of the image of a reactionary, undemocratic, oligarchic south that perverted national ideals and values. At the same time, growth of racial liberalism within the Democratic Party and the national temper generated its own response in the South, especially after 1945. Strom Thurman's Dixiecrat rebellion in 1948 over the civil rights plank in the party platform that year demonstrates that reaction. If it did nothing else, Thurman's abortive campaign helped guarantee the popular identification of the South with the forces of radical reaction.

Although the image of a wickedly wayward South had a venerable history that even pre-existed the abolitionist movement of the 1830s, the nature of national and regional politics after World War II gave that image new force and validity. Despite personal honor and even political integrity, Southern politicians became linked in the public mind with some combination of Senator Claghorn and L'il Abner at best, and with Rod Steiger's pot-bellied Dixie sheriff at his worst. While national opinion has generally been of two minds about the region— fear and loathing on the one side, romanticizing and idealization on the other—the former attitude dominated throughout the war and the postwar period, peaking in the horror of the Selma marches and the Birmingham police riots of the mid-sixties. Indeed, the national-regional polarity became so fixed that one's attitude about the South became something of a barometer of one's patriotism and commitment to national values between 1945 and 1964.

All this had its effect on Margaret Mitchell's novel.

With Southernism in foulest odor, the preeminent novel about and from the South suffered accordingly. Too, the novel's identification with the film exaggerated the tendency to read the book as a romantic evocation of the Lost Cause plantation South, something, of course, that Mitchell herself abjured. Some regional writers, like Lillian Smith and William Faulkner, avoided the prejudice. They did so in part, like Smith, by attacking the Southern system as violently as any national critic and by building their fiction around the themes of Southern racial, patriarchal horror. The very obscurity of Faulkner's purposes also allowed more liberal reading of his fictions. In Malcolm Cowley, too, he had a powerful advocate in the very inner sanctum of the postwar literary establishment in New York. Actually, Smith's and Faulkner's national and even international celebration contributed to Mitchell's critical decline. If they were the "good" Southerners, she, perforce, represented all the values at the other pole. In this scenario, Smith represented the crusading realism and political sensitivity of both the national and regional conscience, and Faulkner personified the Modernist temper whose Southern setting was incidental or even irrelevant to his place in the great ebb and flow of international culture between the two world wars. That such an interpretation distorted Smith and Faulkner hardly less than *Gone with the Wind* is almost beside the point.

Far more than political issues, however, governed the altered reception of Mitchell's work in the decades after World War II. Indeed, while new political values might have undermined the novel's critical repute from one side, radical changes within literary criticism condemned the novel from another perspective entirely. Since World War I, literature had been disordered along with the rest of Western civilization. The collapse of social and political order and the disintegration of Victorian verities in that conflict had spawned cynicism, pessimism, materialism, and hedonism among the children of the Treaty of Versailles. Darwinian biology and Freudian psychology provided models and explanations of human conduct. The literary criticism that matched this climate flowered fully in the United States in the mid-thirties, and the next twenty-five years witnessed its triumph in American letters. And all this had the most far-reaching effects on the critical reception of Mitchell's novel.

Beginning in the 1930s, the New Criticism, as it was called, rewrote the definitions of literary merit. Enunciated most clearly by Southerners like Robert Penn Warren, Allen Tate, John Crowe Ransom, and Caroline Gordon, the new standards emphasized art for itself, celebrated form over content, exaggerated themes of irony and paradox, challenged the idea of any political or moral meaning in literature at all, and basically agreed on the essential difficulty and mystery of the creative act and of the creation itself. Art was mysterious; appreciation came hard. Art was rarified; common accessibility was a phantom. Art was sacred, not profane. The artist, then, was godlike, and critics served as explicator-priests. The New Critics abstracted art from time and place and even from the artist. By such values, biography and history could teach little about the work studied. By the same token, history and historical fiction lost place among critics, too.[3]

Gone with the Wind plopped down into the center of this revolution in literary criticism. It did not escape unscathed. When *Gone with the Wind* first appeared, the New Criticism was only in its infancy; the modern novel, however, was going full tilt. Those skeptical of the trends in contemporary fiction offered Mitchell's work as an alternative. They helped define the battle lines that later critics manned with a vengeance. In one of the earliest reviews of Mitchell's work, Edwin Granberry crowed that Mitchell had tossed down the gauntlet to modernity. He praised Mitchell's clear characterization and sharp story line, for example, in specific contrast to the confused, obscure, and overly complex "moodiness" of the modern novel. Celebrating the story, effectively, above the artistry of its telling, he separated Mitchell's work from the main currents of contemporary fiction and the Modernist temperament. While early exponents of the new mode, like John Crowe Ransom, actually liked the novel, this did not hold true for its later adherents. As the "new formalism" swept the field, its practitioners simply reversed Edwin Granberry's commendation to find in *Gone with the Wind* everything they loathed. And the New Critics carried the day. Mitchell's epic became a touchstone of what to avoid in novel writing.

Even the novel's advocates had frequently noted lapses in Mitchell's prose, her use of stock figures and stereotypical settings, her lack of innovation, and her reliance on traditional forms and structures. But they had then generally insisted, like Henry Steele Commager, that the work "rises triumphantly over this material and becomes, if not a work of art, a dramatic re-creation of life itself." Obviously, given the new formalism's supreme emphasis upon art as art, even such otherwise lavish praise only damned the novel more. Cataloguing the stereotypicality, stock types, and all the rest did no more than confirm the bias of the New Critics. Indeed, few critics ever really differed significantly about the nature of Mitchell's work. They broke ranks almost exclusively on question of the significance or insignificance of the narrative form of the novel. Mitchell's notions of artlessness, her dislike of style *qua* style, and her efforts at artistic self-effacement might have succeeded in her novel, but they all ran counter to the currents of the modern age.

Extraliterary considerations also sustained the opponents' arguments. The publishing world had seen nothing like this novel's popularity, and very quickly, marketplace success fed critics' profoundest doubts about the novel. As the New Criticism assumed the difficulty and obscurity of art, popularity, in contrast, was *prima facie* evidence of failure. "The size of its public is significant," Bernard De Voto proclaimed in 1937; "the book is not."[4] Thirty-three years after the editor of the *Saturday Review* thus dismissed the novel, the Old Guard of the New Criticism proclaimed the connection still more boldly and waved aside the epic still more grandly: "Great literature can occasionally be popular, and certainly popular literature can occasionally be great. But with a few notable exceptions, such as the Bible but not *Gone with the Wind*, greatness and popularity are more likely to be contradictory than congenial."[5] And the popularity of the novel has hardly abated after half a century, with the book reportedly selling close to 40,000 hardcover copies a year and 250,000 paperbacks.

As Mitchell's novel seemed incapable of sustaining any sort of legitimate scholarly inquiry, the investigation of the author herself suffered accordingly. Her estate complicated the difficulty. Almost as private and certainly as stubborn and resistant as his sister, Stephens Mitchell expressed the strongest commitment to guarding her reputation and fulfilling her wish for privacy. Intensely skeptical of the trends of modern biography, too, he did not encourage the free inquiry into the writer's life, although he donated the writer's enormous and rich archives to the University of Georgia in 1970. If scholars ignored the author, though, popular interest in her never faltered. This, however, also complicated the novelist's reputation. On the one side, the regular appearance of biographical articles in the likes of the *Readers' Digest, McCall's,* and the Sunday supplements and magazines of daily newspapers confirmed academic prejudices against the author; at the same time, such essays tended to confuse even the facts of Mitchell's life.

All this began to change by the mid-1970s. Since then, academics turned in increasing numbers to consider the novel's merits and demerits for themselves. While in the period before 1973, scholars ignored Mitchell and her work almost completely, the period since 1975 has witnessed a proliferation of studies of the novel.[6] Little consensus has emerged from this growing academic debate, except for the idea that the novel is indeed worthy of study and examination. What has never been in question, however, is the continuing and extraordinary popular affection for Mitchell's work. As it did in 1936, this devotion puts *Gone with the Wind* in a category all by itself, and with it, its creator. After fifty years, the novel still galvanizes people's imagination.

Nineteen eighty-six marked the fiftieth anniversary of the publication of *Gone with the Wind*. The event won wide notice. The Post Office gave the author a commemorative stamp, even if its portrait bore little resemblance to any known likeness. Newspapers, magazines, and other popular journals published innumerable articles about the novel and its author, while television and radio programs noted the occasion, too. Most phenomenally, the novel leapt back onto the *New York Times* bestseller list for two Sundays running.

It all rather embarrassed Mitchell's native city. Even in her lifetime, many Atlantans had not known what exactly to do with Margaret Mitchell. The problem grew with time. The press quoted Mayor Andrew Young as saying that black America had little to celebrate in the anniversary of *Gone with the Wind*, but his general skepticism of the festivities was actually characteristic of reactions of many others in the city. Atlanta's suburbs teemed with transplants from the wilds of Ohio, Maine, and North Dakota, to whom Margaret Mitchell's novel might be, if anything, a product of another planet. Then, too, official and unofficial Atlanta, ever anxious as of old to assert its loyalty to the new, feared that *Gone with the Wind* represented rather too much nostalgia to fit its upscale, uptown image.

Still, some celebration took place, almost in spite of all the skepticism. Out-of-towners organized some events. Private parties and some public agencies sponsored tours, lectures, and exhibitions of one kind or another. Unofficial or not, however, even these affairs drew devotees from the woodwork. Folks flocked in from California, New Mexico, Pennsylvania, and from the boondocks of the Georgia–Carolina countryside as well. They brought their copies of the novel itself; some new, some venerable. They also stood in line to buy copies of various texts and books on the novel and queued good-naturedly to have the authors autograph their monographs. Some people had actually purchased copies long before, and while the authors scribbled some inscription on the flyleaf, the purchasers asked intelligent questions about the texts. They listened attentively to scholarly expositions about the author's life and bent their minds to understand the place of *Gone with the Wind* in the Southern Literary Renaissance, though some of them had never heard the term before. After fifty years, the old excitement still charged the popular response.

In a question-and-answer period after one of these sessions, one of the faithful confirmed the speaker's assertion of the resentment and anger that lurked just beneath the ladylike surface of Margaret Mitchell's life. When queried about the reason for her confirmation, the woman deflected the question. Pressed, she paused, smiled shyly, looked away, then up again, and finally admitted her source. "It may well be," she conceded in embarrassed pride, "that you are speaking to Margaret Mitchell at this moment. My evidence leads me to believe that Margaret Mitchell inhabits this body." There followed, then, her story of the Mitchell typewriter that spoke again at the touch of those fingers, the flowers that appeared mysteriously on the grave . . . and the other spectral evidence that confirmed for her that she was indeed Margaret Mitchell reincarnated.

On the evening of August 11, 1949, John Marsh consented to his wife's entreaties to attend the movies with her. *The Canterbury Tales* was showing at the Arts Theatre. They took the car from their apartment and drove the short distance through Ansley Park to Peachtree. Their route passed spots that had been home and second home to her for nearly forty years. The Marshes parked on the east side of the street, got out, and prepared to cross. They waded halfway through the light evening traffic, pausing in the middle of Peachtree Street. At that moment, they looked up to see a car roaring towards them that the curve in the street had hidden. This was the old nightmare: the speeding autoist; the drunken driver. The two of them stood in the middle of the street, but not for long. John stood still; she bolted. Overweight, bad feet and all, she dashed for the curb. The driver slammed on brakes, but too late. She had dashed into the path of the oncoming taxi.

The photographer and the curious spectators swarmed. She loathed gawkers and sensationalism, but she did not revive to mock or shoo them off. The ambulance arrived soon after. With siren screaming, it rushed her to Grady Hospital. The attending intern proved to be none other than the son of her old, dear, debutante friend, Lethea Turman Lockridge, one of her fellow radicals with whom she talked about "coming down off the auction block." But then, of course, she would surely have known some nurse, some physician or orderly, given her fifty-year residence in the city and regular visits to the hospitals. Young Dr. Lockridge discovered the car had done the severest damage. Atlanta, and indeed much of the world, read about the concussion and the coma that followed. Telegrams and letters poured in from everywhere. The telephone switchboard at Grady went crazy.

The swelling inside her cranial cavity did not go down, and five days later, at noon on August 16, the brain damage cost her her life.

Oakland Cemetary was home to half of Atlanta, or so it seemed; not merely the dead but the living. Like all great urban cemetaries in old towns, this one served as park as much as burying ground. Sightseers came and went, kids rode bicycles through the grounds, and strollers admired and read the markers for recreation. Margaret Mitchell had known the place as well as she knew her own backyard. She had biked through here as a little girl, and had visited it to place flowers on her mother's grave for thirty years of Sunday mornings. It held literally scores of other relatives and other folks she knew. City notables had buried one another here for nearly a century since its opening in 1854. The Civil War had greatly expanded its population and spawned the rows of white markers, many of them anonymous, to both Union and

Confederate soldiers who had fallen in those gruesome days eighty-five years before, when Sherman had besieged the town. Atlanta was just a village then. Some of these dead had surely seen their last light through the windows of the big wooden house on Jackson Hill when old Annie Stephens's mansion had served as Confederate field hospital in August 1864. Since the dreadful conflagration of 1917, that house, without other particular distinction, lived only in fading memories.

The living presence of that war itself was almost as faint in August 1949. At the premiere of *Gone with the Wind*, only four old veterans remained. The intervening decade claimed all of them. But there were the monuments. Oakland boasted one of the finest. All Atlanta knew the great recumbant stone lion commemorating the fallen Southern dead. Margaret and Stephens both were old enough to remember, too, the ceremonies of its erection and dedication in 1905. She knew the contours of the beast as surely as she knew the shape of her own face. This monument, evocative of King Philip's marker at the battlefield of Chaeroneia, symbolized the old Confederate authority that every Southern schoolchild of that generation had graven on the heart.

The funeral cortège skirted past it and wound by the serried ranks of anonymous markers, too. It threaded through the fantasy of funereal art of high nineteenth-century bourgeois culture, Atlanta-style: monumental crosses, broken columns, grieving angels, and sleeping lambs, such as marked the Porters' and the Coupers' plots and the graves of Hillyers, Newmans, and De Gives; then, too, there was the profusion of those with Hebrew letters and stars of David where her friend Elsas Phillips's family lay, near her old employer from the *Journal*, Major Cohen. The hearse passed near the Stephens plot; it did not stop. Soon before his own death, old Mr. Mitchell had disinterred his wife's remains from the hated in-laws' last resting place. He had removed them to a site not far away. The Mitchells rested now in a separate plot, together again since 1944. And with them lay their first child, who had died in infancy in 1893. Near here, the diggers had prepared another hole, the dread bounty of purple-red earth now nicely concealed beneath the mortician's artificial grass.

The cars debouched their passengers into the heat of a typically stifling, mid-August Atlanta day, and the company gathered grimly around the casket resting on its straps above the pit. Dean Raimundo De Ovies of Atlanta's Episcopal Cathedral conducted the service. On the day before, John had suggested this family friend to Stephens, who had called the minister to lead the service on the seventeenth. Dean De Ovies read from the Book of Common Prayer, the service for the dead. That was fitting. Though religion had remained irrelevant to the author, the rolling cadences of the Episcopal liturgy spoke powerfully to her. The fatal sensibilities of the funereal psalms—*Dixi, custodiam; Domine, refugium; De profundis;* and all the rest—moved her deeply. She had proclaimed her devotion to all the psalms. How much she loved the 103rd, she had exclaimed.

> The days of man are but as grass; for he flourisheth as a
>   flower of the field.
> For as soon as the wind goeth over it, it is gone; and the
>   place thereof shall know it no more.
> But the merciful goodness of the LORD endureth for ever and
>   ever upon them that fear him; and his righteousness upon
>   children's children;
> Even upon such as keep his covenant, and think upon his com-
>   mandments to do them.

It ended shortly. The family returned to the house at Peachtree Street again, and left Oakland to the folks. Hundreds visited the site. As they left, they took blossoms from the flower tributes as mementos. Security guards shooed them off until Stephens heard about it. Never mind, he said; they deserve something tangible.

Within a year, Stephens Mitchell and his boys made a second trip to Oakland to bury Carrie Lou. Her health was bad, as her sister-in-law always knew. Then on the morning of May 5, 1952, when she checked on him for his breakfast, Bessie Jordan found John Marsh dead. He was fifty-six. Two days later, the grave diggers buried him next to his wife. Stephens Mitchell lived to bury his second wife, and his sons conducted their father's simple Catholic services in 1983; his days stretched almost as long as his Grandmother Stephens', whom he, like his sister, disliked to the last.

The fall before she died, Margaret Mitchell had made a will. She was the same age then—forty-seven—as her mother the year that May Belle Mitchell died. She was thinking of mortality—the motif never really left her. Not long before the drunken driver ended her life, her very loyal churchman-brother Stephens had appealed to her to return to the mother church. She remained stubbornly committed to her course. "When you have made a bargain with the devil," she informed him flatly,

> you had better stick to your bargain. I may have made one, but whenever
> I give my word on something, or whenever I take a course of action, I
> am not going to try to crawl out of that course of action because I may
> have made a mistake in starting it. It is not the fair thing to do.[7]

She did not utter the name "Faust," but the imagery is fitting. She lived in the realm of myth and mystery, and her work and life tapped those same qualities for millions. And so they do still.

Notes

๏๏๏๏

Prologue: City of the Tribe

1. "Personality: Keeper of the Legend" [Interview with Stephens Mitchell], *Atlanta Constitution,* Oct. 1, 1979.

2. For the background of the cityscape, see Atlanta Urban Design Commission, *Atlanta Historic Resource Workbook* (Atlanta: Atlanta Urban Design Commission, 1981); Elizabeth M. Sawyer and Jane Foster Matthews, *The Old in New Atlanta* (1976; revised and expanded edition, Atlanta: JEMS Press, 1978); and Sarah Sims Edge, *Joel Hurt and the Development of Atlanta* (Atlanta: Atlanta Historical Society, 1955).

Chapter I: Rebels, Patriarchs, and Ladies

1. Eugene Mitchell to May Belle Stephens, Jan. 5, 1892, in the Margaret Mitchell Marsh Papers, Hargrett Rare Book and Manuscript Library, The University of Georgia Libraries, the University of Georgia, Athens, Georgia (hereafter, Mitchell Marsh, UGa).

2. *Atlanta Constitution,* Nov. 8, 9, 1892.

3. For the Watson threat in the countryside, see C. Van Woodward, *Tom Watson: Agrarian Rebel* (New York: Macmillan, 1938).

4. Unless otherwise noted, the Mitchell family history is drawn chiefly from Stephens Mitchell, "History of Mitchell Ancestors" in the Mitchell file of the Georgia Department of Archives and History; and Stephens Mitchell, "Memoir," in Mitchell Marsh, UGa. The latter, also quoted extensively by Finis Farr in his biography of Margaret Mitchell, *Margaret Mitchell of Atlanta,* was intended originally as a biography of the novelist herself. Stephens Mitchell dictated much of this material in the late 1950s and a ghost writer was working it up into a publishable form. Her death prevented its completion. While the portions of the memoir dealing with the Mitchells' childhood exists, complete with Stephens Mitchell's corrections and changes, the later parts, treating the twenties, no longer exist in the Mitchell archive.

5. Stephens Mitchell, personal interview with the author.

6. Margaret Mitchell to Helen and Clifford Dowdey, May 13, 1943, in Richard B. Harwell, editor, *Margaret Mitchell's "Gone with the Wind": Letters, 1936–1949* (New York: Macmillan, 1976), p. 369; also S. Mitchell, "Memoir," p. 41.

7. S. Mitchell, "Memoir," p. 41.

8. Mitchell to Dowdey, in Harwell, *Letters*, p. 369.

9. S. Mitchell, "History of Mitchell Ancestors," p. 32.

10. S. Mitchell, "Memoir," p. 46, with emendations, entry of June 3, 1959. While Stephens Mitchell's ghost writer apparently composed this version of the story, Mr. Mitchell left another account as an emandation in the same record, pp. 45–46.

11. For the Rice data, see Janet V. Lundgren, "Frank P. Rice and the Political Culture of Late Nineteenth-Century Atlanta," *Atlanta Historical Journal* XXIX (Fall 1983), pp. 27–34.

12. Dewey Grantham, *Hoke Smith and the Politics of the New South* (Baton Rouge: Louisiana State University Press, 1958), p. 21.

13. S. Mitchell, "History of Mitchell Ancestors," p. 33.

14. Ibid., pp. 23, 29, 33.

15. Mitchell had her own version of this family tale as well: see Margaret Mitchell to Clifford Dowdey, May 13, 1943, in Harwell, *Letters*, pp. 369–70.

16. Eugene Mitchell to May Belle Mitchell, July 6, 1889, Mitchell Marsh, UGa.

17. R. C. Mitchell to Emma [Mitchell] Lott, Nov. 7, 1882, Mitchell Genealogical File, Atlanta Historical Society, Atlanta, Georgia (hereafter cited as Mitchell, AHS).

18. S. Mitchell, "History of Mitchell Ancestors," p. 37; see also a surviving report card in Mr. Mitchell's scrapbook in Mitchell, AHS; and Eugene Mitchell to Mrs. R. C. Mitchell, Oct. 5, 1884, also Mitchell, AHS.

19. Eugene Mitchell to Mrs. R. C. Mitchell, Mitchell, AHS.

20. Finis Farr, *Margaret Mitchell of Atlanta*, (1965; reprint, New York: Avon, 1974), p. 31.

21. Eugene Mitchell to May Belle Stephens, July 27, 1892, Mitchell Marsh, UGa.

22. Franklin Garrett, personal interview with the author. See also Farr, *Margaret Mitchell*, pp. 31–32, for Mr. Mitchell's character.

23. Mrs. Ira A. Ferguson, personal interview with the author.

24. Courtenay Ross McFedyen, personal interview with the author.

25. The information here is drawn chiefly from an unsigned, untitled record [Sarah Fitzgerald?], ["Fitzgerald Family Record"]; S. Mitchell, "Memoir"; and another unsigned, untitled document that seems clearly the work of the author of *Gone with the Wind* herself, hereafter cited as [Mitchell], "Fitzgerald"—all in Mitchell Marsh, UGa. The latter has been published in Alice Copeland Kilgore, Edith Hanes Smith, Frances Part Tuck, et al., *History of Clayton County, Georgia, 1821–1983* (Roswell, Ga.: W. H. Wolfe, 1983). See also Mary Kane Stephens Graham (the sister of John Stephens), "The Stephens of Gloster, King's County Ireland, as told by Mary Kane Stephens Graham, Augusta, Georgia, December 1896," Mitchell Marsh, UGa.

26. Southern Catholicism forms a lamentable lacuna in Southern historiography. What was the role of Catholicism in the general patterns of Southern religion? How much prejudice did Catholics endure? Although the anonymous

family historian (Sarah Fitzgerald) records nameless liabilities Phillip Fitzgerald endured because of his religion, little specific evidence of anti-Catholicism exists prior to the Watson era. Random documentary evidence also confirms the absence of religious prejudice. I cite the sermon preached at the funeral of my own ancestor, Judge Abner Darden in 1874, a document in my possession. Judge Darden (1812–1874), a friend of Alexander Stephens and minor Whig politician from Taliaferro and Polk counties, Georgia, attended a "classical" school run by Taliaferro Catholics, among them Mitchell's McGahan ancestors. Darden's school experience instilled in him a great appreciation of learning and a high regard for Catholics as well, without affecting his profound commitment to his native Baptist faith. The Baptist minister who preached his funeral sermon in 1874 dwelt at length on Darden's commitment to and interchanges with his Catholic fellow countrymen.

27. Immigrants to the South also need study. For a beginning of such an examination, see Edward Ayers, *Vengeance and Justice: Crime and Punishment in the Nineteenth-Century South* (New York: Oxford University Press, 1984); also Richard Hopkins, "Status, Mobility, and the Dimensions of Change in a Southern City," in Kenneth T. Jackson and Stanley K. Schultz, eds., *Cities in American History* (New York: Alfred Knopf, 1972), pp. 216–31; and Eugene J. Watts, "The Police in Atlanta, 1890–1905," *Journal of Southern History* 39 (May 1973), pp. 164–82. Such studies explore the part of the mostly anonymous poor, among them the immigrant Irish; the Catholic gentry, like the Stephenses, Flynns, Spauldings, and De Gives—specifically of Atlanta—have yet to find their historian.

28. S. Mitchell, "Memoir," p. 56.

29. Ibid., p. 58.

30. For this particular story, see [Mitchell], "Fitzgerald," pp. 4–5. For the historical background that illuminates such anecdotes, see Steven Hahn's excellent monograph, *Roots of Southern Populism: Yeomen Farmers and the Transformation of the Georgia Upcountry* (New York: Oxford University Press, 1983).

31. In addition to the Fitzgerald material, see John Stephens's obituary in Mitchell, AHS; Margaret Mitchell to Mr. and Mrs. John S. Graham, Aug. 27, 1937, Mitchell Marsh, UGa: also the *Atlanta City Directory* for the years between 1866 and 1896. Farr, *Margaret Mitchell*, p. 38.

32. [Mitchell], "Fitzgerald," p. 11.

33. For his political engagements, see his correspondence with May Belle while she was in convent school in Canada; for example, John Stephens to May Belle Stephens, Nov. 8, 1885; John Stephens to May Belle Stephens, Feb. 2, 1886; and John Stephens to May Belle Stephens, Aug. 6, 1886; all Mitchell Marsh, UGa.

34. See Graham, "The Stephenses," Mitchell Marsh, UGa, for the celebration of family bookishness and cultural proclivities even in Ireland. See also John Stephens to May Belle Stephens, Mar. 9, 1886, Mitchell Marsh, UGa.

35. John Stephens to May Belle Stephens, Mar. 9, 1886, Mitchell Marsh, UGa.

36. Clarence Durham to Margaret Mitchell, Sept. 1, 1937, Mitchell Marsh, UGa.

37. S. Mitchell, "Memoir," p. 55.

38. [Mitchell], "Fitzgerald" p. 10.

39. S. Mitchell, "Memoir," p. 55.

40. Ibid., pp. 20A–21.

41. John Stephens to May Belle Stephens, Nov. 8, 1885, and Feb. 2, 1886, Mitchell Marsh, UGa.

42. S. Mitchell, "Memoir," p. 54.

43. See the general files of lawsuits in the Fulton county court records.

44. Stephens Crockett, personal interview with the author.

45. Sam Heyes, personal interview with the author; and David Crockett, personal interview with the author.

46. Farr, *Margaret Mitchell*, pp. 69, 70. Also Margaret Mitchell Marsh to Harvey Smith, March 15, 1933, The Margaret Mitchell Collection, Special Collections, Emory University, Atlanta, Georgia. Hereafter, Mitchell Emory.

47. Harvey Smith, personal interview with the author.

48. S. Mitchell, "Memoir," p. 19; also the *Atlanta City Directory*, 1880, 1881, 1882.

49. [Mitchell], "Fitzgerald," p. 10.

50. Margaret Mitchell to Mrs. Harry E. Ransford, Feb. 2, 1937, Mitchell Marsh, UGa.

51. [Mitchell], "Fitzgerald," p. 10.

52. Mitchell to Ransford, Feb. 2, 1937; and Mitchell to Lucille Kennan, June 21, 1938, both Mitchell Marsh, UGa. See also [Mitchell], "Fitzgerald," p. 5.

53. John Stephens to May Belle Stephens, Nov. 28, 1886, Mitchell Marsh, UGa.

54. John Stephens to May Belle Stephens, Nov. 8, 1886, Mitchell Marsh, UGa.

55. May Belle Stephens to John Stephens, Oct. 28, 1885, Mitchell Marsh, UGa.

56. Ibid.

57. Ibid.

58. May Belle Stephens to John Stephens, Dec. 1, 1885, Mitchell Marsh, UGa.

59. John Stephens to May Belle Stephens, Feb. 2, 1886, Mitchell Marsh, UGa.

60. John Stephens to May Belle Stephens, July 22, 1886, Mitchell Marsh, UGa.

61. John Stephens to May Belle Stephens, Feb. 2, 1886, and Sept. 16, 1886, Mitchell Marsh, UGa.

62. John Stephens to May Belle Stephens, June 9, 1887; and also John Stephens to May Belle Stephens, Aug. 6, 1886, Mitchell Marsh, UGa.

63. John Stephens to May Belle Stephens, Feb. 2, 1886, Mitchell Marsh, UGa.

64. John Stephens to May Belle Stephens, June 9, 1887, Mitchell Marsh, UGa.

65. John Stephens to May Belle Stephens, Feb. 2, 1886, Mitchell Marsh, UGa.

66. Thomas Carlyle, *Sartor Resartus*, Book 2, pp. 133, 143, quoted in W. E. Houghton, *The Victorian Frame of Mind, 1830–1870* (New Haven and London: Yale University Press, 1957), pp. 392–93.

67. Eugene Mitchell to May Belle Stephens, Jan. 5, 1892, Mitchell Marsh, UGa.

68. Ibid.

69. Eugene Mitchell to Mrs. Mary Walker, June 7, 1942, Mitchell Marsh, UGa.

Chapter II: Jimmy

1. "How *Gone with the Wind* Was Written," *The Atlanta Journal Magazine,* May 23, 1937.

2. For the description of the Mitchell house, see Stephens Mitchell, "Margaret Mitchell and Her People," *Atlanta Historical Bulletin* IX (May 1950), p. 15 (hereafter abbreviated as *AHB*); Stephens Mitchell, "Her Brother Remembers Margaret Mitchell's Childhood," *Atlanta Constitution,* "Margaret Mitchell Memorial Issue," Dec. 23, 1949; and Mitchell, "Memoir," Mitchell Marsh, UGa.

3. S. Mitchell, "Memoir," p. 24. The only source of this incident, Stephens Mitchell, left two accounts, one published in "Margaret Mitchell and Her People," and the fuller unpublished version in his memoir in Mitchell Marsh, UGa. Anne Edwards, in *Road to Tara: The Life of Margaret Mitchell, Author of "Gone with the Wind"* (New Haven: Ticknor and Fields, 1983), apparently missed them both and created a bizarrely fanciful version that violates common sense as well as this clear documentary evidence. Thus, for example, she has the fire coming through forced air grills rather than the open fireplace of fact. She also completely fictionalizes the child's injuries. Stephens Mitchell asserts clearly that no one suffered any physical damage. Edwards also fictionalizes the consequences of the affair, having both May Belle Mitchell and Annie Stephens nurse the injured girl. While grievous enough on their own, such fictionalization also leads to other errors. Annie Stephens and May Belle Mitchell, for example, were not nurturers by any stretch of the facts. The distortions in the treatment of the fire represent the general errors of fact and the still more general distortions in interpretation of this entire biography.

4. S. Mitchell, "Margaret Mitchell," *AHB*, pp. 16–17.

5. S. Mitchell, "Memoir," p. 24.

6. David Crockett interview; Stephens Crockett interview.

7. S. Mitchell, "Margaret Mitchell," *AHB*, pp. 15, 16–17; also, for her love of horses see "Personality: Keeper of the Legend," *Atlanta Constitution;* and Margaret Mitchell to Martha Angley, Apr. 25, 1936, Mitchell Marsh, UGa; also Margaret Mitchell to Harvey Smith, May 24, 1933, Mitchell Emory. For Mrs. Mitchell's anxiety about her children's reckless horsemanship, see Mrs. S. E. Breeden [a cousin] to Margaret Mitchell, Nov. 5, 1936, Mitchell Marsh, UGa.

8. "How *Gone with the Wind* Was Written," *Atlanta Journal.*

9. In two different sources, Mitchell's brother maintains that she did not play with dolls—S. Mitchell, "Memoir," p. 24; and that she did play with dolls—S. Mitchell, "Margaret Mitchell," *AHB*, p. 15.

10. S. Mitchell, "Memoir," p. 25.

11. S. Mitchell, "Margaret Mitchell," *AHB*, p. 17.

12. S. Mitchell, "Memoir," p. 25.

13. Margaret Mitchell to Elinor Hillyer, July 7, 1930, Elinor Hillyer von Hoffman, private papers of Elinor Hillyer von Hoffman (hereafter, von Hoffman).

14. Eugene Mitchell to May Belle Mitchell, Sept. 29, 1906, Mitchell Marsh, UGa.

15. S. Mitchell, "Memoir," pp. 22, 61.

16. Margaret Mitchell to Herschel Brickell, May 25, 1938, in Harwell, *Letters*, p. 204.

17. S. Mitchell, "Memoir," p. 16.

18. William Faulkner, *Absalom, Absalom!* (New York, 1936: Vintage Books, 1972, reprint), p. 16.

19. S. Mitchell, "Memoir," p. 15.

20. Margaret Mitchell to Mrs. Julia Collier Harris, Apr. 28, 1936, in Harwell, *Letters*, p. 3.

21. Ibid., p. 4.

22. "Keeper of the Legend," *Atlanta Constitution.*

23. Faulkner, *Absalom, Absalom!*, p. 9.

24. Margaret Mitchell to Harriet Ross Colquitt, Aug. 7, 1936, in Harwell, *Letters*, p. 50.

25. "Mitchell, Eugene Muse," in Allen D. Candler and Clement A. Evans, eds., *Cyclopedia of Georgia*, 3 vols. (Atlanta: State Historical Association, 1906) II, 602–5.

26. See Grantham, *Hoke Smith;* and "Mitchell," *Cyclopedia of Georgia.*

27. "Mitchell," *Cyclopedia of Georgia.*

28. See his articles in the *Atlanta Historical Bulletin:* also records of his genealogical researches in the Mitchell files at the Georgia Department of Archives and History. For his daughter's version of his genealogical concerns, see Farr, *Margaret Mitchell*, pp. 30–31.

29. Margaret Mitchell to Edwin Granberry, July 8, 1936, in Harwell, *Letters*, p. 29; also Margaret Mitchell to C. P. Howard, June 22, 1942, Mitchell Marsh, UGa.

30. Mitchell to Father J. M. Lelen, Sept. 5, 1936, Mitchell Marsh, UGa.

31. *Atlanta Constitution*, Jan. 26, 1919.

32. Margaret Ransford to Margaret Mitchell, Aug. 31, 1939, Mitchell Marsh, UGa.

33. For the passing reference to her disaster work, see Faith Baldwin, "The Woman Who Wrote *Gone with the Wind:* An Exclusive and Authentic Interview," *Pictoral Review*, March 1937.

34. See Chapter IV.

35. Mitchell to Smith, Mar. 15, 1933, Mitchell, Emory.

36. Heyes interview.

37. See Farr, *Margaret Mitchell*, p. 35.

38. Edward L. Cashin, "Thomas E. Watson and the Catholic Layman's Association of Georgia" (Ph.D. diss., Fordham University, 1962)

39. Cited in Farr, *Margaret Mitchell*, p. 35.

40. Jill Franco, *"GWTW* Author Was a Libber Brother Says," undated clipping, in *Road to Tara* Collection, Atlanta Historical Society. Anne Edwards deposited all of her research materials for her biography in this collection. While her book has little merit as a factual account of Margaret Mitchell's life, she collected useful data, particularly clippings and published material, but especially personal interviews and inquiries. This collection of material is im-

portant to any research on the Atlanta writer. Hereafter, references to this material are cited as Tara, AHS.

41. "Keeper of the Legend," *Atlanta Constitution.*

42. Another area needing more research, the suffrage movement in Georgia is sketched in two venerable essays by A. Elizabeth Taylor, "The Origins of the Woman Suffrage Movement in Georgia," *Georgia Historical Quarterly* XXVII (1944): 63–80; and "Revival and Development of the Women's Suffrage Movement in Georgia," *Georgia Historical Quarterly* XLII (1958), 351–52.

43. "Notes on Woman's Suffrage, National, State and Local," *Atlanta Constitution*, Jan. 31, 1915, in "Women's Suffrage," Atlanta Historical Society (hereafter cited as "Notes," AHS). The other officers listed were, besides Mrs. Mitchell (named second): Mrs. Frances Smith Whiteside, Mrs. Elizabeth McCarthy, Miss Laura Berrien, Mrs. W. Yeandle, Mrs. Jack Hawkins, Miss Ethel Merk, Mrs. Adell G. Helmer, Mrs. Lollie B. Wylie, Miss Mary C. Barker, Mrs. T. Moody, Miss Marion Morris, Mrs. M. S. Yeates.

44. "Keeper of the Legend," *Atlanta Constitution.*

45. Stephens Mitchell interview.

46. While Margaret Mitchell never mentioned her mother's health, her brother discussed her diabetes and her other unnamed illnesses that called for "rest cures" or "milk cures" in the North. She stayed at the "American Hygenic Institute" in New Jersey, for example: see E. M. Mitchell to May Belle Mitchell, Sept. 3, 1906; June 10, 1910; June 29, 1910; all Mitchell Marsh, UGa.

47. Martin Shartar, "The Winds of Time and Chance: Stephens Mitchell Surveys Seven Decades in Atlanta," *Atlanta* XIV (July 1974), 100.

48. "Keeper of the Legend," *Atlanta Constitution.*

49. See Joel Williamson, *The Crucible of Race: Black–White Relations in the American South Since Emancipation* (New York: Oxford University Press, 1984), for the ways that the women's suffrage movement intersected with racial values in the state, at least by way of Mrs. Felton.

50. See both Taylor articles. Even in the 1920s, Eugene Mitchell also continued to contribute to the League of Women Voters.

51. See, for example, S. Mitchell, "Memoir"; Stephens Mitchell's failure to address his father—in contrast to his mother—was especially glaring here, so much so that when Stephens Mitchell submitted his memoir to his son, the younger Mitchell noted it as a shortcoming or imbalance. Stephens Mitchell demonstrated the same tendency in "Keeper of the Legend," *Atlanta Constitution*, and in his interview with the author when he adverted again and again to Mrs. Mitchell while virtually ignoring his father.

52. Quoted in Farr, *Margaret Mitchell*, p. 37.

53. Margaret Mitchell to Mrs. Harry E. Ransford, Sept. 7, 1939, Mitchell Marsh, UGa.

54. Mitchell to Smith, Mar. 15, 1933, Mitchell, Emory.

55. Interpreting Mitchell's letters and style, as here, poses a significant problem to biographers. Like her literary character Rhett Butler, Mitchell often undercut her meaning by tone or detail. She might speak truly, but exaggerate or inflate the figure to make a statement literally incredible. She did so purposefully. In one of the most succinct and self-conscious expressions of the technique, for example, after discussing psychoanalyzing her friends, she added

in literal parentheses, "(I mean that as a joke of course but I mean it seriously, too)": Margaret Mitchell to Dr. Mark Allen Patton, July 11, 1936, in Harwell, *Letters*, p. 42. At other times, she simply fabricated information. As a result, she created a kind of halflight world where fiction and reality flowed almost inseparably together. As suggested by Carleton Perry Lentz in his excellent analysis of *Gone with the Wind*, "Our Missing Epic: A Study of the Novels About the American Civil War" Ph.D. diss., Vanderbilt University, 1970), this ebbing and flowing of true and false, myth and reality, high and low art, emerges as the very essence of both the style and the content of Mitchell's novel. This same sort of play in her letters lends itself to psychological interpretation and scrutiny. The methodology is especially appropriate because of Mitchell's intense interest in psychoanalytic theory and her own propensity to apply psychological insights to behavior. Moreover, she wrote so much and so rapidly that her letters generally follow a pattern of free association. In this stream-of-consciousness approach to correspondence, fairly consistent patterns do emerge. They invite analysis. Her contradictions are so profound, in any case, that her life makes little sense without this sort of interpretation. See Chapter XVI for a discussion of her letter-writing from a literary perspective.

56. Gretchen Finletter, "Parents and Parades," *Atlantic Monthly* 176 (1945): pp. 80–84.

57. Quoted in Farr, *Margaret Mitchell*, p. 36.

58. Mitchell generally paired her virtuous women with a wrathful "double." Sandra M. Gilbert and Susan Gubar, *Madwoman in the Attic: The Woman Writer and the Nineteenth-Century Literary Imagination* (New Haven and London: Yale University Press, 1979), introduce particularly useful and appropriate variations on this theme in the context of feminist theory. Their work has illuminated my general understanding of the relationship between patriarchal cultural values and individual psychology; it has added even more to my particular understanding of Mitchell's life. For a still more destructive example of a Southern woman doubling back against herself, see my "Nell Battle Lewis (1896–1956): To Be a Southern Woman," *Social Studies Perspectives on the South* 3 (1982), pp. 63–85.

59. She recounted the affair first at a notable luncheon at the Macon Writers' Club on the eve of the publication of her book in 1936. For a local newspaper report, see Blythe M'Kay, "Mrs. Marsh Is Honored at Writers' Breakfast," *Macon Telegraph and News*, Apr. 4, 1936. The author gave still another written account in a letter to Henry Steele Commager, July 10, 1936, published in Harwell, *Letters*, pp. 38–39.

60. M'Kay, "Mrs. Marsh Is Honored."

61. Mitchell to Commager, in Harwell, *Letters*, p. 38.

62. Margaret Mitchell, *Gone with the Wind*, p. 772.

63. Mitchell to Commager, in Harwell, *Letters*, p. 38. See also the section on Mitchell in Anne Jones, *Tomorrow Is Another Day: The Woman Writer in the South, 1859–1936* (Baton Rouge: Louisiana State University Press, 1981).

64. S. Mitchell, "Memoir," p. 21.

65. Ferguson interview.

66. Margaret Mitchell to Herschel Brickell, Sept. 4, 1937, in Harwell, *Letters*, pp. 166–67; and Chapter III.

67. M'Kay, "Mrs. Marsh Is Honored."

68. S. Mitchell, "Memoir," pp. 27–28, 39.

69. Ibid., p. 27.

70. Farr, *Margaret Mitchell*, p. 26. See also S. Mitchell, "Memoir"; and Chapter III.

71. S. Mitchell, "Memoir," p. 27.

72. Ibid., p. 2.

73. Ibid., p. 30.

74. McFedyen interview.

75. Ferguson interview.

76. Mitchell repeatedly claimed her mother had mathematical "genius," while just as often she noted her own inability to master even the most rudimentary arithmetic computations. In her letter to Henry Steele Commager that described the Jonesboro Road confrontation, for example, she concluded her version of the affair, "Well, I never could learn the multiplication table above the sevens but I was frightened and impressed enough by her words to learn enough rhetoric to land a job on a newspaper some years later!" (Mitchell to Commager, in Harwell, *Letters*, p. 38.)

77. See her juvenile stories in Mitchell Marsh, UGa; also the long story in Mitchell, AHS, for the handwriting, the spelling, the wildly lined notebooks, and the incompletion. Her spelling never improved, so that her husband, and later private secretary Margaret Baugh, would function indispensably as proofreaders for Mitchell's letters after she achieved fame.

78. S. Mitchell, "Memoir," p. 31.

79. Margaret Mitchell to Donald Adams, July 9, 1936, in Harwell, *Letters*, p. 32.

80. Margaret Mitchell to Father J. M. Lelen, June 6, 1936, in Harwell, *Letters*, p. 19.

81. Margaret Mitchell, "Two Little Folk," Mitchell Marsh, UGa.

82. Margaret Mitchell, "Knighthood," Mitchell Marsh, UGa.

83. Margaret Mitchell, "The Little Pioneers," Mitchell Marsh, UGa.

84. These homemade books survive in Mitchell Marsh, UGa; and Mitchell, AHS.

85. Manuscript in the Mitchell papers at the Atlanta Historical Society, which I discovered and brought to the attention of the staff. This little bound manuscript has no author and no title; its literary form, style, handwriting, and binding, even, are unmistakably the same as those of the author of "The Little Pioneers." It has been edited by Jane Powers Weldon as "Through the Eyes of a Youth: A Civil War Story," *Atlanta Historical Journal* XXIX (Winter 1985–86), 47–59.

86. Quoted in Farr, *Margaret Mitchell*, p. 48. Farr cites this reference apparently from the flyleaf of some additional childhood story. As mentioned below, he seemed to have had access to other juvenile fiction no longer existing in the Mitchell archives at the University of Georgia.

Chapter III: Shero

1. Mrs. Eva Wilson Paisley to Margaret Mitchell, Oct. 19, 1936, Mitchell Marsh, UGa.

2. Howard L. Preston, *Automobile Age in Atlanta* (Athens: University of Georgia Press, 1979), pp. 98–101.

3. S. Mitchell, "Memoir," p. 68.

4. S. Mitchell, "Margaret Mitchell," *AHB*, p. 17.

5. S. Mitchell, "Memoir," p. 66.

6. Ibid., p. 67.

7. Farr, *Margaret Mitchell*, p. 47.

8. S. Mitchell, "Memoir," p. 66.

9. DeWitt Alexander to Margaret Mitchell, Jan. 18, 1937, Mitchell Marsh, UGa.

10. Farr, *Margaret Mitchell*, pp. 47–48; and the photographic album, Mitchell Marsh, UGa; also S. Mitchell, "Margaret Mitchell," *AHB*, p. 23.

11. Lucille Little to Margaret Mitchell, Sept. 26, 1936, in Mitchell Marsh, UGa.

12. Margaret Mitchell to Thomas Dixon, Aug. 15, 1936, in Harwell, *Letters*, pp. 52–53.

13. Scrapbook, Courtenay Ross McFedyen, private collection.

14. Margaret Mitchell to Lucille Little, Sept. 29, 1936, Mitchell Marsh, UGa.

15. McFedyen scrapbook; also McFedyen interview.

16. McFedyen interview.

17. Ibid.

18. Ibid.

19. Jane Bonner Peacock, ed., *Margaret Mitchell, Dynamo Going to Waste: Letters to Allen Edee, 1919–1921* (Atlanta: Peachtree Publishers, 1985). p. 13.

20. McFedyen interview, also personal communication to the author, Apr. 25, 1986.

21. Peacock, *Dynamo*, p. 16; see also McFedyen interview.

22. Berry Fleming to Margaret Mitchell, Oct. 23, 1936, in Mitchell Marsh, UGa.

23. Little to Mitchell, Sept. 26, 1936, Mitchell Marsh, UGa.

24. Margaret Mitchell, "(Seen) Scene at a Soiree," Mitchell Marsh, UGa.

25. See Peacock, *Dynamo*, pp. 70, 103, for Mitchell's later references to McCullough's real-life gullibility.

26. The issues of costume and disguise in particular played a critical role in Mitchell's life. Even by age fifteen, she is a virtual model of the arguments about disguise, the woman's voice, and the woman writer's condition as presented by Gilbert and Gubar in *Madwoman in the Attic*.

27. Margaret Mitchell to Herschel Brickell, Sept. 4, 1937, in Harwell, *Letters*, pp. 166–67.

28. Margaret Mitchell to the Very Rev. Mons. James H. Murphy, Mar. 4, 1937, in Harwell, *Letters*, p. 127.

29. Margaret Mitchell to Mr. and Mrs. Stephen Vincent Benet, July 23, 1936, in Harwell, *Letters*, p. 44.

30. See Chapter VII.

31. Ferguson interview. Caroline Tye was one of Mitchell's girlhood friends who went away to boarding school in the nation's capital.

32. Courtenay McFedyen Leet, personal interview with the author. The daughter of Courtenay Ross McFedyen, Mrs. Leet attended Washington Seminary in the 1930s, and as a non-Atlantan of a very international background

(having lived abroad with her military family), she testified to the school's provincialism and suggested that the narrow, cultural Christocentrism of the institution militated against Catholics as well as Jews and probably helped account for some of Mitchell's difficulties there a generation earlier.

33. Quoted in Martha Angley, "Margaret Mitchell," in Mitchell Marsh, UGa. A high school student in Atlanta in the 1930s, Miss Angley discovered Mitchell just before the publication of *GWTW*, when the author was still liberal with herself and interviews. Miss Angley maintained a correspondence with the author afterward, and she summarized all this information in her essay. It is particularly interesting and revealing. While the student failed to put quotation marks on everything, many of her observations bear the author's unmistakable stamp. It is an important source for stories of Mitchell's school days.

34. For her grades, see "Certificate of Candidate for Admission, copy" for Smith College, Mitchell Marsh, UGa.

35. The long and carefully illustrated notebook is in Mitchell Marsh, UGa.

36. "Certificate of Candidate," Mitchell Marsh, UGa.

37. Angley, "Margaret Mitchell," Mitchell Marsh, UGa.

38. E. W. Paisley, *Sanctuary* (New York: E. P. Dutton, 1940).

39. Paisley, *Sanctuary*, pp. 111–12.

40. Margaret Mitchell to Eva Wilson Paisley, Dec. 23, 1940, Mitchell Marsh, UGa.

41. Mitchell to Paisley, Oct. 23, 1936, Mitchell Marsh, UGa.

42. Ibid.

43. Ibid.

44. E. W. Paisley to Margaret Mitchell, Oct. 19, 1936, Mitchell Marsh, UGa.

45. Anne Equen, "Margaret Mitchell's Story for Annual Once Rejected," *Atlanta Constitution*, Dec. 11, 1939.

46. Margaret Mitchell to Paisley, Oct. 23, 1936, Mitchell Marsh, UGa.

47. McFedyen interview.

48. McFedyen scrapbook.

49. "Washington Seminary" (clipping), McFedyen scrapbook.

50. Quoted in Farr, *Margaret Mitchell,* p. 53.

51. Peacock, *Dynamo,* p. 16.

52. Smith interview.

53. See Peacock, *Dynamo,* pp. 16–17; McFedyen interview; McFedyen scrapbook, and the school yearbook, *Facts and Fancies: 1914, 1915, 1916, 1917, 1918,* Mitchell Marsh, UGa.

54. McFedyen scrapbook.

55. Little to Mitchell, Sept. 26, 1936, Mitchell Marsh, UGa.

56. Elinor Hillyer von Hoffman, personal interview with the author.

57. *The Missema* [the school paper], Vol. 15, no. 2, Washington Seminary, Atlanta, Georgia, Mitchell Marsh, UGa.

58. McFedyen scrapbook.

59. Ibid.

60. "Washington Seminary" (clipping), McFedyen scrapbook.

61. "First Annual Debate" (program); see also the poem scribbled on the program; and "Second Annual Debate" (program), both in McFedyen scrapbook; also Equen, "Margaret Mitchell's Story."

62. *The Missema*, Mitchell Marsh, UGa.

63. Equen, "Margaret Mitchell's Story."

64. Farr, *Margaret Mitchell*, pp. 48–49. Farr seems to have seen a copy of this manuscript when he was writing the biography. Mitchell's secretary, Margaret Baugh, remembered it even though she was less familiar with the manuscript. Correspondence about the work between Lois Cole and Baugh while the Farr biography was being proofread suggests the manuscript survived the destruction of Mitchell's unpublished stories under John Marsh's direction after Mitchell's death, although this is not absolutely clear. The early work does not, in any case, survive in the public realm. See M. Baugh, "Answer to LDC [Lois Dwight Cole] questions *re* Farr Biography," Oct. 12, 1964; and similar correspondence of May 21, 1964, both in Mitchell Marsh, UGa; also Mitchell, Emory. The quotation is from Miss Baugh, Mitchell's secretary.

65. Equen, "Margaret Mitchell's Story."

66. Margaret Mitchell, "Little Sister," *Facts and Fancies*, 1917 (n.p.).

67. "Sergeant Terry," *Facts and Fancies*, 1918 (n.p.).

68. Here again, Mitchell provides a good example of the issues concerning the woman's narrative voice as analyzed by Gilbert and Gubar, *Madwoman in the Attic*.

69. Farr, *Margaret Mitchell*, p. 49.

Chapter IV: "Where Do We Go from Here?"

1. "July Umpteenth," 1927, Mitchell, Emory.

2. See Steve B. Campbell, "The Great Fire of Atlanta, May 21, 1917 (An Official Record)," *AHB* XIII (June 1968): 9–48; and S. Mitchell, "Margaret Mitchell," *AHB*, p. 18.

3. Baldwin, "Exclusive Interview." See also Farr, *Margaret Mitchell*, pp. 50–51.

4. McFedyen scrapbook.

5. Ibid.

6. Ibid.

7. Ibid.; also McFedyen interview.

8. McFedyen scrapbook.

9. Quoted in Farr, *Margaret Mitchell*, p. 51.

10. [——] Powell, "Meet Peggy Marsh of Atlanta," unpublished manuscript of 4/16/42, filed under "Ward Greene" in Mitchell Marsh, UGa.

11. Margaret Mitchell to Susan Myrick, Feb. 10, 1939, quoted in Harwell, *Letters*, p. 250.

12. Quoted in Farr, *Margaret Mitchell*, p. 49.

13. Ibid., p. 50.

14. Margaret Mitchell to Harvey Smith, Mar. 5, 1933, Mitchell, Emory.

15. When Harvey Smith donated his collection of Mitchell letters to Emory, he accompanied each with fair to very elaborate notes. Hereafter, these are cited as his glosses with the letter's date, as follows: Smith (gloss on letter of May 24, 1933), Mitchell, Emory.

16. Quoted in Farr, *Margaret Mitchell*, p. 54.

17. See the Mitchell photographic collection, Special Collections, the Atlanta Public Library, Atlanta, Georgia.

18. This biographical information is drawn from the following sources: *Harvard, Class of 1918, 25th Anniversary Report* (Cambridge, 1943), pp. 369–72; "Harvard Degree to One Absent Boy," *New York Post*, June 19, 1919, in Quinquennial File, Harvard University Archives, Harvard University, Cambridge, Mass.; *Harvard Album, 1918*, Vol. XXIX (Cambridge, Mass.: 1918); and Mark De Wolfe Howe et al., *Memoirs of Harvard Dead in the War Against Germany*, Vol. V (Cambridge, Mass.: 1924), Harvard University Press. See also Farr, *Margaret Mitchell*, p. 64.

19. McFedyen scrapbook.

20. Quoted in Farr, *Margaret Mitchell*, p. 55.

21. Quoted in S. Mitchell, "Memoir," p. 4A.

22. See Mitchell's summary of the trip in the letter to her grandmother and father of Sept. 8, 1918, quoted in Farr, *Margaret Mitchell*, pp. 54–55.

23. Ibid., p. 60. See later in this chapter for a full treatment of this letter.

24. S. Mitchell, "Memoir," pp. 68–69.

25. See Farr, *Margaret Mitchell*, p. 63; also Margaret Mitchell to Allen Edee, July 31, 1920, in Peacock, *Dynamo*, p. 104.

26. Quoted in Medora Field Perkerson, "Twenty-fifth Anniversary of *Gone with the Wind*," *Atlanta Journal and Constitution*, May 16, 1954.

27. Margaret Mitchell to Grandma and Father, Sept. 8, 1918, Mitchell Marsh, UGa. Farr quotes a portion of this important letter in *Margaret Mitchell*, pp. 54–55; he omitted this critical section and others.

28. Margaret Mitchell to Grandma and Father, Sept. 8, 1918, in Farr, *Margaret Mitchell*, p. 55.

29. Smith College yearbook, 1919. See also Mrs. Grierson to Mrs. Parker, n.d.; Mrs. Doris J. Carl to Mrs. Parker, Jan. 16, 1951; Martha Cole to Mrs. Parker, Jan. 15, 1951. Typescripts of letters in the Medora Field Perkerson Papers, Hargrett Rare Book and Manuscript Library, University of Georgia Libraries, University of Georgia, Athens, Georgia (hereafter, Perkerson, UGa). After Mitchell's death in 1949, Mrs. Parker, another Smith graduate, sought to create a scholarship in Mitchell's name. As a part of the fund-raising campaign that followed, she solicited letters of recollection from Mitchell's old housemates and classmates. Perkerson, in turn, made copies of all these and used them in various articles she wrote about her old friend. These quotations and those that follow are taken from the typescript copies of the letters in Perkerson's archive.

30. Smith College yearbook, 1922. See also the photographs in the Mitchell scrapbook from these years: Mitchell Marsh, UGa.

31. See Florence C. Grandin to Mrs. Parker, n.d., Perkerson, UGa; and snapshots in the Mitchell scrapbook, Mitchell Marsh, UGa.

32. See for example, Margaret Mitchell to Dr. Mark Allen Patton, July 11, 1936, in Harwell, *Letters*, p. 42; and Margaret Mitchell to Mrs. Julia Collier Harris, Apr. 28, 1936, in Harwell, *Letters*, p. 4. See also her statement to the high school student Martha Angley in May 1936 to the same effect, in Mitchell Marsh, UGa. Farr, *Margaret Mitchell*, p. 54, treats the medical career as a matter of fact; so does Stephens Mitchell in his memoirs.

33. These interests make a constant thread in her letters. Her friends often spoke of her passions in this regard as well. Her psychology books constituted one of the single largest sections of her library. In addition to Krafft-Ebing and all the works of Havelock Ellis, she owned volumes by Karen Horney, Rieff, and others. Two inventories of her books after her husband's death confirm her interest. (See the inventories in the private papers of Frances Marsh Zane in the possession of Roland Zane (hereafter, Marsh Zane).

34. Martha Cole to Mrs. Parker, Jan. 15, 1951, Perkerson, UGa.

35. William Morris to Margaret Mitchell, Aug. 25, 1936, quoted by Richard Harwell, "A Striking Resemblance to a Masterpiece," in Darden Asbury Pyron, ed., *Recasting: "Gone with the Wind" in American Culture* (Gainesville, Fla.: University of Florida Press, 1984), p. 39.

36. Margaret Mitchell to Allen Edee, Oct. 21, 1919, in Peacock, *Dynamo*, p. 42. See also Chapter V, where she repeated the assertion about writing to a news reporter. She would support herself, she insisted, by writing comedies and short stories. Medora Field, "What Atlanta Debutantes Think," *Atlanta Journal*, Apr. 10, 1921, in Mitchell scrapbook, Mitchell Marsh, UGa.

37. Margaret Mitchell to Mrs. Minnie Hale Daniel, Jan. 6, 1937, Mitchell Marsh, UGa.

38. Margaret Mitchell to Mrs. Eva Wilson Paisley, Oct. 23, 1936, quoted by Harwell, "Masterpiece," in Pyron, *Recasting*, p. 43.

39. Madelaine Baxter to Mrs. Parker, n.d., Perkerson, UGa.

40. Margaret Mitchell to Sally Vanderbilt, Oct. 19, 1936, Mitchell Marsh, UGa; and also her correspondence with Mrs. Paisley.

41. Florence Grandin to Mrs. Parker, n.d., Perkerson, UGa.

42. In the process of writing his book *A Southerner Discovers the South*, Jonathan Daniels made a flying tour of the region, interviewing many famous and not-so-famous Southerners, among them Peggy Mitchell. While his work contains the distillation of that interview, Daniels's notes of that interview record this information about the history-teacher affair. See his notes for his book, p. 102, in Papers of Jonathan Worth Daniels, The Southern Historical Collection, Wilson Library, University of North Carolina, Chapel Hill, N.C. (hereafter, SHC). I appreciate my friend George Brown Tindall's bringing this document to my attention.

43. Madelaine Baxter to Mrs. Parker, n.d.; Florence Grandin to Mrs. Parker, n.d.; Barbara Smith to Mrs. Parker, Jan. 18, 1951; Marie G. Bobbage to Mrs. Parker, Jan. 17, 1951; all Perkerson UGa.

44. In this regard, an interesting sequence of snapshots exists in Mitchell's scrapbook, in Mitchell Marsh, UGa. In the final shot, the group of girls is smiling, neat, and well composed. Mitchell sits demurely in the center. In the earlier sequences, however, she dominates the picture with grand poses and gestures, one hand clasped to her bosom, the other thrust high into the air. From this period on, Mitchell seems particularly self-conscious before cameras and she perpetually struck the most artificial and dramatic poses. She invariably attracted attention to herself. Her old friend Harvey Smith argued that such poses—which he characterized as "camp"—were typical of her, especially whenever she considered herself "onstage." The pose both mocks itself and attracts attention.

45. Perkerson, UGa.

46. Carl to Mrs. Parker, Jan. 16, 1951, Perkerson, UGa.

47. See, for example, Mitchell to Allen Edee, Aug. 21, 1921, in Peacock, *Dynamo*, p. 123; also Mitchell to her father, quoted in Farr, *Margaret Mitchell*, pp. 63–66; and Chapter VIII.

48. See Virginia (Morris) Nixon, no title [1939], in Mitchell Marsh, UGa. Ginny Morris had been one of Mitchell's few close friends at Smith and one of the two women, the other was Madelaine "Red" Baxter, with whom Mitchell continued to correspond over the years. They visited one another in the twenties, too. A freelance writer, Mrs. Nixon prepared this story for publication after the release of *Gone with the Wind*, over Mitchell's specific objections. The novelist still managed to kill the story, and the Morris–Mitchell friendship died in the process. For Mitchell's smoking and profanity, see Chapter VII.

49. Mitchell to Madelaine Baxter, June 22, 1944, Mitchell Marsh, UGa.

50. Cole to Mrs. Parker, Jan. 15, 1951, Perkerson, UGa.

51. Ibid.

52. Grandin to Mrs. Parker, n.d., Perkerson, UGa.

53. Quoted in Peacock, *Dynamo*, p. 61.

54. Margaret Mitchell to Allen Edee, Aug. 21, 1921, in Peacock, *Dynamo*, p. 123.

55. Unless otherwise noted, all the following references are from this letter, Margaret Mitchell to Harvey Smith, "July Umpteenth," 1927, Mitchell, Emory.

56. Unless otherwise noted, the references to this return visit are from Margaret Mitchell to Harvey Smith, Mar. 15, 1933, Mitchell, Emory.

57. Margaret Mitchell, *Gone with the Wind*, p. 434.

58. Quoted in Farr, *Margaret Mitchell*, pp. 59–60.

59. Von Hoffman interview.

60. While her agnostic father converted to Catholicism in 1940 and her brother never faltered in his staunch adherence to the church, Mitchell remained equally steadfast in her refusal to return. See Farr, *Margaret Mitchell*, pp. 262–63. In an interview with the author, Stephens Mitchell also related that he had spoken with his sister about this matter not long before her death, and she still refused to budge on her renunciation of the faith.

61. Margaret Mitchell to Harvey Smith, "July Umpteenth," 1927, Mitchell, Emory.

62. Ellen Bayuk Rosenman, *The Invisible Presence: Virginia Woolf and the Mother–Daughter Relationship* (Baton Rouge: Louisiana State University Press, 1986), has worked out some of the issues as they affected Woolf's writing and career. They apply with almost equal force to Mitchell.

63. Margaret Mitchell to Mrs. Eva Wilson Paisley, Oct. 23, 1936, and Dec. 23, 1940, both Mitchell Marsh, UGa.

64. Stephens Mitchell interview.

65. Smith interview. No examples of the plate survive that I have been able to discover.

Chapter V: First or Nothing

1. Apr. 28, 1920, in Peacock, *Dynamo*, p. 92.

2. Margaret Mitchell to Harvey Smith, Mar. 15, 1933, Mitchell, Emory.

3. Quoted in Farr, *Margaret Mitchell*, p. 63.

4. Margaret Mitchell to Allen Edee, Sept. 13, 1919, in Peacock, *Dynamo*, p. 33.

5. Margaret Mitchell to Allen Edee, July 31, 1920, in Peacock, *Dynamo*, p. 104.

6. See the references in Peacock, *Dynamo*, pp. 32, 71, 104.

7. See Virginia Morris (Nixon), unpublished typescript quoted by Harwell, "Masterpiece," p. 41.

8. Margaret Mitchell to Allen Edee, Mar. 13, 1920, in Peacock, *Dynamo*, p. 69.

9. July 21, 1919, in Peacock, *Dynamo*, p. 29.

10. Margaret Mitchell to Allen Edee, Mar. 26, 1920, in Peacock, *Dynamo*, p. 78.

11. Margaret Mitchell to Allen Edee, n.d., in Peacock, *Dynamo*, p. 97.

12. Margaret Mitchell to Allen Edee, Mar. 13, 1920, in Peacock, *Dynamo*, p. 72.

13. Margaret Mitchell to Elinor Hillyer, "Friday, Aug Umpeith, '30," von Hoffman.

14. S. Mitchell, "Memoir," p. 17.

15. Julia Memminger Riley, personal interview with the author.

16. Frances Marsh Zane, Tara, AHS

17. Peggy Mitchell, "Just Like a Woman; Ditto for Men," *Atlanta Journal Magazine*, Mar. 23, 1923.

18. Margaret Mitchell to Allen Edee, Dec. 21, 1921, in Peacock, *Dynamo*, pp. 130–31.

19. Margaret Mitchell to Allen Edee, Oct. 15, 1919, in Peacock, *Dynamo*, p. 42.

20. Oct. 21, 1919, in Peacock, *Dynamo*, p. 42.

21. See Margaret Mitchell to Allen Edee, Oct. 12, 1919, and Nov. 15, 1919, in Peacock, *Dynamo*, pp. 38 and 47; also pp. 35–36.

22. For one of the rare, even singular explorations of the phenomenon, see Louise H. Loomis, "Debutante Clubs: A Comparative Study of an Old [Savannah] and a New [Atlanta] City" (unpublished manuscript prepared for Dr. R. L. Simpson, May 1961, Sociology 96), SHC. Although focusing on contemporary debuting practices of the late 1950s and colored with undergraduate condescension, this essay generally confirms the structures and meaning of the clubs as described later.

23. See Peacock, *Dynamo*, p. 111.

24. Ferguson interview.

25. "Debs Give Up Bridge for Civics," *Atlanta Journal Magazine*, September 28, 1924, clipping in Mitchell scrapbook, Mitchell Marsh, UGa.

26. See Peacock, *Dynamo*, p. 107.

27. See Medora Field, "What Debs Think," *Atlanta Journal*, Apr. 10, 1921, clipping in Mitchell scrapbook, Mitchell Marsh, UGa.

28. See, for example, Peacock's coverage of the press reports in *Dynamo*, pp. 107–111.

29. For this judgement about Eugene Mitchell, see Farr, *Margaret Mitchell*, p. 67.

30. Smith interview.

31. See for example, Peggy Mitchell, "Belgian Prince Praises Atlanta Girls," *Atlanta Journal Magazine*, June 15, 1924: an interview with the nobleman who was visiting her kinsmen.

32. Quoted in Peacock, *Dynamo*, p. 113.

33. Oct. 21, 1919, in Peacock, *Dynamo*, p. 42.

34. Quoted in Farr, *Margaret Mitchell*, p. 67.

35. Mar. 4, 1920, in Peacock, *Dynamo*, p. 63.

36. "Polly Peachtree," *Hearst Sunday American*, "10/17/20," clipping, in Mitchell, Emory.

37. Field, "What Debs Think."

38. Quoted in Farr, *Margaret Mitchell*, p. 67. See also Cynthia Lee, "Will Girls Wear Knickerbockers?" *Atlanta Journal*, Oct. 9, 1921, clipping in Mitchell scrapbook, Mitchell Marsh, UGa.

39. Field, "What Debs Think."

40. Margaret Mitchell to Allen Edee, Oct. 21, 1919, in Peacock, *Dynamo*, p. 40.

41. See Peacock, *Dynamo*, pp. 111–12; also Farr, *Margaret Mitchell*, p. 71.

42. "That Debutante Dance," clipping in Mitchell scrapbook, Mitchell Marsh, UGa.

43. Quoted in Peacock, *Dynamo*, p. 112.

44. Quoted in Farr, *Margaret Mitchell*, p. 71.

45. Ibid.

46. Field, "What Debs Think."

47. Perkerson, "When Margaret Mitchell Was a Girl Reporter," *Atlanta Journal Magazine*, Jan. 7, 1945.

48. Smith (gloss on the letter of "1927–28–29"), in Mitchell, Emory.

49. Smith interview.

50. Margaret Mitchell to Sue Myrick, Feb. 23, 1939, Mitchell Marsh, UGa.

51. Margaret Mitchell to Frances Marsh [April–June, 1926], Marsh Zane.

52. Von Hoffman interview.

53. Quoted in Farr, *Margaret Mitchell*, p. 53.

54. Anne Hart later married Dr. Murdock Equen, and she figured again in the Mitchell story via the article she wrote for the *Atlanta Constitution* in 1939. See Chapter III. For a long discussion of "the Equen Affair" among Mitchell's friends and family, see the notes on Fanis Farr's manuscript, in Mitchell, Emory.

55. Margaret Mitchell to Allen Edee, May 9, 1920; and July 31, 1920; in Peacock, *Dynamo*, pp. 94, 98. For earlier references, see ibid., pp. 31, 62, 87.

56. Margaret Mitchell to Allen Edee, Aug. 1 or 2, 1921, in Peacock, *Dynamo*, p. 116.

57. Margaret Mitchell to Allen Edee, n.d., in Peacock, *Dynamo*, p. 113; see also S. Mitchell, "Margaret Mitchell," AHB, pp. 22–23.

58. Margaret Mitchell to Allen Edee, Dec. 1921, in Peacock, *Dynamo*, p. 131.

59. See Peacock, *Dynamo*, passim; she regularly stayed up half the night and often used the hours to write—letters to Edee, notably, but also to Courtenay Ross, Virginia Morris, and other friends—also diary entries, short stories, and other literary endeavors.

60. See, for example, John Marsh's notes on the essay written by Edwin Granberry for *Collier's* in Mitchell Marsh, UGa.

61. Margaret Mitchell to Allen Edee, in Peacock, *Dynamo*, pp. 64–65.

62. Margaret Mitchell to Allen Edee, Dec. 1921, in Peacock, *Dynamo*, pp. 128–29.

63. Margaret Mitchell to Allen Edee, Mar. 26, 1920, in Peacock, *Dynamo*, pp. 83–84.

64. Margaret Mitchell to Allen Edee, Nov. 18, 1919, in Peacock, *Dynamo*, p. 50.

65. Allen Edee. Her father preserved the letters she sent him from college and before, and these existed at least up to the time that Finis Farr wrote his biography in the mid-sixties. These letters do not survive in the Mitchell Marsh archives at the University of Georgia now, however. According to Margaret Baugh, Mitchell's secretary, some old stories survived into this time as well, and she suggested that Stephens Mitchell was still destroying Mitchell papers at least into the fifties. At the same time, Mitchell's brother and literary executor was also turning items over to the University of Georgia in the seventies.

66. Margaret Mitchell to Allen Edee, Mar. 4, 1920, in Peacock, *Dynamo*, p. 63.

67. Mar. 13, 1920, in Peacock, *Dynamo*, p. 70.

68. Mar. 26, 1920, in Peacock, *Dynamo*, p. 83.

69. Ibid., p. 81.

70. Ibid.

Chapter VI: The Baby-Faced Vamp

1. N.d. [Mar.–Apr. 1926], Marsh Zane.

2. "Polly Peachtree," "A Stunning Surprise Coming," *The Atlanta Journal*, July 23, 1922.

3. Margaret Mitchell to Harvey Smith, Mar. 15, 1933, Mitchell, Emory.

4. Margaret Mitchell to Allen Edee, Mar. 26, 1920, in Peacock, *Dynamo*, 76–77.

5. Margaret Mitchell to Allen Edee, Aug. 21, 1921, in Peacock, *Dynamo*, p. 125.

6. Ibid.

7. Margaret Mitchell to Allen Edee, Mar. 26, 1920, in Peacock, *Dynamo*, p. 75.

8. Baxter to Mrs. Parker, n.d., Perkerson UGa.

9. Barbara Smith to Mrs. Parker, Jan. 18, 1951, Perkerson, UGa.

10. See Chapter V.

11. Margaret Mitchell to Allen Edee, Nov. 15, 1919, in Peacock, *Dynamo*, p. 50.

12. Mitchell quoted her diary entry of June 5, 1919, in her letter to Edee of Jan. 12, 1919 [1920], in Peacock, *Dynamo*, pp. 60–61.

13. Margaret Mitchell to Allen Edee, Oct. 21, 1919, in Peacock, *Dynamo*, p. 45.

14. Margaret Mitchell to Allen Edee, Jan. 12, 1919 [1920], in Peacock, *Dynamo*, pp. 57, 59.

15. Margaret Mitchell to Allen Edee, Aug. 21, 1921, in Peacock, *Dynamo*, p. 121.

16. Margaret Mitchell to Allen Edee, Oct. 21, 1919, in Peacock, *Dynamo*, pp. 44, 45, 46.

17. Margaret Mitchell to Allen Edee, Jan. 12, 1919 [1920], in Peacock, *Dynamo*, p. 59.

18. Margaret Mitchell to Allen Edee, Jan. 12, 1919 [1920]; Oct. 12, 1919; and n.d. [probably May 1921]; all in Peacock, *Dynamo*, pp. 40, 59, 115.

19. Margaret Mitchell to Allen Edee, Nov. 18, 1919; also see her account of sneaking in late in her letter to Edee, Jan. 12, 1919 [1920], both in Peacock, *Dynamo*, pp. 51, and 59–60.

20. Margaret Mitchell to Allen Edee, Dec. 1, 1919, in Peacock, *Dynamo*, p. 55.

21. Diary entry, quoted in Margaret Mitchell to Allen Edee, Jan. 12, 1919 [1920], in Peacock, *Dynamo*, p. 61.

22. Margaret Mitchell to Allen Edee, Sept. 13, 1919, in Peacock, *Dynamo*, p. 31.

23. Margaret Mitchell to Allen Edee, Aug. 1 or 2, 1921, in Peacock, *Dynamo*, 118–19.

24. Margaret Mitchell to Allen Edee, Oct. 12, 1919, in Peacock, *Dynamo*, pp. 37–38.

25. Margaret Mitchell to Allen Edee, Mar. 26, 1920, in Peacock, *Dynamo*, p. 81.

26. Margaret Mitchell to Allen Edee, Dec. 1, 1919, in Peacock, *Dynamo*, p. 55.

27. Ibid.

28. Margaret Mitchell to Allen Edee, Mar. 4, 1920, in Peacock, *Dynamo*, p. 65.

29. Margaret Mitchell to Allen Edee, Mar. 26, 1920, in Peacock, *Dynamo*, p. 77.

30. Margaret Mitchell to Frances Marsh, [*ca.* Apr.–June 1926], Marsh Zane.

31. Smith interview.

32. Margaret Mitchell to Frances Marsh, [*ca.* Apr.–June 1926], Marsh Zane.

33. Margaret Mitchell to Allen Edee, Mar. 26, 1920, in Peacock, *Dynamo*, pp. 78–79.

34. "Courtenay's Letter," in Peacock, *Dynamo*, pp. 85–86.

35. Mar. 26, 1920, in Peacock, *Dynamo*, p. 80.

36. "Courtenay Letter," in Peacock, *Dynamo*, pp. 86–87.

37. Ibid., p. 87.

38. Ibid., pp. 88–89.

39. Margaret Mitchell to Frances Marsh, [Apr.–June 1926], Marsh Zane. See above for the fuller quotations of these passages.

40. Margaret Mitchell to Allen Edee, Mar. 26, 1920, in Peacock, *Dynamo*, p. 75.

41. Margaret Mitchell to Allen Edee, Mar. 4, 1920, in Peacock, *Dynamo*, p. 66.

42. Margaret Mitchell to Allen Edee, July 20, 1921, in Peacock, *Dynamo*, p. 104.

43. Margaret Mitchell to Allen Edee, Nov. 15, 1919, in Peacock, *Dynamo*, pp. 50, 52.

44. Sept. 13, 1919, in Peacock, *Dynamo*, p. 32.

45. Margaret Mitchell to Allen Edee, Sept. 13, 1919, in Peacock, *Dynamo*, p. 32.

46. Mar. 4, 1920, in Peacock, *Dynamo*, p. 65.

47. Margaret Mitchell to Allen Edee, Oct. 21, 1919, in Peacock, *Dynamo*, pp. 42–43.

48. Margaret Mitchell to Allen Edee, Aug. 21, 1921, in Peacock, *Dynamo*, p. 125.

49. Aug. 1 or 2, 1921, in Peacock, *Dynamo*, p. 119.

50. Margaret Mitchell to Allen Edee, Sept. 13, 1919, in Peacock, *Dynamo*, p. 33.

51. In a state of disintegration, the booklet exists in the Mitchell scrapbook, in Mitchell Marsh, UGa.

52. Helen Turman Markey, Tara, AHS.

53. Margaret Mitchell to Allen Edee, Aug. 1 or 2, 1921, in Peacock, *Dynamo*, p. 116.

54. John Marsh to Frances Marsh, Jan. 18, [1922], Marsh Zane. This is the earliest letter in the Marsh Zane collection. Mrs. Zane dated the letter 1918, but this is impossible as her brother did not move to Atlanta until two years after that. The next letter is dated April 1922 in the correspondence. Finally, as Mitchell had subtracted two years from her age, Marsh's reference to "a girl of twenty" would also make the letter 1922.

55. See the Upshaw files at the North Carolina Department of Archives and History, Raleigh, North Carolina; also Susan Jeffries, "First Husband of Margaret Mitchell Was a Raleigh Man," *Raleigh News and Observer*, n.d., clipping, Mrs. Courtenay D. Egerton and Mrs. Herbert Lamson, Jr., private collection; also personal communication with the author, Oct. 7, 1986, Mrs. Egerton and Mrs. Lamson are the half-sisters of Berrien Upshaw.

56. McFedyen scrapbook.

57. For Upshaw's naval career, see Barbara Weeks, Assistant Registrar, United States Naval Academy, to the author, Sept. 30, 1986; and W. W. Upshaw to the author, Dec. 9, 1986, both in the possession of the author.

58. See *Atlanta City Directory:* 1919, 1920, 1921, 1922, AHS.

59. Quoted in Jeffries, "First Husband."

60. McFedyen interview.

61. Augusta Dearborn Edwards, Tara, AHS.

62. Helen Turman Markey, Tara. AHS.

63. Yolande Gwin, Tara, AHS.

64. Egerton and Lamson correspondence, Oct. 7, 1986.

65. Jeffries, "First Husband."

66. William F. Upshaw to Margaret Mitchell, July 13, 1936, Egerton Lamson, copy in the possession of the author.

67. Farr, *Margaret Mitchell*, pp. 74–75.

68. Mrs. Sydney B. Van Lear, Feb. 12, 1987, in possession of the author.

69. See Chapters VII and IX.

70. McFedyen interview.

71. Margaret Mitchell to Allen Edee, Apr. 28, 1920, in Peacock, *Dynamo*, pp. 89–90.

72. Margaret Mitchell to Allen Edee, Apr. 28, 1920, in Peacock, *Dynamo*, pp. 100–101.

73. John Marsh to Frances Marsh, Jan. 18, [1922], Marsh Zane.

74. John Marsh to Frances Marsh, Mar. 27, 1922, Marsh Zane.

75. Frances Marsh Zane, "To J. R. M." (unpublished manuscript), p. 2, Marsh Zane.

76. John Marsh to Frances Marsh, Mar. 27, 1922; John Marsh to Frances Marsh, Jan. 18, [1922], and Margaret Mitchell to Frances Marsh, [Apr.–June, 1926], Marsh Zane.

77. "The Choice of Chums," clipping, Marsh Zane.

78. Clipping, n.d., Marsh Zane.

79. Frances Marsh Zane, Tara, AHS.

Chapter VII: The Lion's Den

1. Medora Field Perkerson, "When Margaret Mitchell Was a Girl Reporter," *Atlanta Journal Magazine*, Jan. 7, 1945.

2. Ferguson interview.

3. John Marsh to Mrs. M. F. Marsh, Sept. 6, 1922, Marsh Zane.

4. *Atlanta Constitution*, Sept. 2, 1922.

5. John Marsh to Mrs. M. F. Marsh, Sept. 6, 1922, Marsh Zane.

6. See *Atlanta City Directory: 1922, 1923.*

7. Von Hoffman interview.

8. John Marsh to Frances Marsh, July 30, 1923, Marsh Zane.

9. Although Farr and others date the separation from the time the wife went to work in December, the evidence does not support this conclusion. The couple did not separate until July, seven months after the bride drew her first paycheck: see Upshaw *versus* Upshaw, in the Probate Records of Fulton County, Atlanta, Georgia; also John Marsh to Frances Marsh, July 30, 1923, Marsh Zane.

10. John Marsh to Frances Marsh, July 30, 1923, Marsh Zane.

11. Ibid.; also Upshaw *versus* Upshaw.

12. Quoted in Julia Kirk Blackwelder, "Mop and Typewriter: Work in Early Twentieth-Century Atlanta," *Atlanta Historical Journal* 27 (Fall 1983): 27.

13. For these articles, see Mitchell scrapbook, Mitchell Marsh, UGa; also Chapter VIII.

14. See John A. Salmond, "Miss Lucy of the C.I.O.: A Southern Life," in Bruce A. Clayton and John A. Salmond, eds., *The South Is Another Land: Essays on the Twentieth-Century South* (Westport, Conn.: Greenwood, 1987); and Katharine DuPre Lumpkin, *The Making of a Southerner* (New York: Alfred A. Knopf, 1948).

15. See Grantham, *Hoke Smith.*

16. Clement Hunt, Jr., to Margaret Mitchell, Jan. 10, 1940, Mitchell Marsh, UGa.

17. Martha Angley, "Margaret Mitchell Marsh," Mitchell Marsh, UGa.

18. Margaret Mitchell to Elinor Hillyer, Friday, "August Umpteenth, 1930," von Hoffman.

19. Margaret Mitchell to Mrs. Julia Collier Harris, Apr. 28, 1936, in Harwell, *Letters*, pp. 4–5.

20. Augusta Dearborn Edwards, personal interview with the author.

21. See Anne Waldron, *Caroline Gordon and the Southern Literary Renaissance* (New York: G.P. Putnam's Sons, 1987); and Veronica Makowsky, *Caroline Gordon: A Biography* (New York: Oxford University Press, 1989).

22. See Pyron, "Nell Battle Lewis."

23. Willie Snow Ethridge, personal interview with the author. Ethridge herself fits the same pattern, although she was married to the editor she slept with.

24. A fascinating character in her own right, Susan Myrick figures prominently, and hilariously, later in Mitchell's story; see especially Chapter XVIII. The biographical information here is drawn in passing from the Mitchell–Myrick correspondence, in Mitchell Marsh, UGa; Harwell, *Letters;* also Richard B. Harwell, personal interview with the author.

25. Margaret Mitchell to Katharine Brown, Feb. 14, 1937, in Harwell, *Letters*, pp. 119–20.

26. John Marsh to Frances Marsh, Mar. 27, 1922, Marsh Zane.

27. William Howland, "Peggy Mitchell, Newspaperman," *AHB*, "Margaret Mitchell Memorial Issue," p. 47.

28. Margaret Mitchell to John T. Carleton, Nov. 19, 1942, Mitchell Marsh, UGa.

29. Quoted in Howland, "Newspaperman," p. 47.

30. Margaret Mitchell to Harris, Harwell, *Letters*, pp. 4–5; see also Angley, "Margaret Mitchell," Mitchell Marsh, UGa, for another version of the tale.

31. Edwards interview.

32. Quoted in Howland, "Newspaperman," p. 56.

33. Perkerson, "When Margaret Mitchell Was a Girl Reporter."

34. Margaret Mitchell to Frances Marsh, [Mar.–Apr. 1926], Marsh Zane.

35. See Perkerson, "Girl Reporter."

36. Howland, "Newspaperman," pp. 48–49.

37. Ibid., pp. 49–50.

38. Daughter of Judge and Mrs. William T. Newman (one of Atlanta's most aristocratic families), a professional librarian, a member of the avant-garde, a book reviewer and journalist, and author of two notorious novels in the twenties that brought her national fame and local infamy, Frances Newman deserves a biography of her own. See Edwin Mims, *The Advancing South: Stories of Progress and Reaction* (Garden City, N.J.: Doubleday, Page & Co., 1926).

39. Howland, "Newspaperman," p. 61.

40. Ibid., p. 60.

41. Fred B. Moore, Tara, AHS.

42. Margaret Mitchell to Elinor Hillyer, Sunday, Oct. 19, 1930, von Hoffman.

43. Howland, "Newspaperman," pp. 60–61.

44. Perkerson, "When Margaret Mitchell Was a Girl Reporter."

45. Erskine Caldwell, Tara, AHS.

46. Howland, "Newspaperman," p. 54.

47. Hunt Clement to Margaret Mitchell, Jan. 10, 1940, Mitchell Marsh, UGa.

48. Margaret Mitchell to Jessie [Mrs. Basil] Stockbridge, July 27, 1936, Mitchell Marsh, UGa.

49. Clipping in Mitchell scrapbook, Mitchell Marsh, UGa.

50. Erskine Caldwell, Tara, AHS.

51. Willie Snow Ethridge interview.

52. Smith (gloss on letter of May 24, 1933), Mitchell, Emory.

53. Notes for *Southerner Discovers the South*, p. 102, Daniels, SHC.

54. Mitchell scrapbook, Mitchell Marsh, UGa.

55. Margaret Mitchell to Elinor Hillyer, July 7, 1930, von Hoffman.

56. Margaret Mitchell to Harvey Smith, July 23 or 24, 1927, Mitchell, Emory.

57. Smith (gloss on letter of Mar. 1, 1933), Mitchell, Emory.

58. Smith interview.

59. Margaret Mitchell to Elinor Hillyer, Sunday, Oct. 19, 1930, von Hoffman.

60. Smith (gloss on letter of July 13, 1927), in Mitchell, Emory.

61. Elinor Hillyer von Hoffman to the author, Jan. 7, 1987.

62. Margaret Mitchell to Harvey Smith, July 23 or 24, 1927, Mitchell, Emory.

63. Riley interview.

64. Margaret Mitchell to Frances Marsh, [Mar.–Apr., 1926], Marsh Zane.

65. Lamar Ball, Oct. 12, 1946, clipping in Mitchell Marsh, UGa.

66. Frank Daniel, personal interview with the author.

67. Stephens Mitchell interview; and Margaret Mitchell to Cary Wilmer, May 11, 1943, Mitchell, Emory.

68. McFedyen interview.

69. Howland, "Newspaperman," p. 53.

70. Quoted in Howland, "Newspaperman," p. 55.

71. Margaret Mitchell to Henry Steele Commager, July 10, 1936, in Harwell, *Letters*, p. 39.

72. Von Hoffman interview.

73. Howland, "Newspaperman," p. 62.

74. Ibid., p. 63.

75. Ibid., p. 61.

76. Margaret Mitchell to Harlee Branch, Feb. 9, 1937, in Harwell, *Letters*, p. 117.

77. Peggy Mitchell, "Former Policewoman, Held in Shooting, Needs the Help She Gave to So Many Girls," *Atlanta Journal*, Aug. 30, 1923, p. 1: clipping, Mitchell scrapbook, Mitchell Marsh, UGa.

78. Quoted by Margaret Baugh, "Notes," May 21, 1965, Mitchell, Emory.

Chapter VIII: The Whole Story

1. Perkerson, "Girl Reporter."

2. Medora Field Perkerson, unpublished memoir of Peggy Mitchell, Perkerson, UGa.

3. Margaret Mitchell to Willie Snow Ethridge, May 15, 1941, Mitchell Marsh, UGa.

4. John Marsh to Frances Marsh Zane, quoted in Ellen Paullin, ed., "The

Scarlett Letters," "Northeast," *The Hartford Courant*, July 9, 1989. My appreciation to Craig K. Zane for bringing this reference to my attention.

5. Medora Field Perkerson, "Margaret Mitchell's *Journal Magazine* Stories," *Atlanta Journal Magazine*, Dec. 18, 1949.

6. See Nancy Chodorow, *The Reproduction of Mothering: Psychoanalysis and the Sociology of Gender* (Berkeley: University of California Press, 1978).

7. Perkerson, "Memoir."

8. Howland, "Newspaperman," p. 63.

9. Peggy Mitchell, "Camping Out on $7 a Week," July 8, 1923, *Atlanta Journal*. Unless otherwise noted, all references in this chapter refer to the *Atlanta Journal Magazine;* the unbylined pieces are identified from Mitchell's scrapbook in her archives and are so noted.

10. Peggy Mitchell, "Where Women Still Use Curl Papers," Sept. 28, 1924.

11. "Police Station 31 Years Old and Shows It," Aug. 12, 1923, Mitchell scrapbook, Mitchell Marsh, UGa.

12. Peggy Mitchell, "Will One-Eyed Connelly Crash the Pearly Gates?" Nov. 9, 1924.

13. Peggy Mitchell, [review] *"A Pocket Full of Posies,"* (by Anne Parish), July 1, 1923.

14. "Girls Used as 'Blinds' by Rum-Runners," October 19, 1924, Mitchell Scrapbook, Mitchell Marsh, UGa.

15. Mitchell, "Policewoman Needs Help."

16. Peggy Mitchell, "Shot Three Times and Missed Him—Divorced," Feb. 8, 1925.

17. Peggy Mitchell, "Georgia Bids Goodbye to Elopements," Sept. 14, 1924.

18. Peggy Mitchell, "Honest Man Wakes Up to Find Himself a Thief," July 19, 1925.

19. Peggy Mitchell, "Atlanta Subdebs Pass Up Tutankhamen," Mar. 11, 1923.

20. Peggy Mitchell, "Has the Day of Miracles Passed?" Aug. 12, 1923.

21. Peggy Mitchell, "What Keeps Women New?" Aug. 5, 1923.

22. Peggy Mitchell, "Maxim Talks of Perfume, War, and Poetry," March 4, 1923.

23. These two actually constitute a series of four articles on Georgia history. Three bear no byline: those of May 6, May 13, and May 27, but Mitchell preserved them in her scrapbook with the rest of her journalism.

24. When Anne Edwards, in *Road to Tara*, dealt with this article, she ignored the Mitchell scrapbook that contained the other essays in the sequence. Assuming that the others never appeared, she created a completely fictional episode of public reaction against the reporter. She invents an angry Angus Perkerson who, in response to the supposed public outcry, kills the later installments of the series. Besides being simply untrue in its details, this fictional history falsifies how newspapers worked and distorts Mitchell's character in particular. Indeed, by claiming this one essay and failing to sign the other three, Mitchell could be seen asserting her will in a way exactly opposite Edwards's reconstruction.

25. Perhaps it makes too much of the description, but the specific reference to the "impassioned speech" and the subject's "bi-lingualism," if nothing else, recalls Mitchell's references to her own mother. The connections, of course,

are not irrelevant, especially in the context of Mitchell's ambivalence towards the character, too.

26. Peggy Mitchell, "Where Flappers Wear Pigtails Until 21," Dec. 7, 1924.

27. Peggy Mitchell, "English Girls Are Out of Hand, Baronet Says," May 24, 1925.

28. Peggy Mitchell, "No Dumbbells Wanted," Jan. 28, 1923; "Pep, Brains and Clothes Win in Beauty Contest," May 23, 1923; "Debs Keep House While Mothers Are Away," Sept. 9, 1923; and the unbylined pieces from her scrapbook: "What Makes the Pretty Girl Pretty?" Mar. 22, 1925; and "Debs Give Up Bridge for Civics," Sept. 28, 1924, all in Mitchell Marsh, UGa.

29. "No Flattery When Junior Follies Rehearse," May 13, 1923; and "Off-Stage with Atlanta's Own Stars," June 3, 1923," Mitchell scrapbook, Mitchell Marsh, UGa; Peggy Mitchell, "$500 Gowns to Be Worn in Junior League Follies," Jan. 25, 1925; "Junior League to Stage $100,000 Follies," Mar. 28, 1926; "Six Hundred Costumes for Junior League," Apr. 4, 1926.

30. Mitchell, "Subdebs Pass Up Tutankhamen."

31. Perkerson, "Girl Reporter."

32. Peggy Mitchell, "Spirited Heroines and Knee-Length Skirts," January 31, 1925. Mitchell devoted most of the essay to talking with the magazine's literary editor, Willa Roberts, who reviewed and accepted or rejected all the fiction that came to the magazine. She discussed the contemporary heroine in fiction and the changes in the presentation of women in the twentieth century. She also treated these subjects within the broad context of literary history. The article is especially important in understanding values in popular literature, but also in appreciating Mitchell's knowledge of those values.

33. Peggy Mitchell, "Jobs Before Marriage for High School Girls," Apr. 27, 1924.

34. Peggy Mitchell, "Do Working Girls Make the Best Wives?" July 13, 1924.

35. Peggy Mitchell, "Pulling Teeth in a Harem," June 22, 1924.

36. Peggy Mitchell, "Tech Boys Tell Why Girls Are Rushed," June 3, 1923.

37. Peggy Mitchell, "Sheiks, Presidents, and Poets at Boys' High," May 4, 1924.

38. Peggy Mitchell, "Leave Latin Lovers on the Screen," Mar. 9, 1924. For a further treatment of this episode in the development of Mitchell's ideas, see Chapter IX.

39. Peggy Mitchell, "Just Like a Woman; Ditto for Men," Mar. 18, 1923.

40. Marginal notes on clipping, "When Mrs. Bell Ruled the 'Bell House Boys,'" *Atlanta Journal*, June 24, 1923, Mitchell scrapbook, Mitchell Marsh, UGa.

41. Marginal notes on galley proofs of "Just Like a Woman, Ditto for a Man," *Atlanta Journal*, Mar. 18, 1923; and also "Off-Stage with Atlanta's Own Stars," *Atlanta Journal*, June 3, 1923, both, Mitchell scrapbook, Mitchell Marsh, UGa.

42. Margaret Mitchell to Martha Angley, Apr. 25, 1936, Mitchell Marsh, UGa.

Chapter IX: St. John

1. The University of Kentucky yearbook, Lexington, Kentucky, 1916, p. 70. I appreciate the University of Kentucky Office of Alumni Affairs providing me copies of this and other related information on Marsh and his siblings.

2. Marginal notes on Peggy Mitchell, "Camping Out on $7 a Week," *Atlanta Journal*, July 8, 1923, Mitchell scrapbook, Mitchell Marsh, UGa.

3. Riley interview.

4. Ethridge interview.

5. Fergurson interview.

6. Smith interview; and Harvey Smith (gloss on letter of May 24, 1933), Mitchell, Emory.

7. Margaret Mitchell to Frances Marsh, "Saturday January the something 1926," Marsh Zane.

8. Margaret Mitchell to Frances Marsh, Friday [Feb. 6, 1925], Marsh Zane.

9. John Marsh to Mary Marsh, Sept. 6, 1922, Marsh Zane.

10. John Marsh to Mrs. M. F. Marsh, Jan. 20, 1925, Marsh Zane.

11. Roland Zane personal interview with the author.

12. Although Mitchell and her brother related stories that went back generations, their first cousin Stephens Crockett could do the same thing. In a personal interview with the author, this octogenarian related family tales that went back to the mid–eighteenth century.

13. John Marsh to Florence Adkins Nelcamp, Dec. 20, 1936, Mitchell Marsh, UGa.

14. The Marsh family history is drawn chiefly from the Zane interview.

15. Zane interview. See also Marianne Walker, "Mr. Margaret Mitchell," the *Courier-Journal Magazine*, Feb. 15, 1987; Frances Marsh Zane, Tara, AHS; and Frances Marsh Zane, "To J. R. M.," unpublished manuscript, Marsh Zane.

16. Zane, "To J. R. M."

17. Henry Marsh file, Alumni Office, University of Kentucky, Lexington, Ky.

18. John Robert Marsh file, Alumni Office, University of Kentucky, Lexington, Ky.

19. Corporal John R. Marsh, "Barrow Hospital Unit Busy in England," clipping, Dec. 23, 1918, Marsh Zane.

20. Margaret Mitchell to Judge Paxon, June 27, 1937, Mitchell Marsh, UGa.

21. Margaret Mitchell to Herschel Brickell, Sept. 10, 1936, Mitchell Marsh, UGa.

22. Margaret Mitchell to Frances Marsh, "Saturday, January the something 1926," Marsh Zane; see also Margaret Mitchell to Harvey Smith, Apr. 21, 1933, Mitchell, Emory.

23. Frances Marsh Zane, Tara, AHS. Stephens Mitchell interview; Roland Zane interview. Also Edwin Granberry, personal interview with the author.

24. Margaret Mitchell to Herschel Brickell, Sept. 10, 1936, Mitchell Marsh, UGa.

25. While his wedding announcement gave the date as 1919, he himself never referred to any date other than 1920.

26. John Marsh to Randolph Fort, June 24, 1936, Mitchell Marsh, UGa; also John Marsh to Frances Marsh, Aug. 11, 1922, Marsh Zane.

27. John Marsh to Frances Marsh, July 30, 1923; also idem, Jan. 18, [1922], both Marsh Zane.

28. John Marsh to Frances Marsh, [July 1922], Marsh Zane.

29. John Marsh to Frances Marsh, Aug. 11, 1922, Marsh Zane.

30. Ibid.
31. John Marsh to Mary Marsh, Sept. 6, 1922, Marsh Zane.
32. Ibid.
33. John Marsh to Frances Zane, July 30, 1925, Marsh Zane.
34. Edwards, *Road to Tara*, suggested the idea of this affair as rape. Others have picked up this interpretation and it has acquired something of a life of its own: see, for example, Helen Taylor, *Scarlett's Women: "Gone with the Wind" and Its Female Fans* (New Brunswick, N.J.: Rutgers University Press, 1989). Besides the reference to the bed in the divorce proceedings, the stronger evidence for the conclusion of rape lies in the more general predisposition to identify Berrien Upshaw with Rhett Butler. The fictional character, however, had nothing in common with Mitchell's first husband: birth, breeding, size, looks, mind, or character. For more critical sources for Rhett's character, see Chapter XIII.
35. Upshaw *versus* Upshaw.
36. S. Mitchell, "Memoir."
37. Margaret Baugh to Lois Cole, Oct. 12, 1964, Mitchell, Emory.
38. Margaret Mitchell to Harvey Smith, June 29, 1933, Mitchell, Emory.
39. Margaret Mitchell to Frances Marsh, Friday [Feb. 6, 1925], Marsh Zane.
40. Margaret Mitchell to Harvey Smith, June 29, 1933, Mitchell, Emory.
41. Mitchell, "Leave Latin Lovers on the Screen," *Atlanta Journal Magazine*, March 9, 1924.
42. Margaret Mitchell to Harvey Smith, June 29, 1933, Mitchell, Emory.
43. Virginia Woolf, *A Room of One's Own* (New York: Harcourt Brace, 1929).
44. Margaret Mitchell to Harvey Smith, June 29, 1933, Mitchell, Emory.
45. For these judgments on his abortive career with the Associated Press in Washington, see John Marsh to J. L. Morgan, Aug. 23, 1937; and J. L. Morgan to John Marsh, Aug. 19, 1937, both Mitchell Marsh, UGa; and Frances Marsh Zane, Tara, AHS.
46. John Marsh to Mary Marsh, Jan. 20, 1925, Marsh Zane.
47. Margaret Mitchell to Frances Marsh, Monday [Feb. 2, 1925], Marsh Zane.
48. John Marsh to Mary Marsh, Jan. 20, 1925, Marsh Zane.
49. Margaret Mitchell to Frances Marsh, Monday [Feb. 2, 1925], Marsh Zane.
50. Peggy Mitchell, "What Causes Hiccoughs," *Atlanta Journal Magazine*, Dec. 28, 1924.
51. Margaret Mitchell to Frances Marsh, Monday [Feb. 2, 1925], Marsh Zane.
52. Margaret Mitchell to Frances Marsh, Monday [Feb. 23, 1925], Marsh Zane.
53. Mitchell scrapbook, Mitchell Marsh, UGa.
54. Margaret Mitchell to Frances Marsh, Friday [Feb. 6, 1925], Marsh Zane.
55. Margaret Mitchell to Frances Marsh, Mar. 7, 1925, Marsh Zane.
56. Margaret Mitchell to Frances Marsh, Monday [Feb. 23, 1925], Marsh Zane.
57. Margaret Mitchell to Frances Marsh, Thursday [Mar. 2, 1925], Marsh Zane.
58. Ibid.
59. Augusta Dearborn Edwards, Tara, AHS.
60. Ibid.
61. Margaret Mitchell to Judge Paxon, June 27, 1936, Mitchell Marsh, UGa.
62. *Atlanta Constitution*, July 5, 1925.

63. Edwards interview.

64. Medora Field Perkerson, undated manuscript, Perkerson, UGa.

65. John Marsh to Mary Marsh, Jan. 20, 1925, Marsh Zane.

66. Perkerson, manuscript, Perkerson, UGa.

67. Margaret Mitchell to Frances Marsh Zane, Friday [*ca.* Oct.–Nov. 1928], Marsh Zane.

68. Frances Marsh Zane, Tara, AHS.

69. Margaret Mitchell to Harvey Smith, June 29, 1933, Mitchell, Emory.

Chapter X: Hell in Narrow Quarters

1. Peggy Mitchell, "Matrimonial Bonds," *The Open Door,* Tara, AHS.

2. Edwards interview; Riley interview; Stephens Mitchell interview.

3. Margaret Mitchell to Frances Marsh, "Monday morning," [Apr.–June 1926], Marsh Zane.

4. Margaret Mitchell to Frances Marsh Zane, [Oct.–Nov. 1928], Marsh Zane.

5. Margaret Mitchell to Elinor Hillyer, "Friday, Aug. Umpteenth, '30," von Hoffman.

6. See Kenneth Lynn, *Hemingway* (New York: Simon & Schuster, 1987).

7. Whether Mitchell knew it or not, midwives by tradition also served as abortionists, but the novelist's linking of these two roles was no accident in any case. In *Gone with the Wind*, the character of Prissy also represents "perverted midwifery." And to underline the personal identity of herself with that part in the letter about Evelyn Lovette, Mitchell assumes a special identity with the character of Prissy in her novel, too: see Chapter XIII.

8. Harvey Smith (gloss on letter of 21 Apr. 1933), Mitchell, Emory.

9. Riley interview.

10. See Harvey Smith interview; also Erskine Caldwell, Tara, AHS.

11. Margaret Mitchell to Frances Marsh, Friday [Apr.–June 1926], Marsh Zane.

12. Margaret Mitchell to Frances Marsh, Friday [Oct.–Nov. 1928], Marsh Zane.

13. Margaret Mitchell to Frances March, Aug. 28 [1928], Marsh Zane. For a parallel to the Mitchell–Marsh bonding in illness, see Linda A. Davis, *Onward and Upward: A Biography of Katherine S. White* (New York: Harper & Row, 1987). Contemporaries of Peggy and John Marsh, Dorothy and T. S. White, both of *New Yorker* fame, were bound by the same sorts of extraordinary bouts with illness, accident, and physical misfortune.

14. Margaret Mitchell to Frances Marsh, "Monday morning," [Apr.–June 1926], Marsh Zane.

15. Ibid.

16. Margaret Mitchell to Frances Marsh, [Apr.–June 1926], Marsh Zane.

17. Margaret Mitchell to Frances Marsh, [Mar.–Apr. 1926], Marsh Zane. The League produced its show on April 4, 1926.

18. Richard Harwell, the late Mitchell expert, turned up this publication in the late seventies. When Anne Edwards was writing *Road to Tara*, he gave her a copy, which she used and quoted in her text, p. 114; inexplicably, she gets the month and year wrong, placing the date of publication before the Mitch-

ell–Marsh wedding, when it actually appeared nine months after. In terms of its larger biographical significance, the error is considerable.

19. John Marsh, quoted in Medora Perkerson, "Was Margaret Mitchell Writing Another Book?" *Atlanta Journal Magazine*, Dec. 18, 1949.

20. Quoted in Farr, *Margaret Mitchell*, p. 96.

21. "Notes by M[argaret] B[augh]," May 21, 1965, Mitchell, Emory.

22. Lois Dwight Cole to Margaret Mitchell, Jan. 7, 1936, quoted in "Notes by M. B.," Mitchell, Emory.

23. Farr, *Margaret Mitchell*, p. 97.

24. Edwards, *Tara*, pp. 129–130.

25. Joel Williamson, "How Black Was Rhett Butler?" in Numan V. Bartley, ed., *The Evolution of Southern Culture* (Athens: University of Georgia Press, 1988), pp. 87–107.

26. Harold Latham to Margaret Mitchell, Aug. 15, 1935, The Macmillan Company Records, Rare Books and Manuscript Division, The New York Public Library, Astor, Lenox and Tilden Foundations, New York, New York (hereafter, Macmillan, NYPL).

27. "Notes by M. B.," Mitchell, Emory.

28. L[ois] D[wight] C[ole] to M[argaret] B[augh], Oct. 21, 1964, Mitchell, Emory.

29. Harvey Smith interview. Also, Harvey Smith, "Miss India Is Dead!" (manuscript in the possession of the author.)

30. As late as the 1960s and 1970s such places still existed everywhere. As a boy and young man, I was very interested in history and in architecture and I wandered through many of the old houses myself. In rural Taliaferro County, Georgia, I discovered an old Asbury house on lands now owned by a great paper company. One of its columns had fallen across the unkempt yard; hollow, it had broken apart amid the boxwoods. I stood on the porch and hallooed. The occupant greeted me, the literally snaggle-toothed, coveralled resident. He lived here at the suffrance of West Virginia Pulp and Paper because he had discovered a forest fire in these vast, mostly uninhabited acres, had reported the conflagration and won the commendation of the company—thus getting this roof over his head. I saved one boxwood for my own garden.

I cite one more example. My oldest surviving great-grandmother, Annie Desma Fogle Fulmer, passed most of her life in the same house. She died in 1959 at the age of almost ninety. In 1973, I went back to her village to visit my family there, and stopped by her old house on Main Street. I walked around her broad porch where four generations in my family had sat in their rocking chairs and talked in the sweltering heat of August dusks. I peered into the windows of the front rooms that opened onto the porch. Through the dirty glass I saw that my great-grandmother's furniture, much of it as I remembered it, was still in place. The window had no catch. I climbed through. Inside my great-grandmother's bedroom, I discovered her pictures still hanging on the walls, her clothes still hanging in the closets, and even the straw hat she wore against the sun still sitting on her shelf. I cannot verify it myself as the yard now has sprouted an impenetrable tangle of growth, but as far as I know, at this writing in 1990, all remains there still.

31. Harvey Smith (gloss on letter of "1929, 30, 31"); see also Margaret Mitchell to Harvey Smith, May 24, 1933, both Mitchell, Emory.

32. See Margaret Mitchell to Harvey Smith, Apr. 21, 1933, Mitchell, Emory; and Harvey Smith interview.

Chapter XI: Labor Pains

1. Margaret Mitchell to Mrs. Bolen, July 25, 1936, Mitchell Marsh, UGa.
2. Harvey Smith (gloss on "Tallulah Falls Note," n.d.), Mitchell, Emory.
3. Lethea Turman Lockridge, Tara, AHS.
4. Margaret Mitchell to Mrs. Julia Collier Harris, Apr. 28, 1936, in Harwell, *Letters*, p. 6.
5. John Marsh to Mrs. Thomas R. Underwood, Oct. 14, 1936, Mitchell Marsh, UGa.
6. Margaret Mitchell to Frances Marsh, Saturday, Aug. 28, 1926, Marsh Zane.
7. Margaret Mitchell to Frances Marsh Zane, Friday [Oct.–Nov. 1928], Marsh Zane.
8. Margaret Mitchell to Frances Marsh, Aug. 23, 1926, Marsh Zane.
9. McFedyen interview.
10. S. Mitchell, "Memoir," p. 21.
11. Margaret Mitchell to Herschel Brickell, Mar. 19, 1938, in Harwell, *Letters*, p. 189.
12. Edwards interview; Daniel interview.
13. Bessie Jordan to Medora Perkerson, July 6, 1936, quoted in Frank Daniel, "Margaret Mitchell Files Open for Biographers," clipping, June 10, 1964, Tara, AHS.
14. Riley interview.
15. Lois Dwight Cole, "The Story Begins at a Luncheon Bridge in Atlanta," in Harwell, *Book and Film*, p. 57.
16. "Going Like the Wind," *Scribner's Magazine* 100 (1936): 16.
17. Smith interview.
18. Margaret Mitchell to Harry Slattery, Oct. 3, 1936, in Harwell, *Letters*, p. 70.
19. Margaret Mitchell to Mrs. Julia Collier Harris, Apr. 28, 1936, in Harwell, *Letters*, p. 5.
20. Margaret Mitchell to Frances Marsh Zane, Friday [Oct.–Nov. 1928], Marsh Zane.
21. Margaret Mitchell to Harold Latham, July 27, 1935, Macmillan, NYPL.
22. John Marsh to Edwin Granberry, Nov. 17, 1936, copy in Tara, AHS.
23. Margaret Mitchell to Mrs. Julia Collier Harris, Apr. 21, 1936, in Harwell, *Letters*, p. 1.
24. Margaret Mitchell to Mrs. Julia Collier Harris, Apr. 28, 1936, in Harwell, *Letters*, p. 5.
25. Margaret Mitchell to Mrs. Bolen, July 25, 1936, Mitchell Marsh, UGa.
26. Margaret Mitchell to W. B. Elwell, June 18, 1936, Mitchell Marsh, UGa.
27. Margaret Mitchell to Gilbert Govan, Jan. 20, 1942, Mitchell Marsh, UGa.
28. *GWTW*, p. 1,025.
29. Lamar Q. Ball, "Writing of 'Gone with the Wind' Beset by Difficulties, Says Author," *Atlanta Constitution*, Nov. 9, 1936.

30. Margaret Mitchell to Frances Marsh Zane, Friday [Oct.–Nov. 1928], Marsh Zane.

31. Margaret Mitchell to Harvey Smith, Monday [from internal evidence, the letter is 1929, pre-August, probably late spring or early summer].

32. Margaret Mitchell to W. B. Elwell, June 18, 1936, Mitchell Marsh, UGa.

33. Ball, "Beset by Difficulties."

34. See reverse pages of Margaret Mitchell to Elinor Hillyer, July 7, 1930, von Hoffman.

35. Margaret Mitchell to Stark Young, Sept. 29, 1936, in Harwell, *Letters,* p. 65.

36. Margaret Mitchell to Harold Latham, Apr. 16, 1935, Macmillan, NYPL.

37. John Marsh to Lois Dwight Cole, Feb. 13, 1936, Macmillan, NYPL.

38. Quoted in Farr, *Margaret Mitchell,* pp. 139–40.

39. Ball, "Beset by Difficulties."

40. Margaret Mitchell to Harold Latham, July 27, 1935, Macmillan, NYPL.

41. Margaret Mitchell to Harold Latham, Apr. 16, 1935, Macmillan, NYPL.

Chapter XII: History Riddled

1. "Going Like the Wind," *Scribner's Magazine,* p. 16.

2. W. J. Cash, *The Mind of the South* (New York: Alfred A. Knopf, 1941; reprint 1961), p. ix.

3. For a summary of my larger interpretations of the regional revival in the interwar years, see my essay, "Gone with the Wind and the Southern Cultural Awakening," *Virginia Quarterly Review* 62 (Autumn 1986): 565–87. Of the virtually innumerable books and articles on the cultural awakening in the interwar years, the one that has proved most relevant to this study is Fred C. Hobson, Jr., *Serpent in Eden: H. L. Mencken and the South* (Baton Rouge: Louisiana State University Press, 1974).

4. Darden Asbury Pyron, "Nell Battle Lewis (1896–1955): The Dilemmas of Southern Womanhood," *Social Science Perspectives on the South: An Interdisciplinary Annual* III (1984): 77–99.

5. Cited in George Brown Tindall, *The Emergence of the New South, 1913–1945* (Baton Rouge: Louisiana State University Press, 1967), pp. 293, 297, 299.

6. Cash, *Mind of the South,* p. 15.

7. Margaret Mitchell to Virginius Dabney, July 23, 1942, in Harwell, *Letters,* p. 359.

8. *GWTW,* p. 793.

9. *GWTW,* p. 4.

10. *GWTW,* p. 18.

11. *GWTW,* p. 87.

12. *GWTW,* p. 44.

13. *GWTW,* p. 48.

14. *GWTW,* pp. 710–11.

15. *GWTW,* p. 707.

16. *GWTW,* p. 717.

17. *GWTW,* pp. 34–35.

18. *GWTW*, p. 16.

19. *GWTW*, p. 726.

20. *GWTW*, p. 35.

21. Margaret Mitchell to Ernest V. Heyn, Apr. 15, 1939, Mitchell Marsh, UGa.

22. See Ayers, *Vengeance and Justice*, for the circumstances of the Irish of Savannah.

23. Margaret Mitchell to Harvey Smith, Mar. 15, 1933, Mitchell, Emory.

24. Ibid.

25. Farr, *Margaret Mitchell*, pp. 68–70.

26. Stephens Crockett interview.

27. Margaret Mitchell to Harvey Smith, Apr. 16, 1933, Mitchell, Emory.

28. Margaret Mitchell to Henry Steele Commager, July 10, 1936, in Harwell, *Letters*, p. 38.

29. Margaret Mitchell to Edwin Granberry, July 8, 1936, in Harwell, *Letters*, p. 29.

30. Margaret Mitchell to Astrid K. Hansen, Jan. 27, 1937, in Harwell, *Letters*, p. 112.

31. Margaret Mitchell to the Very Rev. Mons. James H. Murphy, Mar. 4, 1937, in Harwell, *Letters*, p. 127.

32. Mitchell to Murphy, in Harwell, *Letters*, p. 126.

33. Margaret Mitchell to Lois Dwight Cole, Oct. 3, 1935, Macmillan, NYPL.

34. Margaret Mitchell to Harold Latham, Aug. 18, 1941, Macmillan, NYPL.

35. Hervey Cleckley, *The Mask of Sanity: An Attempt to Clarify Some Issues About the So-Called Psychopathic Personality*, fifth ed. (St. Louis: C.V. Mosby, 1976; originally published 1941), pp. 320, 321.

36. Margaret Mitchell to Harold Latham, August 18, 1941, Macmillan, NYPL.

37. Margaret Mitchell to Dr. Hervey Cleckley, quoted in Farr, *Margaret Mitchell*, pp. 192–93.

38. See Chapter VII.

39. See Wilhelm Stekel, *Frigidity in Woman in Relation to Her Love Life*, translated by James S. Van Teslaar, 2 vols. (New York: Boni and Liveright, 1926).

Chapter XIII: The Strange Disappearance of Pansy Hamilton

1. Margaret Mitchell to Mr. A. W. Wootton, Oct. 15, 1936, Mitchell Marsh, UGa.

2. Margaret Mitchell to Harold Latham, July 11, 1935, Macmillan, NYPL.

3. Margaret Mitchell to Harold Latham, July 27, 1935; Harold S. Latham to Margaret Mitchell, Nov. 4, 1935; and Lois Cole to Margaret Mitchell, Nov. 4, 1935, Macmillan, NYPL.

4. See Chapter X.

5. *GWTW*, p. 385.

6. Von Hoffman interview.

7. Margaret Mitchell to Stephen Vincent Benet, July 9, 1936, in Harwell, *Letters*, p. 36.

8. *GWTW*, p. 1,030.

9. *GWTW*, p. 772.

10. Many biographical commentators, in particular, have linked Berrien Upshaw with Rhett Butler through the similarity of their names: Red and Rhett. Their characters differ completely. At the same time, colors do figure significantly in Mitchell's literary imagination, reds especially, but the color identification applies to the mother–daughter relationship in Mitchell's life as much as or more than the husband and wife one. Mitchell and her mother both had red hair, and the writer spoke of it as her favorite color of tresses. At the same time, Mitchell identified her parent with the color in special ways when she refers to her as a redhead with a temper to match. Mitchell's treatment of all the red-headed Tarltons and their particular relationship with their mother also underlines Mitchell's hidden sense of red that the Rhett-"Red" Upshaw association obscures.

11. *GWTW*, p. 389.

12. Ibid.

13. See Andre Bleikasten, *The Most Spendid Failure: Faulkner's "The Sound and the Fury"* (Bloomington and London: Indiana University Press, 1976), pp. 53, 215, and passim.

14. *GWTW*, p. 366.

15. On May 23, 1941, the day my children's mother was born, her grandmother, Ella Warley McGee Geer, purchased one of these dolls for her. She still has it.

16. Margaret Mitchell to Katharine Brown, Aug. 13, 1937, in Harwell, *Letters*, p. 163.

17. Margaret Mitchell to Dr. Mark Allen Patton, July 11, 1936, in Harwell, *Letters*, p. 43.

18. Margaret Mitchell to Miss Sara Helena Wilson, Nov. 3, 1936, in Harwell, *Letters*, p. 85.

19. *GWTW*, p. 392.

20. *GWTW*, p. 398.

21. *GWTW*, p. 414.

22. *GWTW*, p. 415.

23. *GWTW*, p. 420.

24. *GWTW*, p. 428.

25. *GWTW*, p. 434; see also Chapter IV for the way Mitchell's attitude about her own mother—or her mother's attitude about her—echoed in her fiction.

26. *GWTW*, p. 398.

27. *GWTW*, p. 416.

28. *GWTW*, p. 412.

29. *GWTW*, p. 403.

30. *GWTW*, p. 359.

31. *GWTW*, p. 409.

32. *GWTW*, p. 418.

33. *GWTW*, p. 419.

34. *GWTW*, p. 1029.

35. *GWTW*, p. 398.

36. *GWTW*, p. 403.

37. *GWTW*, p. 400.

38. *GWTW*, p. 431.

39. *GWTW*, p. 432.

40. Ibid.

41. *GWTW*, p. 434.

42. Margaret Mitchell to Mrs. Alfred L. Lustig, Jan. 19, 1937, in Harwell, *Letters*, p. 111.

43. Ball, "Beset by Difficulties."

44. *GWTW*, p. 397.

45. *GWTW*, p. 403.

46. *GWTW*, p. 416.

47. "My Old Kentucky Home, Goodnight," *As Sung by Christy's Minstrels.* (New York: Firth, Pond & Co, 1892). I appreciate Larry Gulley of the University of Georgia Archives for having confirmed this source for me and provided copies of the stanza in question.

48. See Chapter I.

Chapter XIV: Lamed Ambition

1. Baldwin, "An Exclusive Interview."

2. See *Atlanta City Directory:* 1925–1933.

3. See Farr, *Margaret Mitchell*, p. 108.

4. Augusta Dearborn Edwards, "My Most Unforgetable Character," *Readers' Digest*, Mar. 1962, p. 119. Also see Farr, *Margaret Mitchell*, pp. 101–2.

5. Baldwin, "Exclusive Interview."

6. See Chapter XI.

7. Margaret Mitchell to Elinor Hillyer, Oct. 22, 1930, von Hoffman.

8. Margaret Mitchell to Elinor Hillyer, Dec. 3, 1930, von Hoffman.

9. Margaret Mitchell to Elinor Hillyer, July 7, 1930, von Hoffman.

10. Margaret Mitchell to Elinor Hillyer, Dec. 3, 1930, von Hoffman.

11. John Marsh to Frances Marsh Zane, Sept. 20, 1931, Marsh Zane.

12. Helen Turman Markey, Tara, AHS.

13. Margaret Mitchell to Elinor Hillyer, Dec. 3, 1930, von Hoffman.

14. Margaret Mitchell to Harvey Smith, July 14, 1932, Mitchell, Emory.

15. Margaret Mitchell to Dr. Mark Allen Patton, July 11, 1936, in Harwell, *Letters*, p. 42

16. Margaret Mitchell to Harvey Smith, May 24, 1933, Mitchell, Emory.

17. Zane interview.

18. Smith interview; also Riley interview.

19. Graham was Captain John Stephens's nephew, the son of his favorite sister, and May Belle Mitchell's first cousin. Born in 1859, he had served Alexander H. Stephens as private secretary. After Stephens's death, he became secretary to the justices of the Georgia Supreme Court in 1887, and from 1897 to his death in 1935 held the position of assistant reporter of the Supreme Court. See "John M. Graham, Veteran State Official, Dies," *The Atlanta Georgian*, clipping, [Sept. 1935]; also Margaret Mitchell to Elinor Hillyer, Sept. 15, 1935; both von Hoffman.

20. John R. Marsh to Eugene M. Mitchell, Apr. 10, 1935, Mitchell Marsh, UGa.

21. Margaret Mitchell to Frances Marsh, "Monday morning" [Apr.–June 1926], Marsh Zane.

22. John R. Marsh to Eugene M. Mitchell, Apr. 9, 1934, and Apr. 10, 1934, Mitchell Marsh, UGa.

23. Smith interview.

24. John R. Marsh to Eugene M. Mitchell, Apr. 9, 1934, and Apr. 10, 1934, Mitchell Marsh, UGa. Despite Harvey Smith's recollection and the independent evidence of John Marsh's letter to Mitchell & Mitchell, no evidence of the Marshes' legal action against the driver, Littlejohn, survives in the Fulton County Court records.

25. Harold S. Latham, *My Life in Publishing* (New York: E. P. Dutton, 1965), p. 49.

26. *Atlanta Journal*, Apr. 13, 1935.

27. Latham, *My Life*, p. 50.

28. Quoted in Farr, *Margaret Mitchell*, p. 112.

29. Latham, *My Life*, p. 50.

30. Ibid., p. 51.

31. Ibid.; Farr, *Margaret Mitchell*, p. 143.

32. Quoted in Lois Dwight Cole, "The Story Begins at a Luncheon Bridge in Atlanta," in Harwell, *Book and Film*, pp. 58–59.

33. Latham gave several versions of the affair; most notably, "How the Publisher Secured the Book," in "Margaret Mitchell and Her Novel, 'Gone with the Wind,' (a booklet compiled in response to a flood of requests from readers all over the country for information about the author and her book, by the Macmillan Company, N.Y., 1936)." Annotated copy in Mitchell Marsh, UGa, and Latham, *My Life*, p. 52.

34. Latham, *My Life*, p. 52.

35. Margaret Mitchell to Harold Latham, Apr. 16, 1935, Macmillan, NYPL.

36. Ibid.

37. Margaret Mitchell to Harold Latham, July 9, 1935, Macmillan, NYPL.

38. John Marsh to Lois Cole, Feb. 9, 1936, Macmillan, NYPL. For the description of these chapters, see Chapter XV.

39. John Marsh to Lois Cole, Feb. 9, 1936, Macmillan, NYPL.

40. Margaret Mitchell to Harold Latham, July 27, 1935, Macmillan, NYPL.

Chapter XV: Bloody Work Done

1. Margaret Mitchell to Stark Young, Sept. 29, 1936, in Harwell, *Letters*, p. 65.

2. The Mitchell archive does not contain the first two letters, and the third exists only in published form in Farr, *Margaret Mitchell*, pp. 116–17; Harold Latham to Margaret Mitchell, Apr. 18, 1935.

3. Harold Latham to Margaret Mitchell, July 15, 1935, Macmillan, NYPL.

4. Harold Latham, undated memorandum, Macmillan, NYPL.

5. Harold Latham to Margaret Mitchell, July 22, 1935, Macmillan, NYPL.

For biographical data on the evaluator, see "Charles W. Everett File," Columbiana Collection, Columbia University, New York City.

6. This report does not seem to exist in the Macmillan archives nor the Mitchell papers; these excerpts are quoted in Farr, *Margaret Mitchell*, p. 124.

7. Quoted in Farr, *Margaret Mitchell*, pp. 120, 123–24.

8. Margaret Mitchell to Harold Latham, July 17, 1935, Macmillan, NYPL.

9. Lois Dwight Cole to Margaret Mitchell, Aug. 5, 1935, Macmillan, NYPL.

10. Margaret Mitchell, notes to Norman Berg, Oct. 22, 29, 1936, Margaret Mitchell, UGa.

11. Margaret Mitchell to Harold Latham, Oct. 30, 1935, Macmillan, NYPL.

12. Lois Cole to Harold Latham, Nov. 4, 1935, Macmillan, NYPL.

13. Harold Latham to Margaret Mitchell, Nov. 4, 1935, Macmillan, NYPL.

14. Margaret Mitchell to Harold Latham, Sept. 3, 1935, Macmillan, NYPL.

15. John Marsh to Lois Cole, Feb. 9, 1936, Macmillan, NYPL. One extended passage of these deletions survived by a curious accident. In writing his story about Mitchell for *Collier's Magazine*, Edwin Granberry (or the publishers) included as an illustration a page from the manuscript. While unidentified, it came obviously from that section of the book when Carreen O'Hara has decided to join a Charleston convent, in the published Chapter XLI. See Edwin Granberry, "The Private Life of Margaret Mitchell," *Collier's*, Vol. 99, March 13, 1937.

16. John Marsh to Lois Cole, Feb. 9, 1936, Macmillan, NYPL.

17. Although critics have regularly overlooked this aspect of the novel, recent interpretation after the mid-seventies has rediscovered this innovation in her work: see, for example, Willie Lee Rose, "Race and Region in American Historical Fiction," in her collection of essays, *Slavery and Freedom*, William Freehling, ed. (New York: Oxford University Press, 1982). For a further discussion of these issues, also see, "Bibliographical Essay" in my *Recasting*.

18. All the following references are from Margaret Mitchell to Harold Latham, July 27, 1935, Macmillan, NYPL.

19. *GWTW*, p. 1,035.

20. *GWTW*, p. 1,034.

21. Margaret Mitchell to Dr. H. P. Stuckey, Feb. 3, 1936, Margaret Mitchell, UGa.

22. Margaret Mitchell to Dr. H. P. Stuckey, Dec. 3, 1935, Mitchell Marsh, UGa. For further evidence of her manic devotion to factual reality, see Lois Cole to Margaret Mitchell, Mar. 4, 1936; Margaret Mitchell to Lois Cole, [early Mar., 1936]; and Margaret Mitchell to Lois Cole, Mar. 18, 1936; all Macmillan, NYPL.

23. Margaret Mitchell to Harold Latham July 27, 1935. Macmillan, NYPL.

24. Margaret Mitchell to Harold Latham, Oct. 30, 1935, Macmillan, NYPL.

25. Harold Latham to Margaret Mitchell, Nov. 4, 1935; also Lois Cole to Margaret Mitchell, Nov. 7, 1935. Both Macmillan, NYPL.

26. Marie Conway Oemler, *A Woman Named Smith* (New York: The Century Company, 1919), p. 3.

27. Margaret Mitchell to Harold Latham, Oct. 31, 1935, Macmillan, NYPL.

28. Marie Conway Oemler, *Slippy McGee, Sometimes Known as the Butterfly Man* (New York: The Century Company, 1917), p. 5.

29. Margaret Mitchell to Harold Latham, Oct. 31, 1935, Macmillan, NYPL.

30. John Marsh to Lois Cole, Feb. 13, 1936; and Lois Cole to John Marsh, Feb. 15, 1936; both Macmillan, NYPL.

31. Lois Cole to Margaret Mitchell, Feb. 6, 1936; quoted in Margaret Baugh, notes to LDC, Oct. 13, 1964, Mitchell, Emory.

32. John Marsh to Lois Cole, Feb. 9, 1936, Macmillan, NYPL.

33. John Marsh to Lois Cole, Feb. 13, 1936, Macmillan, NYPL.

34. John Marsh to Lois Cole, Jan. 31, 1936, Macmillan, NYPL.

35. Ibid.

36. Margaret Mitchell to Prof. Charles Everett, quoted in Farr, *Margaret Mitchell*, p. 140.

37. Grace Duggan to her mother, Nov. 15, 1936, copy in Mitchell Marsh, UGa.

38. Margaret Mitchell to Ruth Hinman Carter, "Monday," [*ca.* Jun. 1936], Mitchell Marsh, UGa.

39. Margaret Mitchell to Mrs. K. D. Smith, Jul. 29, 1936, Mitchell Marsh, UGa.

40. Elaine Dillashaw, personal interview with the author; Peggy Palmer, personal interview with the author; see also Margaret Mitchell to Katharine Brown, Feb. 14, 1937, in Harwell, *Letters*, p. 118.

41. Margaret Mitchell to Lois Cole, Apr. 27, 1936, Macmillan, NYPL.

42. As quoted in Farr, *Margaret Mitchell*, p. 141: that biographer and Lois Cole bowdlerized both Myrick and Mitchell. She never uttered expressions like "goldarned." For her original usage, see the copy of the original letter in LDC to Stephens Mitchell, Oct. 12, 1964, in Mitchell Marsh, UGa.

43. Margaret Mitchell to Lois Cole, Apr. 14, 1936, quoted in Farr, *Margaret Mitchell*, pp. 141–44.

44. Farr, *Margaret Mitchell*, p. 144, omitted the final disclaimer; see the copy of the original letter in LDC to Stephens Mitchell, Oct. 12, 1964, Mitchell Marsh, UGa.

45. Blythe M'Kay, "Mrs. Marsh Is Honored at Writers' Breakfast," *Macon Telegraph and News*, Apr. 4, 1936; also Marian Elder Jones, " 'Me and My Book,' " *Georgia Review* XVI (Spring 1962): 180–86.

46. See, for example, W. A. R. Collins to Harold Macmillan, May 8, 1936; and Harold Macmillan to W. A. R. Collins, May 26, 1936; in Macmillan, NYPL; also Chapter XX.

47. Quoted in Farr, *Margaret Mitchell*, p. 146.

48. *New York World Telegram*, Quoted in Farr, *Margaret Mitchell*, p. 147.

49. Ibid.

50. Margaret Mitchell to Lois Cole, May 5, 1936, Macmillan, NYPL.

51. Constance Lindsay Skinner to Lois Dwight Cole, June 20, 1936, typescript copy in Mitchell Marsh, UGa.

52. See Anne C. Loveland, *Lillian Smith: A Southerner Confronting the South* (Baton Rouge: Louisiana State University Press, 1986).

53. Lillian Smith to Margaret Mitchell, May 16, 1936, Mitchell Marsh, UGa.

54. Lillian Smith to Margaret Mitchell, May 18, 1936, Mitchell Marsh, UGa.

55. Margaret Mitchell to Lillian Smith, May 21, 1936, Mitchell Marsh, UGa.

56. See Richard King, "The 'Simple Story's' Ideology," in Pyron, *Recasting*, p. 169. Without reference to the personal exchanges between the two women,

King here takes Smith at her word, and uses her to bolster his argument for the reactionary quality of Mitchell's novel. See "Dope with Lime," *Pseudopodia*, July 1936. Copy in the papers of Lillian Smith, Special Collections, University of Georgia Libraries, University of Georgia, Athens.

57. Margaret Mitchell to Harold Latham, May 21, 1936, Macmillan, NYPL. Eight years later, the Mitchell-Marshes still grumbled about this incident. After the publication of *Strange Fruit* and its effusive front-page *New York Times* Sunday book review, John Marsh wrote his sister:

> Miss Smith and her sidekick, Paula Snelling, are the editors of a little magazine in the Georgia mountains originally called "Pseudopodia" and now "The North Georgia Review." We have met them only once. Shortly after GWTW was published, they wrote Peggy asking if they could come to see her for an interview. As the afternoon dragged on in general conversation, Peggy served them tea and finally told them goodbye, wondering why they had come. A few days later, she received a letter from them asking her if *she* would please write the interview for them, something around 5,000 words—there had been so many questions they had intended to ask but they had just forgotten to do it. Since then, as ex-members of the working press, we have never thought very highly of them.

(John Marsh to Frances Marsh, Mar. 4, 1944, in Marsh Zane.)

Chapter XVI: Ground Exceeding Fine

1. Feb. 11, 1939, clipping in Mitchell Marsh, UGa.

2. For the description of this ritual see the five–part series in the *Atlanta Constitution* by Lamar Q. Ball in Nov. of 1936.

3. For a sampling of the multitudinous concerns summarized in these paragraphs, see her letters in passing for late October and November 1936, in Harwell, *Letters*, pp. 80–97, especially in the context of the Ball *Atlanta Constitution* series.

4. Quoted in Harwell, *Book and Film*, p. 19.

5. Ibid., pp. 25, 26, 27.

6. Edwin Granberry, "Book of the Day," *New York Sun*, June 30, 1936.

7. J. Donald Adams, "A Fine Novel of the Civil War," *New York Times Book Review*, July 5, 1936.

8. Lois Dwight Cole to Margaret Mitchell, April 29, 1936, Macmillan, NYPL.

9. For a fuller treatment of Adams and the novel, see Richard A. Dwyer, "The Case of the Cool Reception," in Pyron, *Recasting*, pp. 22–23.

10. Henry Steele Commager, "The Civil War in Georgia's Red Clay Hills," reprinted in Pyron, *Recasting*, p. 12. In a later review, the Agrarian and Fugitive New Critic John Crowe Ransom noted the same quality in both book and regional culture as he commended the novel's realism. What troubled Isabel Paterson about the novel—a certain cultural shallowness—Commager and Ransom singled out for special praise as a peculiar and distinctive attribute of regional culture. See Ransom, "Fiction Harvest," *Southern Review* 2 (1936–37): 407–8.

11. Reprinted in Harwell, *Book and Film*, pp. 19–21.

12. Undated clipping in Mitchell Marsh, UGa.

13. See Evelyn Scott, *Background in Tennessee: A Facsimile Edition, with an Introduction by Robert L. Welker* (Nashville: University of Tennessee Press, 1980), originally published in 1937; and D. A. Callard, *"Pretty Good for a Woman": The Enigmas of Evelyn Scott* (New York: W. W. Norton, 1985); also Robert K. Welker, "Evelyn Scott: A Literary Biography" (Ph.D. diss., Vanderbilt University, 1958).

14. Evelyn Scott, "War Between the States," *The Nation*, July 4, 1936; see also Belle Rosenbaum, "Why Do They Read It?" *Scribner's* 99 (1937), 23–24, 69–70, for another reviewer's connection of the novel with the literature of the twenties.

15. Mitchell hated this piece. For her very thinly veiled hostility, see her letter to Stark Young, Sept. 29, 1936, in Harwell, *Letters*, pp. 66–67.

16. John Peale Bishop, "All War and No Peace," *New Republic*, July 15, 1936. 1936.

17. Margaret Mitchell to Stark Young, Sept. 1, 1936, in Harwell, *Letters*, p. 59.

18. Margaret Mitchell to Stark Young, Sept. 29, 1936, in Harwell, *Letters*, pp. 66, 67.

19. Malcolm Cowley, "Going with the Wind," in Pyron, *Recasting*, pp. 18–19.

20. Quoted in Dwyer, "The Cool Reception," in Pyron, *Recasting*, p. 26.

21. Cowley, "Going with the Wind," in Pyron, *Recasting*, p. 20.

22. Herschel Brickell to John Marsh, "Friday" [*ca.* Aug. 12, 1936], Mitchell Marsh, UGa.

23. John Marsh to Herschel Brickell, Aug. 14, 1936, Mitchell Marsh, UGa.

24. For the foreign sales, see Chapter XX.

25. Edwin Granberry, "The Private Life of Margaret Mitchell," *Collier's*, Mar. 13, 1937.

26. Marjorie Kinnan Rawlings to Herschel Brickell, n.d., quoted in Herschel Brickell to John Marsh, "Friday" [*ca.* Aug. 12, 1936], in Mitchell Marsh, UGa.

27. Gordon Ray Young to Mrs. Margaret Mitchell Morse [*sic*], July 24, 1936, Mitchell Marsh, UGa.

28. Granberry, "Private Life."

29. For the information on the mail of Harris and Eleanor Roosevelt, see Robert S. McElvaine, ed., *Down and Out in the Great Depression: Letters from the Forgotten Man* (Chapel Hill: University of North Carolina Press, 1983), and John Erwin Talmadge, *Cora Harris* (Athens: University of Georgia Press, [1968]).

30. When Edwin Granberry wrote this essay, he submitted it to the Marshes for their approval. The novelist made a few changes, but her husband added a great deal, which Granberry then incorporated *in toto* into the essay. For John Marsh's additions and alterations in the draft, see the Granberry file, Mitchell Marsh, UGa.

31. Granberry, "Private Life."

32. See Steven M. Stowe, *Intimacy and Power in the Old South: Rituals in the Lives of the Planters* (Baltimore: Johns Hopkins University Press, 1987). I have also profited from Steve Stowe's formal and informal discussions on this

topic of epistolary forms and their particular meaning for regional culture. I add evidence from my own family. Born in 1942, I grew up surrounded by letters. Everyone seemed to save them. I have beside me at this moment an envelope, and on the outside, in my father's distinctive hand, the notation "family letters." It contains the most motley collection of epistles, some of which I added after my father gave the envelope to me twenty–five years ago. A dozen or more antedate the Civil War, including one series from my great– great–grandfather's brother who went to California in the Gold Rush. They also include letters with Confederate stamps, which especially attracted my father as a lad, and his hand again marked them, this time with current prices that such documents would fetch. I found other such documents tucked away among my grandmother's things after her death, and my uncle's death uncov- ered boxes of these documents, which included perhaps 200 letters written between my great–grandmother and my great–grandfather in the 1890s from her hometown of Thompson, Georgia. These catalogue the history of the Pop- ulist Party in that hotbed of dissension at the height of Tom Watson's early career. On the other side of my family, my grandmother and mother each preserved their letters to and from each other as my mother went away from home to attend college in the mid–thirties. Letter-writing formed an essential part of my own childhood, and the form dominated Mitchell's culture even more.

33. See Chapter IX. The clipping has been preserved in Marsh Zane.

34. Although Farr cites the letter extensively, he omits the final admonition. See Margaret Mitchell to Father and Grandmother, Sept. 8, 1918, Mitchell Marsh, UGa.

35. Margaret Mitchell to Harvey Smith, July 14, 1932, Mitchell, Emory.

36. Bessie Jordan to Medora Perkerson, July 6, 1936, quoted in Frank Dan- iel, "Margaret Mitchell Files Open for Biographers," June 10, 1964, clipping, Tara, AHS.

37. John Marsh, notes on Granberry articles, Granberry file, Mitchell Marsh, UGa; see also Chapter XIX.

38. John Marsh wrote these lines and Granberry used them in his *Collier's* article.

39. Margaret Mitchell to Edwin Granberry, July 8, 1936, in Harwell, *Letters,* p. 27.

40. Margaret Mitchell to Herschel Brickell, July 7, 1936, in Harwell, *Letters,* pp. 20–21.

41. For the published letters to Brickell, see Harwell, *Letters,* pp. 19–21, 59, 62–63, 73–75, 80–82, 86–89, 100–101, 108–11, 115–17, 122, 137–39, 143–45, 147–49, 153–54, 166–67, 173–76, 188–92, 199–208, 211–13, 217–20, 223–25, 231–32, 296–97, 299–300, 320. These letters hardly exhaust the correspon- dence: see the Brickell file, Mitchell Marsh, UGa. For other biographical infor- mation on the reviewer, see "Herschel Brickell Is Called a Suicide," *New York Times,* May 30, 1952.

42. Margaret Mitchell to Clifford Dowdey, July 22, 1937, in Harwell, *Letters,* p. 157.

43. Ball, "All Records Smashed," *Atlanta Constitution,* Nov. 9, 1936.

44. Margaret Mitchell to Herschel Brickell, Nov. 13, 1936, in Harwell, *Let- ters,* p. 87.

45. Margaret Mitchell to Herschel Brickell, Feb. 8, 1937, in Harwell, *Letters*, p. 116.

46. Margaret Mitchell to Herschel Brickell, Sept. 9, 1936, Mitchell Marsh, UGa.

47. Ball, "Fame's Tempo," *Atlanta Constitution*, Nov. 13, 1936.

48. Quoted by Grace Duggan in her letter to her mother, Nov. 15, 1936, Mitchell Marsh, UGa.

49. Granberry, "Private Life."

50. Ball, "Fame's Tempo."

51. Margaret Mitchell to Mrs. Julia Collier Harris, June 29, 1936, in Harwell, *Letters*, p. 17.

Chapter XVII: Hollywood Follies

1. July 26, 1940, Mitchell Marsh, UGa.

2. Margaret Mitchell to Katharine Brown, Mar. 8, 1937, in Harwell, *Letters*, pp. 131–32.

3. Margaret Mitchell to Lois Dwight Cole, Mar. 14, 1936, Macmillan, NYPL.

4. Lois Dwight Cole to Margaret Mitchell, Apr. 9, 1936, Macmillan, NYPL.

5. Margaret Mitchell to Lois Cole, Apr. 27, 1936, Macmillan, NYPL.

6. Lois Dwight Cole to Margaret Mitchell, May 2, 1936, Macmillan, NYPL.

7. Margaret Mitchell to Lois Dwight Cole, May 5, 1936; and Margaret Mitchell to Annie Laurie Williams, May 5, 1936, Macmillan, NYPL.

8. Margaret Mitchell to Harold Latham, May 25, 1936, Macmillan, NYPL.

9. Harold Latham to George Brett, May 20, 1936; and Margaret Mitchell to Harold Latham, May 21, 1936; also Annie Laurie Williams to Harold Latham, May 19 and May 29, 1936, Macmillan, NYPL.

10. Annie Laurie Williams to Harold Latham, May 27, 1936, Macmillan, NYPL.

11. Margaret Mitchell to Lois Dwight Cole, July 3, 1936, Macmillan, NYPL.

12. Lois Dwight Cole to Margaret Mitchell, July 8, 1936, Macmillan, NYPL.

13. Roland Flamini, *Scarlett, Rhett, and a Cast of Thousands: The Filming of "Gone with the Wind"* (New York: Collier Books, 1975), pp. 12–13.

14. John Marsh to Margaret Mitchell, July 15, 1936, Mitchell Marsh, UGa.

15. Lois Dwight Cole to Margaret Mitchell, July 13, 1936, Macmillan, NYPL.

16. John Marsh to Lois Cole, July 13, 1936, Macmillan, NYPL.

17. Margaret Mitchell to Harold Latham, May 25, 1936, Macmillan, NYPL.

18. John Marsh to Margaret Mitchell, July 15, 1936, Mitchell Marsh, UGa.

19. John Marsh to Margaret Mitchell, July 15 and July 17, 1936, Mitchell Marsh, UGa.

20. Margaret Mitchell to Herschel Brickell, quoted in Farr, *Margaret Mitchell*, p. 173.

21. Stephens Mitchell to George Brett, Jr., Sept. 21, 1936, Macmillan, NYPL.

22. Margaret Mitchell to Harold Latham, Aug. 13, 1936, in Harwell, *Letters*, p. 51.

23. Quoted in Farr, *Margaret Mitchell*, p. 175.

24. John Marsh to Herschel Brickell, Aug. 14, 1936, Mitchell Marsh, UGa.

25. Margaret Mitchell to Herschel Brickell, Sept. 1, 1936, Mitchell Marsh, UGa.
26. George Brett, Jr., to John Marsh, Sept. 3, 1936, Macmillan, NYPL.
27. Margaret Mitchell to Allan Taylor, Oct. 5, 1936, Mitchell Marsh, UGa.
28. Margaret Mitchell to Harold Latham, Sept. 23, 1936, Macmillan, NYPL.
29. Margaret Mitchell to Harold Latham, Sept. 25, 1936, Macmillan, NYPL.
30. Harold Latham to Margaret Mitchell, Oct. 6, 1936; see also Henry W. Taft to George P. Brett, Oct. 6, 1936; both Macmillan, NYPL.
31. For the full discussion of the results of this fight, see Chapter XXI.
32. Lamar Q. Ball, "Margaret Mitchell Is Hands-Off on GWTW Screening," *Atlanta Constitution*, Nov. 12, 1936.
33. Quoted in Ball, "Hands-Off."
34. Margaret Mitchell to Lois Dwight Cole, July 3, 1936, Macmillan, NYPL.
35. Margaret Mitchell to Katharine Brown, Oct. 6, 1936, in Harwell, *Letters*, p. 71.
36. Ball, "Hands-Off."
37. Ibid.
38. Margaret Mitchell to Katharine Brown, Oct. 6, 1936, in Harwell, *Letters*, p. 72.
39. Margaret Mitchell to Katharine Brown, Nov. 18, 1936, in Harwell, *Letters*, p. 90.
40. Margaret Mitchell to Sidney Howard, Nov. 21, 1936, in Harwell, *Letters*, p. 94.
41. Margaret Mitchell to David Selznick, Oct. 19, 1936, in Harwell, *Letters*, p. 79.
42. Margaret Mitchell to Katharine Brown, Nov. 18, 1936, in Harwell, *Letters*, pp. 90–91.
43. Margaret Mitchell to Russell Birdwell, Nov. 24, 1936, in Harwell, *Letters*, p. 96.
44. Margaret Mitchell to Russell Birdwell, Dec. 5, 1936, in Harwell, *Letters*, pp. 99–100.
45. Her dispatches have been republished in Susan Myrick, *White Columns in Hollywood: Reports from the "GWTW" Sets*, edited with an introduction by Richard Harwell (Macon: Mercer University Press, 1982).
46. Margaret Mitchell to Katharine Brown, Mar. 16, 1938, in Harwell, *Letters*, p. 188; see also Margaret Mitchell to Katharine Brown, Aug. 13, 1937, and July 7, 1938, in Harwell, *Letters*, pp. 163, 209.
47. Susan Myrick to Margaret Mitchell, Jan. 11, 1939, Mitchell Marsh, UGa.
48. Susan Myrick to Margaret Mitchell, Feb. 12, 1939, Mitchell Marsh, UGa.
49. Susan Myrick to Margaret Mitchell, May 28, 1939, Mitchell Marsh, UGa.
50. Ibid.
51. Susan Myrick to Margaret Mitchell, Feb. 12, 1939, Mitchell Marsh, UGa.
52. Margaret Mitchell to Sue Myrick, Feb. 15, 1939, Mitchell Marsh, UGa.
53. Susan Myrick to Margaret Mitchell, Feb. 23, 1939, Mitchell Marsh, UGa.
54. Ibid.
55. Susan Myrick to Margaret Mitchell, Jan. 15, 1939, Mitchell Marsh, UGa.
56. Susan Myrick to Margaret Mitchell, Feb. 2, 1939; also, Susan Myrick to Margaret Mitchell, Feb. 12, 1939; both Mitchell Marsh, UGa.

57. Susan Myrick to Margaret Mitchell, May 28, 1939, Mitchell Marsh, UGa.
58. Susan Myrick to Margaret Mitchell, Jan. 15, 1939, Mitchell Marsh, UGa.
59. Susan Myrick to Margaret Mitchell, May 28, 1939, Mitchell Marsh, UGa.
60. Susan Myrick to Margaret Mitchell, Jan. 15, 1939, Mitchell Marsh, UGa.
61. Margaret Mitchell to Susan Myrick, Apr. 17, 1939, in Harwell, *Letters*, p. 271.
62. Margaret Mitchell to Susan Myrick, Feb. 28, 1939, Mitchell Marsh, UGa.
63. Margaret Mitchell to Susan Myrick, Jan. 19, 1939, Mitchell Marsh, UGa.
64. Margaret Mitchell to Susan Myrick, Mar. 1, 1939, Mitchell Marsh, UGa.
65. Margaret Mitchell to Colonel Telamon Cuyler, Feb. 17, 1939, in Harwell, *Letters*, pp. 255–56; see also Margaret Mitchell to Susan Myrick, Apr. 17, 1939, in Harwell, *Letters*, p. 271.
66. Margaret Mitchell to Susan Myrick, Jan. 19, 1939, Mitchell Marsh, UGa.
67. Margaret Mitchell to Susan Myrick, Feb. 10, 1939, in Harwell, *Letters*, pp. 249–50.
68. Margaret Mitchell to Stephen Vincent Benet, July 9, 1936, in Harwell, *Letters*, p. 36.
69. Margaret Mitchell to Herschel Brickell, Apr. 8, 1937, in Harwell, *Letters*, p. 137.
70. Margaret Mitchell to Susan Myrick, Feb. 10, 1939, in Harwell, *Letters*, pp. 249–50.
71. Margaret Mitchell to Jere Moore, Feb. 16, 1939, in Harwell, *Letters*, p. 255.

Chapter XVIII: Pee Soup

1. Jan. 11, 1939, Mitchell Marsh, UGa.
2. Jack Spauling, "Glamour Wins Over Sentiment, *Atlanta Constitution*, Dec. 16, 1939, clipping in scrapbook, Margaret Mitchell Collection, Atlanta Public Library, Atlanta, Georgia.
3. Margaret Mitchell to Katharine Brown, Apr. 17, 1939, in Harwell, *Letters*, p. 271.
4. Margaret Mitchell to Katharine Brown, Jan. 31, 1939, in Harwell, *Letters*, p. 247.
5. Margaret Mitchell to Lois Cole Taylor, July 18, 1936, in Harwell, *Letters*, p. 284.
6. David Selznick to Katharine Brown, Nov. 27, 1939, in *Memo from David O. Selznick*, selected and edited by Rudy Behlmer with an introduction by S. N. Behrman (New York: Viking Press, 1972), pp. 233, 234.
7. David Selznick to Katharine Brown, Nov. 28, 1939, in Behlmer, *Memo*, pp. 234–35.
8. Margaret Mitchell, interview with Miss Grinnell, Sept. 5, 1941, Macmillan, NYPL.
9. Margaret Mitchell to George Brett, May 12, 1939, in Harwell, *Letters*, p. 276.
10. Medora Perkerson, "Original," (manuscript), Perkerson, UGa.
11. Quoted in Farr, *Margaret Mitchell*, p. 21.

12. Ibid., p. 23.

13. David Selznick to Katharine Brown and Mr. Cooper, Oct. 8, 1936, in Behlmer, *Memo*, p. 141.

14. David Selznick to Sidney Howard, Jan. 6, 1937, in Behlmer, *Memo*, pp. 145, 146, 147.

15. Ibid.

16. Ibid.

17. Sidney Howard to Margaret Mitchell, June 5, 1937, in Richard B. Harwell, editor, *GWTW: The Screenplay, by Sidney Howard* (New York: Macmillan, 1981), p. 15.

18. Sidney Howard to Margaret Mitchell, Oct. 7, 1937, in Harwell, *Letters*, p. 168.

19. Sidney Howard to Margaret Mitchell, Nov. 26, 1937, in Harwell, *Screenplay*, p. 17.

20. David Selznick to George Cukor, Feb. 25, 1938, in Behlmer, *Memo*, pp. 154, 155.

21. David Selznick to Sidney Howard, Jan. 6, 1937, in Behlmer, *Memo*, p. 146.

22. Ibid.

23. David Selznick to Miss MacConnell, Dec. 5, 1938, in Behlmer, *Memo*, pp. 177–78.

24. Quoted in Harwell, *Screenplay*, p. 17.

25. David Selznick to John Hay Whitney and Katharine Brown, Oct. 12, 1938, in Behlmer, *Memo*, pp. 164–65.

26. Roland Flamini, *Scarlett, Rhett, and a Cast of Thousands: The Filming of "Gone with the Wind"* (New York: Macmillan, 1975), p. 201.

27. David Selznick to [Daniel] O'Shea, Nov. 11, 1938, in Behlmer, *Memo*, p. 169.

28. David Selznick to Daniel T. O'Shea, Nov. 20, 1938, in Behlmer, *Memo*, p. 174.

29. David Selznick to Katharine Brown, Dec. 6, 1938, in Behlmer, *Memo*, pp. 178, 179.

30. Ben Hecht, quoted in Flamini, *Filming of GWTW*, p. 196.

31. F. Scott Fitzgerald to Scottie Fitzgerald [Winter, 1939], in *The Letters of F. Scott Fitzgerald*, edited and with an introduction by Andrew Turnbull (New York: Scribner's, 1963; Bantam edition, 1971), pp. 50–51.

32. Quoted in Harwell, *Screenplay*, p. 34.

33. F. Scott Fitzgerald to Maxwell Perkins, Feb. 25, 1939, in Turnbull, *Letters*, p. 289.

34. F. Scott Fitzgerald to Scottie Fitzgerald, Oct. 5, 1940, in Turnbull, *Letters*, p. 97.

35. See Behlmer, *Memo*, p. 184.

36. Susan Myrick to Margaret Mitchell, Feb. 14, 1939, in Harwell, *Screenplay*, p. 25; see also Behlmer, *Memo*, pp. 191–92.

37. Flamini, *Filming of GWTW*, p. 238.

38. Ben Hecht, *Child of the Century* (New York: Simon and Schuster, 1954), pp. 488–89.

39. David Selznick to Ben Hecht, Sept. 25, 1939, in Behlmer, *Memo*, p. 214.

40. Margaret Mitchell to Mr. and Mrs. Wilbur Kurtz, Mar. 11, 1939, in Harwell, *Screenplay*, pp. 29–30.

41. Harwell, in *Screenplay*, lists them, p. 30: in addition to Howard, Selznick, Fitzgerald, Stewart, Hecht, Garrett, and Barbara Keon (the "script girl"), he names John Balderston, Michael Foster, Wilbur Kurtz, Val Lewton, Charles MacArthur, John Lee Makin, Edwin Justus Mayer, Winston Miller, Jo Swerling, and John van Druten.

42. Margaret Mitchell to Susan Myrick, [*ca.* Apr. 11, 1939], in Harwell, *Screenplay*, p. 30.

43. Flamini, *Filming of GWTW*, p. 307; also pp. 296, 305.

44. For a further discussion of race and Selznick's film, see Thomas Cripps, "Winds of Change: *Gone with the Wind* and Racism as a National Issue," in Pyron, *Recasting*; also Leonard J. Leff, "David Selznick's *Gone with the Wind*: 'The Negro Problem,' " *Georgia Review* 38, 1 (1984), pp. 146–64.

45. See Burl Noggle, "With Pen and Camera: In Quest of the American South in the 1930's," in Bruce Clayton and John A. Salmond, *The South Is Another Land: Essays on the Twentieth-Century South* (Westport, Conn.: Greenwood University Press, 1987). Although he fails to deal with *Gone with the Wind*, Noggle provides a fine examination of the forces that helped ensure the film's success.

46. See Thomas H. Pauly, "Hollywood Histories of the Depression," reprinted in Harwell, *Book and Film*.

47. See Ronald Smothers, "Scarlett and Rhett Take Atlanta Again," *New York Times*, Dec. 16, 1989.

48. Judith Crist, *The Private Eye, the Cowboy, and the Very Naked Girl: Movies from Cleo to Clyde*. (New York and Chicago: Holt, Rinehart and Winston, 1968), p. 189.

Chapter XIX: Hawk and Buzzard Time

1. Dec. 4, 1947, Macmillan, NYPL.

2. Margaret Mitchell interview with Miss Grinnell, Sept. 5, 1941, Macmillan, NYPL.

3. Margaret Mitchell to George Brett, June 9, 1941, Macmillan, NYPL.

4. Margaret Mitchell interview with Miss Grinnell, Sept. 5, 1941, Macmillan, NYPL.

5. Margaret Mitchell to Harold Latham, Dec. 26, 1941, Macmillan, NYPL.

6. Margaret Mitchell to Lt. K. H. Kalmbach, Mar. 7, 1942, in Harwell, *Letters*, p. 356.

7. Margaret Mitchell to Captain and Mrs. S. P. Jenkins, Dec. 26, 1941, in Harwell, *Letters*, p. 352.

8. Margaret Mitchell to Mr. and Mrs. Charles W. Bryan, Jr., Aug. 26, 1943, in Harwell, *Letters*, p. 375.

9. Margaret Mitchell to Helen Dowdey, Jan. 29, 1942, Mitchell Marsh, UGa.

10. Margaret Mitchell to Clifford Dowdey, Mar. 9, 1942, Mitchell Marsh, UGa.

11. Margaret Mitchell to Helen Dowdey, Nov. 2, 1942, Mitchell Marsh, UGa.

12. Margaret Mitchell to Clifford Dowdey, Jan. 12, 1942, Mitchell Marsh, UGa.

13. Margaret Mitchell to Leodel Coleman, n.d., Mitchell Marsh, UGa.

14. Margaret Mitchell to Cary Wilmer, Mar. 17, 1943, Mitchell, Emory.

15. Margaret Mitchell to Mrs. Charles Killette, Dec. 9, 1944, in Harwell, *Letters*, p. 384.

16. Margaret Mitchell to Clifford Dowdey, Nov. 18, 1943, Mitchell Marsh, UGa.

17. Margaret Mitchell to Helen Dowdey, Feb. 21, 1945, Mitchell Marsh, UGa.

18. Margaret Mitchell to Harold Latham, Aug. 20, 1942, Macmillan, NYPL.

19. See the entire Wilmer file on deposit in Mitchell, Emory; in particular, Margaret Mitchell to Cary Wilmer, Jan. 4, 1943.

20. Mr. Coleman deposited the originals in the Georgia Southern College Library, Statesville, Georgia; the Mitchell Marsh Collection at the University of Georgia contains the carbons.

21. Margaret Mitchell to Jay McGahee, Nov. 8, 1945, and July 6, 1945, in Mitchell Marsh, UGa.

22. Margaret Mitchell to Helen Dowdey, June 13, 1940, Mitchell Marsh, UGa.

23. Margaret Mitchell to Clifford and Helen Dowdey, July 1, 1940, Mitchell Marsh, UGa.

24. Margaret Mitchell to Clifford and Helen Dowdey, May 19, 1941, Mitchell Marsh, UGa; see also Margaret Mitchell to George Brett, June 9, 1941, Macmillan, NYPL.

25. Margaret Mitchell to Harold Latham, Dec. 10, 1938, Macmillan, NYPL.

26. Margaret Mitchell to Harold Latham, Nov. 3, 1938, Macmillan, NYPL.

27. Margaret Mitchell to Helen Dowdey, May 6, 1944, Mitchell Marsh, UGa.

28. Eugene Mitchell to Mrs. Mary Walker, June 7, 1942, Mitchell Marsh, UGa.

29. Margaret Mitchell to Clifford Dowdey, Jan 8, 1943, Mitchell Marsh, UGa.

30. Margaret Mitchell to Dr. Warde B. Allen, Feb. 15, 1943, Mitchell Marsh, UGa.

31. Dr. Warde B. Allen to Margaret Mitchell, Dec. 11, 1942; also Dr. Walter Dandy to John Marsh, June 1, 1943, both Mitchell Marsh, UGa.

32. Besides the Mitchell correspondence, the information on the neurosurgeon is drawn from William Lloyd Fox, *Dandy of Johns Hopkins* (Baltimore: Williams and Wilkins, 1984); and J. DeWitt Fox, "Walter Dandy—Super-Surgeon," *Henry Ford Hospital Medical Journal* 25 (1977): 149–70.

33. Dr. Warde Allen to Margaret Mitchell, Dec. 11, 1942, Mitchell Marsh, UGa.

34. Margaret Mitchell to Clifford and Helen Dowdey, May 13, 1943, Mitchell Marsh, UGa.

35. Margaret Mitchell to Dr. Walter Dandy, [*ca.* Jan. 20, 1945, not sent] Mitchell Marsh, UGa.

36. Margaret Mitchell to Helen and Clifford Dowdey, Aug. 21, 1943, Mitchell Marsh, UGa.

37. John Marsh to Dr. Frank J. Otenasek, May 18, 1943, Mitchell Marsh, UGa.

38. John Marsh to Dr. Walter Dandy, July 16, 1943, Mitchell Marsh, UGa.

39. John Marsh to Dr. Frank J. Otenasek, May 18, 1943, Mitchell Marsh, UGa.

40. Margaret Mitchell to Clifford and Helen Dowdey, June 29, 1943, Mitchell Marsh, UGa.

41. Margaret Mitchell to Helen Dowdey, Oct. 22, 1943, Mitchell Marsh, UGa.

42. Dr. Walter Dandy to John Marsh, June 1, 1943, Mitchell Marsh, UGa.

43. Dr. Walter Dandy to John Marsh, July 17, 1943, Mitchell Marsh, UGa.

44. Margaret Mitchell to Dr. Walter Dandy [Jan. 20, 1945, not sent], Mitchell Marsh, UGa.

45. Margaret Mitchell to Helen and Clifford Dowdey, June 29, 1943, Mitchell Marsh, UGa.

46. Margaret Mitchell to Walter Dandy, [ca. Jan. 20, 1945, not sent], Mitchell Marsh, UGa.

47. Margaret Mitchell to Dr. Walter Dandy, Jan. 2, 1945, Mitchell Marsh, UGa.

48. Margaret Mitchell to "Dear Pat,", May 16, 1944, Mitchell Marsh, UGa.

49. Margaret Mitchell to Clifford and Helen Dowdey, Apr. 21, 1943, Mitchell Marsh, UGa.

50. His response to Edwin Granberry's article commissioned by *Collier's* typified this chore he set for himself. After producing a draft of the piece, Granberry submitted it to the author. She gave it to her husband. He studied it line by line and produced a twenty–page critique that included alternative drafts of entire passages. See Chapter XVI. John Marsh's notes on the essay in the Edwin Granberry file, Mitchell Marsh, UGa.

51. Lee Fuhrman, "Margaret Mitchell Hungers for 'Cyclone Cellar' Refuge," *Atlanta Constitution*, Apr. 17, 1938; clipping in Margaret Mitchell to Harold Latham, Apr. 18, 1938, Macmillan, NYPL. For two versions of this same affair, see Harwell, *Letters*, pp. 194–95. Harwell reproduces the letter to Harold Latham of April 18, although he deletes Mitchell's outburst against the press; at the same time, he includes a third-party retelling of the confrontation.

52. Margaret Mitchell to Clifford and Helen Dowdey, Apr. 1, 1940, also Mar. 22, 1940, Mitchell Marsh, UGa.

53. Margaret Mitchell to Clifford and Helen Dowdey, June 7, 1940, Mitchell Marsh, UGa.

54. Margaret Mitchell to Helen Dowdey, Dec. 7, 1945, Mitchell Marsh, UGa.

55. John Marsh to Dr. Theodore J. C. von Storch, Apr. 3, 1946, Mitchell Marsh, UGa.

56. Margaret Mitchell to John S. Graham, Oct. 14, 1947, Mitchell Marsh, UGa.

57. Margaret Mitchell to Helen Dowdey, Feb. 14, 1947, Mitchell Marsh, UGa.

58. Margaret Mitchell to Clifford Dowdey, Apr. 9, 1946; also Margaret Mitchell to Helen Dowdey, May 10, 1946; both Mitchell Marsh, UGa.

59. Margaret Mitchell to Helen Dowdey, Feb. 14, 1947, Mitchell Marsh, UGa.

60. Margaret Mitchell to Clifford Dowdey, Dec. 3, 1946, Mitchell Marsh, UGa.

61. Margaret Mitchell to Dr. Walters, Dec. 26, 1946; and Margaret Mitchell to Helen Dowdey, Nov. 7, 1946; both Mitchell Marsh, UGa.

62. Margaret Mitchell to Helen Dowdey, Nov. 7, 1947, Mitchell Marsh, UGa.

63. Margaret Mitchell to Helen Dowdey, Feb. 14, 1947, Mitchell Marsh, UGa.

64. Margaret Mitchell to Harold Latham, July 11, 1945, Macmillan, NYPL.

65. Margaret Mitchell to Deon Ward, Sept. 16, 1947, Mitchell Marsh, UGa.

66. Margaret Mitchell to Miss Stone, Mar. 27, 1947, Macmillan, NYPL.

67. Jordan, "My Dear Employer," *Atlanta Journal Magazine*, Aug. 16, 1951.

68. Margaret Mitchell to Charles A. Ward, July 10, 1946, Mitchell Marsh, UGa.

Chapter XX: Wildcats of the World, Unite!

1. Margaret Mitchell to George Brett, Feb. 25, 1946, Macmillan, NYPL.

2. W. A. R. Collins to Harold Macmillan, May 8, 1936; see also Harold Macmillan to W. A. R. Collins, May 26, 1936; both Macmillan, NYPL.

3. *Manchester Guardian*, Oct. 13, 1936, and Dec. 24, 1936; and *London Times*, Oct. 4, 1936; manuscript copies in Macmillan, NYPL.

4. George Brett to John Marsh (never sent), Mar. 14, 1944; see also George Brett to John Marsh, Mar. 15, 1944, for the letter he actually dispatched in reply to Marsh's tirade; both Macmillan, NYPL.

5. Marion Saunders to Margaret Mitchell, Sept. 18, 1936; quoted in John Marsh to George Brett, Mar. 4, 1944; Macmillan, NYPL.

6. See John R. Marsh to George Brett, Mar. 4, 1944, Macmillan, NYPL.

7. George Brett to John Marsh, Apr. 29, 1940, Macmillan, NYPL.

8. Margaret Mitchell to George Brett, Nov. 8, 1938, Macmillan, NYPL.

9. Margaret Mitchell to Dr. Wallace McClure, July 28 and Oct. 9, 1939, in Harwell, *Letters*, pp. 285, 287–89.

10. Margaret Mitchell to Dr. Wallace McClure, Aug. 8, 1940, in Harwell, *Letters*, p. 313.

11. Margaret Mitchell to Dr. Wallace McClure, Aug. 16, 1940, and Oct. 9, 1939, in Harwell, *Letters*, p. 287, 313.

12. Margaret Mitchell to Katherine Gauss, Nov. 18, 1948, Macmillan, NYPL.

13. Margaret Mitchell to Dr. W. B. Burke, May 14, 1947, in Harwell, *Letters*, p. 403.

14. Margaret Mitchell to Dr. Wallace McClure, Aug. 8, 1940, in Harwell, *Letters*, p. 312.

15. Margaret Mitchell to Dr. Wallace McClure, Aug. 16, 1940, in Harwell, *Letters*, p. 314.

16. Margaret Mitchell to Dr. Wallace McClure, Aug. 8, 1940, in Harwell, *Letters*, p. 312.

17. See Pierre Assouline, *Gaston Gallimard: A Half-Century of French Publishing*, translated by Harold J. Salemson (New York, San Diego London: Harcourt Brace Jovanovich, 1988). While Assouline's biography illuminates the general problems Mitchell confronted in the world, his judgments about Gallimard and buying *Gone with the Wind* seem a little fabulous. Either he, the French publishers, or both ignore the furor over the novel, not only in the United States and Great Britain, but also on the Continent. By Assouline's account, for example, news of Selznick's film hardly filtered through to Paris until after 1938, when news of the Hollywood production had been exciting trans-continental cables for nearly two years.

18. Margaret Mitchell to Harold Latham, Mar. 15, 1939, Macmillan, NYPL.

19. Steen Hasselbalch, the publisher, actually got the figure less than half right: by 1948, he had printed over 90,000 copies. See below.

20. Quoted in Margaret Mitchell to George Brett, Nov. 11, 1938, Macmillan, NYPL.

21. Margaret Mitchell to Harold Latham, July 15, 1940, Macmillan, NYPL.

22. John Marsh to George Brett, Mar. 4, 1944, Macmillan, NYPL.

23. Ibid.

24. Margaret Mitchell to Dr. Charles A. Thomson, Oct. 14, 1944, in Harwell, *Letters*, pp. 381–84. See also Assouline, *Gallimard*.

25. Margaret Mitchell to Clifford Dowdey, Nov. 15, 1945, Mitchell Marsh, UGa.

26. Margaret Mitchell to Helen Dowdey, May 10, 1946, Mitchell Marsh, UGa.

27. Margaret Mitchell to Mrs. Isabel Paterson, Oct. 21, 1946, in Harwell, *Letters*, p. 399.

28. Margaret Mitchell to George Brett, Apr. 11, 1947, Macmillan, NYPL.

29. Ibid.

30. Margaret Mitchell to George Brett, Apr. 21, 1947, Macmillan, NYPL.

31. Ibid.

32. Margaret Mitchell to George Brett, July 4, 1946, Macmillan, NYPL.

33. Ibid.

34. Margaret Mitchell to George Brett, Apr. 11, 1947, Macmillan, NYPL.

35. Ibid.

36. Margaret Mitchell to George Brett, Mar. 16, 1948, Macmillan, NYPL. For the general history of her wrangling with the German question, see her series of letters to Dr. Wallace McClure of the State Department, Mar. 31 and July 1, 1947, in Harwell, *Letters*, pp. 401–3 and 404–6.

37. Margaret Mitchell to George Brett, May 14, 1947, Macmillan, NYPL.

38. Margaret Mitchell to George Brett, Jan. 15, 1947, Macmillan, NYPL.

39. Mauricio Fabry to the Macmillan Company, Nov. 26, 1948; and Margaret Mitchell to Mauricio Fabry, Dec. 8, 1948; both Macmillan, NYPL.

40. See Margaret Mitchell to George Brett, Mar. 18 and Apr. 6, 1948, Macmillan, NYPL.

41. Margaret Mitchell to Miss Gauss, Nov. 18, 1948; also memo from Harold Latham, Oct. 18, 1948, Macmillan, NYPL.

42. Margaret Mitchell to George Brett, Jan. 15, 1947, Macmillan, NYPL.

43. Ibid.

44. Margaret Mitchell to Harold Latham, Dec. 12, 1946, Macmillan, NYPL.

45. Ibid.

46. Margaret Mitchell to Dr. Wallace McClure, Mar. 2, 1948, in Harwell, *Letters*, pp. 409–10.

47. Margaret Mitchell to Malcolm Cowley, Sept. 6, 1945, in Harwell, *Letters*, p. 394.

48. Margaret Mitchell to Mrs. William L. Plummer, Dec. 11, 1944, in Harwell, *Letters*, p. 385.

49. Margaret Mitchell to Katherine Gauss, Nov. 18, 1948, Macmillan, NYPL.

50. Margaret Mitchell to Madame Renee Roussell, Sept. 27, 1945; also Dr. Needham B. Bateman to Mrs. Florence S. Bateman, Aug. 25, 1945; both in Harwell, *Letters*, p. 395.

51. Margaret Mitchell to George Brett, Apr. 6, 1948, Macmillan, NYPL.

Chapter XXI: A Strange, Dark Country

1. July 12, 1949, Macmillan, NYPL.

2. Margaret Mitchell to Mrs. Mark Ethridge, Mar. 10, 1938, in Harwell, *Letters*, p. 185.

3. Stephens Mitchell, quoted by Keith Runyon in "Mr. Mitchell Remembers Margaret," in Harwell, *Book and Film*, p. 82.

4. Clifford Dowdey to the author, Sept. 27, 1977.

5. Margaret Mitchell to Herschel Brickell, May 25, 1938, in Harwell, *Letters*, p. 204.

6. Margaret Mitchell to Dr. Henry C. Link, July 23, 1941, Mitchell Marsh, UGa.

7. Margaret Mitchell, memorandum, (filed under "George Biggers"), Oct. 28, 1942, Mitchell Marsh, UGa.

8. Margaret Mitchell to Senator Walter George, June 3, 1944, Mitchell Marsh, UGa.

9. Margaret Mitchell to Herschel Brickell, May 25, 1938, in Harwell, *Letters*, p. 204.

10. Margaret Mitchell to Senator Walter George, Feb. 28, 1945, Mitchell Marsh, UGa.

11. See the notice in his regular column: Heywood Broun, "It Seems to Me," *New York World Telegram*, Sept. 19, 1936.

12. Howard Rushmore, "Life on *The Daily Worker*," *American Mercury* 50 (June 1940): 215–21.

13. "Topic of the Times," *New York Times*, June 9, 1937.

14. See, for example, "Southern Belle," Oct. 4, 1938; Samuel Sillen, "History and Fiction," Aug. 3, 1943; and Rob F. Hall, "Wrestling with Jim Crow," Aug. 3, 1943; all *New Masses*. Also see Carlton Moss, "An Open Letter to Mr. Selznick," *The Daily Worker*, Jan. 9, 1940, reprinted in Harwell, *Book and Film*, pp. 156–59.

15. Margaret Mitchell to George Brett, Jan. 15, 1947, Macmillan, NYPL.

16. Although her biographer discounts Smith's complaints, the author of *Strange Fruit* ultimately came to see much of the black equality movement subverted by the Communists and Communist-front organizations for their own ends in this same general period: see Anne Loveland, *Smith*, passim.

17. See, for example, Westbrook Pegler, "Our Second Reconstruction," *American Opinion* XI (Apr. 1963), reprinted in Harwell, *Book and Film*, pp. 108–14.

18. Margaret Mitchell to Eugene Lyons, Feb. 5, 1947, Mitchell Marsh, UGa.

19. Margaret Mitchell to Isaac Don Levine, Apr. 1, 1947, Mitchell Marsh, UGa.

20. Margaret Mitchell to George Brett, Apr. 6, 1948, Macmillan, NYPL; also Margaret Mitchell to Governor James M. Cox, July 28, 1949, in Harwell, *Letters*, p. 425.

21. Margaret Mitchell to Dr. Wallace McClure, July 1, 1947, in Harwell, *Letters*, p. 406.

22. Margaret Mitchell to Dr. Wallace McClure, July 26, 1949, in Harwell, *Letters*, p. 424.

23. Margaret Mitchell to George Brett, Mar. 16, 1948; also Apr. 6, 1948, Macmillan, NYPL.

24. George Brett to Margaret Mitchell, Mar. 19, 1948, Macmillan, NYPL.

25. George Brett to Margaret Mitchell, Feb. 18, 1944, Macmillan, NYPL.

26. John Marsh to George Brett, Mar. 4, 1944, Macmillan, NYPL.

27. Margaret Mitchell to Miss Grinnell, Oct. 9, 1944, Macmillan, NYPL.

28. Margaret Mitchell to George Brett, Oct. 23, 1944; also George Brett to Margaret Mitchell, Oct. 26, 1944, Macmillan, NYPL.

29. John Marsh to George Brett, Sept. 17, 1947; and George Brett to John Marsh, Sept. 23, 1947, Macmillan, NYPL.

30. John Marsh to George Brett, Oct. 29, 1947, Macmillan, NYPL.

31. George Brett to John Marsh, Oct. 31, 1947, Macmillan, NYPL.

32. John R. Marsh to George Brett, Nov. 28, 1947, Macmillan, NYPL.

33. Memorandum, Latham to Brett, Dec. 4, 1947; and the undated draft to "Dear John," both Macmillan, NYPL.

34. See Walbridge Taft to John R. Marsh, Sept. 27, 1938, Macmillan, NYPL.

35. George Brett to Margaret Mitchell, May 18, 1938, Macmillan, NYPL.

36. Margaret Mitchell to George Brett, May 20, 1938, Macmillan, NYPL.

37. Margaret Mitchell to Harold Latham, Nov. 18, 1937, Macmillan, NYPL.

38. Margaret Mitchell to Joseph Henry Jackson, Apr. 19, 1938, in Harwell, *Letters*, p. 197.

39. Walbridge Taft to J. A. Fruin, Oct. 6, 1941, quoted in Walbridge Taft to Stephens Mitchell, Nov. 14, 1946; both Macmillan, NYPL.

40. See Margaret Mitchell to George Brett, Feb. 19, 1945, Macmillan, NYPL.

41. Margaret Mitchell to George Brett, May 17, 1946, Macmillan, NYPL.

42. Margaret Mitchell to George Brett, May 24, 1946; see also the reply, George Brett to Margaret Mitchell, June 6, 1946; both Macmillan, NYPL.

43. Margaret Mitchell to George Brett, June 3, 1946, Macmillan, NYPL.

44. Margaret Mitchell to George Brett, May 24, 1946; see also the reply, George Brett, to Margaret Mitchell, June 6, 1946, both Macmillan, NYPL.

45. Walbridge Taft to Stephens Mitchell, Nov. 14, 1946, Macmillan, NYPL.

46. Margaret Mitchell to George Brett, Dec. 8, 1948, Macmillan, NYPL.

47. Margaret Mitchell to the Editor, *The Saturday Review*, Jan. 5, 1946, Mitchell Marsh, UGa.

48. Margaret Mitchell to Granville Hicks, Feb. 7, 1949, Mitchell Marsh, UGa.

49. Margaret Mitchell to Harold Latham, Jan. 12, 1948, Macmillan, NYPL.

50. Virginia Patterson to Harold Latham, June 7, 1948; see also Margaret Mitchell to the *San Antonio Light*, Dec. 23, 1947, clipping in Macmillan, NYPL.

51. See Chapter XX.

52. Margaret Mitchell to Harold Latham, July 2, 1949, Macmillan, NYPL.

53. Margaret Mitchell to Harold Latham, July 12, 1949, Macmillan, NYPL.

54. Margaret Mitchell to Bob Collins, Aug. 4, 1949, Mitchell Marsh, UGa.

Epilogue: A Story Told

1. *Domine, refugium*, Psalm xc, The Book of Common Prayer (1928), The Order for the Burial of the Dead.

2. Quoted in Morton Sosna, "The War Within a War: Views of the Civil War

During World War II," unpublished essay presented at the Fifth Citadel Conference on the South, Charleston, South Carolina, April 9–11, 1987.

3. Of the virtually numberless accounts of the New Criticism, the one most important to this analysis is Michael O'Brien, "Introduction: On the Mind of the Old South and Its Accessibility," in his *All Clever Men Who Make Their Way: Critical Discourse in the Old South.* (Fayetteville: The University of Arkansas Press, 1982). This essay sustains and amplifies my own evaluations of the movement's intellectual history.

4. Quoted in Richard Dwyer, "The Case of the Cool Reception," in Pyron, *Recasting,* p. 29. I consider this essay one of the most illuminating in defining the place of Mitchell's work in the history of literary criticism.

5. Floyd C. Watkins, *"Gone with the Wind* as Vulgar Literature," reprinted in Harwell, ed., *Book and Film,* p. 210; for a fuller treatment of "popularity" as a determining characteristic in otherwise aesthetic judgment, see Dwyer, "Cool Reception."

6. I note the double exception of Robert Y. Drake, "Tara Twenty Years After," *Georgia Review* 12 (Summer 1957): 142–50, notable for its merit as well as for its mere existence; see also the survey of this literature in Pyron, *Recasting,* pp. 209–14.

7. Quoted by Stephens Mitchell in Farr, *Margaret Mitchell,* p. 263.

Index